## Instructions Grouped by Function (*continued*)

| Group | Instruction | Description |
|---|---|---|
| **Transfer** | CALL dest | CALL subprogram |
| | INT number | INTerrupt |
| | IRET | Interrupt RETurn |
| | JA dest | Jump if Above |
| | JAE dest | Jump if Above or Equal |
| | JB dest | Jump if Below |
| | JBE dest | Jump if Below or Equal |
| | JC dest | Jump if Carry |
| | JCXZ dest | Jump if CX is Zero |
| | JE dest | Jump if Equal |
| | JG dest | Jump if Greater |
| | JGE dest | Jump if Greater or Equal |
| | JL dest | Jump if Less |
| | JLE dest | Jump if Less or Equal |
| | JMP dest | JuMP unconditionally |
| | JNA dest | Jump if Not Above |
| | JNAE dest | Jump if Not Above or Equal |
| | JNB dest | Jump if Not Below |
| | JNBE dest | Jump if Not Below or Equal |
| | JNC dest | Jump if Not Carry |
| | JNE dest | Jump if Not Equal |
| | JNG dest | Jump if Not Greater |
| | JNGE dest | Jump if Not Greater or Equal |
| | JNL dest | Jump if Not Less |
| | JNLE dest | Jump if Not Less or Equal |
| | JNO dest | Jump if No Overflow |
| | JNP dest | Jump if No Parity |
| | JNS dest | Jump if Not Sign |
| | JNZ dest | Jump if Not Zero |
| | JO dest | Jump if Overflow |
| | JP dest | Jump if Parity |
| | JPE dest | Jump if Parity Even |
| | JPO dest | Jump if Parity Odd |
| | JS dest | Jump if Sign |
| | JZ dest | Jump if Zero |
| | LOOP dest | LOOP |
| | LOOPE dest | LOOP if Equal |
| | LOOPNE dest | LOOP if Not Equal |
| | LOOPNZ dest | LOOP if Not Zero |
| | LOOPZ dest | LOOP if Zero |
| | RET | RETurn to calling program |
| | RET source | RETurn and adjust stack |
| **Miscellaneous** | CLI | CLear Interrupt flag |
| | IN acc,port | INput from port |
| | NOP | NO oPeration |
| | OUT port,acc | OUTput to port |
| | STI | SeT Interrupt flag |

# PC Assembly Language

# PC Assembly Language

## An Introduction to Computer Systems

**Paul Morneau**
**Adirondack Community College**

**WEST PUBLISHING COMPANY**
Minneapolis/St. Paul   New York   San Francisco   Los Angeles

Borland products are trademarks or registered trademarks of Borland International, Inc.

Hercules, Hercules Graphic Card, and Hercules Graphic Adapter are registered trademarks of Hercules Computer Technology.

Intel is registered trademark of Intel Corporation.

IBM, IBM PC, PC/AT, and AT are registered trademarks of, and PC/XT, MDA, EGA, VGA, OS/2, and PC-DOS are trademarks of, International Business Machines Corporation.

Lotus is a registered trademark of Lotus Development Corporation.

Microsoft, MS-DOS, and Codeview are registered trademarks of, and Quick Pascal and Windows are trademarks of, Microsoft Corporation.

**WEST'S COMMITMENT TO THE ENVIRONMENT**

In 1906, West Publishing Company began recycling materials left over from the production of books. This began a tradition of efficient and responsible use of resources. Today, up to 95 percent of our legal books and and 70 percent of our college texts are printed on recycled, acid-free stock. West also recycles nearly 22 million pounds of scrap paper annually—the equivalent of 181,717 trees. Since the 1960s, West has devised ways to capture and recycle waste inks, solvents, oils, and vapors created in the printing process. We also recycle plastics of all kinds, wood, glass, corrugated cardboard, and batteries, and have eliminated the use of styrofoam book packaging. We at West are proud of the longevity and the scope of our commitment to our environment.

Production, Prepress, Printing and Binding by West Publishing Company.

Artwork: Publication Services, Inc.
Copyediting: Publication Services, Inc.
Design: Publication Services, Inc.
Typesetting: Publication Services, Inc.
Cover Photograph: Lucy Paine Kezar

Copyright © 1993 by WEST PUBLISHING CO.
                           610 Opperman Drive
                           P.O. Box 64526
                           St. Paul, MN 55164-0526

All rights reserved
Printed in the United States of America

00 99 98 97 96 95 94 93     8 7 6 5 4 3 2 1 0

**Library of Congress Cataloging-in-Publication Data**

Morneau, Paul.
    PC assembly language : an introduction to computer systems / Paul Morneau.
       p.      cm.
    Includes bibliographical references and index.
    ISBN 0-314-01003-3
    1. Assembler language (Computer program language)
2. Microcomputers—programming.   I. Title.
QA76.73.A88M67   1992                      92-29595
005.26′2—dc20                 CIP

*To Susan*

# Brief Contents

Preface    xxi
Acknowledgments    xxvii
Chapter 1    Matters of Perspective    1
Chapter 2    Introduction to Computer Organization    21
Chapter 3    Assembly-Language Programming    59
Chapter 4    Integers    97
Chapter 5    Control Structures    135
Chapter 6    Bit Operations and Boolean Data    180
Chapter 7    Subprograms I    215
Chapter 8    Subprograms II    261
Chapter 9    Interrupts and I/O    302
Chapter 10    Memory    351
Chapter 11    Program Translation    366
Chapter 12    Macroinstructions    414
Chapter 13    Arrays    442
Chapter 14    Records    495
Chapter 15    Character Strings    522
Chapter 16    Decimal Data    566
Chapter 17    Floating-Point Data    615
Appendix 1    Input and Output Routines    A.1
Appendix 2    Extended ASCII Character Set    A.12
Appendix 3    Instructions    A.15
Appendix 4    Directives and Operations    A.26
Appendix 5    Microsoft Software    A.29
Appendix 6    Borland Software    A.51
Appendix 7    High-Level Language Information    A.66
Glossary    A.73
Bibliography    A.83
Index    A.85

# Contents

**Preface**   xxi

**Acknowledgments**   xxvii

**Chapter 1   Matters of Perspective   1**
   1.1   Algorithms, Programs, and Abstractions   2
      Algorithms   2
      Programs   3
      Procedural Abstraction   5
      Data Abstraction   6
      Exercises 1.1   7
   1.2   The Programmer's View   7
      Hardware   8
      Software   10
      Exercises 1.2   11
   1.3   Number Systems   11
      The Decimal System   12
      The Binary System   13
      The Hexadecimal System   16
      Exercises 1.3   19
   \*   Key Points   20

**Chapter 2   Introduction to Computer Organization   21**
   2.1   A Calculator Analogy   21
      The User View of a Calculator   21
      The Hardware View of a Calculator   22
      Comparing the Hardware and User Views   24
      Exercises 2.1   24
   2.2   Computer System Hardware   25
      Memory   25
      Central Processing Unit   31
      Peripherals   34
      The Bus   38
      Interrupts   39
      Survey of the 8086 Family   40
      Exercises 2.2   41
   2.3   Instructions   42
      Number of Operands   42
      Operand Types   48
      Instruction Representation   52
      Exercises 2.3   54
   \*   Key Points   56
   \*   PC System Summary   57

## Chapter 3  Assembly-Language Programming  59

### 3.1 Assembly-Language Notation  59
Statement Format  60
Program Format  61
Exercises 3.1  63

### 3.2 Symbolic Operands  63
Operands in Registers  63
Operands in Memory  63
Implied Operands  64
Immediate Operands  65
Operand Expressions  65
Exercises 3.2  65

### 3.3 Directives  66
Segment Ordering  66
Segment Definition  66
Segment Addressing  67
Data Declarations  68
External Definitions  69
Module Termination  70
Exercises 3.3  70

### 3.4 Input and Output  70
Input and Output Routines  70
A Simple Program  73
Exercises 3.4  77

### 3.5 Assembling, Linking, and Executing  77
Assembling  77
Linking  85
Executing  87
Exercises 3.5  87

### 3.6 Examining Memory with DEBUG  88
Exercises 3.6  93
* Key Points  94
* PC System Summary  95

## Chapter 4  Integers  97

### 4.1 Representation  97
Sign and Magnitude  98
Logical Complement  98
Radix Complement  100
Exercises 4.1  101

### 4.2 Operations  102
Move Operations  102
Arithmetic Operations  102
Exercises 4.2  110

### 4.3 Instructions  110
Move Instructions  111

**Contents**

    Conversion Instructions 114
    Arithmetic Instructions 115
    Example Programs 121
    Exercises 4.3 131
 *  Key Points 132
 *  PC System Summary 133

**Chapter 5 Control Structures 135**

  5.1 Tests and Relations 135
    Saving Test Results 136
    Compare Instruction 136
    Interpreting Test Results 137
    Exercises 5.1 142
  5.2 Transfer of Control 142
    Jumps and Branches 143
    Jump Instructions 143
    Relative Addresses 147
    Exercises 5.2 148
  5.3 Selection 148
    Selection with Two Sequences 148
    Selection with One Sequence 152
    Nested Selection Structures 155
    Exercises 5.3 157
  5.4 Repetition 158
    WHILE Loop Structure 159
    REPEAT-UNTIL Loop Structure 162
    FOR Loop Structure 164
    Mixed Loops 172
    Exercises 5.4 175
 *  Key Points 176
 *  PC System Summary 177

**Chapter 6 Bit Operations and Boolean Data 180**

  6.1 Shift Operations 180
    Logical Shifts 181
    Arithmetic Shifts 182
    Rotates 184
    Exercises 6.1 185
  6.2 Shift Instructions 186
    Logical Shifts 187
    Arithmetic Shifts 187
    Rotates 189
    Exercises 6.2 191
  6.3 Boolean Data Representation 192
    Exercises 6.3 196
  6.4 Boolean Operations 196
    AND 196

           OR     197
           XOR    197
           NOT    198
           Exercises 6.4   198
    6.5  Boolean Instructions   199
           The and Instruction   199
           The test Instruction   200
           The or Instruction   202
           The xor Instruction   202
           The not Instruction   203
           Exercises 6.5   204
    6.6  Applications   204
           Converting Flags to Boolean Values   204
           Evaluating Compound Boolean Expressions   206
           Counting One-Bits   208
           Exercises 6.6   210
    *   Key Points   212
    *   PC System Summary   213

**Chapter 7   Subprograms I   215**

    7.1  Addresses and Indirection   215
           Direct Memory Addresses   215
           Indirect Memory Addresses   216
           Register-Direct Operands   218
           Register-Indirect Operands   218
           Uses for Indirect Addressing   220
           Exercises 7.1   221
    7.2  Scope of Identifiers   221
           Internal and External Subprograms   222
           Local and Global Data   224
           Exercises 7.2   225
    7.3  Transfer of Control   225
           Saving the Return Address   225
           Location Counter Symbol   227
           The ptr Operator   228
           Exercises 7.3   230
    7.4  Arguments and Parameters   231
           Types of Arguments   231
           Transferring Arguments by Value   231
           Transferring Arguments by Reference   235
           Exercises 7.4   239
    7.5  The Stack   240
           The 8086 Stack Segment   240
           Operations on a Stack   241
           Transfer of Control   242
           Argument Transfer   243

**Contents**　　　　　　　　　　　　　　　　　　　　　　　　　　　　　　　**xiii**

     Using the Base Pointer 246
     Local Variables 252
     Stack Frames 253
     Exercises 7.5 254
  7.6 Saving the Caller's State 254
     Which Registers to Save 255
     When to Save Registers 255
     Where to Save Registers 256
     Saving Data Registers 256
     Saving Base and Flag Registers 257
     Exercises 7.6 258
  &ast; Key Points 259
  &ast; PC System Summary 260

**Chapter 8 Subprograms II 261**
  8.1 Near and Far Pointers 261
     Accessing Data 262
     Transfer of Control 266
     Exercises 8.1 266
  8.2 External Subprograms 267
     Importing Symbols 267
     Exporting Symbols 268
     Referencing an External Name 268
     Declaring an External Procedure 268
     Exercises 8.2 272
  8.3 Nested Calls 273
     Exercises 8.3 279
  8.4 Linking with High-Level Languages 279
     Segments 280
     Data Types 280
     Arguments 281
     Saving the Caller's State 281
     Example Programs 282
     Exercises 8.4 285
  8.5 Reentrant and Recursive Subprograms 286
     Non-reentrant Procedures 286
     Reentrant Procedures 288
     Recursive Procedures 289
     Tail Recursion 295
     Recursion versus Iteration 298
     Exercises 8.5 299
  &ast; Key Points 300
  &ast; PC System Summary 301

**Chapter 9 Interrupts and I/O 302**
  9.1 Interrupts 302
     External Interrupts 302
     Internal Interrupts 303

The 8086 Interrupts   304
Exercises 9.1   306
- 9.2 DOS and BIOS Services   306
  Which Services to Use   306
  Functions as Interrupts   307
  Using Interrupts   308
  Exercises 9.2   314
- 9.3 User I/O   314
  Device Descriptions   315
  DOS I/O Services   315
  BIOS Keyboard Services   318
  BIOS Video Services   320
  Exercises 9.3   330
- 9.4 Disk I/O   330
  Device Descriptions   330
  DOS File Services   332
  DOS Directory Services   337
  BIOS Disk Services   342
  Exercises 9.4   344
- 9.5 Communications   345
  Ports   345
  Controllers   346
  DMA   348
  Exercises 9.5   348
- \* Key Points   348
- \* PC System Summary   349

## Chapter 10 Memory   351

- 10.1 Real Mode (8086)   351
  Segments   351
  Addresses   352
  Expanded Memory   353
  Exercises 10.1   354
- 10.2 Protected Mode (80286)   355
  Addresses   355
  Extended Memory   357
  Virtual Memory   357
- 10.3 Linear Memory Mode (80386)   358
  Addresses   358
  Pages and Virtual Memory   359
  Exercises 10.3   361
- 10.4 Memory Hardware   361
  RAM and ROM   361
  Cache Memories   362
  Exercises 10.4   363
- \* Key Points   364
- \* PC System Summary   364

**Contents**

**Chapter 11 Program Translation 366**
- 11.1 Binding 367
  - Exercises 11.1 368
- 11.2 Assemblers 368
  - Instruction Specifications 369
  - The Two-Pass Assembler 370
  - Exercises 11.2 393
- 11.3 Translating High-Level Languages 394
  - Compilers 394
  - Interpreters 395
  - Preprocessors 396
  - Exercises 11.3 397
- 11.4 Linkers 398
  - Linker Operation 398
  - Linker Fixups 405
  - Exercises 11.4 407
- 11.5 Loaders 408
  - Program Header 408
  - Loader Fixups 409
  - Initializing Registers 409
  - Program Segment Prefix 409
  - Exercises 11.5 411
- 11.6 Debuggers 411
  - Exercises 11.6 412
- \* Key Points 413
- \* PC Systems Summary 413

**Chapter 12 Macroinstructions 414**
- 12.1 Macro Concepts 414
  - Macro Definition 415
  - Macro Expansion 416
  - Comments in Macros 416
  - Include Files 417
  - Exercises 12.1 418
- 12.2 Macros with Parameters 418
  - Parameters and Arguments 418
  - Multiple Parameters 420
  - Side Effects in Macros 422
  - Macros versus Subprograms 423
  - Exercises 12.2 424
- 12.3 More About Macros 424
  - Labels 425
  - The Substitute Operator 427
  - Exercises 12.3 431
- 12.4 Conditional Assembly 432
  - Using Assembler Symbols 432
  - Conditionals in Macros 436

## xvi Contents

     Exercises 12.4  440
 * Key Points  440
 * PC System Summary  441

### Chapter 13 Arrays  442

  13.1 Representation  442
     Declaring Arrays  443
     Arrays with Explicit Lower Bounds  443
     Arrays with Initial Values  444
     Exercises 13.1  445
  13.2 Addressing  445
     Using Direct Addresses with Arrays  445
     Using Indirect Addresses with Arrays  447
     Index Registers and Indexed Addressing  449
     Exercises 13.2  451
  13.3 Operations  452
     Processing a Whole Array  452
     Processing Individual Elements  457
     Exercises 13.3  461
  13.4 Arrays as Arguments  462
     Passing Arrays by Reference  462
     Passing Arrays by Value  467
     Passing Part of an Array  467
     Exercises 13.4  470
  13.5 Multi-Dimensional Arrays  471
     Declaring Two-Dimensional Arrays  471
     Representation in Memory  472
     Two-Dimensional Arrays as Arguments  473
     Examples  474
     Arrays with More than Two Dimensions  481
     Exercises 13.5  482
  13.6 The SET Data Type  483
     Representation  484
     Operations  484
     An Application  486
     Exercises 13.6  492
 * Key Points  492
 * PC System Summary  494

### Chapter 14 Records  495

  14.1 Representation  495
     Declaring Records  495
     Records with Initial Values  498
     Exercises 14.1  499
  14.2 Addressing  499
     Accessing Fields  499

Record Arguments 504
Arrays of Records 507
Exercises 14.2 511
14.3 Linked Lists 511
Record Description 512
Pointer Variables 514
Dynamic Memory Allocation 519
Exercises 14.3 520
* Key Points 520
* PC System Summary 521

**Chapter 15 Character Strings 522**
15.1 Representation 522
Character Codes 522
Strings in Memory 524
String Length 525
Exercises 15.1 525
15.2 Specification 526
String Constants 526
String Variables 527
Exercises 15.2 528
15.3 Operations 528
Input and Output 528
Finding the Length of a String 531
Copying a Substring 531
Concatenating Two Strings 536
Comparing Strings 536
Matching a Substring 540
Exercises 15.3 541
15.4 Instructions 542
String Pointers 542
Direction Flag 542
Repeat Prefixes 543
Move Instructions 545
Compare Instructions 552
Conversion Instruction 561
Exercises 15.4 563
* Key Points 563
* PC System Summary 564

**Chapter 16 Decimal Data 566**
16.1 Representation 566
Strings of Digits 567
Unpacked BCD 568
Packed BCD 568
Numbers with Fractions 568
Exercises 16.1 568

## Contents

16.2 Specification   569
  Unpacked BCD   569
  Packed BCD   570
  Exercises 16.2   570
16.3 Operations   571
  Conversions   571
  Arithmetic   573
  Comparing Decimal Numbers   575
  Exercises 16.3   575
16.4 Instructions and Procedures—Unpacked BCD   575
  Input and Output   576
  Move and Clear Operations   580
  Arithmetic Instructions   581
  Computing With BCDs   596
  Exercises 16.4   602
16.5 Instructions and Procedures—Packed BCD   602
  Conversions   603
  Arithmetic Instructions   606
  Other Operations   612
  Exercises 16.5   612
  * Key Points   613
  * PC System Summary   613

## Chapter 17  Floating-Point Data   615

17.1 Representation   615
  Converting Real Numbers   616
  Floating-Point Numbers in Memory   619
  Exercises 17.1   625
17.2 Specification   626
  Exercises 17.2   627
17.3 Operations   628
  Moving and Rounding   628
  Conversions   629
  Arithmetic   630
  Comparing Floating-Point Numbers   633
  Exceptions   634
  Exercises 17.3   635
17.4 The 8087 Coprocessor   636
  Data Registers   636
  Control, Status, and Tag Registers   636
  Exception Pointers   638
  Coordinating 8086 with 8087   639
  Exercises 17.4   639
17.5 Instructions   639
  Move Instructions   640
  Arithmetic Instructions   642
  Comparison Instructions   649

## Contents

|  |  |
|---|---|
| | Control Instructions 652 |
| | Transcendental Instructions 655 |
| | Exercises 17.5 655 |
| 17.6 | Applications 656 |
| | FOR Loops 656 |
| | Testing for Equal 657 |
| | Example Programs 659 |
| | Exercises 17.6 672 |
| * | Key Points 673 |
| * | PC System Summary 674 |

**Appendix 1**   **Input and Output Routines**   **A.1**

**Appendix 2**   **Extended ASCII Character Set**   **A.12**

**Appendix 3**   **Instructions**   **A.15**

**Appendix 4**   **Directives and Operations**   **A.26**
Directives   A.26
Operators   A.28

**Appendix 5**   **Microsoft Software**   **A.29**
MASM 5.1   A.29
MASM 6.0   A.30
LINK   A.32
LIB   A.33
DEBUG   A.35
Code View 2.2   A.35
Code View 3.14   A.45
Programmer's Workbench   A.50

**Appendix 6**   **Borland Software**   **A.51**
TASM   A.51
TCREF   A.52
TLINK   A.53
TLIB   A.56
TURBO DEBUGGER   A.57
TDUMP   A.63

**Appendix 7**   **High-Level Language Information**   **A.66**
PASCAL   A.66
C   A.68
FORTRAN   A.70

**Glossary**   **A.73**

**Bibliography**   **A.83**

**Index**   **A.85**

# Preface

## OBJECTIVES

This text is intended for use in introductory assembly-language and computer systems courses. Its principal objectives are to examine computer systems as machines and to show how the various structures and abstractions of computing are realized.

In recent years, first courses in computing have emphasized problem solving, structured programming, procedural abstraction, data abstraction, program verification, basic data structures, and the software life cycle. With the increased emphasis on abstractions has come decreased emphasis on the underlying computer systems.

The abstractions studied in first courses can, however, provide a rich background against which to present computer systems. In this setting, assembly language provides a useful vehicle for studying the structure and capabilities of computers, and for understanding data representation, instruction representation and execution, program translation, subprogram linkage and communication, and data structure implementation.

Courses in assembly language and computer systems may place different relative importance on computer systems and assembly-language programming, depending on the objectives of the curriculum and the department offering the course. This text can accommodate a wide variation in emphasis and should be especially useful in courses where the emphasis may be changing as curricula evolve.

## PHILOSOPHY

Two principles that have greatly influenced the writing of this text make it different from its competitors.

First, a study of computer systems should not be an isolated experience. The concepts presented in such a study must be connected to the background students bring with them. New concepts must develop from the foundation laid in the first courses and must widen that foundation for later courses to build on.

Using assembly language as a tool, we can study the software as well as the hardware of a computer system. We can show the connections between hardware and assembly language and those between high-level languages and assembly language. In stages, we can connect the abstract models used by high-level-language programmers to the hardware and software that implement those models.

By helping students to make such connections now, this text can prepare them to continue making connections in more advanced study. The study of computer systems can thus serve as a unifying experience for much of the study of computing.

Second, even though assembly language is used in this study—and I believe that programming in assembly language is an important experience that must be included in it—developing assembly-language programming skills is only a secondary objective. Understanding computer systems in general is more important than mastering the myriad details of some particular assembler.

Assembly language is more dependent on the particular computer system used than most other topics studied in computing. It is important to guard against becoming preoccupied with assembly-language details at the expense of more general concepts.

This text strives to balance the general concepts that are the primary interest and the system-dependent details needed to illustrate them.

## TEXT ORGANIZATION

Within this text, topics are presented at several levels of abstraction. Hardware descriptions include the models used by high-level-language programmers, block diagrams showing components connected by a bus, and the registers within the processor. Software descriptions include the operations provided in high-level languages, the instructions supported by the processor, high-level system support in the form of program loaders and library managers, and low-level system support in the form of DOS and BIOS service routines.

Presenting this material effectively requires a carefully organized approach. The topics in this text are arranged so that relevant matters from previous coursework are reviewed and a few important concepts are introduced before starting assembly language. These concepts are then reinforced as we begin to study assembly-language programming. The text proceeds from elementary programming through separately translated subprograms, examining how the computer works and how high-level-language features are implemented along the way.

Once that base is well established, it is used to discuss system interrupts, input and output, and memory. Assembling, linking, loading, and executing a program are examined in some detail, as are macroinstructions and conditional assembly, followed by an examination of the simple data structures provided in many high-level languages (arrays, records, and strings) and two other numeric data types (decimal and floating point).

## COURSE ORGANIZATION

There is more material in this text than can be covered thoroughly in one term. The first eight chapters provide a solid foundation in the fundamentals; the remaining nine chapters provide many choices for building a well-rounded course. Figure P.1 shows the prerequisites for the later chapters, with Chapter 8 partitioned into three parts.

Section 8.5 is optional. This material, which is not difficult, provides a good opportunity to reinforce the use of recursion and to examine the costs involved.

Chapters 9 and 10 can be studied at any time after Section 8.1. Chapter 11 can be studied at any time after Section 8.4. Chapter 12 can be studied at any time after Chapter 7. The material in these chapters is not required in any other chapter, so they may be presented in order, or skipped, according to local needs.

Chapter 13 and most of Chapter 17 can be studied any time after Section 8.4. Chapter 13 is required before Chapters 14 and 15, and before one example of Chapter 17. Chapter 15 is required before Chapter 16. The first few sections of any of the last five chapters can be presented earlier, with careful planning and alternative examples.

## PREREQUISITES

This text assumes that students have had one or more semesters of programming in a modern high-level procedural language, including an introduction to simple data structures

**Prerequisites**

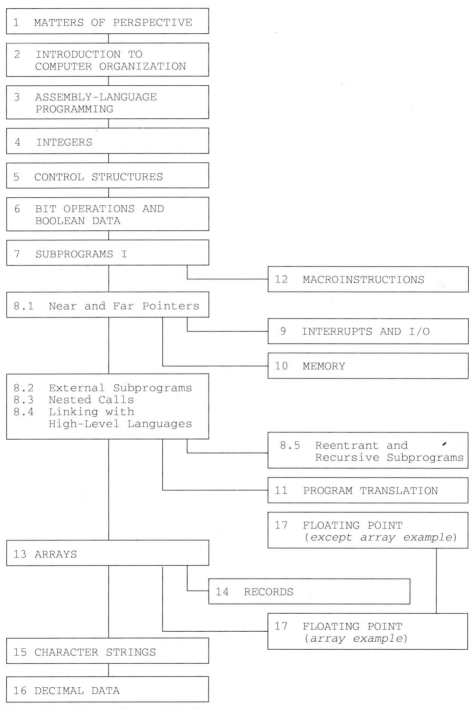

**Figure P.1  Chapter Prerequisite Structure**

(especially arrays, records, strings, and stacks). The mathematical preparation generally required for introductory programming classes is sufficient.

## RESOURCES NEEDED

Assembly-language programming is an essential component of studying computer systems. The programming projects in this text require access to a PC or compatible computer using any processor in the 8086 family, PC-DOS or MS-DOS, an assembler (Microsoft Macro Assembler, Borland Turbo Assembler, or compatible), a debugger (DEBUG, CodeView, or Turbo Debugger), and a linker. Other utilities, such as LIB and TDUMP, are useful but not required. A math coprocessor is needed for the programs in Chapter 17.

Many of the examples in the later chapters are written as assembly-language subprograms that can be linked to programs written in assembly language or Turbo Pascal. Other high-level languages can be used, but changes to the subprograms may be required.

The appendixes provide reference material, and students should have ready access to the reference manuals for the particular hardware and software used.

## TEXT FEATURES

### Program Disk

All programs that appear in this text are provided in source form on the disk that accompanies the text. The disk also includes drivers for all subprograms for which a driver is not printed in the text and data files for programs that read more than a few inputs. See the "read me" file for information on the organization of the disk.

### Input and Output Facilities

A set of input and output procedures is provided on the disk included with the text. These procedures are much simpler to use than those provided by the computer and the operating system; they enable students to include reasonable I/O with even their first programs.

### Compatibility

All assembly-language programs included in the text are compatible with Microsoft Macro Assembler versions 5.1 and 6.0 and with Borland Turbo Assembler version 2.0 (in MASM mode). All programs were individually tested with all three assemblers; no changes are needed to switch between assemblers. Writing programs that are compatible with all three assemblers restricted our choice of syntax in only a few cases; the ability to do so reflects the focus on the enduring characteristics of the computer system rather than trends in assembler features.

### Programming Style

The programs in this text feature a style designed to improve readability and comprehension. Much of the documentation is in the form of comments that resemble high-level-language statements. Sequences of assembly-language instructions are indented following the statement they implement. This style helps reinforce the connections between high-level-language statements and the instructions that implement them.

### Data Abstraction

Data types are presented using a framework similar to that used in presenting abstract data types: The representation and the set of values that define the type are followed by the operations on the type supported by high-level languages, the instructions that implement the operations, and finally examples that use the type.

### Structured Programming

Structured programming is generally accepted and encouraged, but altogether too many assembly-language texts revert to unstructured styles. This text not only carefully shows how the major control structures are implemented, but also uses those implementations consistently throughout the text. This approach, combined with other matters of style, reinforces the ideas of structured programming.

### Careful and Complete Subprogram Presentation

Transfer of control and communication between a program and a subprogram can be overwhelming if presented hastily. This text takes a deliberate, carefully paced approach to these topics. Each activity associated with calling and returning from a subprogram is discussed separately. Each activity is added to the total processing one at a time. The result is a discussion that leads gently from saving a return address to implementing reentrant and recursive subprograms.

### Program Translation by Example

The translation of assembly-language programs into machine instructions is explored first in an informal trace of a simplified two-pass assembler. Following each pass, an algorithm for that pass is provided. There is sufficient detail that writing a simplified assembler can be assigned as a project. The translation process does not stop with assemblers; how the linker resolves external references, how the loader copies the program into memory, and how the operating system passes control to it are also traced.

## PEDAGOGY

### Chapter Introductions

Each chapter begins with a list of the sections and a brief introduction to focus attention on the topics of the chapter.

### Examples

The text includes many examples to illustrate new concepts as they are presented. The examples may be a few lines of code, or a simple calculation, to illustrate a point and help students absorb and understand the material.

### Programs

Extensive programming examples are provided in all chapters that present data types, data structures, or procedural matters. These example programs are provided on the disk included with the text so that students can run or modify them.

### Instruction Summaries

As instructions are presented, they are summarized in displays within the text. These displays include the syntax of the instruction, the processing performed by the instruction, the form of operands allowed, and the effect of the instruction on the flags. The instructions are also tabulated in the PC System Summary at the end of the chapter.

### Exercises

Most sections end with a selection of exercises. Depending on the topics in the section, the exercises may include simple practice problems, review questions, discussion questions, program analysis problems, program modification problems, and programming projects. Generally, the exercises appear more or less in the order just stated. In some cases, analysis and discussion questions depend on completion of programming projects. For easier identification, exercises that involve programming are marked with a triangle (▶).

### Key Points

At the end of each chapter is a list of the key points of the chapter. The key points are general in nature, rather than specific to PC Systems or DOS.

### PC System Summary

At the end of each chapter, except the first, is a separate summary of important features and details specific to PC Systems.

### Reference Material

The appendixes include listings, summaries, and tutorials that are useful in this study. Appendix 1 contains listings of the I/O routines used in the text. Appendix 2 contains a table of the extended ASCII character set, which can also be used for converting numbers less than 256 between decimal, binary, and hexadecimal. Appendixes 3 and 4 summarize all instructions, directives, and operators presented in the text. Appendixes 5 and 6 provide tutorials on Microsoft and Borland assemblers, linkers, debuggers, and selected other utilities. Appendix 7 contains selected information on high-level languages.

## SUPPLEMENTS

An Instructor's Manual, containing more detailed ideas on course organization, chapter overviews with some teaching suggestions, and transparency masters, is available upon adoption. The Instructor's Manual also includes a discussion of possible laboratory projects.

# Acknowledgments

Several years ago, I proposed to write a text that would have been very different from the book in front of you. Nonetheless, that proposal was the spark that led to this book. Although I have changed much of what was in the original proposal, the underlying philosophy—that the concepts and their connections to the knowledge that students bring to the course are more important than the details of a specific assembler—has not changed.

From initial conception to finished text, many people have contributed to this project.

First, I want to thank Jay Ricci, former editor at West. Jay convinced me to write a book based on an earlier proposal, and later persuaded me to rewrite it to use 8086 assembly language. The changes in scope and direction that have led to this book were started under his advisement.

Next, I want to thank Peter Gordon and Sharon Adams, both editors at West, who provided direction, experience, and guidance during major revisions of the manuscript. Their many suggestions helped give the book its final form. Their advice was always welcome; their encouragement was always appreciated. I also want to thank the staffs at West and Publication Services for their effort and cooperation in the production of this book.

Every author of a college text benefits from serious review of the work by experts in the field. Since two very different manuscripts were reviewed, I have benefited twice. For their comments, suggestions, criticisms, compliments, and encouragement, I want to recognize the following reviewers:

| | |
|---|---|
| Keith Barker | University of Connecticut |
| Robert Broschat | South Dakota State University |
| Ken Chen | University of North Carolina-Charlotte |
| Randy Chow | University of Florida |
| Chris Edmondson-Yurkanan | University of Texas-Austin |
| Steven R. Eisenbarth | Baylor University |
| Milton R. Haase | Georgia State University |
| Philip J. Hatcher | University of New Hampshire |
| Donald L. Henderson | Mankato State University |
| Kathleen Keil | Ball State University |
| L. Carl Leinbach | Gettysburg College |
| Bernard W. Lovell | University of Connecticut |
| George Markowsky | University of Maine |
| Duane Overgaard | San Joaquin Delta College |
| George A. Rice | DeAnza College |

| | |
|---|---|
| Jerome Rothstein | Ohio State University |
| Al Saber | Friends University |
| Sushil K. Sachdev | Eastern Michigan University |
| John Sigle | Louisiana State University-Shreveport |
| James L. Silver | Indiana University-Purdue University-Fort Wayne |
| Edward W. Smith | Albright College |
| Gurindar S. Sohi | University of Wisconsin-Madison |
| Barry Irvin Soroka | California State Polytechnic University |
| Jeanne Spicer | Pennsylvania State University |
| David Straight | University of Tennessee-Knoxville |
| Benjamin F. Varn | Wofford College |
| Ambrish Vashishta | Wayne State University |
| F. Y. Wang | Livingston University |

I want to thank Adirondack Community College for its support, and the members of the Mathematics, Engineering, and Computer Science division in particular for their encouragement. I also want to thank the many students who expressed interest and provided inspiration over the years.

I want to thank Phil Coleman for his effort. His enthusiasm and patience are appreciated.

My greatest thanks goes to my family. Without their love, encouragement, and support I would not have been able to finish this book. Words cannot convey how much I appreciate their patience, tolerance, and understanding.

# Matters of Perspective  1

- ◆ **Algorithms, Programs, and Abstractions**
- ◆ **The Programmer's View**
- ◆ **Number Systems**

In beginning to study computers and programming, we learn little about the computer system that executes our programs. We are introduced to problem solving as we learn one or two high-level languages and use them to write modest programs.

With the trend in recent years toward increased structure and abstraction in procedures and data, we no longer need to know many details about our specific computer; we may therefore think about problems and algorithms in more natural terms. For many—probably most—applications, the mechanisms that implement the structures and abstractions take care of hardware details adequately. Occasionally, however, we must implement the structures and abstractions as part of our work, so we might have to know and understand the limits of a given computer or language. A knowledge of how computers implement software is thus important to practicing computer scientists.

This text addresses the area of computer science where algorithms and machines meet. We will see how

- Major components of a computer system are organized
- Instructions are represented and executed
- Data are represented and manipulated
- Control structures of high-level procedural languages are implemented
- Control and data are passed between procedures
- Simple data structures are represented and manipulated

This material will also be connected to the concepts of procedural and data abstraction with which you are already familiar.

In this chapter we review the relationships between algorithms and programs, between programs and computers, and between abstractions and implementations. We review computer hardware and software from a high-level-language programmer's perspective, and the chapter also provides an important background in number systems.

## 1.1 ALGORITHMS, PROGRAMS, AND ABSTRACTIONS

The first steps in programming are analyzing the problem to be solved and developing an algorithm based on that analysis. During the problem analysis and algorithm design steps, the focus is on solving the problem.

The next steps are expressing the algorithm in a programming language and arranging for the computer to execute it. While working on these steps, we must consider the characteristics of our computer and programming language. By using a high-level language, we can concentrate on the problem and its solution rather than on the details of our computer. In this section we review properties of algorithms and programs and consider the layers of abstraction inherent in a high-level-language environment.

### Algorithms

An **algorithm** is a sequence of unambiguous and executable steps that solves a specific class of problems in a finite period of time. It cannot include impossible steps (such as "express $\sqrt{2}$ as a rational number"), nor can it be vague (such as "choose best pair of factors"). Furthermore, it must solve the class of problems, not just a special case; for example, a method to calculate the cosine of one particular angle is unacceptable—to be considered an algorithm, it must calculate the cosine of any angle.

Without a carefully designed and correct algorithm, no amount of program coding will solve a user's problem. The algorithm should be expressed in a way that lends itself to analysis: It may be studied to prove that it solves the problem; it may be analyzed to determine its time and space requirements; and it may be used as a prototype for other programs. The effective use of a system's resources depends on well-planned implementations of carefully designed algorithms.

When working with algorithms, we attempt to keep the design and analysis free of machine-dependent details. Implied, however, is a set of characteristics assumed to be common to all computers. In comparing two sorting algorithms, for example, we usually consider how the number of comparisons changes as the number of elements to sort increases. We include the cost of the other operations in the algorithm, such as swapping values and accessing memory, with the cost of performing the comparison. We know that the time to sort is greater than the time required to compare values, but we assume it is proportional. This is a good assumption, based on the way computers execute programs. The important characteristics that affect this analysis tend to be similar in most computers. We will investigate many of these characteristics in this text.

One of the most important tools we use when designing an algorithm is stepwise refinement. The first level of design is expressed in terms of the major tasks to be performed. As we work on the algorithm, we refine each of those tasks into several smaller tasks, and possibly repeat this process for several stages of refinement. The algorithm can then be easily translated into a high-level-language program.

Operations in an algorithm that are not available in the programming language or the computer system used must be translated into operations that are. If we find in the algorithm a data type or structure that is not supported by our programming language, we write the necessary procedures and functions to implement that data type or structure with the data types that are available. Thus, in the later stages of algorithm development, we begin to consider the programming environment in which we work.

## Programs

Most programs are written in high-level languages that reflect the structure of algorithms and are independent of computer systems. However, programs in high-level languages must be translated before they can be executed.

A **compiler** is a program that translates another program into instructions that the computer can execute. The original program, written in a high-level language, is called the **source program.** The compiler reads the source program and generates an equivalent program, in the form of machine-dependent instructions, called the **object program.** The compiler itself does not perform the operations specified in the source program. An **interpreter,** on the other hand, reads the source program and executes the machine instructions that implement the specified operations as it analyzes the program. It generates no equivalent program, but appears to execute the source program directly. For convenience, we will assume the use of a compiler in the following discussion.

Statements in a high-level-language program can be partitioned into two groups: some are translated into machine instructions, and some specify information that controls the translation process. A simple high-level-language program consists of prologue documentation, a program heading, declarations, executable statements, and an end (see Figure 1.1). The details of this organization are specified by the syntax rules of the programming language used.

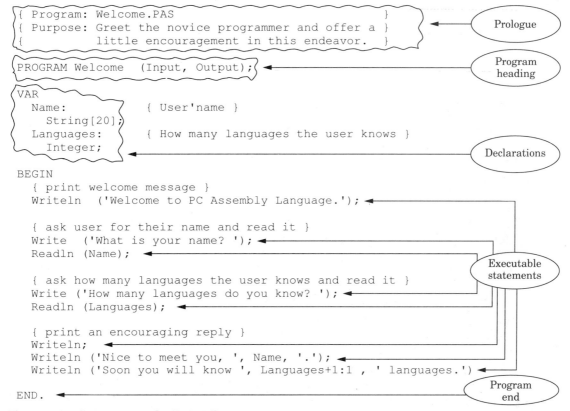

Figure 1.1  Components of a Pascal Program

The **prologue,** written as program comments in a natural language (such as English), is for the benefit of people who may have to read or revise the program. Comments within a program are set off from program text by some means so they will not be examined by the compiler during program translation (braces in Figure 1.1). The prologue may document what problem the program solves, how it solves the problem, what assumptions are made, who wrote and who revised the program, which references they used, and when they wrote it. A glossary of the variables used may be part of the prologue or may be combined with the declarations.

In addition to the prologue, there may be other comments. Blocks of program code are often preceded by one or more lines of comments that describe the task the block performs. These comments serve as an outline of the program and may also explain any special features of the block.

The program heading and program end are explicitly identified for the benefit of the compiler. The **program heading** indicates the entry point, which is used by the operating system to start executing a program and which must usually begin with instructions to accept control of the computer from the operating system. The conventions for the entry point of a program vary from system to system; we will examine the processing required upon entry to a program in Chapter 3. The compiler also generates instructions to return control of the computer to the operating system at the **program end.**

The declarations include information for use by the compiler during translation of the rest of the program. The declarations do not specify explicit operations, such as arithmetic, so the compiler does not generate instructions from them.

The executable statements can be partitioned into two groups:

1. Statements in the first group manipulate data. Arithmetic, relational, logical, character (or string), and input and output operations are commonly available.
2. Statements in the second group control the execution of statements in the first group. These control statements implement repetition structures (WHILE, FOR, REPEAT-UNTIL) and selection structures (IF-THEN-ELSE, CASE).

Used together, the two groups of executable statements allow implementation of any algorithm as a complete program.

Many programs invoke **subprograms** to perform some tasks. These subprograms, which may be either functions or procedures, may be included within the scope of the main program or be completely independent of it. It is useful to consider subprograms as separately written extensions of the programming language because doing so allows us to include them in our programs as operations and data types beyond those included in the programming language.

The distinction between a main program and a subprogram is somewhat artificial. A subprogram resembles a program in that it includes a prologue, heading, declarations, executable and control statements, and an end. A subprogram may also invoke other subprograms, or even itself. Many operating systems invoke a main program as if it is a subprogram. The program header of a main program usually differs from procedure or function headers in the number and type of arguments listed, but all headers identify the entry point for the compiler and operating system. The end statements all return control to the invoking program unit.

## Procedural Abstraction

All tasks specified in a program must be implemented using only the operations available in the original programming language and on the computer used. There are three levels here: at the lowest level, computers perform operations defined by the hardware (such as addition); on the next level, programming languages allow operations to be written in a more useful form (such as arithmetic expressions); and on the highest of the three levels, the use of subprograms allows coherent chunks of programs to be defined as language extensions (such as a function for finding the date some number of days after a given date; see Figure 1.2).

When writing a program, we often think in terms of an **abstract machine** (also called a **virtual machine**), which is represented by the programming language and extensions defined as subprograms. We also make further extensions, adding new layers of abstraction as our programs become larger and more complex. No matter how many layers of programming we implement, every operation must be executed by a machine with a fixed repertoire of instructions.

One of the goals in this text is to learn about these instructions. We will study the Intel 8086 processor family in detail and write assembly-language programs for it.

A programmer should know in a general way how computers execute programs, what restrictions computers impose on operations, and how features of high-level languages are implemented.

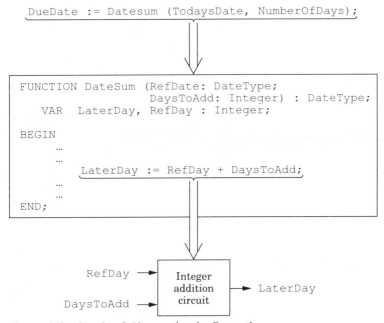

**Figure 1.2** Levels of Abstraction in Operations

## Data Abstraction

Data types processed by programs can be either atomic (single-valued) or structured. They can be provided by the high-level language or implemented as an extension. Operations on the various types may be defined by the programming language or by user-written subprograms. There is much current interest in abstract data types, where the properties of and operations on a data type are clearly defined but the programmer is not given access to the actual implementation of the type. In a sense, some atomic data types and most structured data types are similarly implemented by the programming language using a few primitive data types supported by the hardware.

Data types, like the operations defined on them, also define a system with three levels: on the lowest level, a few simple data types (such as integers) are provided directly by the hardware; on the next level, programming languages provide an implementation of other general-purpose data types (such as an array of integers); and on the highest of the three levels, programmers define other types that can be implemented using those already provided (such as a queue represented by an array of integers; see Figure 1.3).

When programming, we use whatever data types are natural for the problem we are solving. If those data types are already available, we use their definitions; if not, we

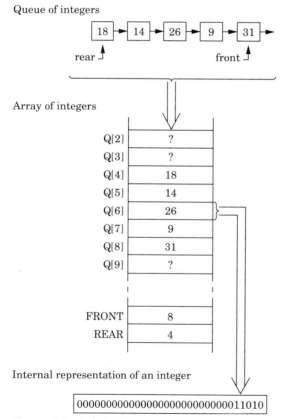

**Figure 1.3** Levels of Abstraction in Data

## 1.2 The Programmer's View

define and implement them ourselves. No matter how complex the data types or their implementation, the data themselves must be represented by a machine with a fixed repertoire of data types.

Another goal in this text is to learn about these data types. The data types supported by the Intel 8086 and 8087 processors will be considered in depth, as will the simpler, common data structures provided in many high-level languages.

A programmer should know in a general way how simple data types are implemented by hardware, what limits are imposed by the implementation, and how high-level languages implement some data types not provided directly by the hardware.

## EXERCISES 1.1

1. Are all algorithms computer programs? Explain.
2. Are all computer programs algorithms? Explain.
3. There is at least one very useful program that is not an algorithm in the strictest sense. What is it, and what property of an algorithm does it not have?
4. Get a printout of a high-level-language program and identify three examples of each of the following:
   (a) A comment
   (b) A declaration
   (c) An executable statement that manipulates data
   (d) An executable statement that controls execution
5. Give an example of a statement in your favorite high-level programming language that
   (a) Reads data from an input device
   (b) Reads data from a storage device
   (c) Writes to an output device
   (d) Writes to a storage device
6. How do the statements you gave for answers to Exercises 5$a$ and 5$b$ differ? How are the operations performed for the two statements similar? How are they different?
7. How do the statements you gave for answers to Exercises 5$c$ and 5$d$ differ? How are the operations performed for the two statements similar? How are they different?
8. List the control statements provided in your favorite high-level language. If you could have only one form of each control structure (that is, one repetition statement and one selection statement), which would you choose? Show how to implement the others using the ones you choose.
9. List the data types provided in your favorite high-level language. Which of these do you think are supported directly in hardware and which do you think are supported using software?

## 1.2 THE PROGRAMMER'S VIEW

Programmers write programs for abstract machines defined by the high-level language they use. For example, a Pascal programmer works as if a "Pascal machine" were available to execute the program. This provides a useful model of computer hardware and software, which we review here.

## Hardware

The principal hardware components of a computer system are

- main (or primary or internal) memory
- auxiliary (or secondary or external) storage
- central processing unit
- input and output devices

**Main memory,** usually referred to simply as **memory,** is used for storing programs and the data they operate on while the programs are executing. **Auxiliary storage,** referred to simply as **storage,** is used for storing inactive programs and data for long periods of time. The **central processing unit (CPU)** executes the program's instructions and controls the computer hardware. The **input** and **output (I/O) devices** provide for communication between the computer and the user. The programmer's view of computer hardware is shown in Figure 1.4. In this model, the arrows indicate the primary data paths.

Programmers working in a high-level language have few hardware-dependent concerns. For example, a program that reads input from a keyboard should print a prompting message, whereas one that reads input from a file stored on disk might echo the input values. However, many of the details of using different devices are hidden by the high-level programming language.

Consider execution of this program fragment:

```
READ (InDevice, Quantity, UnitCost);
ExtendedCost := Quantity * UnitCost;
WRITE (OutDevice, ExtendedCost)
```

The first statement accepts two values from `InDevice` and saves them in memory cells named `Quantity` and `UnitCost`. The second statement multiplies these values together and copies the result into the memory cell named `ExtendedCost`. The third statement sends the value of `ExtendedCost` from memory to `OutDevice`. In this fragment,

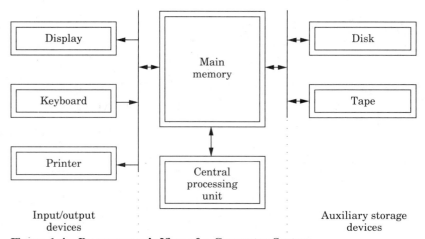

**Figure 1.4  Programmer's View of a Computer System**

`InDevice` and `OutDevice` could be input and output devices or storage devices; the programmer is able to treat these devices the same way.

We now look at each of the components in more detail, beginning with memory.

### Memory

A high-level-language programmer sees memory organized as a collection of named **memory cells,** each of which can store one value of some specific type. The size of a cell depends on the data type to be stored there. Details about the cell—such as its exact placement within memory, its size, its capacity, and how the value it contains is coded—are hidden from the high-level-language programmer. The programmer need not be concerned with these matters unless problems arise, such as those caused when a value exceeds the capacity of the cell.

The instructions in a program are also stored in memory. Details about the instructions, such as their placement in memory and how they are coded, are also hidden from the programmer. Unless there is a problem with the implementation of the language or some special need, the programmer need not be concerned with these details, either.

In the management of system resources, memory is considered not in terms of individual cells but in groups of cells. The groups may be as small as a few cells or as large as a few million cells. To be executed, a program and the data it processes must be present in memory. Allocating memory for programs and data is the responsibility of the operating system. The programmer usually need not be concerned with the details of memory management.

### Storage

Because memory is a limited resource, programs and data are copied to a storage device, usually magnetic disk or tape, when they are to be inactive for a period of time. Data and programs in storage are organized as files. Many programmers are familiar with the major features of data files but are less sure about how programs are represented after translation and how they are copied between memory and storage. These details are also left to the operating system.

### CPU

The central processing unit controls the operation of the computer system and executes the instructions in a program. The CPU performs data move, arithmetic, relational, logical, and data conversion operations. It also controls the sequence in which instructions are executed. The statements in a high-level language hide many details of the processor, letting the programmer control it with a "natural" notation.

### I/O devices

The input and output devices provide communication links between a computer and its users. There is a considerable amount of conversion involved in even the simplest input or output operation. High-level languages not only hide the details of the hardware operation, but also provide any needed conversions. Programmers working in a high-level language tend to take input and output operations for granted.

Some models of computers treat auxiliary storage devices as input and output devices. Others, like the model presented in this section, separate them because storage devices transmit data in two directions (between memory and storage), whereas input and output

## Chapter 1 Matters of Perspective

devices transmit data in only one direction (from an input device or to an output device).

## Software

An application programmer writes a program in a high-level language, then enters it as text using an editor. This text is saved as a file, called the **source file** (Figure 1.5a). The editor is also used to examine and modify this source file during program maintenance. The source file is the only form of the program that can be easily read by a person.

The source file cannot be executed by the processor as text; it must first be translated into machine-dependent instructions. A compiler is a program that reads the source file and generates another file, called an **object file,** that contains an equivalent set of machine

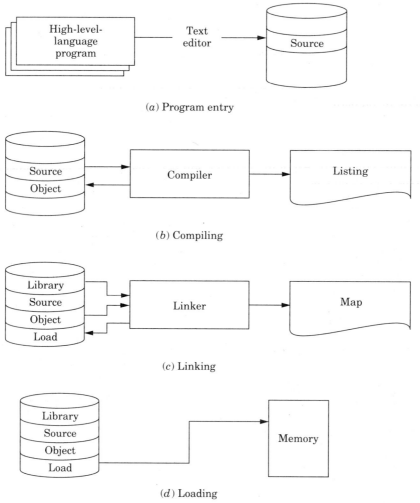

Figure 1.5   Steps in Preparing a High-level-Language Program for Execution

instructions. The source file is unchanged by the compiler. The compiler may also create an annotated listing of the program (Figure 1.5*b*).

The object file by itself is incomplete. Some operations, such as reading numeric data from a terminal or printing a character string, that are directly specified in a high-level language take many machine instructions to implement. The compiler does not translate each such statement directly into the many machine instructions required. These operations are instead implemented as calls on system subprograms that perform the operations. The object code must be combined with the needed system subprograms identified by the compiler before the program can be executed.

The **linkage editor,** or **linker,** combines the object file with system subprograms to create an executable version of the program. This final form has several names, including **run image** and **load module,** depending on how it was produced and the computer system used. Whatever its name, this is the form of the program that can be executed. The linkage editor may also print a **load map** of the program, showing where in memory each module is to be loaded (Figure 1.5*c*).

In order to be executed, the run image must be copied from storage into memory by a **loader** (Figure 1.5*d*). (*Linking loaders* combine the object code and system subprograms into memory directly, so there is only one link-and-load step; some systems also integrate a linker with a compiler.) Although the programmer may specify exactly where in memory to load the run image, the loader usually handles all such details.

The steps in preparing a high-level-language program for execution involve a lot of work, but much of it is done by system programs.

To simplify the procedure for executing a program written in a high-level language, many systems provide a means of automating the compiling, linking, loading, and executing steps in a single command. All of the steps are still performed, but the programmer doesn't have to issue each command separately each time. The result is a simpler to use, yet more abstract, environment for the programmer. Just as a high-level language hides details of computer hardware operation, an automated command hides the details of translating and loading a high-level language. On a PC, such capability is easily provided as a batch file.

Not all programming languages are translated by compilers. An interpreter does much the same analysis of the source file as a compiler, but rather than generating an object file, it performs the indicated operations as they are encountered.

## EXERCISES 1.2

1. What commands do you use to
   - (*a*) Invoke the text editor?
   - (*b*) Invoke a high-level-language compiler?
   - (*c*) Invoke the likage editor?
   - (*d*) Invoke the loader?
   - (*e*) Execute a loaded program?
   - (*f*) Interrupt a program stuck in a loop?

▶2. Write a batch file program to automate the sequence of commands for compiling, linking, and executing a high-level-language program.

## 1.3 NUMBER SYSTEMS

Computers represent information using collections of two-state devices. We represent the states of individual devices using the two symbols of the binary number system, 0 and 1.

The states of a collection of such devices can be represented as a string of binary digits. That string in turn represents a number written in the binary system.

Since long binary numbers are awkward for people to use, they are often expressed as octal or hexadecimal numbers. These provide a more compact representation. The binary, octal, and hexadecimal number systems all share several properties with the decimal number system that we use every day. These properties are reviewed in the following discussion.

## The Decimal System

The decimal system uses ten symbols, the digits 0 through 9. It is a positional system; that is, the value that each digit represents depends on its position within a number. Each digit in a number represents a multiple of a power of 10.

Consider the number 1503. It can be expanded as

$$1503 = 1 \times 1000 + 5 \times 100 + 0 \times 10 + 3 \times 1$$

or

$$1503 = 1 \times 10^3 + 5 \times 10^2 + 0 \times 10^1 + 3 \times 10^0$$

The terms in the second line of the expansion start on the right with a factor of $10^0$. The exponent increases as we move to the left in the number. Zero is used to fill the tens position, since there are no tens in the number 1503. All positions to the left of the most significant digit are blank. They contribute nothing. They could be written as zeros without changing the number; the number 00001503 is the same as 1503.

A number with $n$ digits can take on $10^n$ different values. These values range from a string of $n$ zeros, representing 0, to a string of $n$ nines, representing $10^n - 1$. Another way to state this relationship is that it takes $\lceil \log_{10} n \rceil$ digits to represent $n$ different values. (The ceiling function, written $\lceil x \rceil$, computes the smallest integer greater than or equal to $x$.)

The **radix** of a number system determines the number of symbols in the system, and the base used in the expansion of a number. The use of position to indicate relative value, the use of 0 to fill unused positions, and the relationships between the range of values and the number of digits all apply to the other number systems in which we are interested. Only the radix changes.

A problem that arises when discussing numbers in systems other than decimal is how to indicate the radix. By convention, the radix is always written in decimal, and numbers not in decimal will have a decimal subscript that specifies the radix.

Our review of the decimal number system can be stated in terms of an arbitrary radix, denoted by $r$. A number is written as a string of digits, where each digit is denoted $d_j$. The subscript $j$ indicates the position of the digit. Each number has an origin indicated with a period—called the radix point—or implied to the right of the least significant digit of an integer. The subscript $j$ is 0 for the position to the left of the origin; it increases as we move to the left. An $n$-digit number written as

$$(d_{n-1} d_{n-2} \cdots d_2 d_1 d_0)_r$$

can be expanded as

$$d_{n-1} \times r^{n-1} + d_{n-2} \times r^{n-2} + \cdots + d_2 \times r^2 + d_1 \times r^1 + d_0 \times r^0$$

## 1.3 Number Systems

The largest number that can be represented with $n$ digits in base $r$ is given by the number in which each of the digits $d_j$ is $(r - 1)$. This largest number can also be written as $r^n - 1$. It takes $\lceil \log_r n \rceil$ digits in base $r$ to represent $n$ different values.

### The Binary System

The binary number system uses 2 as the radix. The two symbols of this system, 0 and 1, are frequently referred to as **bits**, from the term *binary digits*. Positional values are based on powers of 2. The number $101001_2$ is a binary number, read as "one zero one zero zero one, base two."

The number of values that can be represented in binary with $n$ bits is $2^n$. As nonnegative integers, they range from 0 (a string of $n$ zeros) to $2^n - 1$ (a string of $n$ ones). It takes $\lceil \log_2 n \rceil$ bits to represent $n$ different values. For example, to represent 300 different values in binary requires $\lceil \log_2 300 \rceil = \lceil 8.229 \rceil = 9$ bits.

### Converting binary to decimal

To convert a binary number to its decimal equivalent, we can expand it as a sum of powers of 2. Consider the number $101001_2$. It can be expanded as

$$101001_2 = 1 \times 2^5 + 0 \times 2^4 + 1 \times 2^3 + 0 \times 2^2 + 0 \times 2^1 + 1 \times 2^0$$

or

$$101001_2 = 1 \times 32 + 0 \times 16 + 1 \times 8 + 0 \times 4 + 0 \times 2 + 1 \times 1$$
$$= 32 + 0 + 8 + 0 + 0 + 1$$

So $101001_2 = 41$.

Another method for converting a number to decimal uses synthetic division. To perform synthetic division, write the number, leaving some space between digits. Skip a line, and copy the most significant nonzero digit onto the next line. For example:

```
 1   0   1   0   0   1
_____
 1
```

Now multiply the number just written below the line by the radix (2 in this example), and record the result under the next digit to the right in the original number:

```
 1   0   1   0   0   1
     2
_____
 1
```

Add the numbers in the column just completed:

```
 1   0   1   0   0   1
     2
_____
 1   2
```

Repeat the preceding two steps for the remaining digits:

```
 1   0   1   0   0   1
     2   4  10  20  40
_____
 1   2   5  10  20  41
```

The final result is the decimal equivalent of the original binary number. Note that all arithmetic is carried out in decimal. The method works for any radix.

The synthetic division method for converting a number to decimal is easily implemented on a calculator. The algorithm is

Result := most significant nonzero digit
WHILE there are more digits
   Result := Radix × Result + next digit

To implement this algorithm on a calculator, start by entering the most significant (leftmost) nonzero digit. This takes care of the first line in the algorithm. Now, working left to right, for each digit multiply the value in the calculator display by the radix, and add the digit. When the last (rightmost) digit of the original number has been added, the display will contain the decimal equivalent. The algorithm is given in terms of an arbitrary radix; it can be used to convert a number from any base to decimal.

## Converting decimal to binary

To convert a decimal number to binary, find the powers of 2 in the expansion by subtraction. Repeat, subtracting (and recording) the largest powers of 2 possible, until the difference is 0. Then write the decimal number as a string of ones for the powers subtracted, filling in zeros for powers that are skipped. For example, consider converting the number 26 to binary. The largest power of 2 that is less than 26 is 16 ($= 2^4$). Subtracting, $26 - 16 = 10$. The largest power of 2 that is less than 10 is 8 ($= 2^3$). Subtracting and continuing, we get

$$26 = 16 + 8 + 2$$
$$= 2^4 + 2^3 + 2^1$$

Filling in the missing powers of two, we find

$$26 = 1 \times 2^4 + 1 \times 2^3 + 0 \times 2^2 + 1 \times 2^1 + 0 \times 2^0$$

Writing this in positional notation gives

$$26 = 11010_2.$$

This method will also work for converting numbers from decimal to any other radix. When converting to a system other than binary, it is necessary to subtract multiples of the powers of the radix, as well as to keep track of the multiples.

An easier way to convert numbers from decimal to another radix uses repeated division. To use this method, divide the number by the radix to get a quotient and a remainder. Then divide that quotient by the radix to get another quotient and remainder. Continue to divide each succeeding quotient by the radix until you obtain a quotient of zero. The number is written in the new radix as the remainders in reverse order of calculation from left to right. For example, consider again the conversion of 26 to binary:

$$26 \div 2 = 13, \text{ with remainder } 0$$
$$13 \div 2 = 6, \text{ with remainder } 1$$
$$6 \div 2 = 3, \text{ with remainder } 0$$
$$3 \div 2 = 1, \text{ with remainder } 1$$
$$1 \div 2 = 0, \text{ with remainder } 1$$

## 1.3 Number Systems

The binary equivalent of 26 is found to be $11010_2$. Note that had we kept dividing, we would get

$$0 \div 2 = 0, \text{ with remainder } 0$$

repeating indefinitely. These zero remainders contribute nothing to the number; they are leading zeros. Often we will write binary numbers with leading zeros to make them a fixed length.

### Arithmetic in binary

Now consider addition, subtraction, and multiplication in binary. Some familiarity with these operations will help in understanding the discussion of machine arithmetic later.

Addition is performed using Table 1.1. The entry in the bottom right of the table shows that $1_2 + 1_2 = 10_2$. In decimal we carry to the left when the sum exceeds 9. In other words, with radix $r$ we carry to the left when a sum exceeds $r - 1$. In binary, therefore, we carry when a sum exceeds 1.

Consider adding $101001_2$ and $11010_2$, shown here with the carries on the top, and the decimal equivalents on the right:

$$
\begin{array}{rr}
11 & \\
101001_2 & 41 \\
+\quad 11010_2 & +26 \\
\hline
1000011_2 & 67
\end{array}
$$

Starting on the right, the first three binary additions present no difficulties. The fourth column from the right illustrates a result bit of 0 and a carry bit of 1. The carry into the fifth column from the right produces another carry, and so on.

Subtraction in binary involves borrowing a power of 2. Consider subtracting $10100_2$ from $1001001_2$. The first few steps give an intermediate result:

$$
\begin{array}{r}
1001001_2 \\
-\quad 10100_2 \\
\hline
?0101_2
\end{array}
$$

The subtractions in the first two columns from the right were trivial. The next step involved borrowing from the fourth column, giving the result shown for those two columns. The next subtraction requires borrowing from two columns away: The intermediate column becomes one, just as an intermediate column in a decimal borrow becomes nine. The final result, with decimal equivalent, is

$$
\begin{array}{rr}
1001001_2 & 73 \\
-\quad 10100_2 & -20 \\
\hline
110101_2 & 53
\end{array}
$$

**Table 1.1 Binary Addition**

| + | 0 | 1 |
|---|---|----|
| 0 | 0 | 1 |
| 1 | 1 | 10 |

**Table 1.2  Binary Multiplication**

| × | 0 | 1 |
|---|---|---|
| 0 | 0 | 0 |
| 1 | 0 | 1 |

Multiplication in binary uses Table 1.2. Longhand multiplication in binary can be performed by copying the multiplicand once for each 1 bit in the multiplier, aligned so that the least significant bit of the multiplicand is under the corresponding 1 bit in the multiplier, then adding.

Consider the following multiplication of $11010_2$ by $1101_2$:

$$\begin{array}{r} 11010_2 \\ \times \quad 1101_2 \\ \hline 11010 \\ 11010 \phantom{0} \\ 11010 \phantom{000} \\ \hline 101010010_2 \end{array}$$

There are three 1 bits in the multiplier. The multiplicand is copied three times between the lines, once for each 1 bit in the multiplier. These copies are aligned so that the rightmost bit is directly below a 1 bit of the multiplier. That much of the multiplication is easy. Adding these three copies together is a little harder, as the carry could be greater than 1 (although it isn't in this example).

## The Hexadecimal System

The hexadecimal number system uses 16 symbols: the digits 0 through 9 and the letters A through F. The value of each position is a power of 16. The usefulness of the hexadecimal system can be seen if we consider groups of four bits. There are 16 ($2^4$) patterns possible with four bits. These patterns represent the numbers 0 through 15, the same as the digits in the hexadecimal system. These patterns and their decimal and hexadecimal equivalents are shown in Table 1.3.

### Converting between hexadecimal and binary

Table 1.3 can be used to convert numbers between binary and hexadecimal. For example, consider the number $111101110100010_2$. First, extend it with leading zeros so that its length is a multiple of 4. Then partition it into groups of four bits, and replace each group with the corresponding hexadecimal digit. This is illustrated here:

$$\begin{aligned} 111101110100010_2 &= 0111 \quad 1011 \quad 1010 \quad 0010_2 \\ &= \phantom{0}7 \quad\quad\; B \quad\quad\;\; A \quad\quad\;\; 2_{16} \end{aligned}$$

We find that $7BA2_{16}$ is the hexadecimal equivalent of the binary number $111101110100010_2$.

## 1.3 Number Systems

Table 1.3 Decimal and Hexadecimal Equivalents of Patterns of Four Bits

| Pattern of Four Bits | Decimal Equivalent | Corresponding Hexadecimal Digit |
|---|---|---|
| 0000 | 0 | 0 |
| 0001 | 1 | 1 |
| 0010 | 2 | 2 |
| 0011 | 3 | 3 |
| 0100 | 4 | 4 |
| 0101 | 5 | 5 |
| 0110 | 6 | 6 |
| 0111 | 7 | 7 |
| 1000 | 8 | 8 |
| 1001 | 9 | 9 |
| 1010 | 10 | A |
| 1011 | 11 | B |
| 1100 | 12 | C |
| 1101 | 13 | D |
| 1110 | 14 | E |
| 1111 | 15 | F |

Even though using the symbols A through F to represent digits takes some getting used to, the hexadecimal number is easier to write and copy.

To convert a number from hexadecimal to binary, we replace each hexadecimal digit with the corresponding group of four bits. For example, the number $D23F_{16}$ can be converted to binary as follows:

$$D23F_{16} = \quad D \quad\quad 2 \quad\quad 3 \quad\quad F_{16}$$
$$= 1101 \quad 0010 \quad 0011 \quad 1111_2$$

The binary equivalent of $D23F_{16}$ is $1101001000111111_2$.

### Converting between hexadecimal and decimal

To convert between decimal and hexadecimal, use the same algorithms as the conversions between decimal and other systems, except that the radix is now 16. When converting to decimal, multiply by 16. There is a little extra complication involving the use of A through F as digits. You may find it easier to replace them with (10) through (15) as an intermediate step. To illustrate, let's convert $3FA2_{16}$ to decimal using synthetic division. The second line shows the intermediate step where the hexadecimal symbols F and A are replaced by the numbers (15) and (10).

```
    3     F      A       2     original number
    3    (15)   (10)     2     using decimal digits
         48    1008    16288
    ─────────────────────────
    3    63    1018    16290
```

This shows that 16290 is the decimal equivalent of $3FA2_{16}$.

When converting from decimal to hexadecimal, divide by 16. Let's convert 2003 to hexadecimal:

$$2003 \div 16 = 125, \text{ with remainder } 3$$
$$125 \div 16 = 7, \text{ with remainder } 13$$
$$7 \div 16 = 0, \text{ with remainder } 7$$

Writing 13 as $D_{16}$, this gives $7D3_{16}$ as the hexadecimal equivalent of 2003.

## Arithmetic in hexadecimal

Addition in hexadecimal uses the values shown in Table 1.4. Hexadecimal addition proceeds in the same manner as decimal addition, except that carries occur when a sum exceeds 15.

For example, consider the addition of $3C45_{16}$ and $AE9_{16}$, shown here with carries and their decimal equivalents:

$$
\begin{array}{r}
11 \\
3C45_{16} \\
+\ AE9_{16} \\
\hline
472E_{16}
\end{array}
\qquad
\begin{array}{r}
111 \\
15429 \\
+\ 2793 \\
\hline
18222
\end{array}
$$

Starting on the right, the first hexadecimal addition step can be read directly from the table. The next two additions each generate a carry.

Subtraction in hexadecimal is also based on the table. When it is necessary to borrow, however, it is a power of 16 that is being borrowed, as illustrated in this example:

$$
\begin{array}{r}
F3D6_{16} \\
-\ 6B7_{16} \\
\hline
ED1F_{16}
\end{array}
\qquad
\begin{array}{r}
62422 \\
-\ 1719 \\
\hline
60703
\end{array}
$$

Table 1.4  Hexadecimal Addition

| + | 0 | 1 | 2 | 3 | 4 | 5 | 6 | 7 | 8 | 9 | A | B | C | D | E | F |
|---|---|---|---|---|---|---|---|---|---|---|---|---|---|---|---|---|
| 0 | 0 | 1 | 2 | 3 | 4 | 5 | 6 | 7 | 8 | 9 | A | B | C | D | E | F |
| 1 | 1 | 2 | 3 | 4 | 5 | 6 | 7 | 8 | 9 | A | B | C | D | E | F | 10 |
| 2 | 2 | 3 | 4 | 5 | 6 | 7 | 8 | 9 | A | B | C | D | E | F | 10 | 11 |
| 3 | 3 | 4 | 5 | 6 | 7 | 8 | 9 | A | B | C | D | E | F | 10 | 11 | 12 |
| 4 | 4 | 5 | 6 | 7 | 8 | 9 | A | B | C | D | E | F | 10 | 11 | 12 | 13 |
| 5 | 5 | 6 | 7 | 8 | 9 | A | B | C | D | E | F | 10 | 11 | 12 | 13 | 14 |
| 6 | 6 | 7 | 8 | 9 | A | B | C | D | E | F | 10 | 11 | 12 | 13 | 14 | 15 |
| 7 | 7 | 8 | 9 | A | B | C | D | E | F | 10 | 11 | 12 | 13 | 14 | 15 | 16 |
| 8 | 8 | 9 | A | B | C | D | E | F | 10 | 11 | 12 | 13 | 14 | 15 | 16 | 17 |
| 9 | 9 | A | B | C | D | E | F | 10 | 11 | 12 | 13 | 14 | 15 | 16 | 17 | 18 |
| A | A | B | C | D | E | F | 10 | 11 | 12 | 13 | 14 | 15 | 16 | 17 | 18 | 19 |
| B | B | C | D | E | F | 10 | 11 | 12 | 13 | 14 | 15 | 16 | 17 | 18 | 19 | 1A |
| C | C | D | E | F | 10 | 11 | 12 | 13 | 14 | 15 | 16 | 17 | 18 | 19 | 1A | 1B |
| D | D | E | F | 10 | 11 | 12 | 13 | 14 | 15 | 16 | 17 | 18 | 19 | 1A | 1B | 1C |
| E | E | F | 10 | 11 | 12 | 13 | 14 | 15 | 16 | 17 | 18 | 19 | 1A | 1B | 1C | 1D |
| F | F | 10 | 11 | 12 | 13 | 14 | 15 | 16 | 17 | 18 | 19 | 1A | 1B | 1C | 1D | 1E |

## 1.3 Number Systems

Starting on the right, the first subtraction involves borrowing. The rightmost two digits of the first number, D6, can be thought of as decimal (13) and (6) before the borrow, and as (12) and (22) after the borrow. Then subtract 22 − 7 = 15, which we write as F in the difference. The subtraction in the $16^2$ position also involves a borrow. We leave it to the reader to verify this borrow and the final difference.

For our purposes, multiplication in hexadecimal is not worth the effort to master. Addition and subtraction in hexadecimal is worth learning, even though it takes some practice to master.

In assembly-language programs, hexadecimal numbers are followed by the letter $h$ rather than a subscript. We will adopt this convention in later sections of this text. The example $3FA2_{16}$ that was used in this section will be written as 3FA2h in later sections.

### EXERCISES 1.3

1. How many values can be represented with
   (a) 18 bits?
   (b) 24 bits?
   (c) 3 hexadecimal digits?
   (d) 4 decimal digits?

2. What is the fewest number of bits that can be used to represent
   (a) The 7 days of the week?
   (b) The 12 months of the year?
   (c) The 26 lower case letters?
   (d) The 52 cards in a deck?
   (e) The 435 members of the House of Representatives?
   (f) The 100 members of the Senate?

3. Convert the following numbers from decimal to binary.
   (a) 47
   (b) 98
   (c) 63
   (d) 64
   (e) 65
   (f) 66
   (g) 255
   (h) 257

4. Convert the following numbers from binary to decimal.
   (a) 11111
   (b) 100000
   (c) 100001
   (d) 1110010
   (e) 100000000000
   (f) 100000000111

5. Convert the following numbers from binary to hexadecimal.
   (a) 110001111
   (b) 101000011010
   (c) 1101011111
   (d) 10011011011111

6. Convert the following numbers from hexadecimal to binary.
   (a) CB3
   (b) D030
   (c) FACE
   (d) 9038

7. Convert the numbers in Exercise 3 from decimal to hexadecimal.

8. Convert the numbers in Exercise 6 from hexadecimal to decimal.

9. Perform the indicated operations in binary.
   (a) 10010101 + 101101
   (b) 11100011 + 110101
   (c) 10010101 − 101101
   (d) 11100011 − 110101
   (e) 10010101 × 1101
   (f) 11100011 × 1011

10. Perform the indicated operations in hexadecimal.
    (a) 23B2 + 92A
    (b) BEAD + BED
    (c) 23B2 − 92A
    (d) BEAD − BED

## KEY POINTS

- An algorithm is a sequence of unambiguous, executable steps that solves a class of problems in a finite time.
- The design of an algorithm that is to be implemented as a computer program is influenced by the properties of computers and programming languages.
- Programs written in high-level languages must be translated into machine-dependent instructions in order to be executed.
- The statements in a program can be partitioned into declarations that control the translation and executable statements.
- The executable statements can be partitioned into those that manipulate data and those that control the instructions that manipulate data.
- All tasks specified in a program must ultimately be implemented using the operations provided by the processor. There may be several intermediate levels of abstraction in the implementation, such as procedures implemented as statements implemented as machine instructions.
- All data processed by a program must ultimately be represented in the data types supported by the processor. There may be several levels of abstraction in the representation, such as a queue of integers represented using an array of integers represented in binary.
- A high-level-language programmer treats memory as being partitioned into cells. Each cell has a name and can store one value, usually of one particular data type.
- Auxiliary storage is used for long-term storage of inactive programs and data files.
- The central processing unit can copy data between memory cells and perform arithmetic, relational, logical, and data conversion operations. It also controls the sequence in which instructions are executed.
- The input and output devices provide a means of communication between the computer and users.
- A source file is program text created by the programmer using a text editor.
- A compiler translates the source file into an object file containing machine instructions.
- A linkage editor combines the object files of all the routines needed to make an executable version of the program, called a run image.
- A loader copies a run image into memory and transfers control to it.
- All data and instructions in a computer are represented in binary. They are often written in octal or hexadecimal for convenience.
- The radix of a number system determines the number of digits in the system; it is the base used in the expansion of a number.
- The number of values that can be represented in $n$ digits with radix $r$ is $r^n$. Conversely, to represent $n$ different values in radix $r$ requires at least $\lceil \log_r(n) \rceil$ digits in radix $r$.
- Conversion of a number in another base to decimal can be performed by synthetic division; conversion of a decimal number to another base can be performed by repeated division.
- Arithmetic operations can be performed in any base.

# Introduction to Computer Organization  2

- ♦ A Calculator Analogy
- ♦ Computer System Hardware
- ♦ Instructions

As programmers working with a high-level language, we have an abstract model of the computer that executes our programs. We know that the statements in our programs are translated into sequences of machine instructions, but as yet we know very little about those instructions and about the computer that executes them. This chapter will explore the subject of computer hardware and instructions.

The chapter begins by examining a simple electronic calculator. Two models of the calculator are described and compared, and several important new terms are introduced. Although computers are significantly more complex, the calculator models provide a familiar starting point. The chapter then describes the major hardware components of computers in general and the organization of the 8086 in particular.

This leads to a consideration of instructions, including what they look like, how much processing each can perform, how they are represented, and how much variation exists in instructions from different machines. To emphasize this last point, instructions with various numbers of operands are considered. The different types of possible operands are also examined. The chapter closes with a discussion of how 8086 instructions are represented.

## 2.1 A CALCULATOR ANALOGY

Computers are machines that manipulate data. Programs specify which operations to perform, in what order, and on what data. Together the computer hardware and software form a very powerful, complex system. Before attempting to understand such a complex system, we will examine a similar but simpler one: a typical electronic calculator.

### The User View of a Calculator

Consider the assignment statement

A := B + C

implemented using a calculator to do the arithmetic, and paper and pencil for recording the values of A, B, and C. A casual user could list the steps needed to implement this process as

1. Enter the value of B.
2. Add the value of C.
3. Record the result.

Note that this description says nothing about how the calculator operates.

A more careful description identifies the various parts of the assignment statement and relates them to the major hardware components of the calculator and, by analogy, to a computer. The values of A, B, and C are recorded on paper so that the user can access them when desired. This corresponds to how data are stored in a computer's main memory. Arithmetic is performed by the calculator, under the control of the user. The central processor of a computer consists of two major units: One performs arithmetic and related operations; the other controls the computer system. The calculator is analogous to the arithmetic unit. The user, operating the calculator and using the paper, acts like the control unit.

Now let's examine the user's description of the processing in more detail. The first step requires the user to find the value of B on the paper and enter it into the calculator. The calculator will display this value. The value of B on the paper is not affected by this operation. The second step requires the user to press the addition (+) key, find the value of C on the paper, and enter it into the calculator. The calculator display is cleared when the user starts to enter the value of C and displays the value of C as it is entered. As before, the value of C on the paper is not affected. The third step requires the user to press the equal (=) key and copy the result shown in the display onto the paper. This value would replace the former value of A, which is erased before writing the new value.

An equivalent program for a computer would proceed as follows. First, it copies the value from the memory cell associated with the name B into a register in the arithmetic unit. A **register** is essentially a very fast memory, built directly into the processor. Registers are used for operands and intermediate results of operations. The memory cell is not changed when its contents are copied into the register. Next, the computer copies the value from the memory cell associated with the name C into another register. As before, the memory cell is unchanged. The computer then adds the values in the two registers, leaving the sum in one of them (or possibly in another register). The final step is to copy the result of the addition from the arithmetic unit into the memory cell associated with the name A.

There are two differences between the computer and calculator operations described here. The computer version has four steps: two copies, an addition, and another copy; the calculator version has only three steps. The computer version also refers to at least two registers, while the calculator has only one display. We could dismiss these differences as inherent in the devices, but that would be unsatisfactory. Actually, the discrepancy is in the level of description used: The calculator has been described from the user's perspective, and the computer from a hardware perspective. Let's look inside the calculator.

## The Hardware View of a Calculator

Consider a more detailed description of the calculator. The keyboard is the input device. The display is the output device. The calculator displays all input operations as they

## 2.1 A Calculator Analogy

proceed. Imagine that there is a register connected to the display and that whatever is stored in the register is also displayed. This register acts as a buffer for all input and output operations, and a second register in the calculator is used in performing arithmetic. To distinguish between them, we refer to them as the display register and the arithmetic register. In many calculators, the arithmetic register can handle more digits than the display register. There is a third, small register that keeps track of the pending operation. In more sophisticated calculators there are sets of pending operation and arithmetic registers, but these will not be discussed here.

In the calculator model shown in Figure 2.1 the digit, decimal point, and clear (c/e) keys are connected to the display register, while the arithmetic ($+$, $-$, $\times$, $\div$) and equal ($=$) keys are connected to the pending operation register. Let's examine the operation of this calculator in more detail, using the same assignment statement used earlier.

When the user presses the clear key, the display register is cleared and the display shows zero. A second press clears the arithmetic and pending operation registers. When the user enters the first number (the value of B in the assignment statement), the keystrokes are recorded in the display register and displayed. When the user presses the addition ($+$) key (or any arithmetic operation key), the value in the display register is copied into the arithmetic register and the keystroke is recorded in the pending operation register. When the user starts to enter the second number, the display register (and display) is cleared and the keystrokes are again recorded in the display register and display. Finally, the user presses the equal ($=$) key. The calculator performs the operation indicated by the pending operation register, using the arithmetic and display registers as operands. The result is left in the display register (and is displayed). The arithmetic and pending operation registers are cleared. These steps are illustrated in Figure 2.2, using 42 and 15 as the values of B and C.

This discussion does not consider all details about the calculator, such as how numbers are represented in the registers and how arithmetic is performed using those representations. Some of these issues are left to later chapters, and some to other texts.

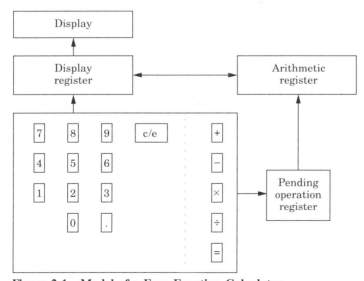

**Figure 2.1** Model of a Four-Function Calculator

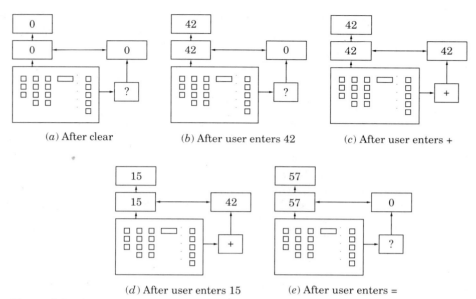

**Figure 2.2** Addition of Two Numbers Using Calculator Model

## Comparing the Hardware and User Views

The foregoing two discussions show the same calculator from two different viewpoints and two possible levels of description. The first takes the user's point of view and shows the implementation of the assignment statement as consisting of three steps. The second takes an internal point of view and shows more detail and a corresponding smaller unit of work as more individual operations are visible. The total amount of processing is the same in both; the amount of processing performed by a single step depends on the number of steps into which the total processing is partitioned.

Similarly, there are many possible levels of detail when discussing computer operation. You are already familiar with the high-level-language model of computing. The next lower level includes a description of the registers and machine instructions. This corresponds roughly to the second model of the calculator, and is the focus of this text.

Still lower levels of description might consider how machines—both calculators and computers—actually perform arithmetic operations. For example, they could discuss circuits such as half-adders and full-adders; at a more detailed level they could address the way in which adders and other circuits are built from gates, how gates are built from transistors, and ultimately how transistors and other components work. While there is certainly much to be learned from studying so many levels of detail, they should be pursued one level at a time.

## EXERCISES 2.1

1. Consider the assignment statement

    Y := (3 * X - 2) * X + 1

    Write the sequence of steps needed to implement this statement with a simple calculator.

2. Using a table, show the effect of each step in your answer to Exercise 1 on the display and registers of the calculator. Assume X = 5. The first two lines are given to help you get started.

| Step | Display | Buffer Register | Arithmetic Register | Pending Operation |
|---|---|---|---|---|
| Clear | 0 | 0 | 0 | ? |
| User enters 3 | 3 | 3 | 0 | ? |
| ⋮ | ⋮ | ⋮ | ⋮ | ⋮ |

3. Many calculators have a square root key. Pressing it computes the square root of the number that is displayed. Modify the description of the calculator of Figure 2.1 to include a square root key. Do not be concerned with how the calculator actually computes the root, but explain how pressing that key would affect the various registers.
4. Calculators more sophisticated than the one presented in this section allow expressions such as $7 + 10 \times 23$ to be entered from left to right but perform the multiplication before the addition. Such calculators compute 237 for this expression, while the one in this chapter computes 391. How could such a calculator be built? Draw a diagram like Figure 2.1 and describe the actions produced by each keystroke.
5. Some calculators require that expressions be entered in reverse notation. To compute $7 + 10 \times 23 = 237$, the user must press the sequence of keys: 7, enter, 10, enter, 23, enter, ×, and +. How could such a calculator be built? Draw a diagram like Figure 2.1 and describe the actions produced by each keystroke.

## 2.2 COMPUTER SYSTEM HARDWARE

This section will consider hardware in more detail. It is difficult to appreciate and understand computer organization before programming in assembly language; it is also difficult to program in assembly language before understanding something of computer organization. This section presents enough on computer hardware to enable you to start programming in the next chapter, but leaves much for later as well.

The major components of a computer system are the memory, the central processor, the input and output devices, and the storage devices. Figure 2.3 shows these components and other supporting hardware as they are used in a typical microcomputer.

### Memory

In the abstract model presented by high-level programming languages, memory is treated as a collection of named cells. Each cell is logically defined in terms of the data type associated with its name. The translator is responsible for mapping the abstract model onto the actual computer system, managing such things as the size of a cell, the operations allowed on it (as implied by the data type), and its actual location. This section will consider some characteristics of memory.

### Bits

Memory is constructed of many two-state devices. We represent the two states of a single device by the binary digits 0 and 1. As noted in Chapter 1, each 0 or 1 is called a bit.

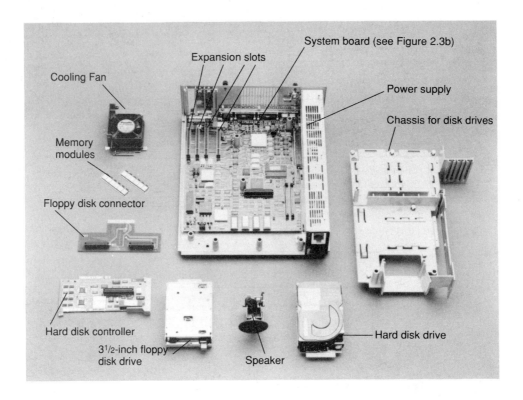

The bits in memory are logically grouped to form characters, numbers, other data types, and instructions. Bits are physically grouped to form bytes, words, segments, and other units. Figure 2.4 summarizes how bits are physically grouped in 8086 systems.

## Bytes

A **byte** is a group of bits used to represent a character. Typically, this is eight bits. Systems that use the 8086 use 8-bit bytes. Some other systems use only six or seven bits to represent a character; the term byte might not be used with these. A few other computers allow a byte to be defined as any contiguous group of bits.

## Words

A **word** is a group of bits that represents a number or an instruction. This definition is simplistic; many computers use a different number of bits for different types of numbers as well as for different types of instructions. Most transfers between memory and the central processing unit involve a word of data, but other quantities can also be transferred. Registers in the central processing unit are generally the same size as a word.

Word sizes vary from 8 bits to over 60 bits, with 16- and 32-bit words common. The 8086 uses 16-bit words, consisting of two consecutive bytes. It is possible to access each byte of a word separately, as well as to access the entire word as a unit.

## 2.2 Computer System Hardware

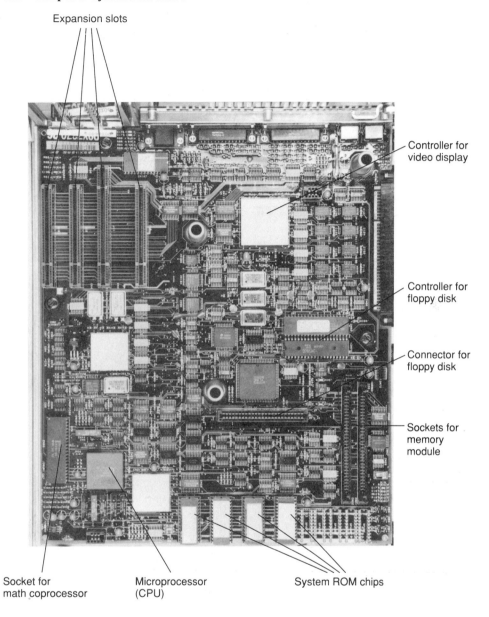

## Larger units

For data types that need more memory, two consecutive words (four bytes in the 8086) can be treated as a doubleword; four consecutive words (eight bytes in the 8086) can be treated as a quadword. The 8086 also has a 10-byte data type. For even larger data, such as character strings, longer sequences of bytes can be used.

There are three other units that are useful in discussing 8086 memory organization, although they are not usually associated with data types. A paragraph is 16 bytes, a page is 256 bytes, and a segment can be as large as 65,536 bytes. These units, especially segments, are discussed below.

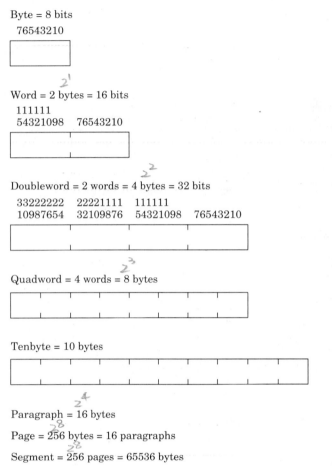

**Figure 2.4  Units of Physical Memory Organization in 8086 Systems**

## Capacity

Memory capacity is measured in multiples of $2^{10}$ (1024), $2^{20}$ (1,048,576), and $2^{30}$ (1,073,741,824) bytes. These units are abbreviated using the letters K, M, and G, from the prefixes kilo-, mega-, and giga-, respectively. Thus, 4M stands for four megabytes of memory.

Few computers today have memory capacities smaller than 64K, and many have potential memory capacity measured in megabytes. Virtual memory (discussed in Chapter 10) and storage capacities are often expressed in gigabytes.

## Addresses

Groups of bits are arranged sequentially in memory. To enable direct access, a number, called an **address,** is associated with each group. Addresses start at zero and increase for successive groups. The term *location* is also used to refer to a group of bits with a unique address. The address is used by the hardware when it accesses the location.

## 2.2 Computer System Hardware

Many computers, including those that use the 8086, associate addresses with each byte of memory. The first byte of memory has address zero, the next byte has address one, and so on up to the last byte of memory. Although some byte-addressed computers require that words begin on an even address, that doublewords begin on an address that is a multiple of four, and so on, the 8086 imposes no such restriction.

Many instructions include one or more addresses coded in binary. An important design trade-off is how small a unit of memory can be addressed directly, compared to how many bits are needed to specify an address. For example, to access 1024 ($2^{10}$) bytes of memory, where each byte has a unique address, requires 10 bits for the address. To access the same memory organized as 256 ($2^8$) words of four bytes each, where only words have addresses, requires only 8 bits for the address. The ability to address individual bytes in memory is often useful, but requires larger address fields in instructions. The trend is to use byte addressing in general-purpose computers. The memory in an 8086-based system is organized to provide access to up to four regions of memory while keeping the address field in the instructions manageable.

## Segments

Programs tend to access locations in memory that are close together. The instructions that a program executes are stored sequentially in memory; the data that those instructions access are also stored more or less together in another region of memory. As the instructions are brought from memory into the processor, the address of the next instruction varies very little from that of the current instruction; similarly, the addresses of the data vary little. Thus the addresses of the instructions tend to have the same most significant digits; the addresses of the data also tend to have the same most significant digits, although not necessarily the same as the instructions.

Memory in an 8086-based system is logically partitioned into **segments.** A program can access up to four different segments directly. In small programs, one segment is used for instructions, another for data. In larger programs, the instructions and data may occupy several segments each, although only one segment of instructions may be accessed at a time.

Each segment may be as large as 65,536 (64K) bytes of memory. To access a particular byte, a 16-bit quantity called an **offset** is used to specify the location of the desired byte within the segment (Figure 2.5). Usually, the segments of a program are adjacent to one another. There is nothing that prevents one segment from overlapping another; for example, if a small program uses only part of a segment for its instructions, its data segment could overlap the unused region of the instruction segment.

There is a maximum of one megabyte of memory in an 8086 system. (Chapter 10 will discuss how to get around this limit with expanded memory.) To access one megabyte of memory requires a 20-bit address. This 20-bit address is called the **physical address.** The 8086 computes a physical address from a 16-bit **segment selector** and a 16-bit offset. The offset has been discussed already; the segment selector, or simply selector, requires a little explanation.

Segments must start at a physical address that is a multiple of 16. Such an address, also called a **paragraph boundary,** is a 20-bit number that is a multiple of 16. As a multiple of 16, the four least significant bits are zeros. If we discard these four zeros and retain only the other 16 bits, we obtain a 16-bit segment selector.

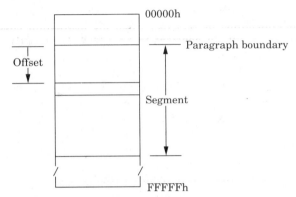

**Figure 2.5** Segmented Addressing

Let's consider this from another point of view. A physical address is computed by multiplying a segment selector by 16 and adding an offset. The multiplication is easily performed by appending four 0 bits to the selector. For example, given the selector 2B08h and the offset 30A4h, we find the physical address as follows:

$$\begin{array}{rl} & 2B080h \\ + & 30A4h \\ \hline & 2E124h \end{array} \qquad \begin{array}{rl} & \text{selector} \times 16 \\ + & \text{offset} \\ \hline & \text{physical address} \end{array}$$

Note that although physical addresses are unique, there are many combinations of segment selector and offset that yield the same physical address. For example, the physical address 2E124h can also be computed from segment selector 1F12h and offset F004h, as in Figure 2.6.

All memory accesses use selectors and offsets. Once the selector has been established, the offset can be specified directly or indirectly. With **direct addressing,** the offset of an operand in memory is coded as part of an instruction. The offset is determined during translation and is coded in the instruction as a constant. With **indirect addressing,** the

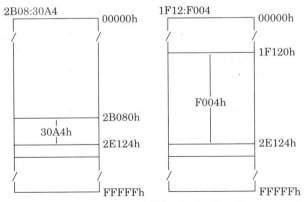

**Figure 2.6** Two Segment:Offset Pairs for the Same Physical Address

## 2.2 Computer System Hardware

offset of an operand in memory cannot be determined by the translator. Rather, it depends on values stored in other memory locations or registers when the instruction executes. The translator may include a displacement—a constant to be added during calculation of an indirect address—in the instruction generated. There are several forms of indirect addressing; the manner in which they are coded will be introduced later in this chapter. Relative addresses will be further examined in Chapter 5, indirect addresses in Chapter 7, and indexed addresses in Chapter 13.

## Central Processing Unit

The central processing unit (CPU) is the center of activity in a computer system. It consists of a control unit and an arithmetic logic unit. The **control unit** fetches instructions from memory, decodes them, and generates the control signals that cause other components to perform the operations. It also supervises the transfer of data within the system. The **arithmetic logic unit** performs arithmetical, relational, and logical operations. The 8086 contains both a control unit and an arithmetic logic unit. The 8087 is a coprocessor that performs operations on floating-point data. The 8086 is discussed in this chapter and throughout the text; the 8087 is discussed in detail in Chapter 17.

The most visible components of a processor are its registers. Registers are very fast memory cells used for performing operations on data and storing intermediate results. The 8086 registers shown in Figure 2.7 can be grouped into five sets. **General registers** provide storage for operands and results of arithmetic and logical operations. **Segment registers** provide the selectors for up to four of the segments that the program is using. **Pointer** and **index registers** are used in forming indirect addresses. The **instruction pointer (IP)** provides the offset of the next instruction. Finally, the **flags register** records status information and controls some aspects of the processor's operation.

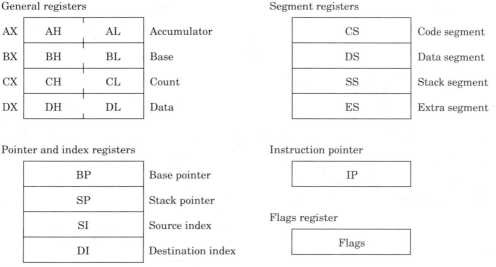

**Figure 2.7  8086 Registers**

## General registers

The 8086 has four 16-bit general registers, named AX, BX, CX, and DX. Each of these can also be used as two 8-bit general registers. As an 8-bit register, the high (more significant) byte of the AX register is named AH; the low (less significant) byte is named AL. This convention also applies to the other registers, giving BH, BL, CH, CL, DH, and DL.

With few restrictions, the general registers can be used for operands or results of addition and subtraction operations, or for moving data between memory locations. Each register also has specific functions that make it unique.

The "A" in AX (and AL) refers to that register's use as an accumulator: It is intended for use in integer arithmetic operations. Arithmetic instructions that use AX or AL as the register operand are more efficient and compact. The AX (or AL) register must be used with multiplication, division, and certain input and output operations.

The "B" in BX refers to that register's use as a base register in some forms of indirect addressing. The "C" in CX (and CL) refers to that register's use as a counter in certain iterative and conditional instructions. The "D" in DX refers to the register's use as a data storage register. DX is also used in some multiplication, division, and input and output operations.

## Segment registers

The 8086 has four segment registers, named CS, DS, SS, and ES. The CS register contains the selector for the current **code segment.** The code segment contains the instructions. The DS register contains the selector for the current **data segment.** The data segment contains data used by the program. The SS register contains the selector for the **stack segment.** Although a stack segment will be declared in the programs in this text, no explicit use will be made of it until Chapter 7, when the topic of subprograms is introduced. The ES register contains the selector of the extra segment. The extra segment can be a second data segment or an alias for the first data segment. The ES register is also used with string instructions.

## Pointer and index registers

The 8086 includes two pointer registers, BP and SP. Although they can be used for other purposes, convention dictates that they be used only with the stack. These two registers are discussed further in Chapter 7.

The 8086 has two index registers, SI and DI. They are used with indexed addressing, and together with the DS and ES registers in processing strings. The index registers are discussed further in Chapter 13.

## Instruction pointer

The instruction pointer, IP, contains a 16-bit offset that is combined with the segment selector in the CS register to form the physical address of the next instruction. The IP register is used by the processor to control the sequence in which instructions are executed.

## 2.2 Computer System Hardware

Instructions are stored in memory. During execution, each instruction is copied into the control unit one at a time. The control unit decodes the instruction to determine which signals to generate. The processing indicated by the instruction is performed, either by the control unit, the arithmetic logic unit as directed by the control unit, or some input or output device. The next instruction is then copied into the control unit, and the cycle repeats.

Before executing a program, the CS register is loaded with the selector of the code segment, and the IP register is loaded with the offset of the first instruction. To execute the program, the control unit repeats the following steps indefinitely:

Fetch      Copy the instruction from the memory location specified by the instruction pointer into the control unit;

Increment  Add the size of the instruction just fetched (in bytes) to the instruction pointer;

Execute    Decode the instruction and perform the specified processing.

This sequence is called the **fetch-execute cycle.**

The instruction may have to be at least partially decoded to determine its length before the increment step can be performed. Alternatively, the increment step may be repeated as each piece of a long instruction is brought into the processor. In the latter case, the IP register points to the next piece of the instruction at each stage. The net effect of the increment step is to adjust the instruction pointer so that it contains the offset of the next instruction during execution of the instruction that was just fetched.

Some instructions change the IP register as part of their operation. This subject will be discussed further in Chapter 5.

## Flags register

The last register to be considered is the flags register. It is a collection of information about the active program, the processor state, and the result of recently executed instructions. Figure 2.8 shows the individual fields of the flags register.

| F | E | D | C | B | A | 9 | 8 | 7 | 6 | 5 | 4 | 3 | 2 | 1 | 0 |
|---|---|---|---|---|---|---|---|---|---|---|---|---|---|---|---|
|   | NT | IOP | | OF | DF | IF | TF | SF | ZF |   | AF |   | PF |   | CF |

| Bit | | Meaning |
|---|---|---|
| F | | (not used) |
| E | NT | Nested task (286, 386 only) |
| CD | IOP | I/O protection level (286, 386 only) |
| B | OF | Overflow flag |
| A | DF | Direction flag |
| 9 | IF | Interrupt enable flag |
| 8 | TF | Trap flag |
| 7 | SF | Sign flag |
| 6 | ZF | Zero flag |
| 5 | | (not used) |
| 4 | AF | Auxiliary carry flag |
| 3 | | (not used) |
| 2 | PF | Parity flag |
| 1 | | (not used) |
| 0 | CF | Carry flag |

**Figure 2.8  Flags Register**

Three of the flags are control flags: The programmer can set (to 1) or clear (to 0) these flags in order to control the operation of the processor. They are the following:

- DF controls direction of string operations; see Chapter 15.
- IF controls whether interrupts will be recognized or ignored; see discussion of interrupts below.
- TF controls whether an interrupt is generated after each instruction; see discussion of interrupts below.

The other six flags record information about the result of an operation. Not all instructions affect all flags, and not all flags are always meaningful. How the flags may be affected is presented with each instruction throughout this text. Briefly, the status flags are the following:

- OF set if a result is too large or too small. *(overflow)*
- SF set if the sign of a result is negative. *(sign)*
- ZF set if a result is 0. *(zero)*
- AF set if an operation generates a carry out of the four least significant bits of a result.
- PF set if the low order byte of a result has an even number of one bits.
- CF set if an operation generates a carry out of a result. *(carry)*

An instruction might clear (to 0), set (to 1), affect (make 0 or 1 depending on result), ignore, or destroy any of the flags.

## Peripherals

Devices in a computer system other than memory and the processor are called **peripherals**. This section will examine some common input, output, and storage devices. It will consider how they are seen by a high-level-language programmer and a little of how they actually operate.

## Keyboard

The typical computer system that uses the 8086 processor has a keyboard with about 88 or about 101 keys—there are many variations. While keyboard input seems simple enough, two particular aspects of it will be discussed here.

First, consider the Pascal program statement

```
Read (Code);
```

where `Code` is a `Char` variable. Any character typed at the keyboard satisfies this `Read` statement—whatever key the user taps, the internal representation of that character is stored in `Code`. This is simple, except that the keyboard may not generate the internal character codes directly.

In PC systems, the keyboard generates a code, called a **scan code**, when a key is pressed; it generates a different code when the key is released. The scan codes are processed by the system hardware and software, which ultimately place ASCII or extended codes in the input buffer. An application program can "read" the keyboard by removing ASCII or extended codes from the buffer.

## 2.2 Computer System Hardware

For example, when the user taps the ENTER key, two codes are generated (one when it is pressed, another when it is released). When the second code is received, the system puts the ASCII CR character in the input buffer. The application program can then "read" the CR character. Similarly, when the user holds down one of the CTRL keys, taps ENTER, and releases the CTRL key, a more complex sequence of operations occurs. First, when the CTRL key is pressed, a scan code is generated; when the system receives this code, it records in a flag that the CTRL key is being held down. Then, when the second of the two codes for the ENTER key is received, the system examines the flag and puts the ASCII LF character into the input buffer. When the CTRL key is released and the code for this is received, the system clears the flag.

Second, consider the statement

```
Read (Factor)
```

where `Factor` is a `Real` variable. Depending on the language implementation used, the exact sequence of characters that satisfy this read varies. Even after the conversion of the scan codes to characters, the Read statement is not finished with the input. The characters are not stored, but are used to generate the internal representation of a real number. Unlike the conversion of scan codes, which is performed by the system, conversion of characters to reals must be performed by applications (often using libraries supplied with language products). This is quite involved. In some programs, the conversions between characters and numbers account for a significant fraction of the total resources used by the program.

### Printer

To print a character string, the program must send the ASCII codes for the characters in the string to the printer. For every code the printer receives, it performs some action. For many codes, the printer generates a character on the paper and advances to the next position. For some codes, such as LF (0Ah) or BS (08h), the printer changes positions by advancing to a new line or moving back one character.

Some actions, such as selecting a special font or enhancement, require sending a sequence of several codes to the printer. The first of these codes is usually the ESC (1Bh) character. As the codes that control printer features are not standardized, each application that uses special printer features must be able to send different codes depending on the printer in use. Usually the application keeps track of enhancements in some generic fashion, then uses a program called a driver to convert the generic codes to the particular codes for the selected printer as it sends the document to the printer.

### Video display

The video display is quite different from the printer. In standard text mode—the only mode we consider here—the display consists of 25 lines of 80 characters. This is 2000 characters. There is a block of 2000 words of memory associated with the display, one word for each position on the display. One byte of the word contains the code for the character to be displayed; the other byte specifies properties such as intensity, inverse video, and so on.

There are system routines for managing the video display. The high-level-language program does not write directly to the video display, but calls the appropriate system routine with the text and attributes to display. The video routines interpret the characters and attributes passed to them and update the display hardware accordingly. Some applications bypass the system video routines and manipulate the video display directly, in order to improve performance.

## Disk drives

Magnetic disks are **direct access** devices, which means that data stored on them can be accessed in any order. In contrast, data stored on a sequential medium can be accessed only in the order in which it is written.

Disk drives (Figure 2.9) consist of one or more circular platters that rotate at a fixed speed. The flat surfaces of the platter are coated with a magnetic medium. For each surface, a read/write head, much like the recording and playback head in a cassette deck, is positioned on a movable arm called an access arm. As a platter rotates with the read/write head in a fixed position, the portion of the surface that can be read or written is called a circular **track**. If the access arm is moved, the read/write head also moves and a different circular track can be read or written.

In a disk drive with more than one platter, the tracks on all platters that line up with each other are called a **cylinder**. There is a separate recording and playback head for each surface. The access arms for all heads are physically connected to each other, so that all tracks in a cylinder can be accessed without moving any heads. Large files that require more than one track are best recorded on the tracks of one cylinder. Each track on a disk is further divided into **sectors** or blocks (Figure 2.10). Disks used with microcomputers often have sectors that store 512 bytes.

Disk drives are sufficiently complex that the control unit does not oversee every operation and check every signal. Instead, there is a separate controller, with which the central processor and low-level software communicate, that manages the details specific to the drive. To access a particular sector on a disk, the track and sector numbers, and possibly the surface number as well, are sent to the disk controller. The controller then moves the head(s) to the requested track, waits for the disk to rotate until the desired sector passes

**Figure 2.9 A Hard Disk Drive**

## 2.2 Computer System Hardware

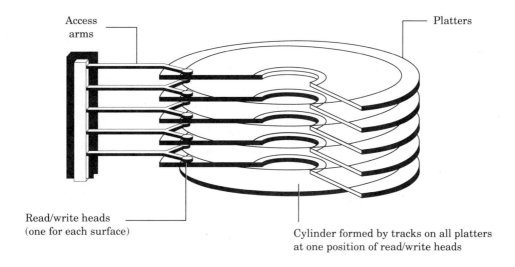

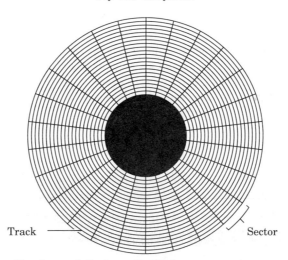

**Figure 2.10** Cylinders, Tracks, and Sectors of a Disk

under the head, and then reads or writes the data on that sector. To access another sector on the same track, the heads do not have to be moved, but the disk must rotate to the beginning of the new sector.

Each access transfers a whole number of sectors of data between the disk and memory. The data transferred is called a **physical record.** Often a program expects to read or write some other quantity of data, based on the logical organization of the data, called a **logical record.** For example, an inventory control program might define a logical record containing a stock number, a description, a supplier number, the quantity on hand, and perhaps a few other data; together, these define a logical record that might use only 60 bytes.

There is potential mismatch in the sizes of logical and physical records. If a logical record requested by a program happens to be the same size as a sector, no other processing of the physical record is required. However, when the logical record is of a different size than a physical record, the operating system or another utility program must read physical records into a buffer and extract logical records from the buffer for the program to read, or accept logical records written by the program and package them into physical records that are written to the disk. In addition to managing the mismatch between record sizes, the operating system must update the disk directory as files are added, modified, and deleted.

## The Bus

The components of a computer system must communicate with each other and with the outside world. Although it might be possible to connect each component to the central processing unit separately, as a practical matter this would require too many physical connections. To keep the number of connections manageable, the processor is connected to memory and all peripherals using a **bus.** A bus is nothing more than a bunch of wires—and electrical paths on the printed circuit board—to which everything in the system is connected. The bus contains three major parts: the data bus, the address bus, and the control lines. Figure 2.11 shows a simplified diagram of a computer system, including the three busses.

The address bus of an 8086 system is 20 bits wide; it contains one wire for each bit of a physical address. Addresses 0 through 640K (00000h through AFFFFh) refer to memory; addresses from 640K through 1M (B0000h through FFFFFh) refer to input and output devices and system ROM (read-only memory, in which the lowest-level system software is stored). The processor can write to the address bus: To access a device or a memory location, the processor first writes the address of the device or memory location to the address bus. All devices monitor the address bus and ignore references to other devices. The data bus of an 8086 system is 16 bits wide; it contains one wire for each bit of a word of data or instruction. Most devices can read from and write to the data bus. The control lines carry control signals between the processor and the other devices on the bus.

For the processor to receive a word of data from a device or memory location, it writes the address of the device or location on the address bus and sends a control signal to the device. When the device senses its address on the address bus and receives the control signal, it writes the requested data on the data bus. The processor then reads the data bus to get the value.

## 2.2 Computer System Hardware

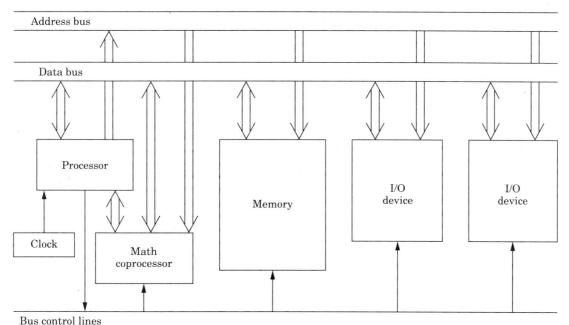

**Figure 2.11 The Bus**

For the processor to send a word of data to a device or memory location, it writes the address of the device or location on the address bus and the data to be sent on the data bus, and then sends a control signal to the device. When the device senses its address on the address bus and receives the control signal, it reads the data from the data bus.

The clock keeps the system synchronized. For purposes of simplicity, Figure 2.11 shows the clock connected only to the processor; in reality, however, clock signals are also available to the other devices. Input and output devices, and their operation, will be examined in more detail in Chapter 9.

### Interrupts

An **interrupt** is a signal to the processor that an event needing immediate attention has occurred. The processor responds by suspending the program that is executing and transferring control to a special program that services the interrupt. When the interrupt service routine terminates, control is returned to the interrupted program.

An **external interrupt** is initiated outside the CPU. Most external interrupts are generated by input, output, and storage devices. Other external interrupts detect hardware faults such as failure of power supplies, or operator-initiated shutdown of the system.

An **internal interrupt** is initiated within the CPU as the result of an error, or by an instruction intended to generate an interrupt. Interrupts that are caused by errors are also called **traps.** Among the errors that can generate interrupts are overflow, attempted division by 0, an invalid operation, and so on. Instructions that produce an interrupt can be used to invoke the services of the operating system or hardware. Several of these instructions will be used in programs in the text.

Certain error conditions generate interrupts that are intended to terminate the interrupted program. In all other cases, except for a slight delay, the processing of an interrupt should have no effect on the program that is executing when the interrupt occurs. Most computers do not interrupt an instruction once it begins execution; instead, the control unit checks for an interrupt signal before fetching each instruction. If there is an interrupt, the control unit saves the instruction pointer and flags, determines which interrupt service routine is needed, and invokes that routine.

Interrupt service routines are much like subprograms, except that they have special calling and return requirements. The values in any registers that the service routine needs to use are first saved. When the service routine is finished, it restores the saved values to the registers and returns control to the interrupted program by restoring the saved flags and the instruction pointer. Interrupts will be discussed in depth in Chapter 9.

## Survey of the 8086 Family

The Intel 8086 was one of the first 16-bit microprocessors available. Since its introduction in 1978, the 8086 and its siblings and descendants have been the dominant microprocessor architecture.

The 8086 has 16-bit registers and a 16-bit data bus. Its address bus is 20 bits wide, allowing a 1M address space. A year after the 8086 was introduced, Intel introduced the 8088. The 8088 is essentially an 8086 modified to use an 8-bit data bus. The 8088 fetches words of data as two separate fetches of one byte each. The instruction set of the 8088 is the same as that of the 8086; the multiple fetches required for word operands are handled transparently by the hardware. IBM used the 8088 in their PC and PC/XT systems.

In 1983 Intel introduced the 80186 and 80188 processors. These are enhanced versions of the 8086 and 8088.

Also in 1983, Intel introduced the 80286. The 80286 has the same register set as the 8086 and is often used as a fast 8086. The 80286 also has additional system registers for implementing a 24-bit protected addressing mode. Its address bus is 24 bits wide, allowing access (in protected mode) to 16M of memory. In protected mode, it provides support for virtual memory and multitasking. IBM used the 80286 for their PC/AT (Advanced Technology) systems.

More recently, Intel introduced the 80386 and 80486 processors. These processors have 32-bit registers, a 32-bit data bus, and a 32-bit address bus. The 80386 and 80486 support page-mode virtual memory, a more sophisticated protection scheme than that provided by the 80286, and a huge 4G address space.

Throughout the development of the 8086 and newer processors, clock speeds have increased. The first 8088 processors used by IBM had a clock speed of 4.7 MHz. Today, 80386 and 80486 processors running with clock speeds of 33 MHz and faster are available.

Along with the 8086 processors, Intel makes coprocessors for floating-point operations. These are the 8087 (for 8086 computers), the 80287 (for 80286 computers), and the 80387 (for 80386 computers). The 80486 has the capabilities of a floating-point math processor built in. Each coprocessor is designed for a particular bus structure and clock speed.

There are also SX versions of the 80386 and 80486 processors. The 80386 SX is essentially an 80386 that uses a 16-bit data bus; it typically runs at slower clock speeds as well. The 80486 SX is essentially an 80486 without the floating-point math processor.

## 2.2 Computer System Hardware

### EXERCISES 2.2

1. What is the difference between a cell and a word?
2. The memory of an 8086 computer is addressed by bytes. What do you think the "address of a cell" is?
3. How many bits are there in a byte? In a word?
4. How many bytes are there in a word? In a paragraph?
5. How large can a segment be?
6. Compute the 20-bit physical address specified by the following selectors and offsets:
   (a) selector: 3F20h  
       offset: 0037h
   (b) selector: 0020h  
       offset: FE00h
   (c) selector: 6442h  
       offset: 3202h
   (d) selector: 35ADh  
       offset: 2977h
7. Determine the offset needed to access the physical address specified with the selector given:
   (a) address: 20216h  
       selector: 2000h
   (b) address: 426BAh  
       selector: 423Ah
   (c) address: 3B42Ah  
       selector: 3A96h
   (d) address: 7CCCCh  
       selector: 7BBBh
8. Determine the offset needed to access physical address 34A26h with each of the following segment selectors:
   (a) 34A2h
   (b) 3400h
   (c) 30A2h
   (d) 24A3h
9. How many different combinations of segment selectors and offsets can specify the same physical address?
10. The *canonic frame number* is the largest segment selector that can be used to specify a particular physical address. Find the canonic frame number for the following addresses:
    (a) 23456h
    (b) 4DFA0h
    (c) FFFFFh
    (d) 00321h
11. For the canonic frame numbers in Exercise 10, give the offset needed to specify the given physical address.
12. Name the general registers of the 8086 and give their general uses.
13. Name the segment registers of the 8086 and describe the contents of the related segments.
14. Name the pointer and index registers of the 8086.
15. What would happen if an instruction modified the instruction pointer by writing a new offset to it?
16. What would happen if an instruction added some small constant—such as 1 or 2—to the instruction pointer (in addition to the increment performed as part of the fetch-execute cycle)?
17. What would happen if a one-byte instruction subtracted 1 from the instruction pointer after the increment performed as part of the fetch-execute cycle?
18. Which flag bits represent state information? Which flag bits represent control information?
19. What peripherals are part of the computer system that you will use with this text?
20. What is a bus? What advantage does it provide over directly connecting every device to the processor? What disadvantages? Can you think of an analogy from everyday life that describes how a bus works?
21. What is an interrupt? Can you think of an analogy from everyday life that illustrates the processing performed when an interrupt occurs?

## 2.3 INSTRUCTIONS

The first part of this chapter showed how the statement

A := B + C

could be implemented using a simple calculator. Two views of the calculator's operation were considered, each with a different number of steps and a different amount of processing performed in each step. Similarly, the instructions of different computers perform different amounts of processing. There are computers in which the example assignment statement is implemented with a single instruction. There are other computers in which the example assignment statement requires three instructions very similar to the three steps performed by the calculator user. There are still other computers in which the example assignment statement requires four instructions very similar to the four steps outlined earlier.

Every instruction sequence that implements the same assignment statement performs the same processes. How the total task is partitioned into individual instructions is one of the things that differentiate computer systems. This section explores several possible instruction sets, considers the parts of an instruction in general, and examines the format of 8086 instructions in some detail.

### Number of Operands

**Operands** specify the values an instruction is to operate on, and where the result is to be stored. An addition instruction might use three operands, for example, where two of the operands provide values to be added together and the third operand specifies where the sum is to be stored. One such instruction could implement the simple assignment statement that was used in the calculator example.

Instruction sets are sometimes classified by the number of operands used in arithmetic instructions. For example, instructions like the one just mentioned are called three-operand instructions. There are also two-operand, one-operand, and zero-operand instruction sets. However, many computers, including the 8086, deviate from this scheme by using instructions with different numbers of operands.

The same assignment statement used for the calculator example will be used again to illustrate several different instruction sets. It is repeated here for reference:

A := B + C  (2.1)

A more complicated assignment statement will also be used:

Y := (X + D) * (N + 1)  (2.2)

### Three-operand instructions

In instructions that have three operands, one of the operands specifies the destination as an address where the result is to be saved. The other two operands specify the sources, either as addresses of memory locations or constants.

The instruction for adding two numbers has the form

ADD    *destination, source1, source2*

The word ADD specifies the operation. Instructions for performing other arithmetic operations are similar.

## 2.3 Instructions

Assignment Statement 2.1 is implemented as one instruction:

ADD      A, B, C

Assignment Statement 2.2 requires that intermediate results be stored in memory. We use the names T1, T2, and so on for intermediate results. A sequence of three instructions that implement Statement 2.2 is

ADD      T1, X, D
ADD      T2, N, 1
MUL      Y, T1, T2

Figure 2.12 illustrates the execution of these three instructions, assuming that X, D, and N have initial values 13, 3, and 5, respectively. Figure 2.12a shows the initial state of the memory. The first instruction,

ADD      T1, X, D

adds the values of X and D together and saves the sum in T1 (Figure 2.12b). Note that T1 now contains 16. The second instruction adds 1 to N and saves the result in T2. T2 now contains 6 (Figure 2.12c). The last instruction multiplies together the two intermediate

Main memory

| | |
|---|---|
| D | 3 |
| N | 5 |
| X | 13 |
| Y | ? |
| T1 | ? |
| T2 | ? |

(a) Before execution

Main memory

| | |
|---|---|
| D | 3 |
| N | 5 |
| X | 13 |
| Y | ? |
| T1 | 16 |
| T2 | ? |

(b) After ADD T1, X, D

Main memory

| | |
|---|---|
| D | 3 |
| N | 5 |
| X | 13 |
| Y | ? |
| T1 | 16 |
| T2 | 6 |

(c) After ADD T2, N, 1

Main memory

| | |
|---|---|
| D | 3 |
| N | 5 |
| X | 13 |
| Y | 96 |
| T1 | 16 |
| T2 | 6 |

(d) After MUL Y, T1, T2

**Figure 2.12** Execution of Three-Operand Instructions for Statement 2.2

results, T1 and T2, and saves the product in Y. (Refer to Figure 2.12d, where Y contains the product 96.)

## Two-operand instructions

Next we consider instructions that have two operands. Both operands specify sources. The first operand also specifies the destination address where the result is to be saved. The first operand must be an address in memory, but the second may be an address or a constant.

The instruction for adding two numbers has the form

ADD     *destination, source*

Instructions for performing other arithmetic operations are similar.

To add two numbers without replacing either of them by the sum, we need to copy one of them to another location and use the copy as the first operand of the ADD instruction. The copy operation is performed by a MOV (move) instruction, which has the form

MOV     *destination, source*

It copies the value of the source operand to the destination. The former value of the destination operand is lost.

Assignment Statement 2.1 is implemented by the two instructions

```
MOV     A, B
ADD     A, C
```

The final destination, A, is used as the destination in the MOV instruction. Since the original value of A will be lost by the assignment statement and it is not needed to evaluate the expression, we can use A this way.

Assignment Statement 2.2 is implemented by the sequence of instructions

```
MOV     T1, X
ADD     T1, D
MOV     Y, N
ADD     Y, 1
MUL     Y, T1
```

Figure 2.13 illustrates execution of these instructions, with the same values as before. Figure 2.13a shows the initial state of the memory. The first MOV instruction copies the value of X to T1, shown in Figure 2.13b. The first ADD instruction adds the value of D to T1, shown in Figure 2.13c. The next pair of MOV and ADD instructions do the same operations using N, 1, and Y. See Figures 2.13d and 2.13e. The MUL instruction multiplies the value of Y by T1, leaving the product in Y (Figure 2.13f).

In the examples of three-operand and two-operand instructions, all operands have been specified either in memory or as constants. Some computers that use these instruction forms have several general-purpose registers available for use with operands. Using registers for intermediate results is more efficient than using memory. A few computers, including the 8086, allow only one operand to be in memory; all others must be in registers.

## One-operand instructions

Some computers have only one general-purpose register, usually called an accumulator. It is implied as one of the source operands and the destination operand in many instructions. The other source operand is specified in the instruction as a location in memory.

## 2.3 Instructions

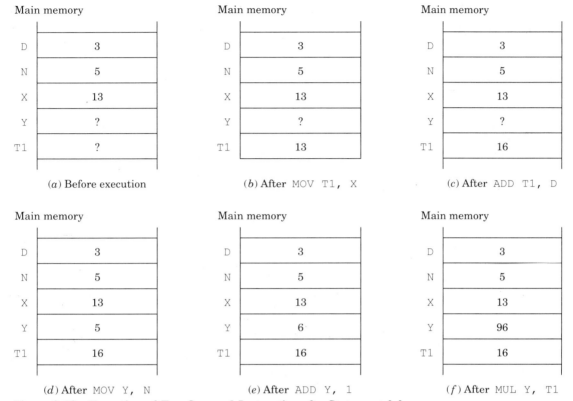

**Figure 2.13** Execution of Two-Operand Instructions for Statement 2.2

The instruction for performing addition has the form

ADD    *source*

Instructions for performing other arithmetic operations are similar.

There are also instructions for copying values between the accumulator and memory. One of these is

LDA    *source*

where LDA stands for LoaD Accumulator. This instruction copies a value from memory into the accumulator. The other is

STA    *destination*

where STA stands for STore Accumulator. It copies the value from the accumulator into memory.

Assignment Statement 2.1 is implemented as three instructions

LDA    B
ADD    C
STA    A

Compare these to the first description of the calculator in Section 2.1.

**46** Chapter 2 Introduction to Computer Organization

Assignment Statement 2.2 is implemented by the instruction sequence

```
LDA  X
ADD  D
STA  T1
LDA  N
ADD  1
MUL  T1
STA  Y
```

Since both additions must use the accumulator, the result of the first ADD must be saved temporarily in T1.

Figure 2.14 shows the memory used for the data and the accumulator (ACC) during execution of these instructions, with the same values as before. Initially, as in Figure

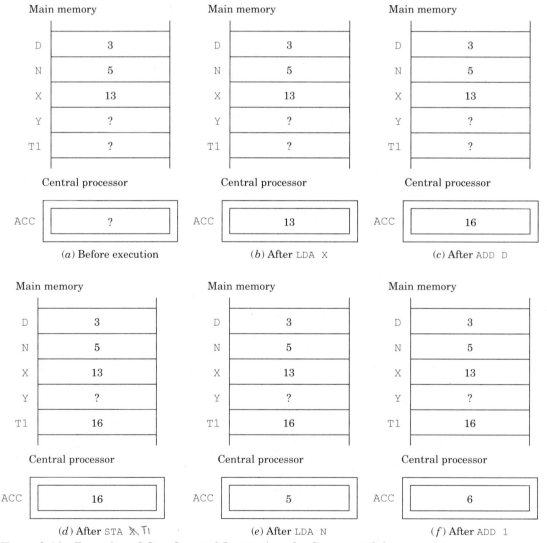

**Figure 2.14** Execution of One-Operand Instructions for Statement 2.2

### 2.3 Instructions

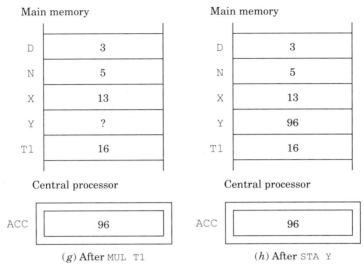

(g) After MUL T1

(h) After STA Y

**Figure 2.14** *(continued)*

2.14a, the values in Y, T1, and ACC are unknown. The first LDA instruction copies the value of X into ACC (Figure 2.14b). The first ADD instruction adds the value of D to ACC, then the STA instruction saves the sum in T1 (Figures 2.14c and 2.14d). The next two instructions add the values of N and 1, leaving the sum in ACC (Figures 2.14e and 2.14f). The next instruction multiplies the value in ACC by the value saved in T1 (Figure 2.14g). The last instruction copies the product from ACC to Y (Figure 2.14h).

## Zero-operand instructions

Some computers have arithmetic instructions in which all operands are implied. These zero-operand instructions use a stack. A **stack** is a list structure in which all insertions and deletions occur at one end; the elements on a stack may be removed only in the reverse of the order in which they were entered. The process of inserting an item is called pushing; removing an item is called popping.

Computers that use zero-operand instructions for arithmetic operations also use one-operand PUSH and POP instructions to copy values between memory and the stack. The instruction

PUSH    *source*

pushes the value of the memory operand onto the top of the stack. The instruction

POP    *destination*

pops the value from the top of the stack and copies it into the memory operand.

The 8087 math coprocessor can be programmed as a zero-operand computer, although the instructions are not the same as those presented here. The 8087 will be discussed in detail in Chapter 17.

The arithmetic instructions pop source operands from the top of the stack, perform the operation, and push the result back onto the stack. For example, the instruction

ADD

pops the top two values off the stack, adds them, and pushes the sum back onto the stack. The stack is one element smaller as a result.

Assignment Statement 2.1 is implemented as the sequence

```
PUSH    B
PUSH    C
ADD
POP     A
```

Assignment Statement 2.2 is implemented as the sequence

```
PUSH    X
PUSH    D
ADD
PUSH    N
PUSH    1
ADD
MUL
POP     Y
```

Figure 2.15 shows the region of memory used for the data and the stack during execution of the above sequence, with the same values as before. The stack is assumed to be empty initially; when the instruction sequence above finishes, the stack will again be empty. Refer to Figure 2.15a for the initial values.

The first two instructions are PUSH instructions, which push the values of X and D onto the stack. See Figures 2.15b and 2.15c. The first ADD instruction pops the top two values off the stack, adds them, and pushes the sum back onto the stack. In Figure 2.15d the value at the top of the stack is 16, the sum of 3 and 13. Two more PUSH instructions push the values of N and 1 onto the stack (Figures 2.15e and 2.15f). Another ADD instruction adds these values together, pushing the sum back onto the stack (Figure 2.15g). The MUL instruction then pops the top two values off the stack, multiplies them, and pushes the product back onto the stack (Figure 2.15h). Finally, the POP instruction pops the value from the top of the stack and saves it in Y (Figure 2.15i).

## Operand Types

The operand(s) of an instruction can be

- in a register
- in memory
- implied by the instruction
- coded as part of the instruction

Some operands in memory are specified using a data structure that includes the starting location and length of the operand.

### Operands in registers

Operands in registers are typically the same length as the register, which is also the same length as a word of memory. In some cases, operands might be only half as long as a

## 2.3 Instructions

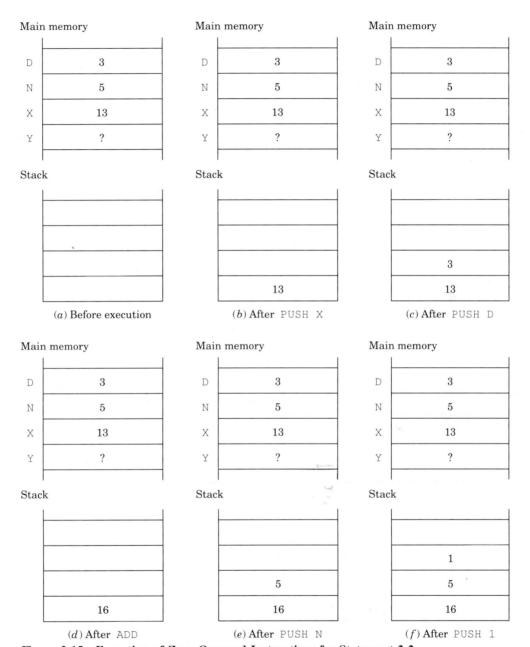

**Figure 2.15** Execution of Zero-Operand Instructions for Statement 2.2

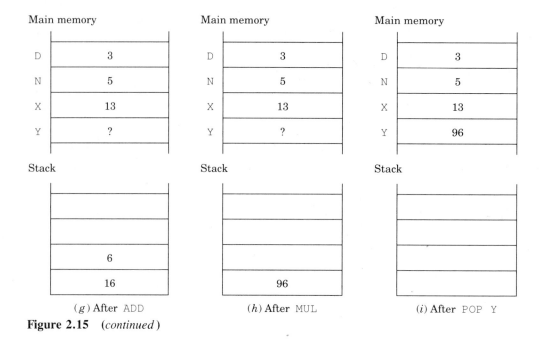

**Figure 2.15** (*continued*)

word and use only half of a register. In other cases, operands might be two words long and use a pair of registers.

An important advantage of using registers for operands is that memory need not be accessed to fetch or store the operand. Accessing a register within the processor is much faster than accessing memory.

The number of registers available is limited because they are relatively expensive to include in the processor. There is a design trade-off between increasing the number of registers to improve performance and keeping the cost of the hardware reasonable.

When using registers for operands, the programmer or the compiler must keep track of which registers are available and which have an intermediate result that will be needed again. A number of strategies for allocating and reclaiming registers and for evaluating expressions have been explored, attempting to optimize their use. A full study of register allocation is beyond the scope of this section.

## Operands in memory

Since all data is stored in memory, it must be possible to use memory directly for operands. Data of the standard types will typically occupy one byte, word, or doubleword, and should be useful as operands.

If the user is willing to write the necessary sequences of instructions to process data of unusual length, operands in memory can be of any length up to the maximum size of a memory segment. It is normally not worth the trouble to define 13-bit integers when using a machine that provides 16-bit integers—the memory saved does not justify the complexity of the programs. However, on the same machine, eleven 16-bit words might be used to implement 176-bit integers. This would be useful if an application required the equivalent of 50-digit integers. Character strings are another example of operands that can have arbitrary lengths.

Operands in memory allow the data in any location or group of locations to be manipulated. During program execution, the addresses of the operands must be determined and the values fetched or stored, all of which take time. Also, coding a memory address as part of an instruction makes the instruction longer than coding a register operand in the instruction would do.

## Implied operands

Some operands are small constant values that can be generated by the processor faster than they could be fetched from memory or a register. Some values typical of this type of constant are 0, 1, and other small powers of 2. As implied operands, these constants are coded as part of the operation.

Consider adding 1 to the value in a register, using an instruction with an implied operand. This instruction for a computer with several general-purpose registers might be

INC    reg

Here, INC stands for INCrement and the operand specifies which register. There is an implied operand of 1.

## Immediate operands

A more general way to use small constants as operands is to include the operand value directly in the instruction. The part of the instruction normally used for an operand address or offset is instead used for the constant.

For example, to add a small constant to a register using an immediate operand, we could write an instruction such as

ADD    reg, const

Here, the second operand is a constant, written as an immediate operand, to be added to the register specified by the first operand.

Immediate operands are faster than memory reference instructions, since the operand is fetched as part of the instruction. It does not require a separate address computation and fetch. Since they allow a greater range of constant values to be used, immediate operands are more general than implied operands. However, an immediate operand cannot be used for an operand that is changed by an instruction.

## Structures as operands

The operand of an instruction can also be a reference to a data structure in memory. Some instructions need more operand information than can be coded within them. For example, an instruction to compare two character strings needs the starting addresses and the lengths of the two strings. There are not enough bits in the instruction to code two addresses and two integers, and so some other mechanism must be used. Typically, either a data structure with all operand information is created in memory and the address of that structure is used as the operand of the instruction, or each operand is implied in a fixed register when the instruction executes.

## Instruction Representation

Instructions are represented as binary numbers. Every instruction includes a code that specifies the operation it performs. That part of the instruction is called the **operation code,** or simply **opcode.** The rest of the instruction specifies operands: the number of operands, the locations of the operands, and possibly the data types of the operands.

Methods to code and combine the various pieces of information in an instruction range from fairly simple to quite complicated, from regular to nearly chaotic. The coding scheme used for 8086 instructions can overwhelm the user who tries to ferret out every detail, so only the general form will be looked at here.

Many of the instructions of the 8086 have the basic format shown in Figure 2.16. There are many variations used: Some fields have different purposes and some fields are not used in some instructions, depending on the number and type of operands. A survey of instruction formats in the 8086 references shows over a dozen variations of this basic format. Here the general format shown in Figure 2.16 will be described; some specific examples will be seen later in the text.

Few instructions require all six bytes; many use just three or four, and a fair number use only one or two. All instructions start with an opcode; this is usually six bits, or seven bits if the *d* bit is not used, or eight bits if the *w* bit is also not used.

The *d* bit is called the direction bit. Consider a MOV instruction with one operand in memory and one in a general register. The 8086 instructions code the register and memory locations in the same fields, regardless of which is the source and which is the destination. If the *d* bit is set, the register is the destination operand; if the *d* bit is cleared, the register is the source operand.

The *w* bit is called the *word/byte* bit. It specifies whether the instruction is to use byte operands or word operands. If this bit is set, word operands are used; if this bit is cleared, byte operands are used. In most instructions with two operands, both operands must be the same size.

In the second byte, the three-bit *reg* field specifies which register is used as an operand. If there is only one register operand, the *d* field specifies whether it is a source or desti-

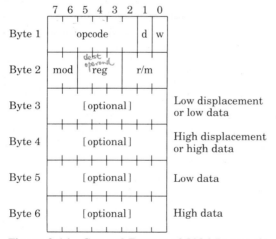

**Figure 2.16 General Format of 8086 Instructions**

## 2.3 Instructions

Table 2.1. Interpretation of *reg* Field of Instruction

| reg | w = 1 | w = 0 |
| --- | --- | --- |
| 000 | AX | AL |
| 001 | CX | CL |
| 010 | DX | DL |
| 011 | BX | BL |
| 100 | SP | AH |
| 101 | BP | CH |
| 110 | SI | DH |
| 111 | DI | BH |

nation operand; if there are two register operands, the *reg* field specifies the destination operand. The registers are coded as shown in Table 2.1. Some instructions with no register operands use the *reg* field for an opcode extension.

The *r/m* field (Table 2.2) specifies the registers used to compute the address of an operand in memory, or the register used for a second register operand. The notation *r/m* stands for *register/memory*. The interpretation of this field depends on the value in the mode (*mod*) field. The simplest case occurs when *mod* = 11: *r/m* specifies a register using the same codes as the *reg* field.

When the *mod* and *r/m* fields specify an operand in memory, it can be specified as a direct address or as an indirect address. In a direct address, an offset is coded in the instruction. In an indirect address, the offset is computed at execution time from information coded in the instruction and registers.

The combination *mod* = 00 and *r/m* = 110 specifies direct addressing. In this mode, the third and fourth bytes of the instruction contain a 16-bit offset. This offset is combined directly with the DS register (except in special cases when another segment register is used, which will not be discussed now) to form the physical address of the operand.

All remaining combinations of *mod* and *r/m* (that is, all combinations other than *mod* = 11, and *mod* = 00 with *r/m* = 110) specify indirect addresses. With indirect addressing, the offset is the sum of one or two base, pointer, or index registers and an optional displacement. The *mod* field gives the size of the displacement in bytes. The actual displacement is coded in the third or third and fourth bytes of the instruction. The combinations of registers used with indirect addresses are coded as shown in Table 2.3.

Table 2.3 appears to lack an indirect addressing mode that uses an offset in BP with no displacement; the likely code for this mode specifies direct addressing instead. It is

Table 2.2. Addressing Modes Coded by *mod* and *r/m* Fields

| mod | r/m | Addressing mode |
| --- | --- | --- |
| 00 | 110 | Direct, word offset |
| 00 | other than 110 | Indirect, no displacement (see Table 2.3) |
| 01 | all | Indirect, byte displacement (see Table 2.3) |
| 10 | all | Indirect, word displacement (see Table 2.3) |
| 11 | all | Register (see Table 2.1) |

Table 2.3. Indirect Address Formulas Coded by *r/m* and *mod* Fields of Instruction

| r/m | Segment | mod = 00 | mod = 01 or mod = 10 |
|---|---|---|---|
| 000 | DS | BX + SI | BX + SI + disp |
| 001 | DS | BX + DI | BX + DI + disp |
| 010 | SS | BP + SI | BP + SI + disp |
| 011 | SS | BP + DI | BP + DI + disp |
| 100 | DS | SI | SI + disp |
| 101 | DS | DI | SI + disp |
| 110[a] | | | BP + disp |
| 111 | DS | BX | BX + disp |

[a] With *r/m* = 110 and *mod* = 00, the instruction contains a 16-bit offset that is used with DS to form the physical address. With *r/m* = 110 and *mod* = 01 or *mod* = 10, an offset is computed from BP and a displacement; the offset is used with SS to form the physical address.

doubtful that such an indirect address would be useful (Section 7.5 will explain why), but if it is necessary to use BP without a displacement, the same effect can be achieved by using *mod* = 01 and *r/m* = 110 and specifying a zero displacement.

The 8086 supports the use of immediate operands in some instructions. The value of the immediate operand is coded in the third or third and fourth bytes if the other operand is a register, or in the fifth or fifth and sixth bytes if the other operand is in memory.

In addition to the instructions that can be coded using variations of the format shown in Figure 2.16, there are many instructions that have only implied operands. These are coded as either an 8-bit opcode or a 16-bit opcode. There are also some instructions that use only four or five bits of the first byte for the opcode. However, this will be sufficient detail for now. In the next chapter, after we write our first assembly-language program, we will examine some of the instructions in it, referring back to the information in this section.

## EXERCISES 2.3

1. Consider the following assignment statements:
   (*a*) R := (F - S) / G
   (*b*) W := (3 * T + Q + H) / 5
   (*c*) X := (X + A / X) / 2

   Write a sequence of instructions that implements each of these for a computer that uses
   (*i*) three-operand instructions
   (*ii*) two-operand instructions
   (*iii*) one-operand instructions
   (*iv*) zero-operand instructions

   Define subtraction and division instructions that are consistent with the instructions presented in the text. Assume that division produces only a quotient.

2. Using a series of diagrams like those in Figures 2.12 through 2.15, trace the sequences of instructions that you wrote for Exercise 1.

3. How does the number of instructions needed to implement an assignment statement depend on the number of operands in an instruction? Use the two assignment statements in the examples of this section and the three assignment statements of Exercise 1 for data. Is there a clear relationship between the number of operands in an instruction and the number of instructions needed to implement a statement? If so, what is it?

## 2.3 Instructions

4. Repeat Exercise 3, but also compare the time to execute the instructions. Assume the following:
   - accessing a register takes one time unit whether getting or saving a value;
   - accessing memory requires three time units, whether getting an instruction, getting a value, or saving a value;
   - addition and subtraction each require two time units;
   - multiplication and division each require ten time units.

   For example, the instruction

   ADD    reg, mem

   requires ten time units: 3 to fetch the instruction, 1 to get the first operand value from a register, 3 to get the second operand value from memory, 2 to add, and 1 to save the result in the register.

   Is there a clear relationship between the number of operands in an instruction and the time required to execute the sequence of instructions for implementing an assignment statement? If so, what is it?

5. How sensitive is the analysis in Exercise 4 to the assumptions about how long it takes to perform each task? That is, if you change the assumptions a little, do the execution times and your conclusions change very much?

6. Suppose we have a program in which we need to add 7 frequently. There is no instruction that adds 7 as an implied operand. Give the advantages and disadvantages of each of the following strategies:
   (a) load 7 once into a register and keep it there so that a register can be used for the operand in the ADD instructions;
   (b) store the 7 in memory and use it for the operand in the ADD instructions;
   (c) use the constant 7 as an immediate operand in the ADD instructions.

7. If all instructions used exactly the format shown in Figure 2.16, how many different instructions could there be?

8. If bit 7 of the first byte of an instruction specifies whether the instruction uses the format shown in Figure 2.16, or is a one-byte opcode with implied operands, how many of each type of instruction can there be? How many instructions in all?

9. A fictitious computer has a single general-purpose register and instructions coded as follows:

   | Bits  | Use |
   | --- | --- |
   | 15–11 | Opcode |
   | 10    | Mode |
   | 9–8   | Segment or extension |
   | 7–0   | Displacement or immediate value |

   If the mode bit is 0, bits 9–8 specify a segment register and bits 7–0 specify a displacement. If the mode bit is 1, bits 9–8 are an extension of the opcode and bits 7–0 are an immediate operand.
   (a) How many instructions are possible with mode = 0?
   (b) How many instructions are possible with mode = 1?
   (c) Assume there are four segment registers, and that the displacement can be relative to any of them. How many memory locations can be referenced using this coding?

10. Imagine a computer with variable-length instructions. A program fragment could consist of instructions with, say, 23, 76, 28, 43, 28, and 11 bits each. These would not be padded to make them multiples of 8. What problems would such programs present to the hardware designer? To a programmer?

11. We mentioned using eleven 16-bit words to implement 50-digit integers. Show that 11 words is the minimum needed to represent an integer with 50 digits. (Hint: use logarithms.)
12. How many 16-bit words are needed to implement 64-digit integers? 24-digit integers?

## KEY POINTS

- Computers are machines that manipulate data under the control of a program.
- The user's description of the processing performed by a computer is algorithmic; it examines the major tasks performed, the inputs, and the outputs.
- The hardware description of the processing performed by a computer is mechanical; it examines the instructions and how they affect the hardware.
- A cell is the memory used by a high-level-language program for one value of a specific type. It is referenced by an identifier. The size of a cell has little relationship to memory organization.
- Information in memory is represented in binary. The smallest unit of memory is a binary digit, or bit.
- A byte is a group of bits used to represent a character, usually eight bits.
- A word is a fixed number of bits typically used to represent one number or one instruction in memory. Word sizes vary from eight bits to over sixty bits.
- Memory capacity is measured in kilobytes ($K = 1024$), megabytes ($M = 1024K$), and gigabytes ($G = 1024M$).
- Numerical addresses are associated with groups of bits in memory. In some computers, every byte has an address; in others, only words have addresses.
- The hardware uses the address of a location in memory to access its contents. Addresses are coded as part of instructions.
- Addresses of items in the same region of memory are similar. This leads to partitioning memory into segments, with separate segments for data and instructions.
- The address of a particular location is found by adding the address of the segment boundary and the offset from the start of the segment of the desired location.
- With direct addressing, the offset of an operand is coded as a constant in an instruction.
- With indirect addressing, the offset is computed from the contents of base, pointer, and index registers during program execution.
- The central processing unit consists of an arithmetic logic unit, which performs the arithmetic, relational, and logical operations, and a control unit, which oversees the computer system hardware.
- Registers in the processor are used for data, addresses, and control information. The number and type of registers available determine many other characteristics of the processor.
- General registers are used in arithmetic, relational, and logical operations.
- Address registers include the segment, pointer, index, and instruction pointer registers.
- The instruction pointer register contains the offset of the next instruction to be executed.
- The flags register contains information about the program that is currently running: the results of tests the program performs, the sign of arithmetic results, whether a result is too large to be represented, and so on, as well as other system information.
- The peripherals of a computer system include the input, output, and storage devices.
- The keyboard generates a scan code for each key pressed and released. Software must convert these scan codes into characters or extended codes.

- Printers accept streams of codes and convert them into images of characters on paper.
- The video display uses an area of memory to represent the display, with one byte for each character displayed and another for its attributes.
- Disk drives store data magnetically, on the surfaces of rotating platters. The platter is formatted into circular tracks divided into sectors. The sectors can be accessed in any order, but each read or write must access an entire sector.
- Peripherals and memory are connected to the processor using a bus. The bus is divided into three parts: address, data, and control.
- Peripherals and memory are accessed by writing the desired address on the address bus and sending the appropriate control signal on the control lines.
- The data bus is used to transfer data between the processor, the memory, and peripherals.
- An interrupt is a signal to the processor to temporarily stop the running program and execute a special routine.
- External interrupts are generated by peripherals or by special circuits that monitor the computer hardware.
- Internal interrupts are generated by software or error conditions that occur during program execution.
- Instructions can be classified by the number of operands they have. Many modern computers have instructions that have different numbers of operands.
- Three-operand arithmetic instructions specify two source operands and a separate destination operand.
- Two-operand arithmetic instructions specify one combined source and destination operand, and a second source operand.
- One-operand arithmetic instructions specify an explicit source operand. The other source operand, and the destination operand, is implied by the instruction.
- Zero-operand arithmetic instructions pop two values off a stack for use as source operands, and push the result of the operation back onto the stack. Computers that use these instructions for arithmetic use one-operand instructions for pushing data from memory onto the stack and for popping data off the stack into memory.
- Operands can be in registers, in memory, coded directly as part of the instruction, or implied by the instruction.
- Instructions always specify at least an operation. This is coded in binary, and is called an opcode.
- Each operand is also coded as part of an instruction.

## PC SYSTEM SUMMARY

- The memory units of the 8086 are
  byte = 8 bits
  word = 2 bytes (16 bits)
  doubleword = 4 bytes
  quadword = 8 bytes
  tenbyte = 10 bytes
  paragraph = 16 bytes
  page = 256 bytes
  segment = 64K bytes

## Chapter 2  Introduction to Computer Organization

- Addresses are specified as a 16-bit offset from the start of a segment.
- Segments must begin on a paragraph boundary; the 16 most significant bits of the address where the segment starts are used as a selector in a segment register.
- The four general registers can be treated as either 16- or 8-bit registers:

| 16-bit | 8-bit |
|---|---|
| AX | AH, AL |
| BX | BH, BL |
| CX | CH, CL |
| DX | DH, DL |

- The four segment registers are the following:

| Register | Selector |
|---|---|
| CS | Code segment |
| DS | Data segment |
| SS | Stack segment |
| ES | Extra segment |

- The two pointer registers are BP and SP.
- The two index registers are SI and DI.
- The instruction pointer, IP, is the offset from CS of the first byte of the next instruction.
- The flags register contains three control flags and six status flags:

| Flag | Interpretation |
|---|---|
| DF | Direction for string operations |
| IF | Interrupt enable |
| TF | Trap following every instruction |
| OF | Overflow flag |
| SF | Sign flag |
| ZF | Zero flag |
| AF | Auxiliary carry flag |
| PF | Parity flag |
| CF | Carry flag |

- The general form of an 8086 instruction consists of some or all of the following fields:

| Field | Meaning |
|---|---|
| *opcode* | Operation to perform |
| *d* | Destination in register or memory |
| *w* | Word or byte operands |
| *mod* | Address mode for memory operand |
| *reg* | Register operand |
| *r/m* | Register or memory operand |
| *disp* | Displacement of memory operand |
| *data* | Immediate operand |

In some instructions, some fields are used for other purposes. There are also a number of other formats for some groups of instructions.

# Assembly-Language Programming    3

- ◆ **Assembly-Language Notation**
- ◆ **Symbolic Operands**
- ◆ **Directives**
- ◆ **Input and Output**
- ◆ **Assembling, Linking, and Executing**
- ◆ **Examining Memory with DEBUG**

When we program in a high-level language, we depend on a compiler or an interpreter to translate our programs into machine instructions. High-level languages resemble natural languages, mathematical notation, or combinations of these, but they require much more precision. For example, to find the average of a list of numbers, we might start with the description "add them up and divide by how many there are." To write a program for this in a procedural language requires a more detailed description, written according to the syntax rules of the language.

To program in assembly language, we need to describe procedures in even greater detail. The exact level of detail necessary varies among computers. Working in assembly language brings the programmer closer to the machine, so the programmer can exert more control over the machine. With the added control come added responsibilities, but less support.

In this chapter, we examine common characteristics of assembly languages in general and of the 8086 assembly language in particular. The chapter presents the input and output routines provided on the disk packaged with this text and used in many of the programs. We look at a simple program that illustrates many of the requirements and features of assembly language. Included is a tutorial on using Microsoft's MASM 5.1, LINK, and DEBUG to assemble, link, execute, dump, and trace our example program.

## 3.1   ASSEMBLY-LANGUAGE NOTATION

Details of an assembly-language program vary from one computer to the next even though the basic format and many of the underlying concepts are the same. The following introduces a subset of 8086 assembly language that will allow us to examine all of the important concepts without getting mired in too many details.

## Statement Format

An assembly-language program is a sequence of lines that contain either comments or statements. Blank lines are also allowed.

Comments document a program: who wrote it, when they wrote it, what it does, how it does it, what input is required, what output is generated, which formulas and algorithms are used, what assumptions are made, and so on. Comments are also useful for breaking a program into blocks of code that reflect the higher levels of the algorithm design. In 8086 assembly languages, comments begin with a semicolon and may start anywhere on a line. All text following the semicolon and up to the end of the line is treated as a comment.

There are four types of statements:

> executable instructions
> assembler directives
> macroinstruction definitions
> macroinstruction calls

Each type of statement will be described in detail shortly.

Each statement can consist of up to four fields. From left to right, the fields are

> name    mnemonic    operand(s)    comment

The fields are separated from each other by one or more spaces. A few assemblers require that each field begin in a certain fixed column; even in the absence of such a requirement, some assembly-language programmers align the fields into columns. We will use a style in which blocks are indented in a manner similar to that often used with high-level languages.

Statements contain a combination of standard and user-defined symbols. A **symbol** is an identifier that can represent a named constant, an address, a register, an operation, a directive, or a macroinstruction. Symbols must start with a letter and must contain only letters, digits, and a few special characters. One of the special characters is an underscore, which can also be used as the first character. Lowercase letters are usually converted internally to capital letters, unless an optional parameter in the assembler command disables that feature. Only the first 31 characters of a symbol are used; longer symbols are allowed but are impractical.

The name field of a statement is used to associate a symbolic name with a constant, a macroinstruction, a procedure, or a memory location. These objects are defined using assembler directives in the mnemonic field. The name field is also used to associate a label with the address of an instruction when used with a mnemonic that represents an instruction. Names used as labels on instructions are followed by a colon, while names of objects are not. Names may be placed on a line without a mnemonic; the assembler will process it as if it is part of the next line that contains a mnemonic.

The mnemonic field may represent an assembler directive, an instruction to be translated into binary, or the name of a previously defined macroinstruction. Assembler directives require the assembler to perform tasks such as reserving memory for variables and constants. A macroinstruction is a named block of text that can be substituted for the name

### 3.1 Assembly-Language Notation

by the assembler during program translation. (Macroinstructions are discussed in Chapter 12.) Each instruction and assembler directive has a mnemonic, which can be an abbreviation (such as sub for SUBtract), an acronym (such as jnc for Jump if Not Carry), or a combination of letters (such as cmp for CoMPare).

If the instruction, directive, or macroinstruction requires any operands, they are coded in the operand field. Depending on the operation, operands may be symbolic names or expressions that we have previously associated with instructions, data, constants, bit patterns, addresses, displacements, or control information. Multiple operands are separated by commas.

Each line may also contain a comment field. It is separated from the operand field, or operation field if there are no operands, by a semicolon.

In many assembly languages, it is possible to pack two or more statements per line and to continue a statement onto more than one line. We will not have need of these capabilities.

### Program Format

A high-level-language program contains documentation, a program heading, declarations, processing statements, and an end. An assembly-language program also has all of these elements. The program heading, declarations, and end of a high-level-language program are specified using keywords reserved for that purpose. In an assembly-language program, they are specified using assembler directives.

Assembler directives—which are sometimes called pseudo-operations, or pseudo-ops—control the translation process, storage allocation, constant definition, and so on. Some directives require a name, some may have a name as an option, and some cannot have a name. There may be any number of operands, some of which may have default values if omitted. A detailed description of specific directives is deferred until later in the chapter, but a few of them are included here in a program shell that illustrates program format.

Figure 3.1 shows the general form of an assembly-language program for the 8086. The program begins with a comment that represents the usual placement of prologue comments describing the program, identifying the author, and so on. They are followed by the definition of any named constants in the program. The DOSSEG directive on the next line specifies the segment order desired in the final executable program. The next three lines define a typical stack segment; nnn represents the number of words reserved for it. The next four lines define a data segment that includes a one-word variable named VarInit, and a one-byte variable named VarUnInit. VarInit is initialized with the value specified by the operand, and VarUnInit is not initialized with a specific value. The rest of the program shell is the code segment, where the executable instructions are written.

A Pascal program shell, roughly equivalent to the assembly-language shell, is given in Figure 3.2. The correspondence between the two program shells may not be as obvious as we would hope for. For one thing, the Pascal program makes no explicit mention of a stack segment, even though it uses one. Although the data declarations in the two shells are similar, Pascal does not provide initialized variables. Further, the declarations of variables in assembly language refer only to the size of an object, not to how values are encoded. The declarations in Pascal specify a data type that implies encoding and

## Chapter 3 Assembly-Language Programming

```
; prologue comments

; constants
   ConName      equ      value

DOSSEG

_STACK SEGMENT para stack 'stack'
             dw      nnn dup (?)
_STACK ENDS

_DATA SEGMENT word public 'data'
   VarInit     dw      value    ;initialized ...
   VarUnInit   db      ?        ;uninitialized ...
_DATA ENDS

_TEXT SEGMENT word public 'code'
     assume  cs: _TEXT

Shell:                          ;entry point
   ...
   ...                          ;instructions
   ...

_TEXT ENDS
END    Shell
```
**Figure 3.1  Assembly-language Program Shell**

allowable operations as well as size. The Pascal compound statement that contains all executable statements roughly corresponds to the code segment.

Although the shell in Figure 3.1 does not convey all of the information needed to start writing programs, neither does the shell in Figure 3.2. These shells are intended to give you a framework to build on as assembly-language programs are discussed in more detail throughout this chapter.

```
PROGRAM Shell (Input, Output);

(* prologue comments *)

CONST
   ConName = value;

VAR
   VarInit  : WORD;   (* NOT initialized *)
   VarUnInit: BYTE;

BEGIN (* Shell *)
   ...
   ...     (* executable statements *)
   ...
END.  (* Shell *)
```
**Figure 3.2  Pascal Program Shell**

## EXERCISES 3.1

1. Examine a simple assembly-language program from a later chapter in this text or from your instructor. Identify the components in it that correspond to those given in the shell of Figure 3.1.
2. For the program in Exercise 1, identify
   (*a*) The instruction and directive mnemonics
   (*b*) The names and labels
   (*c*) The operands
   (*d*) The comments
▶3. For the program in Exercise 1, based on what you can determine from the comments and general format of the program, write an equivalent program in a high-level language.

## 3.2 SYMBOLIC OPERANDS

In the previous chapter the general form of instructions and operands was considered. We saw that an operand can be in a register, it can be in a memory cell, it can be implied by the instruction, or it can be coded as part of the instruction itself. Now we examine operands again, this time considering their symbolic form in an assembly-language program.

### Operands in Registers

To specify a register as an operand we simply write the register name in the operand field. The register names recognized by 8086 assemblers are AX, BX, CX, and DX for 16-bit general registers and AL, AH, BL, BH, CL, CH, DL, and DH for 8-bit general registers. For example, to increment the contents of the AX register, we can write

inc     ax

The segment registers are named CS, SS, DS, and ES. Only a few instructions can operate directly on a segment register. The pointer registers are named BP and SP; the index registers are named SI and DI. The pointer and index registers are used for writing indirect references to memory. We cannot use the instruction pointer or flags register directly as operands. Although most operands can be written as registers, there are a few situations for which a register cannot be used. In some instructions, only one type of register or one specific register is allowed.

### Operands in Memory

Data in memory can be used as operands. There are two aspects to using memory for operands: declaring the name and size of the data object and using the name as an operand.

To define an object in memory, we use a directive like dw or db with the name of the object in the name field. The size of the object is specified by the directive. These declarations are usually written in the data segment. Examples of this were shown in Figure 3.1. Once declared, an object in memory can be used as an operand by writing its name in the operand field. For example, we might have a variable named Count declared as

Count     dw        ?

To increment the value stored in memory associated with the name Count, we use the instruction

```
inc     Count
```

The assembler associates a displacement with each name in a segment. For example, assume that Count above is the fifth word of data defined in the segment. The assembler would then associate a displacement of 8 (the number of bytes that precede Count in the segment) with the name Count. That displacement is coded as part of the increment instruction. (Actually, it is more complicated than this, but until we study assemblers and linkers and loaders in Chapter 11, this is a reasonable simplification.) The assembler, in effect, translates the symbolic name into a displacement.

During instruction execution, the offset by itself is inadequate for forming the physical address. A segment register value is also needed. We must include a directive to associate a segment register with the segment in which Count is declared and arrange for the segment register to be loaded with the appropriate selector. These are not difficult tasks, and a complete example is given later in this chapter.

In some situations, we may need to specify the segment as well as the displacement of a memory operand. This is done by writing the segment register name, and a colon, before the operand field. For example, we can rewrite the increment instruction above as

```
inc     ds:Count
```

In this example, including the segment register explicitly will not affect the assembled instruction.

Some instructions transfer control from one part of a program to another part. (This is the assembly-language version of the infamous GOTO statement.) To do so we write a label in the name field of the destination instruction and use the label as an operand in the instruction that transfers control. For example, the instruction

```
jmp     Store
```

transfers control to the following instruction (in the same code segment)

```
Store:
    mov     Result, ax
```

The displacement of Store from the jmp instruction is computed differently than the displacement of objects in data segments, since both the instruction and the operand are in the same segment. Details of how this displacement is computed are not yet important.

## Implied Operands

The 8086 has a number of instructions that have implied operands. For example, the instruction to convert a signed integer (how integers are stored is examined in the next chapter) from 8 bits to 16 bits is

```
cbw
```

It has no explicit operands. It converts the byte in the AL register to a word in AX.

## Immediate Operands

Many of the 8086 instructions allow the use of immediate operands. An immediate operand is written as a constant in the operand field of the instruction. The assembler generates the constant as part of the instruction, using the field normally used for a displacement. For example, to add four to Count we could use an instruction like

```
add     Count, 4
```

in which the constant 4 is an immediate operand.

## Operand Expressions

In some cases, we must write an expression in the operand field. These expressions consist of constants, symbolic names, and operators. The particular set of operators available and the rules for evaluating complex expressions depend on the assembler used. This subsection considers only a few operators and simple expressions.

Some operators are evaluated during the assembly process to produce constant immediate operands. The first two operators considered here determine the segment or the offset of a physical address. The seg operator returns (with the help of the assembler, linker, and loader) the segment selector of the symbolic operand that follows it. For example, the instruction

```
mov     ax, seg _DATA
```

copies the selector portion of the address where the segment named _DATA begins into the AX register during execution. The instruction

```
mov     ax, offset Count
```

copies the displacement of Count from the start of the segment it is in into the AX register. Note that in both of these examples, the AX register receives part of an address.

Other operators, like dup, act like embedded directives that affect how the assembler treats the operand. dup specifies multiple values in constant declarations. In the program shell of Figure 3.1, we had

```
        dw      nnn dup (?)
```

In an actual program, nnn is replaced with a number like 256. This then means to duplicate the uninitialized value (specified by the question mark) 256 times, thus reserving 256 words of memory for the stack segment.

There are dozens of other operators that we can use in operand expressions, including arithmetic and logical operators. Some will eventually be introduced.

## EXERCISES 3.2

1. Copy an assembly-language program from a later chapter or from your instructor. Examine it and locate an operand
   (*a*) Specified in a register

(b) Specified directly in memory
(c) Implied (this could be difficult)
(d) Specified as an immediate constant

2. For the program in Exercise 1, identify any operand expressions other than simple names or constants. For each, give the operator and what you think the operator does.

3. Consider your favorite high-level language. Does it have anything like the operand expression operators seg, offset, or dup presented in this section? For those that it does have, give an example; for those it does not have, explain why.

## 3.3 DIRECTIVES

This section presents nine assembler directives that will allow us to start writing programs.

### Segment Ordering

The first directive we use is DOSSEG. It specifies that segments in the executable file will follow the Microsoft conventions for segment order, which will be discussed when we examine linking and loading. DOSSEG takes neither a name nor any operands; it is used only in the main module of a stand-alone assembly-language program and is the first statement other than comments and constant declarations.

### Segment Definition

The SEGMENT and ENDS directives define a segment. The syntax is

*seg_name*    SEGMENT  [*align*]  [*combine*]  [*wordsize*]  [*class*]
    ... contents of segment
[*seg_name*]  ENDS

The name of the segment is required in the name field of the SEGMENT directive; it may be required or optional in the name field of the ENDS directive, depending on the assembler used. Here it is included in all examples. Together, SEGMENT and ENDS mark the beginning and end of a logical segment. All instructions and directives on lines between them are assembled into the named segment.

The optional operands of the SEGMENT directive specify the segment's alignment in memory, combine type, word size (32-bit processors only), and class name. The ENDS directive has no operands.

Segments can be aligned in memory on a byte, word, doubleword, paragraph, or page boundary. These correspond to addresses that are multiples of 1, 2, 4, 16, or 256, respectively, and are specified by the operands byte, word, dword, para, or page. The default is para. By convention, the stack segment is aligned on a paragraph boundary and all other segments on a word boundary.

The **combine type** specifies how segments with the same name from different modules are to be combined. The combine types are public, stack, common, and private. Segments specified as public are concatenated to form one contiguous segment. Segments

## 3.3 Directives

specified as stack are also concatenated to form one contiguous segment, but unlike public segments, addresses in stack segments are always relative to the stack segment (SS) register. Segments specified as common are all located at the same memory address, so that all common segments with the same name refer to the same block of memory. FORTRAN programs use COMMON blocks implemented in common segments, for example, to share data between subprograms without passing arguments. Segments defined without a combine type are assigned the private type and are not combined with any other segments.

The word-size operand specifies whether a 32-bit processor (80386 and later) is to operate with 16-bit words for compatibility with earlier processors or to use 32-bit words. Here we use the default 16-bit words.

The **class name** affects how segments are combined. It is more important than segment name in determining segment order, but the interaction of segment name, combine type, class name, and DOS segment ordering can be overwhelming (especially before seeing our first complete program). For now, we will use the class name 'stack' for the stack segment, 'data' for the data segment, and 'code' for the instruction segment. Note that the class name must be enclosed in quotation marks or apostrophes.

Segment attributes for small stand-alone programs are fairly flexible. Segment attributes for larger programs and for programs written in more than a single language are more restricted. For now, our conventions, consistent with most of the conventions used with the Microsoft small memory model and with the simplified directives (which hide some details that we want to discuss), are as follows: The stack segment will be named _STACK, will be aligned on a paragraph boundary, will have combine type stack, and will have 'stack' for its class name. (Naming the segment as STACK, which is the name used in the Microsoft small memory model, will cause a warning message with some assemblers; for consistency with other segment names and to avoid the warning message, we choose _STACK.) The segment used for static data will be named _DATA, will be aligned on a word boundary, will have the public combine type, and will have 'data' for its class name. The segment used for the executable instructions is named _TEXT, is aligned on a word boundary, has the public combine type, and has 'code' for its class name.

## Segment Addressing

The fourth directive we consider is assume. The syntax is

assume   *segreg: seg_name*

It associates, for the benefit of the assembler, a segment register with a segment name. Following the assume directive, the assembler can build addresses as offsets from the selector that (we assume) will be present in the segment register.

The assume directive is not used with the stack segment (SS) register, as the system always uses the SS register for the stack segment selector. The assembler makes no assumptions about the contents of the other segment registers, so we must use assume with them.

The selector is not actually loaded into the segment register by assume; that cannot be done at assembly time. In the case of the code segment (CS) and stack segment (SS) registers, the loader assigns the registers after it has loaded the program into memory and before turning control over to it. The program itself must load the data segment (DS) and extra segment (ES) registers, using immediate operands provided by the loader.

## Data Declarations

The next three directives correspond to the declarations of variables and named constants in a high-level language.

Storage for variables is reserved with define byte (db) and define word (dw) directives. The name field provides a symbolic name for the location. The operand specifies an initial value or indicates that the variable is uninitialized.

Integer values can be written as operands of db or dw directives in several forms. The simplest way is to write the value in decimal. To write an integer in any other base requires that we follow the last digit with a character that specifies the radix: b for binary, q or o for octal, or h for hexadecimal. For example

```
Ex1     dw      42
Ex2     dw      101010b
Ex3     dw      52q
Ex4     dw      2Ah
```

define four one-word constants with names Ex1, Ex2, Ex3, and Ex4. Each is also initialized with the value 42. Hexadecimal numbers must start with a digit: A leading zero is required if the most significant digit is any of A through F. This requirement allows the assembler to distinguish hexadecimal numbers from symbolic names. For example, to distinguish the name D2h from the number D2h, the number must be written 0D2h.

Storage for uninitialized variables is also reserved with the db and dw directives, with a question mark in the operand field. For example,

```
Var1    db      ?
Var2    dw      ?
```

define two variables named Var1 and Var2. The first of these is allocated one byte of memory; the second is allocated one word. Note that there is no provision for specifying the data type — integer, real, or whatever — in this directive. A data type defines the operations that can be performed and how the value is coded. These issues are the programmer's responsibility in assembly language; the processor can perform any operation on any data of the right length for the operation, without regard to what we intend the data to represent.

We can also reserve memory for character strings and other blocks larger than one byte or word. For example,

```
String1     db      "This is a string"
```

reserves 16 bytes of memory and initializes it to the string given. The name String1 is associated with the first byte.

The dup operator is used to provide multiple copies of an operand, as in

```
String2     db      80 dup ("*")
```

## 3.3 Directives

which allocates 80 bytes, initializes each to an asterisk, and associates the name `String2` with the first byte. And

```
String3      db         80 dup (?)
```

reserves a block of 80 bytes of memory with no initial value. In each of these examples, the use of db implies a 1-byte length when the names are used as operands.

To define named constants, we use the equ directive. The equ directive causes the assembler to associate a value with a symbolic name during the assembly process. The name is written in the label field, and the value is written in the operand field. The assembler treats the value as text. For example, if we define two named constants as

```
PageWidth    equ        80
PageLength   equ        66
```

we can then use `PageWidth` and `PageLength` as operands. The assembler substitutes 80 for each occurrence of `PageWidth` and 66 for each occurrence of `PageLength` during translation. Unlike variables, there is no size associated with these constants (it is possible to associate a size with a constant, but that will be described later).

Code that uses named constants is more readable and easier to maintain than code that uses literal constants. Consider two programs, one that uses the names given above and one that uses the constants directly. To change the page width from 80 to 66, we change the operand of the equ in one, but we must search for all occurrences of 80 in the other. Then, perhaps a few days later, to change page length from 66 to 60, we change the operand of the equ in one, but we must search for all occurrences of 66 in the other and decide whether each refers to page width or page length.

## External Definitions

The assembler expects every user-defined symbol used as an operand to be defined within the program module. A symbol that is used in the name field of a statement is so defined. Some symbols, however, are defined externally; they do not appear as names or labels within the program. The extrn directive informs the assembler that a symbol is defined externally and specifies the type of the symbol. The only type of external symbol we will use is a procedure name, which we specify as PROC in the extrn directive.

In our programs, we use a small set of input and output routines that are provided on the disk that accompanies this text. We will use a linker to combine the input and output routines with the object files that the assembler generates when it translates our programs. The assembler must be told that the names of these subprograms are externally defined, or it will generate error messages and not create the object file. For example, one of the output routines provided is named `PutStr`. To allow a program to call `PutStr`, we include the directive

```
extrn    PutStr: PROC
```

within the code segment that includes the call to it. PROC defines `PutStr` as a procedure. We can define several external symbols with a single extrn directive, but the type of each must be given separately.

## Module Termination

The last directive introduced in this section is END. It identifies the end of the program. In the main module of a stand-alone assembly-language program, the operand of the END directive is the label of the first instruction. In a subprogram, the END directive has no operand.

These directives are sufficient for writing simple main programs in assembly language. The next section introduces our input and output subprograms and the instruction sequences used to invoke them.

### EXERCISES 3.3

1. Examine an assembly-language program from a later chapter of this book or from your instructor. Identify at least one instance of each directive presented in this section.
2. Write the directives necessary to declare
   (a) A stack segment that contains 256 words
   (b) A data segment with four 1-word variables
   (c) A data segment with your name in a string variable
   (d) A data segment with a single block of uninitialized memory 512 bytes long
   (e) A data segment with 16 variables initialized to the values 0 through 15, as bytes, with names *Zero, One,* and so on.
3. There is no restriction against using several different data segments within one program—indeed, if the total memory needed for the data exceeds 64K, more than one segment is required. What problems does using more than one data segment pose?

## 3.4  INPUT AND OUTPUT

There is, unfortunately, very little uniformity in low-level input and output facilities from one computer system to the next. A detailed treatment of input and output processing is inappropriate at this point; however, we do need some way to interact with our programs. This section illustrates some simple input and output routines for use with this text.

### Input and Output Routines

Communicating with an input or output device can be a very complex process. Fortunately, the operating system often handles most or all of the details, allowing the use of a few simple subprograms for elementary input and output operations. The disk included with this text contains a set of procedures that we will use to read input from the keyboard and write output to the video display. The source files for the procedures are included in the subdirectory named IO; a library file named IO.LIB is in the root directory. Listings of these procedures are also included in Appendix 1; features of these routines are discussed at various places within the text. The input and output procedures are invoked by a `call` instruction. Examples of calling each of the routines in this chapter are given. The `call` instruction is explained in detail in Chapter 7. Until then it is sufficient to follow the examples presented in this chapter.

## 3.4 Input and Output

Since input and output is tedious in assembly language, even with the provided routines, we will settle for less than ideal prompt messages and output messages.

There are six procedures available for use in the programs. Four of these display a character, a character string, a return/linefeed pair, or a 16-bit signed integer. The other two read a single character or a 16-bit signed integer from the keyboard. There are also two other procedures that are used internally and that are not intended to be called directly from an application program.

All arguments are passed in registers. Except for the values returned by the input routines, no registers are changed by the procedures. With one exception, all procedures return to the calling program normally. The exception occurs when invalid data are encountered in reading a numeric value, as will be discussed shortly.

### PutChar

The `PutChar` procedure displays a single character at the position of the cursor on the display then advances the cursor to the next position on the line. `PutChar` takes one argument: the character to display in the DL register. For example, the program fragment

```
    mov     dl, "?"
    call    PutChar
```

displays a question mark.

### PutStr

To display a character string, we could call `PutChar` with each character of the string. Instead, we provide a procedure, `PutStr`, which displays a string starting at the position of the cursor on the display. It leaves the cursor positioned immediately after the last character displayed. `PutStr` takes two arguments: the length of the string as an integer in the CX register and the offset of the string in the BX register. For example, given the definitions

```
String      db      "Computer Science"
Length      dw      16
```

the fragment

```
    mov     cx, Length
    mov     bx, offset String
    call    PutStr
```

displays the string `Computer Science` and leaves the cursor following the final "e" of the string. This is similar to the Pascal statement

```
Write ('Computer Science')
```

### PutCrLf

To move the cursor to the beginning of the next line, it is necessary to send two characters to the display: a carriage return and a linefeed. The `PutCrLf` procedure does this. It takes no arguments. The instruction

```
    call    PutCrLf
```

invokes this procedure. This is similar to the Pascal statement

```
Writeln
```

## PutDec

The PutDec procedure displays a 16-bit signed integer right-justified in a field of six characters. It takes one argument, the integer to display, in the AX register. Given the declarations above, the fragment

```
    mov     ax, Length
    call    PutDec
```

displays the string     16 and leaves the cursor following the 6 with no trailing space. The fragment

```
    mov     ax, -123
    call    PutDec
```

displays the string   -123 with the minus sign immediately preceding the most significant digit. These are similar to the Pascal statements

```
Write (Length:6);
Write (-123:6)
```

## GetChar

The GetChar procedure reads one character from the keyboard and returns it to the calling program in the AX register. It does not change any other registers.

GetChar actually returns two separate values, one in the AH register and the other in the AL register. To digress, note that some of the combinations of keys that can be pressed generate codes that are not simple characters. These codes are called *extended codes*. If a normal character is read from the keyboard, GetChar returns 0 in AH and the character in AL; if an extended code is read, GetChar returns 1 in AH and the extended code in AL. The instruction

```
    call    GetChar
```

waits for the user to tap a key and returns the character or extended code in AL and 0 or 1 in AH. The GetChar procedure is similar to the Pascal statement

```
Read (Ch)
```

where Ch is a Char variable, except that GetChar leaves the character in AL rather than saving it in memory.

## GetDec

The GetDec procedure reads a signed integer from the keyboard and returns it as a 16-bit number in AX. The input can consist of leading spaces, a leading minus sign, and digits; a trailing space or the RETURN key terminates the input.

The BACKSPACE key cannot be used to correct faulty input. Any incorrect character—anything other than those just listed, in that order—in the input will generate an error

## 3.4 Input and Output

message and terminate the program. If the number entered is out of the allowed range for signed integers, the procedure does return a value, though not the same one that a high-level language might return. The instruction

       call    GetDec

reads a string that represents a signed integer from the keyboard and converts it to the internal 16-bit integer format. The result is returned in the AX register.

   We have procedures to display a single character, display a string, and to read a single character; why not a procedure to read a string? There are many variations possible regarding treatment of extended codes and how to cope with input strings that are longer or shorter than the specified length passed as an argument: That discussion is postponed until Chapter 15.

## A Simple Program

Sufficient description has been given to write a complete program. It appears as Program 3.1. It prints a welcome message, asks the user a simple question, reads an integer, and prints that integer and the next larger one in a short sentence. Execution of the program might result in the following exchange

```
A> welcome
Welcome to 8086 Assembly Language.
How many languages do you know? 2
     2 is a good start.  Soon you'll know        3
A>
```

In this example, the user enters the digit 2 followed by a space in response to the prompt.

### Program 3.1

```
; Program 3.1          Welcome.ASM
; Prints a welcome message, reads how many languages the
;   user knows, and prints a message increasing it by 1.

; DOS function and status parameters
DosFunc         equ     21h     ; invoke a DOS function
ExitToDos       equ     4Ch     ; terminate prog & exit to DOS
NoErrors        equ     00h     ; signal successful completion

       DOSSEG
_STACK SEGMENT para stack 'stack'
               dw      100h dup (?)
_STACK ENDS

_DATA SEGMENT word public 'data'
       Languages   dw   ?
       HelloMsg    db   "Welcome to 8086 Assembly Language."
       HelloLen    dw   34
       PromptMsg   db   "How many languages do you know? "
       PromptLen   dw   32
```

## Program 3.1 (continued)

```
        ReplyMsg   db    " is a good start.  Soon you'll know "
        ReplyLen   dw    36
_DATA ENDS

_TEXT SEGMENT word public 'code'   ; defines the segment
        assume  cs: _TEXT          ; informs the assembler when exe begins, CS reg contains the selector for code seg.
        extrn   PutStr: PROC, PutCrLf: PROC   ; } declare 4 input & output procedures
        extrn   GetDec: PROC, PutDec: PROC    ;

Welcome:                           ; used as operand on the END directive.
; (loads the ds reg with the seg no. of the start of the data seg)
; set up ds register to point to _DATA
        mov     ax, seg _DATA      ; copy seg no. of _DATA first into AX
        mov     ds, ax             ; & then into DS
        assume  ds: _DATA          ; inform assembler that it can use offsets relative to the DS reg to access data in the
                                   ;   directive contain correct segment selector

; print ("Welcome to 8086 Assembly Language.")
        mov     cx, HelloLen       ; mov cx, Length
        mov     bx, offset HelloMsg ; mov bx, offset string
        call    PutStr              ; call PutStr
        call    PutCrLf             ; move the cursor to the beginning of next line

; print ("How many languages do you know? ")
        mov     cx, PromptLen
        mov     bx, offset PromptMsg
        call    PutStr

; read (Languages)
        call    GetDec              ; invoke GetDec to accept a signed integer from the user & returns in AX
        mov     Languages, ax       ; copy the input into the variable Languages

; print (Languages, " is a good start.  Soon you'll know ")
        call    PutCrLf
        call    PutDec              ; mov ax, integer -: is still in reg

        mov     cx, ReplyLen
        mov     bx, offset ReplyMsg
        call    PutStr

; Languages := Languages + 1
        inc     Languages           ; adds one to the value of Languages in memory

; print (Languages)
        mov     ax, Languages
        call    PutDec
        call    PutCrLf

; exit to DOS
        mov     ah, ExitToDos       ; operands
        mov     al, NoErrors
        int     DosFunc

_TEXT ENDS        ; terminate code segment
END     Welcome   ; terminate source file
```

## 3.4 Input and Output

The first lines of the program are comments that state the purpose of the program. The next block defines three named constants that we will use in every stand-alone assembly-language program. The constant `DosFunc` is the interrupt number that we must issue in order to invoke a DOS function. `ExitToDos` is the number of the function we must invoke to terminate our program and exit to DOS gracefully. `NoErrors` is a parameter we provide to the `ExitToDos` function to signal successful completion. These names will be seen again at the end of the program.

The constant declarations are followed by the DOSSEG directive. The next block, three lines in length, declares the stack segment and allocates 100h (256) words for it. The next block, of nine lines, declares the data segment. It specifies the contents of the data segment as an integer variable named `Languages` and three strings, each followed by a word that gives its length.

The rest of the program, except the last line, is the code segment containing the instructions to execute. The first few lines of the code segment are directives. The first defines the segment. The `assume` directive informs the assembler that when execution begins, the CS register will contain the selector for the code segment. The `extrn` directives declare the four input and output procedures that the program uses. The next line consists of the label `Welcome`, followed by a colon, on a line by itself. This label, which is associated with the next instruction and is also used as an operand on the END directive, establishes the entry point.

The next block, of three lines,

```
mov     ax, seg _DATA
mov     ds, ax
assume  ds: _DATA
```

loads the DS register with the segment number of the start of the data segment. The two `mov` (move) instructions copy the segment number of _DATA first into AX and then into DS. The goal is to copy the segment number into DS, but this cannot be done in a single `mov` instruction. The `seg` operator returns the segment part of the address of its argument, in this case _DATA. Once we know that the DS register will contain the correct segment selector, we inform the assembler with the `assume` directive that it can use offsets relative to the DS register to access data in the _DATA segment.

The next block, containing four instructions,

```
mov     cx, HelloLen
mov     bx, offset HelloMsg
call    PutStr
call    PutCrLf
```

prints the welcome message and advances the display to the next line. The `offset` operator returns the offset of its argument; in this case, the offset of `HelloMsg` from the start of the _DATA segment is 2. As explained earlier, the `PutStr` procedure takes two arguments: the length of the string in the CX register and the offset of the first byte of the string in the BX register. The two `mov` instructions set up the CX and BX registers for the call to `PutStr`. The call to `PutCrLf` advances the output to the beginning of the next line.

The next block, having three instructions,

```
mov     cx, PromptLen
mov     bx, offset PromptMsg
call    PutStr
```

prints the prompt string. Following this, the instructions

```
call    GetDec
mov     Languages, ax
```

invoke GetDec to accept a signed integer from the user and copy it to the variable Languages.

The next block of instructions

```
call    PutCrLf
call    PutDec
mov     cx, ReplyLen
mov     bx, offset ReplyMsg
call    PutStr
```

advances the output to the beginning of the next line—in case the user typed a space following the number entered—and prints the number that the user just entered. Since that number is still in the AX register, no mov instructions are needed to set up the argument to PutDec. The program then prints the middle part of the output message.

The next instruction

```
inc     Languages
```

adds one to the value of Languages in memory. The next block, with three instructions,

```
mov     ax, Languages
call    PutDec
call    PutCrLf
```

prints the new value of Languages, then advances the output to the beginning of the next line. The last block, having three instructions,

```
mov     ah, ExitToDos
mov     al, NoErrors
int     DosFunc
```

returns control to DOS. We use the three named constants defined at the beginning of the program as operands. This is how an assembly-language program should terminate. It is very important that programs return control to the operating system correctly, or the computer may lock up or do other unpleasant things. (The return mechanism will eventually be explained in detail.) Finally, the last two lines of Program 3.1 terminate the code segment and then terminate the source file. Note that the label associated with the first instruction is used as the operand on the END directive.

In order to execute Program 3.1, we must assemble it and then link the object file with the input and output routines. These steps are the subject of the next section and of Appendixes 5 and 6.

## EXERCISES 3.4

▶1. Write a program in a high-level language that performs the same tasks as Program 3.1. Compare it to Program 3.1 in terms of
   (a) Number of source lines
   (b) Readability
   (c) Ease of modification
   (d) Restrictions on output format
   (e) Error handling

2. What do you think would happen if the length of a string passed to PutStr was not correct, that is, if CX contained a number other than the length of the string passed through BX? Consider both cases: CX less than the actual length and CX greater than the actual length.

3. The example execution of Program 3.1 in the text assumes that the user types a space following the numeric input. How would the example appear different if the user taps the ENTER key instead?

In Exercises 4 through 8, write an assembly-language program using the routines presented in this section. It is not necessary to assemble or execute these programs (yet).

4. Write a program that prints your initials in large block letters. Use a separate string for each line of your initials.

5. Write a program that asks for the user's age and prints what the user's age will be next year.

6. Write a program that prints a quotation from your favorite author or public figure. Be sure to give credit.

7. Write a program that asks for the number of computing courses the user has completed and prints how many the user will have completed after finishing this course.

8. Write a program that prints three copies of your name and address, in a format like that used on a mailing label. (The output should resemble three mailing labels, one above the other.)

## 3.5 ASSEMBLING, LINKING, AND EXECUTING

The preceding sections have shown instructions, operands, directives, and the organization of an assembly-language program. We have a set of input and output procedures; we have written a complete program; and now we want the computer to execute it. The mechanics are described here, using the Microsoft Macro Assembler, version 5.1, and supporting utilities. More information on the Microsoft assemblers (5.1 and 6.0) and utilities is included in Appendix 5. Information on Borland's Turbo Assembler and utilities can be found in Appendix 6.

### Assembling

After entering the program as a source file using a text editor, the next step is to translate the program into the binary codes that correspond to machine instructions and data. This process, called *assembling*, is performed by a program called an **assembler.** By convention, the source file for an assembly-language program has an .ASM extension. The files created by the assembler have the same base name, with different extensions that indicate the contents of each.

When we invoke the assembler, we can include all file specifications and options on the command line or issue just the command and specify the files and options interactively. Options consist of a slash followed by one or more letters or digits. At most installations, the assembler is configured so that it is not necessary to enter options except in special cases. This book assumes that the reader's installation is so configured.

To invoke the assembler with options on the command line, type MASM followed by the options and tap ENTER. One of the options, /H, displays the syntax of the command line and lists the options with a brief explanation of each. To see this, enter

```
C>MASM /H
```

Note that the /H option is not used when assembling a program.

To assemble a program using the interactive form of the command, enter MASM and any options other than /H, then tap the ENTER key. The assembler prompts for the source filename by displaying

```
Source filename [.ASM]:
```

Type the name of your source file; the assembler assumes the extension .ASM if no extension is entered. For the rest of this example, assume your program is named WELCOME.ASM, as in Program 3.1. You would type WELCOME in response to the prompt. Then the assembler prompts for the object filename by displaying

```
Object filename [WELCOME.OBJ]:
```

If you want the default filename for the object file, tap ENTER. Otherwise, type the filename you want to use for the object file. Next the assembler prompts for the listing filename by displaying

```
Source listing [NUL.LST]:
```

If you do not want a listing file, tap ENTER. The NUL base filename implies that the file is not to be created. To specify a name for the listing file, type the base part of the name (typically the same as the base of the source filename) and tap ENTER. The assembler appends the .LST extension for you. You can specify a different extension if desired.

Finally, the assembler prompts for the cross-reference filename by displaying

```
Cross reference [NUL.CRF]:
```

If you do not want a cross-reference listing file, tap ENTER, and none will be created. To specify one with the .CRF extension, type the base filename and tap ENTER.

The assembler then reads your source file. If the program contains no syntax errors, the assembler generates all of the requested files. If there are syntax errors, no object file is created. The assembler reports on the amount of symbol space available, the number of errors, and the number of warnings. The symbol space is separated into near space, which is limited to 64K, and far space, which is limited only by available memory. These numbers are useful with large programs that consume nearly all available memory, but that should not be a problem with the programs in this text.

To summarize, the process of assembling Program 3.1, WELCOME.ASM, is shown interactively in Figure 3.3. In the figure, both the listing file and the cross reference file are

## 3.5 Assembling, Linking, and Executing 79

```
C>MASM
Microsoft (R) Macro Assembler Version 5.10
Copyright (C) Microsoft Corp 1981, 1988.  All rights reserved.

Source filename [.ASM]: WELCOME
Object filename [WELCOME.OBJ]:
Source listing  [NUL.LST]: WELCOME
Cross-reference [NUL.CRF]: WELCOME

  47356 + 305872 Bytes symbol space free

      0 Warning Errors
      0 Severe  Errors

C>
```

**Figure 3.3** Assembling WELCOME.ASM

requested. The same result can be achieved by entering the filenames on the command line, as

`C>MASM WELCOME,,WELCOME,WELCOME`

Note in this example that it is unnecessary to specify the listing file; it defaults to WELCOME.LST.

We can omit any filename for which we accept the default (as shown in the interactive prompt) as long as we use commas to indicate which filenames are omitted. We can also omit trailing commas by using a semicolon. So, to assemble WELCOME.ASM and create only the object file, we can use the command

`C>MASM WELCOME;`

If we forget the semicolon, or leave off a comma, the assembler interprets as much of the command line as it can and then prompts for any remaining filename(s).

Now that the mechanics of assembling have been shown, consider the files generated by the assembler. The object file contains the instructions and data coded in binary. It can be examined with any program that can dump the contents of a file in hexadecimal, but it won't make much sense yet: Chapter 11 describes an object file in detail, but one can get an idea of its contents from the listing file.

The listing file produced when WELCOME.ASM is assembled is shown in Figure 3.4. A new directive has been added to the first line of this program so that the listing (and cross-reference) file(s) would print in a form more suitable for reproduction. The PAGE directive specifies the number of lines per page and the number of characters per line for the output files. We specified 100 characters per line, instead of the default 80, so that longer lines would not wrap at the right end, and we specified 56 lines per page, instead of the default 50. The default line and page lengths print normally on $8.5 \times 11$ paper but wrap long lines. Depending on your printing facilities, some other values might be more appropriate.

The listing file contains all of the original source program, with several columns of numbers inserted on the left side. The first column shown in Figure 3.4 contains line

## 80  Chapter 3  Assembly-Language Programming

```
Microsoft (R) Macro Assembler Version 5.10               1/13/92 09:32:31
                                                         Page     1-1


 1                              PAGE 56,100
 2                              ; Program 3.1        Welcome.ASM
 3                              ; Prints a welcome message, reads how many languages the
 4                              ;   user knows, and prints a message increasing it by 1.
 5
 6                              ; DOS function and status parameters
 7 = 0021                       DosFunc     equ     21h
 8 = 004C                       ExitToDos   equ     4Ch
 9 = 0000                       NoErrors    equ     00h
10
11                              DOSSEG
12
13 0000                         _STACK SEGMENT para stack 'stack'
14 0000  0100[                               dw      100h dup (?)
15            ????
16                                ]
17
18 0200                         _STACK ENDS
19
20 0000                         _DATA SEGMENT word public 'data'
21 0000  0000                   Languages   dw      ?
22 0002  57 65 6C 63 6F 6D      HelloMsg    db      "Welcome to 8086 Assembly Language."
23       65 20 74 6F 20 38
24       30 38 36 20 41 73
25       73 65 6D 62 6C 79
26       20 4C 61 6E 67 75
27       61 67 65 2E
28 0024  0022                   HelloLen    dw      34
29 0026  48 6F 77 20 6D 61      PromptMsg   db      "How many languages do you know? "
30       6E 79 20 6C 61 6E
31       67 75 61 67 65 73
32       20 64 6F 20 79 6F
33       75 20 6B 6E 6F 77
34       3F 20
35 0046  0020                   PromptLen   dw      32
36 0048  20 69 73 20 61 20      ReplyMsg    db      " is a good start.  Soon you'll know "
37       67 6F 6F 64 20 73
38       74 61 72 74 2E 20
39       20 53 6F 6F 6E 20
40       79 6F 75 27 6C 6C
41       20 6B 6E 6F 77 20
42 006C  0024                   ReplyLen    dw      36
43 006E                         _DATA ENDS
44
45 0000                         _TEXT SEGMENT word public 'code'
46                                   assume  cs: _TEXT
47                                   extrn   PutStr: PROC, PutCrLf: PROC
48                                   extrn   GetDec: PROC, PutDec: PROC
49
50 0000                         Welcome:
51
52                              ; set up ds register to point to _DATA
```

**Figure 3.4  Listing File**

## 3.5 Assembling, Linking, and Executing

```
Microsoft (R) Macro Assembler Version 5.10            1/13/92 09:32:31
                                                      Page     1-2

 53 0000  B8 ---- R              mov     ax, seg _DATA
 54 0003  8E D8                  mov     ds, ax
 55                              assume  ds: _DATA
 56
 57                           ; print ("Welcome to 8086 Assembly Language.")
 58 0005  8B 0E 0024 R           mov     cx, HelloLen
 59 0009  BB 0002 R              mov     bx, offset HelloMsg
 60 000C  E8 0000 E              call    PutStr
 61 000F  E8 0000 E              call    PutCrLf
 62
 63                           ; print ("How many languages do you know? ")
 64 0012  8B 0E 0046 R           mov     cx, PromptLen
 65 0016  BB 0026 R              mov     bx, offset PromptMsg
 66 0019  E8 0000 E              call    PutStr
 67
 68                           ; read (Languages)
 69 001C  E8 0000 E              call    GetDec
 70 001F  A3 0000 R              mov     Languages, ax
 71
 72                           ; print (Languages, " is a good start.  Soon you'll know ")
 73 0022  E8 0000 E              call    PutCrLf
 74 0025  E8 0000 E              call    PutDec
 75
 76 0028  8B 0E 006C R           mov     cx, ReplyLen
 77 002C  BB 0048 R              mov     bx, offset ReplyMsg
 78 002F  E8 0000 E              call    PutStr
 79
 80                           ; Languages := Languages + 1
 81 0032  FF 06 0000 R           inc     Languages
 82
 83                           ; print (Languages)
 84 0036  A1 0000 R              mov     ax, Languages
 85 0039  E8 0000 E              call    PutDec
 86 003C  E8 0000 E              call    PutCrLf
 87
 88                           ; exit to DOS
 89 003F  B4 4C                  mov     ah, ExitToDos
 90 0041  B0 00                  mov     al, NoErrors
 91 0043  CD 21                  int     DosFunc
 92
 93 0045                         _TEXT ENDS
 94                              END     Welcome
```

**Figure 3.4** (*continued*)

numbers in decimal. These are included only if a cross-reference file is also requested. These numbers refer to the lines as printed, not to their positions in the source file. These line numbers are used for reference in this discussion.

The second column contains 4-digit hexadecimal numbers. These are either the values of constants or the displacements within the current segment of the start of the code generated for each line. For example, on lines 7 through 9 we see the values of the three constants. On line 35, we see the displacement of PromptLen from the beginning of the data segment is 0046h, or 70 bytes. Note that PromptLen follows Languages (2 bytes), HelloMsg (34 bytes), HelloLen (2 bytes), and PromptMsg (32 bytes), which

```
Microsoft (R) Macro Assembler Version 5.10           1/13/92 09:32:31
                                                     Symbols-1


Segments and Groups:

                N a m e                 Length   Align   Combine  Class

_DATA  . . . . . . . . . . . . .         006E     WORD    PUBLIC   'DATA'
_STACK . . . . . . . . . . . . .         0200     PARA    STACK    'STACK'
_TEXT  . . . . . . . . . . . . .         0045     WORD    PUBLIC   'CODE'

Symbols:

                N a m e                 Type     Value    Attr

DOSFUNC  . . . . . . . . . . . .         NUMBER   0021

EXITTODOS  . . . . . . . . . .           NUMBER   004C

GETDEC . . . . . . . . . . . . .         L NEAR   0000    _TEXT    External

HELLOLEN . . . . . . . . . . . .         L WORD   0024    _DATA
HELLOMSG . . . . . . . . . . . .         L BYTE   0002    _DATA

LANGUAGES  . . . . . . . . . . .         L WORD   0000    _DATA

NOERRORS . . . . . . . . . . . .         NUMBER   0000

PROMPTLEN  . . . . . . . . . . .         L WORD   0046    _DATA
PROMPTMSG  . . . . . . . . . . .         L BYTE   0026    _DATA
PUTCRLF  . . . . . . . . . . . .         L NEAR   0000    _TEXT    External
PUTDEC . . . . . . . . . . . . .         L NEAR   0000    _TEXT    External
PUTSTR . . . . . . . . . . . . .         L NEAR   0000    _TEXT    External

REPLYLEN . . . . . . . . . . . .         L WORD   006C    _DATA
REPLYMSG . . . . . . . . . . . .         L BYTE   0048    _DATA

WELCOME  . . . . . . . . . . . .         L NEAR   0000    _TEXT

@CPU . . . . . . . . . . . . . .         TEXT    0101h
@FILENAME  . . . . . . . . . . .         TEXT    welcome
@VERSION . . . . . . . . . . . .         TEXT    510


     76 Source Lines
     76 Total  Lines
     26 Symbols

  47356 + 303825 Bytes symbol space free

      0 Warning Errors
      0 Severe  Errors
```

**Figure 3.4**  (*continued*)

## 3.5 Assembling, Linking, and Executing

occupy the first $2 + 34 + 2 + 32 = 70$ bytes of the segment. The numbers in the second column also start at zero for each SEGMENT definition (lines 13, 20, and 45) and give the size of each segment at the ENDS directive (lines 18, 43, and 93).

With a few exceptions, the rest of the information to the left of the original source line is the hexadecimal representation of the code generated by the assembler for the line. This is a simplified representation of the object file. Let's look at several lines, starting with some data.

The value assembled for the variable Languages is 0000h, shown in line 21. This was uninitialized in the source program. The assembler may specify zero for the value of an uninitialized variable in some circumstances. We should not assume this will occur in general; we should initialize each variable to whatever value we need or assume it is not initialized.

Lines 22 through 27 give the hexadecimal codes for the characters in HelloMsg. That is, W is represented by 57h, e by 65h, and so on. (See Appendix 2 for a table of all character codes.) Note that each byte is listed separately, in the order (left to right) in which the characters are stored (at increasing displacements). The object file contains these same codes in the same order.

Line 28 lists displacement 0024h in the data segment, which contains the word 0022h. Note that 0022h is just 34, the value specified for HelloLen. Similarly, line 35 shows the value assembled for PromptLen is 0020h, or 32. Word values are listed with the more significant byte on the left and the less significant byte on the right. The assembler displays these together without a space on the listing; in the object file, the bytes are reversed with the less significant byte at the smaller displacement.

Now let's consider some instructions. Line 54 shows that the internal representation of the instruction

```
    mov     ds, ax
```

is 8ED8h. Instructions with a segment register as one operand are coded using a variation of the format shown in Figure 2.16. The segment register is coded in the *reg* field, and the AX register is coded in the *mod* and *r/m* fields; the direction bit specifies the direction of the move.

Most of the other instructions shown on the listing are followed by either E or R. The instructions followed by R have displacements that are relative to the start of a segment in this program; these displacements may be modified during linking. This happens when a main program and a subprogram share the same segments: the final displacements in the latter will have to be adjusted by the size of the segments in the former. The instructions followed by E have displacements that refer to externally defined objects. The linker will supply displacements for these instructions.

There is an interesting situation in line 53. The instruction starts with B8, which is the code for a mov instruction with AX for the destination operand and an immediate constant for source operand. The assembler cannot determine where _DATA will be loaded, so it cannot compute the segment number to code in the data field. The linker cannot do this either. These two programs pass on the responsibility for this operand to the loader, which fills the data field of this instruction with a constant value that corresponds to the segment number where _DATA is loaded.

Now let's look at the stack segment. Lines 14 through 16 show the contents of the object file for the stack segment as a repeat count of 0100h and a value indicated by ????, which is an uninitialized word. Note that 0100h words is 0200h bytes, the size of the stack segment shown on line 18.

Following the end of the program, there are two tables printed as part of the listing file. The first table lists all segments and groups. Groups are not discussed in this text. There are three segments in the program WELCOME. They are summarized in the table, based on information specified in the SEGMENT directives and the segment lengths. The length of a segment is just the number of bytes assembled for it. The second table describes all symbols used in the program, along with a few symbols the assembler generated. The symbols are sorted alphabetically.

For constants, the type column specifies NUMBER, and the value column gives the value in hexadecimal.

For all other symbols defined in WELCOME, the type column indicates that they are labels (indicated by L; there is no distinction here between label and name). Targets of transfers of control are given as NEAR since they are in the same code segment, and data are given as either WORD or BYTE. The value column gives the displacement (in hexadecimal) from the beginning of the segment named in the first attribute column. The second attribute column indicates which symbols are external.

The symbols generated by the assembler are TEXT symbols, in which the value is given directly either as a number or a character string. The value of @CPU, 0101h, indicates that the program was assembled for the (default) configuration of 8086 processor and 8087 coprocessor. @FILENAME gives the base part of the source filename, and @VERSION indicates that the program was assembled by version 5.10 of MASM.

There are other possible values that can appear in the symbol table. Watch for them in future programs and try to determine what each new entry you see means.

The last few lines of the listing report give the number of lines and symbols, the remaining memory, and the number of warnings and errors.

The other file created by the assembler, when requested, is the cross-reference file. MASM creates this file in binary, but the CREF utility converts it into printable form with the same page specification as the listing file. The CREF utility takes two filenames as parameters: the file generated by the assembler with .CRF extension and the output file that it will generate with .REF extension. The extensions need not be entered if the defaults are acceptable. The CREF program prompts for filenames if they are not entered on the command line.

The output of CREF for the WELCOME program is shown in Figure 3.5. It lists the symbols in sorted order, though different from the symbol table of the listing file. Following each symbol are the line numbers—on the listing file, not in the source file—where the symbol appears. The line where the symbol is defined is indicated by #. Lines where the value associated with the symbol can be changed are indicated by +. For example, Languages is defined on line 21 and referenced on lines 70, 81, and 84; its value can be changed on lines 70 and 81 but not on line 84.

Note that segment names as well as segment class names are included. For example, CODE occurs (but is not defined) on line 45, while _TEXT is defined on line 45. Also notice that the symbols @CPU and @VERSION appear to be defined on line 1; the assembler assumes these default values during startup.

### 3.5 Assembling, Linking, and Executing

```
Microsoft Cross-Reference   Version 5.10      Mon Jan 13 09:32:53 1992

    Symbol Cross-Reference            (# definition, + modification)      Cref-1

   @CPU . . . . . . . . . . . . .    1#
   @VERSION . . . . . . . . . . .    1#

   CODE . . . . . . . . . . . . .    45

   DATA . . . . . . . . . . . . .    20
   DOSFUNC. . . . . . . . . . . .    7#     91

   EXITTODOS. . . . . . . . . . .    8#     89

   GETDEC . . . . . . . . . . . .    48#    69

   HELLOLEN . . . . . . . . . . .    28#    58
   HELLOMSG . . . . . . . . . . .    22#    59

   LANGUAGES. . . . . . . . . . .    21#    70+    81+    84

   NOERRORS . . . . . . . . . . .    9#     90

   PROMPTLEN. . . . . . . . . . .    35#    64
   PROMPTMSG. . . . . . . . . . .    29#    65
   PUTCRLF. . . . . . . . . . . .    47#    61     73     86
   PUTDEC . . . . . . . . . . . .    48#    74     85
   PUTSTR . . . . . . . . . . . .    47#    60     66     78

   REPLYLEN . . . . . . . . . . .    42#    76
   REPLYMSG . . . . . . . . . . .    36#    77

   STACK. . . . . . . . . . . . .    13

   WELCOME. . . . . . . . . . . .    50#    94

   _DATA. . . . . . . . . . . . .    20#    43     53     55
   _STACK . . . . . . . . . . . .    13#    18
   _TEXT. . . . . . . . . . . . .    45#    46     93

   23 Symbols
```

**Figure 3.5  The Output of CREF**

The cross-reference listing is useful when tracking down the cause of a variable that changes unexpectedly.

## Linking

Once assembled, the program must be linked with the modules that define all external references within the program. The Microsoft Linker, LINK, has a command line structure similar to the assembler. The filenames can be specified on the command line or in response to prompts. There are also a number of options, including a HELP option that lists all available options. To link the WELCOME program with the input and output routines and

## Chapter 3 Assembly-Language Programming

generate the optional MAP file, using the interactive form of the command, enter LINK and tap the ENTER key. The linker prompts for the object filenames by displaying

```
Object Modules [.OBJ]:
```

Type the names of your object files separated by spaces; the linker assumes the extension .OBJ if you omit it. Note that if you have more than one object module, such as a main program in one module and subprograms in another, you must enter all of the filenames on one line. In this example, we would type WELCOME and tap ENTER.

Then the linker prompts for the executable filename by displaying

```
Run File [WELCOME.EXE]:
```

The linker uses the first object filename as the default base name for the executable file. If you want to use this, tap ENTER. Otherwise, type the filename you want for the executable file. Next the linker prompts for the map filename by displaying

```
List File [NUL.MAP]:
```

If you do not want a map file, tap ENTER. To specify a name for the map file, type the base part of the name (typically the same as the base of the executable file), and tap ENTER. The linker appends the .MAP extension for you.

Finally, the linker prompts for the names of any libraries you want to use by displaying

```
Libraries [.LIB]:
```

Type the path to the library files you want to use. Assuming that you have copied the file IO.LIB from the floppy disk that accompanies this text to a directory named \LIB on the current drive, you would respond by typing \LIB\IO. Then the linker reads the object and library files. If all external references are resolved, the linker produces the executable and map files. If there are any errors, the linker displays appropriate messages.

The whole dialogue is presented in Figure 3.6 for reference. The same result could be achieved by typing all entries on the command line, as

```
C>LINK WELCOME,,WELCOME,\LIB\IO
```

Again, if we want to use any of the defaults as shown in the dialogue, we can omit the filename; we must include the comma to show the skipped field.

```
C>LINK

Microsoft (R) Overlay Linker   Version 3.64
Copyright (C) Microsoft Corp 1983-1988.  All rights reserved.

Object Modules [.OBJ]: WELCOME
Run File [WELCOME.EXE]:
List File [NUL.MAP]: WELCOME
Libraries [.LIB]: \LIB\IO

C>
```

**Figure 3.6 Linking WELCOME Program**

### 3.5 Assembling, Linking, and Executing

```
Start   Stop    Length  Name                Class
00000H  00179H  0017AH  _TEXT               CODE
00180H  0037FH  00200H  _STACK              STACK
00380H  00419H  0009AH  _DATA               DATA
```

Program entry point at 0000:0010

**Figure 3.7** WELCOME.MAP

An executable file will be examined in Chapter 11. But let's look at the map file now. Figure 3.7 shows the map file produced by the linker for the program WELCOME. There are three segments in three classes in WELCOME.EXE. The first segment is named _TEXT, of class CODE. The linker has combined the _TEXT segment from WELCOME and the _TEXT segment from IO.LIB to form one segment. When it did that, it had to change some of the references within the copy of IO.LIB. The _DATA segments were also combined to form one segment.

Along with the segment names and classes, the map lists the displacements of the first and last byte of each segment within the executable image of the program, and the length of each segment. The last line of the map indicates that the entry point is at displacement 0010h in the CODE segment. Microsoft linkers write the first instruction with this displacement in the CODE segment for compatibility with their other languages. Other linkers may write the first instruction at displacement 0. We will refer back to this map in the next section when we examine memory during execution with DEBUG.

## Executing

Our program started as a text file, was transformed into codes representing the instructions and data by the assembler, and was combined with other codes by the linker. The net result is that we now have an executable file on the disk. In order to execute that file, two things are necessary: to copy the file into memory (and make any final changes to it based on where in memory the program is copied) and to transfer control to the entry point.

The operating system accepts commands from the keyboard and arranges for the program that performs the requested task to be executed. For example, to format a disk, we type FORMAT at the DOS prompt. FORMAT is an external command, so DOS must copy the FORMAT program into memory and give control to it. When the FORMAT program terminates, it returns control to DOS, which then reads the next command, and so on.

To DOS, a program we write and have converted to an executable file is no different from any other external command. So, to execute our program, we type WELCOME at the DOS prompt. This was illustrated in Section 3.4, in which the WELCOME program was first introduced.

### EXERCISES 3.5

▶1. If you did any of the exercises in the previous section that asked you to write a program, now assemble, link, and execute it. Also print the listing, cross-reference, and map files, and determine the following:
   (*a*) Size of your program's code segment

(b) Size of your program's data segment
(c) Size of the code segment, including I/O procedures
(d) Size of the data segment, including I/O procedures
(e) Which symbol is referenced the most times
(f) Which symbols may be changed during execution
(g) Which symbols cannot be changed during execution
(h) Longest instruction
(i) Shortest instruction

2. Examine the listing file for WELCOME, in Figure 3.4.
   (a) How are the characters "8086" in HelloMsg coded?
   (b) Why is there no code shown for line 50?
   (c) What is the significance of 0200 in the code column of line 13?
   (d) The operand fields of the instructions on lines 55 and 56 are both 0000; the operands in the source program are different, so they can't be coded the same. Explain what these 0000 entries mean.

3. Examine the code generated for the mov instructions in the listing of Figure 3.4. What do you think the assembler would code for the following instructions?
   (a) mov    al, 32
   (b) mov    ah, 32h
   (c) mov    ax, 0
   (d) mov    al, 100h

4. Compare the length of the _TEXT segment given in the segments table of the listing file (Figure 3.4) with the length of the same segment given in the map file (Figure 3.7). How many bytes of instructions are there in WELCOME? In IO.LIB?

## 3.6 EXAMINING MEMORY WITH DEBUG

It is useful to look into memory while a program is executing. Doing so enables one to see what the executable program looks like and to watch how instructions affect the various registers and flags. It is also a useful technique for locating some errors in a program.

When looking at memory dumps, we must interpret each byte carefully. We know, from the map and symbol tables, what each byte of memory represents. We can ask DEBUG to interpret any byte as a character, as part of an integer, or as part of an instruction. In the latter two cases, a starting address must be carefully specified, or DEBUG will produce incorrect results. There is no way for DEBUG or the processor to determine what type of information a byte represents.

There are many tools available that allow us to examine memory while a program is executing. This section uses DEBUG, a utility supplied with DOS, to examine WELCOME.EXE. (The appendixes discuss Microsoft CodeView and Borland Turbo Debugger.) DEBUG is a general-purpose utility: It can be used to examine, modify, trace, and execute programs and to modify binary files on disks. Of all these capabilities, we will use it only to examine and trace programs in memory. Consult your DOS User's Reference manual for other features and capabilities of DEBUG.

We start DEBUG with the command

```
C>DEBUG WELCOME.EXE
```

### 3.6 Examining Memory with DEBUG

It prints a hyphen as its prompt and waits for us to enter a command. The first command we issue is D, for dump. This dumps the first 128 (80h) bytes of the program in hexadecimal and ASCII. The first column lists addresses in segment:offset format. Each address is followed by 16 bytes in hexadecimal (the dash in the middle is for reference) and as ASCII characters, with control and extended characters shown as dots. Note: the address where a program is loaded depends on the size of other programs already loaded; the starting address of the data segment will vary accordingly.

```
C>DEBUG WELCOME.EXE
-D
30B2:0010  B8 EA 30 8E D8 8B 0E 24-00 BB 02 00 E8 37 00 E8   ..0....$.....7..
30B2:0020  4C 00 8B 0E 46 00 BB 26-00 E8 2A 00 E8 C9 00 A3   L...F..&..*.....
30B2:0030  00 00 E8 39 00 E8 46 00-8B 0E 6C 00 BB 48 00 E8   ...9..F...l..H..
30B2:0040  14 00 FF 06 00 00 A1 00-00 E8 32 00 E8 1F 00 B4   ..........2.....
30B2:0050  4C B0 00 CD 21 00 50 53-51 52 B4 02 83 F9 01 7C   L...!.PSQR.....|
30B2:0060  07 8A 17 CD 21 43 E2 F9-5A 59 5B 58 C3 00 50 52   ....!C..ZY[X..PR
30B2:0070  B4 02 B2 0D CD 21 B2 0A-CD 21 5A 58 C3 00 50 53   .....!...!ZX..PS
30B2:0080  51 52 3D 00 00 7D 07 F7-D8 B5 2D EB 03 90 B5 20   QR=..}....-....
```

Recall from the map in Figure 3.7 that the first instruction is at displacement 0010h. The first byte dumped is at location 30B2:0010, which corresponds to the first instruction of WELCOME. From the listing file, shown in Figure 3.4, the first instruction,

      mov    ax, seg _DATA

was assembled as B8 followed by an unspecified word. The first three bytes of the dump are B8, EA, and 30. Words are stored with the less significant byte first, so the data in this instruction is 30EAh. Now, the map shows _DATA at offset 0380h. The program starts at 30B20h (the segment number shifted four bits to the left). If we add 30B20h and 0380h, we get 30EA0h, which corresponds to segment 30EAh. We'll return to this number soon.

Let's look at a couple of instructions to see how they are coded. The first instruction, given above, is not coded using the format of Figure 2.16. There is a special short-form instruction for mov when the destination is a register and the source is an immediate value. In the short form, bits 4 through 7 are Bh; bit 3 indicates whether the data is a word or byte (the $w$ bit of Figure 2.16). Bits 0 through 2 specify which register, using the same codes as given in Table 2.1. Since the data is a word, bit 3 is 1. The code for AX is 000. Putting the pieces together, we get 1011 1 000, or B8h, for the first byte of the instruction. The data word is stored with less significant byte in the second byte of the instruction and more significant byte as the third and final byte of the instruction.

The instruction at offset 0012 in the program is

      mov    cx, PromptLen

From the listing file, we see that it is coded using four bytes. Looking at the dump, we see (at 30B2:0022) the four bytes are 8B 0E 46 00. This instruction does follow the format given in Figure 2.16. Writing the first two bytes in binary and separating the fields, we get

```
    8       B       0       E
  1000    1011    0000    1110

100010    1    1    00    001    110
opcode    d    w    mod   reg    r/m
```

The register operand, according to Table 2.1, is the CX register (specified by the *reg* field, 001). The *r/m* operand is a direct memory reference, the special case of *mod* = 00 and *r/m* = 110. Since the *d* bit is 1, the register is the destination. Since the *w* bit is 1, the data is a word. The third and fourth bytes give the low and high bytes of the offset of the memory location from which the operand value is copied. The opcode specifies a move operation.

Let's look at the program another way. We can ask DEBUG to "unassemble" the instructions of WELCOME with the U command. We specify the starting location as 30B2:0010, which we already determined to be the location of first instruction. We also specify the number of bytes to unassemble as 45h, which is just the length of the _TEXT segment used by WELCOME, as given in the first table in the listing file.

```
-U 30B2:0010 L45
30B2:0010 B8EA30        MOV     AX,30EA
30B2:0013 8ED8          MOV     DS,AX
30B2:0015 8B0E2400      MOV     CX,[0024]
30B2:0019 BB0200        MOV     BX,0002
30B2:001C E83700        CALL    0056
30B2:001F E84C00        CALL    006E
30B2:0022 8B0E4600      MOV     CX,[0046]
30B2:0026 BB2600        MOV     BX,0026
30B2:0029 E82A00        CALL    0056
30B2:002C E8C900        CALL    00F8
30B2:002F A30000        MOV     [0000],AX
30B2:0032 E83900        CALL    006E
30B2:0035 E84600        CALL    007E
30B2:0038 8B0E6C00      MOV     CX,[006C]
30B2:003C BB4800        MOV     BX,0048
30B2:003F E81400        CALL    0056
30B2:0042 FF060000      INC     WORD PTR [0000]
30B2:0046 A10000        MOV     AX,[0000]
30B2:0049 E83200        CALL    007E
30B2:004C E81F00        CALL    006E
30B2:004F B44C          MOV     AH,4C
30B2:0051 B000          MOV     AL,00
30B2:0053 CD21          INT     21
```

The unassembled listing shows all instructions using the mnemonics for the operations and hexadecimal numbers for the operands. The bytes of the immediate constants are shown in normal order; for example, the constant in the first instruction is given as 30EAh. (We saw this number earlier, and we'll see it again.) We examined the coding of this instruction above.

Some operands are given in square brackets. These are offsets. For example, the second mov instruction we coded above specified an operand in memory at offset 0046h. This instruction is at 30B2:0022. The unassembled version of it is

```
mov     cx, [0046]
```

There are also a few minor features that have not yet been introduced, such as the ptr operator, that will be skipped for now. The unassembled listing shows the final values of the operands that the assembler did not completely specify and that were provided either by the linker or by the loader.

### 3.6 Examining Memory with DEBUG

Now let's look at the registers as they are when the program is loaded, before executing the first instruction. DEBUG will show all the registers when given the R command.

```
-R
AX=0000  BX=0000  CX=041A  DX=0000  SP=0200  BP=0000  SI=0000  DI=0000
DS=30A2  ES=30A2  SS=30CA  CS=30B2  IP=0010     NV UP EI PL NZ NA PO NC
30B2:0010 B8EA30          MOV     AX,30EA
```

DEBUG shows the contents of the general registers and the pointer and index registers on the first line. It shows the four segment registers, the instruction pointer, and the flags register on the second line. Note that CS:IP is 30B2:0010, the entry point of the program. On the third line, DEBUG prints, in the unassembled format, the instruction pointed to by CS:IP. The states of the flags (except the trap flag, which DEBUG uses) are given in symbolic form, with a 2-letter code for each flag. The interpretation of the codes is given in Table 3.1.

Notice that in the register dump DOS has initialized DS and ES to point to a location 100h bytes before the start of the program. As shown in Chapter 11, DOS creates a prefix for each program as it loads it. The prefix is 100h bytes long and contains the text of the command line and other things.

Now let's watch the computer execute our program. The T (trace) command in DEBUG executes a single instruction and then displays the registers in the same format as the R command.

```
-T
AX=30EA  BX=0000  CX=041A  DX=0000  SP=0200  BP=0000  SI=0000  DI=0000
DS=30A2  ES=30A2  SS=30CA  CS=30B2  IP=0013     NV UP EI PL NZ NA PO NC
30B2:0013 8ED8            MOV     DS,AX
```

The computer executed the first mov instruction. Note that the AX register now contains the constant 30EAh, and the instruction pointer has been advanced by three bytes (the size of the first mov instruction). DEBUG also displays that location and the next instruction in hexadecimal and unassembled. Let's execute the second mov with another T command.

```
-T
AX=30EA  BX=0000  CX=041A  DX=0000  SP=0200  BP=0000  SI=0000  DI=0000
DS=30EA  ES=30A2  SS=30CA  CS=30B2  IP=0015     NV UP EI PL NZ NA PO NC
30B2:0015 8B0E2400        MOV     CX,[0024]                          DS:0024=0022
```

**Table 3.1  Codes Displayed for Flags**

| Flag Bit | Cleared | Set |
|---|---|---|
| overflow | NV | OV |
| direction | UP | DN |
| interrupt enable | DI | EI |
| trap | not shown by DEBUG | |
| sign | PL | NG |
| zero | NZ | ZR |
| auxiliary carry | NA | AC |
| parity | PO | PE |
| carry | NC | CY |

Note that the DS register now is also 30EAh. The instruction pointer has been advanced to the next instruction. The second operand of this instruction is the offset 0024h. DEBUG also shows, near the right end of the line, the current value stored at offset 0024h from the DS register. The value is 0022h.

The two instructions that we traced have moved a constant provided by DOS into the DS register. That constant is the segment boundary where _DATA begins. Now let's dump the _DATA segment. (This could be done at any time; it is not necessary to trace the first couple of instructions before examining the data segment.) We issue a D (dump) command with the starting location of the _DATA segment, 30EA:0000, and the length, 6E, given on the map.

```
-D 30EA:0000 L6E
30EA:0000  00 00 57 65 6C 63 6F 6D-65 20 74 6F 20 38 30 38   ..Welcome to 808
30EA:0010  36 20 41 73 73 65 6D 62-6C 79 20 4C 61 6E 67 75   6 Assembly Langu
30EA:0020  61 67 65 2E 22 00 48 6F-77 20 6D 61 6E 79 20 6C   age.".How many l
30EA:0030  61 6E 67 75 61 67 65 73-20 64 6F 20 79 6F 75 20   anguages do you
30EA:0040  6B 6E 6F 6F 77 3F 20 20 20 00-20 69 73 20 61 20 67 6F  know?   . is a go
30EA:0050  6F 64 20 73 74 61 72 74-2E 20 20 53 6F 6F 6E 20   od start.  Soon
30EA:0060  79 6F 75 27 6C 6C 20 6B-6E 6F 77 20 24 00         you'll know $.
```

The _DATA segment contains the values we specified in our program. Note that the dollar sign two bytes from the end of the dump is just the less significant byte of ReplyLen. The ASCII code for the dollar sign happens to be 24h. Now let's trace the next couple of instructions.

```
-T

AX=30EA  BX=0000  CX=0022  DX=0000  SP=0200  BP=0000  SI=0000  DI=0000
DS=30EA  ES=30A2  SS=30CA  CS=30B2  IP=0019   NV UP EI PL NZ NA PO NC
30B2:0019 BB0200          MOV     BX,0002
-T

AX=30EA  BX=0002  CX=0022  DX=0000  SP=0200  BP=0000  SI=0000  DI=0000
DS=30EA  ES=30A2  SS=30CA  CS=30B2  IP=001C   NV UP EI PL NZ NA PO NC
30B2:001C E83700          CALL    0056
```

The third instruction moved 0022h into CX, and the fourth moved 0002h into BX. These are the instructions that set up the arguments to PutStr. The next instruction is the call to PutStr. We could trace into PutStr and watch it execute, but that is a little beyond our scope right now. This is where another DEBUG command is useful. The P command will execute through a procedure (or certain repetitive blocks of instructions) as though the procedure were a single instruction. We try it with the call to PutStr.

```
-P
Welcome to 8086 Assembly Language.
AX=30EA  BX=0002  CX=0022  DX=0000  SP=0200  BP=0000  SI=0000  DI=0000
DS=30EA  ES=30A2  SS=30CA  CS=30B2  IP=001F   NV UP EI PL NZ NA PE NC
30B2:001F E84C00          CALL    006E
```

The call to PutStr printed the message Welcome to 8086 Assembly Language. and returned to the next instruction in the main program. DEBUG then stopped the program

### 3.6 Examining Memory with DEBUG

to display the registers and the next instruction. The next instruction is a call to `PutCrLf`, so we issue another P command.

```
-P
AX=30EA  BX=0002  CX=0022  DX=0000  SP=0200  BP=0000  SI=0000  DI=0000
DS=30EA  ES=30A2  SS=30CA  CS=30B2  IP=0022   NV UP EI PL NZ NA PE NC
30B2:0022 8B0E4600      MOV     CX,[0046]                         DS:0046=0020

-Q
C>
```

The call to `PutCrLf` advanced the output to a new line. DEBUG then displayed the registers and the next instruction. We don't need to trace the rest of the program at this point. We have seen enough for our purposes here. The Q (quit) command is issued to terminate DEBUG.

There are more sophisticated techniques we can use with DEBUG. For example, if we want to trace only a selected portion of a program, we can start DEBUG, set a breakpoint just before the region we want to trace, and then have DEBUG execute the program up to the breakpoint. We do not have to watch it execute every instruction, nor do we have to get a display of the registers after each instruction. Once control reaches the breakpoint, DEBUG will stop to display the registers and next instruction; then it will prompt for a command. The command summary in Appendix 5 includes the setting of breakpoints with DEBUG.

More sophisticated debugging utilities use the instructions in the executable file and the original program in the source file—and information provided by the assembler and linker—in a way that allows the programmer to watch the execution of a program at the source statement level. These utilities allow the user to set breakpoints and watch the values of variables using the symbolic names in the original source program.

Another useful tool for learning about the operation of a computer is an emulator, which is a program that runs on one computer to make it appear that it is another computer. There are emulators available that display the registers and relevant regions of memory as a program executes. These are not meant to execute programs in a production environment, as they interpret the programs rather than allow them to be executed directly by the computer. Some emulators do not support all of the features of a real computer, but are still quite useful in a learning environment. Emulators are especially helpful when the target computer is not available, such as when a proposed new design is being tested.

## EXERCISES 3.6

▶1. If you did Exercise 1 of Section 3.5, use DEBUG to unassemble the instructions and to dump the data segment of your program.

▶2. If you did Exercise 1 of Section 3.5, use DEBUG to trace the execution of the first few instructions of your program. Explain what they do.

▶3. Assemble, link, and execute WELCOME using DEBUG. What differences are there between your output and that shown in this section? Can you explain the differences?

▶4. Execute WELCOME or your own program using DEBUG. Trace into procedure PutCrLf. Does PutCrLf invoke PutStr with a string of two characters (Cr and Lf), does it invoke PutChar twice, or does it do something else?

5. What would happen if a programmer did not set up the DS register but simply had the assembler assume that DS pointed to the appropriate segment? Consider the program WELCOME, for example. Try to be explicit.

▶6. Write an assembly-language program that includes all of the mov instructions of Exercise 3 of Section 3.5. Use DEBUG's U command to verify your answers.

▶7. Use DEBUG's U command to interpret the data segment of WELCOME.EXE as instructions. What does DEBUG display for bytes that it cannot interpret as instructions? What do you think would happen if the computer attempted to execute the data segment by mistake?

▶8. Invoke DEBUG with WELCOME.EXE, but follow the command by two filenames (the files need not exist for this experiment) and some other text, like parameters. For example, try

   C>DEBUG WELCOME.EXE Filename.001 File2.xxx some parms

   Issue a D command to dump 100h bytes of the region initially pointed to by DS and ES.
   (a) The filenames are saved somewhere in this region in modified form. Where? How are they modified?
   (b) Most of the command line is also saved in this region. Where? Is it modified? What part of the command line is not saved? How many characters from the command line can be saved in this region?

## KEY POINTS

- Comments are used to document a program and to break a program into blocks that reflect its high-level design.
- Statements in an assembly-language program can be executable instructions, assembler directives, macroinstruction definitions, or macroinstruction calls.
- Assembly-language statements contain up to four fields: a label, a mnemonic for the operation, operands, and a comment.
- A symbol is an identifier that represents a constant, an address, a register, an operation, a directive, or a macroinstruction. Some symbols are defined by the assembler; others are defined by the programmer.
- A name is a symbol associated with a constant, a macroinstruction, a procedure, or a block of memory used for a variable or a segment.
- A label is a symbol associated with an instruction in memory.
- Assembler directives control the translation of a program, the allocation of memory, the initialization of constants, and other aspects of the assembly process.
- A macroinstruction is a named block of text that can be substituted for the name by the assembler during program translation.
- Operands can be in registers, in memory, implied by an instruction, or included as part of an instruction.
- Operands in registers are specified by the register name.
- Operands in memory are specified symbolically.
- Immediate operands are constants that are coded in the instruction.
- Operands can be written as expressions with operators that are applied during the assembly process.

- Input and output operations provided by the operating system and hardware are usually fairly primitive.
- The assembler reads the source file and generates an object file that contains the coded instructions and the optional listing and cross-reference files.
- A listing file contains a copy of the original source file with the code generated by the assembler and the tables built during the assembly process.
- A cross-reference table shows, for each symbol in the program, where the symbol is defined, modified, and referenced.
- The linker combines the object file(s) produced by the assembler with library procedures to create the executable file. It can also generate a map file.
- A map shows all of the segments in an executable file and where they will be loaded relative to the beginning of the program.
- Memory dumps are useful in tracing the execution of a program and in finding errors in a program.
- Some dump utilities can partially unassemble instruction segments. These give the displacement of operands in numerical form rather than in symbolic form.
- Some dump utilities, when used with assemblers and linkers that preserve symbolic information, can include symbolic names in the disassembly listing.
- Some dump utilities allow us to set breakpoints in a program. When a breakpoint is encountered, the program is stopped so that the memory can be examined; then the breakpoint can be reset, and the program can resume execution.

## PC SYSTEM SUMMARY

- Comments begin with a semicolon; all text following a semicolon on the line is ignored during program translation.
- Assemblers for the 8086 do not impose a particular line format. The fields in a statement must be separated from each other by one or more spaces.
- User-defined symbols must usually start with a letter and contain only letters, digits, and a few special characters, such as the underscore. Usually all letters are converted to uppercase internally.
- Three segments are needed in a main program: one for the stack, one for the data, and one for the instructions.
- To use a register as an operand, write its name in the desired operand position.
- To use a value in memory as an operand, write the name that is associated with the value in the db or dw directive.
- Constants written in the operand field are treated as immediate data. Constants are written in decimal or another base if a radix specifier immediately follows the last digit. The radix specifiers are b, q, and h for binary, octal, and hexadecimal, respectively.

Directives presented in this chapter:

| | |
|---|---|
| assume | Informs the assembler that a particular segment register is available for use in addressing |
| db | Reserves byte(s) of memory |
| DOSSEG | Specifies DOS segment order |

| | |
|---|---|
| dw | Reserves word(s) of memory |
| END | Declares the end of a program module |
| ENDS | Declares the end of a segment |
| equ | Associates a symbolic name with a constant |
| extrn | Declares an external name |
| PAGE | Specifies number of lines per page and characters per line in listing files |
| SEGMENT | Declares beginning of a segment, its alignment, combine type, and class name |

Procedures presented in this chapter:

| | |
|---|---|
| GetChar | Reads a character from the keyboard |
| GetDec | Reads an integer in decimal from the keyboard |
| PutChar | Displays a single character |
| PutCrLf | Advances output to the beginning of next line |
| PutDec | Displays an integer in decimal |
| PutStr | Displays a character string |

Operators presented in this chapter:

| | |
|---|---|
| dup | Repeats its following operand the number of times specified by its leading operand |
| offset | Returns offset of the operand |
| seg | Returns segment of the operand |

# Integers

4

- **Representation**
- **Operations**
- **Instructions**

Integers are the simplest type of number to work with and the most useful data type to learn about first. Many of the operations on integers have counterparts for other data types. Integers are also used in manipulating addresses and in building many kinds of structures.

When learning a high-level language, we usually begin with simple input and output operations, assignment statements, and arithmetic expressions. These topics are also appropriate in the early stages of learning an assembly language. Although high-level languages allow expressions with more than one type of number, we will begin with just one type of number, the integer.

This chapter will consider how integers are represented and the limits imposed by this representation. It will also examine operations on integers and how errors can occur and be detected. In addition, a few general-purpose instructions will be introduced, as well as those that perform operations on integers.

## 4.1 REPRESENTATION

In Chapter 1 we saw how positive whole numbers can be written in binary. We will now examine how a subset of the integers, including negative values, can be written in binary and represented in a computer.

Memory consists of many two-state devices, each of which is represented by a single bit, grouped to form words. Typically, an integer is stored in a word of memory. The range of integers that can be represented depends on the number of bits in a word; with an $n$-bit word, there are $2^n$ bit patterns possible. Computers that use 8086 processors have 16-bit words.

Ordinarily, half of the bit patterns are used for nonnegative integers. These $2^{n-1}$ patterns represent the integers 0 through $2^{n-1} - 1$. Positive integers are stored as their binary equivalent with leading zero bits to fill the word. For example, the number 41 in binary is $101001_2$; it is stored as 0000000000101001 in a 16-bit word.

The other half of the bit patterns are used for negative integers. There are three conventions for representing negative integers. The representation used affects how the computer performs arithmetic and the range of negative values allowed.

## Sign and Magnitude

The simplest representation of negative integers uses sign and magnitude notation. In this convention, one bit, typically the leftmost (most significant) bit, represents the sign of the integer. Positive is denoted by 0, negative by 1. The remaining bits of the word represent the magnitude of the number. For example, the 16-bit sign and magnitude representation of the integers 41 and −41 are:

$$0000000000101001 \quad (+41)$$

and

$$1000000000101001 \quad (-41)$$

Since one bit is used for the sign, $n-1$ bits are available for the magnitude. Thus the magnitude can range from zero to $2^{n-1} - 1$, and integers can range from $-(2^{n-1} - 1)$ to $+(2^{n-1} - 1)$.

There are two disadvantages to sign and magnitude representation. First, there are two representations for 0, essentially $+0$ and $-0$. This must be accounted for when counting from one side of 0 to the other. Second, the addition of numbers with different signs must be performed as subtraction. For instance, $+23 + (-14)$ must be computed as $+23 - (+14)$. The hardware must examine the signs of the operands as well as the instruction to determine which operation to actually perform. There must be separate circuits for subtraction and addition.

The advantage of sign and magnitude representation is its simplicity. Negative integers can be interpreted as easily as positive integers.

## Logical Complement

Another representation of negative integers uses the logical complement of the magnitude. This is also called **one's complement** notation. To find the logical complement of a number, simply complement each bit of the number: Replace each zero bit with a one bit, and each one bit with a zero bit. For example, the 16-bit logical complement representations of 41 and −41 are

$$0000000000101001 \quad (+41)$$

and

$$1111111111010110 \quad (-41)$$

We use the first bit to distinguish positive values from negative. Consider, for example, the number 1111110000000011. Interpreted as a 16-bit positive integer, it represents 64,515; interpreted as a negative number in logical complement notation, it represents $-0000001111111100_2$, or $-1020$. To avoid confusion, the established convention is that if the leftmost bit is 0 the number is positive, and if it is 1 the number is negative. Note that the signs are also complements of each other.

## 4.1 Representation

Like sign and magnitude notation, logical complement notation has two representations of 0: +0 is all zero bits and −0 is all one bits. The range of values that can be stored with logical complement notation is also the same as with sign and magnitude notation.

Arithmetic is simpler with numbers represented using logical complement notation than with sign and magnitude notation. Numbers can be added directly regardless of sign. However, an additional step is necessary. Consider the following examples. First let's add +9 and −41:

$$
\begin{array}{rr}
0000000000001001 & 9 \\
1111111111010110 & -41 \\
\hline
1111111111011111 & -32
\end{array}
$$

The result is correct. Now let's add −9 and +41:

$$
\begin{array}{rr}
1111111111110110 & -9 \\
0000000000101001 & 41 \\
\hline
10000000000011111 & 32
\end{array}
$$

The result is not correct. We started with two 16-bit numbers, but have a 17-bit result because there is a carry in the last step. If we ignore that carry the result looks like +31, which is still not correct.

When adding integers represented in logical complement form, we must take the carry from the most significant bit position and add it to the least significant bit position. With this extra step included, the last example becomes

$$
\begin{array}{rr}
1111111111110110 & -9 \\
0000000000101001 & 41 \\
\hline
\text{(1)}0000000000011111 & \\
\quad\quad\quad\quad\quad\quad\rightarrow +1 & \\
\hline
0000000000100000 & 32
\end{array}
$$

This is now the correct sum. Note that in the first example, when we added +9 and −41, the carry from the most significant position was 0. The addition of this carry, not shown in the example, will have no effect on the result.

All additions of integers represented in logical complement generate a carry, which can be 0 or 1, out of the most significant bit. This carry must be added to the least significant bit of the result. This in turn may produce a carry of 1 into the next bit position, which must be added as well, and which may produce another carry of 1, and so on. However, this carry of 1 cannot propagate through the entire word and out of the most significant position again. Thus, the addition of two integers in logical complement form requires adding the two numbers directly and adding the carry to the result.

Subtraction can be implemented as addition of the logical complement of the subtrahend. For example, to compute 38−16, the hardware can instead form −16 by taking the logical complement of 16, and then add this to 38. Unlike computers that use sign and magnitude notation, no separate circuit is needed for subtraction. The advantage of this notation is that it is easy for a computer to take logical complements.

## Radix Complement

The radix complement of an $m$-digit number in base $r$ can be found by subtracting the number from $r^m$. The sum of a number and its radix complement is $r^m$, which has $m + 1$ digits.

Consider the following examples of four-digit decimal numbers. To represent $-1268$ as the ten's complement of 1268, subtract 1268 from $10^4$: $10000-1268=8732$. To represent $-4444$ as the ten's complement of 4444, subtract: $10000-4444=5556$. This method of representing numbers requires a convention to distinguish positive numbers from negative ones. For these four-digit decimal examples, this discussion will adopt the convention that 0000 through 4999 represent positive numbers, while 5000 through 9999 represent the negative values $-5000$ through $-1$, respectively. Note that 9999 represents $-1$, while 5000 represents $-5000$. There are 10,000 numbers that can be represented with four digits. Using this convention, the range of integers from $-5000$ through 4999 has been chosen for this discussion.

If we add a number and its opposite we expect a sum of 0. The sum of 1268 and $-1268$ is, of course, 0. Using ten's complement notation, the result

```
  1268
  8732
------
 10000
```

is obtained. The sum is not a four-digit number but is the five-digit result expected from the definition of a radix complement. By choosing to ignore the last carry that made the result five digits, we obtain the correct sum.

Computers represent data in binary. This fact leads to a consideration of **two's complement** notation. The two's complement of an $n$-bit integer can be found by subtracting that number from $2^n$. For example, consider the representation of $-41$ in 16-bit two's complement. We saw earlier that $+41$ is represented as 0000000000101001. The subtraction step, which starts with a borrow from the $2^{16}$ position, gives

```
  10000000000000000
-  0000000000101001
-------------------
   1111111111010111
```

Now, there would be no gain by using radix complements if the computer had to perform a subtraction to represent a negative number. However, there is a special relationship between the logical (or one's) complement and the two's complement of a binary number: Given the one's complement of a binary number, it is possible to determine the two's complement by simply adding 1. Consider the following sequence of steps for determining the two's complement representation of $-41$:

```
      0000000000101001     representation of +41
      1111111111010110     logical complement
 +                   1     add 1
     ------------------
      1111111111010111     two's complement for -41
```

### 4.1 Representation

Taking the logical complement and adding 1 to a number are both operations that a computer can perform quickly.

An advantage of two's complement notation is that it has just one representation for 0: a sequence of bits that are all 0. Consider what happens if we attempt to form $-0$. Start with 16 zero bits:

$$0000000000000000$$

Its logical complement is 16 one bits:

$$1111111111111111$$

When we attempt to add 1 to this, we get

$$\begin{array}{r} 1111111111111111 \\ +\qquad\qquad\qquad 1 \\ \hline 10000000000000000 \end{array}$$

This is a 1 followed by 16 zero bits. The 1 is generated by a carry out of the most significant bit. We do not keep it as part of the result; we keep only the less significant 16 bits. Thus, we have a unique representation for 0.

Other advantages of two's complement notation are that integers can be added without regard for their signs, and that subtraction can be performed by adding the complement of the subtrahend. The extra step of adding the carry when adding numbers in one's complement form is not required when adding numbers in two's complement form. A disadvantage of two's complement notation is that negative numbers are difficult to interpret directly.

The first bit of the number indicates its sign in all representations. In sign and magnitude form, all of the fill bits (those between the sign and the most significant one-bit of the magnitude) are 0. In the complement forms, all fill bits are copies of the sign bit. For example, recall that the binary representation of 41 requires only six significant bits: $101001_2$. In 16-bit words, we saw ten leading 0 bits in the representation of $+41$, and ten leading 1 bits in complement representations of $-41$. This is called the **sign bit extension**; its use will be seen shortly.

The 8086 uses two's complement representation for signed 8-bit and 16-bit integers. It also supports unsigned 8-bit and 16-bit integers.

### EXERCISES 4.1

1. Show how each of the following numbers is represented in 16 bits using sign and magnitude notation.
   (a) 58  (b) $-58$
   (c) $-133$  (d) $-180$
   (e) $-32766$  (f) $-2$
2. Repeat Exercise 1 using one's complement notation.
3. Repeat Exercise 1 using two's complement notation.

**102**    Chapter 4    Integers

4. Interpret each of the following numbers as an integer in sign and magnitude notation.
   (a) 1000000000000111
   (b) 1000000011100000
   (c) 0000000010011001
   (d) 0000000011100001
   (e) 1111111111111111
   (f) 1111111111111100
5. Interpret each of the numbers of Exercise 4 as an integer in one's complement notation.
6. Interpret each of the numbers of Exercise 4 as an integer in two's complement notation.
7. Explain why, in one's complement, the addition of the carry to the least significant bit of the sum cannot itself produce another carry of 1 out of the most significant bit.
8. What is the range of signed integers that can be represented
   (a) in 32 bits using two's complement?
   (b) in 24 bits using sign and magnitude?
   (c) in 36 bits using one's complement?
   (d) in 18 bits using two's complement?
9. What is the range of integers that can be represented
   (a) in 8 bits using two's complement?
   (b) in 16 bits using two's complement?
   (c) in 8 bits using all bits for a positive magnitude?
   (d) in 16 bits using all bits for a positive magnitude?

## 4.2   OPERATIONS

The discussion now turns to typical operations on integers. This section will relate these operations to the capabilities of the processor, discuss errors that can occur, and examine processor characteristics not apparent to a high-level-language programmer.

### Move Operations

One of the simplest statements in a high-level language is the assignment of a value to a variable. Such a statement can be used to initialize a counter, as in

`Count := 0`

or to save the value of a variable before it is used in further calculations, as in

`Copy := Value`

No arithmetic is needed. The computer simply copies the value from wherever it is into the memory cell named by the receiving variable.

    These simple assignment statements are implemented by move instructions. There are two operands: One specifies the source value or its address and the other specifies the destination address. Depending on whether the values are in registers, in memory, or can be coded as immediate operands, as well as on the instruction formats supported, the assignment statements above can be implemented with one or two move instructions.

### Arithmetic Operations

Arithmetic on integers in a high-level-language program is specified using expressions to be evaluated. Arithmetic expressions can be used as the right side of an assignment statement,

## 4.2 Operations

in an output statement, as an argument to a subprogram, or as an index expression. The operations specified in an expression can be as simple as a single addition to increment a counter, or as complicated as the rules of the programming language allow.

This section will examine addition, subtraction, multiplication, division (including the use of remainders), and negation of integers. Other operations considered will include the conversion of integers between different lengths and extended precision addition.

Some languages include an exponentiation operator. This is implemented either as repeated multiplication or as calls on logarithmic and exponential functions, rather than as a primitive operation provided by the processor. Exponentiation will not be discussed further in this chapter.

### Addition

Addition of two integers gives an integer sum. There are, however, two situations that require special attention: overflow and carry.

Overflow occurs when the sum of two integers is outside the range of integers that can be represented. The sum of two $n$-bit integers can require $n + 1$ bits to represent. For example, with 16-bit signed integers, the largest value that can be represented is $2^{15} - 1$, or 32,767. There are many sums of two numbers, each less than 32,767, that exceed this value. None, however, exceeds $2^{16} - 2$.

Overflow is a potential problem with all representations. It is inevitable when the same number of bits is used to represent a sum as is used for the addends. Overflow cannot occur when adding two numbers with different signs. However, when two numbers with the same sign are added, overflow causes a carry into the sign bit of the result. Consider the following addition, shown with the unsigned decimal equivalents of the binary addends:

```
  0110001000000000       25088
+ 0010000000110001     + 8241
  ----------------       -----
  1000001000110001       33329
```

The first bit of the result is a 1, which indicates a negative value. Using two's complement notation, the sum represents $-32207$, which is not equivalent to the value obtained in decimal.

A flag usually records whether overflow has occurred in the most recent arithmetic operation. Addition instructions set the overflow flag to 1 if overflow occurs, or clear it to 0 if overflow does not occur. It is up to the programmer to include code to check the overflow flag and to take corrective action in programs where overflow is likely to cause problems; this is hard to do in high-level languages because they cannot usually check the flags directly.

A carry occurs in every addition. For example, consider the following using 16-bit two's complement notation:

```
  1111111111111111       -1
+ 0000000000000100       +4
  ----------------       --
 10000000000000011        3
```

The carry out of the sign bit is not saved as part of the result, as it is a 17th bit. Ignoring this carry does give the correct sum.

The carry itself represents information that can be useful when implementing addition on multiple-word integers. The flags register contains a bit, the carry flag, which is used to record the carry out of the sign bit. This flag can be tested and can be used as an implied operand in some instructions. This subject will be covered later in the section on extended precision arithmetic.

With unsigned representations, overflow during addition is signaled by a carry of 1. The 8086 uses the carry flag to record overflow with unsigned operands and the overflow flag to record overflow with signed operands.

## Subtraction

Subtraction is implemented as addition of a complement regardless of the signs of the numbers involved. Overflow in subtraction is the same as in addition. The carry flag indicates whether a borrow is needed. This is useful in working with multiple-word integers; it also records overflow with unsigned representations. Note that if you compute a difference by adding a complement it is necessary to complement the carry out of the result.

## Multiplication

Multiplication of two integers gives an integer result. However, the product of two $n$-bit integers can be large enough to require $2n - 1$ bits to represent. Consider the square of the largest $n$-bit integer:

$$(2^{n-1} - 1)(2^{n-1} - 1) = 2^{2n-2} - 2^n + 1$$

The square of the smallest $n$-bit integer in two's complement representation is actually larger:

$$(-2^{n-1})(-2^{n-1}) = 2^{2n-2}$$

These values require $2n - 1$ bits to represent.

Let's consider the consequences of providing only $n$ bits for the product of two $n$-bit factors. That is, multiplication generates a product with $2n - 1$ bits, but only $n$ bits of the product are retained in the result. Which bits should be kept and which discarded?

Consider first a multiplication where the product can be represented in $n$ bits. For example, in multiplying 41 by 3 we get

```
  000000000101001            41
× 000000000000011          ×  3
  ―――――――――――――――          ―――――
  000000001111011           123
```

The product is in the least significant bits; the most significant bits are all zeros. Now consider multiplying 41 by −3, using two's complement representation:

```
  000000000101001            41
× 111111111111101          × −3
  ―――――――――――――――          ―――――
  111111110000101          −123
```

## 4.2 Operations

The product is again in the least-significant bits; the most significant bits are all ones. In both examples, the leading bits are merely the sign extension. It makes sense in these cases to save the least significant bits of the result with sign extension to fill the word.

However, when the product exceeds the capacity of the word used for the result, problems with overflow can occur. Consider multiplying 1250 by 30 as 16-bit integers.

$$
\begin{array}{rr}
0000010011100010 & 1250 \\
\times\ 0000000000011110 & \times\ \ \ \ 30 \\
\hline
1001001001111100 & 37500
\end{array}
$$

As a two's complement number, the product appears to be $-28{,}036$. This is clearly incorrect. The overflow flag is set to indicate the error.

To summarize, when multiplication is specified without providing extra bits for the product, the least significant part of the product is saved as the result. If any significant bits are discarded or the sign is changed, the overflow bit of the flags register is set.

Many computers avoid overflow in integer multiplication by using two consecutive words of memory (or two registers) for the product. Since the product of two $n$-bit integers cannot require more than $2n - 1$ bits, using $2n$ bits for the product allows one bit more than is strictly needed. This is convenient and ensures that overflow does not occur.

In a high-level language, however, a statement like

```
Space := Size * Count
```

where `Space`, `Size`, and `Count` are all defined as integers, the product must have the same number of bits as a standard integer. That is, the most significant bits of the product cannot be stored even if they are computed by the multiplication operation. We therefore need a way to convert a double-length product to a single-length integer.

The conversion can be as simple as merely taking the least significant half of the product as the result. With two's complement, sign extension ensures the correct sign of the result when there is no overflow.

There may be instructions for converting integers from one length to another. The advantage of these conversion instructions is that they may also indicate any loss of significance that occurs by setting the overflow flag. Overflow is indicated if any of the discarded bits differ from the sign bit. The example in Figure 4.1 indicates overflow when

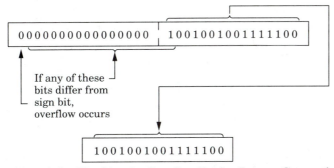

**Figure 4.1** Checking for Overflow During Integer Conversion

37500 (from the previous example) is converted from 32 bits to 16 bits. The carry flag is usually meaningless following a multiplication instruction.

Consider what happens when a user tries to enter a number that is too large with the GetDec procedure. GetDec reads the input one character at a time, converting each digit to internal integer form. It keeps track of the value entered in one word, initialized to 0. As digits are entered, the old value is multiplied by 10 and the new digit (in integer format) is added. Both the multiplication and the addition can produce overflow, but GetDec ignores it. GetDec returns the least significant 16 bits of the last value that is computed. When there are repeated overflows, the result is not related to the user's value in any simple way.

## Division

Division of an integer $m$ (the dividend) by a nonzero integer $n$ (the divisor) gives two integers Q (the quotient) and R (the remainder) such that

$$m = nQ + R$$

There are infinitely many pairs of integers Q and R that satisfy this definition for any values of $m$ and $n$. For example, consider dividing 13 by 3. The following results are possible:

$$13 = 3 \times 4 + 1 \qquad Q=4, R=1$$
$$13 = 3 \times 5 - 2 \qquad Q=5, R=-2$$
$$13 = 3 \times 3 + 4 \qquad Q=3, R=4$$

and so on. To make the definition unambiguous, it is necessary to specify a restriction on either Q or R. The most frequently used condition requires

$$m = nQ + R \text{ and sign}(R) = \text{sign}(m), |R| < |n|$$

Here, the remainder has the same sign as the dividend and has a magnitude that is less than the magnitude of the divisor. This restricts our solution of $13 \div 3$ to the first example given. There are other possible conditions that specify a unique quotient and remainder, but they are not widely used.

The uniqueness condition requires that the sign of the remainder is the same as the sign of the dividend. The quotient is positive if the divisor and dividend have the same sign, negative if the divisor and dividend have different signs.

Many languages also provide a remainder operation, denoted as *rem*. The *rem* operator produces the remainder consistent with the restricted definition of division just given; in symbols, $m \text{ rem } n = R$. Continuing the example,

$$13 \text{ rem } 3 = 1$$

and

$$-13 \text{ rem } 3 = -1$$

Many languages also provide a *mod* operator, and this is sometimes mistaken for a remainder. Actually, $m \text{ mod } n$ is defined only for $n > 0$ and is always nonnegative. For

$m \geq 0$, $m$ *mod* $n$ and $m$ *rem* $n$ give the same result. For $m < 0$, $m$ *mod* $n$ = R + $n$. Continuing the example,

$$13 \ mod \ 3 = 1$$

and

$$-13 \ mod \ 3 = 2$$

Unfortunately, some systems return the remainder for the *mod* operator regardless of sign.

Division by 0 is not defined, and an attempt to divide by 0 generates an interrupt. The routine invoked by the interrupt usually terminates the program with an error message. However, in some systems the routine that services the divide by 0 interrupt sets the quotient and remainder to the dividend and divisor values, sets the overflow flag, and continues execution of the program.

Overflow can occur when dividing, but depends on the length of the dividend. When overflow does occur, both the quotient and remainder are usually meaningless.

The quotient can be no larger in magnitude than the dividend, and the remainder no larger in magnitude than the divisor. If the dividend and divisor are the same length, overflow can occur only with two's complement representation and only when dividing the smallest integer ($-2^{n-1}$) by $-1$. The true quotient is $2^{n-1}$, but this is too large to represent in $n$ bits. Instead, the result will be the original dividend, with the overflow flag set.

Many computers that use two words for the product of two single-word factors also require two words for dividends that are to be divided by single-word divisors. Following the division, one word of the dividend is usually replaced by the quotient and the other word by the remainder.

Overflow is more likely to occur when the dividend is longer than the quotient. Consider dividing any two-word dividend by 1. The quotient will be the same as the dividend, so if the dividend is too large to be stored in one word, overflow occurs. There are many other instances where the quotient is too large for one word, and overflow occurs.

Since the remainder will always be smaller in magnitude than the divisor, it will always fit into one word (assuming the divisor is a word). There is no possible overflow of the remainder.

Converting an integer from one word to two for use as a dividend is accomplished with a special instruction. This instruction copies the original value to the less significant of the two words and extends the sign bit into every bit of the more significant word (Figure 4.2).

## Negation

To negate an integer expression in a high-level language, a unary negation operator is used. Some novice programmers negate an expression by multiplying it by $-1$, or by subtracting it from 0, both of which are more complex operations than necessary.

With two's complement representation, negation requires that every bit in the integer be complemented and that 1 be added to the result. Overflow can occur in one special case: The range of integers in two's complement is not symmetrical, being $-2^{n-1}$ to $2^{n-1} - 1$ for an $n$-bit word. The smallest integer, $-2^{n-1}$, is a 1 bit followed by $n - 1$ 0 bits. When we try to take its two's complement, we can take the logical complement (a 0 followed

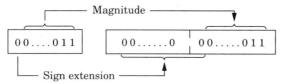

**Figure 4.2** Converting a Short Integer to a Long Integer

by $n - 1$ ones), but adding one generates a sequence of carries and a final result equal to the number with which we started. For example, in 16 bits

$$
\begin{array}{rl}
 & 1000000000000000 \quad -2^{15} \\
 & 0111111111111111 \quad \text{logical complement} \\
+ & \phantom{0000000000000001}1 \quad \text{add } 1 \\
\hline
 & 1000000000000000 \quad -2^{15} \text{ again}
\end{array}
$$

When we attempt to negate the smallest integer in two's complement, we get that smallest integer as a result. The overflow flag is also set.

## Extended arithmetic

The use of products and dividends that are twice as long as the other numbers involved in the operations, as well as the presence of the carry flag, leads us to consider implementing arithmetic on two-word or longer integers. For example, it might be useful to be able to add a series of products in two-word form and then to divide when computing a weighted average. That is, when we have a calculation such as

```
A := (W1*T1 + W2*T2 + W3*T3)/3
```

we want to add the three two-word products and divide without any conversions. We do not want to convert each product to one word, add, and convert the sum to two words before dividing. Any overflow during the conversion to one-word products would lose significance that would not be lost if these conversions were avoided.

Arithmetic on arbitrarily long integers is useful in some applications. Consider finding the sum of two 50-digit integers. To represent a 50-digit integer in binary requires 167 bits. If we use eleven 16-bit words for each integer, we would have to provide routines to copy eleven-word integers, perform arithmetic on them, and read and print them. Only addition will be considered now.

Since using eleven 16-bit words for each operand and for the result would lead to rather cumbersome examples, consider the addition of three-word integers on a computer with four-bit words. This should be easier to follow, although these concepts also apply to other word sizes and operand lengths. Only one example will be considered in detail, and that in two's complement form. The problem is to add 1683 and $-4$. In 12-bit two's complement form, the problem is

$$
\begin{array}{rr}
 0110\ 1001\ 0011 & 1683 \\
+1111\ 1111\ 1100 & +\ \ -4 \\
\hline
 0110\ 1000\ 1111 & 1679
\end{array}
$$

## 4.2 Operations

In this example the numbers have been partitioned to show how each piece would be stored in four-bit words. Note that taken alone, the second word of the first operand, all words in the second operand, and the second word of the sum appear to be negative quantities.

The first step needed to add the two three-word integers is to add the least significant words. Then add the carry from that first addition along with the middle words of the operands. Finally, add the carry from the second addition along with the most significant words. This procedure is shown in Figure 4.3. Note that to perform the first addition the carry flag must either be ignored or first cleared to zero.

Problem:

$$\begin{array}{r} 0110\ 1001\ 0011 \\ +\ 1111\ 1111\ 1100 \\ \hline \end{array}$$

Step (1) add least significant words:

$$\begin{array}{r} 0011 \\ 1100 \\ \hline 0\ 1111 \end{array}$$
carry ↗

Step (2) add middle words and carry from step 1:

$$\begin{array}{r} 0 \\ 1001 \\ 1111 \\ \hline 1\ 1000 \end{array}$$
carry ↗

Step (3) add most significant words and carry from step 2:

$$\begin{array}{r} 1 \\ 0110 \\ 1111 \\ \hline 1\ 0110 \end{array}$$
carry ↗
(ignored)

Solution:

$$\begin{array}{r} 0110\ 1001\ 0011 \\ +\ 1111\ 1111\ 1100 \\ \hline 0110\ 1000\ 1111 \end{array}$$

**Figure 4.3  Addition of Multiple Word Integers**

## EXERCISES 4.2

1. Can multiplication by 1 be used to convert an integer to a longer form on a computer that gives a product that is twice as long as the factors? How could a separate conversion instruction be different?
2. Can division by 1 be used to convert an integer to a shorter form on a computer that gives a quotient that is half as long as the dividend? How could a separate conversion instruction be different?
3. The carry bit is also useful as a borrow bit. Show how the carry bit is used in subtracting multiple-word integers in two's complement.
▶4. Write a program (in a high-level language) that reads and prints integers. What is the largest integer that can be read and printed? Explain what happens when a larger value is entered.
▶5. Repeat Exercise 4 using assembly language and the input and output procedures provided with this text.
▶6. Write a program (in a high-level language) that computes and prints successive powers of 2 until overflow occurs. How can the program detect overflow?
▶7. Write a program (in a high-level language) that attempts to compute and print the following values (`MaxInt` is the largest integer represented): `MaxInt+1`, `MaxInt*2`, `-MaxInt`, `-MaxInt-1`, and `-MaxInt*2`. Explain the behavior of the program.
▶8. Write a program (in a high-level language) that computes and prints the sum of odd integers. The program should print each odd integer along with the sum of all odd integers printed so far, until overflow occurs. How can the program detect overflow?
9. What is the sequence of numbers generated by the sums in Exercise 8?

## 4.3 INSTRUCTIONS

We now examine the move, arithmetic, and conversion instructions available in the 8086 processors for working with integers. In this chapter we consider only those instructions available in all processors in the 8086 family, not those available only in later processors.

As new instructions are presented, the operation(s) they perform are described based on an earlier discussion of the operations, the operands, and the results. It will be noted when an instruction affects any of the bits of the flags register. The discussion may also include other unique, interesting, or merely curious facts about the instruction, as well as any special uses or pitfalls. Many of the instructions presented here are used in programs throughout the text. All instructions are included in displays in the text where they are first presented. Summaries of the instructions can also be found in Appendix 3.

The notation used in these displays and summaries can be described as follows. The first line is a description of the instruction as a phrase in English, with the letters used in the mnemonic in capital letters. This is followed by the syntax of the instruction and a symbolic description of the processing it performs. The latter is written in the form of assignment statements where possible. When two or more activities occur simultaneously they are combined by an ampersand (&). When they occur in a definite sequence they are separated by semicolons (;) and are numbered in the order they occur. Activities that could occur in any sequence—or simultaneously—are separated by semicolons and are not numbered.

## 4.3 Instructions

Next, the flags affected by the instruction are summarized. Each line of the display for the flags includes one-letter names for flags affected, dots for flags not affected, and the effect. For example, the two lines

> flags:     O...SZAPC modified for result
>              .DIT..... unchanged

indicate that the Overflow, Sign, Zero, Auxiliary carry, Parity, and Carry flags are modified according to the result of the operation, while the Direction, Interrupt enable, and Trap flags are unchanged.

The allowed combinations of operands are then given. The abbreviations used in this section of the display are

| | |
|---|---|
| *reg* | any general-purpose register |
| *segreg* | any segment register (CS, DS, ES, SS) |
| *accum* | either AL or AX register |
| *mem* | an operand in memory |
| *label* | a labeled location in code segment |
| *src* | memory operand used as source in a string operation |
| *dest* | memory operand used as destination in a string operation |
| *immed* | a constant used as immediate operand |

Occasionally, the size of an operand is specified as a numerical suffix added to the operand.

Instructions are grouped by the type of operation they perform or by the type of value they manipulate. The instructions introduced in this section move data, clear an operand, convert an integer from one length to another, and perform integer arithmetic.

## Move Instructions

The first instructions to be discussed will be instructions that copy values. The mov instruction copies the value from one register to another register, or between a register and a location in memory. The previous contents of the destination register or memory location are lost; the contents of the source register or memory location are unchanged. The flags are unaffected.

> **MOVe data**
> syntax:     mov *destination, source*
> action:     *destination* := *source*
> flags:     ODITSZAPC unchanged
> operands:     *reg,reg*        *mem,reg*        *reg,mem*
>                 *reg,immed*     *mem,immed*     *accum,mem*
>                 *reg16,segreg*    *mem16,segreg*    *mem,accum*
>                 *segreg,reg16*    *segreg,mem16*

The mov instruction cannot copy a value between two locations in memory, or from an immediate operand to a segment register. These must be implemented as a sequence of two moves—first into a general register and then into the desired destination. For example, the assignment

Copy := Value

where both Copy and Value are declared with dw directives, is implemented as

```
mov     ax, Value
mov     Copy, ax
```

This is illustrated in Figure 4.4a. As another example, the first pair of instructions in a main program establishes the DS register using

```
mov     ax, seg _DATA
mov     ds, ax
```

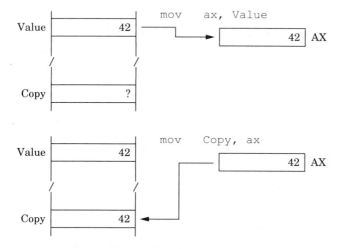

(a) Copying from one memory location to another

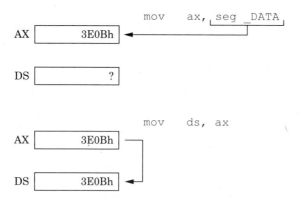

(b) Moving a constant into a segment register

**Figure 4.4  Overcoming Restrictions on Move Instruction Operands**

as illustrated in Figure 4.4b. When the program is loaded into memory prior to execution, the segment number associated with _DATA is provided as an immediate operand for the first of these moves.

The operands of mov can be either bytes or words as long as both operands are the same size. Often, the assembler can determine the size of an operand from the context: The name of a register indicates its size, and the declaration of a variable with db or dw indicates its size. The assembler checks that both operands of a move instruction are the same size. Immediate data, on the other hand, has no defined size. If the assembler can determine the length of the other operand, the immediate data is assumed to be the same length.

There is another instruction for copying data between two registers or between a register and memory. The exchange (xchg) instruction copies the values of each operand to the other without destroying either operand.

---

**eXCHanGe data**

    syntax:      xchg   *destination1, destination2*

    action:       *destination1 := destination2*
                  &*destination2 := destination1*

    flags:        ODITSZAPC unchanged

    operands:   *reg,reg*       *mem,reg*     *reg,mem*
                     *accum,reg16*  *reg16,accum*

---

At least one operand of xchg must be in a general register. The other operand may be in another register or in memory. The xchg instruction is handy for swapping two values. For example, to swap the values in the AX and BX registers, we can use

```
xchg    ax, bx
```

as shown in Figure 4.5a. To do this without xchg, we would need a sequence of three move instructions and a spare register:

```
mov     dx, ax
mov     ax, bx
mov     bx, dx
```

This uses the DX register for an intermediate copy of AX; the original value in DX is lost (Figure 4.5b).

To swap two values in memory, we need three exchange instructions and a register. For example, the sequence

```
xchg    al, Byte1
xchg    al, Byte2
xchg    al, Byte1
```

uses the AL register to exchange the contents of Byte1 and Byte2 (Figure 4.6). Note that the initial value in the AL register is restored by the third instruction. This memory-to-memory exchange could also be implemented as four move instructions that use and change two registers.

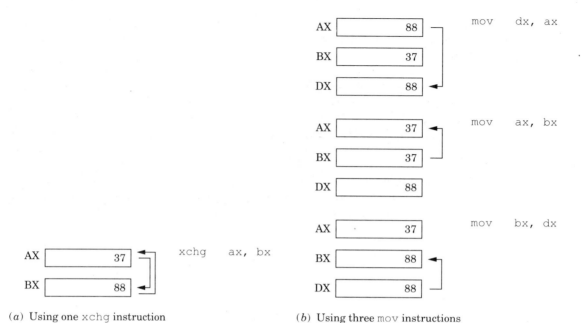

(a) Using one xchg instruction    (b) Using three mov instructions

**Figure 4.5** Swapping the Contents of Two Registers

The 8086 processor does not have specific instructions for clearing a register or an operand in memory. There are several ways to accomplish this, however. One way is simply to move an immediate data value of 0 into the register or into the memory operand. A better way to clear registers will be shown later.

## Conversion Instructions

There are two instructions available on the 8086 processors that increase the length of a signed integer. Both use the accumulator (AL or AX) as an implied operand. The conversion is performed in place, with the result replacing the source operand.

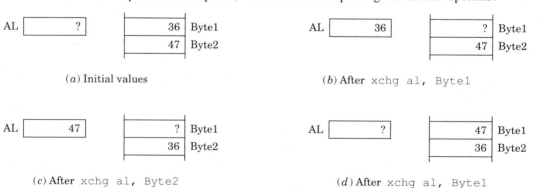

(a) Initial values    (b) After xchg al, Byte1

(c) After xchg al, Byte2    (d) After xchg al, Byte1

**Figure 4.6** Swapping Values of Two Memory Locations Using an xchg Instruction

## 4.3 Instructions

The cbw instruction converts an 8-bit integer in the AL register into a 16-bit integer in the AX register. It does this by extending the sign bit of AL into all bits of AH.

**Convert Byte to Word**
syntax:   cbw
action:   ax := al, sign extended
flags:    ODITSZAPC unchanged

The cwd instruction converts a 16-bit integer in the AX register into a 32-bit integer in the combination of the DX and AX registers. It does this by extending the sign bit of AX into all bits of DX.

**Convert Word to Double**
syntax:   cwd
action:   dx: ax := ax, sign extended
flags:    ODITSZAP unchanged

The cbw and cwd instructions are useful for converting a dividend to the correct length before a division instruction.

There are no instructions for converting signed integers to shorter lengths, as we can simply use the less significant portion of the original number. We can check for overflow by inspecting the more significant portion of the original number for any value other than the expected sign extension. (Test instructions, however, will not be considered until the next chapter.) To convert unsigned integers to a longer length, move zeros into the more significant part of the destination. For example, to convert the 8-bit unsigned (or positive) integer in BL into a 16-bit unsigned integer in BX, move zeros into BH.

## Arithmetic Instructions

Many arithmetic instructions operate on two values and produce one result. These are written with two operands, with the first operand also replaced by the result. A few instructions have only one operand to which an operation is applied. Most arithmetic instructions affect the flags.

## Addition

Addition instructions can have one or two operands. The two-operand instructions add the value of the second operand to the first. There are two of these: One also adds the carry flag to the sum, and the other does not. These can be used with signed or unsigned integers.

**ADD integers**
    syntax:      add  *destination, source*
    action:      *destination* := *destination* + *source*

**ADd integers with Carry**
    syntax:      adc  *destination, source*
    action:      *destination* := *destination* + *source* + carry flag
    flags:       O...SZAPC modified for sum
                   .DIT..... unchanged
    operands:   *reg,reg*      *mem,reg*      *reg,mem*
                    *reg,immed*   *mem,immed*   *accum,immed*

There are three instructions that are used when preparing to use the adc instruction (as well as the similar subtract instruction, which will be discussed later). These instructions clear, set, or complement the carry flag.

**CLear Carry flag**
    syntax:      clc
    action:      carry flag := 0

**SeT Carry flag**
    syntax:      stc
    action:      carry flag := 1

**CoMplement Carry flag**
    syntax:      cmc
    action:      carry flag := 1 − carry flag
    flags:       ODITSZAP. unchanged
                  ........C (see action)

It is often necessary to add a small constant, typically 1, to an operand. Applications that count or search a list sequentially are common uses of this operation. The 8086 provides an instruction just for this purpose. This is the only one-operand addition instruction.

**INCrement integer**
    syntax:      inc  *destination*
    action:      *destination* := *destination* + 1
    flags:       O...SZAP. modified for sum
                  .DIT....C unchanged
    operands:   *reg*     *mem*

### 4.3 Instructions

The operand of inc can be a signed or unsigned integer in a general register or memory location. The carry flag is not added to the sum and is not affected by the sum.

## Subtraction

Subtraction instructions can have one or two operands. With two operands, the instruction computes the difference of two numbers and replaces one of them with the difference. Since subtraction is not commutative, we need to be careful about the order of the operands. The two-operand subtraction instructions subtract the second operand from the first and save the difference in the first operand. As with addition, there are two versions of this instruction: One subtracts the carry flag from the difference, and the other does not. These instructions work with signed and unsigned integers.

---

**SUBtract integers**
- syntax: sub *destination,source*
- action: *destination* := *destination* − *source*

**SuBtract integers with Borrow**
- syntax: sbb *destination,source*
- action: *destination* := *destination* − *source* − carry flag
- flags: O...SZAPC modified for difference
  .DIT..... unchanged
- operands: *reg,reg*    *mem,reg*    *reg,mem*
  *reg,immed*  *mem,immed*  *accum,immed*

---

The subtraction instruction is often used to clear a register to 0. The result of subtracting the contents of a register from itself will always be 0. For example,

```
sub     ax, ax
```

clears the AX register. This is more efficient than

```
mov     ax, 0
```

It differs, however, in that the sub instruction affects the flags while the mov instruction does not.

It is often necessary to subtract a small constant, typically 1, from an operand. The dec instruction is similar to the inc instruction.

---

**DECrement integer**
- syntax: dec *destination*
- action: *destination* := *destination* − 1
- flags: O...SZAP. modified for difference
  .DIT....C unchanged
- operands: *reg*    *mem*

## Chapter 4 Integers

The operand can be a signed or unsigned integer in a general register or a memory location. The carry flag is not subtracted from the difference and is not affected by the difference.

## Multiplication

The multiplication instructions of the 8086 processor have one explicit source operand; the destination operand and other source are implied. When the explicit operand is a word, the other source is the AX register and the product is left in the combination of the DX and AX registers. Overflow and carry flags are set if the product is larger than a word. When the explicit operand is a byte, the other source is the AL register and the product is left in the AX register. Overflow and carry flags are set if the product is larger than a byte.

There are separate multiplication instructions for signed and unsigned integers. The signed instruction extends the sign through all leading bits, while the unsigned instruction clears all leading bits.

**MULtiply (unsigned)**
    syntax:    `mul` *source*

**Integer MULtiply (signed)**
    syntax:    `imul` *source*
    action:    ax := al * *source8*
    or    dx:ax := ax * *source16*
    flags:    O.......C    modified for product
                ....SZAP.    undefined
                .DIT.....    unchanged
    operands:    reg    mem

The examples in Figure 4.7 illustrate signed and unsigned multiplication with byte operands, with and without overflow. In each, the AL register contains 42 before the multiplication. The AH and AL registers and the overflow and carry flags are shown following each multiplication. Note that the correct product is always formed in the AX register; the overflow and carry flags indicate whether the value in AL by itself is correct.

## Division

Like multiplication, the division instructions of the 8086 processor have one explicit operand, the divisor. The dividend is implied and is replaced by the quotient and the remainder. When the divisor is a word, the DX:AX register pair is used as the dividend; the quotient is left in AX and the remainder is left in DX. When the divisor is a byte, the AX register is used as the dividend; the quotient is left in AL and the remainder is left in AH.

There are separate division instructions for working with signed and unsigned numbers.

## 4.3 Instructions

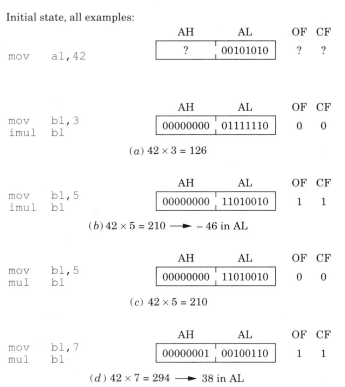

**Figure 4.7 Examples of Multiplication**

---

**DIVide (unsigned)**
    syntax:    `div` *source*

**Integer DIVide (signed)**
    syntax:    `idiv` *source*
    action:    al := quotient of ax ÷ *source8*
             & ah := remainder of ax ÷ *source8*
    or         ax := quotient of dx:ax ÷ *source16*
             & dx := remainder of dx:ax ÷ *source16*
    flags:     O...SZAPC  undefined
             .DIT.....  unchanged
    operands:  *reg*   *mem*

---

The examples in Figure 4.8 all divide 512 (0200h) in AX by an eight-bit number in BL. In the first two examples the divisor is 0Fh, which is 15 whether interpreted as a signed or unsigned number; `idiv` and `div` both give 34 for the quotient and 2 for the remainder. In the last two examples the divisor is F1h. As a signed integer F1h represents −15; `idiv` gives −34 for the quotient and 2 for the remainder. As an unsigned integer F1h represents 241; `div` gives 2 for the quotient and 30 for the remainder.

Initial state, all examples:

```
mov    ax,0200h
```

|   AH   |   AL   |
|--------|--------|
|00000010|00000000|

```
mov    bl,0Fh
idiv   bl
```

|   AH   |   AL   |
|--------|--------|
|00000010|00100010|

(a) 512 ÷ 15 ⟶ Q=34, R=2

```
mov    bl,0Fh
div    bl
```

|   AH   |   AL   |
|--------|--------|
|00000010|00100010|

(b) 512 ÷ 15 ⟶ Q=34, R=2

```
mov    bl,0F1h
idiv   bl
```

|   AH   |   AL   |
|--------|--------|
|00000010|11011110|

(c) 512 ÷ −15 ⟶ Q=−34, R=2

```
mov    bl,0F1h
div    bl
```

|   AH   |   AL   |
|--------|--------|
|00011110|00000010|

(d) 512 ÷ 241 ⟶ Q=2, R=30

**Figure 4.8  Examples of Division**

When the quotient is outside the range that can be represented by the destination, an interrupt is generated; the handler for this condition usually terminates the program with an error message. An attempt to divide by 0 also generates this interrupt.

## Negation

The negation instruction has only one operand. It subtracts the operand from 0 and replaces the operand with the result. The carry flag is set unless the operand is 0; the other flags are affected based on the result of the subtraction. With integers represented in two's complement form, an attempt to negate the smallest integer can produce overflow.

**NEGate**

- syntax: *neg destination*
- action: *destination := 0 − destination*
- flags: O...SZAP.   modified for result
  ........C   set if destination <> 0
  .DIT.....   unchanged
- operands: *reg   mem*

The operand can be a register or a memory location.

## Other instructions

Two other instructions will be mentioned before turning to some example programs. The `call` instruction invokes a procedure. The `int` instruction generates an interrupt. Both of these instructions were used in the program of Chapter 3. The displays for these instructions are presented here; the instructions themselves will be discussed in more detail later.

**CALL procedure**
   syntax:    `call` *procedurename*
   action:    invoke the named procedure
   flags:     ODITSZAPC   unchanged by instruction, may be modified by procedure
   operand:   *label*

**INTerrupt**
   syntax:    `int` *interruptnumber*
   action:    invoke interrupt handler
   flags:     ..IT.....   cleared
              OD..SZAPC   unchanged
   operand:   *immed*

These instructions allow us to start writing programs that operate on integers.

## Example Programs

The programs given here combine the move, length conversion, and integer arithmetic instructions with the input and output routines presented earlier. They illustrate many of the integer arithmetic instructions and show how they are used to evaluate arithmetic expressions.

### Temperature conversion

The first program converts a temperature from Fahrenheit to Celsius. The formula for this conversion is

$$C = 5/9 \times (F - 32)$$

where C and F represent the temperatures on the Celsius and Fahrenheit scales, respectively.

The parentheses around F − 32 indicate that the subtraction is to be performed before the multiplication. This leaves two choices for which operation to perform second: multiplication or division. If we evaluate the formula from left to right, we should next divide 5 by 9. As integers—the only data type we have so far—the quotient will be 0. This in turn will give 0 for the Celsius temperature regardless of the Fahrenheit temperature.

It makes sense, therefore, to multiply the difference by 5 before dividing by 9. Not only will this give a correct answer, it saves two length conversions that would be needed if we divided first. In effect, we are rewriting the formula as

$$C = ((F - 32) \times 5)/9$$

To make the problem more interesting, let's round the result to the nearest integer. The last operation, division, gives a quotient that is incorrect by $r/9$, where $r$ is the remainder. To round the quotient to the nearest integer, we need to adjust it by 1 if the magnitude of the error is more than 0.5. The adjustment should have the same sign as the quotient. For convenience, assume that the dividend and divisor are positive. The adjustment can be written as

$$\text{adjustment} = \begin{cases} 0, & \text{if } 0 \leq r/9 < 0.5, \\ 1, & \text{if } 0.5 \leq r/9 < 1 \end{cases}$$

Now multiply through the inequalities by 2 to clear the decimals. This gives

$$\text{adjustment} = \begin{cases} 0, & \text{if } 0 \leq 2r/9 < 1, \\ 1, & \text{if } 1 \leq 2r/9 < 2 \end{cases}$$

Note that because $0 \leq r < 9$, $2 \times 0/9 \leq 2r/9 < 2 \times 9/9$, or $0 \leq 2r/9 < 2$. Thus, the result of computing $2r/9$ using integer division can only be 0 or 1. The Celsius temperature can therefore be rounded simply by computing $2 \times r/9$ and adding this adjustment to the previous result.

This rounding method works in general, even with a negative dividend or divisor. Since the remainder has the same sign as the dividend, the adjustment—based on the quotient of the second division—will have the same sign as the quotient it adjusts.

This rounding will not be perfect, however. In the event that the remainder is exactly half the divisor (when the divisor is even), 1 should be added to the quotient only if the quotient is odd; the method just presented does not check whether the quotient is odd when the remainder is half the divisor.

Program 4.1 converts a temperature from Fahrenheit to Celsius, with the result rounded to the nearest integer. It begins with prologue comments and the stack segment declaration, followed by the data segment declarations. The data segment defines two variables, Fahrenheit and Celsius, as well as two strings with their lengths.

## Program 4.1

```
; Program 4.1        FToC.ASM
; Convert a temperature from Fahrenheit to Celsius,
;     rounding the result to the nearest integer.

; DOS function and status parameters
    DosFunc      equ      21h
    ExitToDos    equ      4Ch
    NoErrors     equ      00h

DOSSEG
```

### 4.3 Instructions

**Program 4.1 (continued)**

```
_STACK SEGMENT para stack 'stack'
            dw      100h dup (?)
_STACK ENDS

_DATA SEGMENT word public 'data'
  Fahrenheit   dw      ?
  Celsius      dw      ?
  PromptMsg    db      "Enter Fahrenheit temperature: "
  PromptLen    dw      30
  AnswerMsg    db      " degrees Celsius."
  AnswerLen    dw      17
_DATA ENDS

_TEXT SEGMENT word public 'code'
    assume   cs: _TEXT
    extrn    PutStr: PROC, PutCrLf: PROC
    extrn    GetDec: PROC, PutDec: PROC

FToC:

; set up ds register to point to _DATA
    mov     ax, seg _DATA
    mov     ds, ax
    assume  ds: _DATA

; print ("Enter Fahrenheit temperature: ")
    mov     cx, PromptLen
    mov     bx, offset PromptMsg
    call    PutStr

; read (Fahrenheit)
    call    GetDec
    mov     Fahrenheit, ax

; Convert Fahrenheit to Celsius.
    mov     ax, Fahrenheit   ;   Fahrenheit
    sub     ax, 32           ;   Fahrenheit-32
    mov     bx, 5            ;  (Fahrenheit-32)       5
    imul    bx               ;  (Fahrenheit-32) *  5
    mov     bx, 9            ;  (Fahrenheit-32) *  5      9
    idiv    bx               ;  (Fahrenheit-32) *  5  /  9
    mov     Celsius, ax      ; Celsius := (Fahrenheit-32) * 5 / 9

; Compute rounding adjustment, add it to Celsius.
    mov     ax, 2            ;                        2
    imul    dx               ;                        2 * remainder
    idiv    bx               ;                        2 * remainder / 9
    add     Celsius, ax      ; Celsius := Celsius + 2 * remainder / 9

; print (Celsius, " degrees Celsius.")
    call    PutCrLf
    mov     ax, Celsius
    call    PutDec
```

**Program 4.1 (continued)**

```
        mov     cx, AnswerLen
        mov     bx, offset AnswerMsg
        call    PutStr
        call    PutCrLf

; exit to DOS
        mov     ah, ExitToDos
        mov     al, NoErrors
        int     DosFunc

_TEXT ENDS
END     FToC
```

The code segment starts with the usual assume and extrn directives, followed by instructions to set up the DS register. This is followed by six blocks of instructions, each preceded by a comment that explains the processing it performs. Two small blocks of instructions prompt for and read a temperature in Fahrenheit.

The next block of instructions computes a Celsius temperature from the input Fahrenheit temperature, without the extra rounding steps. The comment fields of the instructions in this block show an assignment statement being built step by step, with the contribution of each instruction added at each step. The first mov instruction copies the value of Fahrenheit into the AX register. The sub instruction subtracts the immediate value 32 from it. The next mov instruction copies the immediate value 5 into the BX register, in preparation for the imul instruction, which multiplies the value in the AX register by 5, giving the product in the DX:AX registers. (The imul instruction cannot have an immediate operand.) The product is then divided by 9 (which was moved into BX since idiv also cannot have an immediate operand), leaving the quotient in the AX register and the remainder in the DX register.

The next block of instructions computes the rounding adjustment, and is also documented as a built-up assignment statement in the comment field. The block begins by moving the constant 2 into AX, in preparation for multiplying the remainder, which is still in DX. The imul instruction gives the product in DX:AX; this is then divided by 9 (still in BX). The quotient of this division is finally added to the value of Celsius.

All multiplications and divisions in Program 4.1 are written using the signed versions of these instructions, since the temperatures are signed numbers. The last blocks of instructions print the rounded Celsius temperature and terminate the program.

## Calculating seconds since midnight

The next program is to compute the number of seconds elapsed since midnight, given the time of day as three integers representing hours, minutes, and seconds. We assume a valid input time using a 24-hour clock. To compute the seconds since midnight, multiply the hours by 3600 to convert to seconds, multiply the minutes by 60 to convert to seconds, then add these results to the seconds part of the input. For example, at ten minutes and twelve seconds past 2 in the afternoon, the time is 14:10:12. This is $14 \times 3600 + 10 \times 60 + 12 = 51{,}012$ seconds past midnight.

### 4.3 Instructions

However, at 23:59:59 the number of seconds is 86,399, which is too large for a 16-bit integer. Note that the number of seconds in 59 minutes and 59 seconds is 3599 (one less than the number of seconds in an hour, 3600). The number of minutes since midnight fits safely into a 16-bit integer; only the final result requires a longer integer. The computation can be written as two formulas:

$$\text{number\_of\_minutes} = \text{hour} \times 60 + \text{minute}$$

and

$$\text{number\_of\_seconds} = \text{number\_of\_minutes} \times 60 + \text{second}$$

The result of the first formula is a 16-bit integer, and the result of the second is a 32-bit integer. Program 4.2 implements the latter solution.

## Program 4.2

```
; Program 4.2        Seconds.ASM
; Given a time of day in hours, minutes, and seconds, compute
;   the number of seconds since midnight using the formula
;   Number_of_seconds := ((Hour * 60) + Minute) * 60 + Second

; DOS function and status parameters
    DosFunc     equ     21h
    ExitToDos   equ     4Ch
    NoErrors    equ     00h

DOSSEG

_STACK SEGMENT para stack 'stack'
            dw      100h dup (?)
_STACK ENDS

_DATA SEGMENT word public 'data'
    Hour        dw      ?       ;hour component of input time
    Minute      dw      ?       ;minute component of input time
    Second      dw      ?       ;second component of input time
    PromptHour  db      "  Hour = "
    PromptMin   db      "Minute = "
    PromptSec   db      "Second = "
    PromptLen   dw      9
    ResultMsg   db      " seconds since midnight."
    ResultLen   dw      24
_DATA ENDS

_TEXT SEGMENT word public 'code'
    assume  cs: _TEXT
    extrn   PutStr: PROC, PutCrLf: PROC, PutChar: PROC
    extrn   GetDec: PROC, PutDec: PROC

Seconds:

; set up ds register to point to _DATA
    mov     ax, seg _DATA
    mov     ds, ax
    assume  ds: _DATA
```

## Program 4.2 (continued)

```
        ; Read time as hours, minutes, and seconds.
        ; print (" Hour = ")
            mov     cx, PromptLen
            mov     bx, offset PromptHour
            call    PutStr

        ; read (Hour)
            call    GetDec
            mov     Hour, ax

        ; print ("Minute = ")
            mov     bx, offset PromptMin
            call    PutStr

        ; read (Minute)
            call    GetDec
            mov     Minute, ax

        ; print ("Second = ")
            mov     bx, offset PromptSec
            call    PutStr

        ; read (Second)
            call    GetDec
            mov     Second, ax

        ; Compute seconds since midnight.
        ; number_of_minutes := Hour * 60 + Minute
            mov     bx, 60
            mov     ax, Hour
            mul     bx
            add     ax, Minute

        ; number_of_seconds := number_of_minutes * 60 + Second
            mul     bx
            add     ax, Second
            adc     dx, 0

        ; Divide number_of_seconds by 1000, so that we can print it
        ; with a comma between the thousands and hundreds positions
        ; (12345 will be printed as "   12,  345").
        ; thousands_of_seconds := number_of_seconds div 1000
        ; remaining_seconds := number_of_seconds mod 1000
            mov     bx, 1000
            div     bx

        ; print (thousands_of_seconds, ",", remaining_seconds)
            call    PutDec           ;print thousands_of_seconds
            mov     ax, dx           ;save remaining_seconds
            mov     dl, ','          ;print comma
            call    PutChar
            call    PutDec           ;print remaining_seconds
```

## 4.3 Instructions

**Program 4.2 (continued)**

```
        ; print (" seconds since midnight.")
            mov     cx, ResultLen
            mov     bx, offset ResultMsg
            call    PutStr
            call    PutCrLf

        ; exit to DOS
            mov     ah, ExitToDos
            mov     al, NoErrors
            int     DosFunc

_TEXT   ENDS
END     Seconds
```

The input values are read as three integers and saved in the variables Hour, Minute, and Second. The first formula is implemented by the block of instructions

```
mov     bx, 60
mov     ax, Hour
mul     bx
add     ax, Minute
```

Since the product is less than 1440 for valid input, the more significant part in the DX register is 0. The addition of Minute cannot affect DX, as the sum is less than 1500 for valid input.

The second formula is implemented by the instructions

```
mul     bx
add     ax, Second
adc     dx, 0
```

The multiplication converts the number of minutes into seconds. This product could be as large as 86,340 and must therefore be treated as a 32-bit integer. Adding the value of Second to this requires that it be added to the less significant part of the number of seconds computed so far. This could generate a carry, which must be added to the more significant half of the result. The last instruction in the block adds the carry (and 0) to DX.

Now consider printing the result. PutDec can print a 16-bit integer in decimal, but not a 32-bit integer. The contents of each register could be printed separately, but the user would have to multiply the first number by 32768 and add the second number to get the result as a single number. PutDec also assumes that the integer is a signed number, so the less significant half of the positive result might be printed as a negative number, which would clearly be unacceptable.

Another way to print the result as two numbers is to divide it by 1000 and print both the quotient and the remainder, with a comma between them. For example, if the time in seconds is 12345, it is printed as "    12,   345" where 12 is the quotient from the division by 1000 and 345 is the remainder. The extra spaces are part of the fixed six-character field that PutDec uses. Still, the user can ignore the spaces and read the result as 12,345 seconds.

**128**  Chapter 4  Integers

The two instructions

```
mov     bx, 1000
div     bx
```

compute the quotient, which is left in AX and displayed by PutDec. The remainder is moved from DX into AX before calling PutChar to print the comma, because the DL register is needed for the argument to PutChar. After displaying the comma, the remainder and a brief message are displayed.

Note that in Program 4.2 the multiplications and divisions are performed using the instructions for unsigned numbers. If the input values are valid, all quantities will be positive.

## Calculating the time of day

The final example computes the time of day as three integers representing hours, minutes, and seconds, given the number of seconds since midnight (Program 4.3).

### Program 4.3

```
; Program 4.3        DayTime.ASM
; Given the number of seconds since midnight, convert it to
;    the time of day expressed as hr:min:sec.  Formulas used:
;          SEC := seconds rem 60
;          MIN := (seconds div 60) rem 60
;          HR  := (seconds div 60) div 60
;    Since integer division gives both quotient and remainder,
;    the expressions in all three formulas can be evaluated
;    using just two division instructions.
;    Note: The number of seconds since midnight can be as large
;    as 86399, so we must use a doubleword integer for it.

; DOS function and status parameters
    DosFunc     equ     21h
    ExitToDos   equ     4Ch
    NoErrors    equ     00h

DOSSEG

_STACK SEGMENT para stack 'stack'
            dw      100h dup (?)
_STACK ENDS

_DATA SEGMENT word public 'data'
    KSec        dw      ?       ;thousands of seconds in input
    USec        dw      ?       ;hundreds, tens, and units in input
    Hour        dw      ?       ;hour component in time of day
    Minute      dw      ?       ;minute component in time of day
    Second      dw      ?       ;second component in time of day
    PromptMsg1  db              "Enter seconds, separating thousands from"
    PromptMsg2  db              "hundreds with a space (example: 12 345) "
    PromptLen   dw      40
    AnswerMsg   db              "Time is "
    AnswerLen   dw      8
_DATA ENDS
```

### 4.3 Instructions

**Program 4.3 (continued)**

```
_TEXT SEGMENT word public 'code'
    assume  cs: _TEXT
    extrn   PutStr: PROC, PutCrLf: PROC
    extrn   GetDec: PROC, PutDec: PROC

DayTime:

; set up ds register to point to _DATA
    mov     ax, seg _DATA
    mov     ds, ax
    assume  ds: _DATA

; Get number of seconds since midnight from user.
; print ("Enter seconds, separating thousands from")
; print ("hundreds with a space (example: 12 345) ")
    mov     cx, PromptLen
    mov     bx, offset PromptMsg1
    call    PutStr
    call    PutCrLf
    mov     bx, offset PromptMsg2
    call    PutStr

; read (KSec, Usec)
    call    GetDec
    mov     KSec, ax
    call    GetDec
    mov     USec, ax

; number_of_seconds (in ax:dx)  := KSec * 1000 + USec
    mov     ax, KSec
    mov     bx, 1000
    mul     bx
    add     ax, USec
    adc     dx, 0

; Convert number_of_seconds to time of day.
; Second := number_of_seconds rem 60
; number_of_minutes := number_of_seconds div 60
    mov     bx, 60
    div     bx
    mov     Second, dx

; Minute := number_of_minutes rem 60
; Hour := number_of_minutes div 60
    mov     dx, 0
    div     bx
    mov     Minute, dx
    mov     Hour, ax

; Print time of day in HH MM SS format.
; print ("Time is ", Hour, Minute, Second)
    call    PutCrLf
    mov     cx, AnswerLen
```

**Program 4.3 (continued)**

```
            mov     bx, offset AnswerMsg
            call    PutStr

            mov     ax, Hour        ;print Hour
            call    PutDec

            mov     ax, Minute      ;print Minute
            call    PutDec

            mov     ax, Second      ;print Second
            call    PutDec
            call    PutCrLf

; exit to DOS
            mov     ah, ExitToDos
            mov     al, NoErrors
            int     DosFunc

_TEXT ENDS
END     DayTime
```

---

The first problem is to read the number of seconds since midnight; as in Program 4.2, this number can be too large for a 16-bit signed integer. One solution is to ask the user to enter the number with a space between the thousands and hundreds digits and to read the input as two separate numbers.

The number of seconds is computed by multiplying the first input by 1000 and adding the second input, using the instructions

```
mov     ax, KSec
mov     bx, 1000
mul     bx
add     ax, USec
adc     dx, 0
```

The last of these instructions adds any carry from the first addition to the more significant half of the result.

The conversion to hours, minutes, and seconds is straightforward. The total number of seconds since midnight is divided by 60: The quotient is the number of minutes since midnight, and the remainder is the seconds part of the time of day. The number of minutes since midnight is then divided by 60: The quotient will be the hours part of the time of day, and the remainder will be the minutes part. The formulas are

$$\text{number\_of\_minutes} = \text{number\_of\_seconds } div \text{ } 60$$

$$\text{Second} = \text{number\_of\_seconds } rem \text{ } 60$$

and then

$$\text{Hour} = \text{number\_of\_minutes } div \text{ } 60$$

$$\text{Minute} = \text{number\_of\_minutes } rem \text{ } 60$$

### 4.3 Instructions

The first pair of formulas are implemented by the block of three instructions

```
mov     bx, 60
div     bx
mov     Second, dx
```

Note that the number of minutes since midnight—the quotient—is still in AX. The second pair of formulas are then implemented by the block of four instructions

```
mov     dx, 0
div     bx
mov     Minute, dx
mov     Hour, ax
```

The last blocks of instructions in the program display a brief message and the three components of the time, and then terminate the program.

In this program, the multiplications and divisions are performed using the instructions for unsigned numbers. If the input values are valid, all quantities will be positive.

## EXERCISES 4.3

1. Write a sequence of instructions to exchange two words of memory without using xchg. Use four mov instructions and assume that it is okay to use (and destroy the original contents of) AX and BX.

2. The sub instruction is defined so that

   ```
   sub     reg, mem
   ```

   replaces the contents of the register with the difference (reg - mem). Write a sequence of instructions that replaces the contents of reg with the difference (mem - reg). Do not change any other registers or words of memory.

▶3. Write a program that converts a temperature from Celsius to Fahrenheit. Round the result to the nearest degree.

▶4. Write a program that reads an amount of money in cents and prints the number of quarters, dimes, nickels, and pennies needed to make up that amount. Assume that the amount is less than a dollar.

▶5. Write a program that computes the average speed on a trip, given starting time, ending time, and distance traveled. Both times are given as two integers, representing hours and minutes using a 24-hour clock. Assume that the times are in the same day. In the computation, multiply the distance by 60 and divide by the elapsed time in minutes. For example, if the starting time is 10:40, the ending time is 14:10, and the distance is 147 miles, the average speed is

$$(147 \times 60)/((14 - 10) \times 60 + (10 - 40)) = 8820/(240 - 30)$$
$$= 8820/210$$

or 42 miles per hour.

▶6. Write a program that converts a length measured in centimeters to feet and inches, rounded to the nearest inch. There are 2.54 cm in 1 inch. To implement this, multiply the length by 100 and divide by 254.

**132** Chapter 4 Integers

▶7. Write a program that computes the average of a small fixed number of values. It might average four values, for example, or five values, or some other number of values.

▶8. Write a program that converts an improper fraction to a mixed number, given the numerator and denominator of the fraction. For example, given 27 for the numerator and 6 for the denominator, your program should print    4,    3/    6.

▶9. Write a program that reads three scores and three weights and computes a weighted average. If the scores are S1, S2, and S3 and the weights are W1, W2, and W3, the formula for the weighted average is

$$WtAvg = (S1 \times W1 + S2 \times W2 + S3 \times W3)/(W1 + W2 + W3)$$

Do not round the weighted average.

▶10. Write a program that reads two 2-digit numbers and prints the sum of the digits in the product. For example, if the user enters 12 and 89, your program should compute $12 \times 89 = 1068$, $1 + 0 + 6 + 8 = 15$, and print 15.

## KEY POINTS

- Integers are represented in binary.
- Positive integers are represented with leading zeros to fill a word of memory.
- Sign and magnitude representation uses one bit for the sign (0 for positive, 1 for negative) and the rest of a word for the magnitude.
- Sign and magnitude representation gives a symmetrical range of values, with two representations of 0.
- Sign and magnitude representation requires separate circuits for addition and subtraction; addition of numbers with different signs is implemented as subtraction.
- Logical complement representation of negative values complements each bit of the magnitude of the integer. Logical complement is also called one's complement.
- Logical complement representation gives a symmetrical range of values, with two representations of 0.
- Addition in logical complement representation does not consider the signs of the numbers. Subtraction is implemented as addition of a complement.
- Addition in logical complement representation requires that the carry from the most significant bit of the sum be added to the least significant bit.
- Radix complement representation of negative values subtracts the magnitude from a power of the radix; the power determines the number of digits used. In binary computers, radix complement is called two's complement.
- Radix complement representation gives an asymmetrical range of values. There is a unique 0, but one more negative value than positive.
- Addition in radix complement representation does not consider the signs of the numbers. Subtraction is implemented as addition of a complement.
- In complement representations in binary, the first bit indicates the sign of the integer even though it is not a sign bit. Using bits to the left of the most significant bit of the magnitude (zeros for positive numbers, and ones for negative numbers) is called sign bit extension.
- Move operations copy data from one memory location or register to another.

- Overflow occurs when the result of an operation on integers is outside the range of integers that the computer can represent.
- Addition and subtraction of integers can cause overflow.
- Addition and subtraction of integers can record the carry out of the most significant bit of the sum, which is useful in implementing multiple-word arithmetic.
- Multiplication in some computers gives a product that uses twice as many bits as the factors; there is no overflow with this arrangement. In other computers, the product is the same length as the factors, and overflow is possible.
- Conversion instructions, which change the number of bits used to represent an integer, are used to convert two-word products to a one-word value.
- Division in some computers requires a dividend twice as long as the divisor; in other computers, the dividend can be the same length as the divisor. Some division instructions give a remainder as well as a quotient.
- Division can result in overflow, although this depends on the lengths of the dividend and divisor. An attempt to divide by 0 is always an error.
- Negation can cause overflow only when the operand is the smallest integer in two's complement.
- Extended arithmetic can be used to avoid overflow problems when working with very large numbers. It can also provide greater range for integers in computers with small words.

## PC SYSTEM SUMMARY

- Integers can be signed or unsigned. Unsigned data is always interpreted as positive; signed data uses two's complement representation.
- Integers can be byte, word, or doubleword length.
- The range of integers in each representation is

| | | |
|---|---:|---:|
| signed byte | $-128$ to | 127 |
| unsigned byte | 0 to | 255 |
| signed word | $-32,768$ to | 32,767 |
| unsigned word | 0 to | 65,535 |
| signed doubleword | $-2,147,483,648$ to | 2,147,483,647 |
| unsigned doubleword | 0 to | 4,294,967,295 |

- The same instructions are used in assembly language for operations on byte and word operands. When two operands are used, they must be the same length.
- When there are two operands, the destination is always the first operand. The first operand might also be a source operand as well as the destination.

Instructions presented in this chapter:

Data move:

| | |
|---|---|
| mov | copy from source to destination |
| xchg | copy between source and destination |

Signed integer conversion:

| | |
|---|---|
| `cbw` | convert byte to word |
| `cwd` | convert word to doubleword |
| | (see text for word-to-byte, doubleword-to-word, and unsigned conversions) |

Arithmetic:

| | |
|---|---|
| `adc` | add with carry |
| `add` | add |
| `clc` | clear carry flag |
| `cmc` | complement carry flag |
| `dec` | decrement |
| `div` | unsigned divide |
| `idiv` | signed divide |
| `imul` | signed multiply |
| `inc` | increment |
| `mul` | unsigned multiply |
| `neg` | signed negate |
| `sbb` | subtract with borrow |
| `stc` | set carry flag |
| `sub` | subtract |

Miscellaneous:

| | |
|---|---|
| `call` | invoke procedure |
| `int` | generate interrupt |

# Control Structures 5

- **Tests and Relations**
- **Transfer of Control**
- **Selection**
- **Repetition**

Using the instructions of the previous chapter we can write simple programs that do interesting computations with integers. However, all but the simplest programs require more than a sequence of integer manipulations. Most programs require repetition or selection structures, or both. In this chapter we examine how control structures can be written in assembly language and how they are implemented by language translators. We begin by examining the tests that the hardware can perform on data, such as comparing two values or detecting overflow during an arithmetic operation. We then move on to a discussion of how the result of such a test is recorded and then examine the instructions that transfer control from one part of a program to another, conditionally and unconditionally.

The unrestricted use of instructions that transfer control from one part of a program to another creates programs that are difficult to understand and maintain. Experience with such programs has led to the adoption of control structures in high-level languages. The instructions introduced in this chapter are accompanied by templates for implementing control structures in assembly language. This avoids ad hoc methods of implementing control structures, while providing insight into how a compiler might implement them.

## 5.1 TESTS AND RELATIONS

Tests written in high-level languages compare the values of two expressions to each other, using relational operators. (The logical operators that combine the results of several comparisons are not included in this discussion. They will be considered in Chapter 6.) Some tests, such as the EOF function in Pascal or the END=label option in a FORTRAN READ statement, do not appear to compare two values. Actually, however, they do: They compare a character from an input device to the character code that marks the end of a file. All tests in high-level languages can be treated as comparisons between two values.

In addition to comparisons, computer hardware and assembly language support tests of other properties and conditions. The tests may be implemented as separate operations that save their results for later use by other instructions or as part of conditional instructions.

## Saving Test Results

Operations that compare two values or that test or set other properties and conditions often record their result in one or more flags. As was shown in the previous chapter, arithmetic instructions record overflow, carry, and other properties of the result in flags. A compare instruction is usually nothing more than a subtraction operation that does not save the difference that it computes, but only uses the difference to set or clear flags.

The 8086 saves the results of tests and of arithmetic operations in the flags register. The six flags that record such results are the overflow flag (OF), the sign flag (SF), the zero flag (ZF), the auxiliary carry flag (AF), the parity flag (PF), and the carry flag (CF).

The instruction summaries in this text show the flags that are affected by the instruction. For example, the summary of the add and adc instructions includes the entry

    flags:    O...SZAPC modified for sum

which indicates that the overflow (O), sign (S), zero (Z), auxiliary carry (A), parity (P), and carry (C) flags are set or cleared according to the sum calculated.

## ✓ Compare Instruction

The compare instruction subtracts its second operand from its first operand, sets or clears flags according to the difference, and discards the difference. It does not change either operand. Like the subtraction instruction, the compare instruction works with signed and unsigned numbers.

---

**CoMPare two values**

| | |
|---|---|
| syntax: | cmp *destination, source* |
| action: | compute *(destination − source)* |
| flags: | O...SZAPC modified for difference |
| | .DIT..... unchanged |
| operands: | *reg,reg*    *mem,reg*    *reg,mem* |
| | *reg,immed*   *mem,immed*  *accum,immed* |

---

The instruction

    cmp    ax, Limit

computes the difference AX − Limit. The overflow flag records whether overflow occurs during the subtraction, treating the operands as signed numbers. The sign of the difference is copied into the sign flag. If the difference is 0, which indicates that AX and Limit are equal, the zero flag is set; otherwise it is cleared. Discussion of the auxiliary carry will be deferred until Chapter 16, which covers decimal arithmetic. If the less significant byte of the difference has an even number of set bits (i.e., one bits), the parity flag is set; otherwise it is cleared. The carry flag records whether a borrow has been generated during the subtraction; a borrow also indicates overflow when treating the operands as unsigned numbers.

## Interpreting Test Results

This section will consider the significance of the flags following a cmp instruction. Instructions that inspect flags usually perform a conditional transfer of control. These instructions are available in complementary pairs: One transfers control if some condition is satisfied, while the other transfers control if the complementary condition is satisfied.

Some instructions inspect a single flag; others examine two or more flags at once. Depending on whether the values compared are signed or unsigned data, different flags are used to record the relationship between them. In the following, we discuss how cmp affects the flags with signed data differently than it affects the flags with unsigned data. It is up to the program to inspect the correct flags following the compare instruction.

### Signed data

Three flags are used to record the relationship between two signed values. The zero flag records whether the difference computed by cmp is 0. The sign flag is a copy of the sign bit of the result. These two flags are sufficient to determine the relation between two numbers as long as overflow does not occur during the subtraction.

When overflow occurs during the subtraction, the sign bit of the result is incorrect. It is necessary to check OF as well as SF to determine the relationship between the operands of cmp, as will be shown in the following examples using the AL and BL registers.

In Figure 5.1, BL is subtracted from AL by adding its two's complement in binary. Example 1 has two positive values. The value in AL is greater than the value in BL. The addition of the two's complement of BL to AL clears OF, ZF, and SF: There is no overflow, and AL+(−BL) is neither 0 nor negative. In Example 2 the value in AL is interpreted as a negative number, so it is less than the positive value in BL. The addition of the two's complement of BL to AL clears OF and ZF, and sets SF: There is no overflow, and AL+(−BL) is negative. In Example 3 the value in AL is positive and is greater than the negative value in BL. The addition of the two's complement of BL to AL clears OF, ZF, and SF: There is no overflow, and AL+(−BL) is neither 0 nor negative. In Example 4 the value in AL is positive and is greater than the negative value in BL. The addition of the two's complement of BL to AL overflows. As a two's complement number, the sum can be interpreted as −100, which is 256 less than the true sum. The addition sets OF to record the overflow, clears ZF (since the sum is not 0), and sets SF (since the result appears negative).

In this example, the sum AL+(−BL) can be interpreted as a negative number. This can be written as AL−BL<0, which leads to AL<BL. However, we know the original values in AL and BL and that AL>BL. When overflow occurs, SF by itself gives an incorrect indication of the relation.

Table 5.1 summarizes how ZF, SF, and OF are affected by cmp (or sub) with signed operands. Note that when Dest<Source, OF and SF differ; when Dest>Source, OF and SF are the same.

There are six possible relations to test for when two signed values are compared. These are listed in Table 5.2, along with the states of OF, SF, and ZF that satisfy each test.

**138** Chapter 5 Control Structures

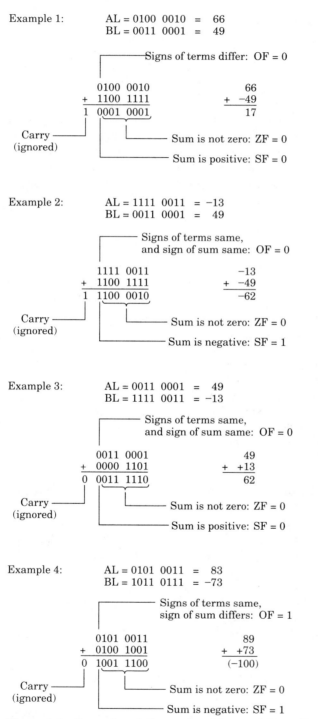

**Figure 5.1 Examples of Computing AL +(− BL) as Signed Integers**

## 5.1 Tests and Relations

**Table 5.1** Effect of cmp with Signed Operands on Zero, Overflow, and Sign Flags

| Relationship of Dest to Source | Result of cmp Dest, Source | | |
|---|---|---|---|
| | **ZF** | **OF** | **SF** |
| Dest = Source | 1 | 0 | 0 |
| Dest < Source | 0 | 0 | 1 |
| | 0 | 1 | 0 |
| Dest > Source | 0 | 0 | 0 |
| | 0 | 1 | 1 |

The table lists each relation twice, and for each it also gives two mnemonics. These mnemonics will become useful shortly.

### Unsigned data

Two flags are used to record the relationship between two unsigned values. The zero flag records whether the difference computed by cmp is 0. The carry flag records whether overflow occurs during the subtraction—that is, whether the result is outside the supported range of unsigned values. This section will refer to this "unsigned overflow" simply as "carry."

The principle can be illustrated using the same examples used for signed data. See Figure 5.2, where BL is subtracted directly from AL. Note that, after the carry flags from Figure 5.1 are complemented, the results are the same in every case. Figure 5.2 shows only ZF and CF. In Example 1 the value in AL is greater than the value in BL. The subtraction of BL from AL clears ZF and CF: There is no overflow, and AL−BL is not 0. In Example 2 the value in AL is also greater than the value in BL. The result is

**Table 5.2** Interpretation of Flags for Signed Conditions

| Condition | Mnemonic | Flags |
|---|---|---|
| Equal | E | ZF=1 |
| Zero | Z | |
| Not equal | NE | ZF=0 |
| Not zero | NZ | |
| Less | L | SF<>OF |
| Not greater or equal | NGE | |
| Less or equal | LE | ZF=1 or SF <> OF |
| Not greater | NG | |
| Greater | G | ZF=0 and SF=OF |
| Not less or equal | NLE | |
| Greater or equal | GE | SF=OF |
| Not less | NL | |

**140**   Chapter 5   Control Structures

Example 1:    AL = 0100 0010 = 66
              BL = 0011 0001 = 49

```
    0100 0010              66
  - 0011 0001            - 49
  0 0001 0001              17
```
              Difference is not zero: ZF = 0
              Borrow is 0: CF = 0

Example 2:    AL = 1111 0011 = 243
              BL = 0011 0001 = 49

```
    1111 0011             243
  - 0011 0001           -  49
  0 1100 0010             194
```
              Difference is not zero: ZF = 0
              Borrow is 0: CF = 0

Example 3:    AL = 0011 0001 = 49
              BL = 1111 0011 = 243

```
    0011 0001              49
  - 1111 0011           - 243
  1 0011 1110            (62)
```
              Difference is not zero: ZF = 0
              Borrow is 1: CF = 1

Example 4:    AL = 0101 0011 = 83
              BL = 1011 0111 = 183

```
    0101 0011              83
  - 1011 0111           - 183
  1 1001 1100           (156)
```
              Difference is not zero: ZF = 0
              Borrow is 1: CF = 1

**Figure 5.2**   Examples of Computing AL − BL as Unsigned Integers

the same as in the first example. Compare this with the second example of Figure 5.1, where the value in AL is interpreted as a negative number. In Example 3 the value in AL is less than the value in BL. The subtraction of BL from AL requires a borrow, so CF is set and ZF is cleared. The difference can be interpreted as 62, which is 256 more than the true difference. In Example 4 the value in AL is again less than the value in BL. The

## 5.1 Tests and Relations

**Table 5.3** Effect of cmp with Unsigned Operands on Zero and Carry Flags

| Relationship of Dest to Source | Result of cmp Dest, Source ||
|---|---|---|
| | ZF | CF |
| Dest = Source | 1 | 0 |
| Dest < Source | 0 | 1 |
| Dest > Source | 0 | 0 |

result is the same as in the third example, with CF set and ZF cleared. The difference can be interpreted as 156, which is again 256 more than the true difference. Table 5.3 summarizes how ZF and CF are affected by cmp (or sub) with unsigned operands.

There are six possible relations to test for when comparing two unsigned values. These are listed in Table 5.4, along with the states of ZF and CF that satisfy each test. Like Table 5.2, this table also lists each relation twice and gives two mnemonics for each. To distinguish signed conditions from unsigned conditions, the unsigned conditions use "above" rather than "greater" and "below" rather than "less."

## Miscellaneous tests

Assembly-language programs can also inspect the other flags. In the spirit of Tables 5.2 and 5.4, Table 5.5 lists all conditions that inspect a single flag, along with the value of the flag that satisfies it and a mnemonic for each condition.

**Table 5.4** Interpretation of Flags for Unsigned Conditions

| Condition | Mnemonic | Flags |
|---|---|---|
| Equal | E | ZF = 1 |
| Zero | Z | |
| Not equal | NE | ZF = 0 |
| Not zero | NZ | |
| Below | B | CF = 1 |
| Not above or equal | NAE | |
| Below or equal | BE | CF = 1 or ZF = 1 |
| Not above | NA | |
| Above | A | CF = 0 and ZF = 0 |
| Not below or equal | NBE | |
| Above or equal | AE | CF = 0 |
| Not below | NB | |

## Chapter 5 Control Structures

Table 5.5  Interpretation of Flags for Single Conditions

| Condition | Mnemonic | Flag |
|---|---|---|
| Equal | E | ZF = 1 |
| Zero | Z | |
| Not equal | NE | ZF = 0 |
| Not zero | NZ | |
| Sign | S | SF = 1 |
| Not sign | NS | SF = 0 |
| Carry | C | CF = 1 |
| Not carry | NC | CF = 0 |
| Overflow | O | OF = 1 |
| Not overflow | NO | OF = 0 |
| Parity | P | PF = 1 |
| Parity even | PE | |
| No parity | NP | PF = 0 |
| Parity odd | PO | |

### EXERCISES 5.1

1. What might the parity flag be used for?
2. A cmp instruction clears the carry flag and overflow flags and sets the sign flag. What can you say about the values compared?
3. Another cmp instruction sets the carry flag and clears the overflow and sign flags. What can you say about the values compared?
4. Are there any combinations of CF, SF, and OF that cannot be the result of a cmp instruction? If so, give an example. If not, explain why not.
5. What is the significance of 256 in the discussions of Example 4 of Figure 5.1 and Examples 3 and 4 of Figure 5.2?

## 5.2 TRANSFER OF CONTROL

We next consider instructions that transfer control within a program. Most of them inspect one or two flags and transfer control only if the desired state is present. Earlier, we saw that the sequence in which instructions are executed can be altered by writing an offset to the instruction pointer (IP). Since IP is the offset in the code segment of the next instruction to be executed, changing IP causes the computer to execute an instruction other than the next one in sequence. The instructions in a program are normally executed one after another in the order in which they are stored. After an instruction is fetched, and before it is executed, IP is incremented by the length of the instruction. Thus, IP has the offset of the next instruction in sequence. When an instruction changes IP, control is transferred to another part of the program.

## 5.2 Transfer of Control

### Jumps and Branches

There are two names for instructions that write new addresses to the instruction pointer: jump instructions and branch instructions. Some instruction sets—including that of the 8086—use one of these names, and other sets use both names. In the latter case, there is some distinction between a jump and a branch. The distinction could be that a branch instruction transfers control within a limited range, such as within the current instruction segment, but a jump instruction can transfer control to any instruction in memory. That is, a branch instruction would be used within a program or subprogram and a jump would be used to transfer control to another program or subprogram. Another possible distinction could be that a conditional jump instruction inspects flags, but a conditional branch instruction performs a new comparison.

Jump and branch instructions can be conditional or unconditional. An unconditional jump always writes an address to IP. A conditional jump first evaluates the specified condition, either by comparing two values or by inspecting one or more of the flags. If the condition is satisfied the conditional jump then writes an address to IP. If the condition is not satisfied the instruction terminates with no further activity, leaving the IP with the address of the next instruction in sequence.

### Jump Instructions

The 8086 has one unconditional and many conditional jump instructions. Jump instructions have just one operand: the address to which control may be transferred. The coding of the address will be discussed after examining the instructions.

The unconditional jump instruction always writes the address given by its operand to the instruction pointer.

**JuMP unconditionally**

| | |
|---|---|
| syntax: | jmp *destination* |
| action: | IP := *destination* |
| flags: | ODITSZAPC unchanged |
| operands: | *label*    *reg*    *mem* |

The conditional jump instructions check one or more flags. Their mnemonics begin with j followed by one to three letters that specify the state of the flags that they check. These additional letters are given in the mnemonic column of Tables 5.2, 5.4, and 5.5. Many of the conditional jump instructions have synonyms; you can use whichever name makes the purpose of the instruction in your program clearer.

Instructions in the first group check for a zero result or equal comparison of two numbers.

**Jump if Equal**
**Jump if Zero**

| | |
|---|---|
| syntax: | je *destination* |
| | jz *destination* |
| action: | if ZF = 1 then IP := *destination* |

**Jump if Not Equal**
**Jump if Not Zero**

   syntax:    jne *destination*
                  jnz *destination*
   action:    if ZF=0 then IP := *destination*
   flags:     ODITSZAPC unchanged
   operand: *label* (short)

---

Instructions in the next group check a relation between unsigned numbers. They are used following compare or arithmetic instructions used with unsigned data.

---

**Jump if Below**
**Jump if Not Above or Equal**

   syntax:    jb *destination*
                  jnae *destination*
   action:    if CF=1 then IP := *destination*

**Jump if Below or Equal**
**Jump if Not Above**

   syntax:    jbe *destination*
                  jna *destination*
   action:    if CF=1 or ZF=1 then IP := *destination*

**Jump if Above**
**Jump if Not Below or Equal**

   syntax:    ja *destination*
                  jnbe *destination*
   action:    if CF=0 and ZF=0 then IP := *destination*

**Jump if Above or Equal**
**Jump if Not Below**

   syntax:    jae *destination*
                  jnb *destination*
   action:    if CF=0 then IP := *destination*
   flags:     ODITSZAPC unchanged
   operand: *label* (short)

---

Instructions in the next group check a relation between signed numbers. They are used following compare or arithmetic instructions used with signed data.

## 5.2 Transfer of Control

**Jump if Less**
**Jump if Not Greater or Equal**
   syntax:     `jl` *destination*
                 `jnge` *destination*
   action:     if SF <> OF then IP := *destination*

**Jump if Less or Equal**
**Jump if Not Greater**
   syntax:     `jle` *destination*
                 `jng` *destination*
   action:     if ZF=1 or SF<>OF then IP := *destination*

**Jump if Greater**
**Jump if Not Less or Equal**
   syntax:     `jg` *destination*
                 `jnle` *destination*
   action:     if ZF=0 or SF=OF then IP := *destination*

**Jump if Greater or Equal**
**Jump if Not Less**
   syntax:     `jge` *destination*
                 `jnl` *destination*
   action:     if SF=OF then IP := *destination*
   flags:      ODITSZAPC unchanged
   operand: *label* (short)

Instructions in the next group inspect one of the flags individually. We have already seen the `jz` and `jnz` instructions, which inspect ZF. The other flags that can be checked are OF, SF, PF, and CF.

**Jump if Overflow**
   syntax:     `jo` *destination*
   action:     if OF=1 then IP := *destination*

**Jump if No Overflow**
   syntax:     `jno` *destination*
   action:     if OF=0 then IP := *destination*

**Jump if Sign**
   syntax:     `js` *destination*
   action:     if SF=1 then IP := *destination*

**Jump if Not Sign**
   syntax:     `jns` *destination*
   action:     if SF=0 then IP := *destination*

**Jump if Parity**
**Jump if Parity Even**
    syntax:    jp *destination*
                jpe *destination*
    action:    if PF = 1 then IP := *destination*

**Jump if No Parity**
**Jump if Parity Odd**
    syntax:    jnp *destination*
                jpo *destination*
    action:    if PF = 0 then IP := *destination*

**Jump if Carry**
    syntax:    jc *destination*
    action:    if CF = 1 then IP := *destination*

**Jump if Not Carry**
    syntax:    jnc *destination*
    action:    if CF = 0 then IP := *destination*
    flags:     ODITSZAPC unchanged
    operand:  *label* (short)

There are also conditional jump instructions that inspect the CX register. Some of them also modify the CX register. These instructions are especially useful when writing loops. The CX register is specially designed for use in counting operations. These conditional jump instructions are part of the extra capability of CX.

The jcxz instruction jumps if the CX register is 0. It does not change the CX register.

**Jump if CX is Zero**
    syntax:    jcxz *destination*
    action:    if CX = 0 then IP := *destination*
    flags:     ODITSZAPC unchanged
    operand:  *label* (short)

Instructions in the final group decrement the CX register, without changing any flags, before testing it. Some of these also inspect ZF, which must be cleared or set by a previous instruction.

**LOOP**
    syntax:    loop *destination*
    action:    (1) CX := CX − 1; (flags unchanged)
                (2) if CX<>0 then IP = *destination*

## 5.2 Transfer of Control

**LOOP if Equal**
**LOOP if Zero**
    syntax:    `loope` *destination*
                  `loopz` *destination*
    action:    (1) CX := CX − 1; (flags unchanged)
                  (2) if CX<>0 and ZF = 1 then IP := *destination*

**LOOP if Not Equal**
**LOOP if Not Zero**
    syntax:    `loopne` *destination*
                  `loopnz` *destination*
    action:    (1) CX := CX − 1; (flags unchanged)
                  (2) if CX<>0 and ZF = 0 then IP := *destination*
    flags:     ODITSZAPC unchanged
    operand:  *label* (short)

The instructions that also check ZF are useful in writing loops in searching applications. Such loops have two termination conditions: The value searched for is found (the `cmp` instruction that checks this sets or clears ZF), or no more locations to search (CX can be used to count how many locations remain to be searched). The last four instructions combine these tests.

## Relative Addresses

Most jump instructions—those of the 8086 and many other computers—are coded differently than other instructions. They have one operand, the label on an instruction. During assembly, the displacement (in bytes) between the instruction following the jump and the label is computed and coded as part of the instruction. This form of address, where the displacement is relative to the instruction Pointer, is called a **relative address**.

When a jump instruction is executed and the jump is made, the instruction pointer is modified. If the instruction uses relative addressing, the displacement field of the instruction is added to the instruction pointer. If the instruction uses some other addressing mode, the physical address is computed and replaces the instruction pointer.

In the 8086, all conditional jump instructions use relative addressing with a one-byte displacement. The displacement is a signed number, which allows backward as well as forward jumps. The range of signed numbers that can be represented in a byte is −128 to +127, so the label must be within −128 to +127 bytes of the instruction that follows the conditional jump. Such a jump is called a *short jump*.

The 8086 unconditional jump can use a relative address with either a byte or word displacement. With a word displacement the label must be within −32768 to +32767 bytes of the instruction that follows the jump; the label can be anywhere in the same segment as the jump. Such a jump is called a *near jump*.

The destination of an unconditional jump can also be in another segment. This is called a *far jump*, which will be discussed later.

Sometimes we need a conditional jump to a destination that cannot be coded as an eight-bit displacement. To overcome this limit, it is possible to use two jump instructions.

For example, if we want to write

```
    js      FarAway
```

where the displacement to FarAway is too large for a signed eight-bit number, we can write

```
    jns     NextInst
    jmp     FarAway
NextInst:
```

We want to jump to FarAway if SF is set. A js instruction is the logical choice, but the displacement is too large for a conditional instruction. Instead, jmp is used to transfer control to FarAway, preceded by jns to skip over the jmp instruction if SF is cleared. The limit on the displacement is the only restriction on conditional jump instructions.

One of the important developments in programming has been the widespread adoption of high-level control structures. The next sections will present ways to implement control structures in assembly language using the jump instructions. There are two reasons for this: When we program in an assembly language, we want to use the control structures as tools; we also want to understand how high-level languages implement the control structures.

## EXERCISES 5.2

1. In terms of programming style, why might we sometimes prefer a mnemonic like jnae to its synonym jb?
2. Examine any programs you have assembled so far; try to determine how many instructions (roughly) occupy 128 bytes. This is the limit of the displacement from a conditional jump to the destination. How often do you think this limit is a problem?
3. There are no instructions for copying between the IP register and another register directly. Would such instructions be useful? How might you use them?

## 5.3 SELECTION

A selection control structure allows a program to execute one of two or more alternative sequences of instructions, based on the data being processed. In its most general form, it consists of two sequences of instructions and a condition that determines which sequence to execute. One variation of it has only one sequence of instructions and a condition that determines whether or not the sequence will be executed. Selection structures can be nested, which makes it possible to implement a structure with an arbitrary number of alternatives.

### Selection with Two Sequences

Pseudocode for the selection structure can be written as

```
IF condition
THEN
   sequence to execute when condition is true
ELSE
   sequence to execute when condition is false
ENDIF
```

## 5.3 Selection

This statement, or one very much like it, is available in most high-level programming languages. The indentation and pseudocode might appear unusual at first, but this arrangement lends itself to translation into assembly language. The sequence of statements following the keyword THEN, executed once when the condition is true, is called the THEN *clause*. The other sequence, executed once when the condition is false, is called the ELSE *clause*.

The selection structure can be implemented in assembly language (Figure 5.3). The keywords of the pseudocode are used either in comments or as labels. Because all labels in a program must be unique, and because some of these keywords are reserved for other uses by 8086 assemblers, sequence numbers are appended to the labels. (These are denoted by nn in Figure 5.3). We also adopt the convention that labels within the code will be on separate lines. This leads to more consistent programs and easier program modification and maintenance.

The first line of the structure is a comment that is the same as the pseudocode, except that a sequence number is appended to IF. This is followed by the instructions that evaluate the condition, and a conditional jump to skip over the THEN clause. The instruction must use the complement of the condition written in the pseudocode. For example, if the condition following IF is $A < B$, we would test for $A \geq B$ in the conditional jump. The jump instruction in Figure 5.3 is given as jn__ and should be replaced with the appropriate conditional jump instruction. The 8086 assemblers provide synonyms that make writing the complement easier; the n as the second letter of the mnemonic provides the complement. To continue the example, if the condition following IF is $A < B$, we would use a jnl instruction to implement the test. The IF statement uses the "Less than" condition, and the instruction uses the "Not Less than" condition.

The THEN clause follows a comment with the word THEN and a sequence number, and with pseudocode that documents the THEN clause. This is followed by an unconditional jump to the end of the structure. This jump skips over the ELSE clause after the THEN clause has executed. The ELSE clause follows a label consisting of the word ELSE followed by a sequence number. This is the target of the conditional jump. The end of the structure

```
; IFnn condition
    ... instructions to
    ... evaluate condition
     jn__    ELSEnn

; THENnn
;    pseudocode for THEN clause
        ... instructions to
        ... implement THEN clause
        jmp      ENDIFnn

 ELSEnn:
;    pseudocode for ELSE clause
        ... instructions to
        ... implement ELSE clause
 ENDIFnn:
```

**Figure 5.3** Implementation of IF-THEN-ELSE Structure

## 150 Chapter 5 Control Structures

has a label consisting of the word ENDIF followed by a sequence number. This is the target of the unconditional jump.

As an example, consider the problem of assigning the larger of $J$ or $K$ to $M$. The pseudocode for this can be written as

```
IF J>=K
THEN
  M := J
ELSE
  M := K
ENDIF
```

This is implemented in Program 5.1. This example takes two instructions to evaluate the condition, because both operands of cmp cannot be in memory. Following cmp, a conditional jump checks the opposite condition. These instructions are

```
; IF01  J >= K
    mov    ax, J
    cmp    ax, K
    jnge   ELSE01
```

## Program 5.1

```
; Program 5.1       Larger.ASM
; Assign M the larger of J or K.

; Dos function and status parameters
    DosFunc     equ     21h
    ExitToDos   equ     4Ch
    NoErrors    equ     00h

DOSSEG

_STACK SEGMENT para stack 'stack'
            dw      100h dup (?)
_STACK ENDS

_DATA SEGMENT word public 'data'
    J           dw      ?       ;first input value
    K           dw      ?       ;second input value
    M           dw      ?       ;larger value
    PromptMsg   db      "Enter two numbers: "
    PromptLen   dw      19
    ResultMsg   db      "The larger is "
    ResultLen   dw      14
_DATA ENDS

_TEXT SEGMENT word public 'code'
    assume   cs: _TEXT
    extrn    PutStr: PROC, PutCrLf: PROC
    extrn    GetDec: PROC, PutDec: PROC
```

## 5.3 Selection

**Program 5.1 (continued)**

```
        Larger:

        ; set up ds register to point to _DATA
                mov     ax, seg _DATA
                mov     ds, ax
                assume  ds: _DATA

        ; print ("Enter two numbers: ")
                mov     cx, PromptLen
                mov     bx, offset PromptMsg
                call    PutStr

        ; read (J, K)
                call    GetDec
                mov     J, ax
                call    GetDec
                mov     K, ax

        ; assign the larger of J or K to M
        ; IF01 J >= K
                mov     ax, J
                cmp     ax, K
                jnge    ELSE01

        ; THEN01
        ;   M := J
                mov     M, ax
                jmp     ENDIF01

        ELSE01:
        ;   M := K
                mov     ax, K
                mov     M, ax
        ENDIF01:

        ; print ("The larger is ", M)
                mov     cx, ResultLen
                mov     bx, offset ResultMsg
                call    PutStr
                mov     ax, M
                call    PutDec
                call    PutCrLf

        ; exit to DOS
                mov     ah, ExitToDos
                mov     al, NoErrors
                int     DosFunc

        _TEXT ENDS
        END     Larger
```

The assignment statements are implemented by one or two mov instructions. Note that the cmp instruction leaves the value of *J* unchanged in the AX register, so only one mov instruction is needed in the THEN clause.

## Selection with One Sequence

A common variation on selection is conditional execution of a sequence of instructions. This can be implemented by omitting the ELSE clause of the selection structure. In assembly language we omit the ELSE clause, change the target of the conditional jump to the end of the structure, and delete the unconditional jump instruction. The implementation of conditional execution is shown in Figure 5.4.

As in the implementation of selection with two alternative sequences, the conditional jump instruction is used to skip over the THEN clause and must use the complement of the condition written in the pseudocode.

For our next example, consider the following structure:

```
IF SideA*SideA + SideB*SideB = SideC*SideC
THEN
   Count := Count + 1
ENDIF
```

This is implemented in Program 5.2. The program reads values for SideA, SideB, and SideC and prints the value of Count after the selection structure. Since Count is initialized to 0 by the operand in the dw directive, the program prints 0 or 1 depending on the outcome of the selection structure.

In evaluating the condition, we leave the products as 32-bit numbers to minimize problems with overflow (which are discussed below). Then we must compare final expressions in two pieces. Since we want to test for equality, it is not necessary to worry about signs and about which piece to test first. The test is implemented using

```
cmp     bx, ax
jne     ENDIF01
cmp     cx, dx
jne     ENDIF01
```

This first compares the less significant words of the expressions and jumps to the end of the structure if they differ. If they are the same, the program then compares the more significant words of the expressions and jumps to the end of the structure if these differ. If these, too, are the same, control flows into the THEN clause.

The three products are computed without overflow. If the condition should be true, overflow cannot occur in the addition either (since there is no overflow in the product SideC*SideC, to which the sum is equal). If overflow does occur in the addition, then SideA*SideA+SideB*SideB should be larger than SideC*SideC, but will appear negative because of the sign change when overflow occurs. However, since we are testing for equality, overflow is not a concern in this example.

## 5.3 Selection

```
; IFnn condition
    ... instructions to
    ... evaluate condition
    jn__     ENDIFnn

; THENnn
;   pseudocode for THEN clause
        ... instructions to
        ... implement THEN clause
ENDIFnn:
```

**Figure 5.4  Implementation of IF-THEN Structure**

## Program 5.2

```
; Program 5.2        RtTriang.ASM
; Increment Count if SideC^2 = SideA^2 + SideB^2.

; DOS function and status parameters
DosFunc     equ     21h
ExitToDos   equ     4Ch
NoErrors    equ     00h

        DOSSEG

_STACK SEGMENT para stack 'stack'
            dw      100h dup (?)
_STACK ENDS

_DATA SEGMENT word public 'data'
    Count       dw      0       ;initialized counter
    SideA       dw      ?       ;length of side A
    SideB       dw      ?       ;length of side B
    SideC       dw      ?       ;length of side C
    PromptMsg   db      "Enter lengths of triangle sides: "
    PromptLen   dw      32
    ResultMsg   db      "Count is "
    ResultLen   dw      9
_DATA ENDS

_TEXT SEGMENT word public 'code'
    assume  cs: _TEXT
    extrn   PutStr: PROC, PutCrLf: PROC
    extrn   GetDec: PROC, PutDec: PROC

RtTriang:

; set up ds register to point to _DATA
    mov     ax, seg _DATA
    mov     ds, ax
    assume  ds: _DATA
```

**Program 5.2 (continued)**

```
    ; print ("Enter lengths of triangle sides: ")
        mov     cx, PromptLen
        mov     bx, offset PromptMsg
        call    PutStr

    ; read (SideA, SideB, and SideC)
        call    GetDec
        mov     SideA, ax
        call    GetDec
        mov     SideB, ax
        call    GetDec
        mov     SideC, ax

    ; Increment Count if SideA^2 + SideB^2 = SideC^2.
    ; IF01   SideA*SideA + SideB*SideB = SideC*SideC
        mov     ax, SideA           ;              SideA
        imul    ax                  ;              SideA * SideA
        mov     bx, ax              ;cx:bx := SideA * SideA
        mov     cx, dx              ;
        mov     ax, SideB           ;              SideB
        imul    ax                  ;              SideB * SideB
        add     bx, ax              ;cx:bx := cx:bx + SideB * SideB
        adc     cx, dx              ;
        mov     ax, SideC           ;              SideC
        imul    ax                  ;dx:ax := SideC * SideC
        cmp     bx, ax              ;(less significant words same?)
        jne     ENDIF01             ;
        cmp     cx, dx              ;(more significant words same?)
        jne     ENDIF01             ;
    ; THEN01
    ;   Count := Count + 1
        inc     Count
    ENDIF01:

    ; print ("Count is ", Count)
        mov     cx, ResultLen
        mov     bx, offset ResultMsg
        call    PutStr
        mov     ax, Count
        call    PutDec
        call    PutCrLf

    ; exit to DOS
        mov     ah, ExitToDos
        mov     al, NoErrors
        int     DosFunc

_TEXT   ENDS
END     RtTriang
```

## 5.3 Selection

### Nested Selection Structures

Some problems require a selection structure with more than two alternative sequences. For example, solving a quadratic equation using the formula requires different processing depending on whether the discriminant is negative, 0, or positive. Assigning letter grades in a class might require from four to more than a dozen alternatives. We can implement these designs as nested selection structures, using each IF statement to partition the sequences into two distinct sets. Each of these sets might require further IF statements to partition again and again.

For example, consider the three values returned by a sign function:

$$\text{Sign}(X) = \begin{cases} -1 & \text{if } X < 0 \\ 0 & \text{if } X = 0 \\ +1 & \text{if } X > 0 \end{cases}$$

This can be written using nested selection structures as

```
IF X < 0
THEN
  Sign := -1
ELSE
  IF X = 0
  THEN
    Sign := 0
  ELSE
    Sign := 1
  ENDIF
ENDIF
```

This is implemented in Program 5.3. This program reads a signed integer for X, determines Sign using the nested selection structures above, then prints the value of Sign.

### Program 5.3

```
; Program 5.3        SignFunc.ASM
; Assign Sign -1, 0, or +1, depending on the sign of X.

; DOS function and status parameters
  DosFunc     equ     21h
  ExitToDos   equ     4Ch
  NoErrors    equ     00h

DOSSEG

_STACK SEGMENT para stack 'stack'
            dw      100h dup (?)
_STACK ENDS

_DATA SEGMENT word public 'data'
  X           dw      ?       ;input value to test
  Sign        dw      ?       ;sign of input value (-1, 0, or +1)
  Prompt      db      "Enter X: "
```

## Program 5.3 (continued)

```
        PromptLen   dw      9
        ResultMsg   db      "Sign is"
        ResultLen   dw      7
_DATA ENDS

_TEXT SEGMENT word public 'code'
        assume  cs: _TEXT
        extrn   PutStr: PROC, PutCrLf: PROC
        extrn   GetDec: PROC, PutDec: PROC

SignFunc:

; set up ds register to point to _DATA
        mov     ax, seg _DATA
        mov     ds, ax
        assume  ds: _DATA

; print ("Enter X: ")
        mov     cx, PromptLen
        mov     bx, offset Prompt
        call    PutStr

; read (X)
        call    GetDec
        mov     X, ax

; assign Sign -1, 0, or +1, depending on the sign of X
; IF01 X < 0
        mov     ax, X
        cmp     ax, 0
        jnl     ELSE01

;   THEN01
;       Sign := -1
        mov     bx, -1
        mov     Sign, bx
        jmp     ENDIF01

    ELSE01:
;       IF02 X = 0
        jne     ELSE02

;       THEN02
;           Sign := 0
        sub     bx, bx
        mov     Sign, bx
        jmp     ENDIF02

    ELSE02:
;           Sign := +1
        mov     bx, 1
        mov     Sign, bx
    ENDIF02:
    ENDIF01:
```

## 5.3 Selection

**Program 5.3 (continued)**

```
; print ("Sign is", Sign)
        mov     cx, ResultLen
        mov     bx, offset ResultMsg
        call    PutStr
        mov     ax, Sign
        call    PutDec
        call    PutCrLf

; exit to DOS
        mov     ah, ExitToDos
        mov     al, NoErrors
        int     DosFunc

_TEXT   ENDS
        END     SignFunc
```

---

Let's trace this program for each of the three cases. If X is negative, the conditional jump instruction in the IF01 block does not jump. Execution continues with the instructions following THEN01, which assign −1 to Sign and leave the structure.

If X is 0, the conditional jump in the IF01 block transfers control to the ELSE01 block, which starts with the IF02 block. Since the result of the cmp instruction is still in the flags register, it is not necessary to repeat the mov and cmp instructions. The conditional jump in the IF02 block does nothing. Execution continues with the instructions following THEN02, which assign 0 to Sign and terminate the structure.

If X is positive, the conditional jump in the IF01 block transfers control to the IF02 block, and the conditional jump there also transfers control to the ELSE02 block. There, 1 is assigned to Sign.

Many high-level languages have additional selection statements, such as the CASE statement in Pascal or the computed GOTO statement in FORTRAN. Some computers even have special instructions for these statements; the 8086 does not. These statements can be implemented using a table of addresses with a jmp instruction, but this will not be implemented here. The additional selection statements can always be rewritten as nested selection structures and implemented using the methods of this section.

## EXERCISES 5.3

1. Some high-level languages include a CASE statement for selection among many alternatives. Show how to implement the following CASE statement in 8086 assembly language:

   ```
   CASE N OF
       1  : P := P + 1;
       2  : P := P - 1;
       3  : P := P + 2;
       4  : P := P - 2;
   ELSE   P := 0        {N not in [1..4]}
   END CASE
   ```

2. Some high-level languages include a computed GOTO, which is a multiway branch. For example, the FORTRAN statement

   GOTO (100, 110, 130, 200, 130), N

   causes execution to continue at the statement with label 100 if the value of N is 1, at 110 if N is 2, at 130 if N is 3 or 5, or at 200 if N is 4. If N is outside the range 1 through 5, control passes to the statement following the GOTO. How can this be implemented using the instructions of this chapter?

3. FORTRAN also contains an older arithmetic IF statement that implements a three-way jump based on the sign of an expression. For example, the statement

   IF (B*B-4*A*C) 310, 320, 400

   evaluates the numeric expression and transfers control to the statement labeled 310 if the value is negative, to the statement labeled 320 if the value is 0, or to the statement labeled 400 if the value is positive. How can this be implemented using the instructions of this chapter?

▶4. Write a program that reads two integers and prints whether the first one entered is larger or smaller than the second.

▶5. Write a program that reads two integers and prints the absolute value of their difference.

▶6. Write a program that reads two integers and prints the sum of their absolute values.

▶7. Write a program that reads three integers and prints them in ascending order. Since we have not seen how to implement the Boolean operators AND and OR, use nested IF statements; design carefully.

▶8. Write a program that reads three integers and prints whether they were entered in ascending order, descending order, or scrambled. Since we have not seen how to implement the Boolean operators AND and OR, use nested IF statements; design carefully.

▶9. Write a program that reads two integers, the smaller one first, and prints whether the second number is an integer multiple of the first number.

▶10. Write a program that reads two integers and prints whether their product exceeds the capacity of a signed 16-bit integer. Be sure to include negative values when you test the program.

## 5.4 REPETITION

Repetition control structures provide a means for the program to execute a sequence of instructions a number of times based on conditions evaluated during execution. Repetition control structures are also called loops.

The sequence of instructions that are conditionally repeated is called the loop body, which may contain other control structures nested within it. The loop body can be skipped completely, or it can be executed one time or many times. Although it may be a little awkward to refer to a sequence of instructions that are not executed or executed only once as part of a repetition structure, that same loop body might be executed many times with different data.

In addition to a loop body, a repetition structure has a condition that controls it. There are three forms of the repetition control structure. In the most general form, the condition is placed before the loop body. In the second form, the condition is placed after the body. In the third form, the condition is implied within the information that specifies a sequence of values for a control variable.

## WHILE Loop Structure

The most general repetition structure is the WHILE loop. In pseudocode, we can write it as

```
WHILE condition
DO
   sequence that constitutes loop body
ENDWHILE
```

The condition is evaluated first. If the condition is true, the loop body is executed and the condition is evaluated again. This cycle is repeated as long as the condition is true. When the condition is false, control passes to the statement following ENDWHILE.

The loop body should change at least one variable that appears in the condition. If it doesn't and the condition is initially true, the condition never becomes false and the loop body then executes over and over until interrupted by some external event.

To implement the WHILE loop, we need a conditional jump to the statement following ENDWHILE when the condition is false, and an unconditional jump from the end of the loop body to the beginning of WHILE. We use the template shown in Figure 5.5, which is similar in style to the templates for selection structures in the preceding section. It starts with a label consisting of WHILE and a sequence number, followed by the condition in a comment (note the semicolon). This is followed by instructions that evaluate the condition, and a conditional jump that tests the complementary condition. A label containing the word DO and the sequence number separates the instructions that evaluate the condition from those that implement the loop body. Following the loop body, an unconditional jump sends control back to the start of the structure. The end of the structure is labeled with ENDWHL, followed by the sequence number.

As an example of a WHILE loop, consider the problem of finding the largest integer $N$ whose square is less than or equal to another integer $M$. That is, given $M$ find the largest integer $N$ such that $N \times N \leq M$. One solution is

```
N := 0
WHILE N*N <= M
DO
   N := N + 1
ENDWHILE
N := N - 1
```

The loop terminates when $N^2 > M$, so we need to subtract 1 from N in the last step. This solution is implemented in Program 5.4.

To evaluate the condition, we compute $N \times N$ in AX, and compare it to the value of $M$ stored in memory, in the block

```
WHILE01:   ;N*N <= M
    mov      ax, N
    imul     ax
    cmp      ax, M
    jnle     ENDWHL01
```

The conditional jump instruction that terminates the repetition is jnle, which tests for the complement of the condition in the WHILE statement. The loop body is to be executed as

## Chapter 5  Control Structures

```
        WHILEnn:   ;condition
           ... instructions to
           ... evaluate condition
           jn__    ENDWHLnn

        ; DOnn
        ;   pseudocode for loop body
           ... instructions to
           ... implement loop body
           jmp     WHILEnn
        ENDWHLnn:
```

**Figure 5.5** Implementation of WHILE Loop Structure

long as $N^2 \leq M$, so the jump instruction causes the loop to terminate when the opposite condition is true.

In the loop body, we increment the value of N using an `inc` instruction. The `jmp` instruction returns control to the beginning of the structure. After the loop terminates, N is adjusted with a `dec` instruction.

## Program 5.4

```
        ; Program 5.4        FindN.ASM
        ; For given M, find the largest integer N such that N*N <= M.

        ; DOS function and status parameters
           DosFunc     equ     21h
           ExitToDos   equ     4Ch
           NoErrors    equ     00h

        DOSSEG

        _STACK SEGMENT para stack 'stack'
                    dw      100h dup (?)
        _STACK ENDS

        _DATA SEGMENT word public 'data'
           M           dw      ?       ;input value
           N           dw      ?       ;result
           PromptMsg   db      "Enter M: "
           PromptLen   dw      9
           ResultMsg   db      "N = "
           ResultLen   dw      4
        _DATA ENDS

        _TEXT SEGMENT word public 'code'
              assume  cs: _TEXT
              extrn   PutStr: PROC, PutCrLf: PROC
              extrn   GetDec: PROC, PutDec: PROC

        FindN:
```

### 5.4 Repetition

**Program 5.4 (continued)**

```
        ; set up ds register to point to _DATA
            mov     ax, seg _DATA
            mov     ds, ax
            assume  ds: _DATA

        ; print ("Enter M: ")
            mov     cx, PromptLen
            mov     bx, offset PromptMsg
            call    PutStr

        ; read (M)
            call    GetDec
            mov     M, ax

        ; Find largest value N such that N*N <= M.
        ; N := 1
            mov     N, 1

        WHILE01: ;N*N <= M
            mov     ax, N
            imul    ax
            cmp     ax, M
            jnle    ENDWHL01

        ; DO01
        ;   N := N + 1
            inc     N
            jmp     WHILE01
        ENDWHL01:

        ; N := N - 1
            dec     N

        ; print ("N = ", N)
            mov     cx, ResultLen
            mov     bx, offset ResultMsg
            call    PutStr
            mov     ax, N
            call    PutDec
            call    PutCrLf

        ; exit to DOS
            mov     ah, ExitToDos
            mov     al, NoErrors
            int     DosFunc

        _TEXT ENDS
        END     FindN
```

## REPEAT-UNTIL Loop Structure

The second repetition structure is the REPEAT-UNTIL loop. It places the condition after the loop body, so that the body will execute at least once. The loop body repeats until the condition is true. In pseudocode this structure is written as

```
REPEAT
   sequence that constitutes loop body
UNTIL condition
```

The key to implementing this structure is a conditional jump from the end of the structure to the beginning when the condition is false. When the condition is true, control passes to the instruction after the loop. In assembly language, the relation used in the jump instruction is again the complement of the condition in the pseudocode. The general implementation of the REPEAT-UNTIL loop is given in Figure 5.6. This template begins with a label consisting of the word REPEAT and a sequence number, followed by the instructions that implement the loop body. In order to separate the loop body from the code that evaluates the condition, an extra keyword TEST may be inserted as a comment in the implementation of this structure. This keyword alerts the reader to the transition from the loop body to the loop condition where it occurs. The condition that controls the loop is given in the comment field on the last line of the template. The condition used in the conditional jump instruction just before it is again the complement of the condition in the UNTIL statement.

As an example of this loop, consider finding the greatest common divisor of two positive integers, $M$ and $N$. An iterative implementation of Euclid's algorithm can be written as

```
REPEAT
   remainder := M mod N
   M := N
   N := remainder
UNTIL N=0
```

This leaves the greatest common divisor in M.

This is implemented in Program 5.5. The first four instructions in the loop body set up and perform the division, leaving the remainder in the DX register. The next two

```
        REPEATnn:
    ;      pseudocode for loop body
               ... instructions to
               ... implement loop body

    ; TESTnn
            ... instructions to
            ... evaluate condition
            jn_     REPEATnn
    ; UNTILnn condition
```

**Figure 5.6** Implementation of REPEAT-UNTIL Loop Structure

### 5.4 Repetition

instructions of the loop body move the value of N from the BX register into M, and the remainder from the DX register into N. The test is implemented by

```
; TEST01
    cmp     dx, 0
    jne     REPEAT01
; UNTIL01 N=0
```

After the loop terminates, the greatest common divisor is copied to memory and printed.

## Program 5.5

```
; Program 5.5        GrComDiv.ASM
; Find the greatest common divisor of M and N.

; DOS function and status parameters
    DosFunc     equ     21h
    ExitToDos   equ     4Ch
    NoErrors    equ     00h

DOSSEG

_STACK SEGMENT para stack 'stack'
            dw      100h dup (?)
_STACK ENDS

_DATA SEGMENT word public 'data'
    M           dw      ?           ;input values whose greatest
    N           dw      ?           ;  common divisor is desired
    GCD         dw      ?           ;greatest common divisor of M and N
    PromptMsg   db      "Enter M and N: "
    PromptLen   dw      15
    ResultMsg   db      "GCD is "
    ResultLen   dw      7
_DATA ENDS

_TEXT SEGMENT word public 'code'
    assume  cs: _TEXT
    extrn   PutStr: PROC, PutCrLf: PROC
    extrn   GetDec: PROC, PutDec: PROC

GrComDiv:

; set up ds register to point to _DATA
    mov     ax, seg _DATA
    mov     ds, ax
    assume  ds: _DATA

; print ("Enter M and N: ")
    mov     cx, PromptLen
    mov     bx, offset PromptMsg
    call    PutStr
```

**Program 5.5 (continued)**

```
        ; read (M, N)
            call    GetDec
            mov     M, ax
            call    GetDec
            mov     N, ax

        ; compute GCD of M and N using Euclid's algorithm
        REPEAT01:
        ;   remainder := M mod N
            mov     ax, M
            cwd                 ; dx=ax:=ax  Convert word to double
            mov     bx, N
            div     bx          ; ax:= quotient of dx:ax ÷ source
                                ; dx:= remainder

        ;   M := N
            mov     M, bx

        ;   N := remainder
            mov     N, dx

        ; TEST01
            cmp     dx, 0
            jne     REPEAT01
        ; UNTIL01 N=0

        ; GCD := M
            mov     GCD, bx

        ; print ("GCD is ", GCD)
            mov     cx, ResultLen
            mov     bx, offset ResultMsg
            call    PutStr
            mov     ax, GCD
            call    PutDec
            call    PutCrLf

        ; exit to DOS
            mov     ah, ExitToDos
            mov     al, NoErrors
            int     DosFunc

_TEXT   ENDS
END     GrComDiv
```

## FOR Loop Structure

Many high-level languages also provide a loop controlled by a counter. Combining features from several languages, pseudocode can be written for a generic version as

## 5.4 Repetition

```
FOR var := exp1 TO exp2 STEP exp3
DO
   sequence that constitutes loop body
ENDFOR
```

When control reaches the FOR statement, the three expressions exp1, exp2, and exp3 are evaluated. The value of the first expression is assigned to the control variable. The values of the other two expressions are saved, but are not accessible to a high-level-language programmer. The cell where the values of the second and third expressions are saved will be referred to as LIMIT and STEP, respectively.

After evaluating the three expressions, the value of the control variable, var, is compared to LIMIT. When STEP is positive and var is less than or equal to LIMIT, the loop body is executed; if var is greater than LIMIT, control is transferred to the instruction after ENDFOR. When STEP is negative and var is greater than or equal to LIMIT, the loop body is executed; if var is less than LIMIT, control is transferred to the instruction after ENDFOR.

When the value of exp3 is positive, this control structure is equivalent to the WHILE loop

```
var := exp1
LIMIT := exp2
STEP := exp3
WHILE var <= LIMIT
DO
   sequence that constitutes loop body
   var := var + STEP
ENDWHILE
```

When the value of exp3 is negative, we must use >= as the condition in the equivalent WHILE loop structure.

Note that not all languages support an arbitrary step size; some restrict it to an integer, others to either +1 or −1. Our version is more general, allowing any numeric expressions (but only integers for now) for exp1, exp2, and exp3. If the STEP exp3 part of the statement is omitted, a default step of 1 is assumed. Also, if either of exp2 or exp3 is a simple constant, it is possible to omit the corresponding variable (LIMIT for exp2, STEP for exp3) and use the constant directly.

As written in the WHILE loop above, if instructions in the loop body change any variable used in exp2 or exp3, the number of times the loop body executes does not change. This is the purpose of the variables LIMIT and STEP in the WHILE loop implementation. Many programmers agree that attempting to change the control information during execution of a FOR loop is poor practice. Should that effect be desired, it is better to use a WHILE loop and make such changes obvious and well documented.

There are two ways to implement counted loops: One implementation is based on the equivalent WHILE statement; the other implementation uses the combined decrement-and-conditional-jump (loop) instruction. The implementation based on WHILE (Figure 5.7) will be discussed first. We define two variables, LIMITnn and STEPnn, in which we save the values of exp2 and exp3. We also include an extra label, TESTnn, as the target of the jmp instruction after the loop body. The code between FORnn and TESTnn corresponds to three assignment statements. If either exp2 or exp3 is a simple constant, the corresponding

```
; FORnn var := exp1 TO exp2 STEP exp3
   ... instructions for
   ... var      := exp1
   ... LIMITnn  := exp2
   ... STEPnn   := exp3

  TESTnn:
     cmp      var,LIMITnn
     j—       ENDFORnn

; DOnn
;    pseudocode for loop body
   ... instructions to
   ... implement loop body

     add      var,STEPnn
     jmp      TESTnn
ENDFORnn:
```

**Figure 5.7** Implementation of FOR Loop Structure

assignment statement is omitted. Figure 5.7 does not specify which conditional jump to use. The instruction to use is affected by the sign of the third expression and by whether the control variable is signed or unsigned (Table 5.6).

As an example of a FOR loop, consider finding the sum of the odd integers from 1 to some given integer $N$. This can be done with

```
Sum := 0
FOR Odd := 1 TO N STEP 2
DO
   Sum := Sum + Odd
ENDFOR
```

This is implemented in Program 5.6. The AX, BX, CX, and DX registers are used for Sum, Odd, LIMIT, and STEP respectively; assigning initial values to these is straightforward. The test to terminate the loop is implemented by the instructions

```
TEST01:
   cmp      bx, cx
   jg       ENDFOR01
```

which compares the values of Odd and LIMIT and jumps out of the loop when Odd > LIMIT.

**Table 5.6** FOR Loop Conditional Jump Instruction

|              | exp3 < 0 | exp3 > 0 |
|--------------|----------|----------|
| Var signed   | jl       | jg       |
| Var unsigned | jb       | ja       |

## 5.4 Repetition

## Program 5.6

```
; Program 5.6        SumOdd.ASM
; Compute the sum of the odd integers 1 + 3 + ... + N.

; DOS function and status parameters
  DosFunc    equ    21h
  ExitToDos  equ    4Ch
  NoErrors   equ    00h

DOSSEG

_STACK SEGMENT para stack 'stack'
            dw      100h dup (?)
_STACK ENDS

_DATA SEGMENT word public 'data'
  N          dw     ?         ;limit on odd numbers to add
  Sum        dw     ?         ;sum of odd numbers from 1 to N
  PromptMsg  db     "Enter N: "
  PromptLen  dw     9
  ResultMsg  db     "1+3+..N = "
  ResultLen  dw     10
_DATA ENDS

_TEXT SEGMENT word public 'code'
      assume  cs: _TEXT
      extrn   PutStr: PROC, PutCrLf: PROC
      extrn   GetDec: PROC, PutDec: PROC

SumOdd:

; set up ds register to point to _DATA
      mov     ax, seg _DATA
      mov     ds, ax
      assume  ds: _DATA

; print ("Enter N: ")
      mov     cx, PromptLen
      mov     bx, offset PromptMsg
      call    PutStr

; read (N)
      call    GetDec
      mov     N, ax

; Compute Sum := 1 + 3 + .. + N.
; Sum (in ax) := 0
      sub     ax, ax            ;subtract dest, source  dest := dest-source

; FOR01 Odd := 1 TO N STEP 2
      mov     bx, 1             ;bx = Odd
      mov     cx, N             ;cx = limit
      mov     dx, 2             ;dx = stepsize
```

**Program 5.6 (continued)**

```
          TEST01:
             cmp      bx, cx
             jg       ENDFOR01

        ; DO01
        ;    Sum := Sum + Odd
             add      ax, bx

             add      bx, dx         ;Odd := Odd + 2
             jmp      TEST01
          ENDFOR01:

        ; save Sum
             mov      Sum, ax

        ; print ("1+3+..N = ", Sum)
             mov      cx, ResultLen
             mov      bx, offset ResultMsg
             call     PutStr
             mov      ax, Sum
             call     PutDec
             call     PutCrLf

        ; exit to DOS
             mov      ah, ExitToDos
             mov      al, NoErrors
             int      DosFunc

        _TEXT ENDS
        END    SumOdd
```

The loop body consists of two add instructions: The first adds Odd to Sum and is the loop body proper; the second adds 2 to Odd and is implicit in the FOR statement.

These are followed by an unconditional jump to TEST01—not to the beginning of the structure. We do not want to start over with the initial value of the loop control variable each time; we want to continue with the next iteration.

The second implementation of a FOR loop uses the combined decrement-and-jump loop instruction. The pseudocode for the counted loop structure is

```
FOR var := exp1 TO exp2 STEP exp3
DO
   sequence that constitutes loop body
ENDFOR
```

This general form can be readily implemented using the loop instruction only when exp1 > 0, exp2 = 1, and exp3 = −1. In this special case, the loop control variable counts by −1 and stops at 0. Note that the body of this loop will be executed at least once. This special counted loop can be implemented as shown in Figure 5.8. This implementation is attractive because of its simplicity. All processing involving LIMIT and STEP is

## 5.4 Repetition

```
; FORnn cx := expl TO 1 STEP -1
   ... instructions for
   ... cx := expl

  DOnn:
;   pseudocode for loop body
      ... instructions to
      ... implement loop body

    loop    DOnn
; ENDFORnn:
```

**Figure 5.8** Implementation of FOR Loop Using `loop` Instruction

eliminated, and all management of the loop control variable is handled by a single instruction once the loop body is entered.

Programs where the loop control variable takes on values that decrease by 1 and end at 1 can be readily implemented with this form. For example, consider raising Base to an exponent Exp, for given values of Base and Exp. Assuming that Exp is positive, we can compute this as

$$\text{Result} = 1 \times \text{Base} \times \text{Base} \times \text{Base} \times \cdots \times \text{Base}$$

where there are Exp factors of Base. This can be written as

```
Result := 1
FOR I := Exp TO 1 STEP -1
DO
   Result := Result * Base
ENDFOR
```

This is implemented in Program 5.7 using the AX register for Result in the loop, and the CX register to control the loop.

## Program 5.7

```
; Program 5.7        PowerCX.ASM
; Compute Base^Exp, for given Base and positive Exp.
;   Returns 0 if Exp <= 0. Base and Exp are signed
;   word integers, as is the result.

; DOS function and status parameters
  DosFunc     equ     21h
  ExitToDos   equ     4Ch
  NoErrors    equ     00h

DOSSEG

_STACK SEGMENT para stack 'stack'
            dw      100h dup (?)
_STACK ENDS
```

**Program 5.7 (continued)**

```
        _DATA SEGMENT word public 'data'
          Base        dw      ?        ;value to be raised to a power
          Exp         dw      ?        ;power to raise to
          Result      dw      ?        ;computed value of Base^Exp
          PromptBase  db      "Enter Base: "
          PromptExp   db      "Enter Exp:  "
          PromptLen   dw      12
          ResultMsg   db      "Result is "
          ResultLen   dw      10
        _DATA ENDS

        _TEXT SEGMENT word public 'code'
            assume  cs: _TEXT
            extrn   PutStr: PROC, PutCrLf: PROC
            extrn   GetDec: PROC, PutDec: PROC

        PowerCX:

        ; set up ds register to point to _DATA
            mov     ax, seg _DATA
            mov     ds, ax
            assume  ds: _DATA

        ; print ("Enter Base: ")
            mov     cx, PromptLen
            mov     bx, offset PromptBase
            call    PutStr

        ; read (Base)
            call    GetDec
            mov     Base, ax

        ; print ("Enter Exp: ")
            mov     bx, offset PromptExp
            call    PutStr

        ; read (Exp)
            call    GetDec
            mov     Exp, ax

        ; IF01 Exp > 0                 ;check for valid inputs
            mov     bx, Exp
            cmp     bx, 0
            jng     ELSE01

        ; THEN01
        ;   Compute Base^Exp using repeated multiplication.
        ;   Result (in ax) := 1
            mov     ax, 1

        ;   FOR02 cx := Exp TO 1 STEP -1
            mov     cx, Exp
```

### 5.4 Repetition

**Program 5.7 (continued)**

```
            DO02:
        ;       Result := Result * Base
                imul    Base

                loop    DO02
        ;   ENDFOR02

        ;   save Result
                mov     Result, ax

                jmp     ENDIF01
            ELSE01:
        ;       Result := 0
                mov     Result, 0
            ENDIF01:

        ;   print ("Result is ", Result)
                mov     cx, ResultLen
                mov     bx, offset ResultMsg
                call    PutStr
                mov     ax, Result
                call    PutDec
                call    PutCrLf

        ;   exit to DOS
                mov     ah, ExitToDos
                mov     al, NoErrors
                int     DosFunc

        _TEXT ENDS
        END     PowerCX
```

In Program 5.7, the loop is written in the THEN clause of a selection that checks for a positive exponent. The setup for the loop consists of the single instruction

```
        ;   FOR02 cx := Exp TO 1 STEP -1
                mov     cx, Exp
```

The body of the loop is a single `imul` instruction. The body is followed by the instruction

```
                loop    DO02
        ;   ENDFOR02
```

which decrements CX, checks whether CX = 0, and, if it does not, jumps back to the start of the loop body.

It is tempting to implement all FOR loops using the `loop` instruction. To do so, there are two concerns that must be addressed: how many times the body of the FOR loop is to be executed, and how to compute the value of the loop control variable from the CX register value. The procedure for implementing an arbitrary FOR loop using the `loop` instruction will be outlined here; the interested reader may write an example and analyze it.

Consider a general counted loop specified as

FOR LCV := First TO Limit STEP Increment

where the values of the expressions for First, Limit, and Increment are evaluated prior to entering the loop. It is assumed that the loop is to be implemented with the condition evaluated before the loop body. The number of times the loop body is to be executed, called the iteration count and denoted as IC, is given by the formula

$$IC = \left\lfloor \frac{\text{Limit} - \text{First}}{\text{Increment}} \right\rfloor + 1$$

If IC is 0 or negative, the loop body should not be executed at all. Notice that those loops where both Limit < First and Increment < 0 will give a positive iteration count.

An arbitrary count-controlled loop can be implemented by computing the iteration count using the formula. If the count is positive, it is loaded into the CX register and the loop instruction is used to control the repetition. Note that the test of whether the iteration count is positive is performed before the loop body is executed the first time. In effect, this makes the loop a pretest loop, as intended.

Many count-controlled loops with arbitrary values for First, Limit, and Increment do need the values for the loop control variable (LCV) implied by the FOR statement. The values that LCV takes on are, in general,

$$LCV = \text{First}, \text{First} + \text{Increment}, \text{First} + 2 \times \text{Increment}, \ldots,$$
$$\text{First} + (IC - 1) \times \text{Increment}$$

The multiples of Increment in this list range from 0 to IC−1. This factor is not difficult to generate: The CX register ranges from IC down to 1 as the loop executes. LCV can be computed as

$$LCV = \text{First} + (IC - CX) \times \text{Increment}$$

Using the formulas for the iteration count and loop control variable, an arbitrary FOR loop using the CX register and the loop instruction can be implemented as shown in Figure 5.9. It gains the efficiency of controlling the loop with a single loop instruction but incurs the cost of computing the iteration count once in the prologue and the loop control variable on every pass. Is this a good trade-off?

## Mixed Loops

In some problems it is necessary to combine the counting features of a FOR loop with the conditional features of a WHILE or REPEAT loop. Many searching problems use this type of loop. Some high-level languages allow both a range and a condition in the loop control statement; others do not. Some programmers code such loops using FOR with a jump out of the loop when the condition is satisfied. This practice is not encouraged.

The 8086 instruction set includes the loope/loopz and loopne/loopnz instructions to implement this type of loop. Until the reader has been introduced to arrays and can write reasonable search routines, there are not many real problems that make effective use of these instructions. Therefore, an invented problem will be presented here.

## 5.4 Repetition

```
; FORnn var := First TO Limit STEP Increment
     ... instructions for
     ... cx := (Limit - First) div Increment + 1

     cmp     cx,0
     jle     ENDFORnn
     mov     ICnn, cx

  DOnn:
     ... instructions for
     ... LCV := (ICnn - cx) * Increment + First

; pseudocode for loop body
     ... instructions to
     ... implement loop body

     loop    DOnn
  ENDFORnn:
```

**FIGURE 5.9** Implementation of FOR Loop Using `loop` Instruction and Formulas for IC and LCV

Consider the task of reading signed integers and keeping a running total of them. We want to stop when the total is exactly 100, or when the user has entered 12 numbers. (Remember, this is a contrived example.) A possible solution might be

```
Sum := 0
Count := 12
REPEAT
  READ N
  Sum := Sum + N
  Count := Count - 1
UNTIL Sum = 100 OR Count = 0
PRINT Sum, (12 - Count)
```

We plan to implement the counter by using the CX register, so we start it at 12 and stop repeating when it is 0 (Program 5.8). The `loopne` instruction is used to control this loop.

## Program 5.8

```
; Program 5.8        Sum100.ASM
; Read and add together signed integers until the sum is 100
;   or the user has entered 12 numbers.

; DOS function and status parameters
  DosFunc      equ     21h
  ExitToDos    equ     4Ch
  NoErrors     equ     00h

DOSSEG

_STACK SEGMENT para stack 'stack'
           dw      100h dup (?)
_STACK ENDS
```

**Program 5.8 (continued)**

```
_DATA SEGMENT word public 'data'
    Count       dw      ?       ;number of values read
    Sum         dw      ?       ;sum of values read
    PromptMsg   db      "Enter numbers, one per line."
    PromptLen   dw      28
    ResultMsg   db      "    SUM      N"
    ResultLen   dw      12
_DATA ENDS

_TEXT SEGMENT word public 'code'
    assume  cs: _TEXT
    extrn   PutStr: PROC, PutCrLf: PROC
    extrn   GetDec: PROC, PutDec: PROC

Sum100:

; set up ds register to point to _DATA
    mov     ax, seg _DATA
    mov     ds, ax
    assume  ds: _DATA

; print ("Enter numbers, one per line.")
    mov     cx, PromptLen
    mov     bx, offset PromptMsg
    call    PutStr
    call    PutCrLf

; Read and add numbers until Sum=100 or 12 numbers have been read.
; Sum := 0
    sub     ax, ax
    mov     Sum, ax

; number of values left to read (in cx) := 12
    mov     cx, 12

  REPEAT01:
;   read number into ax
       call    GetDec

;   Sum := Sum + number read
       add     Sum, ax

;   TEST01
    cmp     Sum, 100         ;test Sum = 100?
    loopne  REPEAT01         ;decrement cx, test for 0
; UNTIL01 Sum = 100  OR  12 numbers read

; Count := 12 - number of values left to read
    mov     ax, 12
    sub     ax, cx
    mov     Count, ax
```

## Program 5.8 (continued)

```
; print ("    SUM         N")
        mov     cx, ResultLen
        mov     bx, offset ResultMsg
        call    PutStr
        call    PutCrLf

; print (Sum, Count)
        mov     ax, Sum
        call    PutDec
        mov     ax, Count
        call    PutDec
        call    PutCrLf

; exit to DOS
        mov     ah, ExitToDos
        mov     al, NoErrors
        int     DosFunc

_TEXT   ENDS
END     Sum100
```

The CX register is used to limit the user to 12 numbers. The conditions specified for repeating the loop are evaluated by the instructions

```
; TEST01
        cmp     Sum, 100
        loopne  REPEAT01
; UNTIL01 Sum = 100  OR  12 numbers read
```

The first of these compares the sum with 100 and sets or clears the zero flag accordingly. The loopne instruction jumps back to the beginning of the loop if the zero flag is cleared and the CX register is not 0. When Sum becomes 100, the zero flag will be set by the cmp instruction and the jump will not be taken. When the CX register becomes 0, the jump will not be taken.

The mixed loop is most accurately written in pseudocode using the REPEAT-UNTIL form, since the tests of CX and of the zero flag are both performed after the loop body is executed.

The loop structures presented in this section, combined with the selection structures of the previous section, make it possible to write readable, well-formed programs. They help to avoid the stray jumps and ad hoc methods that can make reading an assembly-language program very difficult.

## EXERCISES 5.4

1. Compare the two implementations of the FOR loop (the version based on WHILE and the version that uses the loop instruction) in terms of the number of instructions executed once

to set up the control information, and in terms of the number of instructions executed on each iteration (excluding the body of the loop itself).

2. Consider the FOR loop

   FOR K := -20000 TO 20000 STEP 200

   When we try to compare K initially, or when we try to compute the iteration count, we must be careful to recognize overflow. Show how to implement this loop using
   
   (a) our first implementation based on the WHILE loop.
   
   (b) our second implementation based on computing the iteration count and using the loop instruction.

▶3. Implement a general count-controlled loop using the model given in Figure 5.9. Your program should read values for First, Limit, and Increment, and print all values of the loop control variable.

4. Revise Exercise 1 to include your implementation of the loop in Exercise 3.

5. Examine the programs you have written in high-level languages. How many statements are there typically in the blocks following WHILE, FOR, THEN, and ELSE? Using this information, guess how many instructions it takes to implement that number of statements. Then guess how many bytes it takes. How often do you think the jumps that implement control structures can have 8-bit signed displacements?

▶6. Write a program that computes the average of a list of positive integers. The last data value is followed by −1. Use a WHILE loop.

▶7. Write a program that computes the average of a list of positive integers. The last data value is followed by −1. Assume that there is at least one positive value in the list, and use a REPEAT-UNTIL loop.

▶8. Write a program that reads a list of positive integers and prints only those that are even. The last data value is followed by −1. Use a WHILE loop.

▶9. Write a program that reads integers and counts how many integers it reads. It should terminate when the same number is entered twice in succession. Use a WHILE loop.

▶10. Do Exercise 9 using a REPEAT-UNTIL loop. Assume that at least two numbers are entered.

▶11. Write a program that reads a positive integer $N$ and computes and prints $N!$. $N!$ is computed as $N \times (N-1) \times (N-2) \times \cdots \times 2 \times 1$. Use a FOR loop implemented with the loop instruction.

▶12. Write a program that reads two positive integers $M$ and $N$ and computes and prints the sum of all integers between $M$ and $N$. Use a FOR loop implemented with the loop instruction.

13. Program 5.4 uses a WHILE loop to find the largest integer $N$ such that $N \times N \leq M$. Verify that if the user enters a value greater than 32760 for $M$, the loop does not terminate. Why not?

▶14. Modify Program 5.4 to detect the problem discussed in Exercise 13. Your version should terminate gracefully with a suitable message.

## KEY POINTS

- Tests performed in a high-level language generally compare two values.
- In assembly language, a compare instruction compares two values by subtracting the second from the first and setting the flags accordingly, without saving the difference.
- The sequence in which instructions are executed is controlled by the instruction pointer. By changing the instruction pointer, control can be transferred to another part of the program.

- Jump and branch instructions write new values to the instruction pointer. These instructions can be conditional or unconditional.
- Destinations of most jumps are coded as displacements from the instruction pointer.
- Unrestricted use of jump instructions leads to programs that can be difficult to read and understand. Use of these instructions should be restricted to implementing control structures.
- The selection structure with two sequences can be implemented using a conditional jump to skip over the THEN clause and an unconditional jump to skip over the ELSE clause. The condition in the jump is the complement of the condition in the IF statement.
- The selection structure with one sequence can be implemented using a conditional jump to skip over the THEN clause; there is no ELSE clause. The condition in the jump is the complement of the condition in the IF statement.
- Selection structures with more than two alternatives can be implemented as nested selection structures.
- The WHILE loop structure is implemented with a conditional jump to the statement after the structure, and an unconditional jump before the end to jump back to the beginning. The condition that controls the loop is evaluated before the loop body is executed. The condition in the jump is the complement of the condition in the WHILE statement.
- The REPEAT-UNTIL loop structure is implemented with a conditional jump from the end of the structure back to the beginning. The loop body is executed before the condition is evaluated, so the loop body must execute at least once. The condition in the jump is the complement of the condition in the UNTIL statement.
- In one implementation of the FOR loop, we use assignment statements to evaluate the three control expressions, followed by what is essentially a WHILE loop with an assignment statement to increment the control variable.
- In another implementation of the FOR loop, we compute the number of iterations and use a combined decrement-and-conditional-branch instruction to implement the test and jump back to the beginning of the loop body.
- A form of loop that is a mixture of count-controlled and conditional appears in many search algorithms.

## PC SYSTEM SUMMARY

- Some flags are changed by the arithmetic instructions. There is no simple and convenient rule that applies in all cases; the reader should consult instruction summaries in the text and any available reference manuals.
- Relations for unsigned numbers are coded in the zero (ZF) and carry (CF) flags; relations for signed numbers are coded in the zero (ZF), sign (SF), and overflow (OF) flags.
- The states of the overflow, sign, zero, parity and carry flags can be used individually as test results.
- The cmp instruction compares two values and sets the flags as if it subtracted the second operand from the first.
- The 8086 has one unconditional jump instruction, which can transfer control to any real address.

- The 8086 has a number of conditional jump instructions that can transfer control only to an address within −128 to +127 bytes of the next instruction.
- The conditional jump instructions can inspect the flags for signed or unsigned relationships tested with cmp; they can also inspect some of the flags individually.
- There are synonyms for many of the conditional jump instructions, allowing the programmer to choose the mnemonic that best documents the program.
- The 8086 has special loop instructions that support count-controlled loops; there is also an instruction for a mixed count-controlled and conditional loop.

Instructions presented in this chapter:
[Synonyms in brackets]

Comparison:
    cmp     compare two values

Unconditional jump:
    jmp     jump unconditionally

Conditional jump:
  Zero:
    je      jump if equal                  [jz]
    jz      jump if zero                   [je]
    jne     jump if not equal             [jnz]
    jnz     jump if not zero              [jne]

  Unsigned comparison:
    jb      jump if below                  [jnae]
    jnae    jump if not above or equal  [jb]
    jbe     jump if below or equal      [jna]
    jna     jump if not above             [jbe]
    ja      jump if above                  [jnbe]
    jnbe    jump if not below or equal  [ja]
    jae     jump if above or equal      [jnb]
    jnb     jump if not below             [jae]

  Signed comparison:
    jl      jump if less                   [jnge]
    jnge    jump if not greater or equal [jl]
    jle     jump if less or equal       [jng]
    jng     jump if not greater           [jle]
    jg      jump if greater               [jnle]
    jnle    jump if not less or equal    [jg]
    jge     jump if greater or equal    [jnl]
    jnl     jump if not less              [jge]

Individual flags:
- `jo`     jump if overflow
- `jno`     jump if no overflow
- `js`     jump if sign
- `jns`     jump if not sign
- `jp`     jump if parity     [`jpe`]
- `jpe`     jump if parity even     [`jp`]
- `jnp`     jump if no parity     [`jpo`]
- `jpo`     jump if parity odd     [`jnp`]
- `jc`     jump if carry
- `jnc`     jump if no carry

Test cx register for zero:
- `jcxz`     jump if cx is zero

Combined decrement and jump:
- `loop`     decrement cx; jump if cx is not zero
- `loope`     decrement cx; jump if cx is not zero and zero flag set     [`loopz`]
- `loopz`     decrement cx; jump if cx is not zero and zero flag set     [`loope`]
- `loopne`     decrement cx; jump if cx is not zero and zero flag cleared     [`loopnz`]
- `loopnz`     decrement cx; jump if cx is not zero and zero flag cleared     [`loopne`]

# 6  Bit Operations and Boolean Data

- **Shift Operations**
- **Shift Instructions**
- **Boolean Data Representation**
- **Boolean Operations**
- **Boolean Instructions**
- **Applications**

The control structures introduced in the preceding chapter use the result of a comparison between two values to control the order in which instructions are executed. The results of the comparisons are available in the flags register, but only until another instruction alters the flags. What we want to examine now are ways to save the flags in a word of memory and to manipulate bits within a word. These operations provide the programmer with a Boolean data type.

With a Boolean data type, we can consider how to implement control structures with compound conditions. In high-level languages, Boolean values can be combined using the AND and OR Boolean operations. This chapter will also consider how to implement compound conditions.

This chapter examines operations on data at the bit level. These operations include several types of shifts that move the bits within a register, as well as Boolean operations that treat every bit in a register as an individual value. Using these, we see how to save selected flags as Boolean values.

## 6.1  SHIFT OPERATIONS

Shift operations move bits within a register or a memory location. A shift to the left changes each bit to the state of the bit on its right; a shift to the right changes each bit to the state of the bit on its left. It is easier to imagine that in a left shift, for example, each bit moves into the position to its left, hence the name shift. Two questions arise. What happens to the bit or bits that are shifted out of the register or memory location? What happens to the bit positions that are vacated on the other end? To make these questions

## 6.1 Shift Operations

more concrete, consider shifting the contents of a twelve-bit register to the left by three bit positions. The nine bits from the right end of the register are shifted to the left: The fourth bit from the left moves into the bit position at the left end, the fifth bit from the left moves into the second-from-the-left position, and so on, and the bit on the right end moves into the fourth position from the right end. What becomes of the three bits that were originally on the left end? What values do the three bits now on the right end have? (See Figure 6.1.)

The answers to these questions reflect three types of shift operations: logical, arithmetic, and circular. The circular shift operation is also known as a rotate operation. We examine all three types of shift operations in this section and look at 8086 shift instructions in the next section. To achieve consistency in the operations in this section, we use a 12-bit register for all operands. Shift instructions in some computers can also operate on locations in memory. Thus, the use of the word *register* in the discussion that follows implies either a register or memory location.

The number of positions that a bit is shifted is called the **shift count**. All bits in the register participate in the shift; the shift count specifies how far each bit travels. Shift counts are usually specified as operands.

### Logical Shifts

The simplest shift is a **logical shift**, in which the bits shifted out of one end of a register are lost and zeros are supplied for the vacated bit positions on the other end (see Figure 6.2). The logical shift treats each bit as a separate logical value. An unqualified use of the word *shift* often implies a logical shift.

As examples of logical shifts, assume that a 12-bit register initially contains

1010  1111  0011

Spaces have been inserted between every four bits for readability. A logical shift by three bit positions to the left changes the register to

0111  1001  1000

The first three bits on the left, 101, are lost. The other nine bits are shifted to the left, and three zeros are supplied for the right end. A logical shift of the original contents of this register by five bit positions to the right changes it to

0000  0101  0111

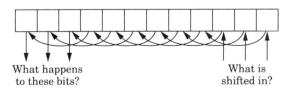

**Figure 6.1** Questions About Shift Operations

**182** Chapter 6 Bit Operations and Boolean Data

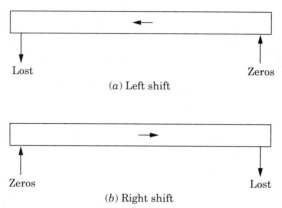

Figure 6.2 Logical Shift Operation

The five bits from the right end, 10011, are lost. The other seven bits are shifted to the right, and five zeros are supplied for the left end.

## Arithmetic Shifts

Note that a logical shift performed on a register that contains a signed integer might change the sign bit. The logical shift treats the sign bit as just another bit. Another type of shift, the **arithmetic shift**, treats the register as a signed number. Arithmetic shifts are useful for multiplying (left shift) and sometimes dividing (right shift) by powers of two. The shift count specifies the power of two by which the register is to be multiplied or divided. The result of a right arithmetic shift, however, is often not the same as the result obtained with a division instruction.

The only bits affected by an arithmetic shift are those to the right of the sign bit. For positive and unsigned numbers, the arithmetic shift supplies zeros for the vacated bits. For negative numbers, however, the operation of arithmetic shift depends on how negative numbers are represented. We consider positive numbers first (see Figure 6.3).

Consider a 12-bit register that contains the value 19:

$$0000 \quad 0001 \quad 0011$$

An arithmetic shift three bit positions to the left gives

$$0000 \quad 1001 \quad 1000$$

Zeros are shifted in, and the three bits to the right of the sign bit are shifted out. A left shift by three bit positions is equivalent to multiplication by $2^3$. The result of the shift is 152, which is $19 \times 8$.

Now consider the same initial value shifted eight bit positions to the left. This gives

$$0011 \quad 0000 \quad 0000$$

The eight bits to the right of the sign bit were lost during the shift. Since the bits shifted out are not all zeros, the most significant part of the number is lost by the shift. As a multiplication, we should get $19 \times 2^8$, or 4864, for the result. But 4864 exceeds the

## 6.1 Shift Operations

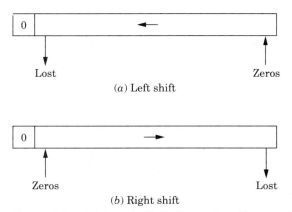

**Figure 6.3** Arithmetic Shift Operation, Nonnegative or Unsigned Integer

capacity of a 12-bit register. The result from the shift, 768, is 4864 mod $2^{12}$. The overflow flag would be set to record the loss of significance.

The same initial value shifted two bit positions to the right gives

$$0000 \quad 0000 \quad 0100$$

Zeros are supplied for the vacated positions to the right of the sign bit. The bits shifted out of the right end of the register are lost. A right shift of two bit positions is equivalent to division by $2^2$. In this example, the result is 4, which is the quotient of $19 \div 4$. Note that the bits shifted out of the register, $11_2$, represent the remainder of $19 \div 4$. Shifting a positive number to the right yields a number that is the correct quotient from dividing by the corresponding power of two; overflow is not possible.

The representation used for negative numbers affects how arithmetic shifts are implemented. Arithmetic shifts of numbers in two's complement form are slightly more complicated than the other shifts. An arithmetic shift to the left supplies zeros for the bit positions vacated at the right end of the register. If any of the bits shifted out by the arithmetic shift differ from the sign bit, there is a loss of significance. An arithmetic shift to the right copies the sign bit into the vacated positions. The bits shifted out of the right end are lost. There is no loss of significance in a right shift (see Figure 6.4).

Consider the same 12-bit register and $-21$ represented in two's complement form

$$1111 \quad 1110 \quad 1011$$

An arithmetic shift five bit positions to the left gives

$$1101 \quad 0110 \quad 0000$$

This is $-672$. Now shifting $-21$ eight bit positions to the left yields

$$1011 \quad 0000 \quad 0000$$

The eight bits to the right of the sign bit are shifted out. One of them is a 0, which is a significant bit in a negative number. The result, interpreted as a two's complement number, is $-1280$. The product of $(-21) \times 2^8$, however, is $-5376$, which exceeds the capacity of this 12-bit register. The result appears to be $-1280$, the 12 least significant bits of $-5376$. The overflow flag would be set to record the loss of significance.

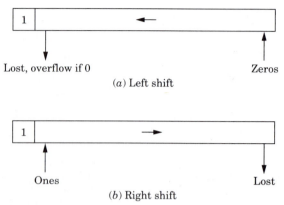

(a) Left shift

(b) Right shift

**Figure 6.4** Arithmetic Shift Operation, Negative Integer in Two's Complement Representation

An arithmetic shift of $-21$ in two's complement form by three bit positions to the right gives

$$1111 \quad 1111 \quad 1101$$

Note that since the sign bit is 1, ones are supplied for the vacated positions on the right. This example has an unexpected result. We shift three bit positions to the right, which is equivalent to dividing by eight. We expect $(-21) \div 8$ to give a quotient of $-2$ and a remainder of $-5$. Instead, the result is the two's complement representation of $-3$ in the register. The bits we shifted out, $011_2$, interpreted as a positive integer, represent 3. These results can be interpreted as $(-21) \div 8 = (-3)$ with remainder 3. We can check this using the (unrestricted) definition of division given in Chapter 4, $-21 = 8 \times (-3) + 3$. It checks, but is not consistent with the results of the division instruction.

## Rotates

In the third kind of shift, a **circular shift**, or **rotate**, the bits that are shifted out one end of the register are brought back into the other end of it (see Figure 6.5).

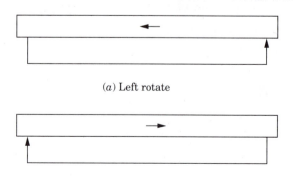

(a) Left rotate

(b) Right rotate

**Figure 6.5** Rotate Operation

## 6.1 Shift Operations

In discussing rotate operations, it is useful to imagine that the ends of the register are connected to each other, as if the register formed a circle. The rotate operations shift the bits around the circle, across the joined ends of the register.

As an example, consider a 12-bit register that initially contains

$$1010 \quad 1111 \quad 0000$$

Rotating by five bit positions to the right gives

$$1000 \quad 0101 \quad 0111$$

Here, the five bits from the right end, 10000, are shifted out and back in on the left end while the other bits are shifted to the right. The rotate operation does not treat the sign bit any differently than the other bits.

Some computers implement the rotate instruction with the carry flag superimposed between the ends of the register. Others do not include the carry flag in the rotate. And some, like the 8086, allow the programmer to specify the instruction either way.

## EXERCISES 6.1

1. Consider a 16-bit register that initially contains

    $$1111 \quad 0000 \quad 1100 \quad 1010$$

    Give its contents after each of the following logical shifts (start each part with the above pattern).
    (*a*) Left four bit positions
    (*b*) Right four bit positions
    (*c*) Left seven bit positions
    (*d*) Right eleven bit positions

2. Consider a 16-bit register that initially contains

    $$1111 \quad 0000 \quad 1100 \quad 1010$$

    and for which the carry flag is 1. Give the register contents and carry flag after each of the following rotates (start each part with the above pattern).
    (*a*) Left six bit positions, exclude carry
    (*b*) Left six bit positions, include carry
    (*c*) Right eight bit positions, exclude carry
    (*d*) Right eight bit positions, include carry
    (*e*) Right eighteen bit positions, include carry

3. Consider a 16-bit register that initially contains

    $$0000 \quad 1111 \quad 0011 \quad 0101$$

    Give the register contents and the overflow flag after each of the following arithmetic shifts (start each part with the above pattern).
    (*a*) Left one bit position
    (*b*) Left one bit position, repeated 3 times
    (*c*) Left one bit position, repeated 5 times
    (*d*) Left five bit positions
    (*e*) Right five bit positions

4. Consider a 16-bit register that initially contains

    1111 0000 1100 1010

    which represents some negative integer in two's complement. Give the register contents and state of the overflow flag after each of the following arithmetic shifts (start each part with the above pattern).
    (a) Left one bit position
    (b) Left one bit position, repeated 3 times
    (c) Left one bit position, repeated 5 times
    (d) Left five bit positions
    (e) Right five bit positions

5. What shift instruction would you use with an integer in a register to
    (a) Multiply it by sixteen?
    (b) Multiply it by eight?
    (c) Divide it by sixteen?
    (d) Multiply it by $\frac{1}{2}$?

6. It is proposed that the result of a right arithmetic shift of a number in two's complement can be made to agree with the quotient from division by adding the sign of the number (as 0 or 1) to the result. Does this work in every case? How can this condition be implemented in assembly language?

7. Assume there is only one rotate instruction. What shift count can be specified to get the same result as a shift of $n$ bits in the other direction? Assume a 16-bit register.

## 6.2 SHIFT INSTRUCTIONS

Shift instructions must specify the register or memory location to shift, the type of shift, the direction of the shift, and the shift count. The register or memory location is specified as the destination operand. The type of shift and the direction are usually part of the instruction mnemonic. The shift count is the most varied aspect of writing a shift instruction.

The instructions of some computers can shift only one bit position at a time. In such cases, the instruction must be repeated three times in order to shift the contents of a register by three positions. Instructions of other computers can specify the shift count as any constant. The most flexible arrangement of all allows the shift count to be placed in a register, thereby creating a variable shift count.

The 8086 uses the first and last methods of specifying a shift count. The newer processors in the family also allow constant shift counts as immediate operands; this feature will not be discussed here.

In the descriptions of the shift instructions, the subscripts denote the position of one bit or a group of bits before and after the instruction executes. The bits are numbered 0 through N, from right to left. N is 7 for a byte operand, or 15 for a word operand. The number of bits is the same on both sides of each assignment statement used to describe a shift instruction except when the expression on the right side of the assignment operator represents one bit and the expression on the left represents more than one bit. In this situation, enough copies of the source bit to fill the destination field are implied. To improve readability, the word *destination* is abbreviated as *dest* in the action descriptions.

## 6.2 Shift Instructions

### Logical Shifts

The 8086 has two logical shift instructions, shl and shr. These instructions have two operands: the destination to be shifted and the shift count. The shift count can be either the constant 1 or the CL register; no other values are allowed.

**SHift Left**
- syntax: shl *destination*, 1
- action: $dest_{N..1} := dest_{N-1..0}$
  & $dest_0 := 0$

**SHift Right**
- syntax: shr *destination*, 1
- action: $dest_{N-1..0} := dest_{N..1}$
  & $dest_N := 0$
- flags: O...SZ.PC modified for result
  ......A.. undefined
  .DIT..... unchanged

**SHift Left**
- syntax: shl *destination*, cl
- action: $dest_{N..cl} := dest_{N-cl..0}$
  & $dest_{cl-1..0} := 0$

**SHift Right**
- syntax: shr *destination*, cl
- action: $dest_{N-cl..0} := dest_{N..cl}$
  & $dest_{N..N-cl+1} := 0$
- flags: ....SZ.PC modified for result
  O.....A.. undefined
  .DIT..... unchanged
- operands: *mem*, 1    *reg*, 1
  *mem*, cl    *reg*, cl

The last bit shifted out of the register or memory location is saved in the carry flag. The other flags that are modified for the result have the same interpretation as they would if the instruction were an unsigned multiplication (or division) by a power of 2. Note that the overflow flag is defined following a shift only if the shift count is 1.

### Arithmetic Shifts

The arithmetic shift instructions for the 8086 parallel the logical shift instructions. Operands specify both which register or memory location to shift and a shift count, which, again, can be 1 or CL.

**188**  Chapter 6  Bit Operations and Boolean Data

The left arithmetic shift works exactly like the left logical shift; it can change the sign bit. The right arithmetic shift acts much like the version described in Section 6.1. The 8086 arithmetic shifts were designed to multiply and divide signed numbers by powers of 2. They achieve this goal as well as can be expected.

---

**Shift Arithmetic Left**

    syntax:      sal *destination*, 1

    action:      $dest_{N..1} := dest_{N-1..0}$
                   & $dest_0 := 0$

    flags:       O...SZ.PC modified for result
                  ......A.. undefined
                  .DIT..... unchanged

**Shift Arithmetic Right**

    syntax:      sar *destination*, 1

    action:      $dest_{N-1..0} := dest_{N..1}$
                   & $dest_N$ unchanged

    flags:       ....SZ.PC modified for result
                  O........ cleared
                  ......A.. undefined
                  .DIT..... unchanged

**Shift Arithmetic Left**

    syntax:      sal *destination*, cl

    action:      $dest_{N..cl} := dest_{N-cl..0}$
                   & $dest_{cl-1..0} := 0$

    flags:       ....SZ.PC modified for result
                  O.....A.. undefined
                  .DIT..... unchanged

**Shift Arithmetic Right**

    syntax:      sar *destination*, cl

    action:      $dest_{N-cl..0} := dest_{N..cl}$
                   & $dest_{N..N-cl+1} := dest_N$

    flags:       ....SZ.PC modified for result
                  O........ cleared
                  ......A.. undefined
                  .DIT..... unchanged

    operands:   *mem*, 1     *reg*, 1
                   *mem*, cl    *reg*, cl

---

The last bit shifted out of the register or memory location is saved in the carry flag. The other flags that are modified for the result have the same interpretation as they would if the instruction were a signed multiplication (or division) by a power of two. Note that

## 6.2 Shift Instructions

the overflow flag is defined following a left arithmetic shift only if the shift count is 1; it is always cleared by a right arithmetic shift.

### Arithmetic by shifts

The use of an arithmetic shift instruction to implement multiplication or division by a power of 2 is generally faster than the corresponding multiplication or division instruction. However, when the dividend is negative and represented in two's complement, the right shift will not give the same result as a division instruction. Arithmetic shifts can be used in place of arithmetic instructions as long as the potential problems with some numbers are understood and all such uses are clearly documented.

Multiplication by numbers other than powers of 2 can be implemented by combining shifts with additions. For example, to multiply an operand by 10, we could shift it left twice (making it four times its original value), add the original value (making it five times its original value), then shift the sum left. Using the AX register to compute 10 times the value of Factor, we can write

```
mov     ax, Factor
sar     ax, 1
sar     ax, 1
add     ax, Factor
sar     ax, 1
```

The sequence of four instructions following mov is 2.5 times longer than an equivalent multiply instruction. The add instruction with an operand in memory is 4 bytes long; each sar instruction is 2 bytes long. The above sequence requires 10 bytes. An equivalent mul or imul instruction is just 4 bytes long.

The shift instructions, though, pay off in execution time. Depending on the processor and value being multiplied, the multiply instruction requires from about 2.5 to 12 times longer to execute than the sequence of shifts and add! Considering how often we might need multiplication by small constants, implementing such multiplications as shifts and additions can significantly reduce the execution time of a program.

The sequence of shifts and add is used to multiply by 10 in the GetDec procedure (see Appendix 1). Multiplication time is not critical in GetDec, as the procedure spends much more time waiting for the user to type a number. The shift and add sequence was used in GetDec for illustration purposes.

There are other ways to build sequences of shift and add instructions to achieve multiplication by 10 and other factors that are not powers of 2. Division by numbers other than powers of 2, however, is best implemented using the division instructions.

### Rotates

The 8086 has four rotate instructions. The rol and ror instructions rotate an 8-bit or 16-bit quantity to the left and right respectively. The destination of these instructions can be in a register or in memory. The rcl and rcr instructions rotate a 9-bit or 17-bit quantity to the left and right respectively. The extra bit involved in rcl and rcr is the carry flag.

These instructions have two operands: the destination to be rotated and the shift count. The shift count can be either the constant 1 or the CL register; no other values are allowed.

Let us look at `rol` and `ror` first.

---

**ROtate Left**
- syntax: `rol` *destination*, 1
- action: $dest_{N..1} := dest_{N-1..0}$
  & $dest_0 := dest_N$

**ROtate Right**
- syntax: `ror` *destination*, 1
- action: $dest_{N-1..0} := dest_{N..1}$
  & $dest_N := dest_0$
- flags: O.......C modified for result
  .DITSZAP. unchanged

**ROtate Left**
- syntax: `rol` *destination*, cl
- action: $dest_{N..cl} := dest_{N-cl..0}$
  & $dest_{cl-1..0} := dest_{N..N-cl+1}$

**ROtate Right**
- syntax: `ror` *destination*, cl
- action: $dest_{N-cl..0} := dest_{N..cl}$
  & $dest_{N..N-cl+1} := dest_{cl-1..0}$
- flags: ........C modified for result
  O........ undefined
  .DITSZAP. unchanged
- operands: *mem*, 1   *reg*, 1
  *mem*, cl   *reg*, cl

---

The last bit rotated out of the register or memory location is saved in the carry flag. A rotate instruction with a shift count of 1 affects the overflow flag the same way that a logical shift instruction would, but it is not clear what overflow means in this case. The overflow flag is undefined following a rotate instruction with a variable shift count.

Now let us look at `rcl` and `rcr`, which include the carry flag as part of the destination.

---

**Rotate with Carry Left**
- syntax: `rcl` *destination*, 1
- action: $dest_{N..1} := dest_{N-1..0}$
  & $dest_0 := CF$
  & $CF := dest_N$

## 6.2 Shift Instructions

**Rotate with Carry Right**
- syntax: `rcr` *destination*, 1
- action: $dest_{N-1..0} := dest_{N..1}$
  & $dest_N := CF$
  & $CF := dest_0$
- flags: O......C modified for result
  .DITSZAP. unchanged

**Rotate with Carry Left**
- syntax: `rcl` *destination*, cl
- action: $dest_{N..cl} := dest_{N-cl..0}$
  & $dest_{cl-1} := CF$
  & $dest_{cl-2..0} := dest_{N..N-cl+2}$
  & $CF := dest_{N-cl+1}$

**Rotate with Carry Right**
- syntax: `rcr` *destination*, cl
- action: $dest_{N-cl..0} := dest_{N..cl}$
  & $dest_{N-cl+1} := CF$
  & $dest_{N..N-cl+2} := dest_{cl-2..0}$
  & $CF := dest_{cl-1}$
- flags: ......C modified for result
  O....... undefined
  .DITSZAP. unchanged
- operands: *mem*, 1    *reg*, 1
  *mem*, cl    *reg*, cl

The last bit rotated out of the register or memory location is saved in the carry flag, by definition. The overflow flag is again modified when the shift count is 1, though it is not clear what overflow means following a rotate instruction.

We will use some of these instructions in programs later in this chapter, along with instructions from Section 6.4. But first, the next section will consider the Boolean data type.

## EXERCISES 6.2

1. Assume that the AX register contains

    1111 0000 1100 1010

    and the CL register contains 4. Give the contents of the AX register and the state of the overflow and carry flags (when defined) following each of the instructions below:

    (a) shl ax, 1    (b) shl ax, cl
    (c) shr ax, cl    (d) shr ah, 1
    (e) sal al, 1    (f) sal ax, cl
    (g) sal ax, cl    (h) sar ax, cl
    (i) rol ax, cl    (j) ror ah, cl
    (k) rcr al, 1    (l) rcl ax, 1
    (m) ror ax, cl    (n) rcr ah, cl

2. Write the 8086 shift (or rotate) instruction(s) you could use to accomplish each of the following tasks.
   (*a*) Multiply the contents of AX by 32
   (*b*) Divide the contents of AH by 2
   (*c*) Exchange AH with AL
   (*d*) Move CF into bit 0 of AL, clear rest of AL
   (*e*) Multiply the contents of AH by 4
3. Write a sequence of shift and add instructions, similar to that given for multiplying by 10, that multiplies Value by each of the following
   (*a*) 12
   (*b*) 20
   (*c*) 15
   (*d*) 18
4. Can you propose a rule for specifying when to add and when to shift to achieve a particular product, based on your solutions to Exercise 3?
5. The arithmetic shifts of the 8086 are designed to operate on signed numbers. Which 8086 shift instructions, if any, could be used to multiply and divide unsigned numbers by powers of 2?

## 6.3 BOOLEAN DATA REPRESENTATION

Many high-level programming languages provide a Boolean (or logical) data type. Variables of this type can have two values: true or false. This section explains how to implement the Boolean data type in assembly language.

A Boolean value can be represented by a single bit. Some languages allow each bit of a word or byte to represent a separate Boolean value. Usually, however, an entire byte or word is used for each value. The criterion for deciding whether to pack more than one Boolean value into a single byte is efficiency. The space saved by packing eight Boolean values in a byte (or 16 in a word) must be compared to the space occupied by the additional instructions needed to extract or change individual Boolean values. The time an application will use executing these additional instructions must also be considered. If a program uses only a few Boolean values, packing is unattractive; but if it uses hundreds of them, packing might be worthwhile.

In this section, we consider only unpacked data and assume that each Boolean value is stored in a separate byte. The bit used and the state that represents each value vary from computer to computer and from language to language. Compilers for different languages on the same computer may use different codings; different compilers for the same language on different computers, and even on the same computers, may also use a different coding. Most likely the first bit or last bit of the word is used, with the rest of the word coded as zeros. Often 0 is used for false and 1 for true, a convention followed in this section.

Using the bit the furthest to the left—the sign bit—for a Boolean value and interpreting the word as a signed integer yields a nonnegative integer for false and a negative integer for true. When the bit the furthest to the right—the least significant bit—is used, an even integer represents false and an odd integer represents true. There are advantages and disadvantages to each scheme.

Many compilers for the 8086 processors use the least significant bit in a byte to represent a Boolean value. Some languages use more than one byte, but usually the leading bytes

## 6.3 Boolean Data Representation

are ignored. Treating the byte that contains the Boolean value as an integer, 0 represents false and 1 represents true.

In our programs we use 0 and 1 as immediate operands as the values for False and True, respectively. To make this convention more readable and self-documenting, names can be associated with these values using the equ directive:

```
; Boolean constants
  True         equ       1
  False        equ       0
```

A mov instruction can be used to assign a value to a Boolean variable. The constant False can be assigned to the Boolean variable Flag using the instruction

```
    mov       Flag, False
```

False is an immediate operand in this example, not a second memory reference.

To copy the value of one Boolean variable to another, one or two mov instructions are used, depending on whether the variables are in registers or memory. A more interesting problem involves assigning the value of a condition to a variable, such as

Found := Left + 1 = Right

where Found is Boolean and Left and Right are integers. This statement can be rewritten as a selection structure with assignment of a constant in each sequence:

```
IF Left + 1 = Right
THEN
   Found := True
ELSE
   Found := False
ENDIF
```

This is implemented in Program 6.1.

---

## Program 6.1

```
; Program 6.1        BooleVar.ASM
; Implement the assignment statement
;     Found := Left + 1 = Right

; DOS function and status parameters
  DosFunc      equ       21h
  ExitToDos    equ       4Ch
  NoErrors     equ       00h

; Boolean constants
  True         equ       1
  False        equ       0

DOSSEG

_STACK SEGMENT para stack 'stack'
            dw        100h dup (?)
_STACK ENDS
```

**Program 6.1 (continued)**

```
        _DATA SEGMENT word public 'data'
          Left       dw      ?         ;input value
          Right      dw      ?         ;input value
          Found      db      ?         ;Boolean variable
          Prompt1    db      "Enter Left:  "
          Prompt2    db      "Enter Right: "
          PromptLen  dw      13
          ResultMsg  db      "Left + 1 = Right : "
          ResultLen  dw      19
        _DATA ENDS

        _TEXT SEGMENT word public 'code'
            assume cs: _TEXT
            extrn  PutStr: PROC, PutCrLf: PROC
            extrn  GetDec: PROC, PutDec: PROC

        BooleVar:

        ; set up ds register to point to _DATA
            mov     ax, seg _DATA
            mov     ds, ax
            assume  ds: _DATA

        ; print ("Enter Left: ")
            mov     cx, PromptLen
            mov     bx, offset Prompt1
            call    PutStr

        ; read (Left)
            call    GetDec
            mov     Left, ax

        ; print ("Enter Right: ")
            mov     bx, offset Prompt2
            call    PutStr

        ; read (Right)
            call    GetDec
            mov     Right, ax

        ; Implement 'Found := Left + 1 = Right' as selection.
        ; IF01 Left + 1 = Right
            mov     ax, Left
            inc     ax
            cmp     ax, Right
            jne     ELSE01

        ; THEN01
        ;   Found := True
            mov     Found, True
            jmp     ENDIF01
```

## 6.3 Boolean Data Representation

**Program 6.1 (continued)**

```
        ELSE01:
;         Found := False
            mov     Found, False
        ENDIF01:

; print ("Left + 1 = Right : ", Found)
            mov     cx, ResultLen
            mov     bx, offset ResultMsg
            call    PutStr
            mov     al, Found
            sub     ah, ah
            call    PutDec
            call    PutCrLf

; exit to DOS
            mov     ah, ExitToDos
            mov     al, NoErrors
            int     DosFunc

_TEXT ENDS
END     BooleVar
```

To use a Boolean variable as a condition in a control structure, we need to compare the variable to one of the symbols True or False, as defined earlier. Consider a WHILE loop in which a previously assigned Boolean variable is the condition, such as the fragment

```
Vacant := True;
WHILE Vacant
DO
  ...
  Vacant := ...
  ...
ENDWHILE
```

where Vacant is a Boolean variable, and the ellipses (...) indicate steps that are irrelevant here.

The assignment to Vacant within the loop can be written using a selection structure. The test in the WHILE statement itself is implemented as

```
; WHILE02 Vacant
    cmp     Vacant, True
    jne     ENDWHL02
DO02:
```

The cmp instruction compares Vacant to True (one) and sets the flags accordingly. If Vacant is False (zero), the conditional jump transfers control past the loop body; if Vacant is True, the jump is not taken, and the loop body is executed.

More complex Boolean expressions will be considered following the discussion of the Boolean operations and instructions in the next sections.

## EXERCISES 6.3

1. Some languages use 0 for False and any nonzero value for True. How does this affect the evaluation of a Boolean variable used to control a structure?
2. Suppose that you need to write routines that convert Boolean variables (as bytes) between the two formats (identified as A and B) given in each problem below. How could the conversions be performed?
    (a) A: (True: bit 7 is 1; False: all bits 0)
        B: (True: bit 0 is 1; False: all bits 0)
    (b) A: (True: any nonzero value; False: 0)
        B: (True: bit 0 is 1; False: all bits 0)
    (c) A: (True: all bits 1; False: all bits 0)
        B: (True: "T"; False: "F")
    (d) A: (True: any bit 1; False: all bits 0)
        B: (True: bit 0 is 1; False: all bits 0)

## 6.4 BOOLEAN OPERATIONS

Most high-level programming languages include three Boolean operators: NOT, AND, and OR. Some languages have a second form of the OR operator, called XOR. The former is the inclusive OR, and the latter is the exclusive OR. We will examine the difference shortly. NOT is a unary operator; it complements the value of its operand. The others are binary operators, combining two operands into a single value. We consider each operation separately.

### AND

The AND operation combines two bits as illustrated in Table 6.1. Combining two bits with AND yields a result of 1 only when both of the bits examined are ones. If either bit is 0, the result is 0. Compare this operation to that of multiplying two bits together; the result is the same.

Depending on the instruction formats available in a given computer, AND operates on every pair of bits in the same position in two registers, in two memory locations, or in a register and a memory location. The examples that follow use an eight-bit register and a byte of memory. If AND is used to combine a register containing 00110011 with a byte

Table 6.1  Logical AND Operation

| AND | 0 | 1 |
|---|---|---|
| 0 | 0 | 0 |
| 1 | 0 | 1 |

## 6.4 Boolean Operations

of memory containing 01010101, the result is 00010001. The operation is easier to see if the values are aligned:

$$\begin{array}{rl} 00110011 & \text{register} \\ \text{AND } 01010101 & \text{memory} \\ \hline 00010001 & \text{result} \end{array}$$

Starting from the left, the first pair of bits are both zero: 0 AND 0 = 0. The next two pairs give 0 AND 1 = 0, and 1 AND 0 = 0. The fourth pair of bits are both ones, so the result is one: 1 AND 1 = 1. The same pattern repeats in the last four bits.

### OR

The OR operation combines two bits according to Table 6.2. The result of combining two bits with OR is 1 if either or both of the bits are 1. Only if both bits are 0 is the result 0. This form of the OR is called the inclusive OR.

Like AND, OR operates on every pair of bits in two operands. The operands can be in registers or memory locations. If OR is used to combine a register containing 00110011 with a byte of memory containing 01010101, the result is 01110111. The operation is easier to see if the values are aligned:

$$\begin{array}{rl} 00110011 & \text{register} \\ \text{OR } 01010101 & \text{memory} \\ \hline 01110111 & \text{result} \end{array}$$

Starting from the left, the first pair of bits are both zero: 0 OR 0 = 0. The next two pairs of bits are each composed of a zero and a one, yielding a result of one: 0 OR 1 = 1 and 1 OR 0 = 1. The fourth pair of bits are both ones, and 1 OR 1 = 1. The same pattern repeats in the last four bits.

### XOR

The XOR operation is the exclusive OR. It differs from the inclusive OR only when both operand bits are one. The inclusive OR gives 1 for this, whereas the exclusive OR gives 0. This pattern is shown in Table 6.3. In words, the XOR of two bits is 1 if either, but not both, of the bits are 1.

Like the AND and the inclusive OR, the exclusive OR operates on every pair of bits in the same position in two registers, in two memory locations, or in a register and a

**Table 6.2 Inclusive OR Operation**

| OR | 0 | 1 |
|---|---|---|
| 0 | 0 | 1 |
| 1 | 1 | 1 |

## Chapter 6 Bit Operations and Boolean Data

Table 6.3 Exclusive OR Operation

| XOR | 0 | 1 |
|---|---|---|
| 0 | 0 | 1 |
| 1 | 1 | 0 |

memory location. Repeating the eight-bit example from the AND and OR discussions yield the result:

```
    00110011   register
XOR 01010101   memory
    ────────
    01100110   result
```

Compare this to the result from the inclusive OR.

## NOT

The Boolean operator NOT is a unary operator. It changes the state of a bit from 1 to 0 or 0 to 1. The result is the complement of the operand (see Table 6.4).

Like the other Boolean operators, NOT operates on every bit of a register or memory location. Using the eight-bit register for another example, the effect of NOT can be seen quite easily

```
NOT 00110101   register
    ────────
    11001010   result
```

Each bit that was originally 1 is cleared to 0, and each bit that was originally 0 is set to 1.

## EXERCISES 6.4

1. Consider a 16-bit register that initially contains

   0000 1111 0011 0011

   Give the contents of the register after each of the following Boolean operations (start each part with the above pattern).
   (a) AND with 1111 1111 0000 0000    (b) AND with 0101 0101 0101 0101
   (c) OR  with 1111 1111 0000 0000    (d) OR  with 0101 0101 0101 0101
   (e) XOR with 1111 1111 0000 0000    (f) XOR with 0101 0101 0101 0101
   (g) NOT

Table 6.4 NOT Operation

|   | NOT |
|---|---|
| 0 | 1 |
| 1 | 0 |

2. How would you clear the middle 8 bits of a 16-bit register to zeros, leaving the first and last four bits unchanged?
3. How would you set the middle 8 bits of a 16-bit register to ones, leaving the first and last four bits unchanged?
4. How would you complement the middle 8 bits of a 16-bit register, leaving the first and last four bits unchanged?

## 6.5 BOOLEAN INSTRUCTIONS

We have seen that the AND operation is similar to multiplication and that the XOR operation is similar to addition (neglecting the carry bit). The instructions for Boolean operations on two values are similar to the instructions for arithmetic operations on two values. The instruction for the Boolean NOT operation is also similar to the instruction for negation.

### The and Instruction

The and instruction is similar in format to the add instruction. Both operands of and can be in registers, or one can be in a register and the other in memory.

**logical AND**
- syntax: and *destination, source*
- action: *destination* := *destination* AND *source*
- flags:
  ....SZ.P. modified for result
  O.......C cleared
  ......A.. undefined
  .DIT..... unchanged
- operands: *reg, reg*  *mem, reg*  *reg, mem*
  *reg, immed*  *mem, immed*  *accum, immed*

The and instruction clears the overflow and carry flags since the result cannot be out of range. The sign, zero, and parity flags are set according to the result.

The and instruction is useful for clearing part, but not all, of a register to 0. This goal is accomplished by creating a mask that has a 0 in each position to be cleared to 0 and a 1 in each position to be left unchanged. The next step is to and the register with the mask. For example, the following instruction will clear all but the four right-most bits of a 16-bit register to 0:

    and     ax, 000Fh

Here the mask is written as an immediate operand in hexadecimal. The mask contains 12 0-bits on the left, so the 12 bits on the left end of the AX register will be cleared. The mask also contains four 1-bits on the right, so the four bits on the right of the AX register will be unchanged.

## The test Instruction

The `test` instruction performs the same operation as the `and` instruction, except that it does not change the destination operand. It is useful for testing an individual bit (or a number of bits together).

---

**logical compare**

    syntax:    `test` *destination, source*

    action:    compute (*destination* AND *source*)

    flags:    ....SZ.P. modified for result
                O.......C cleared
                ......A.. undefined
                .DIT..... unchanged

    operands:    *reg, reg*    *mem, reg*    *reg, mem*
                    *reg, immed*  *mem, immed*  *accum, immed*

---

To illustrate the `test` instruction, we will test the third bit from the right in a 16-bit word named Range. If that bit is 1, the integer variable Scale should be set to 2. The corresponding pseudocode is

```
IF third bit of Range is 1
THEN
   Scale := 2
ENDIF
```

The third bit can have two states, 0 and 1, of course. We can logically and the register with a mask that is all 0 except for the position in the register to be tested; the result will be either all zeros, if the bit to be tested is 0, or a nonzero value that depends on the position of the bit to be tested, if that bit is 1. The actual result of and, however, is not needed. The testing process requires only the state of the zero flag, so the `test` instruction is appropriate.

This is implemented in Program 6.2. The program clears Scale to 0 before testing, so that the result of program can be verified more readily. The mask is the hexadecimal

---

**Program 6.2**

```
; Program 6.2       TestBit.ASM
; Set Scale to 2 if bit 3 of Range is set.

; DOS function and status parameters
   DosFunc      equ       21h
   ExitToDos    equ       4Ch
   NoErrors     equ       00h

DOSSEG
```

### 6.5 Boolean Instructions

**Program 6.2 (continued)**

```
_STACK SEGMENT para stack 'stack'
            dw      100h dup (?)
_STACK ENDS

_DATA SEGMENT word public 'data'
  Range       dw      ?          ;input value
  Scale       dw      ?          ;result
  PromptMsg   db      "Enter Range: "
  PromptLen   dw      13
  ResultMsg   db      "Scale is "
  ResultLen   dw      9
_DATA ENDS

_TEXT SEGMENT word public 'code'
    assume cs: _TEXT
    extrn  PutStr: PROC, PutCrLf: PROC
    extrn  GetDec: PROC, PutDec: PROC

TestBit:

; set up ds register to point to _DATA
    mov     ax, seg _DATA
    mov     ds, ax
    assume  ds: _DATA

; print ("Enter Range: ")
    mov     cx, PromptLen
    mov     bx, offset PromptMsg
    call    PutStr

; read (Range)
    call    GetDec
    mov     Range, ax

; clear Scale for reference
    mov     Scale, 0

; Set Scale to 2 if bit 3 of Range is set.
; IF01 bit 3 of Range = 1
    mov     ax, Range
    test    ax, 0004h
    jz      ENDIF01

; THEN01
;   Scale := 2
    mov     Scale, 2
  ENDIF01:

; print ("Scale is ", Scale)
    mov     cx, ResultLen
    mov     bx, offset ResultMsg
    call    PutStr
    mov     ax, Scale
    call    PutDec
    call    PutCrLf
```

**Program 6.2 (continued)**

```
; exit to DOS
      mov     ah, ExitToDos
      mov     al, NoErrors
      int     DosFunc

_TEXT ENDS
END     TestBit
```

number 0004h. This has a 1-bit in the third bit position from the right; all other bits are 0. The conditional jump instruction, jz, transfers control to the end of the structure if the zero flag is set. This will be the case only if the third bit of the AX register was 0 before the test instruction. If the third bit was a 1, the test operation clears the zero flag, the condition for the jump is not satisfied, and the THEN clause is executed.

## The or Instruction

The or instruction parallels the and instruction. It operates on two values, in registers or memory, and produces one result. The or instruction affects the flags the same way that the and instruction does.

**inclusive OR**

syntax:    or *destination, source*

action:    *destination* := *destination* OR *source*

flags:     ....SZ.P. modified for result
           O.......C cleared
           ......A.. undefined
           .DIT..... unchanged

operands:  reg, reg      mem, reg      reg, mem
           reg, immed    mem, immed    accum, immed

The inclusive or instruction is useful for setting part or all of a register or memory location to 1. This goal is accomplished by creating a mask that has a 1 in each position to be set to 1 and a 0 in each position to be left unchanged. The next step is to or the register with the mask. For example, the following instruction will set alternating groups of four bits of the AX register to 1:

```
or      ax, 0F0Fh
```

## The xor Instruction

The xor instruction is similar to the or instruction. Like and and or, xor clears the overflow and carry flags and sets the sign, zero, and parity flags according to the result.

## 6.5 Boolean Instructions

**eXclusive OR**
- syntax: *xor destination, source*
- action: *destination* := *destination* XOR *source*
- flags:
  - ....SZ.P. modified for result
  - O.......C cleared
  - ......A.. undefined
  - .DIT..... unchanged
- operands:  *reg, reg*   *mem, reg*   *reg, mem*
             *reg, immed* *mem, immed* *accum, immed*

The xor instruction is useful for complementing part or all of a register. This goal is accomplished by creating a mask that has a 1 in each position to be complemented, and a 0 in each position to be left unchanged. The next step is to xor the register with the mask. For example, the following instruction will complement the third through seventh bits from the left of the AX register:

    xor    ax, 3E00h

The mask, partially expanded in binary, is 001111100..02.

Some programmers use the xor instruction to clear a register to 0. For example, to clear AX, they use

    xor    ax, ax

Since the same register is both the source and destination operand, every pair of bits of the source and destination register are the same, so xor clears the corresponding bit of the destination register. This method is neither smaller nor faster than using subtraction, as in

    sub    ax, ax

## The not Instruction

The effect of the NOT operation can be achieved with the xor instruction. If one of the operands of xor is treated as a mask containing some pattern of zeros and ones, then the xor instruction computes the complement of every bit in the other operand for which the mask has a 1-bit. It leaves those bits that correspond to zeros in the mask unchanged. This observation demonstrates that an xor instruction with a mask of all ones can be used to complement every bit in an operand.

The advantage of xor over not is the ability to specify which bits to complement rather than having to complement all of them. On the other hand, not could be slightly faster when complementing all of the bits—the instruction need not fetch or consider the mask in any way.

The not instruction has the same format as the neg instruction. Unlike the other instructions of this section, the not instruction does not affect any of the flags.

**logical complement**

| | |
|---|---|
| syntax: | not *destination* |
| action: | *destination* := NOT *destination* |
| flags: | ODITSZAPC unchanged |
| operands: | *reg*    *mem* |

## EXERCISES 6.5

1. Assume that the AX register contains

   0000   1111   0011   0011

   Give the contents of the AX register after each of the following instructions is executed (start each part with the above pattern).
   - (a) and   ax, 0FF00h
   - (b) and   ax, 00FFh
   - (c) or    ax, 0F0F0h
   - (d) or    ax, 0FF0h
   - (e) xor   ax, 00FFh
   - (f) xor   ax, 0F00Fh
   - (g) not   ax

2. Write an 8086 instruction with an immediate operand that clears the middle eight bits of the AX register to zeros, leaving the first and last four bits unchanged.

3. Write an 8086 instruction with an immediate operand that sets the middle eight bits of the AX register to ones, leaving the first and last four bits unchanged.

4. Write an 8086 instruction that complements the middle eight bits of the AX register, leaving the first and last four bits unchanged.

## 6.6 APPLICATIONS

This section considers methods of converting the various flags into Boolean variables, evaluating compound Boolean expressions, and an application of the shift and Boolean instructions.

### Converting Flags to Boolean Values

Some machines have instructions that assign Boolean values directly. These instructions set or clear a register or memory location, depending on the result obtained from evaluating a condition. Like the conditional jump instructions of the previous chapter, these instructions vary considerably in the kinds of conditions that they can evaluate. The 8086 and 80286 processors do not have such instructions, but the 80386 does.

The 80386 conditional set instructions assign Boolean values to their operand according to the states of selected bits in the flags register. For example,

setnz     al

## 6.6 Applications

sets AL to 1 if the zero flag is clear, or clears AL to 0 if the zero flag is set. The conditional set instructions of the 80386 implement all of the conditions previously shown in Tables 5.2, 5.4, and 5.5 using similar mnemonics.

For the 8086 and 80286, these operations can be implemented two ways: by using a selection structure or by using shift and mask operations on a copy of the flags register. We consider the latter method first.

The initial hurdle is to copy the flags register into a general-purpose register. There are two instructions that transfer information between the AH register and bits 0 through 7 of the flags register. The lahf instruction, which is of primary concern in this discussion, copies bits 0 through 7 of the flags register to the AH register. The sahf instruction copies the contents of the AH register into bits 0 through 7 of the flags register; it has little use here but is presented for general information. Unfortunately, not all of the relevant flags are in the bits that lahf and sahf copy.

**Load AH from Flags**
    syntax:    lahf
    action:    ah := bits 0..7 of flags
    flags:    ODITSZAPC unchanged

**Store AH into Flags**
    syntax:    sahf
    action:    bits 0..7 of flags := ah
    flags:    ....SZAPC copied from ah
              ODIT..... unchanged

There is an indirect way to copy all 16 bits of the flags register into any of the general registers. It involves using the stack, which will be discussed in detail in the next chapter. Because each copy requires two instructions, this method is less efficient than the lahf instruction. This section will use lahf to demonstrate the basic technique of transforming a flag bit into a Boolean value.

The organization of the flags register was given earlier. It is repeated here for easier reference (see Figure 6.6). Now, consider the procedure for assigning the Boolean variable Zip a copy of the zero flag. Zip is a byte in memory; it is necessary to clear bits 1 through 7 and copy the zero flag into bit 0. The zero flag is bit 6 of the flags register. The objective can be accomplished with the following sequence of instructions:

```
lahf
mov     cl, 06h
shr     ah, cl
and     ah, 01h
mov     Zip, ah
```

This sequence starts by copying the flags to AH, and then it shifts the register so that the zero flag is in bit 0. Bits 1 through 7 of the register are then cleared by the logical and instruction. Finally, the result is copied to memory.

```
 F  E  D  C  B  A  9  8  7  6  5  4  3  2  1  0
   |NT| IOP |OF|DF|IF|TF|SF|ZF|  |AF|  |PF|  |CF|
```

| Bit | | Meaning |
|---|---|---|
| F | | (not used) |
| E | NT | Nested task (286, 386 only) |
| CD | IOP | I/O protection level (286, 386 only) |
| B | OF | Overflow flag |
| A | DF | Direction flag |
| 9 | IF | Interrupt enable flag |
| 8 | TF | Trap flag |
| 7 | SF | Sign flag |
| 6 | ZF | Zero flag |
| 5 | | (not used) |
| 4 | AF | Auxiliary carry flag |
| 3 | | (not used) |
| 2 | PF | Parity flag |
| 1 | | (not used) |
| 0 | CF | Carry flag |

**Figure 6.6  Flags Register**

The other method of assigning the Boolean variable `Zip` the value of the zero flag is to use a selection structure such as the following

```
; IF01 ZF=1
      jnz       ELSE01
; THEN01
;   ZIP := True
      mov       Zip, True
      jmp       ENDIF01
  ELSE01:
;   ZIP := False
      mov       Zip, False
  ENDIF01:
```

The first of these two methods, though interesting, does have practical limitations. The overflow flag is bit 11 in the flags register, so the `lahf` instruction does not copy it into AH. Some conditions require that two or three flags be inspected. For example, the unsigned "above" test must check CF and ZF, while the signed "greater" test must check ZF, SF, and OF. These multiple checks are more readily implemented using the conditional jump instructions to control a selection structure.

## Evaluating Compound Boolean Expressions

We now consider evaluating compound conditions that contain a Boolean operator. One way to do this is to perform all arithmetic and relational operations and then apply the Boolean operators to determine the value of the condition. This method is called **full evaluation**. For example, in

Value := (X < Y) OR ((N <> 0) AND (X*Y > 32))

## 6.6 Applications

full evaluation proceeds as if we had written

```
B1 := X < Y
B2 := N <> 0
B3 := X*Y > 32
Value := B1 OR (B2 AND B3)
```

This can be implemented by evaluating each subexpression and assigning the result to the temporary Boolean variables B1, B2, and B3. Then and and or instructions can be used to find the value of the original expression. This is not difficult, but it is long and is thus left as an exercise.

Another way to evaluate a compound condition is to attempt to rewrite it so that a minimum number of instructions must be executed to determine its value. This method is called **partial evaluation**. The basic transformations that can be made involve the following observations. When two Boolean expressions are combined by or, if the first one evaluated is True the other need not be evaluated: The result will be True regardless of the value of the second expression. When two Boolean expressions are combined by and, if the first one evaluated is False the other need not be evaluated: The result will be False regardless of the value of the second expression. When more than two Boolean expressions are combined with the same operator, these cases can be extended.

To illustrate, consider the previous example again:

```
Value := (X < Y) OR ((N <> 0) AND (X*Y > 32))
```

Note that, when X < Y is True, the entire expression will always evaluate to True. Using this observation, we could evaluate X < Y first, and if it is True, we do not need to evaluate the rest of the expression. But if it is False, we must evaluate more of the expression.

We can apply the second observation and evaluate N <> 0 next. If this is False, the value of the whole expression is also False, so we need not evaluate any more of it. But if N <> 0 is True, the value of the whole expression is the same as the value of X*Y > 32.

Putting all of this together, we can write a single selection structure like the following:

```
; IF01 (X < Y) OR ((N <> 0) AND (X*Y > 32))
;   if X < Y expression will be true
        mov     ax, X
        cmp     ax, Y
        jl      THEN01
;   with X >= Y, if N = 0 the expression is false
        mov     ax, N
        cmp     ax, 0
        je      ELSE01
;   with X >= Y and N <> 0, X*Y > 32 determines value
        mov     ax, X
        imul    Y
        cmp     dx, 0
        jg      THEN01      ;X*Y > 2^15, so X*Y > 32
        cmp     ax, 32
        jng     ELSE01      ;X*Y <= 32, expression false
```

```
        THEN01:
;           Value := True
            mov         Value, True
            jmp         ENDIF01
        ELSE01:
;           Value := False
            mov         Value, False
        ENDIF01:
```

Note that there are a number of conditional jumps to THEN01 or ELSE01 throughout the code. These jumps require careful documentation. Also note that THEN01 has been written as a label rather than a comment, as it usually is written.

## Counting One-Bits

An application of shift and Boolean instructions is to count the number of 1-bits in the least significant positions in a word of memory. For example, a word that contains the number 0000111101011111 has five ones on the right end of the register. The algorithm used to count them is

```
Count := 0
Copy := word to test
WHILE least significant bit of Copy is 1
DO
   Count := Count + 1
   shift Copy right one bit position
ENDWHILE
```

This is implemented in Program 6.3, using the AX register for Copy. The program is straightforward.

A test can be made to evaluate whether the least significant bit is one by using the mask 0001h with the test instruction. In the loop, the copy is shifted to the right one bit position, bringing the next bit into position for testing. This loop continues until a 0-bit is eventually found. Such an outcome is guaranteed since the shift instruction provides zeros for the vacated bit positions.

### Program 6.3

```
;   Program 6.3     Low1Bits.ASM
;   Count the number of consecutive 1-bits in a register,
;      starting from the least significant end (bit 0). For
;      example, for 0000000011100011, the count should be 2.

;   DOS function and status parameters
    DosFunc     equ     21h
    ExitToDos   equ     4Ch
    NoErrors    equ     00h

DOSSEG
```

### 6.6 Applications

**Program 6.3 (continued)**

```
        _STACK SEGMENT para stack 'stack'
                dw       100h dup (?)
        _STACK ENDS

        _DATA SEGMENT word public 'data'
            N           dw      ?         ;number to inspect
            Count       dw      ?         ;number of consecutive 1-bits
            PromptMsg   db      "Enter N: "
            PromptLen   dw      9
            ResultMsg   db      " low-order 1-bits."
            ResultLen   dw      18
        _DATA ENDS

        _TEXT SEGMENT word public 'code'
            assume  cs: _TEXT
            extrn   PutStr: PROC, PutCrLf: PROC
            extrn   GetDec: PROC, PutDec: PROC

Low1Bits:

; set up ds register to point to _DATA
            mov     ax, seg _DATA
            mov     ds, ax
            assume  ds: _DATA

; print ("Enter N: ")
            mov     cx, PromptLen
            mov     bx, offset PromptMsg
            call    PutStr

; read (N)
            call    GetDec
            mov     N, ax

; Count number of 1-bits at least significant end of N.
; Count := 0
            mov     Count, 0

; ax := working copy of N
            mov     ax, N

    WHILE01: ;least significant bit of ax = 1
            test    ax, 0001h
            jz      ENDWHL01

;   DO01
;       Count := Count + 1
            inc     Count

;       shift ax right one bit
            shr     ax, 1
            jmp     WHILE01
    ENDWHL01:
```

## Program 6.3 (continued)

```
        ; print (Count, "low-order 1-bits.")
        mov     ax, Count
        call    PutDec
        mov     cx, ResultLen
        mov     bx, offset ResultMsg
        call    PutStr
        call    PutCrLf

        ; exit to DOS
        mov     ah, ExitToDos
        mov     al, NoErrors
        int     DosFunc

_TEXT   ENDS
END     Low1Bits
```

## EXERCISES 6.6

▶1. Write a program that counts the number of bits in a register that are ones. Use the following algorithm:

```
Count := 0
WHILE Register <> 0 DO
   isolate least significant bit
   add least significant bit to Count
   shift register contents right one position
ENDWHILE
```

▶2. A faster algorithm than the one in Exercise 1 works as follows. Assume we can clear the 1-bits of a register to 0, one at a time. Then we can count the ones using

```
Count := 0
WHILE Register <> 0 DO
   clear a one bit to zero
   increment Count
ENDWHILE
```

To clear a 1-bit to 0, consider the expression

```
register AND (register - 1)
```

Subtracting 1 from a register clears the least significant 1 to 0 but sets bits to the right. Combining this with the original register using and clears all bits changed by the subtraction. Write a program that uses this expression in the loop given. Be sure to document it carefully.

▶3. Write a program that reads a positive integer and computes and prints the number of bits needed to represent it.

▶4. Write a program that reads an integer in hexadecimal and converts it into decimal. The input should be a string of hexadecimal digits, read as individual characters. The output can be printed using PutDec.

### 6.6 Applications

▶5. Write a program that reads an integer using GetDec and prints its internal representation in binary.

▶6. Two positive integers can be multiplied together using only addition and shifts of one bit position. The algorithm, multiplying Factor1 and Factor2 to give Product, is

```
Product := 0
WHILE Factor1 > 0
DO
   IF Factor1 is odd
   THEN
       Product := Product + Factor2
   ENDIF
   Factor1 := Factor1 shifted right one position
   Factor2 := Factor2 shifted left one position
ENDWHILE
```

Write a program that reads two integers, multiplies them together using the above algorithm, and prints the product. Product will be the same size as the factors. Can you explain why this algorithm works?

▶7. The 80386 has a pair of instructions, bsf and bsr (Bit Scan Forward and Bit Scan Reverse), that are not available on the 8086. bsf inspects the bits of its source operand, starting with the least significant bit, looking for a 1-bit. If it finds a 1-bit in the source operand, it sets the zero flag and records in the destination operand the position where the first 1 is found. For example, if the source operand is 00010100, bsf sets ZF to 1 and the destination operand to 2. bsr is similar, starting at the most significant end of the source operand.

Write a program that uses 8086 instructions that implement these operations. You need not preserve the other flag bits.

▶8. If text consists of only capital letters and a space, three characters can be packed in a 16-bit word as follows. Each letter can be represented by a five-bit number, using 1 for A, 2 for B, and so on, with 26 for Z. Use 0 for a space; do not use the numbers 27 through 31. Three five-bit codes are packed into a word; the leading bit is not used. For example, the letters ACM would be represented as

$$0 \quad 00001 \quad 00010 \quad 01101$$
$$A=1 \quad C=2 \quad M=13$$

Write a program that reads three capital letters (or spaces) using GetChar, codes and packs them into a word, then prints the word using PutDec.

▶9. Using the scheme of Exercise 8, write a program that reads a number using GetDec, converts it into three characters, and prints the characters using PutChar. Be careful to use good test data.

10. Examine, using a symbolic debugger, the code generated by the high-level-language compilers for evaluating compound Boolean expressions. Do your compiler(s) use full or partial evaluation? Is there a compiler switch or directive that controls this?

11. Write the sequences of instructions needed to evaluate the following Boolean expressions using full evaluation (all variables are signed words):
    (a) (X < Y) OR ((N <> 0) AND (X*Y > 32))
    (b) (X > 0) AND (X < 100)
    (c) ((Min <= Max) AND (Count > 3)) OR (Count = 0)
    (d) ((S > 5) XOR (S < −5)) AND (Plus <> 0)
    (e) (A < B) AND ((A > 0) OR (B < 100))
    (f) (Length + Girth < 100) AND (Weight <= 80)

12. Repeat Exercise 11 using partial evaluation.
13. Compare your answers to Exercises 11 and 12. Which method, full or partial evaluation, requires writing more instructions? Which method usually executes more instructions? On average, what would you estimate as the savings, as a percentage of instructions written? As a percentage of instructions executed?
14. On a given programming project, one programmer has written

    ```
    IF (NOT Found) AND (Left < Right)
    THEN ...
    ```

    Another programmer has written

    ```
    IF NOT Found
    THEN
      IF Left < Right
      THEN ...
    ```

    Assume that the same statements are in both THEN clauses indicated by ellipses. Which program is unaffected by whether the compiler uses full or partial evaluation? The compiler might generate the same instructions for both programs in one mode (full or partial evaluation), but it must generate different instructions for each program in the other mode. For which mode could the instructions be the same? Explain your answers.

## KEY POINTS

- Shift operations move bits within a register or word of memory. The type of shift determines what happens to bits shifted out and what fills vacated positions.
- In a logical shift, bits shifted out are lost and zeros fill the vacated positions.
- In an arithmetic shift, the sign bit is not changed. Bits shifted out are lost. In two's complement, zeros fill positions vacated during left shifts; copies of the sign bit fill vacated positions during right shifts.
- A left arithmetic shift has the same effect as a multiplication by a power of 2; it can set the overflow flag if any significant bits are lost during the shift.
- A right arithmetic shift of a positive number has the same effect as a division by a power of 2; a right arithmetic shift of a negative number has an effect different from division by a power of 2 using an integer division instruction.
- In a rotate, the bits shifted out of one end of the register or memory location fill vacated positions on the other end. Rotates are also called circular shifts.
- The carry bit is sometimes included in the shift and rotate operations.
- Each shift instruction must specify the type of shift, the operand to shift, the direction, and the shift count.
- A Boolean value is represented by a single bit, 0 for False and 1 for True; an entire word or byte is often used.
- Boolean values are copied and moved using the same instructions that copy and move integers.
- Boolean variables can be assigned the value of an expression using a selection structure, with the expression controlling the selection, and statements that copy constants as the two clauses; Boolean variables can also be assigned by special instructions that inspect the flags register.

- The Boolean operations AND, OR, XOR, and NOT operate on every bit in a register or memory location.
- AND yields true in every position of its result where the corresponding bits of both operands are true; it is useful for clearing selected bits of a register.
- OR yields true in every position of its result where the corresponding bit of either operand is true; it is useful for setting selected bits of a register.
- XOR yields true in every position of its result where the corresponding bits of either but not both of its operands are true; it is useful for complementing selected bits of a register.
- NOT yields the complement of every bit of its operand.
- The instructions that perform Boolean operations are similar to those that perform arithmetic operations with the same number of operands.
- Boolean expressions in some high-level languages are always fully evaluated even though their value can be determined by evaluating only a part of the expression. In others, only as much of a Boolean expression as is necessary to determine its value is evaluated.

## PC SYSTEM SUMMARY

- The shift instructions of the 8086 can operate on data in a register or in memory.
- The shift count can be a constant 1 or the number in the CL register. On 80286 and newer processors, the shift count can also be an immediate constant.
- The destination operand of a shift instruction is the register or location to be shifted.
- The last bit shifted out of a register is saved in CF. CF may also be included in a rotate.
- Many compilers for the 8086 code Boolean values using the least significant bit of a byte set to 1 for true or cleared to 0 for false. Some compilers use two or four bytes, ignoring the leading bytes.
- The Boolean and (and test), xor, and or instructions are similar to the integer add instruction; the Boolean not instruction is similar to the integer neg instruction.
- The 80386 and later processors have set instructions that write the Boolean value True or False to a register based on the flags.

Instructions presented in this chapter:

Shift and Rotate:
```
shl    shift left
shr    shift right
sal    shift arithmetic left
sar    shift arithmetic right
rol    rotate left
ror    rotate right
rcl    rotate with carry left
rcr    rotate with carry right
```

Logical:

| | |
|---|---|
| and | logical and |
| or | inclusive or |
| xor | exclusive or |
| not | logical complement |
| test | test bit pattern |

Move flags:

| | |
|---|---|
| lahf | load ah with flags |
| sahf | store ah into flags |

# Subprograms I

- **Addresses and Indirection**
- **Scope of Identifiers**
- **Transfer of Control**
- **Arguments and Parameters**
- **The Stack**
- **Saving the Caller's State**

A useful strategy for solving a large problem is to partition it into smaller subproblems, solve each of the subproblems, and combine the solutions to solve the original problem. When following this strategy in programming, the solutions to the subproblems are written as procedures, subroutines, and functions. These are collectively referred to as subprograms.

There are many issues that arise when implementing subprograms. We must be able to transfer control to the subprogram and to return to the next instruction in the program. We must be able to share data between a main program and a subprogram, using parameters as well as global data. And we must be able to save the state of a program when invoking a subprogram so that it can resume execution properly when control returns to it.

This chapter introduces the indirect addresses that are used in accessing arguments and returning from a subprogram. It discusses scope, including internal and external subprograms; local and global data; subprogram linkage; parameter-passing conventions; and procedures for saving the caller's state. It also examines the stack segment and its role in all aspects of subprogram implementation.

## 7.1 ADDRESSES AND INDIRECTION

In assembly-language instructions, operands in memory are referred to using symbolic names. During the assembly process, the operand names are translated into addresses coded in binary as displacements. When an instruction with an operand in memory is executed, the address of the operand must be computed before it can be fetched. The address computed from the information in an instruction is called the **effective address**. The calculation varies according to the addressing mode used.

### Direct Memory Addresses

A direct memory address is one for which the effective address can be calculated from the information in the operand field of the instruction and a segment register. To compute an effective address for an operand in memory specified with direct addressing on the 8086, the processor extracts the displacement from the operand field and adds it to the result obtained by shifting the segment register four bits to the left.

Once the effective address has been computed, the operand is fetched. The processor does this by writing the effective address to the address bus and the control signals to the control lines. The memory management unit then uses the address on the address bus to fetch the operand, and places it on the data bus. Finally, the processor reads the operand value from the data bus.

## Indirect Memory Addresses

With indirect addressing, the address computed from the displacement field of the instruction and the segment register does not give the effective address of the actual operand. Instead, the calculation gives the address in memory that, in turn, contains the address of the operand.

The intermediate location—the one whose address is coded in the instruction—is called an **indirect pointer.** An indirect pointer may contain a displacement relative to a segment register, or it may contain a complete direct address. Indirect pointers in some machines (not the 8086) contain other information as well. Some have a field that indicates another level of indirection so that it can also refer to another indirect pointer. If the indirect pointer specifies indirection, we say that there are two levels of indirection. Some computers restrict indirection to one level; others allow arbitrarily long sequences of indirect pointers to be chained together.

Following a series of indirect pointers is not as confusing as it first appears. Figure 7.1 illustrates direct addressing and one and two levels of indirect addressing. In the figure, indirect operands are indicated by enclosing them in brackets. Indirect pointers are indicated by a short arrow pointing to an identifier used as a label on another memory location. The mov instruction of the 8086 does not use indirect pointers as shown in these examples; rather, mov is used as a well-understood prototype instruction to illustrate the concept of indirection. Specific features of the 8086 will be discussed later.

We have seen the role of the address and data buses in fetching an operand using direct addressing. Now consider the example of Figure 7.1*b* with one level of indirection. The steps in fetching the operand with one level of indirection are

1. The processor computes an address from the displacement in the operand field of the instruction and the segment register. It writes this address on the address bus, and signals the memory management unit to fetch.

    address bus = address of IPtr

2. The memory management unit fetches the contents of the location specified on the address bus and writes it on the data bus.

    data bus = address of Value

3. The processor reads the indirect pointer from the data bus and writes it on the address bus. It again signals the memory management unit to fetch.

    address bus = address of Value

## 7.1 Addresses and Indirection

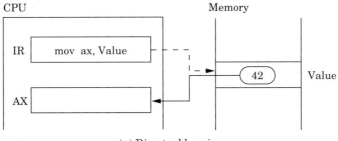

(a) Direct addressing

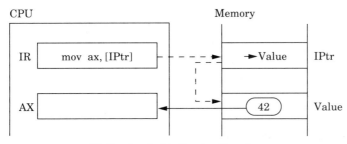

(b) One level of indirect addressing

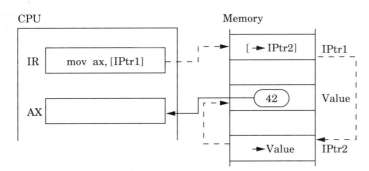

(c) Two levels of indirect addressing

**Figure 7.1** Direct and Indirect Addressing

4. The memory management unit fetches the contents of the location specified on the address bus and writes it on the data bus.

$$\text{data bus} = 42$$

5. The processor reads the value from the data bus into the AX register.

The example of Figure 7.1c, with two levels of indirection, proceeds similarly with one more cycle of fetching and resolving indirection. The steps in fetching the operand in this case are

1. The processor computes an address from the displacement in the operand field of the instruction and the segment register. It writes this address on the address bus and signals the memory management unit to fetch.

$$\text{address bus} = \text{address of IPtr1}$$

2. The memory management unit fetches the contents of the location specified on the address bus and writes it on the data bus.

    data bus = address of `IPtr2`

3. The processor reads the indirect pointer from the data bus and writes it on the address bus. It again signals the memory management unit to fetch.

    address bus = address of `IPtr2`

4. The memory management unit fetches the contents of the location specified on the address bus and writes it on the address bus.

    data bus = address of `Value`

5. The processor reads the indirect pointer from the data bus and writes it on the address bus. Once again it signals the memory management unit to fetch.

    address bus = address of `Value`

6. The memory management unit fetches the contents of the location specified on the address bus and writes it on the data bus.

    data bus = 42

7. The processor reads the value from the data bus into the AX register.

With more levels of indirection, steps 3 and 4 would be repeated for each additional level.

The 8086 restricts indirection to one level; it does not provide any means for an indirect pointer to specify another level of indirection. It is up to the programmer to follow a series of indirect pointers when more than one level of indirection is desired.

## Register-Direct Operands

Operands can also be in registers. The name of the register is used in the operand field to specify its contents as an operand. In the examples of direct and indirect memory operands just discussed, the AX register was used as a register-direct operand.

## Register-Indirect Operands

Indirect pointers can also be in registers. When fetching an operand using register-indirect addressing, the processor reads the contents of the specified register and writes it to the address bus. The memory management unit then fetches the operand value from memory and writes it to the data bus.

The 8086 uses register-indirect addressing. This requires the programmer to write an extra instruction for each level of indirection, but allows an arbitrary number of levels of indirection (although more than two would be rare). A register operand is enclosed in square brackets to indicate that it is an indirect pointer.

To illustrate, instructions are provided for the three examples of Figure 7.1. The first example, shown in Figure 7.1a, uses familiar direct addressing:

```
mov     ax, Value
```

## 7.1 Addresses and Indirection

The second example, shown in Figure 7.1*b*, can be implemented as

```
    mov     bx, IPtr
    mov     ax, [bx]
```

Note the brackets around the register, which indicate its use as an indirect pointer. The second instruction copies the contents of the location whose address is in BX into the AX register. Compare this to

```
    mov     ax, bx
```

which copies the contents of BX to AX.

The BX register is the only general register that can be used in register-indirect addressing. The B in BX stands for "base," and registers used with register-indirect addressing are often called base registers.

The third example, shown in Figure 7.1*c*, can be implemented as

```
    mov     bx, IPtr1
    mov     bx, [bx]
    mov     ax, [bx]
```

The first instruction copies the contents of `IPtr1`, which is the address of `IPtr2`, into BX. The second instruction copies the contents of `IPtr2`, which is the address of `Value`, into BX. Note that it copies the contents of the location referred to by the BX register into the BX register. Without the brackets,

```
    mov     bx, bx
```

copies the contents of BX into itself, accomplishing nothing. The third instruction in the sequence copies the contents of `Value` into the AX register.

Having established how to use an address in a register, consider how the pointers `IPtr`, `IPtr1`, and `IPtr2` in Figure 7.1 get their values. There are two ways to accomplish this, one at assembly time and one at execution time. Setting up pointers at assembly time is quite simple from a programmer's point of view. The declarations

```
_DATA SEGMENT   word public 'data'
  Value     dw      42
  IPtr      dw      Value
  IPtr1     dw      IPtr2
  IPtr2     dw      Value
```

establish everything shown in memory in Figure 7.1. Using the name of another object, such as `Value`, in the operand field of the `dw` directive causes the assembler to build the displacement of that object as the value of the operand. Hence, `IPtr` refers to a word that contains the displacement of `Value` in the _DATA segment. Similarly, `IPtr1` refers to a word that contains the displacement of `IPtr2` in _DATA; `IPtr2` refers to a word that contains the displacement of `Value` in _DATA . It does not matter whether `IPtr1` is defined before or after `IPtr2` .

The second method of setting up the pointers, at run time, uses the `offset` operator. We have been using the `offset` operator to set up the DS register, and with a parameter of the `PutStr` procedure. Offsets are actually computed during assembly and treated as constants. For example, for the instruction

```
    mov     bx, offset PromptMsg
```

the assembler determines the offset of PromptMsg from the segment it is in and builds the instruction as a mov instruction with BX as the destination operand and the offset as an immediate (constant) source operand.

The names in Figure 7.1 can be declared as

```
_DATA SEGMENT  word public 'data'
    Value       dw          42
    IPtr        dw          ?
    IPtr1       dw          ?
    IPtr2       dw          ?
```

Here, the pointers are not set up by the assembler. The offsets can be loaded during execution. To load IPtr, we use the sequence

```
    mov     bx, offset Value
    mov     IPtr, bx
```

To load IPtr1 and IPtr2 without using Iptr, we use the sequence

```
    mov     bx, offset Value
    mov     IPtr2, bx
    mov     bx, offset IPtr2
    mov     IPtr1, bx
```

Generally, we would probably have the assembler set up the pointers in a program as simple as that implied here. However, this method will be used to assign values to pointers during execution.

## Uses for Indirect Addressing

Indirect addressing is needed when the location of an operand cannot be fixed during program translation. The location of an operand of some instructions may vary during program execution, or may not be fixed until program execution begins. The latter occurs with dynamic allocation of memory, a topic that will be deferred until much later in this text. The former situation, where an operand location may vary, occurs frequently with subprograms.

Consider the input and output routines. Each is invoked by a call instruction, and must return control to the instruction following the call that invokes it. The location of the instruction following the call cannot be fixed, as there may be more than one invocation of a subprogram and each will have a different return address. The return address is specified using indirection, with an appropriate pointer set up before or by a call instruction.

Another use of indirect addressing is to pass arguments to a subprogram. The input and output routines provided with this text pass arguments using registers (for simplicity), but this is not the most general technique. Even using registers, however, a form of indirection has been used with PutStr: We pass PutStr an offset, which is merely an indirect pointer. The PutStr routine accesses the string one character at a time, using BX as a register-indirect operand.

## 7.2 Scope of Identifiers

Indirect addressing with subprograms is also used to refer to external symbols, whether they are subprogram entry points or global data. During program translation, the assembler (or compiler) generally does not have the locations of external references. It usually builds indirect references to external symbols and provides information for the linker (or loader) to resolve the references. Some translators make all external references refer to a pointer that the linker will later fill in; others require the linker to fill in all such operand fields.

Finally, one other application of indirection related to subprograms involves interrupts. The `int` instruction has been used to invoke a DOS function that terminates the program. This DOS function is a special kind of subprogram, called an interrupt handler, provided as part of the operating system. To allow revision of the operating system without rewriting every application program, the interrupt number (21h, named DosFunc in the programs) refers to an indirect pointer to the handler. If an interrupt handler is rewritten and the other handlers are moved around in memory, only the values of the indirect pointers need to be changed—not every reference to the handlers.

### EXERCISES 7.1

1. An indirect pointer on the 8086 may contain only an offset, or a segment number as well as an offset. What other information might an indirect pointer (on other systems) include? How might it be useful?
2. One way to implement indirect pointers in memory is to include in each pointer a bit that indicates that the operand is a pointer rather than data. What problem(s) might this present?
3. One way to implement multiple levels of indirection in memory is to include in each pointer a bit that indicates whether it is the final pointer to the data, or a pointer to yet another pointer. What problem(s) might this present?
4. Another way to implement multiple levels of indirection in memory is to include a small field in the instruction that indicates the number of levels of indirect addressing to use (the field would be 0 for direct addressing, 1 for one level of indirection, and so on). What problem(s) might this present?
5. What effect would adding 1 to `IPtr` in Figure 7.1b have on the sequence of instructions that implement it using the BX register on the 8086?
6. What effect would adding 1 to `IPtr1` in Figure 7.1c have on the sequence of instructions that implement it using the BX register on the 8086? What about adding 1 to `IPtr2` instead?

## 7.2 SCOPE OF IDENTIFIERS

A subprogram is a program that is invoked by another program to perform some task for it. The program that invokes the subprogram is referred to as the calling program or simply the caller. The subprogram is the called program or simply the callee. Since subprograms can call other subprograms and possibly themselves, the term calling program is also used to refer to a subprogram that invokes another subprogram. When a subprogram finishes whatever processing it does and gives control back to the calling program, it is said to return.

## Internal and External Subprograms

With most assemblers, the main program (if present) and any subprograms that appear in the same file before the END directive make up a **module**. Note that a file can contain more than one module as long as each module has a separate END directive and would be syntactically correct if it were the only module in the file.

An **internal subprogram** is one that is assembled as part of the same module as the calling program. The assembler translates all programs in a module together. All symbols in every program and subprogram in a module are defined and available everywhere in the module.

For example, consider the segment declarations in Program 7.1. (The jumps between the main program and the subprogram will be examined later, so do not be concerned with these details yet.) On first inspection, it appears that Program 7.1 has five segments: _STACK, _DATA, and _TEXT in the main program and _DATA and _TEXT in the subprogram. Actually, _DATA in the subprogram is a continuation of _DATA in the main program, and _TEXT in the subprogram is a continuation of _TEXT in the main program. Each unique segment must have a unique name. When a segment declaration is repeated with the same name, the alignment, combine type, and class names must agree with those in the first definition. If these fields are omitted, the assembler provides them. Even though the main program's data and code are declared separately from the subprogram's data and code, these are combined to form one data segment and one code segment. The declarations serve only to document our intentions, not to force the separation into distinct segments.

**Program 7.1**

```
; Program 7.1        SubProg1.ASM
; Illustrate a subprogram call that stores the offset
;   of the return address in the subprogram's data area.

; DOS function and status parameters
   DosFunc      equ        21h
   ExitToDos    equ        4Ch
   NoErrors     equ        00h

DOSSEG

_STACK SEGMENT para stack 'stack'
            dw         100h dup (?)
_STACK ENDS

_DATA SEGMENT word public 'data'
   MainMsg     db         "In main program ..."
   MainLen     dw         19
_DATA ENDS

_TEXT SEGMENT word public 'code'
       assume    cs: _TEXT
       extrn     PutStr: PROC, PutCrLf: PROC
       extrn     PutDec: PROC
```

## 7.2 Scope of Identifiers

**Program 7.1 (continued)**

```
Main:

; set up ds register to point to _DATA
    mov     ax, seg _DATA
    mov     ds, ax
    assume  ds: _DATA

; print ("In main program ...")
    mov     cx, MainLen
    mov     bx, offset MainMsg
    call    PutStr
    call    PutCrLf

; call subprogram
    mov     ax, offset Return1
    mov     RetPtr, ax
    jmp     Subprogram

; print ("In main program ...")
Return1:
    mov     cx, MainLen
    mov     bx, offset MainMsg
    call    PutStr
    call    PutCrLf

; call subprogram again
    mov     ax, offset Return2
    mov     RetPtr, ax
    jmp     SubProgram

; print ("In main program ...")
Return2:
    mov     cx, MainLen
    mov     bx, offset MainMsg
    call    PutStr
    call    PutCrLf

; exit to DOS
    mov     ah, ExitToDos
    mov     al, NoErrors
    int     DosFunc

_TEXT ENDS

;;;;;;;;;;;;;;;;;;;;;;; SubProgram ;;;;;;;;;;;;;;;;;;;;;;
; Print the offset of the return address.

_DATA SEGMENT
    RetPtr      dw      ?       ;offset of return address
    SubProgMsg  db      "Offset of return address is: "
    SubProgLen  dw      29
_DATA ENDS
```

**Program 7.1 (continued)**

```
_TEXT SEGMENT

SubProgram:

; print ("Offset of return address is: ", RetPtr)
     mov      cx, SubProgLen
     mov      bx, offset SubProgMsg
     call     PutStr
     mov      ax, RetPtr
     call     PutDec
     call     PutCrLf

; return to main program
     jmp      RetPtr
_TEXT ENDS
END    Main
```

An **external subprogram** is one that is defined in a module other than the one that contains the calling program. Symbols defined in one program can be made available to an external program by using appropriate assembler directives in both programs; otherwise, symbols are not available outside the module in which they are defined.

## Local and Global Data

All data defined in a module are available to every program and subprogram in that module. That is, to the programs in the module they are **global data**. Each symbol defined in a module can be defined only once. Each memory cell used for data has a name, and that name is unique within the module. Each label on an instruction must be unique within the module. The same symbol cannot be used for a name and a label in the same module. References to a symbol by different programs within the module are necessarily to the same symbol. For example, in Program 7.1 the variable `RetPtr` is defined in the data included in the subprogram, yet the main program moves the contents of AX into `RetPtr` just before each jump to the subprogram. This illustrates the global nature of data declarations in a module.

The use of global data makes sharing values between programs in a module easy. However, this sharing is not always a benefit. Consider a program that uses several locations for temporary, intermediate results. If a calculation in a subprogram in the same module uses the same temporary location for an intermediate result that the invoking program uses, there could be conflict between the two programs. If all intermediate results in a subprogram are local to that subprogram, no such conflict will arise.

Modern software design methods warn against using global references. The problems that arise from side effects and their impact on program maintenance far outweigh the convenience of such references. There are occasional uses for global data that are justifiable; however, they are the exception rather than the rule.

When each subprogram is defined in a separate module, the data defined in each program are referred to as **local data** for that program. With this arrangement, there is no chance of two programs accessing the same data item or jumping to the same location simply by using the same symbol. Segments from separate modules may be combined by the linker, but this does not make the symbols used in each module global. The symbols used for names and labels within the segments are known only within the modules that define them.

## EXERCISES 7.2

1. Examine the scope rules for your favorite high-level language. Does it allow global references to all data in a module? What mechanisms does it use to restrict global access to data in the module?
2. Does your favorite high-level language support separately compiled subprograms? What about external references to data? How, other than through argument lists, can a program in your language refer to data in a subprogram, or vice versa?
3. In Program 7.1, could we store the offset of the return address in the main (calling) program's data instead of the subprogram's data? How would that change the program?

## 7.3 TRANSFER OF CONTROL

One of the first problems to consider when implementing subprograms is arranging for each subprogram to return control to the program that invokes it. Each invocation of a subprogram can be from a different program, or from different places in the same program. Each call transfers control to the same instruction—the first one of the subprogram. Each return has to transfer control back to the instruction after the one that invoked the subprogram. This is potentially a different instruction for each call.

### Saving the Return Address

One way to arrange this return is to label the return point and save its address as an indirect pointer. This can be written as shown earlier in Program 7.1.

The first invocation of the subprogram uses the instructions

```
        mov     ax, offset Return1
        mov     RetPtr, ax
        jmp     SubProgram
Return1:
```

to store the offset of the label on the instruction that follows the jump into the subprogram's data area in a location named `RetPtr`. The `jmp` instruction then transfers control to the first instruction of the subprogram. Later, the subprogram returns by means of the instruction

```
        jmp     RetPtr
```

Note that this jump instruction, with a name (not a label) in the operand field, specifies an indirect jump to the location specified in the corresponding word. That is, since `RetPtr` is a name and not a label, the instruction does not transfer control to the data at `RetPtr`, but to the instruction whose address is stored in `RetPtr`.

The second invocation of the subprogram works the same, except that the offset of `Return2` is stored in `RetPtr`. Storing different offsets in `RetPtr` gives the subprogram the capability to return to a different instruction each time it is invoked.

To help reinforce this idea, the subprogram in Program 7.1 prints the offset stored in `RetPtr`. It prints 43 the first time it is invoked and 65 the second. These are the displacements, in bytes, of the return points from the start of the code segment. (Note that 43 and 65 are obtained when the program is assembled with MASM 5.1 and linked with a Microsoft linker. When assembled and linked with MASM 6.0, which optimizes the jump instructions (discussed later), the subprogram prints 42 and 63. When Borland's Turbo Assembler and TLINK are used, the subprogram prints 27 and 49, both of which are 16 less than the MASM 5.1 values; TLINK does not write the first instruction in the executable file at displacement 0010h as the Microsoft linkers do.)

The method Program 7.1 uses to save the return pointer works only with an internal subprogram. The instructions that save the return address need to have access to the word of memory where the subprogram expects this address, so it must be in the same module or made available as an external reference. The fewer symbols a subprogram has to make known externally, the less chance for unwanted side effects to occur. The name of the subprogram, and hence the address of the first instruction of the subprogram, must be known externally for the `jmp` instruction to transfer control to it. The issues involved when the name of a subprogram is made an external symbol will be considered shortly. For now, the discussion will focus on fixing the subprogram return mechanism so that the address of the return pointer need not be made external as well.

When a register in which to keep the return address can be spared, it is not necessary to have the calling program save it in the subprogram's data area. The subprogram can use the return pointer that is in the register. This avoids the need to make the subprogram's data area accessible to the calling program.

Program 7.1 can be modified to use the AX register for the return address by simply removing the two

```
        mov     RetPtr, ax
```

instructions in the main program before the `jmp`s to the subprogram, deleting

```
        RetPtr  dw      ?
```

from the subprogram, and rewriting the last instruction of the subprogram as

```
        jmp     ax
```

Note that this `jmp` instruction transfers control not to the AX register, but to the instruction whose address is in the AX register. Earlier, it was stated that BX is the only general register that can be used for register-indirect addressing. That's true in general, but the 8086 allows any of the general registers to be used as an indirect pointer with the unconditional `jmp` instruction.

The calling program and subprogram must agree on which register to use for the offset of the return address. It is also important not to change the contents of that register within the subprogram. In the proposed modification of Program 7.1, AX was used for the offset of the return address. If BX had been used instead, there would have been a conflict, since BX is needed for the argument to `PutStr`. The conflict would be solved by saving the offset of the return address in `RetPtr`, using the instruction

```
        mov     RetPtr, bx
```

## 7.3 Transfer of Control

immediately upon entry to the subprogram. The return would then be as in the original version of Program 7.1.

## Location Counter Symbol

During translation, the assembler keeps track of the displacement of the next available byte in the current segment, in what is called the **location counter**. Assume that the location counter is 100 when the assembler encounters the directives

```
PromptMsg    db         "Enter X: "
PromptLen    dw         9
```

The assembler associates the displacement 100 with the name PromptMsg, and writes the string into the nine bytes of memory at displacements 100 through 108 in the current segment. It then advances the location counter to 109, associates that displacement with the symbol PromptLen, and writes the internal representation of 9 into the word that starts at displacement 109 in the current segment.

The assembler allows us to access the location counter in our programs. The dollar sign, when used in an operand expression, represents the current value of the location counter. Continuing the preceding example, if we write

```
PromptLen    dw         $
```

it would have the same result as writing

```
PromptLen    dw         109
```

The actual value would change if we added or deleted other declarations before PromptLen. But this is not what we intend as a value for PromptLen. The assembler has already determined that the offset of PromptMsg is 100. So the statement

```
PromptLen    dw         $ - PromptMsg
```

causes the assembler to compute 109 − 100, or 9, for the operand value. This achieves the desired result, as long as PromptLen immediately follows PromptMsg. We will use this in our programs from now on, rather than count the characters.

Now back to the problem of calling a subprogram. The instructions we want to use to copy the return address into the AX register and transfer control are

```
     mov    ax, offset Return1
     jmp    SubProg
Return1:
```

The mov instruction is assembled with the offset coded as a two-byte immediate operand, which makes this instruction three bytes long. The jmp instruction, assuming the default near jump with a 16-bit offset, is also three bytes long. See Figure 7.2.

The Return1 label can be eliminated and the mov instruction rewritten as

```
     mov    ax, offset $ + 6
```

The assembler computes the offset of the instruction following the jmp to the subprogram, based on the determination that the mov and jmp instructions occupy six bytes of memory.

## 228  Chapter 7  Subprograms I

```
Location
counter:
   $     | opcode of mov      |   mov    ax, offset Return1
   $+1   | offset             |
         |   of               |
   $+2   | Return1            |
   $+3   | opcode of jmp      |   jmp    SubProgram
   $+4   | displacement       |
         |   of               |
   $+5   | SubProgram         |
                                  Return1:
   $+6   | opcode ...         |     (next instruction)
```

**Figure 7.2**  Offsets Relative to Location Counter During Translation of mov Instruction

It is important, however, not to put any other instructions between this mov and the jmp to the subprogram, as that will change distance between the mov instruction that saves the offset of the return address in AX and the actual return address.

Recall that the output of Program 7.1 varies with the assembler and linker used. This can now be explained. MASM 5.1 and TASM 2.0 both assume that the jmp instruction will have a two-byte displacement initially; at some point, they change the instruction to 1 with only a one-byte displacement and replace the second byte reserved for the displacement with a one-byte filler instruction. When MASM 6.0 shortens the jmp instruction, it adjusts all of the references that follow it in the program by 1 rather than insert the filler instruction. This explains why the first return address is 1 less and the second is 2 less, with MASM 6.0.

## The ptr Operator

If we depend on the jmp instruction to be a particular size, we must ensure that it is. To do this, we introduce an operator, ptr, that can be used in operand expressions. ptr forces the assembler to use a two-byte displacement in the jmp instruction when written

```
    jmp     near ptr SubProgram
```

(Actually, some assemblers still reduce the instruction to use a one-byte displacement and supply a one-byte filler instruction; the result is three bytes of instructions.) The next few programs in this chapter will adopt this convention. It is shown in Program 7.2.

## Program 7.2

```
; Program 7.2        SubProg2.ASM
; Illustrate a subprogram call that saves the offset
;   of the return address in ax.

; DOS function and status parameters
    DosFunc     equ     21h
    ExitToDos   equ     4Ch
    NoErrors    equ     00h
```

### 7.3 Transfer of Control

**Program 7.2 (continued)**
```
        DOSSEG

        _STACK SEGMENT para stack 'stack'
                    dw      100h dup (?)
        _STACK ENDS

        _DATA SEGMENT word public 'data'
          MainMsg      db      "In main program ..."
          MainLen      dw      $ - MainMsg
        _DATA ENDS

        _TEXT SEGMENT word public 'code'
            assume  cs: _TEXT
            extrn   PutStr: PROC, PutCrLf: PROC
            extrn   PutDec: PROC

Main:

        ; set up ds register to point to _DATA
            mov     ax, seg _DATA
            mov     ds, ax
            assume  ds: _DATA

        ; print ("In main program ...")
            mov     cx, MainLen
            mov     bx, offset MainMsg
            call    PutStr
            call    PutCrLf

        ; call subprogram
            mov     ax, offset $ + 6
            jmp     near ptr SubProgram

        ; print ("In main program ...")
            mov     cx, MainLen
            mov     bx, offset MainMsg
            call    PutStr
            call    PutCrLf

        ; call subprogram again
            mov     ax, offset $ + 6
            jmp     near ptr SubProgram

        ; print ("In main program ...")
            mov     cx, MainLen
            mov     bx, offset MainMsg
            call    PutStr
            call    PutCrLf

        ; exit to DOS
            mov     ah, ExitToDos
            mov     al, NoErrors
            int     DosFunc

        _TEXT ENDS
```

**Program 7.2 (continued)**

```
;;;;;;;;;;;;;;;;;;;;;;;;;; SubProgram ;;;;;;;;;;;;;;;;;;;;;;;;;;
; Print the offset of the return address.

_DATA SEGMENT
    SubProgMsg  db      "Offset of return address is: "
    SubProgLen  dw      $ - SubProgMsg
_DATA ENDS

_TEXT SEGMENT

SubProgram:

; print ("Offset of return address is: ", ax)
    mov     cx, SubProgLen
    mov     bx, offset SubProgMsg
    call    PutStr
    call    PutDec
    call    PutCrLf

; return to main program
    jmp     ax

_TEXT ENDS
END     Main
```

ptr can also be used with other values to force a particular data size. For example, to access the first two characters of PromptMsg as a word, we could use

    mov     ax, word ptr PromptMsg

This overrides the size specified by the db directive. Other uses for ptr will be considered later in the discussion of arguments.

The method of managing the return address shown in Program 7.2 is not recommended for production programs. It will be used only in the next few programs, until the complete subprogram call, return, and argument-passing mechanisms have been presented.

## EXERCISES 7.3

1. What would happen if we insert the following instructions in the beginning of the subprogram in Program 7.2? (Each is inserted separately.)
   (a) sub ax, 6
   (b) add ax, 1
   (c) sub ax, 3
   (d) mov ax, 16  (Microsoft linkers only)
   (e) mov ax, 0   (TLINK only)

▶2. Write a subprogram that uses PutCrLF and PutStr to terminate a paragraph of text and indent the next paragraph. Write a main program that prints a few messages, calling the subprogram as appropriate to format the output as paragraphs.

### 7.4 Arguments and Parameters

▶3. Write a program with two subprograms. The main program should print a message and invoke the first subprogram. The first subprogram should print a message and invoke the second subprogram. The second subprogram should print a message and return to the first. The first should then print another (different) message and return to the main program.

4. Is it possible to write a subprogram that calls another so that, when the second subprogram returns, it returns directly to the program that invoked the first subprogram (rather than returning to the first subprogram)? If so, write such a program. If not, explain carefully why not.

## 7.4 ARGUMENTS AND PARAMETERS

A subprogram performs some operation for the benefit of the program that calls it. In a very few cases, the operation is totally independent of the data in the calling program; an example of such a subprogram is one that advances a printer to a new page. More commonly, however, the subprogram accesses data provided by the calling program.

One way to share data between a program and a subprogram that it calls is to place that data in a global data area. This is easy to do with internal subprograms. Data can also be shared if they are placed in an externally defined shared data area, such as FORTRAN's COMMON block.

Another way that a program can share data with a subprogram is to pass that data as **arguments**. The subprogram defines **parameters** to access the arguments passed to it. In some programming languages and texts, the terms "actual arguments" and "dummy arguments," or "actual parameters" and "formal parameters," or some other variations, are used for what are defined here as "arguments" and "parameters" respectively.

### Types of Arguments

An argument may be passed to a subprogram in several ways. The methods most commonly used today pass the value of the argument or the address of the argument. There are other methods, which are explored briefly in the exercises.

Passing the value of an argument is referred to as **call by value**. In this method, the value of each argument is copied to a corresponding parameter in the subprogram. The parameter is often called a **value parameter**.

Passing the address of the argument is referred to as **call by reference**. In this method, the address of each argument, rather than its value, is copied to the corresponding parameter in the subprogram. The parameter is often called a **variable parameter**. The subprogram can access the value stored in the calling program's data area using indirection. Any changes the subprogram makes this way changes the corresponding arguments.

### Transferring Arguments by Value

Although simply copying the value from one memory location to another within the same program module will work when the argument and parameter can be accessed globally, it is preferable to avoid the use of global data. If global data areas are not used to pass arguments, these methods should work with external subprograms as well as with internal ones.

If there is only one argument, it can be loaded into a register before invoking the subprogram. The subprogram could copy the value from the register to the location reserved for the parameter before doing any other processing. This is a simple and efficient way to pass one value. In Program 7.2, for example, the offset of the return address was passed by value in the AX register.

Functions, which by definition produce exactly one result, return the value of the result to the calling program in a register. In some cases, the function result is a string or another data structure, but it is returned as a pointer (in a register) to the string or structure. By convention in 8086 systems, functions return word results in AX, byte results in AL.

With more than one argument, it might be possible to load each argument value into a separate register before jumping to the subprogram. This is how arguments are passed to the input and output routines. The problem is, of course, that there are likely to be situations in which there are more arguments than registers. In general, not all of the registers are always available for passing arguments, and even if they are, it is still possible to have more arguments than registers. The number of arguments should not be restricted by the number of registers.

Since it is generally impossible to plan on using a separate register for each argument, this discussion will use only one register for passing arguments. That way, the conventions developed will work for any number of arguments.

## Argument lists

The key to passing more than one argument using just one register is to build a list of the argument values and pass the offset of the list in the register. To build the list of argument values, the calling program must define a block of memory for arguments and copy the values there in the order that the subprogram expects them. Just before the jump to the subprogram, the calling program must load the address of the argument list into the appropriate register.

Building the argument list is not too much work for the calling program. With a little planning, the memory locations that will be used for arguments might be defined in consecutive locations, in the order that the subprogram expects them. This will be shown in the next example. The BX register will be used for the offset of the argument list.

Once the argument list is in the calling program's data segment and the offset of the list is in the BX register, the calling program jumps to the subprogram. In the subprogram, BX is used as a base register with indirect addressing to move the argument values from the calling program's data area to the subprogram's data area. In the subprogram, the return address is saved locally in order to make AX available for other uses.

By way of illustration, Program 7.3 reads three values and passes them to a subprogram that prints them in reverse order. After reading the argument values into Arg1, Arg2, and

---

**Program 7.3**

```
; Program 7.3      RevPrint.ASM
; Read three numbers and pass them (by value) to a
;   subprogram that prints them in reverse order.
```

### 7.4 Arguments and Parameters

**Program 7.3 (continued)**

```
        ; DOS function and status parameters
          DosFunc    equ     21h
          ExitToDos  equ     4Ch
          NoErrors   equ     00h
        DOSSEG

        _STACK SEGMENT para stack 'stack'
                      dw      100h dup (?)
        _STACK ENDS

        _DATA SEGMENT word public 'data'
          Arg1        dw      ?       ;first number entered by user
          Arg2        dw      ?       ;second number entered by user
          Arg3        dw      ?       ;third number entered by user
          PromptMsg   db      "Enter 3 numbers: "
          PromptLen   dw      $ - PromptMsg
          EndMsg      db      " are your three numbers reversed."
          EndLen      dw      $ - EndMsg
        _DATA ENDS

        _TEXT SEGMENT word public 'code'
            assume  cs: _TEXT
            extrn   PutStr: PROC, PutCrLf: PROC
            extrn   GetDec: PROC, PutDec: PROC

        Main:

        ; set up ds register to point to _DATA
            mov     ax, SEG _DATA
            mov     ds, ax
            assume  ds: _DATA

        ; print ("Enter 3 numbers: ")
            mov     cx, PromptLen
            mov     bx, offset PromptMsg
            call    PutStr
            call    PutCrLf

        ; read (Arg1, Arg2, Arg3)
            call    GetDec
            mov     Arg1, ax
            call    GetDec
            mov     Arg2, ax
            call    GetDec
            mov     Arg3, ax

        ; RevPrint (Arg1, Arg2, Arg3)
            mov     bx, offset Arg1
            mov     ax, offset $ + 6
            jmp     near ptr RevPrint
```

## Program 7.3 (continued)

```
; print (" are your three numbers reversed.")
    mov     cx, EndLen
    mov     bx, offset EndMsg
    call    PutStr
    call    PutCrLf

; exit to DOS
    mov     ah, ExitToDos
    mov     al, NoErrors
    int     DosFunc

_TEXT ENDS

;;;;;;;;;;;;;; RevPrint (Parm1, Parm2, Parm3 ) ;;;;;;;;;;;;;;
; Print values of parameters in reverse order.

_DATA SEGMENT
  RetPtr        dw      ?       ;offset of return address
  Parm1         dw      ?       ;copy of first argument
  Parm2         dw      ?       ;copy of second argument
  Parm3         dw      ?       ;copy of third argument
_DATA ENDS

_TEXT SEGMENT

RevPrint:

; save return address
    mov     RetPtr, ax

; copy arguments into parameters
    mov     ax, [bx]        ;Parm1 := Arg1
    mov     Parm1, ax
    mov     ax, [bx+2]      ;Parm2 := Arg2
    mov     Parm2, ax
    mov     ax, [bx+4]      ;Parm3 := Arg3
    mov     Parm3, ax

; print (Parm3, Parm2, Parm1)
    mov     ax, Parm3
    call    PutDec
    mov     ax, Parm2
    call    PutDec
    mov     ax, Parm1
    call    PutDec

; return to calling program
    jmp     RetPtr

_TEXT ENDS
END     Main
```

## 7.4 Arguments and Parameters

Arg3, the calling program loads the offset of the list into the BX register, loads the offset of the instruction following the jmp into the AX register, and jumps to the subprogram using the instructions

```
; RevPrint (Arg1, Arg2, Arg3)
    mov     bx, offset Arg1
    mov     ax, offset $ + 6
    jmp     near ptr RevPrint
```

To copy the values of the arguments into the parameters, a series of mov instructions is needed. The first argument requires only the pair of instructions

```
    mov     ax, [bx]
    mov     Parm1, ax
```

For the second argument, it is necessary to add 2 to the offset of the first argument (the arguments are words). This can be done with the instructions

```
    add     bx, 2
    mov     ax, [bx]
    mov     Parm2, ax
```

Actually, it is not necessary to change the contents of BX to reach the second argument; we need only add 2 to the offset used in the mov instruction. This can be done directly in the operand field, as

```
    mov     ax, [bx+2]
```

To get the third argument, we need to add 4 to the offset of Arg1.

## Transferring Arguments by Reference

Now that we know how to pass the address of a list of values using call by value, let's modify the method to pass a list of addresses instead.

For the calling program, the only difference is that it is necessary to build a list of addresses rather than a list of values. This is done with a sequence of mov instructions that copies the offsets of the arguments to a list.

In the following example the list will be built during execution. To illustrate that passing the offset rather than the value allows the subprogram to change the value of an argument, Program 7.4 replaces each of its three arguments with the difference between the argument and the average. That is, if the values 12, 14, and 22 are passed to the subprogram, it should change them to $-4$ ($= 12 - 16$), $-2$ ($= 14 - 16$), and 6 ($= 22 - 16$), since 16 is the average of the three values.

### Program 7.4

```
; Program 7.4       DiffList.ASM
; Read three numbers and print the differences between
;    them and their average. Passes numbers by reference
;    to subprogram that computes average and replaces each
;    value with the difference between it and the average.
```

**Program 7.4 (continued)**

```
        ; DOS function and status parameters
        DosFunc     equ     21h
        ExitToDos   equ     4Ch
        NoErrors    equ     00h

        DOSSEG

        _STACK SEGMENT para stack 'stack'
                    dw      100h dup (?)
        _STACK ENDS

        _DATA SEGMENT word public 'data'
        V2          dw      ?               ;user's second value
        V1          dw      ?               ;user's first value
        ArgList     dw      3 dup (?)       ;offsets of arguments
        V3          dw      ?               ;user's third value
        PromptMsg   db      "Enter 3 numbers: "
        PromptLen   dw      $ - PromptMsg
        ResultMsg   db      "Differences are: "
        ResultLen   dw      $ - ResultMsg
        _DATA ENDS

        _TEXT SEGMENT word public 'code'
            assume  cs: _TEXT
            extrn   PutStr: PROC, PutCrLf: PROC
            extrn   GetDec: PROC, PutDec: PROC

Main:

        ; set up ds register to point to _DATA
            mov     ax, SEG _DATA
            mov     ds, ax
            assume  ds: _DATA

        ; print ("Enter 3 numbers: ")
            mov     cx, PromptLen
            mov     bx, offset PromptMsg
            call    PutStr
            call    PutCrLf

        ; read (V1, V2, V3)
            call    GetDec
            mov     V1, ax
            call    GetDec
            mov     V2, ax
            call    GetDec
            mov     V3, ax

        ; call DiffList (V1, V2, V3)
        ;   build list of argument offsets
                mov     ax, offset V1
                mov     ArgList, ax         ;ArgList := offset V1
                mov     ax, offset V2       ;ArgList+2 := offset V2
```

## 7.4 Arguments and Parameters

**Program 7.4 (continued)**

```
        mov     ArgList+2, ax
        mov     ax, offset V3           ;ArgList+4 := offset V3
        mov     ArgList+4, ax

;   invoke DiffList
        mov     bx, offset ArgList
        mov     ax, offset $ + 6
        jmp     near ptr DiffList

; print ("Differences are: ", V1, V2, V3)
        call    PutCrLf
        mov     cx, ResultLen
        mov     bx, offset ResultMsg
        call    PutStr
        mov     ax, V1
        call    PutDec
        mov     ax, V2
        call    PutDec
        mov     ax, V3
        call    PutDec
        call    PutCrLf

;exit to DOS
        mov     ah, ExitToDos
        mov     al, NoErrors
        int     DosFunc

_TEXT ENDS

;;;;;;;;;;;; DiffList (VAR Parm1, Parm2, Parm3) ;;;;;;;;;;;;
; Replaces each parameter with the difference between it and
;    the average of the three parameters.

_DATA SEGMENT
    RetPtr      dw      ?           ;offset of return address
    Parm1       dw      ?           ;offset of first argument
    Parm2       dw      ?           ;offset of second argument
    Parm3       dw      ?           ;offset of third argument
_DATA ENDS

_TEXT SEGMENT

DiffList:

; save return address
        mov     RetPtr, ax

; copy offsets of arguments into parameters
        mov     ax, [bx]            ;Parm1 := offset Arg1
        mov     Parm1, ax
        mov     ax, [bx+2]          ;Parm2 := offset Arg2
        mov     Parm2, ax
        mov     ax, [bx+4]          ;Parm3 := offset Arg3
        mov     Parm3, ax
```

**Program 7.4 (continued)**

```
; Average (in ax) := (Arg1 + Arg2 + Arg3) / 3
    mov     bx, Parm1
    mov     ax, [bx]            ;       Arg1
    mov     bx, Parm2
    add     ax, [bx]            ;       Arg1 + Arg2
    mov     bx, Parm3
    add     ax, [bx]            ;       Arg1 + Arg2 + Arg3
    cwd
    mov     bx, 3
    idiv    bx                  ;ax := (Arg1 + Arg2 + Arg3) / 3

; compute differences (argument - average)
    mov     bx, Parm1           ;Arg1 := Arg1 - average
    sub     [bx], ax
    mov     bx, Parm2           ;Arg2 := Arg2 - average
    sub     [bx], ax
    mov     bx, Parm3           ;Arg3 := Arg3 - average
    sub     [bx], ax

; return to calling program
    jmp     RetPtr

_TEXT ENDS
END     Main
```

---

The list of offsets is built in the block declared

```
ArgList     dw      3 dup (?)
```

This reserves a block of three words, with the name ArgList associated with the first byte. To help convince skeptics that there are no wonderful coincidences here, the three variables V1, V2, and V3 are declared out of order, with ArgList among them.

To build the argument list, we copy the offset of V1 into ArgList and ArgList+1; the offset of V2 into ArgList+2 and ArgList+3; and the offset of V3 into ArgList+4 and ArgList+5. The first of these offsets is copied by the instructions

```
    mov     ax, offset V1
    mov     ArgList, ax
```

The second offset is copied by the instructions

```
    mov     ax, offset V2
    mov     ArgList+2, ax
```

Note that a displacement can be added directly in the operand field of the mov instruction. The third offset is copied by a similar pair of instructions, using a displacement of 4 in the last mov instruction.

In the subprogram, the offsets must be copied from ArgList into the individual parameters. This can be done using the same sequence of instructions that was used in Program 7.3 to copy values.

### 7.4 Arguments and Parameters

To access the value of an argument, the subprogram copies the offset into the base register (BX) and then uses indirection. For example, to get the value of the first argument, the subprogram uses

```
mov     bx, Parm1
mov     ax, [bx]
```

Similar sequences, used with add and the other arguments, are used in computing the average, which is left in AX.

Once we have the average, we subtract it from all argument values. We again copy the offset into the BX register, and do the subtraction with indirection using instructions such as

```
sub     [bx], ax
```

The list of arguments can also be built by the assembler. We know, at least by name, which arguments to pass to a subprogram when we write the calling program. Rather than use a sequence of instructions to build a list of offsets during execution, we can have the assembler build it since the assembler determines the offsets. The argument list in the main program of Program 7.4 can be specified with declarations such as

```
ArgList     dw      V1
            dw      V2
            dw      V3
```

These tell the assembler to reserve a block of three words, with the label ArgList associated with the first of them. This block is initialized with the offsets of the three arguments. The calling program need only load the BX register with the offset of ArgList before jumping to the subprogram.

The subprogram does not change when the assembler builds the list of offsets. There is no difference between a list of offsets built by the assembler and a list of offsets built during program execution.

The methods used to save the return address, to return control to the calling program, and to pass arguments illustrate some of the tasks that must be performed when invoking a subprogram. The next section will demonstrate how use of the system stack simplifies these tasks.

## EXERCISES 7.4

1. In addition to call by value and call by reference, there is a less-favored technique known as *call by name*. For each argument that uses this method, the entry point of a routine (with no parameters) that computes the current value of the argument is passed. Research the intent and applications of call by name, as well as any advantages or disadvantages that it has.

▶2. Write a program that illustrates call by name (see Exercise 1).

3. Many languages allow passing a function name as an argument. For example, a subprogram that plots a curve on a graphics device might have as one argument the name of the function to plot. Thus,

```
PlotFunction (COS, -3.14, 3.14)
```

would plot the cosine function, whereas

```
PlotFunction (UserF, LowX, HighX)
```

would plot a user-written function named `UserF`. How can this type of argument be implemented?

4. How do the methods of passing arguments in Exercises 1 and 3 differ?
5. In some languages, all arguments are passed by reference. To use value parameters in such a language, it is necessary either to pass copies of the values by reference, or to make local copies of the values passed by reference. Should the copies be made by the calling program or the subprogram? Discuss the advantages and disadvantages of each.
6. What would happen if the argument-passing method used by the calling program were not the method expected by the subprogram? Consider arguments passed by value being treated as references, and arguments passed by reference being treated as values.
▶7. Modify Program 7.4 so that the assembler builds the argument list.
▶8. Write a subprogram that accepts three arguments passed by value. It is to print them in ascending order.
▶9. Write a subprogram that accepts two arguments passed by value. It is to print the absolute value of their difference.
▶10. Write a subprogram that accepts two arguments passed by reference. It is to swap their values if the second is smaller than the first.
▶11. Write a subprogram that accepts three arguments passed by reference. It is to use the subprogram from Exercise 10 to sort the three values. The main program should print the sorted values.

## 7.5 THE STACK

A stack can be useful when implementing some of the steps in calling a subprogram. Earlier, we saw instructions that perform arithmetic using the top elements of a stack. The present discussion will focus on other instructions that operate on a stack, and on how they are used in calling a subprogram.

Stacks can be implemented in many ways. A stack can be a single global structure maintained by the processor in a shared region of memory. It can be a structure local to only one user or one load module—the programs that are linked together and executed as a unit—and maintained by the operating system.

The stack can also be a user-defined data structure implemented in a program's local memory with little system support. Such a stack might be used in an application program, such as traversing a tree structure, and would usually be separate from the one used in implementing subprograms.

### The 8086 Stack Segment

The 8086 processor uses one of its four memory segments as a stack. The programs in this book have declared this stack segment with 256 (100h) words, but have not directly used it. It has, however, been used by the input and output routines.

The stack segment register, SS, contains the segment number of the stack segment. Its initial value is established by the loader when the program is copied into memory. The stack pointer register, SP, contains the offset of the last word pushed onto the stack; this word is also called the top of the stack. The initial value of the SP register is the number of bytes reserved for the stack. When the stack is empty, the SP register has its initial

## 7.5 The Stack

```
_STACK SEGMENT para stack 'stack'
           dw      100h dup (?)
_STACK ENDS
```

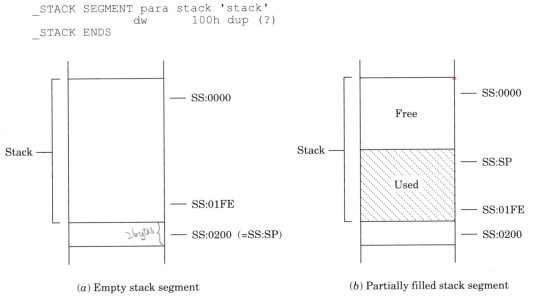

(a) Empty stack segment    (b) Partially filled stack segment

**Figure 7.3  Organization of 8086 Stack Segment**

value (see Figure 7.3a). With just one word on the stack, the SP register is two less than its initial value. As the stack grows, the stack pointer register is decremented (see Figure 7.3b). When the stack is full, the SP register is 0. As we draw memory with the addresses increasing down the page (the way they print in a dump), the stack appears to grow up the page even though the SP register value decreases as the stack expands.

### Operations on a Stack

The basic operations on a stack are to push data onto it and to pop data off of it. These operations will be examined now; operations on data other than the top element will be addressed later.

The stack is a block of words. The push and pop operations work with words of data. To work with a single byte, we must extend the byte to a word; to work with a doubleword, we must work with each word of it separately.

The push instruction moves the top of the stack by one word and enters a value into the new top of the stack.

| PUSH operand onto stack | |
|---|---|
| syntax: | push *source* |
| action: | (1) sp := sp − 2; |
|  | (2) [ss:sp] := *source* |
| flags: | ODITSZAPC unchanged |
| operands: | *reg16*    *mem16*    *segreg* |

The operand of the 8086 push instruction can be any of the 16-bit general-purpose or segment registers, or a word in memory. On later processors, the operand can also be an immediate value.

Note that the push instruction changes the value of the SP register before copying the value of the operand onto the stack. Thus, except when the stack is empty, the SP register points to the top element of the stack, not to the next available word. Also note that push subtracts 2 from the SP register because the source operand is always a word, and the stack grows toward smaller offsets.

If the stack is full when we try to push another word onto it, the SP register changes from 0000h to FFFEh and the processor attempts to copy the operand to the word of memory addressed by SS:SP. The effect is generally unpredictable.

To remove the value at the top from the stack we use a pop instruction:

**POP operand from stack**

| | |
|---|---|
| syntax: | pop *destination* |
| action: | (1) *destination* := [ss:sp]; |
| | (2) sp := sp + 2 |
| flags: | ODITSZAPC unchanged |
| operands: | *reg16*   *mem16*   *segreg* |

The operand of the pop instruction can be any 16-bit general-purpose or segment register, or a word in memory. Note that the pop instruction copies the value from the top of the stack into the destination before it adds 2 to the SP register.

## Transfer of Control

One use for the stack is to save the return address when a subprogram is invoked. We have been passing the offset of the return address to the subprogram in the AX register, in addition to having the subprogram save it in its own data area as necessary.

Consider a program that calls a subprogram, which calls another subprogram, which in turn calls a third, and so on. Each subprogram saves the address of the instruction it returns to in its own local memory. Note that we cannot just leave the return address in a register; the register will be changed when each subprogram calls the next one. These return addresses, although not stored in consecutive locations, form a kind of stack data structure. The first return address to be used at any time is the last one that was saved. This last-saved-first-used property of the return addresses parallels the definition of a stack as a last-in-first-out list.

Rather than have each subprogram save its return address in its own local memory, we can save all return addresses on the stack. Computers that use a stack for the return addresses have an instruction that saves the return address on the stack before jumping to the address given as the operand. On the 8086, the `call` instruction does just that.

We have used the `call` instruction to invoke the input and output routines. The operand can be the label of the subprogram entry point, or it can be a pointer in a register or memory that points to the entry point of a subprogram. The `call` instruction decrements the stack pointer, copies the instruction pointer to the top of the stack, and jumps to the subprogram.

Using the stack for the return address has the advantage that no register or local variable is needed for the return pointer during the jump. Another advantage, which we examine in more detail later, is that saving the return address on a stack satisfies one of the requirements for making a subprogram reentrant.

## 7.5 The Stack

**CALL subprogram**
- syntax: `call` *destination*
- action:
  (1) sp := sp − 2;
  (2) [ss:sp] := ip;
  (3) ip := *destination*
- flags: ODITSZAPC unchanged
- operands: *label   reg   mem*

When the return pointer is saved on the stack, another instruction is used to return to the calling program.

**RETurn to calling program**
- syntax: `ret`
- action:
  (1) ip := [ss:sp];
  (2) sp := sp + 2
- flags: ODITSZAPC unchanged

The `ret` instruction pops the return address off the top of the stack and copies it into the instruction pointer. There is another form of the `ret` instruction that takes an operand and modifies the stack more; we will discuss it later.

## Argument Transfer

In addition to the return pointers, the stack can be used to transfer arguments. Values of arguments to be passed by value, and addresses of arguments to be passed by reference, can be pushed onto the stack before calling the subprogram. In a sense, the argument list is built on the stack instead of being placed somewhere in the calling program's data area. Program 7.5 shows a program that passes two arguments by value and one by reference to a subprogram using this method.

## Program 7.5

```
; Program 7.5       Ratio.ASM
; Illustrate a subprogram call that uses the stack for
;   the return address and three parameters.  Two of the
;   parameters are passed by value; the third by reference.

; DOS function and status parameters
    DosFunc     equ     21h
    ExitToDos   equ     4Ch
    NoErrors    equ     00h

DOSSEG

_STACK SEGMENT para stack 'stack'
            dw      100h dup (?)
_STACK ENDS
```

## Program 7.5 (continued)

```
_DATA SEGMENT word public 'data'
  Dividend    dw    ?        ;user's value for dividend
  Divisor     dw    ?        ;user's value for divisor
  RoundQuot   dw    ?        ;quotient, rounded to nearest
  PromptMsg   db    "Enter two numbers: "
  PromptLen   dw    $ - PromptMsg
  ResultMsg   db    "Ratio is "
  ResultLen   dw    $ - ResultMsg
_DATA ENDS

_TEXT SEGMENT word public 'code'
  assume  cs: _TEXT
  extrn   PutStr: PROC, PutCrLf: PROC
  extrn   GetDec: PROC, PutDec: PROC

Main:

; set up ds register to point to _DATA
  mov     ax, seg _DATA
  mov     ds, ax
  assume  ds: _DATA

; print ("Enter two numbers: ")
  mov     cx, PromptLen
  mov     bx, offset PromptMsg
  call    PutStr

; read (Dividend, Divisor)
  call    GetDec
  mov     Dividend, ax
  call    GetDec
  mov     Divisor, ax

; call Ratio (Dividend, Divisor, RoundQuot)
  push    Dividend            ;by value
  push    Divisor             ;by value
  mov     ax, offset RoundQuot   ;by reference
  push    ax
  call    Ratio

; print ("Ratio is ", RoundQuot)
  mov     cx, ResultLen
  mov     bx, offset ResultMsg
  call    PutStr
  mov     ax, RoundQuot
  call    PutDec
  call    PutCrLf

; exit to DOS
  mov     ah, ExitToDos
  mov     al, NoErrors
  int     DosFunc

_TEXT ENDS
```

## 7.5 The Stack

**Program 7.5 (continued)**

```
;;;;;;;;;;;; Ratio (Num, Den; VAR RoundRatio) ;;;;;;;;;;;;
; Compute RoundRatio := Num/Den rounded to nearest integer.

_DATA SEGMENT
  Num         dw    ?     ;copy of first argument
  Den         dw    ?     ;copy of second argument
  RoundRatio  dw    ?     ;offset of third argument
_DATA ENDS

_TEXT SEGMENT

Ratio:

; get parameters off stack
    pop     ax                    ;save return address
    pop     RoundRatio
    pop     Den
    pop     Num
    push    ax                    ;put return address back

; quotient (in bx) := Num div Den
    mov     ax, Num
    cwd
    idiv    Den
    mov     bx, ax

; adjustment (in ax) = (remainder * 2) div Den
    mov     ax, dx
    mov     dx, 2
    imul    dx
    idiv    Den

; RoundRatio := quotient + adjustment
    add     ax, bx
    mov     bx, RoundRatio
    mov     [bx], ax

; return to calling program
    ret
_TEXT ENDS
END     Main
```

The main program in Program 7.5 pushes the values of Dividend and Divisor, and the offset of RoundQuot, onto the stack and calls the subprogram using the sequence

```
; call Ratio (Dividend, Divisor, RoundQuot)
    push    Dividend
    push    Divisor
    mov     ax, offset RoundQuot
    push    ax
    call    Ratio
```

Note that pushing an offset requires first moving it into a register and then pushing the register onto the stack. The offset is a constant coded as an immediate operand, but the 8086 cannot push immediate operands onto the stack.

The subprogram first pops the return address off the stack into a register for safekeeping. It then pops the third, second, and first parameters, in that order, off the stack. Finally, it pushes the return address back onto the stack. Later, when the subprogram executes the ret instruction, the return address is popped off the stack. That will leave the stack in the same state that it was in before we pushed the arguments onto it in the calling program. It is important that the stack be in the same state after a called subprogram returns that it was in before the call is made. If this is not ensured, the stack will become chaotic and disorganized.

The arithmetic in the subprogram computes the ratio of the first parameter to the second, using the same rounding technique that was used in Program 4.1. The result in this subprogram is stored in the main program's storage for the third argument by the indirect mov

```
mov     bx, RoundRatio
mov     [bx], ax
```

One problem with using the stack as it was used in Program 7.5 is that, when the parameters are popped off the stack, they are in reverse order (compared to the argument list). This is not difficult to correct when implementing a subprogram; however, if overlooked, it can cause troublesome errors. Another problem is that the return address must be popped off the stack before the arguments can be accessed and must be pushed back on before returning. This is awkward. It would be better to leave the arguments on the stack and access them there without popping anything until the subprogram returns. This is the situation for which the BP register is useful.

## Using the Base Pointer

There are two problems connected with directly accessing the parameters in the stack segment without first popping them off. First, the offsets of the parameters must be established from the stack segment register. Second, when the subprogram returns, the stack must be restored to the same state that it was in before the call. Figure 7.4 shows the stack segment upon entry to the subprogram of Program 7.5. The stack pointer refers to the offset of the return address. Two bytes below that is the last parameter (the stack is backward insofar as SP + 2 is "below" SP). Four bytes below, at SP + 4, is the next-to-last parameter, and so on. If we try to use these as operands when referring to the parameters, it can get very confusing if we push anything onto the stack within the subprogram; before such a push, the first parameter is at SP + 6; after one push, it is at SP + 8, after two pushes, it is at SP + 10, and so on.

The base pointer register, BP, can be useful here. It is normally used to specify a reference offset in the stack segment. The BX register, which has also been used for some arithmetic, is intended as a base register in the data segment. That is, for an instruction such as

```
mov     [bx+2], ax
```

## 7.5 The Stack

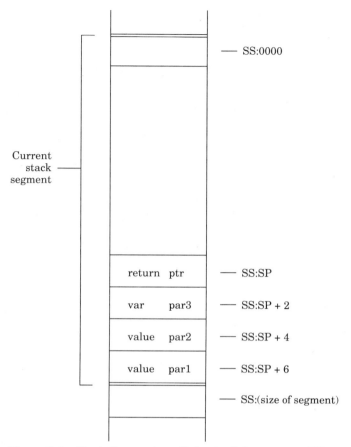

**Figure 7.4** Stack Segment on Entry to Subprogram of Program 7.5

the processor computes the effective address of the destination as DS:BX+2. Similarly, the BP register is intended as a base register in the stack segment. For an instruction such as

    mov     [bp+4], ax

the processor computes the effective address of the destination as SS:BP+4.

Consider what happens if BP is set to the same offset as SP upon entry to a subprogram. No matter how much is pushed onto the stack (or popped off, as long as it is not more than is pushed), the first parameter is at BP+2. This is certainly easier to deal with than keeping track of displacements from a moving top of stack.

Except for one small problem, this approach works so well that most high-level-language compilers use it (actually, they use the correct version being developed here), as do many assembly-language programmers. Since most subprograms use the BP register to point to their parameters, it is important that the BP register be preserved. Each subprogram changes BP to use it in accessing its arguments, but expects any subprograms called to leave BP unchanged. Therefore, before the contents of SP can be copied into BP, it is necessary to save the contents of BP somewhere. BP must then be restored before returning to the calling program.

The most likely place to save BP is, of course, on the stack—and this changes the displacement of the parameters. In Figure 7.5, the state shown is achieved by the sequence of instructions

```
push    bp
mov     bp, sp
```

upon entry to the subprogram. The parameters can then be accessed at BP+4, BP+6, and so on. This is the convention used most often. To restore the BP register before returning to the calling program, the instruction

```
pop     bp
```

can be used before the ret instruction. This takes care of the problem of accessing the parameters.

The second problem in using the stack for passing arguments is that of removing them when the subprogram returns. Other than using a number of pop instructions, there are two solutions to this problem.

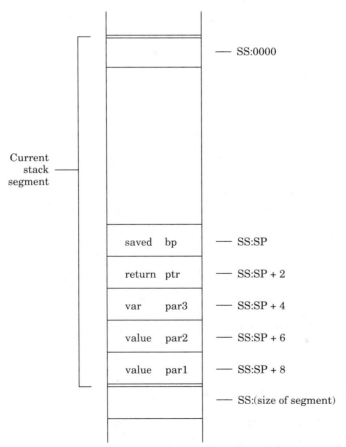

Figure 7.5  Stack Segment after Pushing Base Pointer onto Stack

## 7.5 The Stack

The calling program can adjust the stack after the return by adding the size of the parameter list to the contents of the SP register. For example, if the subprogram leaves three words of parameter information on the stack—which the calling program pushed there in the first place—the calling program can correct SP with the instruction

```
add     sp, 6
```

A complete call of a subprogram with two parameters passed by value would then be

```
push    ValArg1
push    ValArg2
call    SubProg
add     sp, 4
```

This is the convention for adjusting the stack used by C compilers.

The other solution involves a capability of the ret instruction that has not yet been discussed. ret can take an operand that specifies an adjustment to SP.

---

**RETurn to calling program and adjust stack**

| | |
|---|---|
| syntax: | ret *source* |
| action: | (1) ip := [ss:sp]; |
| | (2) sp := sp + 2 + *source* |
| flags: | ODITSZAPC unchanged |
| operand: | *immed* |

---

Specifying an immediate operand with the ret instruction will cause it to adjust the stack for that many bytes of parameters left on the stack. This has the same effect as having the calling program add the constant when the subprogram returns. However, it is more efficient, since it is part of the ret instruction rather than a separate instruction.

There are a few minor details that need to be considered before the BP register is put to work. First, an instruction operand written as [BP+4] has no type: The assembler cannot tell if the operand is a word, a byte, or a doubleword. In some contexts, the assembler will determine this from the other operand or from the instruction mnemonic. For example, if we write

```
mov     ax, [bp + 4]
```

the assembler will assume that the second operand is a word, since the first operand is a word. In other cases, we must help the assembler by specifying the type. We can specify that [BP+4] refers to a single word with the ptr operator and type word. For example,

```
idiv    word ptr [bp + 4]
```

specifies division of a doubleword by a word.

Writing word ptr with some references to parameters and not with others can lead to confusion. Writing it with every parameter reference is tedious, and not very helpful in documenting the program. Instead, we prefer to associate a name with strings such as word ptr [bp + 4] using equ directives. These directives are included at the start of the subprogram.

## 250 Chapter 7 Subprograms I

If the calling program pushes three argument values onto the stack with the instruction sequence

```
push    Left
push    Center
push    Right
```

and we want to access them as First, Middle, and Last, we could name the parameters with the sequence

```
First     equ     word ptr [bp + 8]
Middle    equ     word ptr [bp + 6]
Last      equ     word ptr [bp + 4]
```

Not only does this make the instructions that use the parameters easier to read, it confines the issues of parameter order and type to a few lines. This aids in program maintenance.

Program 7.5 has been rewritten as Program 7.6, and illustrates the procedure for passing arguments onto the stack. It also illustrates the use of the BP register, the use of the equ directive to name the parameters, the use of the ptr operator to associate types with parameters, and the use of the ret instruction with an operand.

## Program 7.6

```
; Program 7.6         RatioBP.ASM
; Illustrate a subprogram call that uses the stack for
;   the return address and parameters, as in Program 7.5.
;   This version uses bp register to access the stack and
;   an operand with the ret instruction.

; DOS function and status parameters
    DosFunc      equ      21h
    ExitToDos    equ      4Ch
    NoErrors     equ      00h

DOSSEG

_STACK SEGMENT para stack 'stack'
            dw       100h dup (?)
_STACK ENDS

_DATA SEGMENT word public 'data'
    Dividend     dw       ?       ;user's value for dividend
    Divisor      dw       ?       ;user's value for divisor
    RoundQuot    dw       ?       ;quotient, rounded to nearest
    PromptMsg    db       "Enter two numbers: "
    PromptLen    dw       $ - PromptMsg
    ResultMsg    db       "Ratio is "
    ResultLen    dw       $ - ResultMsg
_DATA ENDS

_TEXT SEGMENT word public 'code'
    assume   cs: _TEXT
    extrn    PutStr: PROC, PutCrLf: PROC
    extrn    GetDec: PROC, PutDec: PROC
```

## 7.5 The Stack

**Program 7.6 (continued)**

```
Main:
    ; set up ds register to point to _DATA
        mov     ax, seg _DATA
        mov     ds, ax
        assume  ds: _DATA

    ; print ("Enter two numbers: ")
        mov     cx, PromptLen
        mov     bx, offset PromptMsg
        call    PutStr

    ; read (Dividend, Divisor)
        call    GetDec
        mov     Dividend, ax
        call    GetDec
        mov     Divisor, ax

    ; call RatioBP (Dividend, Divisor, RoundQuot)
        push    Dividend            ;by value
        push    Divisor             ;by value
        mov     ax, offset Roundquot   ;by reference
        push    ax
        call    RatioBP

    ; print ("Ratio is ", RoundQuot)
        mov     cx, ResultLen
        mov     bx, offset ResultMsg
        call    Putstr
        mov     ax, RoundQuot
        call    PutDec
        call    PutCrLf

    ; exit to DOS
        mov     ah, ExitToDos
        mov     al, NoErrors
        int     DosFunc

_TEXT ENDS

;;;;;;;;;;;; RatioBP (Num, Den, VAR RoundRatio) ;;;;;;;;;;;;
; Compute RoundRatio := Num/Den rounded to nearest integer.

; Parameters:
  Num           equ     word ptr [bp + 8]
  Den           equ     word ptr [bp + 6]
  RoundRatio    equ     word ptr [bp + 4]

_TEXT SEGMENT

RatioBP:

; save bp, set bp to point to stack top
        push    bp
        mov     bp, sp
```

## Program 7.6 (continued)

```
        ; quotient (in bx) := Num div Den
            mov     ax, Num
            cwd
            idiv    Den
            mov     bx, ax

        ; adjustment (in ax) := (Num mod Den) * 2 div Den
            mov     ax, dx
            mov     dx, 2
            imul    dx
            idiv    Den

        ; RoundRatio := quotient + adjustment
            add     ax, bx
            mov     bx, RoundRatio
            mov     [bx], ax

        ; restore bp, return to calling program
            pop     bp      ←add sp, 8
            ret     6

_TEXT   ENDS
END     Main
```

## Local Variables

The stack is used to save the return address. It is used to pass arguments. It is used to save the value of the BP register so that the subprogram can use the BP register to retrieve the parameters. It can also be used for uninitialized local variables while the subprogram is executing.

Assume that we want to allocate four words on the stack for local variables in a subprogram. To reserve space for them, we could push four words of zeros onto the stack. Later, before the subprogram returns, we would have to pop the four words off the stack. However, pushing zeros and popping final values that we don't care about adds overhead to the program. Since these variables are uninitialized, we could just move the stack pointer by four words to allocate space; this can be done with a single subtraction. Before the return, we would move the stack pointer back with a single addition.

A subprogram that allocates four words on the stack in this manner would include the instruction

```
        sub     sp, 8
```

immediately after moving the contents of the SP register into the BP register. It would also include the instruction

```
        add     sp, 8
```

immediately before popping the stack into BP to restore it.

How are these local variables accessed on the stack? It would certainly not be desirable to be repeatedly popping them off and pushing them back on—that would defeat the

## 7.5 The Stack

purpose of using the stack because we would need space in a data segment to save the popped values. Rather, we can use the same strategy that is used with parameters. If we assume three parameters as in Figure 7.5, after adjusting SP for four words of local variables, the stack appears as in Figure 7.6. Clearly, we can use the BP register to access these local variables in the same way that we access the parameters. We can even name the locals with the equ directives, as in

```
Local1      equ     word ptr [bp - 2]
Local2      equ     word ptr [bp - 4]
```

and so on.

In the discussion of coding instructions in Section 2.3, it was mentioned that there was no way to code an indirect address that uses an offset in BP with no displacement, and that such an indirect address would not be useful. As shown in Figure 7.6, SS:BP will normally point to the saved value of BP on the stack, which is not likely to be used as an operand. The lack of a way to code such an operand without specifying a zero displacement explicitly is not a serious omission.

### Stack Frames

The block of the stack segment used for the subprogram now contains the parameters, the return pointer, the saved BP register, and space for local variables. We may save other

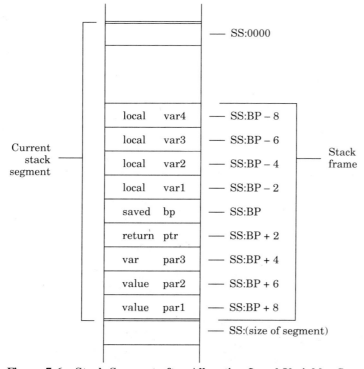

Figure 7.6  Stack Segment after Allocating Local Variables Storage

registers on the stack, either before or after the local variables. Taken together, all of these things define a block, called a **stack frame**, that is used by the subprogram (see Figure 7.6).

A stack frame is used by a single subprogram, and only when the subprogram is active. Before the subprogram is invoked, the data defined in the stack frame is not associated with any memory location. When the subprogram is invoked, the elements in the stack frame are associated with whatever locations are just above the top of the stack. When the subprogram returns, the locations used for the stack frame are released for whatever other use the program might make of them. We say, therefore, that the stack frame consists of **dynamic data**; that is, the data are dynamically allocated as part of calling the subprogram.

In contrast, the locations for the elements in the data segment are associated with specific memory locations when the program is loaded. That is also true for the instructions in the code segment. These data are said to be **static**. (It is true that the stack segment is associated with fixed memory locations at load time, but the stack frames that will occupy those locations within the stack segment are fixed only when the subprograms are active.)

Stack frames play an important part in making subprograms reentrant and recursive. These topics will be discussed further in the next chapter.

## EXERCISES 7.5

1. How large, in words, can a stack be on the 8086?
2. The 8086 pop instruction removes the contents of the top of the stack and places it into a register or memory word. Some applications require that the value at the top of the stack be copied into a register or memory location without being removed from the stack. How can this be accomplished on the 8086?
3. Write a sequence of instructions for exchanging the top element of the stack with the element below it.
4. How many words of stack space are used by Program 7.5 in calling Ratio?
5. How many words of stack space do you think are used in calling the input and output routines provided with the text? How could you determine this?
6. What are some of the advantages of using the stack for the local variables in a subprogram instead of using space in the data segment? What are some of the disadvantages?

In Exercises 7 through 9 follow the conventions of Program 7.6. The main program in each should invoke the subprogram within a loop that executes several times.

▶7. Write a program that passes two arguments by value to a subprogram that prints the magnitude of their difference.
▶8. Write a program that passes two arguments by reference to a subprogram that swaps their values. The main program should print them after the subprogram returns.
▶9. Write a program that passes four arguments by reference to a subprogram. The subprogram is to copy the parameter values into local variables defined on the stack, and replace the arguments with the values in reverse order.

## 7.6 SAVING THE CALLER'S STATE

The calling program and the subprogram use the same registers. How do we prevent the subprogram from changing important data that the calling program left in a register? Either the calling program or the subprogram should save at least some of the registers as part of the call, and restore them as part of the return. But which registers? And which program should save them? And where?

One register, or in some cases one pair of registers, does not need to be saved and restored. This is the register (or pair of registers) in which a function result is returned.

## Which Registers to Save

General-purpose registers can be saved either by the calling program or by the subprogram. We could have either of these save all of the registers (except those used for a function result) every time a subprogram is called, but that usually incurs more overhead than necessary.

To have the calling program save some registers but not all of them, it would either have to know which registers the subprogram changes, or it would have to save those registers that contain values that should not be changed by the subprogram. The former choice presents serious maintenance difficulties: If the subprogram is modified and uses different registers, every program that invokes it has to be changed.

To have the subprogram save registers but not save all of them, it would either have to know which registers the calling program needs preserved, or it would save those registers which it changes (other than a function result). The former choice presents serious design difficulties: if the subprogram can be called by more than one program, it must save the registers needed by all of the programs that call it.

Clearly, whether registers are saved by the calling program or by the subprogram, the selection of registers to save should depend only on which registers are used by the program that saves them. Also, the program that saves them as part of the call should be responsible for restoring the registers as part of the return.

## When to Save Registers

The choice of whether the registers should be saved by the calling program or by the called program is not clear. We expect that the number of registers that need to be saved would be about the same, on average, whether the calling program saves the registers that it needs or the subprogram saves the registers that it changes. For the same number of registers, the calling program and the subprogram would use the same instructions to save the registers and the same instructions to restore them.

There are some situations that influence whether the calling program or the subprogram should save and restore the registers. When the calling program saves and restores the registers that it needs preserved, there is no need to restore and save the registers between calls if some program calls two different subprograms one right after the other. Also, if a subprogram immediately calls another, it doesn't yet have any values of its own in the registers, so no save is needed. The potential saving from these situations may not be great, but should not be neglected in the decision.

On the other hand, when the subprogram saves and restores the registers that it uses, there is a potential saving when the same subprogram is called from more than one location in a program. In this case, the subprogram needs only one copy of the instructions for saving and restoring the registers. When the calling program saves and restores the registers, each place in the program that calls the subprogram has a copy of these instructions. This potential saving also may not be great.

As these two situations probably occur with roughly equal frequency, adopting either strategy is likely to produce the same saving (or incur the same cost) over the long term. In general, there are no obvious reasons to prefer either the calling program or the subprogram for saving and restoring registers.

## Where to Save Registers

Having reached no conclusion about when to save registers, let's turn to the question of where to save registers. There are two choices: in the data area of the program or subprogram doing the save, or on the stack.

Regardless of whether the registers are saved by the calling program or by the subprogram, space in the data segment is allocated at load time. If the space is declared in a subprogram (either because it saves registers when entered or because it saves registers before calling another subprogram), the memory intended for the save area is unavailable for other purposes, even when the subprogram has not been called. In large programs with many levels of subprograms, this can waste a substantial amount of memory.

In contrast, space on the stack is allocated during execution. Using the stack segment for the saved register values limits the amount of memory allocated for saving registers to exactly that which is used for saving registers at the moment. This is a more efficient use of memory.

## Saving Data Registers

How can a program efficiently save the registers? Using the instructions introduced so far, it requires as many push instructions (or mov instructions, if the stack is not used) as there are registers to be saved. It also takes as many pop (or mov) instructions to restore them.

The 8086 programmer must resort to pushing and popping each register individually. The newer processors in the family, starting with the 80186, have two instructions that simplify the process.

---

**PUSH All registers (80186 and later processors)**
    syntax:    pusha
    action:    push ax, cx, dx, bx, sp, bp, si, di
                   onto stack, in that order

**POP All registers (80186 and later processors)**
    syntax:    popa
    action:    pop di, si, bp, sp, bx, dx, cx, ax
                   off stack, in that order
    flags:     ODITSZAPC unchanged

## 7.6 Saving the Caller's State

These instructions save and restore the four general-purpose registers, the two base registers, and the two index registers. They do not save or restore the segment registers, the instruction pointer, or the flags register.

### Saving Base and Flag Registers

In addition to saving the general-purpose registers, various address and control registers might also be saved when invoking a subprogram. The flags register contains information about the calling program that might be needed when control returns to it.

The base registers, especially the BP register used to access parameters in the stack, will likely have different values for the subprogram, so their values in the calling program need to be saved and restored. The base registers can be saved with push and pop, or pusha and popa when available. For example, the subprogram of Program 7.6 started by saving the calling program's BP register and establishing the desired BP register value with the instructions

```
push    bp
mov     bp, sp
```

Later, immediately before the ret instruction, the calling program's BP register was restored with the instruction

```
pop     bp
```

The DS and ES segment registers can be saved with push and restored with pop, which is handy when DS and ES are used with multiple data segments. The SS segment register can be pushed onto the stack, and the stack can be popped into the CS and SS registers, but since there is no need to alter the CS or SS registers directly, it is not necessary to save and restore them using the stack.

The flags register can be saved on the stack using variations of the push and pop instructions.

**PUSH Flags**
- syntax: pushf
- action: push flags register onto stack
- flags: ODITSZAPC unchanged

**POP Flags**
- syntax: popf
- action: pops stack into flags register
- flags: ODITSZAPC restored from stack

These two instructions push and pop all 16 bits of the flags register.

Section 6.6 hinted at a method to copy all 16 bits of the flag register into the AX register using the stack. The flags can simply be pushed onto the stack and the stack popped into the AX register:

```
pushf
pop     ax
```

Note that we did not use the `popf` instruction, because it would copy the word popped off the stack back into the flags register.

Finally, the following conventions for saving and restoring registers will be used in this text. Registers modified by a subprogram are saved and restored in the subprogram. The register or registers used for a function result are not saved or restored. When a subprogram is intended to be called from a high-level language, only those registers modified by the subprogram and required to be saved by the high-level language are saved and restored.

On entry to a subprogram, BP is saved in the stack frame and any space for local variables is reserved there as well. Any other registers that need to be saved are pushed. The saved registers are popped off the stack, and the space for local variables is discarded before popping BP and returning to the calling program.

## EXERCISES 7.6

1. A new computer is proposed. It will have an extra set of registers, which only the operating system can use. What impact might this have on whether the calling program or the subprogram should save the registers?

2. What, other than registers, might be saved when a subprogram is called and restored when the subprogram returns?

3. A new computer is proposed. It will allocate a region of special high-speed memory for saving registers during a subprogram call and will provide special instructions for saving and restoring registers. This special region of memory will be implemented as a stack. Discuss some of the trade-offs of such an approach.

4. The input and output routines provided with this text use some registers for passing arguments, but otherwise leave the contents of the general registers unchanged. Examine the listings of their source files (in Appendix 1) to determine what strategy is used to implement this. Discuss why this strategy is appropriate.

5. A programmer needs to include a call to a subprogram in a program, but does not have access to the source file of the subprogram. The available documentation does not mention whether the subprogram preserves or destroys registers, so the programmer is unsure whether it is necessary to save the registers before the call or if that would be a waste of processor time. How could you determine whether it preserves or destroys the registers?

▶6. Write a program that tests whether a subprogram preserves the general registers.

In the following exercises, write a main program and subprogram(s) that use the calling conventions of this chapter.

▶7. Write a subprogram with two integer parameters passed by value. It should return 1 in AL if the second parameter is a factor of the first, 0 if it is not.

▶8. Write a subprogram with two integer parameters passed by value. It should return in AX the absolute value of the difference of the parameters.

▶9. Write a subprogram with three integer parameters passed by reference. It should change each to the sum of the other two; use the stack for local variables.

▶10. Write a subprogram with one integer parameter passed by reference. It is to print the digits of the argument one per line, and return a number composed of the same digits in reverse order.

## KEY POINTS

- The address computed from the information in an instruction is called the effective address.
- A direct address specifies an address in memory where an operand is stored.
- An indirect address specifies an address in memory where a pointer to the operand is stored.
- A pointer to an operand can also be stored in a register.
- Indirect addressing is used when the location of an operand is not known during program translation, but can be determined during execution. Examples include the return address for a subprogram and the arguments passed to a subprogram.
- A module in assembly language includes everything from the start of the source file to the first END directive, or everything from one END directive to the next.
- An internal subprogram is one that is compiled or assembled as part of the same module as the program that invokes it; all labels and names in the module are available to every (sub)program in it.
- An external subprogram is one that is not defined in the same module as the program that calls it.
- Returning from a subprogram requires that the address of the instruction following the jump to the subprogram be saved where the subprogram can access it. The return is made by an indirect jump to that address.
- Data that a program shares with a subprogram are called arguments. The subprogram refers to these data using parameters.
- In call by value, a copy of the argument value is passed to the parameter. Any change to the parameter affects only the copy, not the original argument.
- In call by reference, the address of the argument is passed to the parameter. The actual argument is referenced through indirection, and any changes affect the original argument.
- A function computes a single value, which it returns in a register.
- A subroutine or procedure returns values by changing the values of one or more of the arguments.
- The stack is used to save the return address when calling a subprogram. To return to the calling program, the subprogram jumps to the address on the top of the stack and pops the stack.
- The stack is used for transferring arguments. The calling program pushes each argument value or address onto the stack before transferring control.
- The stack is used for temporary local memory by the subprogram.
- The block of the stack used by a subprogram for the return pointer, arguments, and local temporary variables is called a stack frame.
- The state of the calling program—its registers and status flags—should be preserved so that, after the subprogram finishes, the calling program can continue without having lost any of its data.
- There is no clear preference, in general, to saving and restoring the calling program's registers in the calling program rather than in the subprogram.
- The calling program's registers are saved by pushing them onto the stack, and restored by popping their values off the stack later.

## PC SYSTEM SUMMARY

- Indirection is implemented by loading the BX register with the offset of the object and using it enclosed in square brackets as a pointer.
- Indirect pointers in memory can be set up at assembly time by using the destination name in the operand field of a dw directive.
- Indirect pointers can be specified using the offset operator.
- When a named location (as opposed to a labeled one) is used as the operand of a jump instruction, it is treated as an indirect pointer.
- The dollar sign ($) used in an operand field refers to the current value of the location counter, which the assembler uses to keep track of the displacement within the current segment.
- The stack pointer register, SP, keeps track of the top of the stack. It is initialized to the size specified in the stack segment declaration. As the stack fills, SP decreases.
- Words of data can be pushed onto and popped off the stack using push and pop instructions.
- Blocks of the stack segment that are used for local temporary variables can be allocated by subtracting the number of bytes from SP.
- The call instruction pushes the instruction pointer onto the stack and jumps to the subprogram.
- The ret instruction pops the return address off the stack and uses it to return control to the calling program. An optional operand specifies how many extra bytes of the stack to de-allocate.
- To pass an argument by value, push its value onto the stack; the subprogram uses the value directly.
- To pass an argument by reference, push its offset onto the stack; the subprogram uses the stack entry as a pointer to the argument.
- The BP register is used in retrieving arguments (values and pointers) within a subprogram.
- Word results of functions are returned in AX; byte results are returned in AL.
- No registers are saved automatically by the call instruction. It is up to the programmer to follow some convention in this matter.

Instructions presented in this chapter:

Stack Manipulation:
```
    push    push operand onto stack
    pop     pop stack into operand
    pusha   push all registers          (80186 and later)
    popa    pop all registers           (80186 and later)
    pushf   push flags onto stack
    popf    pop stack into flags
```

Subprogram Linkage:
```
    call    push IP onto stack and jump to subprogram
    ret     pop stack into IP to return from subprogram
```

# Subprograms II    8

- **Near and Far Pointers**
- **External Subprograms**
- **Nested Calls**
- **Linking with High-Level Languages**
- **Reentrant and Recursive Subprograms**

In the previous chapter we saw the essential concepts needed to implement subprograms in assembly language. Linking subprograms in assembly language with programs in a high-level language is important. Few large programming projects are written completely in assembly language; that level of control is needed in only a few routines typically.

There are a number of issues to consider, including whether subprograms share code and data segments with the calling program, how segment registers are set up when switching segments, how external names are communicated, and how parameters are passed. This chapter considers these and other related issues.

Subprograms often call other subprograms. Although there is little more to this than being careful to pass arguments by reference or by value as expected by each subprogram, an example of nested subprogram calls is given.

No discussion of subprograms would be complete without the ideas of reusable, reentrant, and recursive programs. The chapter closes with an explanation of these topics.

## 8.1   NEAR AND FAR POINTERS

Recall the discussion of relative addresses in Section 5.2, which showed that when the destination of an unconditional jump is in the same segment as the instruction, the displacement can be coded in either a byte or a word. Jumps that transfer control within a segment are called **near jumps** when the displacement is coded in a word or **short jumps** when the displacement is coded in a byte. An unconditional jump can be coded with both a segment number and an offset to transfer control to an instruction in another segment. Jumps that transfer control to another segment are called **far jumps**.

The distinction between near and far—between intrasegment and intersegment—also applies to accessing data and parameters and to transferring control between programs and subprograms. An offset used as an indirect pointer to an item in the same segment is a **near pointer**; a segment and offset pair used as an indirect pointer to an item in a different segment is a **far pointer**. Note that the use of a far pointer does not imply huge distances between the pointer and what it points to; they could be adjacent words of memory that happen to be in logically different segments.

## Accessing Data

To access an operand in a data segment, we first move the segment number into a register, ES or DS, and specify an offset from that register. If we use ES, we must also specify that an instruction is to use ES in computing the effective address of the operand.

So that we can access the data segment with near references, we have been setting up the DS register with the instructions

```
mov      ax, seg _DATA
mov      ds, ax
assume   ds: _DATA
```

The two mov instructions load the DS register with the segment number corresponding to the start of the _DATA segment. The assume directive causes the assembler to use the DS register when accessing names in the _DATA segment. Data in the segment can be accessed with just an offset—a near reference—from the DS register.

To access operands in more than one segment, we must specify the segment and offset of each operand. The segment number must be available in either DS or ES; the offset can be in a general, base, or index register. When the segment number and offset will be available as constants, as in the preceding example, we can use the seg and offset operators to build a far pointer.

When the segment number and offset are available in memory, we can use mov without seg or offset. For example, given the declarations

```
FarValue    dw    201
FarPtr      dd    FarValue
```

we can load the segment and offset of FarValue, available in FarPtr, using

```
mov    ax, word ptr FarPtr + 2
mov    es, ax
mov    bx, word ptr FarPtr
```

Here, the ptr operator with word operand is needed to override the doubleword size in the declaration of FarPtr. Note that the segment number is stored in the word with the higher address.

The 8086 provides instructions that simplify loading a pair of registers with a far pointer. One loads the segment number into DS, the other into ES; both load the offset into the register specified in the destination operand.

---

**Load far pointer into DS**

    syntax:    lds *destination, source*

    action:    DS := segment of *source*
                   *destination* := offset of *source*

**Load far pointer into ES**

    syntax:    les *destination, source*

    action:    ES := segment of *source*
                   *destination* := offset of *source*

    flags:     ODITSZAPC unchanged
    operand:  *reg, far_mem*

### 8.1 Near and Far Pointers

lds and les require that the far pointer that is to be loaded into registers be stored in memory.

Program 8.1 demonstrates many of the concepts of this section. It has two data segments, one named MAIN_DATA and the other named OTHER_DATA. In the main program, we set up DS to point to MAIN_DATA.

**Program 8.1**

```
; Program 8.1        FarDemo.ASM
; Demonstrate far references to data and subprograms.

; DOS function and status parameters
    DosFunc     equ     21h
    ExitToDos   equ     4Ch
    NoErrors    equ     00h

DOSSEG

_STACK SEGMENT para stack 'stack'
            dw      100h dup (?)
_STACK ENDS

MAIN_DATA SEGMENT word public 'maindata'
    UserInput       dw      ?
    PromptMsg       db      "Enter a number: "
    PromptLen       dw      $ - PromptMsg
    ResultMsg       db      "Your number, Counter are "
    ResultLen       dw      $ - ResultMsg
MAIN_DATA ENDS

OTHER_DATA SEGMENT word public 'otherdata'
    Counter         dw      ?
    Four            dw      4
OTHER_DATA ENDS

_TEXT SEGMENT word public 'code'
    assume  cs: _TEXT
    extrn   PutStr: PROC, PutCrLf: PROC
    extrn   GetDec: PROC, PutDec: PROC

Main:

; set up ds register to point to MAIN_DATA
    mov     ax, seg MAIN_DATA
    mov     ds, ax
    assume  ds: MAIN_DATA

; print ("Enter a number: ")
    mov     cx, PromptLen
    mov     bx, offset PromptMsg
    call    PutStr

; read (UserInput)
    call    GetDec
    mov     UserInput, ax
```

## Program 8.1 (continued)

```
        ; set Counter to 60
                mov     ax, seg OTHER_DATA
                mov     es, ax
                mov     es:Counter, 60

        ; call FarSub (UserInput)
                push    ds
                mov     ax, offset UserInput
                push    ax
                call    far ptr FarSub

        ; print ("Your number, Counter are ", UserInput, Counter)
                call    PutCrLf
                mov     cx, ResultLen
                mov     bx, offset ResultMsg
                call    PutStr
                mov     ax, UserInput
                call    PutDec
                mov     ax, es:Counter
                call    PutDec
                call    PutCrLf

        ; exit to DOS
                mov     ah, ExitToDos
                mov     al, NoErrors
                int     DosFunc


;;;;;;;;;;;;;;;;;;;;; FarSub (VAR IntParm) ;;;;;;;;;;;;;;;;;;;
; Add Four to IntParm and increment Counter

        ; Parameter:
          IntParm       equ     dword ptr [bp + 6]

FarSub:

        ; set up bp register to point to parameter
                push    bp
                mov     bp, sp

        ; save callers registers
                push    ax
                push    bx
                push    ds
                push    es

        ; set up ds to point to OTHER_DATA
                mov     ax, seg OTHER_DATA
                mov     ds, ax
                assume  ds: OTHER_DATA

        ; add Four to IntParm
                mov     ax, Four
                les     bx, IntParm
                add     es:[bx], ax
```

## 8.1 Near and Far Pointers

**Program 8.1 (continued)**

```
; increment Counter
      inc     Counter

; restore registers and return
      pop     es
      pop     ds
      pop     bx
      pop     ax
      pop     bp
      retf    4

_TEXT ENDS
END   Main
```

After printing a prompt and reading a number, Program 8.1 then sets Counter, in OTHER_DATA, to 60, using

```
      mov     ax, seg OTHER_DATA
      mov     es, ax
      mov     es:Counter, 60
```

The first two of these move the segment number of OTHER_DATA into the ES register. The third moves 60 into Counter. The use of es: before Counter specifies that the effective address is computed from the offset of Counter and the value in ES, not DS. This notation is used again later in the main program when printing the value of Counter.

The arguments that we have passed by reference so far have been near pointers, consisting of just an offset. To pass an argument by reference as a far pointer, we must push the segment number on the stack before the offset. In Program 8.1, we pass UserInput (in the MAIN_DATA segment, which is pointed to by DS) using

```
      push    ds
      mov     ax, offset UserInput
      push    ax
```

We will examine the call itself shortly.

In the subprogram, we define the parameter as

```
IntParm     equ     dword ptr [bp + 6]
```

This is similar to the parameter declarations of the preceding chapter, except that the displacement is 6, not 4 (you will see why when we look at the call), and the type is defined as a doubleword.

In the subprogram, we save the caller's registers by pushing them on the stack, then set up DS to point to OTHER_DATA. To add Four, in OTHER_DATA, to the value of the argument corresponding to IntParm, we write

```
      mov     ax, Four
      les     bx, IntParm
      add     es:[bx], ax
```

The les instruction copies the far pointer into ES:BX. The add instruction specifies indirection to access the value pointed to, not the pointer itself. The references to Four and

Counter, both in the segment that DS points to, use only the offset specified by the name. We then restore the caller's registers, including BP, and return.

## Transfer of Control

The other area in which far pointers are used is with transfer of control. One form of the unconditional jump instruction takes a far pointer for its operand. In assembly language, we can write

```
jmp     far ptr FarDest
```

where FarDest is a label anywhere in memory. The operand uses the ptr operator with the leading operand far to force a far jump to FarDest.

The jmp instruction to a far label is assembled with four bytes of immediate operands: two for the segment number and two for the offset of the destination. Unlike near and short jumps, which are coded with displacements relative to IP, far jumps are coded with the segment and offset as immediate operands. When executed, such a jump overwrites CS with the segment number and IP with the offset of the destination.

The call instruction can also transfer control to a far label. With a near destination, call pushes IP onto the stack then overwrites IP with the offset coded as an immediate operand in the instruction. With a far destination, call pushes both CS and IP onto the stack and then overwrites them with the segment number and offset coded in the instruction. We can force the assembler to treat the destination as far, as we do in Program 8.1, with

```
call    far ptr FarSub
```

When defining parameters relative to BP in the subprogram, we must account for the word on the stack used for CS with far calls. In Program 8.1, the displacement of the first argument is 6 rather than 4 for this reason.

The return from a subprogram to the calling program must pop IP (for a near call) or CS and IP (for a far call) from the stack. There are actually three mnemonics for the ret instruction: retn, which is always a near return; retf, which is always a far return; and ret, which depends on whether an external subprogram is declared as near or far (all internal subprograms default to near). In Program 8.1, we force a far call, so we force a far return with retf.

The next section examines how to declare an external procedure.

### EXERCISES 8.1

▶1. Rewrite one of your programs so that it uses the ES register and far pointers to access some of its data. How does this change the size of the program? How does this change the execution speed of the program?

2. The short operator is used to force a jump to be assembled with a byte displacement. What happens if the destination is beyond the reach of a byte displacement and the short operator is used?

3. Can some of the jumps to one destination within a program be short and some be near? If so, give an example that assembles correctly. If not, explain why not and give an example that shows the error message(s) from the assembler.
4. What happens when a subprogram invoked using a far call returns with a near ret? When a subprogram invoked using a near call returns with a far ret?
5. When writing a very large program with much data, is it necessary for all references to data to use far pointers? Is it necessary for all jumps (including call, ret, and unconditional jumps) to be far? Explain your answer carefully.
6. Is there a distinction of near or far when passing value parameters? If so, what is it? If not, explain why not.

## 8.2 EXTERNAL SUBPROGRAMS

An external subprogram is one that is not part of the same module as the calling program. The symbols defined in a module are not known outside of the module unless we direct the assembler to make them available to the linker. The symbols in an external subprogram that we might want to access are the entry point and global data.

The problem of accessing an external symbol is the same whether the symbol is an entry point or global data. The only difference is the nature of the access: We use mov to access a global variable and call to transfer control to an entry point. In both cases, the access would be a near reference if the symbol is in the same segment or a far reference if different.

While translating the programs in a module, the assembler builds two lists for the linkage editor to use later when resolving external references. From a module in which external references occur, the linkage editor needs to know the names of external symbols and where they are referenced; one of the lists that the assembler builds contains this information. From a module in which external symbols are defined, the linkage editor needs to know the names of symbols that are to be made available to other modules, and where these symbols are defined; the other list that the assembler builds contains this information. Since a module can reference external symbols and provide symbols for other modules to reference, the assembler may build both lists for each module that it translates.

It is the programmer's responsibility to tell the assembler which symbols referenced in a module are defined externally, and which symbols defined in a module should be made available as external symbols. We do not want the assembler to make every symbol in a module available as an external symbol. Nor do we want it to assume that every symbol that it encounters as an operand but that is not defined in the module is an external symbol. Either of these behaviors would lead to chaos.

### Importing Symbols

We use several directives to declare external references. To tell the 8086 assembler that a symbol is an external one for which the linker should provide an address, we use the extrn directive. The syntax is

extrn    *name*: *type* [, *name*: *type* ... ]

The operands, consisting of a *name* and a *type*, can be repeated. We have used this in our programs to declare the input and output procedures, as in

extrn  GetDec: PROC, PutDec: PROC

The name field of the operand is the name of the external symbol. The type field of the operand specifies whether the external object is the entry to a procedure (PROC) or a datum (byte, word, and so on). Procedures should be declared in the code segment that calls them; data should be declared in a data segment, even if we have to create a dummy data segment with only extrn declarations in it.

## Exporting Symbols

To tell the 8086 assembler that a symbol defined in the module should be made available to other modules as an external reference, we use the public directive. The syntax is just

public    name[, name...]

The operands can be repeated. The public directive can be written anywhere in the module that defines the names being exported; it is preferable to keep it close to the declaration of the symbol.

Note that for a module to access a symbol defined in another module the accessing module must declare the symbol with extrn and the defining module must declare the symbol with public. Both declarations are necessary.

## Referencing an External Name

When transferring control to an internal subprogram was discussed, the symbols in the calling program were treated as separate from those in the subprogram. One small oversight, though, was that the label that the calling program jumped to was within the same module. With external subprograms, the assembler cannot determine the address associated with the entry point. How is the call instruction then translated into the correct machine code?

The assembler can generate the operation code for the call instruction and leave the displacement field of the instruction empty. When the linkage editor combines the object files for the main program and subprograms, it can determine the offset of the entry point and use it to complete the call instruction. The details of this processing by the linkage editor is covered in Chapter 11.

References to external data, other than arguments, are handled in a similar manner. The assembler generates as much of each instruction as it can. It also writes a list of incomplete instructions to the object file for the linker to finish. Later, the linker can determine offsets and fill in the incomplete instructions.

## Declaring an External Procedure

In addition to making the name of an external subprogram public, we must declare whether the subprogram is to be called with a near or far call, whether the return pointer is two or four bytes long.

With 8086 assemblers, the entry point of a subprogram is defined using the PROC directive. To declare the procedure within the same code segment as the program that calls it—a near procedure—we use

ProcName PROC NEAR

## 8.2 External Subprograms

or just

ProcName PROC

Here we use ProcName as the label of the entry to the procedure. To declare the same procedure in a code segment as different from the program that calls it—a far procedure— we use the directive

ProcName PROC FAR

The end of a subprogram, like the end of a segment, must also be declared using the ENDP directive with the same label as the PROC directive.

To illustrate an external subprogram, let's write a function that raises an integer Base to a positive exponent Exp. The calculation performed by the function is the same as in Program 5.7, with the result returned in the AX register. Our external function is given in Program 8.2. It consists of just a code segment, named _TEXT. The public directive makes the entry point symbol, defined as PowerFunc in the PROC and ENDP directives, available as an external symbol.

---

**Program 8.2**

```
;  Program 8.2        PowerFn.ASM
;  Function PowerFunc (Base, Exp : Integer) : Integer;
;     Compute Base^Exp, for positive Exp,  0 for Exp <= 0.
;     Function result is computed and returned in ax.

; Parameters:
  Base          equ     word ptr [bp + 6]
  Exp           equ     word ptr [bp + 4]

_TEXT SEGMENT word public 'code'
      assume  cs: _TEXT
      public  PowerFunc

PowerFunc PROC FAR

; set up bp register to point to parameters
      push    bp
      mov     bp, sp

; save caller's cx and dx registers
      push    cx
      push    dx

; Compute Base^Exp.
; IF01 Exp > 0
      mov     cx, Exp
      cmp     cx, 0
      jng     ELSE01

; THEN01
;    compute Base^Exp using repeated multiplication
;    result (in ax)   := 1
      mov     ax, 1
```

## Program 8.2 (continued)

```
;       FOR02 cx := Exp TO 1 STEP -1
;         (Exp in cx from test in IF01)
        DO02:
;           result := result * Base
            imul    Base

            loop    DO02
;       ENDFOR02

        jmp     ENDIF01

    ELSE01:
;       result := 0
        sub     ax, ax
    ENDIF01:

; restore registers and return with result in ax
        pop     dx
        pop     cx
        pop     bp
        ret     4

PowerFunc ENDP
_TEXT ENDS
END
```

The function first establishes the BP register so that we can use it to access the parameters, which are named with equ directives. Then the function saves two of the registers it changes: CX is used in the loop, and DX is changed by the multiplication. Note that the AX register is not saved; the calling program expects the function to return a result in it. Before the function returns, it pops the three registers it saved off the stack to restore them. As part of the return, the ret instruction also adds 4 to the SP register to effectively remove the arguments.

A simple driver program, in assembly language, is given in Program 8.3. The call and assignment of the result is accomplished by the sequence

```
; Result := PowerFunc (Base, Exp)
    push    Base
    push    Exp
    call    PowerFunc
    mov     Result, ax
```

Note that the operand of the call instruction is the label of the PROC directive in the function.

## Program 8.3

```
; Program 8.3        PowerMn.ASM
; Driver program for use with function PowerFunc.
```

## 8.2 External Subprograms

**Program 8.3 (continued)**

```
; DOS function and status parameters
  DosFunc     equ     21h
  ExitToDos   equ     4Ch
  NoErrors    equ     00h

  DOSSEG

  _STACK SEGMENT para stack 'stack'
              dw      100h dup (?)
  _STACK ENDS

  _DATA SEGMENT word public 'data'
    Base        dw      ?         ;number to raise to power
    Exp         dw      ?         ;power to raise number to
    Result      dw      ?         ;number raised to power
    PromptBase  db      "Enter base: "
    PromptBLen  dw      $ - PromptBase
    PromptExp   db      "Enter exponent: "
    PromptELen  dw      $ - PromptExp
    ResultMsg   db      "Result is "
    ResultLen   dw      $ - ResultMsg
  _DATA ENDS

  _TEXT SEGMENT word public 'code'
      assume  cs: _TEXT
      extrn   PutStr: PROC, PutCrLf: PROC
      extrn   GetDec: PROC, PutDec: PROC
      extrn   PowerFunc: PROC

PowerMain:

; set up ds register to point to _DATA
      mov     ax, seg _DATA
      mov     ds, ax
      assume  ds: _DATA

; print ("Enter base: ")
      mov     cx, PromptBLen
      mov     bx, offset PromptBase
      call    PutStr

; read (Base)
      call    GetDec
      mov     Base, ax

; print ("Enter exponent: ")
      mov     cx, PromptELen
      mov     bx, offset PromptExp
      call    PutStr

; read (Exp)
      call    GetDec
      mov     Exp, ax
```

**Program 8.3 (continued)**

```
; Result := PowerFunc (Base, Exp)
        push    Base
        push    Exp
        call    PowerFunc
        mov     Result, ax

; print ("Result is ", Result)
        mov     cx, ResultLen
        mov     bx, offset ResultMsg
        call    PutStr
        mov     ax, Result
        call    PutDec
        call    PutCrLf

; exit to DOS
        mov     ah, ExitToDos
        mov     al, NoErrors
        int     DosFunc

_TEXT   ENDS
        END     PowerMain
```

(handwritten annotations: "Ret pt / Exp / Base" stack diagram; "far ptr" near mov Result, ax)

---

After assembling both the main program and the subprogram, we link them together with the input and output routines. To do this, with most linkers, we just specify both object files, main program first, separated by a space, when the linker requests the object file. The rest of the linking sequence is the same.

---

## EXERCISES 8.2

1. PROC is both a directive and a type specifier. Give an example of its use as each. How is it different as a directive than a type specifier?

▶2. Write a main program and several subprograms, with different combinations of segment names, combine types, and class names. The subprograms need not perform any useful processing. Assemble, link, and obtain a map. Examine how the segments are ordered and combined. Review Section 3.3, and describe what happened with the segments in your programs.

In Exercises 3 through 8, write a main program and a subprogram in separate modules so that the subprogram will be external.

▶3. Write a function that converts a temperature in Celsius, passed as a value parameter, into the equivalent Fahrenheit temperature, rounded to the nearest degree. Write a main program that reads the Celsius temperature, invokes the function, and prints the function result.

▶4. Write a subprogram with one value parameter, an amount of money in cents, that determines and returns through four variable parameters the number of quarters, dimes, nickels, and pennies needed to make up that amount. Write a main program that reads the amount in cents, invokes the subprogram, and prints the results.

### 8.3 Nested Calls

▶5. Write a function with six value parameters that represent three scores and three weights. It is to compute and return the weighted average. If the scores are S1, S2, and S3 and the weights are W1, W2, and W3, the formula for the weighted average is

$$\text{WtAvg} = (S1 \times W1 + S2 \times W2 + S3 \times W3)/(W1 + W2 + W3)$$

Write a main program that reads the scores and weights, invokes the function, and prints the average.

▶6. Write a subprogram that prints the sum of the digits in a 16-bit (positive) integer passed by value. For example, if the argument is 10972, the subprogram should compute $1 + 0 + 9 + 7 + 2 = 19$, then print 19. Write a main program that reads a number and passes it to the subprogram.

▶7. Write a function that computes the factorial of its integer parameter. The factorial of $N$, written $N!$, is computed as $N \times (N - 1) \times (N - 2) \times \cdots \times 2 \times 1$. Write a main program that reads an integer, passes it to the function, and prints the result.

▶8. Write a subprogram that reads an integer in hexadecimal and converts it into decimal. The input should be a string of hexadecimal digits read as individual characters. The result should be returned through a variable parameter. Write a main program that invokes the subprogram and prints the result using PutDec.

## 8.3 NESTED CALLS

Now that we can write external subprograms, we want to examine nested subprogram calls.

Consider the problems of finding the larger of two integers and the largest of three integers. The first of these is easily solved by a function like

```
Function Max2 (M, N : Integer) : Integer;
BEGIN
  Max2 := M;
  IF M < N
  THEN
    Max2 := N
  ENDIF
END;
```

Once we have this Max2 function, the largest of three could be found in a function that calls it twice, like

```
Function Max3 (M, N, P : Integer) : Integer;
BEGIN
  Max3 := Max2( Max2(M, N), P);
END;
```

Let's start with a main program that calls each of these functions. See Program 8.4. Note that Max2 and Max3 are both declared as external procedures in the beginning of the code segment. In this example, the arguments are passed by value—typical for a function—therefore the calls are simply a sequence of two or three push instructions to copy the argument values onto the stack, a call instruction to invoke the function, and a mov instruction to save the function result in memory. The rest of the main program only reads and prints, to verify that the functions work.

## Program 8.4

```
; Program 8.4         NestdMax.ASM
; Find the larger of two integers, and the largest of
; three integers, using external functions.

; DOS function and status parameters
DosFunc      equ      21h
ExitToDos    equ      4Ch
NoErrors     equ      00h

DOSSEG

_STACK SEGMENT para stack 'stack'
             dw       100h dup (?)
_STACK ENDS

_DATA SEGMENT word public 'data'
    N1           dw       ?       ;user's first number
    N2           dw       ?       ;user's second number
    N3           dw       ?       ;user's third number
    Result       dw       ?       ;larger or largest number
    Prompt2      db       "Enter 2 integers: "
    Prompt3      db       "Enter 3 integers: "
    PromptLen    dw       $ - Prompt3
    Large2Msg    db       "The larger value is "
    Large2Len    dw       $ - Large2Msg
    Large3Msg    db       "The largest value is "
    Large3Len    dw       $ - Large3Msg
_DATA ENDS

_TEXT SEGMENT word public 'code'
     assume   cs: _TEXT
     extrn    PutStr: PROC, PutCrLf: PROC
     extrn    GetDec: PROC, PutDec: PROC
     extrn    Max2: PROC,   Max3: PROC

NestedMax:

; set up ds register to point to _DATA
     mov      ax, seg _DATA
     mov      ds, ax
     assume   ds: _DATA

; Find larger of two inputs.
; print ("Enter 2 integers: ")
     mov      cx, PromptLen
     mov      bx, offset Prompt2
     call     PutStr

; read (N1, N2)
     call     GetDec
     mov      N1, ax
     call     GetDec
     mov      N2, ax
     call     PutCrLf
```

## 8.3 Nested Calls

**Program 8.4 (continued)**

```
        ; Result = Max2 (N1, N2)
            push    N1
            push    N2
            call    Max2
            mov     Result, ax

        ; print ("The larger value is ", Result)
            mov     cx, Large2Len
            mov     bx, offset Large2Msg
            call    PutStr
            mov     ax, Result
            call    PutDec
            call    PutCrLf

        ; Find largest of three inputs.
        ; print ("Enter 3 integers: ")
            mov     cx, PromptLen
            mov     bx, offset Prompt3
            call    PutStr

        ; read (N1, N2, N3)
            call    GetDec
            mov     N1, ax
            call    GetDec
            mov     N2, ax
            call    GetDec
            mov     N3, ax
            call    PutCrLf

        ; Result := Max3 (N1, N2, N3)
            push    N1
            push    N2
            push    N3
            call    Max3
            mov     Result, ax

        ; print ("The largest value is ", Result)
            mov     cx, Large3Len
            mov     bx, offset Large3Msg
            call    PutStr
            mov     ax, Result
            call    PutDec
            call    PutCrLf

        ; exit to DOS
            mov     ah, ExitToDos
            mov     al, NoErrors
            int     DosFunc

        _TEXT ENDS
        END     NestedMax
```

The Max2 function is given in Program 8.5. Since it returns the function value in the AX register, the function starts (after setting up BP) by moving the first parameter value into AX. The selection structure then checks whether the second parameter value is larger; if it is, it is copied into AX. The BP register is restored, and the function returns to the calling program with the larger parameter value in the AX register.

## Program 8.5

```
; Program 8.5         Max2Fn.ASM
; Function Max2 (M, N : Integer) : Integer;
;    Return the larger of M, N in ax.

; Parameters
    M              equ      word ptr [bp + 6]
    N              equ      word ptr [bp + 4]

_TEXT SEGMENT word public 'code'
    assume    cs: _TEXT
    public    Max2

Max2 PROC

    ; set up bp register to point to parameters
        push      bp
        mov       bp, sp

    ; assume M is larger, then check it
        mov       ax, M

    ; IF01 M < N
        cmp       ax, N
        jnl       ENDIF01

    ; THEN01
    ;    return N instead
        mov       ax, N
    ENDIF01:

    ; return with result in ax
        pop       bp
        ret       4

Max2 ENDP
_TEXT ENDS
END
```

The Max3 function is given in Program 8.6. Note that Max2 is declared as an external procedure in Max3. One interesting feature of Max3 is that, as in the design we gave above, it uses the value returned by Max2(M,N) as an argument to another call of Max2. The first call of Max2 is implemented using the instructions

```
    push    M
    push    N
    call    Max2
```

## 8.3 Nested Calls

Since the function value is returned in AX and we are passing parameters by value, we can simply push the function value onto the stack as a parameter for the second call

```
push    ax
push    P
call    Max2
```

Again, Max2 returns the result in AX. Max3 also returns its result in AX, so we just leave it there and return.

---

**Program 8.6**

```
; Program 8.6        Max3Fn.ASM
; Function Max3 (M, N, P : Integer) : Integer;
;   Return the largest of M, N, P in ax.

; Parameters:
  M              equ      word ptr [bp + 8]
  N              equ      word ptr [bp + 6]
  P              equ      word ptr [bp + 4]

_TEXT SEGMENT word public 'code'
     assume   cs: _TEXT
     extrn    Max2: PROC
     public   Max3

Max3 PROC

; set up bp register to point to parameters
     push     bp
     mov      bp, sp

; Max3 := Max2 (Max2 (M, N), P)
     push     M
     push     N
     call     Max2           ;      Max2 (M, N)
     push     ax
     push     P
     call     Max2           ; Max2 (Max2 (M, N), P)

; return with result in ax
     pop      bp
     ret      6
Max3 ENDP
_TEXT ENDS
END
```

---

Now consider the necessary changes to pass the arguments by reference. We would not normally pass arguments to a function by reference, but rather than write a new set of programs we propose to modify the three of this section. First, the main program as given in Program 8.4 needs only the same change in five places: for example, the instruction

```
push    N1
```

which pushes the value of argument N1 onto the stack, would become

```
mov     ax, offset N1
push    ax
```

to push the offset of the argument N1 onto the stack instead.

To change function Max2 so that it accepts parameters passed by reference requires that the offsets passed as parameters be loaded into BX, then used with indirection to access the values of arguments, that is, the instruction

```
mov     ax, M
```

before the selection structure is replaced by

```
mov     bx, M
mov     ax, [bx]
```

Similarly, the compare instruction of the selection structure

```
cmp     ax, N
```

is replaced by

```
mov     bx, N
cmp     ax, [bx]
```

And the instruction in the THEN clause

```
mov     ax, N
```

is replaced by

```
mov     ax, [bx]
```

Note that since the pointer to N is still in BX, there is no need to reload BX with the offset passed as the argument.

To change Max3 is more interesting. The value returned by the first call to Max2 must be saved in the data segment, since Max2 expects an offset relative to DS for the arguments. We can set up a local variable for this result with

```
_DATA SEGMENT word public 'data'
  MaxMandN    dw      ?
_DATA ENDS
```

and inform the assembler of it with the directive

```
assume ds: _DATA
```

Note that it is not necessary to actually load DS with the segment number of _DATA, as the linker will resolve the references when this segment is combined with the data segment of the main program. The first call of Max2 from Max3 is unchanged. The result from the first call is saved in MaxMandN, and the offset of MaxMandN is passed as the first argument in the second call of Max2:

```
call    Max2                ;first call
mov     MaxMandN, ax        ;save result
mov     ax, offset MaxMandN
push    ax
push    P
call    Max2                ;second call
```

### 8.4 Linking with High-Level Languages

Note that the offsets passed to Max3 by the main program can be passed on to Max2 unchanged.

---

**EXERCISES 8.3**

▶1. The algorithm used in Max2 for finding the larger of two integers is not as common as the following one:

```
Function Max2 (M, N : Integer) : Integer;
IF M > N
THEN Max2 := M
ELSE Max2 := N
ENDIF;
```

Implement this algorithm as an external function with parameters passed by value. How does it compare to Program 8.5?

▶2. Implement Max2 and Max3 as external functions with parameters passed by reference, as described in this section.

3. In the revised version of the Max3 program discussed in this section (and implemented in Exercise 2), can the local variable MaxMandN be stored on the stack rather than the data segment? If so, implement Max3 this way. If not, carefully explain why not.

▶4. Rewrite Max2 and Max3 so that they are procedures that return the larger or largest value by changing the value of an extra parameter passed by reference. The input parameters should be passed by value.

▶5. Repeat Exercise 4, passing the input parameters by reference.

6. Why, in the modification to Program 8.4 to use call by reference, do we use a mov instruction instead of just writing

```
push    offset N1
```

to push the arguments on the stack?

## 8.4 LINKING WITH HIGH-LEVEL LANGUAGES

In principle, a program written in any language should be able to call a subprogram written in any language. In practice, there are always some conventions that must be followed for the transition between languages to work.

We are interested in combining subprograms written in assembly language with a program written in a high-level language. By writing the main program in a high-level language, we can take advantage of the input and output facilities available. This arrangement also allows any initialization routines needed to establish the high-level language environment to execute as intended.

The conventions for mixing assembly and high-level language programs involve segments, data types, arguments, and preserving the caller's state. Each of these are considered in turn, and then an example is given. The conventions and requirements of Turbo Pascal 6.0 are given because that language will be used in the examples. In Appendix 7, information on several languages is provided for illustrative purposes. You should check the documentation of your particular compiler for its conventions.

## Segments

In revising Program 8.5 to use parameters passed by reference, we proposed allocating a word of memory for the intermediate result. We declared this variable in a data segment with the same name, align type, combine type, and class name as the data segment in the calling program. This declaration was necessary since the offset of the variable relative to the value of the DS register used by the main program was assumed; we did not set up the DS register, but we used the assume directive to have the assembler build the offsets relative to the start of the segment named _DATA. The linker fixes the offset determined by the assembler when it combines this segment with the one from the main program (and possibly others).

Depending on the language and compiler, you may have to (or want to) use the same segment declarations used by the high-level language. Doing so allows references to be near rather than far, which eliminates the bother of saving, setting up, and later restoring segment registers. On the other hand, some languages or compilers might expect external subprograms to use private segments and far pointers to avoid problems with limits on segment size.

To link an assembly-language subprogram with a main program written in Turbo Pascal 6.0, the following restrictions apply to segment names:

- The instruction segment must be named CODE, CSEG, or a name ending in _TEXT.
- A segment containing initialized local variables, if present, must be named CONST or a name ending in _DATA.
- A segment containing uninitialized local variables, if present, must be named DATA, DSEG, or a name ending in _BSS.

The align type, combine type, and class name operands of the SEGMENT directive are ignored.

## Data Types

We have used byte-sized and word-sized signed and unsigned integers, individual characters as bytes, and character strings as sequences of bytes. When the Boolean data type was discussed, some conventions used in various high-level languages were indicated. Although you can use the range of values supported to guess how various types of integers are stored in some high-level language, the situation is less clear with other data types.

The only data usually accessible by an external subprogram are global variables declared as external (or COMMON in FORTRAN) and arguments. The next subsection discusses arguments, and some external data are considered in Appendix 7. It is suggested that you use the reference manual for your compiler to find more specific information.

In Turbo Pascal, for example, the representations used for the data types we have used are the following:

- ShortInt variables are signed byte integers.
- Byte variables are unsigned byte integers.
- Integer variables are signed word integers.

## 8.4 Linking with High-Level Languages

- `Word` variables are unsigned word integers.
- `LongInt` variables are signed doubleword integers.
- `Char` variables are bytes.
- `Boolean` variables are bytes (0 = False, 1 = True).

### Arguments

Most languages for the 8086 pass arguments on the stack, as we did in the last couple of examples. Additionally, most languages use an operand on the `ret` instruction to remove the arguments as well, although C compilers usually have the calling program adjust the SP register after the return instead.

The size of the data (for parameters passed by value) or the type of pointers (for arguments passed by reference) pushed onto the stack depends on the data type as well as the language and compiler. For example, C compilers pass individual characters as 16-bit words with a leading byte of zeros. Pointers to arguments passed by reference can be offsets from DS (near pointers) or segment:offset pairs (far pointers).

Turbo Pascal pushes value parameters of the types we have seen directly onto the stack. Bytes are extended to words, with the value in the low byte. It pushes far pointers for all variable parameters, regardless of type.

The order in which arguments are pushed onto the stack also varies. Most high-level languages, including Turbo Pascal, push the arguments in the same order, left to right, as they are listed in the argument list. C, on the other hand, generally pushes arguments in reverse order, from right to left. Some languages also pass hidden information along with the arguments; for example, FORTRAN passes the (declared) length of character strings along with the strings, but not as named arguments.

Related to argument-list concerns is the subject of how functions return results. Although there may be variations for some compilers and some data types, byte results are usually returned in AL, word results (values and pointers) in AX, and doubleword results (values and pointers) in DX:AX. Turbo Pascal follows these conventions. For values longer than a doubleword, either a pointer to the result is returned, or the calling program pushes a pointer to the location where the result is to be written for the subprogram to use.

### Saving the Caller's State

It is usually up to each subprogram to save and restore any registers changed that the calling program assumes will not be changed. Of course, the register(s) used for a function result must not be restored. One must refer to each compiler's reference manual to find out which registers must be preserved and which may be changed by your subprograms. The `call` and `ret` instructions preserve CS and IP for every call, if used properly, so these are not usually mentioned in the lists of registers to be saved and restored.

Turbo Pascal 6.0 requires only that the data segment register (DS) and the stack segment and base pointer registers (SS and BP) be preserved. The stack pointer register (SP) must also be restored before returning to the calling program, which is usually accomplished by an operand on the `ret` instruction to discard the arguments. The index (SI and DI), general (AX, BX, CX, and DX), and extra segment (ES) registers can be changed.

## Example Programs

Turbo Pascal is used for several main programs in the rest of this book. Using it will simplify reading and writing the remaining data types and data structures. To show the conventions for calling an assembly-language subprogram from Turbo Pascal, we will write a simple main program to serve as a driver for Program 8.2.

We do not have to make any changes in Program 8.2 to call it from Turbo Pascal. We can remove the operands on the SEGMENT directive, but the information that the assembler writes to the object file for those operands is ignored if we leave it in. We could also delete the instructions that push and later pop CX and DX, but these four instructions do no harm if left in. By not changing Program 8.2, we show how the same subprogram can be called from more than one language (though not optimally).

The main program can be written as shown in Program 8.7. Several features of this program are worth noting. The function is declared just like a Pascal function, with integer parameters and an integer result. The word External following the function type informs the compiler that the function is defined in another, separately compiled or assembled file.

**Program 8.7**

```
{ Program 8.7        PowerMn.PAS                       }
{ Test PowerFunc, which computes Base^Exponent. }

PROGRAM PowerFunctionTest (Input, Output);

VAR
  Base,            { number to raise to power  }
  Exponent:        { power to raise number to  }
    Integer;

FUNCTION PowerFunc (Base, Exp: Integer): Integer; External;
{$L PowerFn.OBJ }

BEGIN { PowerFunctionTest }
  { print title }
  Writeln ('   Test of PowerFunc.   ');
  Writeln ('Computes base^exponent');
  Writeln;

  { get first test case }
  Write ('Enter base: ');
  Readln (Base);
  WHILE Base <> 0 DO
  BEGIN
    Write ('Enter exponent: ');
    Readln (Exponent);

    { validate exponent: it must not be negative }
    IF Exponent < 0
    THEN
      Writeln ('Exponent is negative; function returns zero.');
```

### 8.4 Linking with High-Level Languages

**Program 8.7 (continued)**

```
      { invoke function and print result }
      Write (Base:1, '^', Exponent:1, ' = ');
      Writeln (PowerFunc (Base, Exponent):1);
      Writeln;

      { get next test case }
      Write    ('Enter base (0 to stop): ');
      Readln   (Base)
   END
END.   { PowerFunctionTest }
```

The line following the function declaration,

`{$L PowerFn.OBJ }`

is a compiler directive. The Turbo Pascal compiler also links as it translates the program and generates the executable file. The $L directive causes Turbo Pascal to search the current directory for the object file named and to link it in as part of the executable file. The object file must be prepared by an assembler before Turbo Pascal is invoked.

The assembly-language function can be invoked, just like any other function in Pascal, as part of an expression. We invoke it as a parameter of Writeln to demonstrate this.

Program 8.8 illustrates some of the other conventions of calling a subprogram from Turbo Pascal, such as passing variable parameters and using our input and output routines in the subprogram. This procedure accepts two parameters passed by reference. If the first is less than or equal to the second, it does nothing; if the first is less than the second, it swaps their values and prints (using PutStr) a message to that effect.

**Program 8.8**

```
; Program 8.8        Sort2Int.ASM
; Procedure Sort2Int (VAR Int1, Int2 : Integer);
;    Sort Int1 & Int2, and print status message.

; Parameters
   Int1       equ       dword ptr [bp + 8]
   Int2       equ       dword ptr [bp + 4]

_DATA SEGMENT
   SwapMsg    db        "Swapped values..."
   SwapLen    dw        $ - SwapMsg
_DATA ENDS

_TEXT SEGMENT
   assume   cs: _TEXT
   assume   ds: _DATA
   extrn    PutStr: PROC, PutCrLf: PROC
   public   Sort2Int

Sort2Int PROC
```

**Program 8.8 (continued)**

```
        ; set up bp register to point to parameters
            push    bp
            mov     bp, sp

        ; IF01 Int1 > Int2
            les     bx, Int1
            mov     ax, es:[bx]
            les     bx, Int2
            cmp     ax, es:[bx]
            jng     ENDIF01

        ; THEN01
        ;    swap values of Int1 and Int2
            xchg    ax, es:[bx]
            les     bx, Int1
            mov     es:[bx], ax

        ;    print ("Swapped values...")
            mov     cx, SwapLen
            mov     bx, offset SwapMsg
            call    PutStr
            call    PutCrLf
        ENDIF01:

        ; return
            pop     bp
            ret     8
Sort2Int ENDP
_TEXT ENDS
END
```

In Program 8.8, the parameters are defined as far pointers using dword ptr in the equ directives. To compare their values, we move the value of the first argument into AX and compare it to the second. Each of these steps uses an les instruction first to copy the far pointer into ES:BX. If the values must be swapped, an xchg instruction swaps the value of the first argument in AX with the value of the second argument (pointed to by ES:BX); then we copy the far pointer to the first argument into ES:BX and mov the value of the second argument (in AX as a result of xchg) into the first argument.

To print a message, we first define a string that contains the message in the _DATA segment. In the THEN clause, we call PutStr and PutCrLf in the usual way. It is not necessary to set up DS to point to _DATA, because Turbo Pascal will set up DS to point to its data segment, and _DATA will be combined with it during linking. It is necessary to include an assume directive for DS, however.

Program 8.9 is a Pascal driver that invokes Program 8.8. The subprogram is declared as an external procedure. The $L directive specifies the name of the object file that must be linked, as before.

A new feature in Program 8.9 is the $I directive, which causes the compiler to read the contents of the file IO.INC in the subdirectory \INC and process it as part of the

## Program 8.9

```
{ Program 8.9         SortTwo.PAS                       }
{ Test Sort2Int, which swaps two integer values.        }

PROGRAM SortTwo (Input, Output);

VAR
  I1, I2:   { two integers to sort }
    Integer;

PROCEDURE Sort2Int (VAR Int1, Int2: Integer); External;
{$L Sort2Int.OBJ }
{$I \INC\IO.INC  --- include i/o routines for Sort2Int to use. }

BEGIN { SortTwo }
  { print title }
  Writeln (' Test of Sort2Int ');
  Writeln;

  { get first test case }
  Write ('Enter two different integers: ');
  Readln (I1, I2);
  WHILE I1 <> I2  DO
  BEGIN

    { sort two integers and print results }
    Sort2Int (I1, I2);
    Writeln ('Sorted values: ', I1, ', ', I2);
    Writeln;

    { get next test case }
    Write ('Enter two integers (same to stop): ');
    Readln (I1, I2)
  END
END. { SortTwo }
```

source file. This file contains declarations and $L directives for each of the input and output procedures we have been using. The subdirectory also includes object files, with .OBJ extensions, for these routines. Programs written in Pascal cannot properly invoke the I/O routines provided with this text. However, Turbo Pascal must be able to link the object files for any of the I/O routines that are called by subprograms called from a Pascal program.

## EXERCISES 8.4

1. When given the choice of using the same segments or different segments for the code of an assembly-language subprogram and a high-level-language calling program, what factors might influence your choice?

2. Because C pushes its arguments in right-to-left order, the first argument always begins on the stack at displacement BP+2 regardless of how many arguments there are and how they are passed. How could this be a useful advantage?

3. When passing a character string as an argument, we could push the entire string onto the stack or push a pointer to the string instead. What are the advantages and disadvantages of each method?

4. The input and output routines provided with this text, and the system routines invoked as software interrupts, expect arguments in registers. For example, PutStr expects the length of a character string in CX and the offset of the first character from DS in BX. Why do you think this method was chosen for these routines? Why do compilers for high-level languages (except C, sometimes) not use this method?

▶5. Write a program in a high-level language that invokes Max2Fn and Max3Fn of Section 8.3. Modify copies of those functions if necessary.

▶6. Write a function in assembly language that converts a weight in pounds and ounces, passed as two value parameters, into the equivalent weight in grams. There are 454 grams in a pound. Write a main program in a high-level language to test your function.

▶7. Write a procedure in assembly language that converts a weight in grams, passed as a value parameter, into the equivalent weight in pounds and ounces. The results are to be returned through two variable parameters. Write a main program in a high-level language to test your procedure.

▶8. Write a function in assembly language that determines whether its three value parameters could be the sides of a triangle and that returns the result as a Boolean function value. Each side of a triangle must be shorter than the sum of the other two sides (or, equivalently, the longest side must shorter than the sum of the other two). Write a main program in a high-level language to test your function.

## 8.5 REENTRANT AND RECURSIVE SUBPROGRAMS

This section covers the characteristics of a subprogram that determine whether it can be invoked more than once within a program, whether it can be invoked by another program before it finishes executing a call from one program, and whether a subprogram can invoke itself.

### Non-reentrant Procedures

A segment of code is **non-reentrant** if it changes during execution in such a way that it can be executed reliably only that one time. Any instruction that changes any instructions or data in a segment can render that segment non-reentrant. It does not matter whether the instruction is in the same segment.

As an example of a non-reentrant subprogram, consider the function for raising an integer to a nonnegative power shown in Program 8.10. This is the same function as in Program 8.2, modified to make it non-reentrant. The function uses an iterative algorithm to compute Base^Exp by simply multiplying Result, which is initialized to 1 by the dw directive, by Base in a loop that executes Exp times. The first invocation of this function works correctly. If the values of the parameters are 3 and 4, respectively, the function computes 81 for the value of Result in the loop. The program moves the result into the variable Result whenever a new value is computed.

## Program 8.10

```
;  Program 8.10      NonReEnt.ASM
;  Function PowerFunc (Base, Exp : Integer) : Integer;
;    Compute Base^Exp, for positive Exp,  0 for Exp <= 0.
;    This version is not reentrant.

;  Parameters:
  Base          equ     word ptr [bp + 6]
  Exp           equ     word ptr [bp + 4]

_DATA SEGMENT word public 'data'
  Result        dw      1
_DATA ENDS

_TEXT SEGMENT word public 'code'
        assume  cs: _TEXT
        assume  ds: _DATA
        public  PowerFunc

PowerFunc PROC

; set up bp register to point to parameters
        push    bp
        mov     bp, sp

; save caller's cx and dx registers
        push    cx
        push    dx

; compute Base^Exp
; IF01 Exp > 0
        mov     cx, Exp
        cmp     cx, 0
        jng     ELSE01

; THEN01
;   FOR02 cx := Exp TO 1 STEP -1
;   DO02:
;     Result := Result * Base
        mov     ax, Result
        imul    Base
        mov     Result, ax

        loop    DO02
;   ENDFOR02

        jmp     ENDIF01

  ELSE01:
;   Result := 0
        mov     ax, 0
        mov     Result, ax
  ENDIF01:
```

**Program 8.10 (continued)**

```
        ; restore registers and return with Result (already) in ax
            pop     dx
            pop     cx
            pop     bp
            ret     4

PowerFunc ENDP
_TEXT ENDS
END
```

---

What makes the function non-reentrant is that Result is initialized to 1 by the dw directive during program translation. The first invocation starts with Result as 1. The second invocation, however, starts with Result as its final value from the first invocation. If we compute PowerFunc(3,4) then attempt PowerFunc(2,3), the result is 648. PowerFunc(2,3) should compute 8 ($= 2^3$), but since Result starts at 81 rather than 1, it computes $81 \times 2^3$, or 648. A third invocation, if present, computes with Result starting at 648 and returns a value that would be in error by a factor of 648. This is easily verified by linking it with Program 8.7, which invokes PowerFunc in a loop. (It is necessary to have the assembler use PowerFn.OBJ for the object file, rather than the default NonReEnt.OBJ name that it will generate if not specified, in order to link it.)

To have the function compute correctly, we need to load a new copy of it (or at least its data segment) every time we invoke it. DOS does not do this. DOS loads the program every time we invoke it from the system prompt; as long as we use the function only once in each invocation of the program, it will work okay. This is easily verified by linking it first with Program 8.3, which invokes it once then terminates. To execute it again, DOS must load a fresh copy when we issue the command.

### Reentrant Procedures

There are two kinds of reentrant code. A procedure is **serially reentrant** if each invocation works as expected when it is allowed to return from one invocation before another invocation occurs. There are two ways that a subprogram can be invoked while a previous invocation is still active: sharing the code in a multiprogram system and allowing the subprogram to invoke itself. A procedure is **fully reentrant** if each invocation works as expected regardless of how it is invoked and whether it is invoked again before completion.

A serially reentrant subprogram is described first. The function of Program 8.10 can be made serially reentrant with just one small change. We should initialize Result to 1 before entering the loop. This requires only a couple of instructions like

```
mov     ax, 1
mov     Result, ax
```

(We could also change the operand of the dw directive from 1 to ? so that the value is not initialized until the instructions above do so, but this is not strictly necessary.) With this simple change, the function now computes the correct value regardless of the final value of Result in the previous invocation.

## 8.5 Reentrant and Recursive Subprograms

This newer version still fails if we attempt to share the function between two or more calling programs in a multiprogram environment. When we say "share the function," we mean just that: There is only one copy of the function in memory. Each calling program does have a separate stack segment when it invokes the function. Now, as long as each call of PowerFunc is allowed to complete and return a value before it is called again, there is no difficulty. But imagine that one program has called PowerFunc with arguments 4 and 3, the function starts to compute $4^3$, and the program is interrupted just after saving 16 in Result. Next assume that the program is switched from running to ready, and another program is switched from ready to running; this happens all the time in a multiprogram environment. Further assume that this second program now calls PowerFunc with arguments 5 and 2. PowerFunc initializes Result to 1, then computes $5^2$ correctly. This leaves 25 in Result. Shortly, the second program terminates, and the first regains control. It attempts to finish the computation of PowerFunc(4,3), but the value in Result has been changed from 16 to 25 by the interceding call. The value that PowerFunc returns is not 64, but 100.

To avoid one invocation of a serially reentrant program from affecting any other invocations of it, we can do either of two things. We can simply not share the data segment, forcing each caller to have its own private data segment, as some multiprogram systems do. Or we can put all local data in the stack frame (or registers). Our original version of PowerFunc in Program 8.2, which is fully reentrant, uses registers for all intermediate results—this alternative avoids needing a static data segment.

Normally, there is nothing in a procedure segment except instructions and constants. As long as the instruction sequence does not modify itself as it executes—a dubious practice at best—there is nothing in the procedure segment that changes. Such a segment is called a **pure code segment.** Many of the instruction segments in an operating system are written as pure code. The instructions in ROM are also pure code; ROM cannot be modified, so it can be used only for static information such as instructions and constants.

Placing all local data in the stack frame makes that data temporary, since the stack frame is allocated while the subprogram is active. Occasionally, the local data that a program uses must be static because it is initialized at translation, because it is the previous value of a local variable needed on the next invocation, or because it is shared between several subprograms but cannot be passed between them as arguments. Memory for such static data is not allocated in the stack frame. Instead, we declare the data in another segment, which is allocated when the program is loaded and accessed through another base register.

Implementing the changes to avoid problems with a subprogram being invoked while it is active makes that subprogram fully reentrant. To share a fully reentrant program, only the pure instruction segment is shared. Each caller has a separate stack segment and a separate data segment.

### Recursive Procedures

A subprogram that has been invoked is said to be **active**. One that has not been called is inactive. A **recursive subprogram** is one that calls itself, that calls a second subprogram that in turn calls it, that calls a second subprogram that calls a third that calls it, or the like. The essential aspect of recursion is that it involves calling a subprogram that is already active for the same user.

## Chapter 8 Subprograms II

Each active subprogram has an area that it uses on the stack. With pure instruction segments and private stack segments, we can invoke an already active subprogram in the same way as an inactive one. We need to create a new stack frame for the new invocation of the subprogram. There is no confusion—for the machine, at least—since the base pointer register (BP) for the most recent call provides access to the argument list and local data for the current invocation. The BP register for each earlier invocation was saved along with the other registers when the subprogram called itself or another subprogram.

To see how this works, let's consider a recursive version of PowerFunc. The problem is to compute, for an integer Base and nonnegative Exp, the value of Base^Exp. This can be computed recursively as

```
FUNCTION PowerFunc(Base, Exp)
BEGIN
  IF Exp > 0
  THEN
    PowerFunc := Base * PowerFunc(Base, Exp-1)
  ELSE
    IF Exp = 0
    THEN
      PowerFunc := 1
    ELSE
      PowerFunc := 0
    ENDIF
  ENDIF
END
```

The recursive assembly-language version of this function is given in Program 8.11. The label on the PROC directive defines the entry point of this function for the benefit of any calling program, including itself.

## Program 8.11

```
; Program 8.11      PowerRec.ASM
; Function PowerFunc (Base, Exp : Integer) : Integer;
;   Computes Base^Exp, for positive Exp; returns 0 if Exp <= 0.
;   This version uses the recursive algorithm.

; Parameters:
Base            equ     word ptr [bp + 6]       ;value parameter
Exp             equ     word ptr [bp + 4]       ;value parameter
ExpM1           equ     word ptr [bp - 2]       ;local variable

_TEXT SEGMENT word public 'code'
    assume  cs: _TEXT
    public  PowerFunc

PowerFunc PROC

; set up bp register to point to parameters
    push    bp
    mov     bp, sp

; allocate stack space for local variable
    sub     sp, 2
```

## Program 8.11 (continued)

```
        ; save caller's cx and dx registers
            push    cx
            push    dx

        ; compute Base^Exp
        ; IF01 Exp > 0
            mov     cx, Exp
            cmp     cx, 0
            jng     ELSE01

        ; THEN01
        ;   ExpM1 = Exp - 1
            dec     cx
            mov     ExpM1, cx

        ;   return Base * PowerFunc (Base, ExpM1)
            push    Base
            push    ExpM1
            call    PowerFunc
            imul    Base
            jmp     ENDIF01

        ELSE01:
        ;   IF02 Exp = 0
            jne     ELSE02
        ;   THEN02
        ;       return 1
            mov     ax, 1
            jmp     ENDIF02

        ELSE02:
        ;       return 0
            sub     ax, ax
        ENDIF02:
        ENDIF01:

        ; restore registers and return with result in ax
            pop     dx
            pop     cx
            add     sp, 2
            pop     bp
            ret     4

PowerFunc ENDP
_TEXT ENDS
END
```

When the function is invoked with a negative value for Exp, it loads 0 into AX and returns. When it is invoked with the base case, Exp=0, it loads 1 into AX and returns. For any positive value of Exp, the function computes Exp−1 and saves it in the local variable ExpM1. The function then invokes itself, passing Base and ExpM1 as arguments.

**292  Chapter 8  Subprograms II**

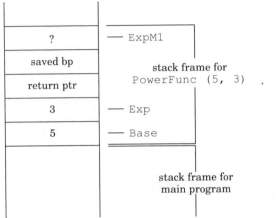

**Figure 8.1  Stack on Entry to** PowerFunc(5, 3)

This call of the function returns control to the imul instruction following call, with its result in the AX register. The function can then multiply that result by the value of Base and return to the calling program with the result in the AX register.

To see more detail in the recursive calls and returns, let's trace execution of PowerFunc. The stack is shown in various stages of the trace in Figures 8.1 through 8.7. Let's start

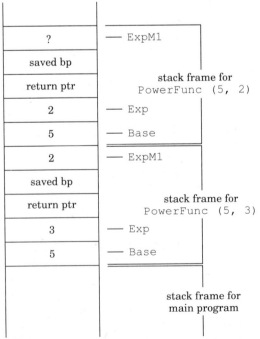

**Figure 8.2  Stack on Entry to** PowerFunc(5, 2)

## 8.5 Reentrant and Recursive Subprograms

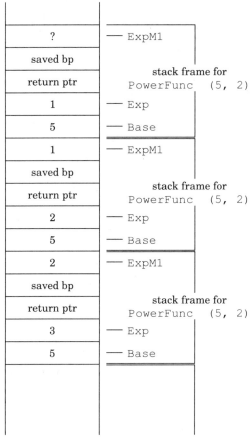

**Figure 8.3** Stack on Entry to PowerFunc(5, 1)

with a calling program invoking this function, passing 5 and 3 for the argument values. The state of the stack on entry to the function for the first time is shown in Figure 8.1. The parameters in the stack frame contain the values passed from the main program. The local variable ExpM1 is allocated space in the stack frame but has not yet been assigned any meaningful value. The top of stack pointer (SP) has been omitted from this series of figures to minimize clutter. In each, the SP register has the address of ExpM1 in the last stack frame shown.

The first invocation of PowerFunc computes a value of 2 for ExpM1 and then invokes itself. This second call of the function creates a new stack frame. The second parameter for the second invocation gets the value of ExpM1 computed by the first call. See Figure 8.2.

A third call of the function works just like the second call, as shown in Figure 8.3. Now the second parameter is the value of ExpM1 computed by the second call of the function.

The fourth call of the function is similar to the previous two calls, with the second parameter getting the value of ExpM1 from the previous call. See Figure 8.4. This invocation, however, executes the base case. The value of ExpM1 in the previous invocation

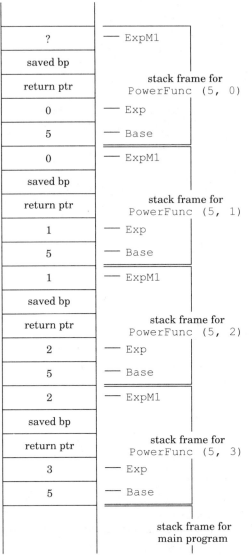

**Figure 8.4** Stack on Entry to PowerFunc(5, 0)

is 0, and this is passed as the value for Exp. This invocation of PowerFunc simply loads 1 into the AX register as the function value and returns to the previous invocation. The stack and AX register are now as shown in Figure 8.5. Note the stack frame for PowerFunc(5, 0) is now considered vacant area.

The previous invocation, PowerFunc(5, 1), now gets control back from PowerFunc(5, 0) with 1 in the AX register. It multiplies this by the value of its first parameter. The result, 5, is left in the AX register as the result for the call of PowerFunc(5, 1). Control then returns to the previous invocation. See Figure 8.6.

## 8.5 Reentrant and Recursive Subprograms

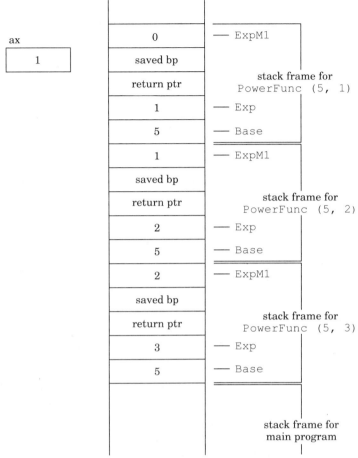

**Figure 8.5** Stack on Return from `PowerFunc(5, 0)`

Once again the result passed back in the AX register is multiplied by the first argument, this time by the invocation of `PowerFunc(5, 2)`. It leaves the product in the AX register and returns control to `PowerFunc(5, 3)`. See Figure 8.7.

Finally, the oldest invocation of `PowerFunc` takes that result and multiplies it by its first parameter. It leaves the product in the AX register and returns to the original calling program. The calling program then gets back the final value of `PowerFunc(5, 3)`, oblivious to all the activity involved in the recursive `PowerFunc` function. The stack is now the same as it was before the original invocation of `PowerFunc`.

### Tail Recursion

Some languages that support or encourage the use of recursion recognize a special case of recursion that can be implemented more efficiently. The special case is called **tail**

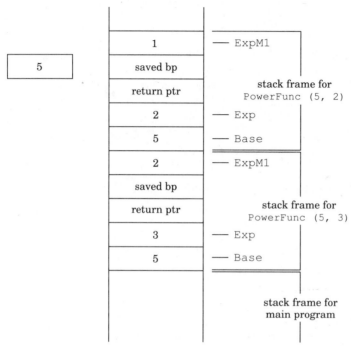

**Figure 8.6** Stack on Return from `PowerFunc(5, 1)`

**recursion,** occuring when a subprogram invokes itself as the last action prior to returning to the program that called it. There is some potential saving with tail recursion since it can be implemented without allocating another stack frame. Of course, the compiler has to determine when, and how, it can treat a recursive call as tail recursion.

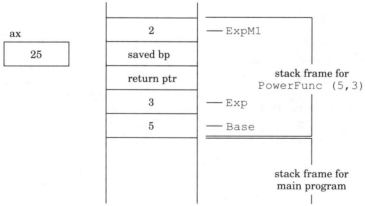

**Figure 8.7** Stack on Return from `PowerFunc(5, 2)`

### 8.5 Reentrant and Recursive Subprograms

As an example of tail recursion, consider the function that computes the greatest common divisor of two integers, using Euclid's algorithm. This can be written as

```
FUNCTION GCD (M, N)
BEGIN
  Remainder := M mod N
  IF Remainder = 0
  THEN
    GCD := N
  ELSE
    GCD := GCD (N, Remainder)
  ENDIF
END
```

When GCD returns to the calling program, possibly itself, from the recursive call in the ELSE clause, it must only leave the result in the appropriate register and return. Compare this to the preceding recursive example, `PowerFunc`, which continues a computation when the function returns to itself.

The GCD algorithm is implemented using tail recursion in Program 8.12. It contains a label, `ReEnter`, and an unconditional jump to that label in the ELSE clause. This essentially converts the selection structure into an unstructured loop. The subprogram can be transformed, with a little more effort, into a neat conditional loop. We did not take that approach because we wanted to keep the sense of the recursion in the ELSE clause of the selection structure.

## Program 8.12

```
; Program 8.12       GCDTail.ASM
; Function GCD (M, N : Integer) : Integer;
;    Computes the greatest common divisor of M and N.
;    Uses recursive algorithm implemented as tail recursion.

; Parameters:
   M           equ       word ptr [bp + 6]
   N           equ       word ptr [bp + 4]
   Remainder   equ       word ptr [bp - 2]

_TEXT SEGMENT word public 'code'
     assume   cs: _TEXT
     public   GCD

GCD PROC

; set up bp register to point to parameters
     push     bp
     mov      bp, sp

; allocate stack space for local variable
     sub      sp, 2

; save caller's dx register
     push     dx
```

**Progam 8.12 (continued)**

```
        ReEnter:    ;re-entry point for tail recursion

        ; Remainder := M mod N
            mov     ax, M
            cwd
            idiv    N
            mov     Remainder, dx

        ; IF01 Remainder = 0
            cmp     dx, 0
            jne     ELSE01

        ; THEN01
        ;    GCD := N
            mov     ax, N
            jmp     ENDIF01

          ELSE01:
        ;    GCD := GCD (N, Remainder)
            xchg    dx, N
            mov     M, dx
            jmp     ReEnter
          ENDIF01:

        ; restore registers and return with result in ax
            pop     dx
            add     sp, 2
            pop     bp
            ret     4

GCD   ENDP
_TEXT ENDS
END
```

The key to implementing tail recursion without the overhead of a `call` instruction and another stack frame is to make all parameters local. We can then change the call to the subprogram into a jump to the beginning of the subprogram. When the subprogram does eventually return, since it never called itself, there are no extra stack frames to release. Thus the jump to ENDIF01 in Program 8.12 passes control to the instructions that release the stack frame and return to the original calling program.

## Recursion versus Iteration

Many subprograms can be written using either recursion or iteration. When should one method be chosen over the other?

In almost every programming-language text that discusses recursion, there is mention that using recursion incurs a penalty in extra overhead. It is not unusual to come away from some of these discussions thinking that recursive programs are incredibly more "expensive" to execute than iterative ones. In fairness, many texts do a good job, considering how

## 8.5 Reentrant and Recursive Subprograms

little of the overhead they can discuss with only a high-level language as background. A few thoughts on the subject are shared here.

First, note that in order for a subprogram to be recursive, it must be fully reentrant. On some systems, for which instructions and data share the same segment (even if there is no explicit mention of "segments"), the way to make a subprogram recursive is to load a new copy of it for every invocation. Loading new copies incurs a hefty penalty in memory use and execution time (which now includes loading multiple copies of the subprogram from relatively slow storage). On other systems, like those that use the 8086, making a subprogram fully reentrant requires only a new stack frame for each invocation.

Compare Programs 8.2 and 8.11, which implement the same computation iteratively and recursively. The iterative version uses two words of stack space to save the CX and DX registers, in addition to the space for the arguments, return pointer, and BP register. Each call of the recursive version uses two words of stack space to save the CX and DX registers and one word for a local variable, in addition to the arguments, return pointer, and saved BP register. Unless there are hundreds of recursive calls before any invocations of the subprogram complete and return, this amount of extra space is not prohibitive (but must be considered when declaring the stack segment). Space is probably not the deciding factor.

The time to execute may be a factor. There are two ways to compare execution time: by analyzing the number of instructions executed or by timing. Counting how many times each instruction is executed for some mix of arguments, though not too difficult, can be tedious. Timing how long each version takes to execute requires that enough executions be performed so that the amount of time measured is much greater than the resolution of the clock. Also important is timing both implementations with the same sets of arguments.

Both programs were run with a variety of arguments for thousands of calls from a main program. In these tests, the recursive implementation required about three times longer to execute than the iterative version. To put that in perspective, consider three applications, in which the time to execute the iterative version of the function accounts for 10%, 2%, and 0.1% of the total execution time. The penalty for using the recursive version of the function would be 20%, 4%, and 0.2% of total time, respectively. Clearly, if we have an application in which the calls on this function represent a significant part of the total program, we should use the iterative version; but if calls on this function account for only a small part of total execution time, the penalty for the recursive version is less important. (We would be spending our time better by looking to improve some other part of the program that does represent a greater part of total execution time.)

Thus, the extra memory used in a recursive subprogram may not be significant as long as the number of calls—and of stack frames—does not get too large. The extra execution time required for the recursive implementation may not be a significant part of the time required for the entire application. But then again, it may.

## EXERCISES 8.5

▶1. Write an assembly-language function that computes $N!$ using the definition

$$N! = \begin{cases} 1 & \text{when } N = 0 \\ N \times (N-1)! & \text{when } N > 0 \end{cases}$$

Implement using recursion. Write a main program to test it.

2. Trace the execution of the recursive function in Exercise 1. Draw a series of diagrams like those of Figures 8.1 through 8.7.

▶3. Write an assembly-language function that computes $N!$ using the definition

$$N! = 1 \times 2 \times 3 \times \cdots \times (N-1) \times N$$

Implement this using a repetition structure. Write a main program to test it (or use the main program of Exercise 1).

4. Compare the time needed to execute the functions of Exercises 1 and 3. Compare the space needed for each. What guidance can you suggest when asked whether to use recursion or iteration?

▶5. Write a recursive assembly-language procedure that reads a series of integers until a zero is entered, then prints the input values in reverse sequence. The procedure is essentially

```
Read (Number)
IF Number <> 0
THEN
    invoke this procedure
ENDIF
Print (Number)
```

Note that each invocation needs a separate local variable (in the stack frame) for the number entered and later printed. Write a main program to test it.

6. Trace the execution of the recursive procedure in Exercise 5. Draw a series of diagrams like those of Figures 8.1 through 8.7.

▶7. Write an iterative assembly-language procedure that reads a series of integers until zero is entered and then prints the input values in reverse sequence. To do so, use a loop to read integers and push them onto the stack until a zero is read, and then use a second loop to pop them off the stack and print them. Write a main program to test it (or use the main program of Exercise 5).

8. Compare the time needed to execute the procedures of Exercises 5 and 7. Compare the space needed for each. What guidance can you suggest when asked whether to use recursion or iteration?

9. Determine the number of instructions executed by Program 8.2 as a function of Exp.

10. Determine the number of instructions executed by Program 8.11 as a function of Exp.

▶11. Write and run your own timing experiments.

12. Compare your results from Exercises 9, 10, and 11 with the results of the timing experiments reported in the text.

## KEY POINTS

- References to external symbols cannot be resolved by an assembler or a compiler; the linker and loader must resolve them.
- Assembler directives are used to declare symbols that are to be made available to the linkage editor and to specify symbols for which the linkage editor must find addresses.
- When one subprogram invokes another, the return address and arguments are handled in the same way as when a main program invokes a subprogram. Care must be taken when passing a reference parameter as an argument to another subprogram.
- A program segment is non-reentrant if it can be reliably executed only once each time it is loaded.

- A program segment is serially reentrant if it can be reliably executed more than once after it is loaded, but only if each invocation is allowed to terminate before another invocation occurs.
- A program segment is fully reentrant if it can be reliably executed regardless of whether there are other invocations that are still active.
- A segment that contains only instructions and constants, in which none of the instructions are modified during execution, is called a pure segment. Pure segments are fully reentrant.
- A program that invokes itself, or another that invokes it in turn, is recursive.
- When the recursive invocation of a program is the last step in it, the call can be replaced by a jump to the entry point. This saves the overhead of allocating another stack frame and copying arguments. This form of recursion is called *tail recursion*.

## PC SYSTEM SUMMARY

- Jumps that transfer control within a segment are called *near jumps* if they use a word displacement or *short jumps* if they use a byte displacement. Those that transfer control to another segment are called *far jumps*.
- References to data in the current data segment, using just an offset, are called *near references*; references to data in another segment, using a segment and an offset, are called *far references*.
- To specify a segment override, we write the segment register with a colon before the operand.
- The `ptr` operator can be used to specify the type of a label as `far` or `near`.
- The `extrn` directive informs the assembler that a symbol is an external reference for which the linker is to provide an offset.
- The `public` directive informs the assembler that a symbol is to be made available to the linker for use in resolving external references from other modules.
- The entry point to a procedure is declared in the procedure with the PROC directive. An optional operand specifies whether it is NEAR or FAR and controls the type of `ret` instruction generated to return control.
- The language-dependent conventions for linking assembly-language subprograms with high-level-language programs involve segments, data types, arguments, function results, and saving the caller's state. (See Appendix 7 for some details.)
- Generally, the segmented structure of 8086 programs helps to separate instructions from data, making pure code segments easier to write. However, segment purity is not enforced.

Instructions presented in this chapter:

    `lds`    loads a far pointer into DS and another register
    `les`    loads a far pointer into ES and another register

Directives presented in this chapter:

    `extrn`    declares an external reference
    `public`    makes a reference available to external modules
    `proc`    defines the start of a subprogram
    `endp`    defines the end of a subprogram

# 9 Interrupts and I/O

- **Interrupts**
- **DOS and BIOS Services**
- **User I/O**
- **Disk I/O**
- **Communications**

Few application programmers want to deal with the many machine-dependent details of communicating with an input or output device. Fortunately, the disk operating system (DOS) and the basic input/output system (BIOS) of the computer system provide a convenient means of using most devices. When a program requests an I/O operation, it invokes the services of DOS, which in turn invokes the services of the BIOS, which in turn accesses the hardware. Sometimes a program accesses the BIOS or hardware directly, trading the overhead of DOS for the responsibility of managing more details.

A peripheral device can also request some processing to be performed by the BIOS (or DOS or an application, if these have been substituted for the BIOS routines that service the device) when an event occurs. Since peripheral devices operate asynchronously from programs, interrupts are used to coordinate them.

This chapter discusses the 8086 interrupt facilities and how to use them for I/O operations. It surveys the characteristics of the keyboard, video display, and disk drives. It also examines the services available from DOS and from the BIOS.

## 9.1 INTERRUPTS

An **interrupt** is a signal to the processor that an event needing immediate attention has occurred. There are two types of interrupts: **external interrupts**, which are generated outside of the CPU by other hardware, and **internal interrupts**, which are generated within the CPU as a result of some operation or instruction. When an interrupt occurs, the program that is running is suspended so that a special program, called an interrupt handler, can service the event that caused the interrupt. When the interrupt handler finishes, control is returned to the program.

### External Interrupts

Most external interrupts are generated by input and output devices. In a multiprogram system, after a program initiates an I/O request the operating system changes its state from running to blocked, since the program will be idle while waiting for the device to respond. It also changes the state of some other program from ready to running. Later, while the second program is running, the device requested by the first program can respond by generating an interrupt. The interrupt handler might acknowledge the device, send another request to it, or accept some input and put it in a buffer.

Timers also generate external interrupts. To prevent programs with potential errors from using too much of the system's resources in the event of an infinite loop, some multiuser systems set a maximum running time for a program when it is started. If the program uses all of the allotted time before it finishes, it is interrupted by a routine that terminates the program and displays an error message.

Another timer interrupt occurs in real-time systems that monitor or control processes. A computer monitoring a chemical process would have a program scan a number of temperature, pressure, and flow rate sensors every few seconds, and then analyze the data obtained. If necessary, the program might make small changes in the process or signal an operator to make changes. When this program is not running, the computer could be executing other programs, perhaps generating reports of plant operation. The program that scans the sensors and analyzes the data is initiated by a timer that interrupts whatever other programs are running.

Other external interrupts involve detection of hardware faults such as a failure of power supplies or an operator-initiated system shutdown.

## Internal Interrupts

Internal interrupts are generated by errors detected by the CPU or by instructions that specifically initiate an interrupt. Internal interrupts generated by errors are also called **traps**, and the routines invoked to service them are called **trap handlers**. Some traps are caused by overflow, an attempt to divide by zero, an invalid operation, or an attempt to access memory other than that allocated for the program.

Overflow occurs when the result of an arithmetic operation is too large. In some systems, there are flag bits that determine whether overflow is to be ignored or is to generate an interrupt; in others, when overflow occurs during an integer operation, the overflow flag is set and execution continues at the next instruction. In the latter type of system, it is up to the programmer to include instructions in the program to check the overflow flag and take appropriate action when overflow could be a problem.

Division by zero is not defined. Some systems may have flags that indicate whether an interrupt should be generated to invoke a trap handler, or whether the divide instruction should just be skipped.

An invalid operation interrupt is generated when the control unit is unable to decode an instruction. In almost every instruction set, there are opcodes or combinations of opcodes and other fields that are not defined. If the processor encounters one of these undefined opcodes, which can happen when a program attempts to execute data, the system has little choice but to terminate the program and display the faulty instruction and its address. Another invalid operation interrupt is generated when a valid instruction is used with invalid data. For example, as we will see in Chapter 17, there are some bit patterns that do not represent valid floating-point data (the REAL data type in many programming languages). When such a pattern is fetched as an operand, the 8087 coprocessor detects it and generates an interrupt.

The last internal interrupt considered here is generated by an attempt to access memory outside of the region allocated to the program in a multiprogram system. Such accesses can be the result of a programmer error or an attempt to violate system security. The interrupt handler for this usually terminates the program with an error message.

## The 8086 Interrupts

The 8086 processor recognizes 256 different interrupts, each identified by a byte of data that accompanies the interrupt signal. There is a table of 256 far pointers (a four-byte segment:offset pair) in memory at addresses 00000h through 003FFh. Each of these pointers is the entry point of the handler for the corresponding interrupt. For example, when DOS or an application requests a BIOS keyboard service by the `int` 16h instruction, the processor computes $4 \times 16h = 58h$ and fetches the far pointer at 0000:0058. It then uses that far pointer to invoke the BIOS routine (see Figure 9.1). (In the figure, the address of the `int` 16h handler is that given in a reference book; it may vary depending on BIOS version and system configuration.)

The 8086 allows most interrupts to be disabled temporarily. An interrupt that can be disabled by setting a control flag is a **maskable interrupt**. The interrupt enable flag (IF)

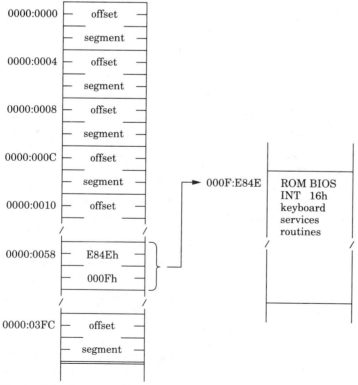

**Figure 9.1** Interrupt Vectors, with INT 16h Vector and Service Routines

## 9.1 Interrupts

controls maskable interrupts: When the flag is cleared, interrupts are not recognized until the flag is set again; when the flag is set, interrupts are serviced as they occur. Some interrupts, notably those that deal with emergencies such as impending power failure, are always enabled; these are called **nonmaskable interrupts**.

There are two instructions for clearing and setting the IF flag.

**CLear Interrupt flag**
- syntax: `cli`
- action: IF cleared

**SeT Interrupt flag**
- syntax: `sti`
- action: IF set
- flags: OD.TSZAPC unchanged
  ..I...... cleared or set

Interrupts should be masked with care and for as short a time as is practical. Disabling interrupts for long periods of time, or without reason, invites disaster.

When an interrupt occurs, assuming that IF is set, the processor finishes the instruction it is executing. Then it pushes the flags, CS, and IP registers onto the stack. These three registers represent the state of the machine that must be restored when the interrupt handler terminates. After saving the machine state, the processor loads CS:IP with the far pointer corresponding to the interrupt that occurred and resumes execution, fetching the first instruction of the interrupt handler.

When the interrupt handler terminates, it returns control to the interrupted program by popping the stack into IP, CS, and the flags registers, using the `iret` instruction. This restores the machine to its state at the time of the interrupt.

**Interrupt RETurn**
- syntax: `iret`
- action:
  (1) pop IP;
  (2) pop CS;
  (3) pop flags
- flags: ODITSZAPC restored from stack

In many ways, an interrupt handler is like a subprogram. It must first carefully save any registers before it changes them and then restore them before returning to the interrupted program. This procedure ensures that it does not adversely affect the interrupted program. Since interrupts can occur at any time, and the event that triggers an interrupt may not be related to the program that is executing, interrupt handlers must leave no sign that they executed except for intended obvious effects (such as displaying an error message or moving an input value to a buffer).

Every program must provide stack space for saving the machine state when an interrupt occurs. It is recommended that at least 128 bytes of stack space be available for the interrupt system. Interrupt handlers that need a large amount of stack space switch to their own stack segments.

Although there is no need to do so, any subprogram could switch stack segments. To do so, another segment must be reserved (different name, not combined with the main stack segment), and SS:SP must be switched to point to the top of the new stack. This procedure raises an interesting problem. Consider moving new values into SS and SP with two mov instructions. If an interrupt occurs between these two instructions, the interrupt handler uses the new SS with the old SP, or vice versa, which is not the top of either stack. To prevent this, the IF flag can be cleared to disable maskable interrupts before the mov instructions, and IF can be set afterward. A better way—implemented in all but the very earliest 8088 and 8086 processors—is for the processor to disable interrupts for one instruction automatically whenever the destination of a mov instruction is the SS register. With this feature, systems just mov the new value for SP into it immediately after they mov the new value into SS.

The basic input/output system (BIOS) and DOS routines are invoked as software interrupts. We have used interrupt 21h to return control to DOS when our programs terminate. Actually, this one interrupt is used to invoke many DOS functions. The next section discusses in greater detail how interrupts are used to access system services.

## EXERCISES 9.1

1. What could happen if an interrupt handler attempted to return by using separate pop instructions rather than iret?
2. Why should interrupts not be disabled arbitrarily for long periods of time?
3. In what ways are interrupts not like conventional subprograms?

## 9.2 DOS AND BIOS SERVICES

Application programmers working in a high-level language take much for granted concerning system support of input and output operations. Between the program's instructions and the hardware are at least two levels of support for input and output operations. These are the disk operating system (DOS) and the basic input/output system (BIOS) (see Figure 9.2).

Consider the task of reading a character from the keyboard. An application program written in a high-level language might use a READ statement. READ invokes a DOS procedure to get the next character from the input buffer associated with the keyboard. DOS, in turn, uses the BIOS routines to check whether a keystroke is available, to get the scan code, to acknowledge the receipt of the code, and so on.

### Which Services to Use

The BIOS provides the lowest level interface to the hardware; DOS provides the next higher level interface to the hardware, as well as an interface to the BIOS. Different computers using the same processor but otherwise different hardware will have slightly different BIOS routines. The interface to these routines is consistent, even though the actual operations performed by the BIOS depend on the hardware. Different computers using the same operating system can use different versions of the BIOS thanks to a common, well-defined interface.

## 9.2 DOS and BIOS Services

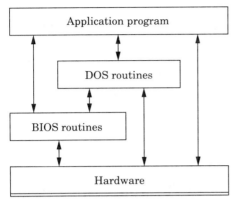

**Figure 9.2** DOS and BIOS Interface to Hardware

Note from Figure 9.2, however, that a program can access the BIOS and the hardware directly, bypassing DOS; likewise, DOS can access the hardware directly, bypassing the BIOS. These capabilities raise questions of when a program should call DOS, call the BIOS, or access the hardware directly. In general, using the highest level of support available hides the most system-dependent details, making the application more portable. This practice, however, sacrifices some control and possibly some efficiency.

There are cases when a program skips over DOS to access the BIOS. Many disk utility packages use BIOS routines directly because they provide more low-level control than do DOS routines. However, for routine file processing, there is no reason to work with BIOS routines rather than DOS routines; to do so entails, in essence, writing the DOS facilities into the program.

There are also cases when a program skips over DOS and the BIOS to access the hardware directly. Many drawing programs write their output directly to the memory that is mapped to the display rather than passing it through DOS and the BIOS. This makes the screen update faster. The delays introduced by passing the drawing information through DOS and the BIOS may be unacceptable in these applications.

A situation in which a program must access the hardware directly occurs when a new device not supported by the BIOS is attached to the computer. The new device requires a software interface called a **device driver**. The device driver must access the new device directly. The programs that use the new device do so by calling the device driver.

In general, applications should use the services that DOS provides rather than access the BIOS. When using DOS is not feasible, the BIOS routines are preferred to accessing the hardware directly. Only when absolutely necessary—and provided that the programmer understands the hardware and the potential side effects—should the hardware be accessed directly.

### Functions as Interrupts

DOS and BIOS functions impose several requirements on a calling program. The interrupt mechanism that invokes DOS and BIOS services meets all of these requirements.

DOS and BIOS routines can be called from any program, anywhere in memory, so the calls and returns must be far. It is unlikely that every call to any of the system routines will be made from the same segment. Since it is inconvenient to vary the use of near and far calls, all calls must be far. The interrupt mechanism uses far pointers and a far return.

Different versions of DOS and variations in BIOS routines exist on different but compatible computers. The different versions of the DOS and BIOS routines vary in size, so the addresses of the routines cannot be fixed in memory. Instead, the system must provide a common, fixed reference for each routine and use indirection to transfer control to it. The BIOS and DOS startup routines set up these fixed references as indirect pointers to the actual routines. A table of far pointers could be used with the `call` instruction but would require a far reference to fetch the pointer followed by a far `call` to transfer control; the extra level of indirection adds to the overhead of invoking the routine. Using the interrupt vector table and the `int` instruction helps to manage the far pointers.

The hardware must be able to invoke some of the BIOS routines directly and immediately. It cannot wait for some application program to check the hardware status. Interrupts constitute the only mechanism that allows hardware to invoke software.

We should also note here that all BIOS and most DOS interrupt service routines preserve all registers except the AX register and any registers used to return results. Most DOS routines that return an error code set the carry flag to indicate an error and return the code in AX; they clear the carry flag if no errors occur.

## Using Interrupts

We now examine some short programs that use DOS and BIOS services. As we will see in the next section, every time a key is pressed or released, the keyboard controller generates interrupt 09h. The handler for this interrupt updates the keyboard status in memory and makes the character code (ASCII or an extended code) available in a buffer. A program can later invoke interrupt 16h to get the character code from the buffer.

To demonstrate the use of interrupts (though not in a useful application), consider a routine that, once installed, monitors how many times keys are pressed or released. The idea is to load a small routine into memory and modify the vector for interrupt 09h so that it invokes the routine. The routine simply increments a counter and then passes control to the BIOS interrupt 09h service routine.

One problem is eventually printing the counter. It is certainly undesirable to print the counter every time a key is pressed or released. The plan is to use a separate routine to return the counter in a register. This second routine will also be loaded into memory and left there. It does not need to use a BIOS interrupt: Interrupts 60h through 66h are reserved for user programs, so interrupt 60h can be designated to retrieve the counter.

Three DOS functions are necessary to install these two routines in memory. The first of these is function 35h: Get Interrupt Vector. It loads ES:BX with the far pointer to the routine that services the interrupt specified in the AL register. The second DOS function is 25h: Set Interrupt Vector. It copies the pointer contained in DS:DX to the interrupt vector associated with the interrupt number specified in AL. The final DOS function used in the program is 31h: Keep Process. It terminates a program but keeps part (or all) of it resident in memory. The DX register specifies how many paragraphs, including the 16 paragraphs used for the program segment prefix (described in Chapter 11), to retain in memory.

### 9.2 DOS and BIOS Services

Program 9.1 contains the preceding two interrupt routines and an installation program. Everything from the beginning of the code segment—including the word of data in the code segment for the counter and the two words for the original interrupt 09h vector—to the label SetUp will remain resident in memory when the installation program terminates. The installation program comprises everything from the label SetUp through the end of the program, as well as the stack segment.

**Program 9.1**

```
; Program 9.1      CountKey.ASM
; Set up a TSR that counts the number of times a key
; is pressed or released.

DOSSEG

TSR_STACK SEGMENT para stack 'stack'
            dw       100h dup (?)
TSR_STACK ENDS

TSR_TEXT SEGMENT word public 'code'
    assume   cs: TSR_TEXT

;;;;;;;;;;;;;;;;;;;;; Resident part ;;;;;;;;;;;;;;;;;;;;

; Data for TSR
    KeyCount    dw      0       ;number of times int 09h issued
    Old09_Off   dw      ?       ;far pointer to original
    Old09_Seg   dw      ?       ;   interrupt 09h handler

; CountKey TSR, invoked by interrupt 09h when any key is
; pressed or released (or held down longer than Typematic
; threshold), increments KeyCount and passes control to
; original interrupt 09h handler.

CountKey:

; save registers
    push    es
    push    ax

; set up es register to point to TSR_TEXT
    mov     ax, seg TSR_TEXT
    mov     es, ax

; increment KeyCount
    inc     es:KeyCount

; restore registers
    pop     ax
    pop     es

; transfer control to original 09h handler
    jmp     dword ptr Old09_Off
```

**310**  Chapter 9  Interrupts and I/O

## Program 9.1 (continued)

```
        ; ReturnCount TSR, invoked by INT 60h issued by a user
        ; program, returns KeyCount in ax.

ReturnCount:

        ; save es, then set it up to point to TSR_TEXT
            push    es
            mov     ax, seg TSR_TEXT
            mov     es, ax

        ; load KeyCount into ax
            mov     ax, es:KeyCount

        ; restore es and return to caller
            pop     es
            iret


;;;;;;;;;;;;;;;;;;;;;; Installation part ;;;;;;;;;;;;;;;;;;;;

        ; SetUp saves far pointer to original int 09h handler, sets
        ; int vector 09h to point to CountKey, int vector 60h to
        ; point to ReturnCount, and terminates with them resident.

        ; DOS function and status parameters
            DosFunc     equ     21h
            SetIntVect  equ     25h
            GetIntVect  equ     35h
            KeepProcess equ     31h

        ; Interrupt vectors changed
            KeyboardInt equ     09h
            RetnCount   equ     60h

SetUp:

        ; set up ds register to point to TSR_TEXT
            mov     ax, seg TSR_TEXT
            mov     ds, ax
            assume  ds: TSR_TEXT

        ; save original int 09h vector
            mov     ah, GetIntVect
            mov     al, KeyboardInt
            int     DosFunc
            mov     Old09_Seg, es
            mov     Old09_Off, bx

        ; set up int 09h to point to CountKey
            mov     dx, offset CountKey
            mov     ah, SetIntVect
            mov     al, KeyboardInt
            int     DosFunc
```

### 9.2 DOS and BIOS Services

**Program 9.1 (continued)**

```
        ; set up int 60h to point to ReturnCount
        mov     dx, offset ReturnCount
        mov     al, RetnCount
        int     DosFunc

        ; compute number of paragraphs to leave resident, as
        ; (size of TSRs + PSP)/16, rounded up
        mov     ax, offset SetUp        ;size of TSRs
        add     ax, 0100h               ;size of PSP
        cwd
        mov     cx, 16
        div     cx
        inc     ax                      ;add 1 for rounding
        mov     dx, ax

        ; terminate, leaving TSRs resident
        mov     ah, KeepProcess
        int     DosFunc

TSR_TEXT ENDS
        END     SetUp
```

The operand of the END directive specifies that execution begins with the instruction labeled SetUp. The first two instructions following that label set the DS register to point to the start of TSR_TEXT, much like the first instructions in any program establishing the data segment, except the data is part of the code segment in this example.

The next five instructions

```
mov     ah, GetIntVect
mov     al, KeyboardInt
int     DosFunc
mov     Old09_Seg, es
mov     Old09_Off, bx
```

use DOS function 35h to retrieve the current vector for interrupt 09h and save it. This far pointer will be used by the CountKey routine to transfer control to the BIOS keyboard routine, which must continue to perform all of its normal processing of each keyboard interrupt.

The following sequence

```
mov     dx, offset CountKey
mov     ah, SetIntVect
mov     al, KeyboardInt
int     DosFunc
```

uses DOS function 25h to set the vector for interrupt 09h to point to the CountKey routine. The next three instructions set the vector for interrupt 60h to point to the ReturnCount routine in the same way.

The sequence

```
mov     ax, offset SetUp
add     ax, 0100h
cwd
mov     cx, 16
div     cx
inc     ax
mov     dx, ax
```

computes the number of paragraphs to leave resident. AX is first loaded with the offset of `SetUp`—nothing further needs to remain in memory. The size of the PSP, 100h bytes (discussed in Chapter 11), is added because the PSP is loaded in memory before the first instruction. The sum is then divided by 16 to convert from bytes to paragraphs; 1 is added to account for any remainder from the division. The result is passed to DOS function 31h, to terminate this program but leave the first part of the code segment resident.

Now consider the two routines in the beginning of the code segment. Remember that they are invoked not from the command prompt but as interrupt handlers. Routine `CountKey` starts by saving the registers it uses and setting ES to point to the `TSR_TEXT` (code) segment where the counter is stored:

```
push    es
push    ax
mov     ax, seg TSR_TEXT
mov     es, ax
```

Using ES as a segment override, the instruction

```
inc     es:KeyCount
```

adds 1 to the counter. Then the routine restores the saved registers and transfers control to the original BIOS interrupt 09h handler:

```
pop     ax
pop     es
jmp     dword ptr Old09_Off
```

This transfer is *not* a `call`; the BIOS routine should not return control to this program. Instead, the BIOS routine ends with an `iret` instruction that transfers control back to whatever program was executing when the keyboard interrupt occurred. The BIOS routine works as if the `CountKey` routine were not present.

Routine `ReturnCount` is invoked by interrupt 60h, which is issued only by user programs. A program for that process will be written shortly. `ReturnCount` saves ES on the stack and sets ES to point to `TSR_TEXT`, just as `CountKey` does. Then, it simply copies `KeyCount` into AX, restores ES from the stack, and returns to the interrupted program by the `iret` instruction. AX is not saved and restored; the invoking program expects the counter returned in AX. Unlike DOS and BIOS routines, neither `ReturnCount` nor `CountKey` returns a status in the carry flag.

When Program 9.1 is executed from the DOS prompt, it installs the new interrupt vectors and terminates with the `CountKey` and `ReturnCount` routines in memory. Program 9.1 should not be executed again unless the system is restarted. (The exercises explore the reason for this.)

## 9.2 DOS and BIOS Services

Now consider Program 9.2, which uses interrupt 60h to access the counter. After the usual instructions to set up DS, the program invokes ReturnCount as an interrupt and prints the value returned using the instructions

```
int     RetnCount
call    PutDec
```

Conveniently, ReturnCount returns the counter in the AX register, where PutDec expects its argument. Then Program 9.2 prints a short message.

---

**Program 9.2**

```
; Program 9.2      PrtCount.ASM
; Print the number of times a key has been pressed or
; released since CountKey was installed.

; DOS function and status parameters
  DosFunc     equ     21h
  ExitToDos   equ     4Ch
  NoErrors    equ     00h

; User-defined interrupt
  RetnCount   equ     60h

DOSSEG

_STACK SEGMENT para stack 'stack'
            dw      100h dup (?)
_STACK ENDS

_DATA SEGMENT word public 'data'
  OutMsg      db      " INT 09h invocations. "
  OutLen      dw      $ - OutMsg
_DATA ENDS

_TEXT SEGMENT word public 'code'
      assume  cs: _TEXT
      extrn   PutStr: PROC, PutCrLf: PROC, PutDec: PROC

PrintCount:

; set up ds register to point to _DATA
      mov     ax, seg _DATA
      mov     ds, ax
      assume  ds: _DATA

; print (KeyCount, " INT 09h invocations. ")
      int     RetnCount       ;invoke ReturnCount as interrupt
      call    PutDec          ;pass count to output routine
      mov     cx, OutLen
      mov     bx, offset OutMsg
      call    PutStr
      call    PutCrLf
```

**Program 9.2 (continued)**

```
; return to DOS
      mov    ah, 4Ch
      mov    al, 00h
      int    21h

_TEXT ENDS
END PrintCount
```

## EXERCISES 9.2

1. How do you interpret the statement that "the DOS routines and the BIOS routines represent different machine models" based on the discussion of this section?
2. Some DOS routines invoke BIOS routines, but no BIOS routines invoke DOS routines. Why not?
3. BIOS routines are provided in read-only memory as part of the system hardware. (Read-only memory is discussed in the next chapter.) DOS routines are usually provided as software on a disk. How is this difference significant?
4. Suppose you want to call a subprogram with a near pointer at some times and a far pointer at other times. Could you do this? If so, show how; if not, explain why not.
5. It is possible to run several different operating systems on an 8086-based computer (although not at the same time, of course). What do you think all of those operating systems must have in common? What else do you think they might have in common?
6. What happens when Program 9.1 is executed more than once? Try it. Use the DOS MEM command (with /DEBUG option if available) after each execution. What happens each time a key is pressed after Program 9.1 has been executed several times?
▶7. Research the DOS functions that remove a resident program (free the memory, reset the interrupt vector, do other needed housekeeping) and write a program that removes CountKey and ReturnCount from memory.
8. The typematic feature generates multiple copies of the same key when that key is pressed and held down. Using Programs 9.1 and 9.2, determine whether the typematic feature also repeats generating codes when the SHIFT, ALT, and CTRL keys are held down.
9. Program 9.1 actually counts the number of times interrupt 09h is invoked by the keyboard controller. If 09h is invoked by both pressing and releasing a key, how can the value printed by Program 9.2 sometimes be even and sometimes be odd?

## 9.3 USER I/O

This section discusses some properties of common input and output devices and demonstrates the routines that DOS and the BIOS provide for using them. The input and output procedures supplied with the text will be examined.

## Device Descriptions

The most common input device is a keyboard. Keyboards used with most personal computers have from about 80 to over 100 keys. Each time a key is pressed, the keyboard generates signals that ultimately may be interpreted as a character in some code. Some keys, such as SHIFT or CTRL, do not represent characters but, rather, modify the codes generated for other keys.

The most widely used output device is a video display. A typical video display works much like the picture tube in a television set: A focused electron beam sweeps across the inside surface of the display, causing the phosphor coating to glow. The position of the beam and its intensity are controlled by signals generated by the computer's video subsystem. In text mode, many video displays show 25 lines of 80 characters, or a total of 2000 characters. In a microcomputer, a region of memory is reserved for a map of the display. Writing a character to a byte of that memory causes the character to appear in a corresponding location on the display. PCs and compatible microcomputers use two bytes of memory for each character cell on the display, one for the character code and one for its color and brightness attributes.

In graphics mode, the video display is mapped to a much larger memory. The display is a grid of many small dots or picture elements, called pixels, or pels. Graphics displays contain from about $300 \times 200$ to over $1280 \times 1024$ pixels. In a monochrome system, each pixel is mapped to a single bit; the pixel is on if the bit is set, off if the bit is cleared. In a color system, as much as a word of memory is used to define the color and brightness of each pixel. Depending on resolution and color attributes, from 8K to over 2M of memory may be needed to represent a graphics image.

Printers are the next most widely used output device. Printers accept a stream of codes from the computer and convert them into signals that control the mechanisms for printing the characters and advancing the paper. There are standard control codes that cause printers to eject to a new page, start a new line, and so on. Control codes are transmitted just like text. To print graphics images, the processor must send each dot on the page to the printer. Except for extra control codes and a greater quantity of data to transmit, communication is the same for printing text and graphics.

There are other, more esoteric input and output devices that will not be presented. Devices such as mice, graphics tablets, scanners, plotters, musical device interfaces, voice systems, and pen-based systems, are beyond the scope of this book.

## DOS I/O Services

DOS provides a dozen functions for handling input and output with "standard" devices. The standard input device is the keyboard, but input can be redirected from another device. The standard output device is the video display, but output can be redirected to another device. For more on standard devices, refer to the MS-DOS reference manual.

All DOS functions are invoked by moving the function number into the AH register and issuing interrupt 21h (named DosFunc in the programs in this book). Other registers are used for additional parameters and results. Table 9.1 lists 12 DOS I/O functions with the parameters expected and values returned. Unless otherwise noted, input functions check for CTRL-C and issue interrupt 23h when detected.

## 316 Chapter 9 Interrupts and I/O

**Table 9.1  DOS Standard I/O Functions**

| DOS function | Description |
| --- | --- |
| 01h Read Keyboard and Echo | Get character from standard input, return it in AL, and display it on standard output. |
| 02h Display Character | Send character in DL to standard output. |
| 03h Auxiliary Input | Get character from auxiliary input and return it in AL. |
| 04h Auxiliary Output | Send character in DL to auxiliary device. |
| 05h Print Character | Send character in DL to standard printer. |
| 06h Direct Console I/O | With DL = FFh (input function): If character is available from standard input, get it, return it in AL, and clear zero flag. If no character is available from standard input, clear AL and set zero flag. [This function does not check for CTRL-C.] With DL < FFh (output function): Send character in DL to standard output. |
| 07h Direct Console Input | Get character from standard input, return it in AL. [This function does not check for CTRL-C.] |
| 08h Read Keyboard | Get character from standard input, return it in AL. |
| 09h Display String | Send string starting at DS:DX to standard output; string must terminate with "$" ("$" not displayed). |
| 0Ah Buffered Keyboard Input | Read string from standard input into the buffer starting at DS:DX; first byte of buffer specifies the maximum length string; second byte of buffer returns the length of the string read. |
| 0Bh Check Keyboard Status | Check whether any characters are available from standard input; return FFh in AL if characters are available, 00h in AL if not. |
| 0Ch Flush Buffer, Read Keyboard | Empty standard input buffer, then invoke function 01h, 06h, 07h, 08h, or 0Ah, based on value in AL. |

The input and output routines provided with this text (`PutStr`, `GetDec`, and so on) use functions 01h, 02h, and 08h. Refer to Appendix 1 for listings of these routines. All output routines use function 02h (named `DispChar` in the program listings).

`PutChar` is simply the sequence

```
push    ax
mov     ah, DispChar
int     DosFunc
pop     ax
ret
```

Note that the input to `PutChar`, the character to display, is expected in the DL register. Function 02h also expects the character to display in that register. The `push` and `pop` instructions preserve the AX register. `PutStr` displays the characters in the argument

## 9.3 User I/O

string, one at a time in a loop, using function 02h; PutCrLf invokes function 02h once with CR (ASCII code 0Dh) and once with LF (ASCII code 0Ah); and PutDec converts the internal representation of a signed integer to six characters, then displays them using function 02h.

GetChar is the most complex procedure in its use of DOS functions. It uses function 01h (named ReadKbdEcho in the program listings) to read a character from the keyboard and echo it. However, if the user enters a key or combination that represents an extended code, such as PAGEUP or CTRL-INSERT, function 01h returns 00h in AL and 01h in AH. The scan code for the extended character can be read (except when executing under control of some debuggers) using function 08h (named ReadKbd in the program listings). The selection structure

```
; IF51 an extended code was entered
      cmp     al, 0
      jne     ELSE51
; THEN51
;     call DOS Read Keyboard to get code byte
      mov     ah, ReadKbd
      int     DosFunc
;     indicate extended character
      mov     ah, 1
      jmp     ENDIF51
  ELSE51:
;     indicate ASCII character
      mov     ah, 0
  ENDIF51:
```

checks the code returned by function 01h and invokes function 08h if needed. It also sets or clears AH to indicate whether the character in AL is an ASCII character or an extended code.

One task remains in reading a character with GetChar. When the user taps the ENTER key, the CR character is read and echoed. However, it is also necessary to echo an LF character using function 02h. This is accomplished in the selection structure

```
; IF52 character is <Enter>
      cmp     al, Cr
      jne     ENDIF52
; THEN52
;     send <Lf> to display
      push    dx
      mov     ah, DispChar
      mov     dl, Lf
      int     DosFunc
      pop     dx
;     return <Cr> in al
      mov     ah, 0
      mov     al, Cr
  ENDIF52:
```

DX is saved before calling function 02h so that DL can be used to pass the LF character to it. The code for CR is moved into AL and 00h into AH before returning from GetChar when CR is read.

GetDec uses GetChar to get the input characters. GetDec ignores any leading spaces. Once another character is read, GetDec checks whether it is a minus sign and saves $-1$ or $+1$ in CL accordingly. Then, it accepts digits and builds the internal representation of the magnitude of the number in a loop. GetDec calls ChkDigit, a routine in the same module, to check that the input is a valid digit. If it is, the previous value is multiplied by 10 using a series of shifts and an add, and the value of the digit is added. The loop terminates when the input is not a digit; if it is anything other than a space or CR, GetDec calls IOError to display an error message and terminate. If the last character is a space or a CR, GetDec moves the magnitude to AX and negates the magnitude if a leading minus sign was entered. Finally, GetDec restores the saved registers and returns.

Although not exhaustive, this discussion should help you to appreciate the DOS services that the input and output routines use for keyboard input and video output.

## BIOS Keyboard Services

The BIOS services for the keyboard and video subsystems are complex. We consider them separately, starting with the keyboard services. Refer to Figure 9.3. Every time a key is pressed or released, the keyboard transmits a one-byte code one bit at a time to a controller in the computer system. The controller packs the bits received from the keyboard into a byte and issues interrupt 09h. The BIOS handler for interrupt 09h examines the bytes from the keyboard controller and processes them as follows:

- For certain key combinations (such as CTRL-ALT-DEL or CTRL-NUMLOCK), corresponding functions (RESET or PAUSE, respectively) are requested.

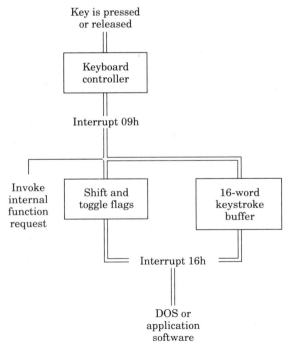

**Figure 9.3** Processing a Keystroke

### 9.3 User I/O

- For shift (SHIFT, CTRL, or ALT) or toggle (INSERT, CAPSLOCK, SCROLL-LOCK, or NUMLOCK) keys, flags in memory are updated.
- For other keys, a word is placed in the keystroke buffer: ASCII code (zero for function and edit keys) in the low byte and the scan code in the high byte.

Recall the two small TSR programs written and installed in Section 9.2. The first one is invoked by interrupt 09h whenever a key is pressed or released. It increments a counter and then passes control to the original handler for this interrupt.

The keystroke buffer is a queue of 16 words. DOS and application software can access the keystroke buffer using interrupt 16h. The functions provided by the BIOS for this interrupt are selected by loading the desired function number into the AH register before issuing it (see Table 9.2).

If the keystroke buffer is empty when function 00h is requested, the program is suspended until a character is available. On AT systems, the operating system may perform another task while waiting for keyboard input. Program 9.3 is a simple function that invokes interrupt 16h and returns the character in AX. This function will be used later in a larger example.

**Program 9.3**

```
; Program 9.3        ReadKey.ASM
; Read one keystroke using BIOS interrupt.

; BIOS interrupt and function
BiosKeybdInt    equ     16h
ReadKeyFunc     equ     00h
```

**Table 9.2 BIOS Keyboard Functions**

| BIOS function | Description |
|---|---|
| 00h Read Keyboard Input (standard)<br>10h Read Extended Keyboard Input (101/102 key) | Copy character code from keystroke buffer to AX, then delete character code from keystroke buffer. |
| 01h Return Keyboard Status (standard)<br>11h Return Extended Keyboard Status (101/102 key) | Check whether a keystroke is present in the buffer. If so, copy it into AX and clear ZF; keystroke buffer is not altered. If no character present set ZF. |
| 02h Return Shift Flag Status (standard)<br>12h Return Extended Shift Flag Status (101/102 key) | Load status of shift and toggle keys into AL; bits of AL correspond to keys as shown in the diagram. A set bit indicates that the lock is active or the key is pressed. |

| 7 | 6 | 5 | 4 | 3 | 2 | 1 | 0 |
|---|---|---|---|---|---|---|---|
| INS | CAPS LOCK | NUM LOCK | SCRL LOCK | ALT | CTRL | LEFT SHIFT | RIGHT SHIFT |

**Program 9.3 (continued)**

```
_TEXT SEGMENT word public 'code'
    assume  cs: _TEXT
    public  ReadKey

ReadKey PROC

; read one keystroke
    mov     ah, ReadKeyFunc
    int     BiosKeybdInt
    ret

ReadKey ENDP
_TEXT ENDS
END
```

In addition to the functions in Table 9.2, there are functions that set the delay and rate at which repeated codes are generated and functions that store character codes into the keystroke buffer from a register.

## BIOS Video Services

Several video adapters can be used in PCs: The monochrome display adapter (MDA) and color graphics adapter (CGA) are supported by the system BIOS, and the enhanced graphics adapter (EGA) and video graphics array (VGA) adapter require a separate ROM BIOS on the adapter card itself. The Hercules display adapter, which provides graphics on monochrome monitors, uses the MDA support of the BIOS for text, but each application program that uses Hercules graphics mode must have its own device driver.

All BIOS routines for video services are invoked by interrupt 10h. The available functions are selected by loading the function number into AH. Brief descriptions of several video functions are given in Table 9.3.

Two procedures that use video functions will now be presented to illustrate the BIOS video services. These procedures will later be combined with Program 9.3 to write a program with simple "window" capabilities. The first procedure, Program 9.4, writes a string on the display. The arguments to the procedure are the row (0 to 24) and column (0 to 79) where the string is to begin, the length of the string, and a far pointer to the string. The program uses the current video page, mode, and text attributes.

Program 9.4 uses function 13h of BIOS INT 10h, the Write String Function, which requires an AT-class or later machine. Using this function is simpler than displaying each character separately and moving the cursor ourselves. Moreover, constructing the program in this manner illustrates its machine dependence. The exercises further explore the issue of machine dependence.

The program saves the registers that it uses, copies the arguments into the necessary registers, copies the function number and CursorMove parameter into registers, and issues the interrupt. When the BIOS routine returns control, this program restores the saved registers and returns.

## 9.3 User I/O

**Table 9.3  BIOS INT 10h Video Functions**

| Function | Description |
|---|---|
| 00h Set Video Mode | Set video registers for operation in the mode specified in AL; if mode is supported by the video hardware installed, then clear the screen, move cursor to (0, 0), and set default colors. |
| 02h Set Cursor Position | Move cursor to row specified in DH (0 = top) and column specified in DL (0 = left side) on page specified in BH. |
| 06h Scroll Page Up | Scroll contents of window defined by CH (top), DH (bottom), CL (left), and DL (right) up the nonzero number of rows specified in AL, or clear the window if AL=0. BH specifies attribute for blanked lines. The display outside the window is not affected. |
| 07h Scroll Page Down | Like function 06h, except that contents of window are scrolled down. |
| 09h Write Character/Attribute | Write character in AL at current cursor position. The CX register specifies a repeat count; the cursor position is not changed unless the same character is repeated. BH and BL specify the page and attributes for text, or colors for graphics. |
| 0Fh Return Video Status | Return current mode in AL, width of display in AH, and active page number in BH. |
| 13h Write String (AT BIOS only) | Write a string to page specified in BH using attributes specified in BL, beginning at position specified by DH (row) and DL (column). ES:BP must point to the first character of string, and CX must contain its length. AL specifies two 1-bit flags:<br><br>bit 0 = 1: cursor remains at last character.<br>bit 0 = 0: cursor returns to original position.<br>bit 1 = 1: characters within the string are followed by their attributes.<br>bit 1 = 0: only displayable characters (no attributes) are within the string. |

## Program 9.4

```
; Program 9.4      WriteStr.ASM
; Write a string at specified position, using current
; page, mode, and text attributes.
; This function works only on AT and newer machines.

; Parameters:
  Row             equ     byte ptr [bp + 12]
  Col             equ     byte ptr [bp + 10]
  OutStrLen       equ     word ptr [bp + 8]
  OutPutStr       equ     dword ptr [bp + 4]

; BIOS interrupt, function, and parameter
  BiosVideoInt    equ     10h
  WriteStrFunc    equ     13h
  CursorMove      equ     01h
```

**Program 9.4 (continued)**

```
        _TEXT SEGMENT word public 'code'
            assume  cs: _TEXT
            public  WriteStr

WriteStr PROC

    ; set up bp to point to parameters
        push    bp
        mov     bp, sp

    ; save registers
        push    ax
        push    cx
        push    dx

    ; Set up parameters for BIOS routine:
    ;   string length in cx
        mov     cx, OutStrLen

    ;   starting position in dh and dl
        mov     dh, Row
        mov     dl, Col

    ;   pointer to string in es:bp
        les     bp, OutputStr

    ;   invoke function, specifying cursor move
        mov     ah, WriteStrFunc
        mov     al, CursorMove
        int     BiosVideoInt

    ; restore registers and return
        pop     dx
        pop     cx
        pop     ax
        pop     bp
        ret     10

WriteStr ENDP
_TEXT ENDS
END
```

The next procedure, Program 9.5, is not only a little more ambitious, but it is much longer. It displays a rectangular window on the display, using the double-rule line-drawing characters in the extended character set, by alternating calls to the Set Cursor Position and Write Character functions.

**Program 9.5**

```
; Program 9.5      Outline.ASM
; Outline a window on screen with double lines, using
; the current video mode, page, and text attributes.
```

**Program 9.5 (continued)**

```
        ; Parameters:
        LeftColumn      equ     byte ptr [bp + 10]
        RightColumn     equ     byte ptr [bp + 8]
        TopRow          equ     byte ptr [bp + 6]
        BottomRow       equ     byte ptr [bp + 4]

        ; Character codes
        TopLeftChar     equ     0C9h        ;"╔" for top left corner
        TopRightChar    equ     0BBh        ;"╗" for top right corner
        HorzLineChar    equ     0CDh        ;"═" for top and bottom lines
        BotLeftChar     equ     0C8h        ;"╚" for bottom left corner
        BotRightChar    equ     0BCh        ;"╝" for bottom right corner
        VertLineChar    equ     0BAh        ;"║" for left and right sides

        ; BIOS interrupts, functions, parameters
        BiosVideoInt    equ     10h
        CursorPosFunc   equ     02h
        WriteCharFunc   equ     09h

_TEXT SEGMENT word public 'code'
        assume  cs: _TEXT
        public  Outline

Outline PROC

        ; set up pointer to parameters
        push    bp
        mov     bp, sp

        ; save registers
        push    ax
        push    cx
        push    dx

        ; print top left corner of outline
        mov     dh, TopRow
        mov     dl, LeftColumn
        mov     ah, CursorPosFunc
        int     BiosVideoInt
        mov     al, TopLeftChar
        mov     cx, 1
        mov     ah, WriteCharFunc
        int     BiosVideoInt

        ; print top line of outline, except corners
        mov     dl, LeftColumn
        inc     dl
        mov     ah, CursorPosFunc
        int     BiosVideoInt
        mov     al, HorzLineChar
        mov     cl, RightColumn
        sub     cl, LeftColumn
        dec     cl
        mov     ah, WriteCharFunc
        int     BiosVideoInt
```

## Program 9.5 (continued)

```
        ; print top right corner of outline
            mov     dl, RightColumn
            mov     ah, CursorPosFunc
            int     BiosVideoInt
            mov     al, TopRightChar
            mov     cx, 1
            mov     ah, WriteCharFunc
            int     BiosVideoInt

        ; print sides of outline, one character at a time
        REPEAT01:

        ;   move down one row
                inc     dh

        ;   print left side
                mov     dl, LeftColumn
                mov     ah, CursorPosFunc
                int     BiosVideoInt
                mov     al, VertLineChar
                mov     ah, WriteCharFunc
                int     BiosVideoInt

        ;   print right side
                mov     dl, RightColumn
                mov     ah, CursorPosFunc
                int     BiosVideoInt
                mov     al, VertLineChar
                mov     ah, WriteCharFunc
                int     BiosVideoInt

        ; TEST01
            cmp     dh, BottomRow
            jne     REPEAT01
        ; UNTIL01 dh = BottomRow

        ; print bottom left corner of outline
            mov     dh, BottomRow
            mov     dl, LeftColumn
            mov     ah, CursorPosFunc
            int     BiosVideoInt
            mov     al, BotLeftChar
            mov     cx, 1
            mov     ah, WriteCharFunc
            int     BiosVideoInt

        ; print bottom line of outline, except corners
            mov     dl, LeftColumn
            inc     dl
            mov     ah, CursorPosFunc
            int     BiosVideoInt
            mov     al, HorzLineChar
            mov     cl, RightColumn
            sub     cl, LeftColumn
```

**Program 9.5 (continued)**

```
            dec     cl
            mov     ah, WriteCharFunc
            int     BiosVideoInt

; print bottom right corner of outline
            mov     dl, RightColumn
            mov     ah, CursorPosFunc
            int     BiosVideoInt
            mov     al, BotRightChar
            mov     cx, 1
            mov     ah, WriteCharFunc
            int     BiosVideoInt

; restore registers and return
            pop     dx
            pop     cx
            pop     ax
            pop     bp
            ret     8

Outline ENDP
_TEXT ENDS
END
```

The Outline procedure in Program 9.5 takes a great amount of code that is more burden than challenge. To display the character for the top left corner, for example, the following sequence is used:

```
mov     dh, TopRow
mov     dl, LeftColumn
mov     al, CursorPosFunc
int     BiosVideoInt
mov     al, TopLeftChar
mov     cx, 1
mov     ah, WriteCharFunc
int     BiosVideoInt
```

The first four instructions move the cursor to the position specified by DH and DL. The last four instructions display the character in AL the number of times specified by CX. The other three corners are displayed using similar sequences.

The top and bottom of the outline are also displayed by a similar sequence. The number of characters to display is calculated as

```
RightColumn - LeftColumn - 1
```

and specified in CL. Earlier, CX was loaded with 1, so CH is still clear; effectively, the number of characters to display is in CX, as expected by the BIOS function.

The sequences for the two sides are similar to the sequence for the corner given previously, with the row number controlling a loop. The CX register has 1 on entry to the loop, so it is not loaded within the loop.

Finally, Program 9.6 illustrates how some of these capabilities might be used in an application. A realistic, working application would be several times larger than Program 9.6,

## Program 9.6

```
; Program 9.6        Window.ASM
; Display a window on screen and scroll text in it.

; Frame of window
  LeftFrame          equ     12
  RightFrame         equ     64
  TopFrame           equ      6
  BottomFrame        equ     18

; Limits of window (within frame)
  LeftLimit          equ     LeftFrame + 1
  RightLimit         equ     RightFrame - 1
  TopLimit           equ     TopFrame + 1
  BottomLimit        equ     BottomFrame - 1

; DOS function and status parameters
  DosFunc            equ     21h
  ExitToDos          equ     4Ch
  NoErrors           equ     00h

; BIOS interrupts, functions, parameters
  BiosVideoInt       equ     10h
  SetModeFunc        equ     00h
  ScrollUpFunc       equ     06h
  ScrollDownFunc     equ     07h
  ClearWinParm       equ     00h

; Text attributes
  HiWhiteOnBlack     equ     0Fh
  WhiteOnBlack       equ     07h
  BlackOnWhite       equ     70h

_STACK SEGMENT para stack 'stack'
           dw       100h dup (?)
_STACK ENDS

_DATA SEGMENT word public 'data'
   VideoMode    db   ?         ;video mode on entry
   VideoPage    db   ?         ;active video page on entry
   Text1Msg     db   "Tap U to scroll up, D to scroll down."
   Text1Len     dw   $ - Text1Msg
   Text2Msg     db   "Tap X to terminate."
   Text2Len     dw   $ - Text2Msg
_DATA ENDS

_TEXT SEGMENT word public 'code'
      assume  cs: _TEXT
      extrn   OutLine: PROC
      extrn   WriteStr: PROC, ReadKey: PROC

Window:

; set up ds register to point to _DATA
      mov     ax, seg _DATA
```

## 9.3 User I/O

**Program 9.6 (continued)**

```
            mov     ds, ax
            assume  ds: _DATA

; save video mode and page for later
            mov     ah, 0Fh
            int     10h
            mov     VideoMode, al
            mov     VideoPage, bh

; set text attribute for frame
            mov     bl, HiWhiteOnBlack

; call Outline (LeftFrame, RightFrame, TopFrame, BottomFrame)
            mov     ax, LeftFrame
            push    ax
            mov     ax, RightFrame
            push    ax
            mov     ax, TopFrame
            push    ax
            mov     ax, BottomFrame
            push    ax
            call    Outline

; set up cx, dx to limits of window, for BIOS routines
            mov     cl, LeftLimit
            mov     dl, RightLimit
            mov     ch, TopLimit
            mov     dh, BottomLimit

; set text attribute for background,
; and clear window via scroll function
            mov     bh, WhiteOnBlack
            mov     ah, ScrollUpFunc
            mov     al, ClearWinParm
            int     BiosVideoInt

; set attribute for text within window,
; and restore video page number in bh
            mov     bl, WhiteOnBlack
            mov     bh, VideoPage

; WriteStr (TopLimit+1, LeftLimit+1, (length),
;           "Tap U to scroll up, D to scroll down.")
            mov     ax, TopLimit
            inc     ax
            push    ax
            mov     ax, LeftLimit
            inc     ax
            push    ax
            push    Text1Len
            push    ds
            mov     ax, offset Text1Msg
            push    ax
            call    WriteStr
```

**Program 9.6 (continued)**

```
        ; change attribute for text within window
              mov     bl, BlackOnWhite

        ; WriteStr (TopLimit+2, LeftLimit+5, (length),
        ;          "Tap X to terminate.")
              mov     ax, TopLimit
              add     ax, 2
              push    ax
              mov     ax, LeftLimit
              add     ax, 5
              push    ax
              push    Text2Len
              push    ds
              mov     ax, offset Text2Msg
              push    ax
              call    WriteStr

        ; get a keystroke
              call    ReadKey

        WHILE01: ;keystroke is not 'X' or 'x'
              cmp     al, 'X'
              je      ENDWHILE01
              cmp     al, 'x'
              je      ENDWHILE01

        ; DO01
        ;     IF02 keystroke is 'U' or 'u'
              cmp     al, 'U'
              je      THEN02
              cmp     al, 'u'
              jne     ENDIF02

        THEN02:
        ;     scroll window up one line
              mov     ah, ScrollUpFunc
              mov     al, 1
              int     BiosVideoInt
        ENDIF02:

        ;     IF03 keystroke is 'D' or 'd'
              cmp     al, 'D'
              je      THEN03
              cmp     al, 'd'
              jne     ENDIF03

        THEN03:
        ;     scroll window down one line
              mov     ah, ScrollDownFunc
              mov     al, 1
              int     BiosVideoInt
        ENDIF03:

        ;     read a keystroke
```

### 9.3 User I/O

**Program 9.6 (continued)**

```
        call    ReadKey
        jmp     WHILE01
ENDWHILE01:

; clear screen by resetting current video mode
        mov     ah, SetModeFunc
        mov     al, VideoMode
        int     BiosVideoInt

; exit to DOS
        mov     ah, ExitToDos
        mov     al, NoErrors
        int     DosFunc


_TEXT ENDS
END Window
```

---

but this program will suffice here. It defines a window on the current video page, outlines the window, clears it, writes text into it, scrolls the text within the window in response to keyboard input, and clears the entire video page before terminating.

The first block of constants in the program defines the coordinates of the window. It does not check for valid values; these values can be changed, although they must be kept within the bounds of the screen and the window must be large enough for the text to be written in it. The fifth block defines attributes for the frame and two lines of text within the window. These are set for monochrome systems and will work with all systems; they can be changed for color systems. The other constants are those that define the limits for text within the outline and those that are associated with the DOS and BIOS functions.

After establishing the DS register, the program invokes function 0Fh of interrupt 10h to get the video mode and page. They are saved in the variables VideoMode and VideoPage for later use. The program then sets the attribute for the frame as high-intensity white characters on a black background and calls the Outline procedure.

After returning from Outline, the program copies the limits of the window within the outline in CL, DL, CH, and DH. From this point on, none of these four registers will be changed; some of the BIOS routines expect the limits of a window to be in these registers, and this program can proceed without changing them. A more serious application, however, could probably not afford to devote these registers to the limits of the text region in the window.

The next block of instructions clears the region inside the frame. This uses function 06h, Scroll Up, with AL (the number of lines to scroll) cleared to zero, which specifies clearing the window instead of scrolling it. Then, the program changes the attribute for text within the window to normal white characters on a black background (turning off the high intensity used for the frame). It also restores the video page to BH, where other BIOS routines expect it. The BH register was used to specify background attributes when clearing the window.

The program then calls WriteStr to display two lines of instructions within the window. These calls require several instructions to set up the arguments on the stack, but they are straightforward. Between the calls, the program changes the text attributes to black text on a white background.

After writing the instructions, Program 9.6 calls ReadKey to read a keystroke. The program then scrolls the contents of the window up or down as requested, until the user taps the X key. Although long, the program is direct; try running it and observing its behavior while you read it.

### EXERCISES 9.3

▶1. Write a program that invokes DOS function 01h (Read Keyboard with Echo) in a loop. Assemble it with debugging information enabled. Execute it from your debugger and watch the contents of AX as you enter different characters. Give the contents of the AX register for each of the following characters entered: a, A, CTRL-a, ALT-a, b, B, CTRL-b, ALT-b, END, PAGEUP, PAGEDOWN.

2. From your observations in Exercise 1, what do you think the codes for the following characters are: c, C, CTRL-c, ALT-c, SHIFT-END, CTRL-END, SHIFT-PAGEUP, SHIFT-PAGEDOWN, CTRL-PAGEUP, CTRL-PAGEDOWN. Run your program again and check your predictions.

3. Why do some word processing applications distinguish PAGEUP from CTRL-PAGEUP, but not SHIFT-PAGEUP?

▶4. Write a program that displays the status of the shift and toggle keys whenever they change. Your program should use the BIOS routine to get the flags, compare them to their previous values, and print whatever key has changed. Repeat this until the combination of NUMLOCK and SCROLLLOCK are both active. Do not print anything when the shift and status keys have not changed since the last scan.

5. What type of display adapter (MDA, CGA, etc.) does your computer system have? What kind of display (CRT, LCD, liquid plasma, etc.)? What are some of the advantages of that combination? Disadvantages?

6. What happens when you try to display a character string using PutStr and the string is longer than a line of the video display?

7. Test Program 9.6 on a variety of computers, noting their class (PC, XT, or AT) and video adapter (MDA, CGA, EGA, VGA). Report any differences in output.

▶8. Revise and test Program 9.6 to determine what happens when the WriteStr procedure displays a string that extends past the right side of the window defined. Explain the program's behavior.

9. Test Program 9.6 to determine what happens when text is scrolled up past the top of the window defined. Does scrolling down bring the text back? Explain the program's behavior.

## 9.4 DISK I/O

The principal storage device used in many computer systems is a magnetic disk. In this section, we examine some of the physical characteristics of disk storage devices and some of the DOS and BIOS disk services.

### Device Descriptions

The two types of disks, floppy and hard, are alike in many ways. Disks, whether flexible or rigid, consist of one or more platters with a coating, much like the coating used for

## 9.4 Disk I/O

cassette tapes, that can store a magnetic field. An access arm in the disk drive supports an electromagnet above the coated surface of each platter. Called a **head**, this electromagnet is used to record (write to disk) and play back (read from disk) magnetic patterns on the surface of the disk. As the disk platters spin, the portion that passes under a head—and can be read or written—is a circular region called a **track**. Disks have from 40 to over 1000 tracks.

In a drive with one platter, both surfaces may be coated. In a drive with multiple platters (which are assembled as a rigid unit and spin together), all platter surfaces may be coated, though the top surface of the top platter and the bottom surface of the bottom platter sometimes are not. When there is more than one coated recording surface, the set of tracks on all surfaces at one fixed position of the heads is called a **cylinder**; if you picture several circular tracks aligned over each other, connected to form a surface, that surface would be a right circular cylinder. There is a head for each recording surface. In a drive with more than one head, all of the heads are physically connected to each other so that all of the tracks in a cylinder can be accessed at the same time. (See Figure 9.4.)

Each circular track on a disk is divided into arcs called **sectors**. Data is recorded as a stream of bits, with each sector typically able to store 512 bytes. Read and write operations transfer data in a whole number of sectors.

Floppy disks consist of a single platter made of a flexible plastic and enclosed in a protective jacket or case. (Some users mistake 3.5-inch floppy disks for "hard" disks because of the case; the platter inside the case is indeed a "floppy" disk.) In most formats, both sides of the platter are used. The coating determines how densely data can be recorded; standard are double density (360K on 5-1/4-inch disks or 720K on 3.5-inch disks) and high density (1.2M on 5-1/4-inch disks or 1.44M on 3.5-inch disks), with higher densities on the horizon (3.5-inch disks with 2.8M have already been introduced). Because floppy disks are removable, the potential capacity of a drive is unlimited.

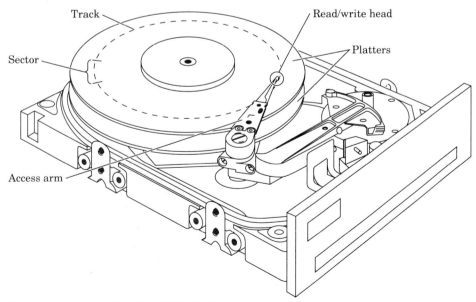

**Figure 9.4  Parts of a Hard Disk Drive**

Hard disks are available in a large number of configurations. Capacities range from 10M for older drives (10M was a large storage capacity when hard disks were introduced to the personal computer market) to over 300M for more recent ones. Because hard disk drives have fixed platters, their capacity is also fixed. However, hard disks are much faster and more convenient than floppy disks.

Magnetic disks are **direct access** devices, so sectors on a disk can be read or written in any order. To access a particular sector, the track, sector, and surface numbers are sent to the disk controller. The controller positions the heads to the requested cylinder (track), waits for the disk to rotate until the desired sector passes under the head, and then reads or writes that sector. To access another sector on the same cylinder, the heads do not have to be moved, but the disk has to rotate to the beginning of that sector. To access a sector on another cylinder, the heads must be repositioned.

## DOS File Services

One of an operating system's jobs is to organize files on disks and maintain the data structures necessary to locate them. An application sees a disk as a collection of files, each of which in turn is a collection of records or a stream of characters. Each file has a name, and any application can access the file by its name, with no hint of cylinders, tracks, sectors, heads, or platters. DOS manages the organization of files on the disk, mapping each file, by name, to the sectors in which it is stored. DOS also records which sectors of the disk are available.

Data is transferred between a disk and memory one or more sectors at a time. (DOS actually reads or writes a cluster, often four sectors, to improve system performance.) An application may work with just a few bytes of data at a time. DOS provides buffers and manages the mismatch between the amount of data a program uses and the amount that is transferred to or from a disk.

DOS provides two methods to access files. The older method uses **file control blocks** (FCBs). With FCBs, programs allocate a region of memory for each open file. This region contains the drive number, filename and extension, current block number (a block is a group of 128 records), record size, file size, date and time of last write, current record number, and relative record number within the block. When a file is opened, DOS sets up some of these fields; as the file is modified, DOS updates them; when the file is closed, DOS updates the directory entry using this data. The program accesses this data to specify which record to access and to modify some parameters if the defaults used by DOS are incorrect.

The newer, preferred method of accessing files uses handles. In this method, DOS maintains a common region of memory for all open files. When a file is opened, DOS returns an integer, called a **handle**, that the program uses to reference the file. The program is not required to maintain any information about the file, simplifying the task of the programmer. However, all files appear as streams of bytes with no record structure.

Associated with each file is an attribute byte that contains information about the basic characteristics of a file. Figure 9.5 illustrates the fields within this byte. The archive bit indicates whether the file has been changed since the last backup. The directory bit indicates whether the file contains directory (or subdirectory) information. The volume name bit indicates whether the entry refers to the volume identification; only

## 9.4 Disk I/O

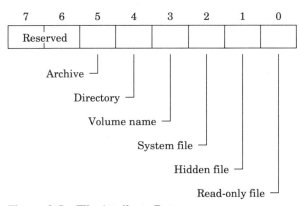

**Figure 9.5** File Attribute Byte

one file in the root directory can have the volume name. The system file and hidden file bits specify whether the files are system or hidden files; such files are not usually listed in directory searches. The read-only bit specifies whether the file is protected against modifications.

The DOS routines for accessing files using handles are shown in Table 9.4. (FCBs will not be considered further.) The functions in Table 9.4 are invoked by loading the function number into AX and issuing int 21h. Filenames and pathnames are specified as ASCIZ strings, each of which is a string of ASCII characters followed by a byte that contains only 0-bits. The offset of the pathname is passed in the DX register. A number of details and other functions are not listed in Table 9.4. More extensive coverage of the DOS file services can be found in the reference manuals.

A program can have up to 20 open handles at one time. Handles 0 through 4 are predefined and refer to the standard I/O devices, leaving 15 handles for disk files. If an application needs more, the number of handles can be increased.

To illustrate the use of file handles, Program 9.7 copies the file TEXTIN.ASC on the A drive to TEXTOUT.ASC on the same drive. As it copies the file, the program converts all lowercase letters to capital letters. The filenames are specified in db directives. To use other filenames, we can modify these directives, then assemble and link again.

After establishing the DS register, Program 9.7 invokes function 3Dh to open the input file. If the file is not found, an error message is displayed in the ELSE01 clause. If there is no disk in the drive, the DOS error handler intervenes. If the input file is successfully opened, its handle is saved.

The program then invokes function 3Ch to create a new file for output. If there is an error, either DOS intervenes or the program displays an error message in the THEN02 clause, depending on the error. If the output file is successfully opened, its handle is saved.

The program next reads a character using function 3Fh, converts it to a capital letter if it is a lowercase letter, and writes it to the output file using function 40h. After each character is read, AX is checked for the end-of-file condition. Processing continues until the end-of-file is encountered.

At end-of-file, both files are closed using function 3Eh. Note where the files are closed; it is important to close the files within the clause that executes when each file is successfully opened. The program should not leave the input file open when an error is encountered in opening the output file.

## Chapter 9 Interrupts and I/O

Table 9.4  DOS File Functions Using Handles

| Function | Description |
|---|---|
| 3Ch Create Handle | Create a file with specified attributes, open it, and return its handle in AX. DS:DX must point to the pathname as an ASCIZ string; CX must contain the file attribute byte (and leading zeros). If file with same name exists, it will be destroyed. |
| 3Dh Open Handle | Open an existing file for input or output. DS:DX must point to the pathname as an ASCIZ string; AL must contain an access code (0 = read, 1 = write, 2 = read/write; other codes available for sharing and inheritance). |
| 3Eh Close Handle | Close a file opened by Create Handle or Open Handle. BX must contain the file handle. |
| 3Fh Read Handle | Read from file (or device) specified by the handle in BX, and return the number of bytes read in AX. DS:DX must point to the buffer; CX must contain the number of bytes to read. |
| 40H Write Handle | Write to the file (or device) specified by the handle in BX, and return the number of bytes actually written in AX. DS:DX must point to the data to be written. |
| 42H Move File Pointer | Move the read/write pointer of the file specified by the handle in BX, and return the new pointer in DX:AX. CX:DX must specify a distance (in bytes) to move the pointer; AL specifies the reference point to which this distance is added (0 = start of file, 1 = current position, 2 = end of file). |
| 5Ah Create Temporary File | Create a file with specified attributes, open it, and return its handle in AX. DS:DX must point to a block containing the pathname, as an ASCIZ string, followed by 13 bytes for the filename; CX must contain the file attribute byte (and leading zeros). |
| 5Bh Create New File | Create a file with specified attributes, open it, and return its handle in AX. DS:DX must point to the pathname as an ASCIZ string; CX must contain the file attribute byte (and leading zeros). File must not already exist. |
| 68h Commit File | Flush all buffers for the file specified by the handle in BX (write all data in the output buffers to the disk file so that it is current) without closing the file. |

## Program 9.7

```
; Program 9.7      CapFile.ASM
; Copy a text file, changing lower case letters to capitals.

; DOS functions and status parameters
    DosFunc         equ     21h
    CreateHandle    equ     3Ch
    NormFileAttr    equ     0000h
    OpenHandle      equ     3Dh
    OpenToRead      equ     00h
    CloseHandle     equ     3Eh
    ReadHandle      equ     3Fh
    WriteHandle     equ     40h
    ExitToDos       equ     4Ch
    NoErrors        equ     00h
```

## Program 9.7 (continued)

```
        DOSSEG

        _STACK SEGMENT para stack 'stack'
                    dw      100h dup (?)
        _STACK ENDS

        _DATA SEGMENT word public 'data'
          PathIn        db      "a:textin.asc",00h
          PathOut       db      "a:textout.asc",00h
          HandleIn      dw      ?       ;handle DOS uses for input file
          HandleOut     dw      ?       ;handle DOS uses for output file
          CharInOut     db      ?       ;char. copied from input to output
          InErrMsg      db      "Error opening input file. "
          OutErrMsg     db      "Error opening output file."
          ErrorLen      dw      $ - OutErrMsg
          SuccessMsg    db      "File copy, capitalization complete."
          SuccessLen    dw      $ - SuccessMsg
        _DATA ENDS

        _TEXT SEGMENT word public 'code'
            assume  cs: _TEXT
            extrn   PutStr: PROC, PutCrLf: PROC

Capfile:

; set up ds register to point to _DATA
        mov     ax, seg _DATA
        mov     ds, ax
        assume  ds: _DATA

; open handle for input file
        mov     ah, OpenHandle
        mov     al, OpenToRead
        int     DosFunc
        mov     HandleIn, ax


; IF01 no error while opening input handle
        jc      ELSE01

; THEN01
;       create handle for output file
            mov     ah, CreateHandle
            mov     cx, NormFileAttr
            mov     dx, offset PathOut
            int     DosFunc
            mov     HandleOut, ax

;       IF02 no error while creating output handle
            jc      ELSE02

;       THEN02
            REPEAT03:
;               read the next character from input
```

## Program 9.7 (continued)

```
                mov     ah, ReadHandle
                mov     bx, HandleIn
                mov     cx, 1
                mov     dx, offset CharInOut
                int     DosFunc

;       IF04 not end of input file
                cmp     ax, 0
                je      ENDIF04

;         THEN04
;           IF05 character is lowercase letter
                mov     ah, CharInOut
                cmp     ah, "a"
                jb      ENDIF05
                cmp     ah, "z"
                ja      ENDIF05

;             THEN05
;               convert it to capital letter
                sub     ah, 20h
                mov     CharInOut, ah
            ENDIF05:

;           write character to output file
                mov     ah, WriteHandle
                mov     bx, HandleOut
                mov     cx, 1
                mov     dx, offset CharInOut
                int     DosFunc
            ENDIF04:

;       TEST03
                cmp     ax, 0
                jne     REPEAT03
;       UNTIL03 end of input file

;       close output file
                mov     ah, CloseHandle
                mov     bx, HandleOut
                int     DosFunc

;       display successful copy message
                mov     cx, SuccessLen
                mov     bx, offset SuccessMsg
                call    PutStr
                jmp     ENDIF02

    ELSE02:
;       display error opening output file
                mov     cx, ErrorLen
                mov     bx, offset OutErrMsg
                call    PutStr
    ENDIF02:
```

### 9.4 Disk I/O

**Program 9.7 (continued)**

```
        ;   close input file
                mov     ah, CloseHandle
                mov     bx, HandleIn
                int     DosFunc

                jmp     ENDIF01
        ELSE01:
        ;   display error message
                mov     cx, ErrorLen
                mov     bx, offset InErrMsg
                call    PutStr
        ENDIF01:

        ; new line
                call    PutCrLf

        ; exit to DOS
                mov     ah, ExitToDos
                mov     al, NoErrors
                int     DosFunc

        _TEXT   ENDS
        END     Capfile
```

## DOS Directory Services

DOS maintains the disk directory. Although we do not consider the details of the directory structure in this text, we do examine some of the functions that DOS provides for working with the directory (see Table 9.5). DOS provides functions for creating and deleting subdirectories, deleting files from a directory, changing the name and attributes of a file, and moving around in the directory structure. DOS employs the concept of a current directory, which it searches first when looking for files. DOS provides functions for changing the current directory, searching for a particular file or set of files, and searching for files with particular attributes.

The search commands record information about the state of the search so that the next invocation can continue where the previous search left off. The area used for this is the data transfer area, or DTA. DOS provides functions, listed in Table 9.6, for accessing the pointer to the DTA. The layout of the data returned by Find First File (function 4Eh), which is used and modified by Find Next File (function 4Fh), is shown in Figure 9.6.

To illustrate the search commands, we include a program that displays the names of all files in a directory along with the total size and number of files in the directory. As written, Program 9.8 will find all normal, system, and hidden files in the current directory. (You can run Program 9.8 from anywhere—even from another drive—as long as you specify its pathname when invoking it.) To restrict the search to files with some particular name or extension, the value declared for DirPath in the _DATA segment can be changed. To find another combination of file types, we can change the attribute byte passed to function 4Eh, Find First File.

## Table 9.5  DOS Directory Functions

| Function | Description |
| --- | --- |
| 39h Create Directory | Create a new subdirectory. DS:DX must point to the subdirectory's pathname as an ASCIZ string. |
| 3Ah Remove Subdirectory | Delete a subdirectory, but only if it contains no files. DS:DX must point to the subdirectory's pathname as an ASCIZ string. The current directory cannot be deleted. |
| 3Bh Change Current Directory | Change the current directory. DS:DX must point to the destination directory's pathname as an ASCIZ string not longer than 64 characters. |
| 41h Delete Directory Entry | Delete a file by erasing its directory entry. DS:DX must point to the pathname of the file to delete as an ASCIZ string; read-only files cannot be deleted. |
| 43h Get/Set File Attributes | Return (AL=0) or set (AL=1) the attributes of a file. DS:DX must point to the pathname of the file as an ASCIZ string. The volume name and directory attribute bits cannot be changed by this function. |
| 47h Get Current Directory | Return the pathname of the current directory. DL must contain the current drive number (0=default, 1=A, and so on); DS:SI must point to a 64-byte buffer in which the function returns the pathname as ASCIZ string. |
| 4Eh Find First File | Search for the first entry that matches the specified pathname and attributes. The pathname can specify a directory as well as a filename; if no directory is specified, the current directory is assumed. The pathname can include DOS wildcard (?=any character, *=any string) characters. DS:DX must point to the pathname as an ASCIZ string; CX must contain the attributes to match. Information is returned in a block stored at the Disk Transfer Address (see Figure 9.4 and Table 9.6). |
| 4Fh Find Next File | Continue a search started by function 4Eh, Find First File, using and updating the information in the DTA. If no more files are found that match, set the carry flag and set AX to 18. |
| 56h Change Directory Entry | Rename a file by changing its directory entry. DS:DX must point to the pathname of the file to be renamed as an ASCIZ string; ES:DI must point to the pathname that the entry is being changed to as an ASCIZ string. |

## Table 9.6  DTA Functions

| Function | Description |
| --- | --- |
| 1Ah Set Disk Transfer Address | Set the Disk Transfer Address pointer to DS:DX. The DTA is used by file functions that use FCBs and by some of the directory functions. If not set by this function, DOS uses offset 0080h from the start of the Program Segment Prefix (see Section 11.5). |
| 2Fh Get Disk Transfer Address | Return the pointer to the Disk Transfer Area in ES:BX. |

## 9.4 Disk I/O

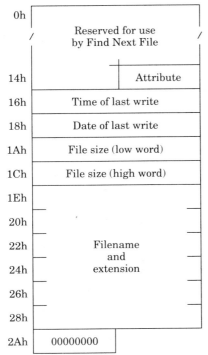

**Figure 9.6** Data Transfer Area Following Find First File

After setting up DS, Program 9.8 sets up the data transfer area. Each field in the DTA is defined using a separate db or dw directive so that it can be easily accessed. The DTA is established by the call to function 1Ah

```
mov     dx, offset DTA
mov     ah, SetDTA
int     DosFunc
```

## Program 9.8

```
;  Program 9.8       FileList.ASM
;  Displays the names of all normal, system, and hidden files
;     in a directory, their total size and number.

;  DOS function and status parameters
    DosFunc     equ     21h
    SetDTA      equ     1Ah
    ExitToDos   equ     4Ch
    NoErrors    equ     00h
    FindFirstFl equ     4Eh
    FileAttrib  equ     0006h       ;system + hidden + normal
    FindNextFl  equ     4Fh

DOSSEG
```

## Program 9.8 (continued)

```
       _STACK SEGMENT para stack 'stack'
                dw      100h dup (?)
       _STACK ENDS

       _DATA SEGMENT word public 'data'
           DirPath      db      "*.*",00h
           FileCount    dw      0           ;number of files ...
           TotalLo      dw      0           ;total size of all files ...
           TotalHi      dw      0           ; with specified attribute
           SizeMsg      db      " bytes in "
           SizeLen      dw      $ - SizeMsg
           CountMsg     db      " files."
           CountLen     dw      $ - CountMsg

       ; *** DTA declarations --- must not be altered ***
           DTA          db      15h dup (?)
           Attrib       db      ?
           Time         dw      ?
           Date         dw      ?
           LoSize       dw      ?
           HiSize       dw      ?
           FileName     db      0Ch dup (00h)   ;initialize to nulls
           Zero         db      ?
       ; *** end of DTA declarations ***

       _DATA ENDS

       _TEXT SEGMENT word public 'code'
           assume  cs: _TEXT
           extrn   PutStr: PROC, PutCrLf: PROC
           extrn   PutDec: PROC, PutChar: PROC

FileList:

       ; set up ds register to point to _DATA
           mov     ax, seg _DATA
           mov     ds, ax
           assume  ds: _DATA

       ; set up DTA for directory search
           mov     dx, offset DTA
           mov     ah, SetDTA
           int     DosFunc

       ; find first file in directory
           mov     dx, offset DirPath
           mov     cx, FileAttrib
           mov     ah, FindFirstFl
           int     DosFunc

       WHILE01: ;more files & no errors
           jc      ENDWHL01

       ; DO01
```

## 9.4 Disk I/O

**Program 9.8 (continued)**

```
        ;   add file statistics
            inc     FileCount
            mov     ax, LoSize
            add     TotalLo, ax
            mov     ax, HiSize
            adc     TotalHi, ax

        ;   display filename
            mov     cx, 0Ch
            mov     bx, offset FileName
            call    PutStr
            call    PutCrLf

        ;   clear filename area for next use
            sub     ax, ax
            mov     word ptr FileName, ax
            mov     word ptr FileName+2, ax
            mov     word ptr FileName+4, ax
            mov     word ptr FileName+6, ax
            mov     word ptr FileName+8, ax
            mov     word ptr FileName+10, ax

        ;   find next file
            mov     ah, FindNextFl
            int     DosFunc
            jmp     WHILE01
    ENDWHL01:

; Display file statistics.
; thousands_of_bytes := total_bytes div 1000
; remaining_bytes := total_bytes mod 1000
            mov     bx, 1000
            mov     ax, TotalLo
            mov     dx, TotalHi
            div     bx

; print (thousands_of_bytes, ",", remaining_bytes)
            call    PutDec          ;print thousands_of_bytes
            mov     ax, dx          ;save remaining_bytes
            mov     dl, ','         ;print comma
            call    PutChar
            call    PutDec          ;print remaining_bytes

; print (" bytes in ", FileCount, " files.")
            mov     cx, SizeLen
            mov     bx, offset SizeMsg
            call    PutStr
            mov     ax, FileCount
            call    PutDec
            mov     cx, CountLen
            mov     bx, offset CountMsg
            call    PutStr
            call    PutCrLf
```

**Program 9.8 (continued)**

```
    ; exit to DOS
        mov     ah, ExitToDos
        mov     al, NoErrors
        int     DosFunc

_TEXT ENDS
END     FileList
```

---

Then, the program uses function 4Eh to find the first file in the directory. The instruction

```
    mov     dx, offset DirPath
```

establishes the directory and pathname to search. This is initialized to *.* so that the program will find all files in the current directory. However, the initialization can be changed to *.asm to find only assembly-language source files. Note that the string is followed by a byte containing zero; DirPath must be an ASCIZ string.

The attribute of the files to search for is 06h, or $00000110_2$. As indicated by Figure 9.5, this pattern includes system and hidden files, but not directories. To include directories, $00010110_2$, or 16h, would be the attribute byte. This byte is loaded into CX, and the Find First File function is invoked.

The Find File functions clear the carry flag if they are successful or set it if either an error occurs or no more files are found. The WHILE loop checks the carry flag. In the body of the loop, the number of files is incremented, and the file size is added to the total size of all files. The loop also displays the name of the file (and clears the name field for the next find operation—the find operations do not pad the names out to the full 12 bytes). After processing each file, DOS finds the next file using the Find Next File function.

The last part of the program prints the number and total size of all found files. Because the total file size is two words long, the program divides it by 1000 and passes the quotient (representing thousands of bytes) and the remainder to PutDec separately. (This procedure was also performed in Program 4.2, Seconds.ASM.) This program, along with Program 9.7, illustrates some of the disk functions that DOS provides.

There are other sets of disk functions that should be briefly mentioned. These include functions that use file control blocks to access files and functions that DOS provides to access the disk directly using clusters (a cluster is a group of contiguous sectors) and what DOS refers to as logical sectors. Low-level DOS treats the disk as a collection of logical sectors, numbered from 1 to the number of sectors on the disk, without reference to cylinders or surfaces. The low-level DOS functions use the logical sector number to access the cluster containing that sector. Application programs have no need to use such functions.

DOS maintains the directory and information about where a file is recorded using logical sectors. There is a file allocation table, FAT, that stores this information in terms of logical sectors. It would take a whole chapter to discuss the directory and FAT structures in detail; that is beyond the scope of this book.

## BIOS Disk Services

This section considers some of the services that the BIOS provides for working with disks. These functions are used by DOS and by some disk maintenance utilities. Because of the

## 9.4 Disk I/O

potential for error and data loss, these functions should not be used casually by novices. When the services of DOS are insufficient, an experienced programmer should consult the reference manuals for the particular system BIOS and drives in use. Sufficient details to invoke the BIOS disk functions are not provided here.

The BIOS does not support a file system. Its model of a disk drive consists of cylinders, heads, tracks, and sectors. It considers the disk as a physical device. The gap between the DOS file and directory functions and the BIOS functions is bridged by some of the lower-level DOS functions that were previously mentioned.

The BIOS disk functions perform the following operations:

- Reset disk
- Read disk status
- Read drive type
- Read sectors
- Write sectors
- Verify sectors
- Format track
- Format cyclinder

These functions are available for both floppy disks and hard disks. Other functions for both types of disks exist as well.

Reset Disk resets both the floppy and fixed disk controllers by reinitializing the drive parameters, thereby recalibrating the read/write head positions to cylinder 0. This is useful with floppy disks when a disk access fails because the drive is not up to full speed at the moment that the access is attempted.

Read Disk Status returns an error code produced by the last requested function. This allows system programmers to write routines for reporting and recovering from errors that are independent of the disk functions.

Read Drive Type returns information about a specified disk. For a floppy disk, it returns whether the drive specified is a valid drive number and, if it is, whether the drive can detect when the door is opened. For a hard disk, it returns whether the drive number is valid and, if it is, whether the selected hard disk is drive 1 or 2 and the number of sectors on the disk. Another function returns some of the drive's parameters: size and capacity, maximum track or cylinder number, number of heads, and address of parameter table. This information can be checked by the system programs before accessing the drive to ensure that the access is successful; it is also used by diagnostic utilities.

Read Sectors copies a number of sectors into a buffer. The address of the buffer, the number of sectors to read, the cylinder number, sector number, head number, and drive number are arguments to the function. The buffer cannot span a segment boundary, so no more than 64K bytes can be read in one access.

Write Sectors copies a specified number of sectors from a buffer in memory to a disk. It takes the same arguments as Read Sectors.

Verify Sectors neither transfers data between the disk and memory nor compares disk data to data in memory. It simply checks that the sectors can be read and that the hardware functions properly. It takes the same arguments, including a buffer in memory, as Read Sectors and Write Sectors.

Finally, Format Track and Format Cylinder write the sector number and track number to each sector on a track. The number of sectors, drive number, head number, track or cylinder number, and address of a buffer are arguments to these functions. The buffer must contain the data for each track: For floppy disks, this consists of a pattern of four bytes (track number, head number, sector number, sector size) for each sector; for hard disks, this consists of a pair of bytes (good/bad flag, sector number) for each sector on the track.

There are many other BIOS disk functions, especially for hard disk systems. It is not necessary to pursue them in order to appreciate the level of support provided by the BIOS.

This completes the discussion of DOS and BIOS services for input and output. The next section will examine communication at the hardware level.

## EXERCISES 9.4

1. For each combination of parameters given below, determine the capacity of the disk. All sectors have 512 bytes. ("Sides" refers to the number of recording surfaces or heads.)

   |     | tracks/side | sectors/track | sides |
   |-----|-------------|---------------|-------|
   | (a) | 40          | 8             | 2     |
   | (b) | 40          | 9             | 2     |
   | (c) | 80          | 15            | 2     |
   | (d) | 80          | 9             | 2     |
   | (e) | 80          | 18            | 2     |
   | (f) | 306         | 17            | 4     |
   | (g) | 733         | 17            | 5     |
   | (h) | 1023        | 17            | 15    |
   | (i) | 977         | 26            | 5     |

▶2. Modify Program 9.7 so that it makes two copies of the source file. In one copy, all letters should be capital letters. In the other, all letters should be lowercase.

▶3. Write a program that counts the number of characters in a text file. Use files that are smaller than 32K bytes long to test it, so that the number of characters can be represented in one word and printed with PutDec.

▶4. Write a program that copies a text file but limits each "line" of text to no more 40 characters. Insert a CR and an LF character whenever 40 characters have been copied to the output file.

▶5. Modify Program 9.8 so that it also prints the size of each file.

▶6. Modify Program 9.8 so that it also prints the date and time each file was last modified. The date is stored in the directory at 18h as follows: bits 0 through 4 are the day (1 to 31); bits 5 through 8 are the month (1 to 12); and bits 9 through 15 are the number of years since 1980 (0 to 119). The time is stored at 16h as follows: bits 0 through 4 are half the seconds (0 to 29, multiply by 2 to get seconds); bits 5 through 10 are the minutes (0 to 60); and bits 11 through 16 are the hours (0 to 24).

▶7. Modify Program 9.8 so that it prints the file attributes. Not all files printed will necessarily have the same attributes. Devise an appropriate coding scheme for your output. Refer to Figure 9.5.

▶8. Combine the enhancements of Exercises 5 through 7 into a single program.

▶9. Write subprograms in assembly language that invoke the DOS directory functions; your subprograms should be callable from your high-level language. Then write a high-level-language program that determines the total size of all files in a directory, including all files in its subdirectories. It should print the name and size of each subdirectory. (Hint: This is a tree traversal problem; the reserved field of the data structure in Figure 9.6 is essentially a pointer (but not the usual simple pointer) to the next node of the tree. Use the techniques you learned when studying trees.)

10. Using the description of BIOS disk services, design a data structure for a disk directory that can be implemented using those functions. Do not attempt to implement it. What are some of the problems such a structure must help solve?

## 9.5 COMMUNICATIONS

We have examined the support provided by DOS and BIOS functions for input and output operations. Now we consider how the processor is connected to the input and output devices and how it communicates with an external device.

### Ports

Communication with an external device can be carried out either by the processor or by separate hardware. The device and memory must be connected, and some means of controlling the interactions must be available. This discussion will start with the processor providing the connection and the control.

When the processor performs an output or input operation, data is transferred to or from the peripheral device through a **port**, a special register with an address much like a memory location. The port address can be in either the range of memory addresses or a separate range used only for ports. Data transfer is limited to the size of the port, usually a byte or a word.

When ports are mapped to memory addresses, they are accessed the same as any other byte or word of memory. Data is moved into and out of ports using mov instructions. It is the responsibility of every programmer to treat the locations that represent ports with special care; using them as memory can play havoc with a system.

When ports are separate from main memory they are accessed only by special instructions. This is the method used with the 8086 processors. The 8086 uses an in instruction to read from a port, and an out instruction to write to a port. These instructions have two forms: direct, where the port number is an immediate byte operand, and indirect, where the port number is given by the contents of DX.

**INput from port**

    syntax:      in *accumulator, port*
    action:      *accumulator := port*
    operands:  *accum, immed*    *accum*,dx

**OUTput to port**

    syntax:      out *port, accumulator*
    action:      *port := accumulator*
    flags:       ODITSZAPC unchanged
    operands:  *immed,accum*    dx,*accum*

The in and out instructions transfer a byte between AL and an 8-bit port, or a word between AX and a 16-bit port.

The ports in an 8086 system are numbered from 0000h to FFFFh (the same as offsets in a segment), though no system uses more than a few hundred ports. In a typical AT, ports

0000h through 00FFh are reserved for the system board and ports 0100h through 03FFh are used for input and output devices.

The data written to a port by out or read from a port by in are moved on the same data bus that connects memory and the processor. The in and out instructions also use the address bus to specify a port number, except only the least significant 16 bits are used. A control line signals whether the address bus references memory or a port. When an in or out instruction is executed, the control line indicates a port; for all other instructions, it indicates memory.

Each input and output device has it own set of ports. The CGA video adapter uses 4 ports; each parallel printer uses 3 ports; each serial communication interface uses 11 ports. (The word *port* is used by some for a communication interface, as in advertisements for computers with "one parallel and two serial ports." Do not confuse this with the use of the word to refer to a register.)

As a simple example, consider the three ports used for a parallel printer. The first port contains the data byte to be sent; the second port contains status information (whether the printer is busy, out of paper, ready for data, and so on); and the third port is used for control. It is possible to send a string to a printer using the algorithm shown in Figure 9.7. The figure omits the details of manipulating the string by using a simple move instruction to copy Char into the AL register to represent the instructions needed to copy the next character of the string into AL. It also omits the details of testing for the end of the string.

The fragment in Figure 9.7 assumes that the printer is on, paper is loaded, and so on. The first four instructions copy the number for the printer status port into DX, read from the port using the in instruction, and test the bit that signals whether the printer is busy. If the bit is set, the read and test are repeated. This loop continues until the printer signals that it is ready by clearing the busy bit.

When the printer is ready, the character to be printed is written to the printer's data port using an out instruction. Then the printer is signaled to read its data port and print the character. To send this signal, called a strobe, the program fragment sets the strobe bit in the control port. It clears the bit after the printer has the data byte.

Several timing issues must be considered. The sequence shown in the program fragment will work with most computers and most printers using a standard parallel interface. To implement the fragment as a program, it is necessary to know which ports to use. Although there are standard port numbers, LPT1 (the name DOS gives to the first printer interface) uses a different set of ports depending on whether it is implemented on a monochrome display adapter or a separate input/output adapter.

The method of transferring data described in Figure 9.7 is far from ideal. A program using it can do no useful processing while waiting for an input or output device to complete an operation: The first loop in Figure 9.7 keeps running until the printer is no longer busy. A better method is to allow the program to initiate an input or output operation and then have some other device monitor the input or output device and inform the program when the device is ready. Such a device is called a controller.

## Controllers

A **controller**, located between the processor and a peripheral device, accepts incoming data or control codes for a device and converts them to the signals used by the device. For

## 9.5 Communications

```
; Send a character string to printer.
; Assumes printer is initialized.
   REPEAT01:
      mov      dx, PrintStatus
   REPEAT02:
      in       al, dx
      test     al, BusyMask
      jnz      REPEAT02
;  UNTIL02 until printer is ready
;  send character to printer
;  (details of moving next character of
;  string into al are omitted)
      mov      al, Char
      mov      dx, PrintData
      out      dx, al
;  send control signals:
;  set strobe
      mov      dx, PrintControl
      mov      al, StrobeOn
      out      dx, al
;  clear strobe
      mov      al, StrobeOff
      out      dx, al
;  check for more characters
;  (details of string manipulation omitted)
      j--      REPEAT01
; UNTIL01 end of string encountered
```

**Figure 9.7 Using IN and OUT to Print a String**

example, a disk controller accepts the head, cylinder, and sector numbers and generates signals that instruct the heads to move to the desired cylinder and then to wait for the disk to rotate to the correct position. The controller also maintains communication with the central processor using ports.

When reading from a disk drive, a program first writes various control data (sector, cylinder, and head numbers, and so on) to the ports associated with the drive and then writes a command to a control port. This last write notifies the drive controller that a read request has been issued. If possible, the program continues whatever it is doing while the drive processes this information. In the meantime, the controller monitors the drive. When the drive is ready to transfer data, the controller generates an interrupt. The interrupt handler copies the data from the drive's data port into the buffer in memory as the data arrives at the port. Depending on the system and the disk, an interrupt handler might accept just one byte and terminate, so that the controller would have to generate an interrupt for each byte of data requested.

The use of interrupts to complete an input or output request allows the program to continue, where possible, with other processing. This yields greater throughput and allows input and output with different devices to occur simultaneously. However, the processor must handle each byte individually. When a large block of data is to be transferred between memory and a relatively fast device such as a disk, the transfer can be made faster if the controller accesses memory directly.

## DMA

If the controller of a fast device is connected to the data and address buses, it can access memory directly and transfer large amounts of data without the help of the processor. Such an arrangement is called **direct memory access**, or **DMA**. To copy several sectors of data from a disk into a buffer in memory, for example, the processor sends the controller the address of the buffer, the number of sectors to transfer, the direction of the transfer, and the head, cylinder, and sector numbers. The processor then signals the DMA controller to transfer the data.

The processor is idle while the DMA controller is active. This is necessary because there is only one path to memory; the processor and the DMA controller cannot use it simultaneously. But while the DMA controller is waiting for the disk, it returns control to the processor.

To keep the central processor busy during transfers of large blocks of data between memory and peripherals, some computers use a separate I/O processor. The I/O processor does more than simply copy streams of data between a peripheral device and memory. It is actually a complete processor designed for and dedicated to tasks associated with input and output processing. It can pack bytes to form words and unpack words to form bytes; it can convert data from one character code to another and perform similar tasks.

The central processor must initiate the operation of the I/O processor, but the I/O processor can then complete the transfer between the memory and the peripheral while the processor continues with the program it is executing. The I/O processor interrupts the central processor only when it needs to access memory. It communicates with the peripheral controller by checking the status port for the controller. When the controller is ready, the I/O processor writes (or reads) data into (or from) the controller's data port. Computers that use the 8086 and newer processors use simple ports for user input and output and DMA with the disk drives; they generally do not include separate, sophisticated I/O processors.

### EXERCISES 9.5

If appropriate reference materials and supervision are available, write a program for one of the following tasks:

▶1. Print the contents of a text file using DOS functions to read the file and using in and out with the printer's ports to print the file.

▶2. Send text typed at one computer to the display of a second computer. Use in and out and the serial ports of the two computers to transmit the data, but use DOS functions to read the keyboard and write to the video display.

## KEY POINTS

- An interrupt is a signal to the processor that an event needing immediate attention has occurred.
- External interrupts are generated outside the CPU by hardware such as input, output, or storage devices.
- Internal interrupts are generated within the CPU, and by instructions that request low-level system operations. Internal interrupts that are the result of errors are called traps.

- When an interrupt occurs, the processor finishes the current instruction and then transfers control to a special type of subprogram called an interrupt handler. The interrupt handler performs the operations needed to service the interrupt and returns control to the program that was interrupted.
- Input and output operations requested by an application are implemented by routines supplied by the operating system and the basic input/output system (BIOS). These routines use interrupts to communicate with the hardware; they are also invoked as interrupts.
- Using the highest level of available support for I/O operations reduces the number of system-dependent details with which the programmer must cope and the amount of control that the programmer has over the system.
- Each time a key is pressed or released, the keyboard transmits a code to a controller on the system board, which packs the code into a byte and generates an interrupt. The BIOS interrupt handler examines the byte of data from the controller and invokes a special function, updates shift and toggle flags, or places data in the input buffer.
- The BIOS video functions establish the video display mode, control the cursor position, and produce output at the cursor position.
- Disk drives contain one or more platters coated with material that can hold a magnetic field. Drives also contain an electromagnet that can alter (write) and detect (read) the pattern of magnetic fields on a platter's surface.
- As it spins, the portion of a platter that can be read or written is a circular track.
- The collection of tracks on all platters at the same position is called a cylinder.
- Tracks are divided into sectors; each read or write operation must transfer a whole number of sectors.
- The operating system maintains the organization of data on a disk as files by providing routines for opening, reading, writing, closing, and deleting files. It maintains a directory of which files exist and where each file is stored. It also maintains a list of available sectors where files can be added.
- The BIOS provides access to the disk drive controller, supporting format, read, write, and verify operations.
- Communications ports are registers in input and output devices (or their controllers) that are accessed much like words of memory. Devices are managed by writing to control ports; their status is checked by reading control ports; and data is transferred via data ports.
- Controllers manage I/O devices, freeing the central processor from that burden. A controller monitors the ports associated with a device and communicates with the processor (using interrupts) when the I/O device needs attention or when memory must be accessed.
- Direct memory access (DMA) uses special controllers that are also connected to the memory address and data buses. These controllers manage all aspects of the transfer of large blocks of data between memory and an I/O or storage device.

## PC SYSTEM SUMMARY

- The 8086 processor recognizes 256 different interrupts, identified by a byte that accompanies the interrupt signal.

- The first 256 doublewords of memory are a table of far pointers. The interrupt number, multiplied by four, is used as an index into this table to get the far pointer to the interrupt handler.
- Most interrupts may be disabled temporarily. Those that can be disabled are referred to as maskable. The interrupt enable flag, IF, specifies whether the maskable interrupts are serviced (IF set) or not (IF cleared) as they occur.
- When invoking an interrupt handler, the processor pushes the flags, CS, and IP registers onto the stack and transfers control to the far address given in the interrupt vector table at the index specified by the interrupt number. The return from an interrupt restores the flags, CS, and IP registers.
- DOS and BIOS services are invoked using the interrupt mechanism. BIOS services are also requested by hardware issuing interrupts.
- DOS provides functions (all using interrupt 21h) for text I/O using the keyboard and video display. See Table 9.1 (p. 316).
- The BIOS uses two interrupts with the keyboard: 09h is issued by the controller every time a key is pressed or released; 16h is used by software to get a character or scan code from the input buffer. The latter provides several functions, as listed in Table 9.2 (p. 319).
- BIOS interrupt 10h provides many services for using the video display. Depending on the video adapter, different systems use different functions; some common functions are listed in Table 9.3 (p. 321).
- DOS provides two methods for file access: file control blocks (FCBs) and the newer, preferred handles. Some functions (of interrupt 21h) that use file handles are listed in Table 9.4 (p. 334).
- DOS provides functions for working with directories. They also use interrupt 21h. See Table 9.5 (p. 338).
- File and path names are specified as ASCIZ strings, which are sequences of ASCII characters followed by a byte of zeros.
- In addition to the DOS file services listed in Tables 9.4 and 9.5, DOS provides both lower-level disk services that work with sector numbers and functions that maintain the directory structures.
- The BIOS disk functions perform low-level operations such as formatting, reading and writing sectors of data, and checking disk status.
- I/O ports are numbered from 0000h to FFFFh, just like offsets within a segment. The in instruction copies data from a port to a register; and the out instruction copies data from a register to a port.

Instructions presented in this chapter:

Interrupt use:
```
    cli    clear interrupt flag
    sti    set interrupt flag
    iret   pop stack into IP, CS, and flags
```

Direct input and output:
```
    in     copy contents of port into AL or AX
    out    copy contents of AL or AX into port
```

# 10
# Memory

- **Real Mode (8086)**
- **Protected Mode (80286)**
- **Linear Memory Mode (80386)**
- **Memory Hardware**

The programs presented in this text do not make many demands of modern computer systems. The intent is to examine through simple examples how programs can be implemented by real computers in general and by the 8086 processor in particular. Example programs do not need to be large to accomplish this task.

However, real applications do require significant system resources. The so-called checklist wars have led to applications so full of features that the small model of a single 64K code segment with another 64K data segment is inadequate. Indeed, some applications have grown beyond the 1 megabyte address space of the original 8086 processor.

In this chapter, the three major addressing modes—real (8086), protected (80286), and linear (80386)—of the 8086 family are examined. Along with these modes, some of the memory management features of the newer processors are presented. Segmented and paged virtual memory, expanded memory, and extended memory are also discussed. The difference between RAM and ROM and the uses for each are given in the last section of this chapter, and the idea of cache memory is introduced.

The treatment of the topics in this chapter is not supposed to be exhaustive; the intention is to impart enough exposure to encourage further study of whatever systems are available.

## 10.1 REAL MODE (8086)

The memory mode used by the 8086 and 8088 processors is called real mode. The newer processors—the 80286, 80386, and 80486—all support real mode to provide compatibility with software developed for the 8086. Many current applications do not take advantage of the advanced features of the newer processors; these applications simply run faster on the newer processors. In this section real mode addressing is examined.

### Segments

Real mode programs use separate segments for instructions, data, and the stack. A fourth segment—called the extra segment—is also available; it is typically used for data.

It is useful to distinguish between physical segments and logical segments. A **physical segment,** also called a **frame,** is a region of 64K of memory address space. Physical segments start on a paragraph boundary in real mode. Physical segments can overlap.

A **logical segment** is a region of memory used for the instructions or data in a program. A program translator typically determines the contents of part of a logical segment as it translates a program. The linker combines logical segments with the same name, combine type, and class name from different programs to form fewer, larger logical segments. The loader copies the logical segments into physical segments prior to execution. A logical segment can be no larger than a physical segment, or 64K.

Many compilers for 8086 systems share a convention for specifying the default sizes of code and data areas. This convention makes use of six different memory models. These models refer to the combined data areas as one unit regardless of segment structure, and they refer to all instructions as the code.

In the tiny model, used for executable programs in a special .COM format, all data and code are combined into a single segment. In the small model, which has been used for the assembly-language programs in this text, all data fits in one 64K segment, and all code fits in a separate 64K segment; all references to data are near. In the medium model, all data fits in a single 64K segment, and references to data are near; code may exceed 64K, and some jumps must be far if it does. In the compact model, the data may exceed 64K, and some references must be far if it does; all code fits in one 64K segment, and jumps are near (or short). In the large model, data and code may each exceed 64K. However, each data array must be smaller than one 64K segment. In the huge model, data and code may each exceed 64K. An array may also exceed 64K.

Many programs use one model for most code and data but selectively use another model for some code or data. Most assemblers provide a set of simplified segment directives that allows the programmer to specify a memory model. The assembler then names the segments and declares their alignment, combine type, and class names based on the memory model. Assembly-language programmers willing to use the full segment declarations—as has been done in this text—are free to write mixed-model programs; they must be careful, though, to use the right type of pointers or jumps.

## Addresses

Physical addresses in real mode are 20 bits long. This size provides access to $2^{20}$ locations, that is, 1 megabyte of memory. When the 8086 was designed, this amount of memory was considered substantial.

The physical address is computed from the segment number and the offset. The segment number is given by only the 16 most significant bits of the address of a paragraph boundary; the four least significant bits of a paragraph boundary are always 0. The offset is a 16-bit number, formed as the sum of one or more of the following: a displacement in an instruction, a base register, or an index register. The 20-bit physical address is computed by multiplying the segment number by 16 and adding the offset. See Figure 10.1.

Actually, the processor does not directly multiply the segment number by 16; it merely shifts the segment number to the left by four positions. This shift is implemented by connecting the "wires" of the segment register to the shifted positions in the 20-bit register

## 10.1 Real Mode (8086)

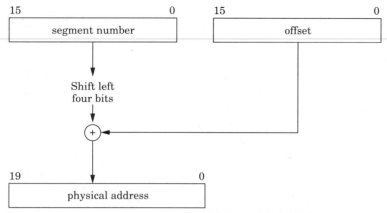

Figure 10.1  Computing a Physical Address, Real Mode

used for computing physical addresses. The offset is added to this register, aligned on the least significant bit. Thus, the calculation is essentially a (shifted) move and unsigned addition.

With only four segment registers available, a maximum of four 64K segments (256K of memory) can be accessed directly. To use more of the 1 megabyte address space, the segment number in one of the segment registers must be changed. It is not difficult to partition the instructions of a program into several code segments, using different segments for different subprograms. Transferring control between such segments is accomplished with far calls and far returns.

Difficulties can arise when a program has more than 64K of data (or 128K if the extra segment is used carefully), all of which must be accessible throughout the whole program. Actually, setting up the DS register to point to a particular data segment is not difficult; this has been done at the beginning of each main program in this text. But an application program is slowed when it has to switch data segments often, and the programmer is required to keep track of which data segment the DS register points to throughout the program.

Much of the software in use today, including PC-DOS and MS-DOS, executes in real mode. Such software makes no direct use of the more advanced features of the newer processors, but it does ensure software compatibility with the earliest processors, making such software usable even after hardware upgrades. However, support software and applications that use the features of the newer processors are available.

## Expanded Memory

The 8086 (and 8088) processors can address 1 megabyte of memory. When these systems were designed, 1 megabyte was considered substantial. A few years later, however, it was considered inadequate by many users.

Manufacturers found a way to add more memory to systems that use the 8086. At first it might seem silly to install more memory than can be addressed directly; after all, no matter what is done to the bus structure and other components of the system, the processor has only 20 bits of address. However, there is a way to use more than 1 megabyte of memory in 8086 and 8088 systems.

The 1 megabyte of address space is partitioned into two regions. The first 640K is used by DOS, application programs, and user data; the remaining 384K is reserved for the video system, input and output ports, and other hardware. But there is a region of 64K within this 384K that is not reserved or used for anything. If memory is installed in that address range—and it is arranged for DOS to make use of it—usable memory can be increased by 64K without exceeding the 1 megabyte address range.

One problem is to "convince" DOS to use that region even though the region is not contiguous with the memory available for applications. This problem was solved, and the solution suggested another possibility, known as expanded memory.

Imagine treating that 64K address range not as one 64K segment but as four 16K regions called banks. Doing so allows for more flexible management of the region: The banks can be treated collectively as one 64K segment, as separate 16K banks, or as some combination of 16K and 32K banks. Expanded memory boards have many distinct 16K banks of memory configured in such a way that any four of their banks can be switched into the four 16K address ranges.

For example, assume an expanded memory board has 32 banks of 16K (a total of 512K). At a given moment, banks 17, 23, 5, and 9 might be mapped, in that order, to the address space. The destination operand of a mov instruction to the tenth byte of the region would be stored in the tenth byte of bank 17. Some time later, bank 17 might be switched out so that bank 6 can be switched in. The data in bank 17 is preserved but is inaccessible until bank 17 is switched in again. Although this example used only 512K, actual expanded memory cards can have as much as 8 megabytes.

The switching requires additional hardware on the expanded memory card and software drivers to enable programs to properly use the 64K region. To make this scheme work with hardware from different manufacturers and software from different publishers, a standard was established by Lotus, Intel, and Microsoft called both LIM memory and EMS (Expanded Memory Specification) 3.2 memory.

Other, more powerful, versions of expanded memory are available that also make use of the idea of switching banks of memory installed on an expansion card into the address space. The newer versions, called EEMS (Enhanced EMS) and EMS 4.0, allow banks of any size to be switched into any region of the 1 megabyte address space. Whole programs can be switched into and out of addressable memory very quickly with these systems, opening the door for some fairly sophisticated user environments.

## EXERCISES 10.1

1. Determine the 20-bit physical address corresponding to the following:
    - (a) segment = 2020h
      offset = 00AAh
    - (b) segment = 00F0h
      offset = 0087h
    - (c) segment = 1230h
      offset = 1056h
    - (d) segment = 8FFFh
      offset = 9876h

2. Determine the offset needed to access physical address 23AF6h using the following segment numbers
   (a) 23AFh        (b) 2300h
   (c) 23A0h        (d) 2222h
3. How many different combinations of segment number and offset refer to the same physical address?
4. What 20-bit physical address do you think is formed from segment number FFF0h and offset 0123h?
5. Describe how you could access more than 64K of data within a program.

## 10.2 PROTECTED MODE (80286)

The 8086 and 8088 were designed to address a maximum of 1 megabyte of memory. With falling memory prices and increasing user expectations, 1 megabyte of memory is often not enough. With the 80286 protected mode, a second memory mode, one that can address 16 megabytes of memory, was introduced.

### Addresses

Like a real mode program, a protected mode program uses separate segments for instructions, data, and the stack, with a fourth extra segment available. The instructions are the same as in real mode, but the calculation of a physical address is different.

An address in protected mode consists of a 16-bit segment selector and a 16-bit offset. The selector is not an address; rather, it contains three fields: A 13-bit index into one of two tables of descriptors and a 1-bit indicator to select which table are used in computing addresses; the other 2-bit field is part of protection mechanism. See Figure 10.2.

A *segment descriptor* is a 64-bit record that contains information about a segment. The layout of a segment descriptor is shown in Figure 10.3. For now, the only field of interest is the base address. The other fields will be presented later.

Programs can access two tables of descriptors. These tables contain segment descriptors as well as other types of descriptors not discussed here. One of the tables, called the local descriptor table, or LDT, is local to the program. The other table, called the global descriptor table, or GDT, is shared by all programs.

Figure 10.4 shows how the selector, offset, and descriptor tables are used in computing a physical address in protected mode. The table indicator bit in the selector specifies whether the selector refers to the LDT or GDT. The 13-bit index specifies which descriptor in the table to use. The 24-bit base address field of that segment descriptor is added to the 16-bit

TI = Table indicator
RPL = Requested privilege level

**Figure 10.2  Format of a Segment Selector**

## 356 Chapter 10 Memory

```
 6      4 4   4 3              1 1
 3      8 7   0 9              6 5      0
┌───────┬─────┬─────────────────┬───────┐
│   0   │Access│  Base address  │ Limit │
└───────┴─────┴─────────────────┴───────┘
```
**Figure 10.3  Format of a Segment Descriptor**

offset (computed from the base and index registers and a displacement, as in real mode). The sum is the 24-bit physical address.

Determining a physical address in protected mode is more complex than in real mode. Fortunately, only the addition of the offset to the base address is needed for most accesses. The 24-bit base address associated with a segment changes only when the corresponding segment register changes. That is, every reference to a location in the data segment

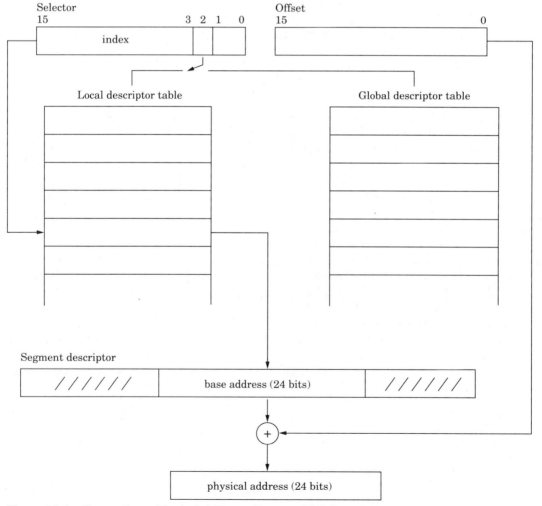

**Figure 10.4  Computing a Physical Address, Protected Mode**

that uses DS as the segment register also uses the same 24-bit base address. The 80286 processor has extra registers called *shadow registers* where four 24-bit base addresses are saved, one for each segment register. When a base address is needed, the value in the shadow register corresponding to the segment register is used without referencing the descriptor table. When a segment register is changed, the processor detects it and updates the corresponding shadow register with the base address from the new descriptor. Thus, the processor accesses the descriptor table relatively few times.

With a 24-bit physical address, $2^{24}$ bytes (16 megabytes) of memory can be accessed. However, physical segments are still limited to 64K by the 16-bit offsets.

## Extended Memory

The 80286 processor can address 16 megabytes of memory, and many computers that use it can have as much as 4, 6, or even 8 megabytes of memory installed without using an expansion card. Only the first megabyte can be accessed in real mode; the 80286 must be in protected mode to access any memory beyond that. (This is a simplification; it is possible to access a 64K segment of memory above the 1 megabyte address by exploiting overflow in address computation, but that idea will not be considered here.)

DOS was written for the 8086, which can access only 1 megabyte of memory. Running DOS on an 80286 system requires running the system in real mode. DOS will not switch the 80286 into protected mode to make use of the larger address space.

For some 80286 systems, memory above 1 megabyte can be configured, with appropriate hardware and software, to work as banks of expanded memory. (See the discussion of expanded memory in the preceding section.)

Another way to use memory above 1 megabyte with DOS is to temporarily switch the processor into protected mode, use the memory in an application, and then switch back to real mode just before invoking any DOS routines. When these steps are taken, the memory above the 1 megabyte limit of real mode is called extended memory. There are standards and conventions for writing programs that use protected mode.

Some compilers can generate object code that can be further processed by what is called a DOS extender to generate protected mode applications that use extended memory. Several utilities and shells are available that utilize extended memory for switching between programs quickly, for spoolers, for disk buffers, and so on. The Microsoft Windows environment, for example, uses extended memory when available for many of these purposes.

Even though expanded memory can be used with any model processor and extended memory requires at least an 80286, the current trend is toward an increased use of extended memory.

## Virtual Memory

As stated earlier, a protected mode physical address has 24 bits. With 24-bit addresses, the processor can reference $2^{24}$ locations, or 16 megabytes of memory. The address is represented using a 13-bit index into a table of segment descriptors, so there can be up to $2^{13}$ descriptors in the table. There are two tables, one of which is selected by the table indicator bit in the selector. So there can be up to $2^{14}$ segment descriptors, each referring to a segment with up to $2^{16}$ (64K) bytes. (Actually, a global descriptor with index 0 is used to provide a null—or uninitialized—descriptor, but this exception will be ignored to simplify the following computation.) With $2^{14}$ segments of $2^{16}$ bytes, there is a potential address space of $2^{30}$ bytes (1 gigabyte).

The address space is much larger than the memory that the 24-bit physical address can access. One way to exploit this huge address space is by means of something called **virtual memory,** a technique in which part of a fast direct-access storage device, typically a hard disk, is used to represent a very large address space. Programs and data are loaded into this very large space, and selected portions are swapped into memory as needed. The swapping, and indeed the fact that the programs and data are on disk rather than in memory, is transparent to the program. Applications, and most of the operating system, can be written as if there is actually 1 gigabyte of memory. In this way, many more programs and much larger programs can appear to be loaded in memory than the physical memory can accommodate.

Recall that a program must be in memory to be executed. In a large program, only the instructions in a small region will be executed in any short period of time. If a program executes only for a short time before relinquishing the system to another program, there is no need for all of the program to occupy memory at that time. The other programs that share the processor also need memory; what one program does not use, another can.

With support from the processor, a multiprogram operating system can swap pieces of a program between the disk and memory. In the 80286, the pieces that can be swapped are segments; the processor helps by providing some status bits in the segment descriptors that the operating system can use. The details of how virtual memory is implemented are beyond the scope of this text.

## 10.3 LINEAR MEMORY MODE (80386)

In this section, the linear memory mode and 32-bit addressing introduced in the 80386 and the paged virtual memory it supports are examined.

### Addresses

An address in the 80386 is specified as a 16-bit segment selector and a 32-bit offset. The selector is very much like a selector in the 80286, except that the segment descriptors specify a 32-bit base address. The sum of the base address and the offset gives a 32-bit address.

Programs written for the 80386 still use one segment for code, one for the stack, and one or two for data. But with 32-bit offsets, a segment can be as large as $2^{32}$ bytes (4 gigabytes, or 4096 megabytes). The problem of needing several segments for data, which occurs when the segments are limited to 64K as in the 8086 and 80286, vanishes for the 80386. But with 32-bit offsets, all references within a segment need 4-byte pointers, while references to other segments need 6-byte pointers. (The terms near pointer and far pointer have different definitions, appropriately, with the 32-bit addressing of the 80386.)

## 10.3 Linear Memory Mode (80386)

Some programs written for the 80386 associate all four segment registers with address 0 and use offsets to specify addresses directly. Doing so simplifies programming somewhat and is especially handy when trying to implement programs written for other, larger computers on an 80386-based microcomputer. Larger computers generally do not impose the limits that the 8086 and 80286 segmentation does; programs written for larger computers require a lot of effort to implement within the restrictions of the smaller segments of the 8086 and 80286. Programs for larger computers can be adapted to 80386-based microcomputers somewhat more easily.

Defining all memory as one large segment, then setting all segment registers to point to it, sacrifices the protection provided by the segments. However, the 80386 implements similar protection measures—on smaller blocks—as part of its virtual memory management.

### Pages and Virtual Memory

With a 32-bit address the 80386 can access $2^{32}$ bytes, or 4 gigabytes, of memory. This value is also the potential size of virtual memory. Note that even though this value is the same size as the range of physical addresses, it is larger than the potential size of virtual memory on the 80286, which has a potential virtual memory size much larger than its range of physical addresses. The address formed by adding the base (from a segment descriptor) and the offset is called the linear address; it refers to a location within virtual memory. Each location in virtual memory is mapped to a location in real memory specified by a physical address.

The memory, both virtual and physical, of the 80386 is divided into one million **pages** of 4K each. The 32-bit address is partitioned into a 20-bit page number and a 12-bit offset relative to the start of the page. (Be careful not to confuse an offset used in discussing pages with offsets used in forming the linear address in the first place. Unfortunately, the word offset is commonly used for both of these.) Virtual memory management and protection on the 80386 works with pages rather than segments.

Note that no computer will actually have all one million pages of real memory (it would be quite expensive and underutilized); the number of pages of real memory is more likely to be several hundred to a few thousand—up to a dozen or so megabytes. The number of pages of virtual memory available depends on the disk capacity devoted to storing pages; the number of pages of virtual memory actually in use varies according to need. Note that the capacity of virtual memory is limited by the amount of disk space available, not by real memory. Of course, we expect to need significantly more pages of virtual memory than of real memory—there would be little reason to bother with virtual memory if we did not.

The mapping of a 20-bit virtual page number into a 20-bit physical page number is a two-step process. The virtual page number is partitioned into two 10-bit indexes. The first index is used with a table called the page directory. The entry in the page directory with the specified index is a pointer to a page table. The second 10-bit index in the virtual page number is used with the page table. The entry in the page table at the specified index gives the physical page number and other information used in managing virtual memory. The 12-bit offset in the linear address is concatenated to the 20-bit physical page number to form the 32-bit physical address. See Figure 10.5.

**360** Chapter 10 Memory

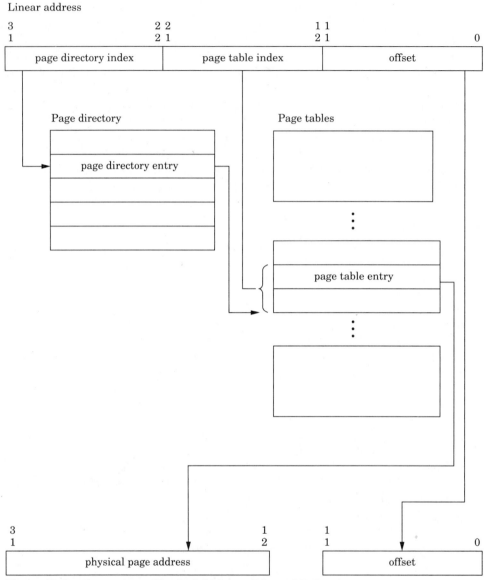

**Figure 10.5 Computing a Physical Address, Linear Mode**

The 80386 is available in two versions: the original model, now called the DX, and a less expensive version called the SX. (Other variations may be introduced, with energy-saving features for use in laptop and notebook PCs; these versions will likely be similar to the SX.) The primary difference between the DX and SX is the size of the data bus: The DX uses 32 bits, while the SX uses only 16 (like the 80286 and 8086). The addressing techniques and virtual memory support are the same.

### EXERCISES 10.3

1. The 80286 manages memory with variable-size, potentially large segments; the 80386 does so with fixed-size, smaller pages. What advantages do you think the use of pages provides?
2. There is a strong relationship between segments and the logical structure of a program, but not between pages and the logical structure of the program. How do you think this difference might affect the virtual memory management algorithms?
3. Investigate how much memory and disk capacity a "typical" 80386 system has. How many pages of virtual and physical memory are available on this system?
4. Why is disk performance so important to the effective use of virtual memory?
5. There are probably more 80386 computers running software written for the 8086 (under DOS) than running software written for the 80386 (under UNIX or DOS extenders). Are experts predicting this situation will change soon? What forces are at work in the marketplace that affect this situation?

## 10.4 MEMORY HARDWARE

Computer memory is available as RAM and ROM. In each of these memory types, there are variations to better match the hardware to a specific application. These memory types are discussed in this section, as is the use of cache memories.

### RAM and ROM

The terms RAM and ROM refer to **Random Access Memory** and **Read-Only Memory,** respectively. These terms do not capture all of the properties of the two memory types, since there are different types of RAM and ROM.

The term random access, when applied to memory, refers to two important properties: (1) the ability to access any location in memory at any time, rather than being restricted to accessing locations sequentially, and (2) the ability to write (change) the contents of a location as well as read (fetch or copy) it. The memory used for data in application programs is RAM.

The most common type of RAM, which is cheaper and smaller, is *dynamic RAM,* or DRAM. Dynamic RAM stores a bit of data as a charge on a capacitor; the capacitors are made as a type of transistor in an integrated circuit or chip. The charge on a capacitor decays with time. To avoid loss of data due to decay, all capacitors in the chip are recharged every few milliseconds. This recharge and other hardware factors beyond the scope of this text limit how quickly the data stored in DRAM can be accessed.

Another type of RAM is called *static RAM,* or SRAM. A static RAM stores a bit of data as the state of a flip-flop. A flip-flop is a logic circuit that remains in one of two possible states until an input pulse causes it to switch to the other state. Static RAM does not need to be recharged periodically like dynamic RAM. Static RAM also provides faster read and write operations. But because flip-flops are more complex than capacitors, SRAM is larger and more expensive than DRAM.

The RAM used for main memory is usually dynamic RAM. The size and cost of static RAM currently prohibits incorporating very much of it into a computer. But there is a way to take advantage of the speed of static RAM using only a modest amount of it, as will be seen later in this section.

The term read-only memory (ROM) refers to memory that can be read (fetched or copied) but not written (changed). Locations in ROM can be accessed in any order; no particular sequence is required. The contents of RAM can be changed, whereas the contents of ROM are permanent. ROM is also nonvolatile; that is, the contents of ROM are not lost when the power is turned off.

Some of the memory in a typical microcomputer is ROM. This ROM typically includes the program that starts the computer; that is, the program that performs the hardware tests when the power is turned on, checks the status of devices connected to the computer, and loads the operating system (or parts of it, at least) from disk into memory and transfers control to it. ROM is also used for the hardware BIOS discussed in Chapter 9.

Since ROM cannot be changed during program execution, the software installed in it must consist only of constants and instructions that are not modified during execution. In other words, segments that are to be installed in ROM must be pure. To write a program with the intent of having it installed in ROM, the program must be partitioned into one or more pure (code) segments and one or more impure (data and stack) segments; only the pure segments can be implemented in ROM.

The contents of ROM must be fully determined before the ROM is manufactured. Once built, there is no way to change its contents. It is very expensive to design and build ROM chips for specific applications. The economics of mass production is required to make the use of ROM a viable option.

To take advantage of the nonvolatile nature of ROM without incurring the high overhead cost of producing application-specific chips, *programmable ROM,* called PROM, has been developed. When PROM is manufactured, all bits of the memory are set to 1. Using a special programmer (a hardware device), individual bits of the PROM can be cleared to 0. This irreversible process is much like breaking an electrical path in the chip by blowing a fuse. But if an error in the program is found, only a few chips need to be discarded, and new chips can be programmed. Doing so is much less expensive than designing a ROM for a particular program. Other variations of ROM include PROMs than can be completely erased and then reprogrammed, and PROMs that can be selectively reprogrammed.

## Cache Memories

Since all data and instructions are stored in memory, a significant part of program execution time is spent accessing memory. Hardware designers devote considerable attention to speeding up memory access time. One approach uses cache memory. **Cache memory** is a very fast type of internal storage. It is a few times faster than main memory, approaching the speed of the processor itself. It is also much more expensive than main memory; usually, only a limited amount of cache memory is installed.

Effective use of cache memory depends on two attributes inherent to most programs. First, instructions tend to be executed in sequence, with relatively few jumps. Thus the location of the next few instructions usually can be predicted easily. By copying a block of instructions into the cache memory when any instruction must be fetched from main memory, there is a good chance that the next several instructions can be fetched from the cache rather than requiring an access of main memory. Second, the same data areas tend to be accessed several times in a short period of time. It's reasonable to expect that data in memory that have been accessed once are more likely to be accessed again soon; the program can then use cache memory for that data as well. When the cache memory allocated for data is full, it swaps the least used data from cache to memory to make room in the cache for data more likely to be accessed.

Managing the instructions and data to keep in cache memory is a hit-or-miss proposition, but the underlying assumptions about program behavior have been shown to be correct: Hit rates (the percentage of memory accesses that can be satisfied by accessing the cache instead of main memory) of 90% have been achieved. Such hit rates produce a significant increase in system performance.

There are several ways to implement cache memories. In one method, called associative mapping, the real memory address is stored in the cache along with the data from that location in memory. When the processor requests data from a particular memory location, that address is used by logic circuits in the cache memory. If that address is found in the cache memory, the corresponding data are returned; otherwise, the data are fetched from main memory. One reason why cache memory is so much more expensive is that logic circuits are required to access data by value—the cache treats the main memory address as data.

There are three levels of memory organization: secondary storage for long-term storage, main memory for short-term use by programs that are loaded, and cache memory for the instructions and data of a program that is running. Just as programs must be loaded from secondary storage to memory for execution, portions of programs are copied between main memory and cache memory for execution. There is special hardware that controls the cache memory and allows the programs and data to remain unaffected by all the copying activity.

Cache memories can be designed as separate chips using static RAM (SRAM). This approach allows for some flexibility in the amount of SRAM installed in any given system, but it requires the use of the system bus to transfer data between the cache and processor. Another approach, used in many of the newer and more powerful processors, is to include the cache and the controlling circuits as part of the CPU chip. This method allows faster and more predictable operation, because the size of the cache is fixed by chip design.

There is much research and engineering work being done on cache memory design and implementation. Although cache memories already provide significant advantages, there is promise for even faster designs and higher hit rates.

## EXERCISES 10.4

1. How much RAM is installed in your computer system? How much ROM? What is the ROM used for?
2. Think about a typical, inexpensive, scientific or business calculator—not a programmable one, but one with a dozen or so special function keys. What would RAM be used for in such a calculator? What would ROM be used for? How much of each do you think such a calculator actually contains?

3. Based on your answers to Exercises 1 and 2, what proportion of the total memory of a computer is RAM? What proportion of the total memory of a calculator is ROM?
4. Does your computer system have any cache memory? If so, how much? How is it implemented?

## KEY POINTS

- Physical segments, also called frames, are regions of memory address space. Logical segments are defined in programs and mapped to physical segments during program loading.
- Virtual memory uses a fast storage device to represent a very large address space. Active programs and data in regions of that address space are copied to real memory, as needed, by the operating system. The programmer then sees a virtual machine with a large address space.
- Pages are fixed-size regions of memory. Programs are partitioned logically into segments, with data separate from code and with large data or code areas split into different segments according to logical structure (as specified by directives in assembly language, for example). Programs are split automatically into pages, however, with no regard to logical organization.
- Virtual memory can be managed as either pages or segments.
- Random access memory (RAM) can be read or written to in any order. Dynamic RAM (DRAM) stores bits as charges that must be refreshed, whereas Static RAM (SRAM) stores bits using flip-flops. DRAMs are cheaper, smaller, and slower than SRAMs.
- Read-only memory (ROM) can be read in any order but not written to. It is manufactured with pure code and constants permanently written into it. Programmable ROM (PROM) can be written to once, allowing prototypes and small production runs to be made less expensively.
- Cache memories are very fast (but small and expensive) storage devices used to improve system performance by providing very quick access to selected instructions and data. The selection algorithms they use consider the frequency and probability that any given word of main memory will be needed soon.

## PC SYSTEM SUMMARY

- Many compilers use standard memory models, which specify how large the data and code of a program can be and what type of references are needed. The six standard models are summarized here:

    Tiny: data and code in same segment, up to 64K; all references near.

    Small: data and code in separate segments, up to 64K each; all references near.

    Medium: data segment up to 64K, using near references; code may exceed 64K, using far jumps.

    Compact: data may exceed 64K, using far references; code segment up to 64K, using near (and short) jumps.

    Large: data and code may each exceed 64K, using far references; no single array may exceed 64K.

    Huge: like large, except arrays may each exceed 64K.

**PC System Summary**

- Programs, especially when written in assembly language, may use more than one memory model.
- Addresses in real mode are 20 bits long, specified as the sum of a shifted 16-bit segment number and a 16-bit offset.
- Addresses in protected mode are 24 bits long, specified as the sum of a 24-bit base address and a 16-bit offset. The base address is retrieved from a table of segment descriptors indexed by a 16-bit segment selector.
- Linear addresses are 32 bits long, specified as the sum of a 32-bit base address and a 32-bit offset. The linear address is converted to a 32-bit physical address using two 10-bit indexes to retrieve a 20-bit page number, to which the remaining 12 bits of the linear address are appended as an offset.

# 11  Program Translation

- ◆ **Binding**
- ◆ **Assemblers**
- ◆ **Translating High-Level Languages**
- ◆ **Linkers**
- ◆ **Loaders**
- ◆ **Debuggers**

One of the objectives of this text is to show how the various data types, data structures, operations, and control structures found in high-level languages are implemented. Assembly language has been used to examine many of the concepts in this study. Assembly-language programs must be translated to machine instructions in order to be executed. Furthermore, no program exists in isolation; all depend on the services of other programs during preparation—text editors, compilers or assemblers, linkers—and during execution—loaders, memory managers, drivers for input and output devices, and so on. Thus, assembly-language programs must be translated and combined with other programs to be useful.

This chapter examines the objects that make up programs, emphasizing the attributes and the point at which the values of the attributes are bound to the objects. The idea of binding attributes to objects (symbols) provides a framework in which to consider the translation and linking processes.

We examine the translation process in some detail by following an assembly-language program through a two-pass assembler. Along the way, we see more of the format of 8086 instructions, the construction and use of the symbol and segment tables, and the role of directives. A draft algorithm for the assembler is also offered. Compilers and interpreters are discussed, but since much of the theory underlying these topics is beyond the scope of this book, no attempt is made to compile an example.

Even after translation of source file to object file, much work may remain before a program can be executed, so we continue to follow the assembled program through a linkage editor. Here, we see it combined with the input and output routines, we see the separate code and data segments combined and displacements adjusted, and we see external references resolved. Finally, we follow the output of the linker into memory, and see how control of the computer system is turned over to it.

No discussion of how programs are transformed from symbolic form to executable form is complete without considering how symbolic debuggers, watching the execution of the

## 11.1 Binding

executable program, can give the programmer some of the original symbolic information. Thus, this chapter ends with a study of the manner in which selected symbolic information is carried along through translation, linking, and loading for use by the debugger.

## 11.1 BINDING

Computer systems consist of objects and actions. Objects include instructions, registers, symbols, and segments. Actions include the execution of instructions. This section is more concerned with the objects that form programs than with actions and objects fixed by the design of a system. Thus, the focus will be on symbols and segments.

Every object (and action) has one or more attributes that define it. Consider the symbol Wave in the statement

```
Wave      dw       ?
```

The attributes of the symbol Wave include its name (Wave), type (word, specified by the dw directive), location in memory, the value stored in that location, and possibly other characteristics. The attributes of a segment include its name, length, alignment, combine type, class name, location in memory, and so on.

Some of the attributes of an object, such as its name, are assigned values when the object is first used. Others are assigned values during program translation, linking, loading, or execution. Whenever it occurs, the process of fixing—even temporarily—the value of an attribute is called **binding**. Binding time refers to the moment when the value of an attribute is fixed. Binding occurs at every stage of program translation from source text to executable file, as well as during program execution.

*Static binding* occurs when a value and an attribute are bound only once, permanently. Associating a type with a name is an example of static binding. *Dynamic binding* occurs repeatedly during execution, with different values bound to the attribute each time. Assigning the value of an expression to a variable is an example of dynamic binding.

The concept of binding provides a good vantage point from which to consider assemblers, linkers, and loaders. These programs process their input files to produce output files (or an image in memory, in the case of the loader) in which more attributes are bound. In the process, they convert a symbolic program into a form that the computer can execute.

One advantage of programming in assembly language instead of coding programs directly in binary is that the programmer can defer specifying exactly which address in memory to use for each instruction and datum. The assembler binds some of the symbols in programs to constants and fixed addresses. However, the assembler also defers binding the location of each instruction in memory, leaving that task to some later step. The linker, when it combines segments from different object files, alters the information regarding the location of the instructions. The loader, when it loads the program into memory, finally binds the location in memory of each instruction. During these processes, enough information from the original source file must be passed along, and modified as needed, by each process until every instruction is bound.

Some attributes are partially bound at various stages in the translation, linking, and loading process. For example, an external reference is noted by the assembler, partially resolved by the linker, and fixed by the loader. In some more complex systems, external references are neither resolved by the linker nor bound to specific locations until the actual reference occurs. In this case, the symbolic reference must be available during execution for use in resolving the reference.

As attributes are bound to values, the information needed to bind the attribute can be discarded. For example, the information describing the type of Wave given earlier as a word is specified in the source file by the dw directive. Once the assembler has finished translating, the type may not be needed explicitly: The fact that the operand is a word has been coded in the instructions that access it.

There are instances when all of the symbolic information in the source file is retained along with the output of the assembler, linker, and loader. The most common reason to retain this information is to make it available to a symbolic debugger like Microsoft's CodeView or Borland's Turbo Debugger. We return to this subject in the last section of this chapter.

The trend in software is to defer binding as long as possible. An example of very late binding is virtual memory—physical addresses are not determined by the hardware until the moment of the actual access. Late binding has the advantage of providing more flexible and powerful environments for programs, but it requires more complex language translators and operating systems.

## EXERCISES 11.1

1. What are some of the attributes of the symbols in the following declarations?

    ```
    PromptMsg    db      "Enter N: "
    PromptLen    dw      $ - PromptMsg
    ```

2. Which of the attributes in your answer to Exercise 1 are bound during assembly? To what values are those attributes bound?

3. Consider a typical university. Like a computer system, a university has certain resources that are fixed, such as library and laboratory buildings, and some resources that are more dynamic, such as faculty and course offerings. Compare the students enrolled in a university to the symbols of a program. What associations made by (or to) students can be explained in terms of binding? What attributes are bound?

4. Can you think of an analogy, like that of Exercise 3, that illustrates binding in a real-life experience?

## 11.2 ASSEMBLERS

Assembly-language programs are written in symbolic form. The symbols used are made up of letters, digits, punctuation, and other special characters to represent data and operations. The symbols must conform to the syntax rules of the language, but generally programmers are quite free to write in a style that they hope is easily understood by other programmers.

Computers, however, can only execute instructions that are coded as strings of bits. Data must also be coded as strings of bits. Programs could be coded directly as strings of bits, but that is too much bother—it is too easy to make errors when coding programs in binary.

## 11.2 Assemblers

A more efficient method is to write programs in symbolic form and have the computer translate them into the strings of bits. The program that translates an assembly-language program into machine-dependent binary codes is called an assembler.

Each executable statement in an assembly language corresponds to one machine instruction, though there are exceptions. Each operand is translated into one reference to a register, a memory location, or a constant, as specified by the programmer and the syntax rules of the assembler.

The assembler must perform much analysis while translating a program from symbols to binary numbers, but a formal treatment of that analysis is beyond the scope of this book. It is best left to a text devoted to program translation. Still, we can trace the action of a typical assembler on a small program.

In this section, we translate a short assembly-language subprogram in much the same way an assembler would. This treatment is not an exhaustive study of assembler techniques; we are more interested in how an assembler works than with how to write a working assembler. We deliberately ignore questions of how the information in various tables is coded and searched, as well as how the assembler reads and analyzes the source file. We also use a textual representation of the object file produced (the object file is used in Section 11.3 in the discussion of linkers).

### Instruction Specifications

To translate an assembly-language program into strings of bits, it is necessary to know how the instructions are coded. Recall the discussion in Section 1.3 and the diagram of Figure 2.16, which is repeated here as Figure 11.1. This figure shows the basic layout used for many, but not all, 8086 instructions.

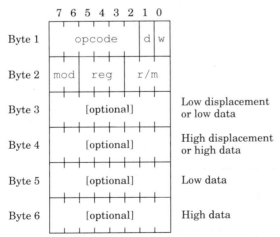

**Figure 11.1   General Format of 8086 Instructions**

Table 11.1  Instruction Table

| Mnemonic | Operands | Length | Coding | | |
|---|---|---|---|---|---|
| add | reg,imm | 3–4 | 100000,s,w | mod,000,r/m | data(1-2) |
| add | acc,imm | 2–3 | 0000010,w | data(1-2) | |
| call | label | 3 | 11101000 | disp(2) | |
| cmp | reg,imm | 3–4 | 100000,s,w | mod,111,r/m | data(1-2) |
| cmp | reg,mem | 3–4 | 001110,d,w | mod,reg,r/m | disp(1-2) |
| cmp | acc,imm | 2–3 | 0011110,w | data(1-2) | |
| cwd | – | 1 | 10011001 | | |
| dec | reg16 | 1 | 01001,reg | | |
| idiv | mem | 4 | 1111011,w | mod,111,r/m | disp(2) |
| imul | mem | 4 | 1111011,w | mod,101,r/m | disp(2) |
| jmp | label | 2 | 11101011 | disp(1) | |
| jmp | label | 3 | 11101001 | disp(2) | |
| jne | label | 2 | 01110101 | disp(1) | |
| jng | label | 2 | 01111110 | disp(1) | |
| jnl | label | 2 | 01111101 | disp(1) | |
| loop | label | 2 | 11100010 | disp(1) | |
| mov | reg,reg | 2 | 100010,d,w | mod,reg,r/m | |
| mov | reg,mem | 3–4 | 100010,d,w | mod,reg,r/m | disp(1-2) |
| mov | reg,imm | 2–3 | 1011,w,reg | data(1-2) | |
| mov | acc,mem | 2–3 | 1010000,w | disp(1-2) | |
| mov | mem,acc | 2–3 | 1010001,w | disp(1-2) | |
| nop | – | 1 | 10010000 | | |
| pop | reg | 1 | 01011,reg | | |
| push | reg | 1 | 01010,reg | | |
| push | mem | 4 | 11111111 | mod,110,r/m | disp(2) |
| ret | imm | 3 | 11000010 | data(2) | |
| sub | reg,reg | 2 | 001010,d,w | mod,reg,r/m | |
| sub | reg,imm | 3–4 | 100000,s,w | mod,101,r/m | data(1-2) |

The assembler uses a table of instruction information during the translation. Part of such a table, in a form convenient to read, is given in Table 11.1. This table shows all of the instruction forms used in the subprogram we plan to assemble, plus a few others to illustrate some of the variation in coding instructions with the same mnemonic but different operands.

## The Two-Pass Assembler

A **two-pass assembler** reads and analyzes the entire program twice. In the first pass, the assembler builds two tables: the **symbol table**, which contains a record for each symbol used in the program, and the **segment table**, which contains a record for each segment used in the program. The entries in these tables record the values of the attributes of the symbols and segments. In the second pass, the assembler analyzes the source program again. Using the information in the tables constructed in the first pass, it generates the object file and optional listing and cross-reference files.

It is possible to write an assembler that requires only one pass, combining the processes of building the tables and generating the object file, but some means of resolving forward

## 11.2 Assemblers

references must be provided. This problem will be easier to understand after we see more of the assembler, so we defer further consideration until later. It is also possible to add features to an assembly language that necessitate a third pass.

We will use a two-pass assembler to translate Program 11.1. Although this short procedure performs no useful processing, it does include a variety of features pertaining to this discussion.

---

**Program 11.1**

```
; Program 11.1      ExSub.ASM
; Subroutine used in discussion of assembling, linking,
;    loading, and debugging.  Performs no useful work.

; Parameters:
  VarParm      equ      word ptr [bp + 6]
  ValParm      equ      word ptr [bp + 4]

_DATA SEGMENT word public 'data'
  LocalVar     dw       ?
  ErrorMsg     db       "Argument is too small."
  ErrorLen     dw       $ - ErrorMsg
_DATA ENDS

_TEXT SEGMENT word public 'code'
      assume   cs: _TEXT
      assume   ds: _DATA
      extrn    PutStr: PROC
      public   ExSub

ExSub PROC

; set up pointer to parameters
      push     bp
      mov      bp, sp

; LocalVar := VarParm
      mov      bx, VarParm
      mov      ax, [bx]
      mov      LocalVar, ax

; IF01 VarParm < 3
      mov      ax, ValParm
      cmp      ax, 3
      jnl      ELSE01

; THEN01
;   print error message
      mov      cx, ErrorLen
      mov      bx, offset ErrorMsg
      call     PutStr
      jmp      ENDIF01
```

**Program 11.1 (continued)**

```
        ELSE01:
;       VarParm := (27 + ValParm) rem LocalVar
            add     ax, 27
            cwd
            idiv    LocalVar
            mov     [bx], dx
        ENDIF01:

;       return
            pop     bp
            ret     4

ExSub   ENDP
_TEXT   ENDS
        END
```

## The first pass

The first pass reads the source program and builds the symbol and segment tables. The records in the symbol table include the following attributes for each symbol: name, type, value, and other type-dependent attributes. The types used in this example are (near) label, (near) procedure, byte, word, and text. The values used in the example are constants (for type text) or offsets (for the other types). The type-dependent attributes are segment name (for values that are offsets), scope (for external and public symbols), and length (for objects). Each of these attributes will be explained as they are encountered in the example.

The records in the segment table include the following attributes for each segment: name, length, alignment, combine type, class name, and register. These attributes, other than length and register, were discussed briefly in Chapter 3, in conjunction with the SEGMENT directive. The length of a segment is its size in bytes; it is determined by the assembler in the first pass and used in the second pass and by the linker and loader. The register attribute specifies which segment register, if any, can be assumed to have the selector for this segment.

As we build the symbol table, we, like an assembler, must constantly be aware of three things:

1. Our position in the program
2. The next available location in each segment
3. The current segment

We keep track of our position in the program informally; an assembler, however, reads the program sequentially, so it has some type of file buffer and pointer to monitor its position. We keep track of the next available location in each segment the same way an assembler does, using the length attribute in the segment table entry for the current segment. Finally, we keep track of the current segment informally; an assembler, however, uses an index into the segment table for this purpose.

Initially both the segment and symbol tables are empty, and the file containing the source program is opened for input. We will imitate the actions of the assembler almost line by line, skipping only blank lines and lines that contain nothing but comments. We also borrow the record notation of Pascal, using `symbol.attribute` to refer to a particular attribute of some symbol.

## 11.2 Assemblers

The first interesting line of the program is

```
VarParm    equ    word ptr [bp + 6]
```

It contains the symbol VarParm. We search the symbol table but do not find VarParm, so we add it to the symbol table. Its attributes (and how we determine them) are

```
name  = VARPARM         (specified in name field)
type  = TEXT            (specified by equ directive)
value = "word ptr [bp + 6]"      (operand)
```

Note that we convert all names to all capital letters.

The next line

```
ValParm    equ    word ptr [bp + 4]
```

also contains a new symbol to add to the symbol table. Its attributes are

```
name  = VALPARM
type  = TEXT
value = "word ptr [bp + 4]"
```

The line

```
_DATA SEGMENT word public 'data'
```

defines a segment. We scan the segment table and do not find this segment in it, so we add the segment with the attributes:

```
name         = _DATA       (specified in name field)
length       = 0           (first declaration of segment)
alignment    = WORD
combine type = PUBLIC
class name   = 'DATA'
register     = none        (no assume directive yet)
```

We also make _DATA the current segment.

The next line

```
LocalVar   dw    ?
```

has a new symbol. We add it to the symbol table with the attributes:

```
name    = LOCALVAR
type    = WORD       (specified by dw)
value   = 00h        (_DATA.length)
segment = _DATA
length  = 2          (a word is two bytes)
```

and add LOCALVAR.length to _DATA.length. When this directive is encountered, the current segment is _DATA, as noted above; the value is the current length of the current segment, _DATA.length, which is 0. The word for this variable will therefore begin with offset 0 in the _DATA segment. The next available byte is then at offset 2 (02h) from the start of _DATA, so we add LOCALVAR.length to _DATA.length, making it 02h.

The next line

```
ErrorMsg   db    "Argument is too small."
```

contains a new symbol to add to the symbol table. Its attributes are

```
name    = ERRORMSG
type    = BYTE      (specified by db)
value   = 02h       (offset; current length of _DATA)
segment = _DATA
length  = 16h       (characters in operand string)
```

Some of these attributes might not be what you anticipated. That the operand is a string of 22 (16h) bytes does not change the type of ERRORMSG, which was declared as byte by the db directive. It does specify the length attribute. When this directive is encountered, the current segment is _DATA, as noted above; the value is the current length of the current segment, _DATA.length, which is 02h. The 22 bytes for this string will therefore begin with offset 02h in the _DATA segment. The next available byte is then at offset 24 (18h) from the start of _DATA, so we add ERRORMSG.length to _DATA.length, making it 18h.

The next line

```
ErrorLen    dw      $ - ErrorMsg
```

has another new symbol. We add it to the symbol table with the attributes:

```
name    = ERRORLEN
type    = WORD      (specified by dw)
value   = 18h       (_DATA.length)
segment = _DATA
length  = 2
```

In processing this symbol, we must determine the value of the length attribute by examining the operand. We do not yet need the value of the operand expression. The expression used requires only one word, so ERRORLEN.length is 2. We add this to _DATA.length, making the latter 1Ah.

The line

```
_DATA ENDS
```

specifies the end of the _DATA segment. We note this by changing the current segment to none.

The line

```
_TEXT SEGMENT word public 'code'
```

starts a new segment. We add a record with the following attributes to the segment table:

```
name         = _TEXT
length       = 0
alignment    = WORD
combine type = PUBLIC
class name   = 'CODE'
register     = none
```

We also make _TEXT the current segment.

The line

```
    assume  cs: _TEXT
```

has no symbol or segment. When we scan it, we simply change _TEXT.register to CS. We do the same with the following line, changing _DATA.register to DS. This information will be used when building instructions.

## 11.2 Assemblers

The line

    extrn   PutStr: PROC

introduces another new symbol. We add a record with the following attributes to the symbol table:

```
name = PUTSTR
type = PROC       (near by default)
value = 0000      (undefined)
segment = _TEXT   (current segment)
other = EXTERNAL
```

The line

    public  ExSub

introduces another symbol but not much information. We add this to the symbol table:

```
name = EXSUB
type = unknown
value = unknown
segment = _TEXT
other = unknown
```

But the next line

ExSub PROC

allows us to bind a few more attributes. We modify the record for this symbol so that it becomes

```
name = EXSUB
type = PROC       (near by default)
value = 0000      (undefined)
segment = _TEXT
length = 0        (see below)
other = GLOBAL
```

The length attribute is temporarily assigned the value of _TEXT.length, which happens to be 0 in this example but could be any value for a second or third procedure in the same module and segment. Later, when we find the end of the procedure, we can subtract the value that was temporarily assigned from _TEXT.length to get the actual length.

For easier reference, the symbol and segment table records are collected in Tables 11.2 and 11.3. The entries in these tables are listed in the order in which the records

**Table 11.2  Symbol Table During Pass One**

| Name | Type | Value | Other attributes |
|---|---|---|---|
| VARPARM | TEXT | "word ptr [bp + 6]" | |
| VALPARM | TEXT | "word ptr [bp + 4]" | |
| LOCALVAR | WORD | 00h | segment = _DATA, length = 2 |
| ERRORMSG | BYTE | 02h | segment = _DATA, length = 16h |
| ERRORLEN | WORD | 18h | segment = _DATA, length = 2 |
| PUTSTR | PROC | 0000 | segment = _TEXT, other = EXTERNAL |
| EXSUB | PROC | 0000 | segment = _TEXT, other = GLOBAL, length = 0 |

**376** Chapter 11 Program Translation

Table 11.3 Segment Table During Pass One

| Name | Length | Align | Combine type | Class name | Register |
|------|--------|-------|--------------|------------|----------|
| _DATA | 1Ah | WORD | PUBLIC | 'DATA' | DS |
| _TEXT | 0 | WORD | PUBLIC | 'CODE' | CS |

were added. In the assembler, these might be inserted to maintain alphabetical ordering by name, which would allow faster searching. We will need to refer to the symbol and segment tables frequently during the analysis of the instructions.

Now back to assembling. The next line

    push    bp

is an instruction. The operand is a register. As shown in Table 11.1, the push instruction is one byte long. We add this length to the length of the current segment, making _TEXT.length 01h.

The next line,

    mov    bp, sp

is also an instruction. mov with two register operands is two bytes long (refer again to Table 11.1). We add 2 to _TEXT.length, making it 03h.

The next line that we consider,

    mov    bx, VarParm

requires a little more work. We must look up the symbol VARPARM to determine its value; we find that it is a text symbol. Thus, the instruction is essentially

    mov    bx, word ptr [bp + 6]

The second operand is an indirect memory reference. According to Table 11.1, this form of the mov instruction requires two bytes plus the size of the displacement. The displacement is 6, which fits in one byte, so the instruction requires three bytes. We add 3 to _TEXT.length, making it 06h.

The next line is

    mov    ax, [bx]

This is the same as the last instruction, except that the displacement is 0. (Of course, an assembler would have to analyze each operand completely before reaching this conclusion.) This instruction takes just two bytes, so we add 2 to _TEXT.length, making it 08h.

The next line is

    mov    LocalVar, ax

We search the symbol table for LOCALVAR and find that it is an offset from _DATA. This operand is a direct address. The register operand is the AX register; the special form of the mov instruction where one operand is the accumulator (AL or AX) and the other is a direct address can be used. This instruction is 1 byte plus the displacement. The displacement given in the symbol table is 00h. The linker, however, may combine the _DATA segment

## 11.2 Assemblers

with other segments, thereby causing the offset of LOCALVAR from the start of the segment to be too large for a 1-byte displacement. Thus, we need to use a 2-byte displacement so that this mov instruction is three bytes long. We add 3 to _TEXT.length, making it 0Bh.

The next instruction,

    mov    ax, ValParm

is similar to the second mov instruction of this section of the program. We add its length of three bytes to _TEXT.length, making the latter 0Eh.

The next instruction is

    cmp    ax, 3

There are two forms of this instruction in the table. The form with accumulator and immediate operands is one byte long plus the size of the immediate data. But the immediate data in this instruction must be the same size as the accumulator. Since the AX register is two bytes long, the instruction is three bytes long. Adding 3 to _TEXT.length makes it 11h.

The jnl instruction in the next line is always two bytes long. Note that the operand symbol ELSE01 is not yet in the table. That does not matter, as all conditional jumps must have 1-byte displacements in the 8086, making the instructions two bytes long. We add 2 to _TEXT.length, making it 13h. We can also add a record to the symbol table for this symbol, but without specifying attributes. Such an entry would be useful in checking for errors, which we have neglected during this discussion. We will, however, defer adding the symbol to the table until we actually find it used as a label or external reference.

The next line is

    mov    cx, ErrorLen

We search the symbol table for ERRORLEN and find that it is an offset from _DATA. This operand is a direct address. The register operand is the CX register, so we cannot use the special accumulator form. This instruction is two bytes plus the size of the displacement from DS. As we saw earlier, the linker may combine the _DATA segment with other segments; again we need a 2-byte displacement. Thus, this mov instruction is four bytes long. We add 4 to _TEXT.length, making it 17h.

The line

    mov    bx, offset ErrorMsg

appears similar to the previous line, but it is actually quite different. The second operand is not a direct address; rather, it is a constant that the linker will fill in later. The second operand is, ultimately, immediate data. This form of the instruction is one byte plus the size of the immediate data. That immediate data is an offset, always two bytes. Thus, we add 3 to _TEXT.length, making it 1Ah.

The call instruction in the next line requires one byte plus the size of the displacement. Since the program doesn't specify the distance to PutStr, it is assumed to be near. Accordingly, this near call has a 2-byte displacement, and the total length of the instruction is three bytes. We add 3 to _TEXT.length, making it 1Dh.

The jump to ENDIF01 in the next instruction could require either two bytes or three bytes to code. We cannot determine this, as the symbol ENDIF01 is not in the symbol table. To be safe, we use the 3-byte form of the instruction. We add 3 to _TEXT.length, making it 20h.

The next line is just

ELSE01:

which is a label. It is not yet in the symbol table, so we add it with the attributes:

name = ELSE01
type = LABEL
value = 20h    (_TEXT.length)
segment = _TEXT

Note that labels have no length, so they do not increase the size of the segment in which they occur.

The next instruction is

    add    ax, 27

Like an earlier mov instruction, this line contains a special accumulator form of the add instruction that is one byte long plus the size of the immediate data (which must be the size of the accumulator register used). Thus, this instruction is also three bytes long. We add 3 to _TEXT.length, making it 23h.

The cwd instruction on the next line is always one byte long, so we increment _TEXT.length to 24h.

The next line is

    idiv    LocalVar

With an operand in memory, regardless of addressing mode, this instruction is four bytes long. We add 4 to _TEXT.length, making it 28h.

The last mov instruction has one operand in a register, and one indirect operand in memory. The displacement of this indirect operand is 0. The instruction is two bytes long, plus no bytes for the displacement. We add 2 to _TEXT.length, making it 2Ah.

The next line is just the label ENDIF01. We searched the symbol table for it earlier but did not find it. Now we add it to the table. Its attributes are

name = ENDIF01
type = LABEL
value = 2Ah    (_TEXT.length)
segment = _TEXT

The pop instruction in the next line is one byte long, so we increment _TEXT.length to 2Bh.

The ret instruction with an immediate operand is three bytes long. We add 3 to _TEXT.length, making it 2Eh.

The next line is

ExSub ENDP

This marks the end of the EXSUB procedure. Now we can subtract the value that we saved in EXSUB.length (when we found the PROC directive earlier) from _TEXT.length, obtaining 2Eh for EXSUB.length.

The line

_TEXT ENDS

specifies the end of the _TEXT segment. We change the current segment to none.

## 11.2 Assemblers

Finally, we reach END in the next line. This almost completes the first pass. If there were no errors found—we certainly weren't looking for any—we open the object file for output. There is information that must be written to the object file now, before we start the second pass. The records that will be written to the object file at this time are shown in Figure 11.2. In the figure, the records are presented in a readable form—not the coded form in which they are actually written.

The first record we write is a header record, containing just the name of the source file. This is followed by a record that contains all of the segment and class names. The linker will need these names, and they can appear frequently in the object file. To provide more organization and use less space, the names are collected into a list in this record. Any subsequent reference to a name can be written simply as the index into this table. The first name is the null string, to provide a valid index for an unnamed combine class.

The next two records are segment definitions. The linker will need all of the information currently in the segment table except the register field, so we code each of the records

```
Header
      name = exsub.ASM
```
```
List of names
      (1) null
      (2) DATA
      (3) CODE
      (4) _DATA
      (5) _TEXT
```
```
Segment definition (1)
      attributes = relocatable, word aligned,
                   combine type is PUBLIC
      length = 0001Ah
      segment name index = 4
      class name index = 2
```
```
Segment definition (2)
      attributes = relocatable, word aligned,
      combine type is PUBLIC
      length = 0002Eh
      segment name index = 5
      class name index = 3
```
```
External names
      name = PUTSTR
```
```
Public names
      segment index = 2
      name = EXSUB
      offset in segment = 0000h
```
```
Comment
      end of pass one; start of pass two
```

**Figure 11.2  Records in Object File, End of Pass One**

in the segment table and write them to the object file. The order in which the segment definition records are written will be used as indexes later, with index 1 referring to the first segment definition record written.

Following the segment definitions, we write the names of any external symbols needed to be found by the linker. To write these records, we scan the symbol table looking for symbols with an attribute set to EXTERNAL. For each of these that we find—only the one for PUTSTR in this example—we write an external definition record to the object file. Later, the linker will use these records to determine which public symbols to search for in other object or library files.

We then scan the symbol table looking for symbols with an attribute set to GLOBAL. For each of these that we find—again we find only one, EXSUB, in this example—we write a public definition record to the object file. Note that the segment index in this record refers to the segment definitions, not the segment names. Later, the linker will use these records to determine which symbols in this object file to make available when searching for external references from other object files.

The last thing we do in the first pass is write a comment record to the object file to mark the end of the first pass and the start of the second pass. The symbol and segment tables are now as complete as they will be. For reference in pass two, these are shown in Table 11.4 and Table 11.5.

Now that we have walked through the processing performed in the first pass, we collect the ideas and sketch an algorithm. We omit details of checking for errors such as an instruction mnemonic not found in the table or a label defined more than once in the program. Of course, such checking must be included when the assembler is implemented.

The overall purpose of the first pass is to build the symbol and segment tables. Some assemblers create an intermediate file to take advantage of the information found in the first pass. If done properly, this can lead to a much faster second pass—most of the searches of the instruction table would not need to be repeated. We did not attempt this here. Only that processing directly related to building the symbol and segment tables was performed in our first pass.

A draft algorithm for the first pass is given in Figure 11.3. There are several deliberate omissions from this algorithm: It does not include the details of the search methods; it assumes that there are no syntax errors in the source file; and it does not specify an implementation for the symbol table.

The main procedure, PassOne, clears all three tables, sets the current segment to null (to indicate no SEGMENT directive encountered yet), and opens the source file. In a loop

**Table 11.4  Symbol Table, End of Pass One**

| Name | Type | Value | Other attributes |
|---|---|---|---|
| VARPARM | TEXT | "word ptr [bp + 6]" | |
| VALPARM | TEXT | "word ptr [bp + 4]" | |
| LOCALVAR | WORD | 00h | segment = _DATA, length = 2 |
| ERRORMSG | BYTE | 02h | segment = _DATA, length = 16h |
| ERRORLEN | WORD | 18h | segment = _DATA, length = 2 |
| PUTSTR | PROC | 0000 | segment = _TEXT, other = EXTERNAL |
| EXSUB | PROC | 0000 | segment = _TEXT, other = GLOBAL, length = 0 |
| ELSE01 | LABEL | 20h | segment = _TEXT |
| ENDIF01 | LABEL | 2Ah | segment = _TEXT |

## 11.2 Assemblers

**Table 11.5 Segment Table, End of Pass One**

| Name  | Length | Align | Combine type | Class name | Register |
|-------|--------|-------|--------------|------------|----------|
| _DATA | 1Ah    | WORD  | PUBLIC       | 'DATA'     | DS       |
| _TEXT | 2Eh    | WORD  | PUBLIC       | 'CODE'     | CS       |

```
PROC PassOne:
  ClearSegmentTable
  ClearSymbolTable
  ClearNamesTable
  CurrentSegment := null
  open source file
  REPEAT
    read line of source file
    IF line is not (comment or blank)
    THEN find Mnemonic
      IF Mnemonic present
        THEN IF Mnemonic is a directive
              THEN ProcessDirective1
              ELSE ProcessInstruction1
             ENDIF
        ELSE ProcessLabel
      ENDIF
    ENDIF
  UNTIL Mnemonic is 'END'
  close source file
  WriteObjectFile1
ENDPROC PassOne

PROC ProcessDirective1:
  SELECT Mnemonic
    assume  : segment.register := register
    dosseg  : note this for later
    db      : find Name and OperandLength;
              AddSymbol(Name, 'byte', OperandLength)
    dw      : find Name and OperandLength;
              AddSymbol(Name, 'word', OperandLength)
    end     : (no processing)
    endp    : compute procedure.length and save it
    ends    : CurrentSegment := null
    equ     : find Name and Value;
              AddSymbol(Name, 'text', Value)
    extrn   : find Name and Type;
              AddSymbol(Name, Type, 'external')
    proc    : find Name;
              AddSymbol(Name, 'proc', null)
    public  : find Name;
              AddSymbol(Name, ?, 'global')
    segment : find Name, Align, Combine, Class;
              AddSegment(Name, Align, Combine, Class);
              CurrentSegment := Name;
              add Name and Class to NamesTable
  ENDSELECT
ENDPROC ProcessDirective1
```

**Figure 11.3 Draft of Pass One of Assembler**

```
PROC ProcessInstruction1:
  find operands and their types
  search instruction table for Mnemonic and the given operand types
  determine instruction length from instruction table and operands
  add instruction length to CurrentSegment.length

ENDPROC ProcessInstruction1

PROC ProcessLabel:
  find Name
  AddSymbol (Name, 'label', null)
ENDPROC ProcessLabel

PROC AddSymbol (Name, Type, Other)
  IF Type = PROC
  THEN Value := 0000
  ELSE Value := CurrentSegment.length
  ENDIF
  search symbol table for Name
  IF Name is found
  THEN compare attributes with arguments, replacing missing attributes with arguments;
    report any errors or inconsistencies
  ELSE write Name, Type, and Value to new record;
    IF Other <> null
    THEN write other attributes to record
    ENDIF
  ENDIF
ENDPROC AddSymbol

PROC AddSegment (Name, Align, Combine, Class)
  search segment table for Name
  IF found
  THEN compare attributes with arguments, replacing missing attributes with arguments;
    report any errors or inconsistencies
  ELSE write arguments to new record;
  ENDIF
ENDPROC AddSegment

PROC WriteObjectFile1:
  IF no errors
  THEN
    open object file
    write header record
    IF dosseg directive encountered
    THEN write comment (dosseg)
    ENDIF
    write list of names record
    FOR each record in Segment Table
      write segment definition record
    write external names record
    write public names record
    write comment (end pass one)
  ENDIF
ENDPROC WriteObjectFile1
```

**Figure 11.3** (*continued*)

that continues until the END directive is found, each line of the source program is read and analyzed: Comments and blank lines are skipped, and separate procedures process directives, instructions, and labels on separate lines. After the loop terminates, `PassOne` closes the source file, opens the object file, and writes the names and segments records.

Procedure `ProcessDirective1` is a multiple branch selection structure with one or two statements to execute for each directive. In many cases, the processing for a directive involves adding a new symbol to the symbol table or a new segment description to the segment table. Procedure `ProcessInstruction1` searches the instruction table for the length of the instruction, based on mnemonic and possibly operand types. That length is added to the size of the current segment. Procedure `ProcessLabel` inspects the line to determine the symbol name and passes that on to `AddSymbol`.

Procedure `AddSymbol` first determines the value and segment attributes, using `CurrentSegment` and `CurrentSegment.length`. It then searches the symbol table for the name passed as an argument. If that name already exists in the symbol table, the other arguments are checked for consistency and used to fill in any empty fields in the table entry. If the symbol is new, a new record is added to the symbol table. Procedure `AddSegment` works much like `AddSymbol`, working with the segment table and slightly different attributes.

Procedure `WriteObjectFile` checks whether any errors were found, a process that we did not cover. Complete and useful error checking is perhaps the most difficult part of designing an assembler; as such, it tends to overshadow those aspects of an assembler relevant to this discussion, so it was left out. Assuming that there are no errors, we open the object file and write a standard header record that identifies the file as containing object code. For a main program that specifies DOS segment order (via DOSSEG), a comment record with the code for this would be written to the object file.

The first unique record that we write to the object file is the list of segment and combine class names. These names are referred to by index throughout the rest of the object file. Then, for each segment, the record from the segment table is written to the object file as a segment definition record. The linker collects all segment definitions from all object and library files in a program and combines them based on their attributes.

Following the segment definition records, we write one record containing all of the external names the linker must resolve for this module. This is followed by one more record containing all of the information available on names within the module that are to be made public. The linker uses the public definition and external name records to resolve all external references between modules.

## The second pass

The second pass of the assembler generates machine instructions and constants and writes them to the object file. Information needed by the linker to resolve external references and to combine segments is also written to the object file.

The second pass opens the source file for input; the object file remains open from the end of the first pass. Before starting to describe the second pass, we note that there are at least two types of data records that can be written to specify the contents of the object—and ultimately the executable—file: logical enumerated data records and logical iterated data records. The former records, the only kind that appears in this example, include every value explicitly, whereas the latter specify a single value and a repeat count. The use of the iterated form makes the object file smaller when there are repeated values.

In describing the second pass, we do not include the process of printing a listing of the program with the object code in a human-readable format. We are interested only in generating the machine-readable object file. It is presented line by line, as was done for the first pass, and then a sketch of the algorithm is given. Again, all comment lines and blank lines are skipped. The lines with the equ directives are also skipped because the values have been recorded in the symbol table.

The line declaring the _DATA segment is read, and we note that _DATA is now the current segment. We also start building an enumerated data record for the object file and indicate that it is specifying the contents of the _DATA (current) segment.

We will also need to record the offset of the data in this enumerated record from the start of the segment, as well as the length of the data in this record. In order to do this, we must write the record into a buffer as we determine its length. Note that a single segment can be described by a combination of enumerated and iterated data records, so we cannot simply assume that the first record describes the entire segment. We will not dwell on the buffering needed here; suffice to say that we write to the object file.

We need to reserve a word of memory in the segment for LocalVar described by

```
LocalVar  dw       ?
```

There are two methods of dealing with an uninitialized variable. One is to terminate the current data record, if there is one, and start the next data record with a larger initial offset so that the loader will skip over one word of memory. The other, more efficient method is to treat the line as though it were written with a zero operand and write a one-word zero value to the object file. This is more efficient because it involves fewer records in the object file, so we write 0000h to the object file.

For the line

```
ErrorMsg  db       "Argument is too small."
```

the operand string is written to the object file.

The line

```
ErrorLen  dw       $ - ErrorMsg
```

includes an expression that must be evaluated now. The $ indicates the current offset, which is recorded in the symbol table as the value of ErrorLen (0018h); the value from the symbol table for ErrorMsg is 0002h. The expression then evaluates to 0018h − 0002h = 0016h. This number is written to the object file, less significant byte first.

The next line terminates the _DATA segment, so we terminate the logical enumerated data record (and copy it from the buffer to the actual file).

Next, the line declaring the _TEXT segment is read. We note that _TEXT is now the current segment. The next few lines, containing assume, extrn, public, and PROC directives, are skipped in this pass. We proceed to the first instruction

```
    push    bp
```

From the instruction table (Table 11.1), we see the format of the push instruction is 01010,reg; the code for the BP register is 101 (refer to the discussion in Section 2.3). Putting these together, we get

```
opcode reg
 01010 101
```

## 11.2 Assemblers

or 55h for this instruction. We create a header for an enumerated data segment that references _TEXT with offset 0, and we write the header and the instruction 55h to the object file. We also keep track of our position in the record, as we'll need this when we process some of the other instructions. The current record is 1 byte long; the next byte will be written at a displacement of 1 from the beginning of this record (actually, 1 plus the size of the record identifier and length bytes). We'll refer to this as the record displacement.

The instruction

```
mov     bp, sp
```

follows the general form shown in Figure 11.1, with no displacement or data bytes (both operands are in registers). The operation code from the instruction table for a register-to-register mov is 100010. Because both operands are words, the w bit is 1. Both operands are registers, so we code the destination in the reg field, the source register in mod and r/m, and set the d bit to 1. The code for the BP register is 101. To code the SP register in the mod and r/m field, with w set to 1, we need mod = 11 and r/m = 100 (again, refer to the discussion in Section 2.3). Putting all of these pieces together, we get the instruction

```
opcode d w  mod reg r/m
100010 1 1   11  101 100
```

or 8BECh. We write these two bytes to the object file and adjust the record displacement to 03h.

The next instruction

```
mov     bx, VarParm
```

uses the same opcode as the previous one. The operands are words, so w is again 1. The destination operand is the BX register, so d = 1 and reg = 011. The source operand is VARPARM, which the symbol table shows to be a text symbol. The text for VARPARM can be substituted into the operand field and the instruction interpreted as

```
mov     bx, word ptr [bp + 6]
```

Here, word ptr specifies that the expression [bp + 6] is a word (as opposed to a doubleword or byte) expression. The displacement is 6, which can be coded as a byte, so the source operand is coded with r/m = 110 and mod = 01. Putting these pieces together we get

```
opcode d w  mod reg r/m    disp
100010 1 1   01  011 110   00000110
```

or 8B5E06h. We write these three bytes to the object file and advance the record displacement to 06h.

The next instruction is

```
mov     ax, [bx]
```

Again, the opcode is 100010, the operands are words so w = 1, and the destination is a register so d = 1. The destination, AX, is coded in the reg field as 000. The source is an indirect reference to memory through the BX register, with no displacement. This combination is coded as r/m = 111 and mod = 00. Putting these together, we get

```
opcode   d w   mod reg r/m
100010   1 1   00  000 111
```

or 8B07h, which we write to the object file and advance the record displacement to 08h.

The next instruction

    mov    LocalVar, ax

can be coded using one of the special shorter format instructions that imply use of the AX or AL register. Looking at Table 11.1, we find the opcode 1010001 for the memory-to-accumulator form of the mov instruction. Looking in the symbol table for LOCALVAR, we find its type is word, so w=1, which is also implied by use of the AX register. The value of LOCALVAR is the offset 00h from the start of _DATA. This offset might change during linking (the next section will explain how this occurs), so we do not know the final offset that will appear in the executable version of this program. For now, we leave the displacement as 0. This gives the instruction as

```
opcode    w   lo disp   hi disp
1010001   1   00000000  00000000
```

or A30000h, which we write to the object file and add 3 to the record displacement to make it 0Bh.

We also start a list of displacements for the linker to resolve. Each adjustment the linker must make is coded in what is called a *fixup record*. The record displacement of the start of this instruction was 08h, so the record displacement of the first byte to be adjusted by the linker is 09h. (This is called the offset in the fixup record.) The field to be adjusted by the linker (called the location in the fixup record) is an offset relative to the start of a segment. Relative to the start of the _DATA segment, the target offset is 0000h; this must be adjusted to account for _DATA being combined with other segments. The first fixup record we build is

```
mode     = segment-relative
location = offset
offset   = 009h
target   = _DATA:0000h
```

Other information is needed in more complex situations that we won't bother with now. We will see how the linker uses the information in these records in Section 11.3. The fixup record is not written to the object file yet, but rather, is saved; it will be written when we close the current data record.

Translating the instruction

    mov    ax, ValParm

follows the same pattern as translating the instruction

    mov    bx, VarParm

with a different destination operand and a displacement of 4. The instruction is coded as 8B4604h, which we write to the object file. We add 3 to the record displacement to make it 0Eh.

## 11.2 Assemblers

The next instruction is

    cmp     ax, 3

The implied-accumulator and immediate value version of this instruction has opcode 0011110. Since the AX register is specified, we need w=1 and a word data value. The instruction is coded as

```
opcode   w   lo data   hi data
0011110  1   00000011  00000000
```

or 3D0300h, which we write to the object file. We also add 3 to the record displacement, making it 11h.

The next instruction is

    jnl     ELSE01

The conditional jump instructions have an 8-bit opcode that includes the relation to test for, as well as an 8-bit relative displacement. Because we have been keeping track of our position in the segment during the translation process—just as we did in the first pass—we know that the jnl instruction starts at displacement 11h. But when it is executing, the instruction pointer will have the offset of the next instruction, or 13h. From the symbol table, we find the value for ELSE01 as 20h. Subtracting, we get 20h − 13h = 0Dh. This difference is the second byte of the instruction; the first byte is 7D from the table. So we write 7D0Dh to the object file and add 2 to the record displacement, making it 13h.

The next instruction,

    mov     cx, ErrorLen

uses the general form of the mov instruction with opcode 100010. The CX register operand is the destination, and it is a word register, so d = 1 and w = 1. The reg field is 001 to code the CX register. We find the other operand, ERRORLEN, in the symbol table: Its value is the displacement 0018h from the start of the _DATA segment. Again, the final displacement in the instruction depends on how the linker combines segments. We code the displacement as 0000h and add this reference to the list for the linker to resolve. The memory reference is direct (it does not involve a base or index register), so it is coded with mod=00 and r/m=110—the special case. The instruction is coded as

```
opcode d w   mod reg r/m   lo disp   hi disp
100010 1 1   00  001 110   00000000  00000000
```

or 8B0E0000h. We write this to the object file and adjust the record displacement to 17h.

We also build a second fixup record for the linker. The displacement field of the instruction just written starts at 15h. The fixup record, saved for later, is

```
mode     = segment-relative
location = offset
offset   = 015h
target   = _DATA:0018h
```

The next instruction

    mov     bx, offset ErrorMsg

is coded with the source operand as an undefined immediate operand that must be filled in when the program is loaded into memory. The opcode for a mov immediate-to-general-register instruction is 1011, followed by the w bit (which is 1, to indicate a word value) and the register number (011 for the BX register). We leave two bytes of zeros for the word of data that the loader will supply. The instruction that we write to the object file is coded as

```
opcode w reg   lo data    hi data
1011   1 011   00000000   00000000
```

or BB0000h. We also adjust the record displacement to 1Ah.

We build another fixup record for the linker. The displacement field of the previous instruction begins at 018h. The target is the third byte of the _DATA segment. Note that the effect of the offset operator in the instruction is to have the offset of ErrorMsg treated as an immediate constant, not as a memory reference. The linker builds the offset for this instruction in the same way as if it were a memory reference instruction. Thus, the fixup record is

```
mode = segment-relative
location = offset
offset = 018h
target = _DATA:0002h
```

This fixup record is also saved for later.

The next instruction is

```
        call    PutStr
```

where PutStr is an external reference. The opcode for call is the byte 11101000, or E8h. This is followed by a word displacement that must be provided by the linker. We write the opcode and two bytes of zeros, E80000h, to the object file. We adjust the record displacement to 1Dh and build another fixup record.

The displacement field of the call instruction starts at 1Bh. The target is the external procedure PutStr; this is coded as an index into the external definitions record. Since we wrote the instruction without an explicit use of the far or near type, the assembler assumed a near call in which the entry point of PutStr will be accessible without changing the value in the CS register. (But note that PutStr is not necessarily in the _TEXT segment; this point is discussed later.) The displacement in the call instruction is relative not to the start of the segment but to the contents of IP when the call is executed; this situation is called a self-relative displacement. The fixup record

```
mode = self-relative
location = offset
offset = 01Bh
target = PUTSTR
```

is built and saved for later.

The next instruction is

```
        jmp     ENDIF01
```

## 11.2 Assemblers

The jmp instruction can be one or two bytes long, depending on the displacement of the destination from the instruction pointer. In the first pass, we could not determine this displacement since the symbol ENDIF01 was undefined when we encountered this instruction. We took the safe approach and allocated two bytes for the displacement. It turns out that the displacement for this jump can be coded in one byte. Now we have three choices: build the instruction with a 1-word displacement; build it with a 1-byte displacement and use the third byte for something else; or build it with a 1-byte displacement and change the size of the program and fix any later symbols in the symbol table. The last option requires a third pass. The second option is attractive, but the only thing we can use the third byte for is a 1-byte nop (No OPeration) instruction. Still, there is a slight timing advantage with this option, so many assemblers use it.

(Recall how the output of Program 7.1 varied depending on the assembler used; the variation was caused by the different approaches used by assemblers to code displacements. Some used the approach we take here, and others used a byte displacement and adjusted all other displacements in that program.)

We code the instruction as EBh (opcode) followed by a 1-byte displacement. When the 2-byte jmp instruction executes, the instruction pointer will contain 001Fh; the value of ENDIF01 from the symbol table is 002Ah. The displacement is thus 2Ah−1Fh=0Bh. The third byte that we reserved for the instruction is filled with the 1-byte nop instruction, 90h. Thus, we write EB0B90h to the object file and add 3 to the record displacement, making it 20h.

The next instruction

```
        add     ax, 27
```

has a special immediate-to-accumulator form. The opcode is 0000010 followed by the w bit and one or two bytes of data. Since the accumulator used is AX, the w bit is 1; two bytes of data follow the opcode. The instruction is thus

```
opcode   w   lo data    hi data
0000010  1   00011011   00000000
```

or 051B00h, which we write to the object file. We add 3 to the record displacement, making it 23h.

The cwd instruction is just the opcode 99h, so we write that to the object file and add 1 to the record displacement.

The idiv instruction with divisor in memory follows the general form with d=1 and the reg field of the second byte used for an opcode extension of 111. The value of the operand LOCALVAR is the displacement 0000h from _DATA. Again, the linker will modify this displacement, so we code it as zeros and build a fixup record for it. The reference is direct (no base or index register) and is coded with the special case mod = 00 and r/m = 110. The instruction is coded as

```
opcode   w   mod ext r/m   lo disp    hi disp
1111011  1   00  111 110   00000000   00000000
```

or F73E0000h. We write this to the object file and add 4 to the record displacement, making it 28h.

**390** Chapter 11 Program Translation

The fixup record we build for this reference is

```
mode = segment-relative
location = offset
offset = 026h
target = _DATA:0000h
```

We save this fixup record for later.
    The next instruction

           mov      [bx], dx

has a register for the source operand and an indirect memory reference for destination operand. From the instruction table, we find the instruction with opcode 100010 and d = 0. The source register is DX, a word, so w = 1 and reg = 010. The indirect reference through BX with no displacement is coded as mod = 00 and r/m = 111. Thus the instruction is coded as

```
opcode d w  mod reg r/m
100010 0 1   00 010 111
```

or 8917h. We write these two bytes to the object file. We also add 2 to the record displacement, making it 2Ah.
    The pop instruction is coded like the push instruction, with 5-bit opcode 01011 and register number 101. So the instruction is just 01011101, or 5Dh, which we write to the object file. We increment the record displacement to 2Bh.
    The last instruction is ret, with immediate operand 4. This instruction is three bytes long: the opcode C2h followed by two bytes of data. So we write C20400h to the object file and add 3 to the record displacement.
    The ENDP directive is skipped. The ENDS directive signals the end of the _TEXT segment, so we can terminate the enumerated data record (and actually write it from the buffer to the file after fixing its length).
    Now we can write the fixup records to the object file. These records refer to the immediately preceding data record using displacements within the record, as well as the indexes into the names record and indexes into the segment definition records. The format of fixup records is quite complex, because of the large number of variations in the tasks that the linker must perform. Our example program illustrates only a few simple cases. The general contents of the fixup records were described as we built each record. These were written to the object file in the order they were built.
    After writing this information to the object file, the assembler resumes reading the source file. It finds the END directive, signaling the end of the module. It writes a record indicating the end of the module to the object file. Then the assembler detects the end of the source file. It closes all files and terminates.
    The records written to the object file in the second pass are shown in Figure 11.4. These records follow those written in the first pass, shown in Figure 11.2.

```
Logical enumerated data
    segment = _DATA
    offset  = 0000
    length  = 001A
    data = 00 00 41 72 67 75 6D 65
           6E 74 20 69 73 20 74 6F
           6F 20 73 6D 61 6C 6C 2E
           16 00
```
```
Logical enumerated data
    segment = _TEXT
    offset  = 0000
    length  = 002E
    data = 55 8B EC 8B 5E 06 8B 07
           A3 00 00 8B 46 04 3D 03
           00 7D 0D 8B 0E 00 00 BB
           00 00 E8 00 00 EB 0B 90
           05 1B 00 99 F7 3E 00 00
           89 17 5D C2 04 00
```
```
Fixup
    009: segment-relative, offset,
         target = _DATA:0000
    015: segment-relative, offset,
         target = _DATA:0018
    018: segment-relative, offset,
         target = _DATA:0002
    01B: self-relative, offset,
         target = PUTSTR
    026: segment-relative, offset,
         target = _DATA:0000
```
```
Module end
```

**Figure 11.4** Records Written to Object File in Pass Two

Now that we have seen the second pass in action, we sketch an algorithm for it in Figure 11.5. Procedure PassTwo is similar in structure to Procedure PassOne. It opens the source file and processes it one line at a time. Comments, blank lines, and most directives are skipped; some directives and all instructions are processed by separate procedures. When the END directive terminates the loop, PassTwo writes the fixup record and a module end record.

Procedure ProcessDirective2 does nothing for directives other than SEGMENT, ENDS, db, and dw. For the latter two, the operands are converted to internal representation and written to the object file. For the SEGMENT directive, the name of the segment is noted for writing to the data record header. For the ENDS directive, the header for the data record is written: This header includes the segment name, offset, and length. Then the actual data record is written. Of course, the information in the data record has been written to a buffer, waiting for the end of the segment (or record) before being written to the actual object file.

```
PROC PassTwo:
   open source file
   REPEAT
      REPEAT
         read line of source file
         IF line is not (comment or blank)
         THEN find Mnemonic
            IF Mnemonic is present
            THEN IF Mnemonic is a directive
                 THEN ProcessDirective2
                 ELSE ProcessInstruction2
                 ENDIF
            ENDIF
         ENDIF
      UNTIL Mnemonic is 'END'
      WriteModuleEnd
   UNTIL end of source file
   close source and object files
ENDPROC PassTwo

PROC ProcessDirective2:
   SELECT Mnemonic
      assume   : (no processing)
      dosseg   : (no processing)
      db       : evaluate operand(s);
                 write operand values to data record
      dw       : evaluate operand(s);
                 write operand values to data record
      end      : (no processing)
      endp     : (no processing)
      ends     : write data record to object file
                 IF any fixup records apply to data record
                 THEN write fixup record to object file
                 ENDIF
      equ      : (no processing)
      extrn    : (no processing)
      proc     : (no processing)
      public   : (no processing)
      segment  : find Name;
                 CurrentSegment := Name
   ENDSELECT
ENDPROC ProcessDirective2

PROC ProcessInstruction2:
   find operands and their types
   search instruction table for Mnemonic and given operand types
   determine instruction format from instruction table
   determine d, w, s, mod, reg, r/m fields, if used
   determine disp and data fields, if used
   assemble instruction
   write instruction to object file
   IF operand reference can be modified by linker
   THEN create fixup record
   ENDIF
ENDPROC ProcessInstruction2
```

**Figure 11.5  Draft of Pass Two of Assembler**

## 11.2 Assemblers

Procedure `ProcessInstruction2` builds the binary coded instructions, using the format and code information from the instruction table. Information about the operands must come from the symbol table. From this information, the procedure builds the instruction and writes it to the object file. It also determines whether a fixup will be needed, and if so, creates a record of the necessary information for later writing to the object file.

We mentioned earlier that some assemblers make only one pass. The dilemma these assemblers face is what to do about symbols that are used as operands before they are defined: The symbol table does not include information about the symbol until it is defined, but the instruction must be written to the object file when it is encountered. One way to solve this problem is to leave the operand field empty and include a fixup record for the linker to fix. This procedure complicates the linker and the format of the fixup records, but it saves the time of a second pass through the source file. It also requires some extra record keeping by the assembler in order to generate the correct fixup records.

### EXERCISES 11.2

1. Trace pass one of the assembler presented here for one of the programs listed below. Show the contents of the object file at the end of the pass.
   (a) Program 8.2
   (b) Program 8.5
   (c) Program 8.11
2. Compare the object file you generated for Exercise 1 with the symbolic dump of the object file printed by Borland's TDUMP with the –O option (if available).
3. Trace pass two of the assembler presented here for the program you used in Exercise 1.
4. Compare the object file you generated for Exercise 3 with the symbolic dump of the object file printed by Borland's TDUMP with the –O option (if available).
5. Consider a program that includes the following declarations in its _DATA segment:

   ```
   Fifty     dw    50
   Sixty     dw    60
   Buffer    db    100 dup (0Fh)
   Message   db    "Buffer Full."
   ```

   This data could be written to the object file as three records: The first enumerates the 50 and 60; the second iterates 100 copies of 0Fh; and the third enumerates the string. How do you think the offset field in the data record is used in this example?
6. If `Buffer` in Exercise 5 was declared with (?) instead of (0Fh), how do you think this would change the contents of the object file?
▶7. Write a subprogram that accepts as arguments the operation code and codes for the various fields of the instructions of Table 11.1 (p. 370). Your program should combine the pieces into an instruction and return it as a result. Do this for the following types of instructions:
   (a) add acc,imm
   (b) cmp acc,imm
   (c) jnl label
   (d) mov reg,reg
   (e) mov reg,mem

   Be sure to document carefully how the arguments are coded for your subprogram. Also write a driver to call your subprogram and display the instruction in hexadecimal.

▶8. Write a program that reads and analyzes an assembly-language program. For each line of the source program, your program should print a summary of the line. For example, your program might print BLANK or COMMENT for those lines, or

SEGMENT: name = _DATA, align = WORD, combine = PUBLIC

and so on for a segment definition, and maybe

INSTR: operation = mov, source = ax, dest = VarParm

for a mov instruction.

This can become a long program, so you should impose some restrictions on the source file to make it manageable. Document the restrictions carefully. Test your program with a source file that satisfies those restrictions. Write this in a high-level language.

▶9. Modify the program you wrote for Exercise 8 to include printing error messages for any line that violates any restriction you imposed on the source file.

## 11.3 TRANSLATING HIGH-LEVEL LANGUAGES

An assembler translates statements written in assembly language into machine instructions coded as binary numbers. In this section, we explore the process of translating statements written in a high-level language into machine instructions. We examine compilers, interpreters, and preprocessors in this discussion.

### Compilers

A compiler is a program that translates a program written in a high-level language. Usually a compiler generates an object file—instructions in machine-executable form that are equivalent to the program being translated. Technically, a compiler could generate an equivalent program in another language, even another high-level language. Some of the earliest compilers generated output in the form of an assembly-language program that was then translated by an assembler.

In earlier chapters, we showed how to implement various expressions and control structures as sequences of assembly-language instructions. We presented algorithms for translating expressions and templates for implementing each of the control structures. Some of these techniques, and many more sophisticated ones, can be used in a program to translate a high-level language into assembly language and, ultimately, into machine instructions. Note that we are skipping many issues, such as recognizing an operand and matching the components of nested control structures.

A substantial body of theory is concerned with language translation. Translating a program from a high-level language into machine instructions involves two principal activities: analysis of the source program and generation of the object program. We do not intend to pursue the analysis of the source program or the theoretical issues regarding the generation of the object program; we do, however, want to make a few observations about the object program.

Each executable statement in the source program, such as an assignment statement or a procedure call, is translated into one or more instructions in the object program. The fact that a high-level-language statement can correspond to many machine-level instructions reflects a basic mismatch between high-level programming languages and the instruction sets of computers. Hopefully it also reflects a better match between programmers and high-level languages.

Some statements correspond to so many instructions that they are translated into calls to subprograms in a library. This avoids duplicating long sequences of instructions many times within a program. Conversion of data from its internal representation to a character string for printing, for example, is often implied as part of a PRINT or WRITE statement but implemented as a call to the appropriate conversion routine.

Some statements require sequences of operations that are so dependent upon hardware that programmers prefer not knowing all of the details. Moreover, these sequences change when different hardware is used, although the operation is conceptually the same. For example, to actually transmit some text to an output device requires a sequence of instructions that varies according to the actual device used. In a high-level language, the process of writing to a data file stored on a disk differs little from the process of writing the same information to a printer. However, the disk drive and the printer require very specific, and different, signals from the computer. These details are implemented by system routines, and the WRITE statements are translated as calls to these routines.

Also implemented as subprograms in libraries are operations that may be tricky to code correctly, that are used frequently, or both. The most obvious examples are the mathematical functions, such as square root or cosine, which are coded as function calls in a high-level language. Similarly, if a particular computer does not directly support a data type in hardware, each operation on that type can be translated as a call to a subprogram. For example, FORTRAN includes a COMPLEX data type. Each value is internally represented by a pair of REAL numbers, but the programmer can operate on them as a single COMPLEX number. The operations may be implemented as calls to subprograms that perform operations on the individual components of the complex numbers.

All of these calls to subprograms are in addition to any calls the programmer requests explicitly. Usually the compiler can generate the appropriate `call` instruction, but it leaves the address of the subprogram unspecified. It becomes the responsibility of the linker to provide the subprogram's addresses as it builds the executable run image.

Programming in a high-level language is much more convenient than programming in assembly language, but a trade-off exists: The object program produced by a compiler is often a little less efficient than an equivalent program written directly in a low-level language. The basic problem is that any optimization strategy a compiler writer develops is limited in application to relatively few computers, because of the variety of instruction sets, registers, addressing modes, data representations, and other processor characteristics. Optimization strategies, however, are part of a good assembly-language programmer's standard techniques. As research continues, compilers improve. Considering the effort it takes for a programmer to master any particular assembly language and computer, most applications are best written in high-level languages.

## Interpreters

An interpreter is a program that inspects another program, often written in a high-level language, and performs the indicated operations. Like a compiler, it performs two major tasks. First, an interpreter performs a program analysis similar to one that a compiler performs. Second, rather than generating object code, an interpreter performs the operations specified in the source program.

An analogy will help distinguish compilers from interpreters. Suppose you have a recipe for a chocolate cake, but it is written in a foreign language that you don't know. You mail the recipe to a friend who does understand that language, and your friend later sends back the original recipe and a copy of it in English. In this case, your friend acted like a compiler; the original recipe corresponds to the source file, and the English version of the recipe corresponds to the object file. You have no cake, but you do have usable instructions for making a cake.

Now suppose instead that your friend comes to visit. You give the recipe to your friend. Your friend goes into the kitchen and bakes the cake for you. Your friend acted like an interpreter; upon reading the directions in the foreign language, your friend carried them out. You do not have a translation of the recipe that you can use, but you do have a cake.

Compared to a compiler, an interpreter is usually easier to write and use. It is also much less efficient when the same program statements are executed frequently. Each time each statement is encountered, the interpreter must analyze it before performing the operations. This can be especially inefficient with repetition structures.

The sequence of instructions that an interpreter executes for a given statement is not much different than that generated by a compiler for the same statement. However, interpreters are very limited in the kinds of code optimization that they can perform. For example, consider the statements

```
FOR I := 1 TO 20 DO
  A := 0
  Print (I, 2*I, I*I)
ENDFOR
```

The statement A := 0 is performed 20 times, even though only the first has any real effect; the other 19 times are wasteful. A good compiler will internally rearrange statements so that A is assigned only once, outside of the loop. An interpreter cannot usually make this kind of change. Even worse, the interpreter must analyze and translate that statement 20 times when once is sufficient.

## Preprocessors

Programming languages continue to evolve. Sometimes they become more like natural languages; sometimes they become more sophisticated; sometimes they become simpler to use; and sometimes they try to become all of these things at once. Whatever direction the evolution of a particular programming language is taking at the moment, its users want the latest features without giving up their investment in the language (their training and the many pages of programs written already). With a preprocessor, however, the user of an older language can write programs with the latest language features and have them translated into a form their older compiler can translate.

For example, early versions of FORTRAN had no WHILE or block IF structures. Programmers altered the sequence in which the statements in a program were executed primarily with the GOTO and logical IF statements. The implementation of control structures in Chapter 5 is based on the experience of trying to implement them using FORTRAN. With the advent of more structured statements to control the flow in a program, many preprocessors for FORTRAN were developed. With one of these, a programmer could write a new program with WHILE and block IF structures in it. The preprocessor would convert these into GOTO and logical IF statements but leave the rest of the program alone. The output of the preprocessor was then used as input to the FORTRAN compiler. The advantage of such a setup was that the new programs were compatible with the older programs, since they were all produced by the same compiler. The disadvantage was that the programmer had an extra step; the better preprocessors did very extensive error checking or were integrated closely with the FORTRAN compiler so that the error messages referred to the original program lines.

Preprocessors differ from compilers by generating high-level-language statements rather than machine instructions. Preprocessors combine their output with those portions of the source program that they do not modify, thereby producing an intermediate source file, which is then compiled normally. Depending on the degree of integration of the preprocessor and compiler, this intermediate file may or may not be available for inspection. In the least-coupled systems, the intermediate file is not only available, but the programmer must issue the command to have it compiled.

As programming languages continue to evolve, they reflect less and less the properties of the computers that execute the programs. The differences between a programming language and the hardware must be managed by layers of translators and related utilities.

## EXERCISES 11.3

Exercises 1 through 3 require either a compiler that has an option to expand the listing file to include a pseudoassembly listing of the object code it is generating or a compiler that can generate symbolic information for one of the symbolic debuggers and the symbolic debugger.

▶1. Write a program that includes an assortment of control structures. Compile it and determine what instructions are generated for each. Compare these to the instructions that you would generate by hand using the templates of Sections 5.3 and 5.4.

▶2. Write a program with several obvious inefficient sequences in it, such as the assignment statement in the loop that was given in the discussion of optimization in the section on interpreters. Compile it and determine which inefficient sequences the compiler can improve. What sequences of instructions are generated in each case? Can you find some inefficient code examples the compiler does not optimize? (Note: Most compilers have an optional command-line switch to control the degree and type of optimization performed.)

▶3. Write a program that uses many of the intrinsic functions and procedures provided in some high-level language. Compile it and determine which functions and procedures are implemented in-line and which are translated into calls to subprograms.

4. If you have access to a compiler and an interpreter for the same language on the same computer, compare the execution times of several programs using the interpreter and the compiler. Try to include programs with many small loops as well as a program with a single large loop. Can you state a factor (or a range) to predict how much faster a compiled program will run compared to an interpreted one?

5. It is often argued that student programs and programs under development should be interpreted and that programs being placed into production should be compiled. What is the reasoning behind this argument? What potential problems does this procedure introduce?

6. It is often argued that most compiler optimization should be disabled during development but should be used when generating the final code before placing a program into production. What is the reasoning behind this argument? What potential problems does this procedure introduce?

## 11.4 LINKERS

The object file written by the assembler is not directly executable. It contains references to external entry points and external data that must be resolved by the linker; it contains displacements that will change when the object file is combined with other object files; and it contains references to addresses that will not be known until the program is actually loaded into memory for execution. All of these must be processed by the linker (and some again by the loader) before the program can be executed.

A linkage editor, or *linker,* is a program that combines separately translated modules into a single load module. Although this processing can also be performed by a loader—or more accurately, by a *linking loader*—on some systems, we will consider linking separately from loading.

### Linker Operation

A linker must perform two major tasks. The first is to concatenate all of the object code into one module, possibly adjusting the displacements that are to be relative to the start of the final module for files other than the first file. In an 8086 system, different segments must be combined or concatenated as part of this task. The other task is to provide the pointers needed for the external references in each module.

A linkage editor works much like a two-pass assembler. In the first pass, it builds a table of the external addresses needed by each module and a table of the external addresses available in each module; in the second pass it copies the modules into one new module, writing the new module to disk. In the second pass the linker also adjusts displacements (if needed) and fills in the addresses for the pointers. The latter process requires searching each table of externals available for each external needed by a module.

We will now examine a specific example of actions performed by the linker, much like we did for the assembler in Section 11.2, but in less detail. We will continue with procedure ExSub of Program 11.1. The object file for this procedure was previously discussed; it is shown in Figure 11.2 (p. 379) and Figure 11.4 (p. 391). Program 11.2 is a driver, ExMain, that calls several of the input and output procedures that we have been using, as well as ExSub.

The object file produced when ExMain is assembled is shown in Figure 11.6. As with the other figures in this chapter, Figure 11.6 is not as detailed as the binary version of the file. The details of the data records generated in the second pass are not shown for the two segments; the details of the fixup records are also not shown.

## Program 11.2

```
; Program 11.2      ExMain.ASM
; Main program for use with EXSUB.ASM, in discussions
;    of assembling, linking, loading, and debugging.

; DOS function and status parameters
  DosFunc      equ      21h
  ExitToDos    equ      4Ch
  NoErrors     equ      00h

DOSSEG

_STACK SEGMENT para stack 'stack'
               dw       100h dup (?)
_STACK ENDS

_DATA SEGMENT word public 'data'
  N            dw       ?
  PromptMsg    db       "Enter N: "
  PromptLen    dw       $ - PromptMsg
  ResultMsg    db       "Final result is "
  ResultLen    dw       $ - ResultMsg
_DATA ENDS

_TEXT SEGMENT word public 'code'
      assume   cs: _TEXT
      extrn    PutStr: PROC, PutCrLf: PROC
      extrn    GetDec: PROC, PutDec: PROC
      extrn    ExSub: PROC

ExMain:

; set up ds to point to _DATA
      mov      ax, seg _DATA
      mov      ds, ax
      assume   ds: _DATA

; print ("Enter N: ")
      mov      cx, PromptLen
      mov      bx, offset PromptMsg
      call     PutStr

; read (N)
      call     GetDec
      mov      N, ax

; call ExSub (N, 5)
      mov      ax, offset N
      push     ax
      mov      ax, 5
      push     ax
      call     ExSub

; print ( "Final result is ", N)
      mov      cx, ResultLen
```

**Program 11.2 (continued)**

```
        mov     bx, offset ResultMsg
        call    PutStr
        mov     ax, N
        call    PutDec
        call    PutCrLf

; exit to DOS
        mov     ah, ExitToDos
        mov     al, NoErrors
        int     DosFunc

_TEXT ENDS
END     ExMain
```

| |
|---|
| Header<br>    name = exmain.ASM |
| Comment<br>    use DOS segment ordering |
| List of Names<br>    (1) null<br>    (2) _STACK<br>    (3) DATA<br>    (4) CODE<br>    (5) STACK<br>    (6) _DATA<br>    (7) _TEXT |
| Segment definition (1)<br>    attributes = relocatable, para aligned,<br>              combine type is STACK<br>    length = 0200h<br>    segment name index = 2<br>    class name index = 5 |
| Segment definition (2)<br>    attributes = relocatable, word aligned,<br>              combine type is PUBLIC<br>    length = 0001Fh<br>    segment name index = 6<br>    class name index = 3 |
| Segment definition (3)<br>    attributes = relocatable, word aligned,<br>              combine type is PUBLIC<br>    length = 00039h<br>    segment name index = 7<br>    class name index = 4 |

**Figure 11.6** Object File for Program 11.2

## 11.4 Linkers

| |
|---|
| External names<br>    name = PUTDEC<br>    name = PUTSTR<br>    name = PUTCRLF<br>    name = EXSUB<br>    name = GETDEC |
| Comment<br>    end of pass one; start of pass two |
| Logical enumerated data<br>    segment = _DATA<br>    offset = 0000<br>    length = 001F<br>    data = (*not shown*) |
| Logical enumerated data<br>    segment = _TEXT<br>    offset = 0000<br>    length = 0039<br>    data = (*not shown*) |
| Fixup<br>    (*14 records, not shown*) |
| Module end |

**Figure 11.6** (*continued*)

When we link the object files produced from ExMain and ExSub to form an executable image, we include the file IO.LIB. A library file is essentially a collection of object files with one additional record that identifies it as a library and another record that signals the end of the library. The contents of this file are shown in Figure 11.7. Again, the details of the data and fixup records are not shown.

| |
|---|
| Library begin |
| Header<br>    name = putchar.ASM |
| Comment<br>    name = putchar |
| List of Names<br>    (1)  null<br>    (2)  CODE<br>    (3)  _TEXT |

**Figure 11.7** Object File for IO.LIB

## Chapter 11 Program Translation

| |
|---|
| Segment definition (1)<br>`attributes = relocatable, word aligned`<br>` combine type is PUBLIC`<br>`length = 0007h`<br>`segment name index = 3`<br>`class name index = 2` |
| Public names<br>`segment = 1; name = PUTCHAR;  offset = 0000h` |
| Comment<br>end of pass one; start of pass two |
| Logical enumerated data<br>    `segment = _TEXT`<br>    `offset = 0000h`<br>    `length = 0007h`<br>    `data =` (*object code of* PutChar) |
| Module end |
| Header<br>    `data = name = putstr.ASM` |
| Comment<br>    `name = putstr` |
| List of Names<br>    (1)  null<br>    (2)  CODE<br>    (3)  _TEXT |
| Segmentation definition (1)<br>    `attributes = relocatable, word aligned`<br>    `             combine type is PUBLIC`<br>    `length = 0017h`<br>    `segment name index = 3`<br>    `class name index = 2` |
| Public names<br>`segment = 1; name = PUTSTR;   offset=000h` |
| Comment<br>    end of pass one; start of pass two |
| Logical enumerated data<br><br>    `segment = _TEXT`<br>    `offset = 000h`<br>    `length = 0017h`<br>    `data =` (*object code of* PutStr) |
| Module end |

**Figure 11.7**  (*continued*)

## 11.4 Linkers

| Header |
|---|
| / / (*similar records for PutCrLf, PutDec,* / / *GetChar modules are present in IO.LIB*) / / |
| Module end |
| Header<br>    name = getdec.asm |
| Comment<br>    name = getdec |
| List of Names<br>    (1)  null<br>    (2)  DATA<br>    (3)  CODE<br>    (4)  _DATA<br>    (5)  _TEXT |
| Segment definition (1)<br>    attributes = relocatable, word aligned<br>               combine type is PUBLIC<br>    length = 007Fh<br>    segment name index = 5<br>    class name index = 3 |
| Segment definition (2)<br>    attributes = relocatable, word aligned,<br>               combine type is PUBLIC<br>    length = 0002Ch<br>    segment name index = 4<br>    class name index = 2<br>External names<br>  name = PUTSTR<br>  name = GETCHAR<br>  name = PUTCRLF |
| Public names<br>segment = 1; name = IOERROR;  offset = 0064h<br>segment = 1; name = CHKDIGIT; offset = 0051h<br>segment = 1; name = GETDEC;   offset = 0000h |
| Comment<br>    end of pass one; start of pass two |
| Logical enumerated data<br>    segment = _TEXT<br>    offset = 0000h<br>    length = 0064h<br>    data = (*object code of* GetDec, ChkDigit) |

**Figure 11.7** (*continued*)

| |
|---|
| Fixup <br>     (5 records, not shown) |
| Logical enumerated data <br>     segment = _DATA <br>     offset = 0000h <br>     length = 002Ch <br>     data = (_DATA *segment of* IOError) |
| Logical enumerated data <br>     segment = _TEXT <br>     offset = 0064h <br>     length = 001Bh <br>     data = (*object code of* IOError) |
| Fixup <br>     (6 records, not shown) |
| Module end |
| Library end |

**Figure 11.7** *(continued)*

Before we discuss how the linker combines the object and library files to form the executable file, consider what an executable program looks like in memory. First, the instructions in the main program, in the subprogram, and in the library routines must all be accessible with the same value in the CS register. Because all of the jumps and calls have been near or short, they change only IP, not CS, and the various code segments must be combined into one unit no more than 64K bytes long. Such a unit is called a frame, or physical segment. By contrast, the named segments defined in a program are called logical segments. The logical data segments, like the code segments, must be combined to form a single physical data segment because we used only near pointers to the data.

Final segment order is determined by a number of factors. The assembler writes the segment definition records either in the sequence in which they occur in the program or, if requested by a directive or assembler command option, alphabetically. The linker determines final segment order based on the combination of order of the object files, segment order within object files, class names, and whether the DOSSEG directive was used in the main program. DOS order is fine for stand-alone assembler programs; use of a high-level language will also usually dictate the final segment order. The order of segments when DOSSEG is specified is as follows: All segments with class name 'CODE' will be in the first frame; other segments will be combined based on combine type and class name and will be written to the .EXE file in the order they appear in the object files and in the order of the files in the command to the linker. The segment order for this example is as follows: The .EXE file has a header followed by all 'CODE' segments (combined), the 'STACK' segment, and finally all 'DATA' segments (combined).

The linker must build the first frame from a number of logical segments. In this example, there will be eight _TEXT data records in the object and library files: one each for the _TEXT segments in ExMain, ExSub, PutStr, PutCrLf, PutDec, and GetDec (and ChkDigit), which are called by ExMain and others; GetChar, which is called by GetDec; and IOError, which is called by GetDec. This will be the order in which

## 11.4 Linkers

the linker combines the segments to produce a single frame. For compatibility with other Microsoft languages, the first instruction of the main program is displaced 10h bytes from the start of the frame.

Using the order given above, and the offsets in the PUBLIC NAMES records of the object files shown in Figures 11.2, 11.6, and 11.7 (and the ones omitted from Figure 11.7), we can determine where each procedure's code segment will be loaded in the frame (see Table 11.6) by concatenating the segments and making sure that each begins on a word boundary (as specified in the SEGMENT directive and recorded in the object file record).

### Linker Fixups

The linker must perform many types of fixups. To keep this presentation at a manageable length, we consider only those needed for the example program. We start with a self-relative fixup.

Consider the instruction

```
call    PutStr
```

at offset 1Ah in _TEXT of ExSub. We assembled that instruction as E80000h, and also wrote a fixup record to the object file for it. That fixup record (the fourth in Figure 11.4) indicates that offset at 1Bh (relative to _TEXT in that module) should be set to the displacement of PutStr relative to IP when the instruction executes. Let's plug in some numbers to make this easier to follow. The offset field that needs to be fixed is at _TEXT + 1Bh in ExSub. Since the _TEXT segment of ExSub starts at 004Ah in the frame, the offset field to be modified is at displacement 004Ah + 001Bh, or 0065h, in the frame. The fixup is self-relative, which means that the offset field of the call instruction contains a displacement relative to IP. When the call instruction executes, IP will be 0067h (the start of the next instruction). From Table 11.6, we find the start of PutStr as 0078h in the frame, so the displacement is 0078h − 0067h, or 0011h. When the linker copies the data record for segment _TEXT from file EXSUB.OBJ into the load module, it must substitute the offset 0011h at displacement 0065h.

Table 11.6  Procedures in CODE Frame

| Module name | Procedure name | Procedure size | Offset in segment | Displacement in frame |
|---|---|---|---|---|
| reserved |  | 10h |  | 0000h_000Fh |
| ExMain.ASM | ExMain | 39h | 0000h | 0010h_0048h |
| unused |  |  |  | 0049h |
| ExSub.ASM | ExSub | 2Eh | 0000h | 004Ah_0077h |
| PutStr.ASM | PutStr | 17h | 0000h | 0078h_008Eh |
| unused |  |  |  | 008Fh |
| PutCrLf.ASM | PutCrLf | 0Fh | 0000h | 0090h_009Eh |
| unused |  |  |  | 009Fh |
| PutDec.ASM | PutDec | 5Bh | 0000h | 00A0h_00FAh |
| unused |  |  |  | 00FBh |
| GetChar.ASM | GetChar | 24h | 0000h | 00FCh_011Fh |
| GetDec.ASM | GetDec | 51h | 0000h | 0120h_0170h |
| GetDec.ASM | ChkDigit | 13h | 0051h | 0171h_0183h |
| GetDec.ASM | IOErrror | 1Bh | 0064h | 0184h_019Eh |

The other fixups in EXSUB.OBJ are segment-relative, and refer to the _DATA segment. The linker will build another frame for the segments with combine class 'DATA', of which there are three, one each in ExMain, ExSub, and IOError (in the GetDec module). The segments will be combined in the order listed. The _DATA segment of EXMAIN is 001Fh bytes long, and occupies the first 001Fh bytes of the DATA frame. The _DATA segment of EXSUB follows, but since it is declared as word-aligned, it actually starts at byte 0020h in the frame.

Now consider the first fixup in EXSUB.OBJ. The offset to be fixed is at 0009h relative to _TEXT of ExSub, or 004Ah + 0009h = 0053h in the CODE frame. The target is _DATA:0000h, but the _DATA segment of ExSub starts at 0020h in the DATA frame. So the linker must add 0020h to the displacement 0000h, resulting in offset 0020h in the DATA frame, and substitute 0020h for the displacement field in the instruction when it copies the data record for _TEXT of ExSub into the load module.

Segment-relative fixups are actually more complicated than the ones in ExSub appear. By coincidence, the _DATA segment of ExSub in the frame starts on a paragraph boundary (a multiple of 10h), simplifying the arithmetic somewhat. When a segment does not start on a paragraph boundary, the displacement computed in the fixup must be relative to the start of the paragraph. Consider the instructions

```
mov     ax, seg _DATA
mov     ds, ax
```

and

```
add     bx, MemOp
```

where MemOp is in the _DATA segment. The offset in the add instruction, at all stages, must be relative to a paragraph boundary because the DS register during execution will point to a paragraph boundary. Thus, even though _DATA is word aligned, the value ultimately assigned to DS during execution must refer to the boundary of the paragraph that contains the first byte of _DATA. The offset computed by the linker must also take this paragraph alignment into consideration.

The other three fixups of ExSub, and most fixups of ExMain and the I/O procedures, are similar to the two just illustrated. Some fixups, however, cannot be resolved fully by the linker and must be completed by the loader. These will be explained in Section 11.5.

Without tracing the operation of a linker or giving an algorithm for it, we have nevertheless demonstrated the processing performed by the linker. The ExMain.EXE file created by the linker for the program consisting of ExMain, ExSub, and the I/O procedures is shown in simplified form in Figure 11.8. In the figure, the fields of the header are expanded by including a brief description of the field; in the actual file, these fields are just two or four bytes. The next section will explain how the loader uses the information in the header. Figure 11.8 also shows the first four instruction and data bytes of each procedure and data segment explicitly, with their displacements in the file given on the side of the figure for reference.

In summary, the linker must read the various object and library files, build a file header for the loader to use, copy the data records for the various segments into the load module in the order specified (or implied), fix the operand references specified in the object files, and record in the header information regarding remaining fixups for the loader.

## 11.4 Linkers

| Header | Offset |
|---|---|
| file type = .exe | 00h |
| bytes in last page = 0006h | 02h |
| no. of pages in file = 0004h | 04h |
| no. of relocation entries = 0002h | 06h |
| no. of paragraphs in header = 0020h | 08h |
| min. paragraphs above end = 0000h | 0Ah |
| max. paragraphs above end = FFFFh | 0Ch |
| initial SS register (+ reloc) = 001Ah | 0Eh |
| initial SP register = 0200h | 10h |
| file checksum = 4B59h | 12h |
| initial IP register = 0010h | 14h |
| initial CS register (+ reloc) = 0000h | 16h |
| offset of relocation table = 001Eh | 18h |
| overlay number = 0000h | 1Ah |
| relocation entry: 0000:0011 | 1Eh |
| relocation entry: 0000:0185 | 22h |
| **Load module** | |
| (first paragraph reserved) | 200h |
| B8 3A 00 8E ... (ExMain _TEXT) | 210h |
| 55 8B EC 8B ... (ExSub _TEXT) | 24Ah |
| 50 53 51 52 ... (PutStr _TEXT) | 278h |
| 50 52 B4 02 ... (PutCrLf _TEXT) | 290h |
| 50 53 51 52 ... (PutDec _TEXT) | 2A0h |
| B4 01 CD 21 ... (GetChar _TEXT) | 2FCh |
| 53 51 52 2B ... (GetDec _TEXT) | 320h |
| 80 FC 00 75 ... (ChkDigit _TEXT) | 371h |
| B8 3A 00 8E ... (IOError _TEXT) | 384h |
| 00 00 00 00 ... (_STACK) | 3A0h |
| 00 00 45 6E ... (ExMain _DATA) | 5A0h |
| 00 00 41 72 ... (ExSub _DATA) | 5C0h |
| 45 52 52 4F ... (IOError _DATA) | 5DAh |

**Figure 11.8** Format of EXMAIN.EXE File

## EXERCISES 11.4

1. Obtain a listing file for one or more programs you have written. How are the various fixups that are required noted and distinguished on the listing file?
▶2. Write a subprogram in which the instructions are in a segment with a unique name but with class name 'CODE'. Where in the load module will the linker put these instructions?
▶3. Write a subprogram in which the instructions are in a segment named _TEXT (as are the instruction segments of the other subprograms and the main program) but with a unique class name. Where in the load module will the linker put these instructions?
4. Does careless use of segment and class names potentially limit the size of a program? Explain.

5. Is it possible to write an assembly-language program (including any subprograms that it calls) that does not require the linker to perform any fixups? If so, write one and explain what limitations such a program has. If not, carefully explain why such a program cannot be written.
6. Compare the tasks performed by an assembler with those performed by a linker. Which program do you think is more complex, based on what you have seen in this chapter? Which do you think has a greater potential impact on system performance?
7. Disassemblers can inspect an executable file and generate a pseudoassembly listing. (DEBUG, CodeView, and Turbo Debugger all have this capability.) They do not reconstruct segment information. Why not? What difficulties would there be in writing a utility that could reconstruct segment information? How could such a utility be useful?

## 11.5 LOADERS

The load module created by the linker can be loaded into memory and executed. A utility called a loader copies the load module into memory. The DOS command processor invokes the program loader routine; no separate load command is necessary. DOS also provides access to the loader as a system function (see interrupt 21h, function 4Bh in your reference manual).

The loader copies the load module according to the parameters specified in the .EXE file header. We will consider what those parameters can specify using the example shown in Figure 11.8 of the preceding section. Once the loader determines how much memory is needed (we'll describe how it does this in a moment) and determines a starting address for the program, it builds a program segment prefix (PSP) in the first 100h bytes of the memory allocated for the program. We will return to the PSP later. First we will explore how the loader uses the information in the header of the .EXE file.

### Program Header

At offset 04h, the loader finds there are four pages in the file; at offset 02h, the loader finds that the last page is only 06h bytes long; from this information, it calculates the length of the file as

Number of full pages × Page size + Size of last page

In this case, the result is (4 − 1) × 0200h + 0006h = 0606h.

At offset 08h, the loader finds the header size as 0020h paragraphs (= 0200h bytes). It can calculate the size of the load module as 0606h − 0200h = 0406h bytes.

The entry at 0Ah specifies that this load module needs no additional memory when loaded, and the entry at 0Ch specifies that this module would like all remaining memory allocated to it. Many MS-DOS programs use this convention. In real mode, only one application is running at a time, and DOS allocates whatever memory is available to it.

The file checksum at displacement 12h is used to verify that the file has been read correctly. As the file is read, all bytes are added together (with overflow ignored). The sum should be zero, so the checksum is simply the complement of the sum of all the other bytes in the file.

The overlay number is used to manage overlays. When a program is too big, the programmer can partition it into a resident module and a number of overlays. At any time, the resident portion and some (but not all) overlays are in memory. When needed, one of the other overlays is brought into memory in place of one or more already there. This

## 11.5 Loaders

is a crude, programmer-managed variation of virtual memory. The role of the loader in managing overlays, however, is beyond the scope of this book.

## Loader Fixups

Another type of entry in the header concerns fixups that depend on load address. One of these fixups was hinted at in the example near the end of Section 11.4. The instruction

```
mov     ax, seg _DATA
```

is assembled with an immediate operand. The value of this operand is the segment number (paragraph boundary) where _DATA begins. The linker determines where _DATA starts relative to the start of the load module but cannot determine the final value for this immediate constant. The loader must add the displacement provided by the linker to the address where it starts loading the module in order to determine the value of the immediate operand. The loader substitutes this value when the instruction is actually copied into memory. This fixup is recorded in the .EXE file as part of the header, in a much simpler form than fixups in object files.

For example, the foregoing instruction occurs in ExMain as the very first instruction. Because the load module starts with a paragraph of zeros, this instruction is at displacement 0010h and the operand field for the constant is at 0011h (refer to Figure 11.8). The first relocation entry in Figure 11.8 specifies this location as 0000:0011. Now, the _DATA segment of ExMain begins at displacement 05A0h in the file or at 03A0h in the load module. The linker wrote the number 003Ah as an intermediate value of the immediate operand at 0011h in the load module.

The loader knows the address in memory where it starts to copy the load module, of course. It uses the relocation entries in the header to find operands that need fixing and proceeds to fix them by adding the paragraph boundary of the starting address to those operands. Thus, if this program is loaded starting at 4A240h, the loader adds 4A24h to 003Ah, obtains 4A5Eh, and writes this at displacement 0011h in the load module, as the immediate operand in the first instruction.

The other fixup in the example—for the instruction that loads the segment number for the _DATA segment in the IOError procedure—is similar.

## Initializing Registers

Now we can consider how the segment registers and the instruction and stack pointer registers are initialized. The initial values for the SP and IP registers are given in the header at 10h and 14h, respectively. The initial values for CS and SS, given in the header at 16h and 0Eh, must be adjusted for the starting address of the load module. To continue the example, if this program is loaded starting at 4A240h, the initial value for the CS register is 0000h (from header) + 4A24h, or 4A24h. The initial value for the SS register would be 001Ah (from header) + 4A24h, or 4A3Eh.

Note that the address we have been using, 4A240h, is where the load module is copied. The program segment prefix for this program would begin at 4A140h and occupy 100h bytes. The loader initializes DS and ES to the paragraph boundary of the PSP, or 4A14h in this example.

After copying the load module, performing the fixups, creating the PSP, and setting the initial values of the registers, control is passed to the program. This transfer is accomplished

## Program Segment Prefix

Now we consider the program segment prefix. Figure 11.9 illustrates the layout of this block (the figure is not to scale).

The first entry in the PSP is an `int 20h` instruction. This can be used to return control to DOS, though this is no longer the recommended way to terminate a program. The second entry is the size of the program in paragraphs. The next six bytes are reserved for DOS to use.

The next 12 bytes are saved interrupt vectors. In the event that a program modifies these interrupt vectors, so that the related interrupts transfer control to a handler provided by the program, these entries allow DOS to restore the normal vectors.

The next block of the PSP is used by DOS. Starting at displacement 5Ch, there is an unopened file control block (FCB), with the drive number corresponding to the first file or path following the program name on the command line, if present. There is a second unopened FCB starting at 6Ch. Note, however, that the block reserved in the PSP for these FCBs is too small to record information for two complete, opened FCBs. Also note that only the drive number is valid, and only if there are filenames or pathnames on the command line.

The second half of the PSP is a copy of the command line following the program name. For example, if we type the command

```
C:\> TRASH BAK 6/90
```

to invoke program TRASH.EXE, the string `'BAK 6/90'` will be copied into the PSP beginning at displacement 81h. The length of this string, 8, will be stored at displacement 80h in the PSP. It is up to the program to access this string and parse it.

| | Offset |
|---|---|
| INT 20h | 00h |
| Size in paragraphs | 02h |
| Reserved | 04h |
| Terminate address (IP,CS) | 0Ah |
| CTRL-C exit address (IP,CS) | 0Eh |
| Critical error exit address (IP,CS) | 12h |
| Used by DOS | 16h |
| Unopened FCB 1 | 5Ch |
| Unopened FCB 2 | 6Ch |
| Length of command string | 80h |
| Command string | 81h |
| | 100h |

**Figure 11.9** Format of Program Segment Prefix

## 11.6 Debuggers

The significance of the PSP is that it is a combination of a saved system state when the program is invoked, a copy of the command line (beyond the command name), and the size of the program. None of the other information from the assembler or linker not explicitly needed in an instruction or operand is present during execution.

### EXERCISES 11.5

1. It was stated that the CS and IP registers are loaded with values from the header (with the starting segment number added to the value for CS) as the last step. Clearly, these must both be loaded as the result of executing the same instruction, or control will jump to some location using a combination of new CS and old IP or old CS and new IP. What instruction can the loader use to change both CS and IP at once?
2. Is it possible to write a program in assembly language such that the loader will not have any fixups (other than initializing CS and SS) to perform? If so, write such a program and describe the limitations imposed. If not, carefully explain why such a program cannot be written.
▶3. Write a program that reads an .EXE file and prints the information contained in the header with descriptions. Note that words are written to the file with least significant byte first. Doublewords are written to the file in order from least significant to most significant. Refer to Figure 11.8 (p. 407).
▶4. Write a program that prints a copy of its PSP. Note that both DS and ES point to the PSP when execution begins. Refer to Figure 11.9 (p. 410). Run your program with extra text typed on the command line.

## 11.6 DEBUGGERS

The assembler, linker, and loader are program development tools. Other tools available to programmers include text editors, make utilities, file managers, project tracking programs, revision control systems, and so on. Most of these are more appropriate to another course of study. One other tool, however, is of interest here because of the requirements that it imposes on assemblers, compilers, linkers, and loaders. This tool is invariably called a *debugger*, though it is also useful in some contexts not associated with finding program errors.

Debuggers are available with a variety of capabilities. Some can do little more than display the contents of a region of memory, leaving it up to the programmer to specify the block of memory by a range of addresses and to interpret the output. At the other extreme, the most powerful debuggers can use information provided by the translator and the linker, along with the original source files, to display selected fragments of a program symbolically. For the remainder of this discussion, we assume some familiarity with either Microsoft's CodeView or Borland's Turbo Debugger. See Appendix 5 or Appendix 6, respectively, for an overview of each tool.

To take full advantage of a symbolic debugger, the load module must contain information regarding the symbolic names used in the source file and where the instructions corresponding to each line in the source file begin in the load module. Such information is written to the object files first and is then included in the executable file by the linker. The object files also contain a comment record—much like the comment that marked the end of pass one—that indicates the presence of the extra line number and symbolic information records.

Consider the line number information first. The assembler (or compiler) can generate a list of pairs of numbers. One number in each pair is a line number in the source file; the other is the displacement in the code segment where the instructions for the line begin. This list is written, as a special segment, to the object file as a separate record. The linker later modifies the displacements in this record to reflect how the code segment is combined with other code segments, and the linker includes the segment in the executable file. The debugger then uses this record together with the source file to show the line that is currently executing, to allow the user to set breakpoints on a given line, and so on.

The symbolic information is more complicated because no standard segment definition for symbolic information exists—each debugger expects the symbolic information in some unique format. Most linkers can process symbolic information in several formats, though they often can generate only the symbolic information required by the same company's debugger. For example, the symbolic information can be coded in the object file as a series of comment records with a comment record for each symbol. The information can also be collected into another special segment and written as enumerated data to the object file.

The information needed for each symbol is usually that listed as attributes in the symbol table: name, type, value, and perhaps some type-dependent attributes. The manner in which these are coded is not important to this discussion. The attributes allow the symbolic debugger and the user to employ symbolic names when setting watches and working with other expressions. The use of symbolic names here is a great advantage of these debuggers over those that require the user to enter memory addresses.

Although not every module must include line number or symbolic information in the executable file in order to use a symbolic debugger, the main program must often do so. Say, for example, that the input and output routines provided in the library have been assembled with neither line number nor symbolic information; when linked with a program that does include these, the resulting executable program can be examined with the symbolic debugger, but the input and output routines can only be examined as disassembled code. Of course, a user would usually "step over" (that is, execute without examining each instruction) these routines when working with an application program that uses them. This latter capability increases efficiency: Once some routines are thoroughly tested and made available for others to use, there should be no need to examine them symbolically during execution.

The line number and symbolic information make the object and executable files larger than those that do not contain this information. Thus, once a program is debugged, it should be assembled (or compiled) and linked again without the debugging information. Some utilities strip the debugging information out of the executable file, so that translation and linking need not be repeated. Either way, the presence of symbolic debugging information in the executable file of a production program is often undesirable, as it just wastes memory and disk space.

## EXERCISES 11.6

1. If you have not done so yet, learn how to use the symbolic debugger available to you.
▶2. Modify a program you have written to include one or more subtle errors. Exchange the source files with another student (or the instructor). Use the symbolic debugger to find the flaws in the other student's program. Share any observations you make about the debugging process with the student whose program you examine.

3. Compare the size of the object files produced for the same programs with no debug information, line numbers only, and full debugging information. How much larger are the files with debug information, as a percentage increase?
4. Repeat Exercise 3 for executable files.

## KEY POINTS

- Attributes are properties or characteristics associated with objects and actions.
- Binding is the process of associating a value with an attribute. Binding time refers to the moment when the value of an attribute is assigned.
- An assembler is a program that translates an assembly-language program into machine-dependent codes. The output of an assembler is called an object file.
- A two-pass assembler reads and analyzes the entire source file twice. During the first pass, it constructs a symbol table and a segment table; during the second pass, it uses the information in the tables to generate the object file.
- A compiler is a program that translates high-level-language programs into other languages; most often, compilers generate sequences of machine-dependent codes, but some generate equivalent programs in other high-level or assembly languages.
- A statement in a high-level language can correspond to many machine instructions; most statements in assembly language correspond to exactly one instruction.
- An interpreter is a program that analyzes the statements in a high-level programming language and performs the indicated operations.
- Preprocessors are available to add statements and data types to existing languages. Programs that use these extra features are first processed by the preprocessor, which generates an intermediate file; the intermediate file is then compiled normally.
- A linker, or linkage editor, is a program that combines object and library files to produce an executable run image. During its processing, the linker resolves the external references and fixes displacements as needed.
- A loader copies into memory a load module produced by a linker, establishes initial register and header area values, and transfers control to the program.
- A symbolic debugger needs attribute information provided by the assembler and linker and included in the run image, as well as the original source file, to match the lines and symbols of the original program to the instructions as they execute.

## PC SYSTEMS SUMMARY

Although much of this chapter involved details of DOS and the 8086 processor, the nature of those details do not lend themselves to simple summary. Such a summary, if undertaken, would be of nebulous value.

One instruction, nop (No OPeration), was introduced as a 1-byte operation code that can be used to pad the object file when an instruction in the second pass is smaller than it was assumed to be during the first pass. This instruction is not normally used in writing programs.

# 12 Macroinstructions

- **Macro Concepts**
- **Macros with Parameters**
- **More About Macros**
- **Conditional Assembly**

Programming in assembly language is more tedious than in a high-level language. It gives the programmer more control over the computer system, but it requires the programmer to accept responsibility for more details.

Early assembly-language programmers recognized that some sequences of instructions occurred frequently. They developed a method whereby they could define such sequences and name them; during translation, the assembler would replace the names with instruction sequences. The sequences were called macroinstructions, or simply macros. Today, macros are used for a variety of text substitutions; they also have parameters and conditionals.

This chapter examines some of the macro capabilities of 8086 assemblers. This chapter is optional in a study of computer systems; however, it is useful in a study of assembly language. For those contemplating a substantial programming project in assembly language, this chapter serves as an introduction; the assembler reference manual should be consulted for the many features omitted.

## 12.1 MACRO CONCEPTS

Assembly-language programs are longer and more tedious to write than equivalent programs in high-level languages. There are several ways that programmers can relieve some of the burden without giving up the control available only in assembly language.

One useful technique is to code large programs using small subprograms. Many of the subprograms written for one project may perform operations common to other projects. The common subroutines are collected into libraries that are linked with the new or unique portions of new programs to produce new applications. Since library routines are in object form, they must be linked as whole subprograms.

The ability to manipulate fragments of assembly-language programs would be useful. Many fragments of assembly-language programs that occur frequently in many programs, perhaps with a few minor changes, would not be appropriate as subprograms. For example, segment directives appear in all programs, but they cannot be made into a subprogram.

One way to manage common fragments of assembly-language programs (or any programs, for that matter) is to keep each fragment in a separate file. When entering the program with a text editor, import each fragment where it is needed. This approach leads to a large collection of fairly small files, which tends to waste much disk space and can be hard to manage. (Each file, though only a few bytes long, usually takes a whole

## 12.1 Macro Concepts

cluster—often 2K—on the disk.) If a fragment to be imported includes labels or operands that should vary from one insertion to another, each insertion requires further editing. These problems can be more frustrating to deal with than simply typing each program from scratch.

Another way to manage fragments of assembly-language programs is to use **macroinstructions** (macros). A macro is a named fragment of program text. It can include operands, labels, conditionals, and several special operators. The assembler—not the text editor—expands each occurrence of the macro name in a program as part of the translation process. The expansion can be as simple as a direct text replacement, can include parameters (possibly a variable number of them), or can involve nested (possibly recursive) macro expansions. The remainder of this section introduces simple macros in detail; later sections describe more advanced features of macros.

### Macro Definition

Each macro must be defined within a program before it is used in that program. Macros unique to one program are usually defined in the source file for the program, at the very beginning of the file; macros useful in many programs are often collected into files of macro definitions that can then be merged into source files during program translation. The former arrangement is used in the first example, and then the latter is considered.

As an example of a fragment that is common to many programs, consider the sequence that returns control to DOS:

```
      mov     ah, 4Ch         ;Exit To Dos function
      mov     al, 00h         ;No Errors
      int     21h             ;Dos function interrupt
```

(We used hexadecimal numbers for the constants in this example, rather than the names we have been using, since the macro will also hide these numbers.) Although it is not hard to write these three instructions at the end of every program, it would be more convenient to write a single instruction that accomplishes the same thing.

Two new assembler directives are needed to define a simple macro. The MACRO directive marks the beginning of a macro definition and specifies the name of the macro. The ENDM directive marks the end of the definition. To define a macro named ExitToDos, which can be used in place of the three instructions, we can include the following in our source file:

```
ExitToDos MACRO
      mov     ah, 4Ch         ;Exit to Dos function
      mov     al, 00h         ;No Errors
      int     21h             ;Dos function interrupt
ENDM
```

The name of the macro is written just like any other name on the same line as the MACRO directive. The instructions that define the macro are written between the MACRO and ENDM directives.

Macros are not limited to sequences of instructions. Any text can be included in the definition of a macro. We will see examples of macros that include other directives and macros that contain no instructions at all.

## Macro Expansion

Once we have defined a macro, we simply use its name later in the program. The assembler expands the macro during translation by inserting the text in the definition into the program where the macro name appears. For example, once we define ExitToDos as given above, to return control to DOS we simply write

ExitToDos

at the place in our program where we want the assembler to insert those instructions.

## Comments in Macros

We will want to include comments in our macros, especially the more complex macros. It is useful to have two types of comments. Some of the comments we want to appear only in the definition of the macro, but other comments we want to appear in the expansion (on the listing file) as well. Most assemblers provide this capability.

In a macro definition, any comment that starts with a single semicolon (;) is included as part of the macro expansion on the listing. Any comment that starts with two consecutive semicolons (;;) appears only in the macro definition and not in the expansions. For example, consider the definition of ExitToDos shown at the beginning of Program 12.1. Only portions of the listing file for the program are shown; the complete program is available on the disk provided with the text.

Compare the comments in the definition of this macro to those in the expansion. The comment immediately following the MACRO directive begins with two semicolons, so it

**Program 12.1**

```
                        ; Program 12.1      FirstMac.ASM
                        ; Illustrate a simple macro.

                        ExitToDos MACRO
                        ;;exit to DOS with return code 0.
                              mov       ah, 4Ch         ;Exit To Dos function
                              mov       al, 00h         ;No Errors
                              int       21h             ;Dos Function interrupt
                        ENDM

                                .
                                .
                                .
000F E8 0000 E                call      PutCrLf

                        ExitToDos
0012 B4 4C          1         mov       ah, 4Ch         ;Exit To Dos function
0014 B0 00          1         mov       al, 00h         ;No Errors
0016 CD 21          1         int       21h             ;Dos Function interrupt

0018                    _TEXT ENDS
                        END       FirstMac
```

is not included in the expansion. The comments on the instructions begin with just one semicolon, so they are included in the expansion. Finally, the MACRO and ENDM directives do not appear in the expansion.

## Include Files

Macros defined at the start of a source file are useful only within that file. Many macros, however, can be useful in many different programs. Clearly, if we have to type each macro as part of the program source file, we would not gain much. And if a program uses a macro defined within it only once, it requires more typing to enter the macro definition than to just enter the corresponding text without using a macro. However, if we gather useful macro definitions in a separate file and insert them as needed into source programs, we can save a lot of typing.

An *include file* is a text file that contains any source statements; files of macro definitions are typical, though files of other text are possible. The assembler provides an INCLUDE directive, which consists of the word INCLUDE followed by the pathname of a file. When the assembler encounters the INCLUDE directive, it copies the contents of the named file into the input buffer for the source file. Then it processes the contents of the include file as if it were part of the original source file (but it does distinguish between the included lines and the original source lines on the listing). When the end of the include file is reached, the assembler resumes processing the source file at the statement after the INCLUDE directive.

All of the macros presented in this chapter are defined in an include file. This file is in the same subdirectory as the programs for this chapter and is named MACROS.INC. To use the macro definitions in sample programs, we use the statement

INCLUDE MACROS.INC

in our programs. To use the file on the disk provided with the book, keep the MACROS.INC file in the same directory as the programs that use INCLUDE to specify it.

As we examine other macro features, we will refer to the macros in the include file as if they were separate programs. The listings printed in the text indicate that the macros are part of the include file. As we progress from one macro to another, our programs use the macros already discussed. For example, the include file contains a macro to establish the DS register. See Program 12.2. We use this macro, along with ExitToDos, in all other programs in this chapter. One interesting result is that as we incorporate more macros—and more complex macros—in our programs, the programs become shorter.

### Program 12.2

```
; Program 12.2       SetUpDs
; Macro definition from file MACROS.INC

SetUpDs    MACRO
;;set up ds to point to _DATA
     mov       ax, seg _DATA
     mov       ds, ax
     assume    ds: _DATA
ENDM
```

A drawback to using a large file of macro definitions is that the assembler must process all of the macro definitions in the file even if only a few of the macros are used in the program. To minimize this, related macros can be grouped into separate files, and separate INCLUDE directives can be used to select only those files with needed macros. A lot of the tedium of programming in assembly language can be relieved by using collections of macros defined in separate files.

Section 12.2 describes macros with parameters.

## EXERCISES 12.1

▶1. Modify the comments in the macro definition of Program 12.1 (FirstMac.ASM), and assemble with the listing file enabled. Examine the listing file, and verify how various comments are included or suppressed in the listing.

▶2. Modify a copy of Program 12.1 so that it does not use the macro facility. Assemble both, obtaining as much information from the assembler as you can. Are the object files for the two versions of this program the same?

▶3. Modify Program 12.1 so that it uses the ExitToDos macro in the include file MACROS.INC. Delete the macro definition in FirstMac.ASM. Assemble and obtain a listing file. How are the included lines marked on the listing? (Note: There are many macros in MACROS.INC that have not yet been shown; do not be overwhelmed by them.)

4. Propose another use for the INCLUDE directive. Give some examples of the text that an include file might have other than macro definitions.

5. Most assemblers allow include files to contain an INCLUDE directive; it is called a nested INCLUDE directive. How could it be useful? How many levels of nesting does your assembler support?

## 12.2 MACROS WITH PARAMETERS

The example macros of the previous section are not very exciting. Every time ExitToDos is expanded, the assembler gives exactly the same three instructions. We would like to be able to write macros having certain parts different in each expansion. The use of parameters with macros gives us that ability.

### Parameters and Arguments

Before proceeding, a potentially confusing use of terms is explained. When we discuss subprograms, we use *argument* to refer to an actual value passed to a subprogram; we use *parameter* to refer to the name by which the subprogram can access an argument. We use the terms *argument* and *parameter* in a similar way when discussing macros, though there are important differences. Parameters are names used in macro definitions that are replaced with arguments when the macro is expanded. Some may object to the use of the same terms with subprograms and macros, but there is enough contextual information that confusion can be avoided.

Let's consider an example macro with one parameter. Many assemblers provide simplified segment directives; we propose a macro that implements a simplified stack directive.

## 12.2 Macros with Parameters

Our stack definitions in this text have been the following:

```
_STACK  SEGMENT  para stack 'stack'
        dw       100h dup (?)
_STACK  ENDS
```

One part of this definition that may change from one program to another is the number of words of stack space to reserve; a program with many nested subprogram calls and many arguments can require a larger stack segment. We can make most of the text of the stack declaration the definition of a macro, and we can use a parameter to represent the size of the stack. Such a definition may be written as in Program 12.3.

### Program 12.3

```
; Program 12.3       DefineStack
; Macro definition from file MACROS.INC

DefineStack MACRO size
;;defines a stack segment for main programs.
;;  size = size of stack segment in words
_STACK  SEGMENT  para stack 'stack'
        dw       size dup (?)
_STACK  ENDS
ENDM
```

To define the stack once the macro is defined, we can simply write

`DefineStack 100h`

The 100h, which can be regarded as a hexadecimal number but which the assembler treats as a string of four characters, is the argument. The assembler substitutes "100h" for size when it expands the definition of DefineStack. To define a larger stack, we can write

`DefineStack 4096`

Here, the argument is also a string even though we can regard it as a decimal number. Program 12.4 illustrates the use of the three macros defined so far and the INCLUDE directive.

### Program 12.4

```
; Program 12.4       StackMac.ASM
; Illustrate simple macros, including arguments.

; Get definitions of macros:
;   DefineStack     declares a stack segment
;   SetUpDS         establishes ds register
;   ExitToDos       terminates with return code 0
INCLUDE MACROS.INC

DOSSEG

    DefineStack 100h
```

## Program 12.4 (continued)

```
_DATA SEGMENT word public 'data'
  ExitMsg    db      " ... returning to DOS."
  ExitLen    DW      $ - ExitMsg
_DATA ENDS

_TEXT SEGMENT word public 'code'
    assume  cs: _TEXT
    extrn   PutStr: PROC, PutCrLf: PROC

StackMac:

  SetUpDS

; display a message, so user knows something happened
    mov     cx, ExitLen
    mov     bx, offset ExitMsg
    call    PutStr
    call    PutCrLf

  ExitToDos

_TEXT ENDS
END     StackMac
```

## Multiple Parameters

We can write macros that have more than one parameter. When we do, the arguments during expansion are associated with the parameters in the definition from left to right.

Consider multiplying a source operand by 10 and putting the product in a destination operand. There is no single 8086 instruction that works like this, so let's define one. Our instruction might be used as

`MulTenW ResultVal, TestVal`

which would implement the assignment statement

`ResultVal := 10 * TestVal`

We cannot really add instructions to the 8086, but we can make it appear that way by defining macros. Program 12.5 shows the definition of the MulTenW macro; it uses word operations, hence the W in the name. It is left as an exercise to implement a byte version of it. The multiplication is performed using shift and addition instructions, as explained in Chapter 6. The destination parameter, first in the definition, is replaced by ResultVal, the first argument in the expansion. The source parameter is replaced by TestVal in the expansion.

## Program 12.5

```
; Program 12.5    MulTenW
; Macro definition from file MACROS.INC
```

## 12.2 Macros with Parameters

**Program 12.5 (continued)**

```
MulTenW MACRO dest, source
;;computes dest := 10 * source using shifts and addition.
;;  dest can be any word register or variable,
;;  source can be any word register except AX, any word
;;  variable or immediate value.
        mov     ax, source
        sal     ax, 1           ;;source * 2
        sal     ax, 1           ;;source * 4
        add     ax, source      ;;source * 5
        sal     ax, 1           ;;source * 10
        mov     dest, ax
ENDM
```

The arguments to `MulTenW` can be any word operands, whether in memory or in registers (except that AX cannot be used as the source). They can be different or the same. Thus

`MulTenW bx, SomeData`

multiplies the value of `SomeData` by 10 and leaves the result in the BX register, and

`MulTenW cx, cx`

multiplies the contents of the CX register by 10. We cannot use the AX register for the source argument: We need the original value of source after AX has been changed by two shift instructions. The source operand, however, can be an immediate operand. Program 12.6 tests the `MulTenW` macro with two operands in memory.

## Program 12.6

```
; Program 12.6         MulTenW.ASM
; Illustrate a macro with two parameters.

; Get definitions of macros:
;   DefineStack     declares a stack segment
;   SetUpDS         establishes ds register
;   ExitToDos       terminates with return code 0
;   MulTenW         computes dest := 10 * source
INCLUDE MACROS.INC

DOSSEG

    DefineStack 100h

_DATA SEGMENT word public 'data'
    TestVal         dw      ?
    ResultVal       dw      ?
    PromptMsg       db      "Enter number to multiply"
    PromptLen       dw      $ - PromptMsg
    ResultMsg       db      " times 10 is "
    ResultLen       dw      $ - ResultMsg
_DATA ENDS
```

**Program 12.6 (continued)**

```
_TEXT SEGMENT word public 'code'
    assume  cs: _TEXT
    extrn   PutStr: PROC, PutCrLf: PROC
    extrn   PutDec: PROC, GetDec: PROC

MulTen:

    SetUpDS

; print ("Enter number to multiply ")
    mov     cx, PromptLen
    mov     bx, offset PromptMsg
    call    PutStr

; read (TestVal)
    call    GetDec
    mov     TestVal, ax
    call    PutCrLf

; ResultVal := 10 * TestVal
    MulTenW ResultVal, TestVal

; print (TestVal, "times 10 is", ResultVal)
    mov     ax, TestVal
    call    PutDec
    mov     cx, ResultLen
    mov     bx, offset ResultMsg
    call    PutStr
    mov     ax, ResultVal
    call    PutDec
    call    PutCrLf

    ExitToDos

_TEXT ENDS
END     MulTen
```

There may or may not be a limit imposed on the number of parameters a macro can have, depending on the assembler. Certainly most assemblers allow enough parameters to enable writing some very powerful macros, more parameters than most programmers would ever need.

## Side Effects in Macros

Macros that implement a sequence of instructions usually change the contents of one or more registers. For example, the MulTenW macro uses the AX register. The statement

```
MulTenW     bx, SomeData
```

### 12.2 Macros with Parameters

computes 10∗SomeData and copies the result into BX; not obvious, however, is that it changes the AX register in the process. This change to AX is called a *side effect*.

Most side effects are unwelcome. An unsuspecting programmer can spend a lot of time and effort finding the cause of the side effect, especially if, by coincidence, the side effect results in only a small change in a value. There are three approaches to dealing with potential side effects in macros.

The first approach is to document every side effect of each macro and expect all programmers to refer to such documentation when using macros. Of course, in an ideal setting, that might actually work. However, it is human nature to refer to documentation only when problems arise; that the documentation provided to avoid side effects is consulted only when a side effect is observed—and not all side effects will be observed immediately—defeats the documentation approach to avoiding side effects.

The second approach is to save every register used in the macro before using it, then restore it afterward. For example, we would add

```
push        ax
```

to the beginning of MulTenW and

```
pop         ax
```

after copying the result to the destination argument. However, this action imposes the restriction that AX, which already cannot be the source argument to MulTenW, now cannot be the destination argument.

The third approach is to revise the macro so that it uses any registers that will be changed intentionally as working registers. For example, MulTenW would test whether the destination argument is a register; if it is, it would use that register for intermediate steps. If it is not, the working register could then be saved and restored as in the second approach. Such tests are not difficult to implement.

Of the three approaches, the first admits of side effects and puts the burden of avoiding problems on the programmer using the macro. The second and third approaches put the burden of not introducing side effects on the programmer writing the macro. Before writing macros, one should determine how side effects will be managed. Before using unfamiliar macros, one should find out how side effects were managed by the programmer who wrote the macros. And we should test programs very carefully.

## Macros versus Subprograms

Macros and subprograms both provide a means of working with pieces of programs; both can be used to simplify writing large programs by making the pieces available as needed; both have a parameter mechanism. However, there are very important differences.

Consider a sequence of instructions that performs a useful calculation, such as computing the absolute difference of two values. Assume this calculation is needed in several places in a program. We can implement this calculation as either a macro or as a function.

As a function, there is exactly one copy of the instructions, and it is used each time the function is invoked. The values are passed as arguments to the function as part of transferring control to it. The function result is left in a register when control is returned to the calling program. The advantage is that there is only one copy of the instructions. The disadvantage is the overhead of calling the function and passing arguments to it.

We can also write this calculation as a macro with parameters. Each expansion of the macro definition may use different arguments, giving slightly different copies of the instruction sequence for each expansion. The macro is defined once and is expanded wherever an absolute difference in the program is needed. The advantage is that there is no overhead during execution to pass arguments or transfer control. The disadvantage is that, for each expansion, there is a separate complete copy of the instructions.

Like so many other aspects of computing, the trade-off exists between execution time and memory space. Macros favor the former and subprograms the latter. It is up to the programmer to choose carefully between macros and subprograms.

Macros, however, are also useful in some situations where subprograms are not. Since macro expansion is essentially the substitution of the text of a definition for a name, macros are not necessarily related to tasks in the way that subprograms are. Consider, for example, the ExitToDos macro again. There is nothing to be gained, in terms of the problem being solved, by writing a subprogram to invoke DOS function 4Ch, but the macro does save some typing effort if the macro definition is in an include file. The following sections give other examples of macros that would not be sensible—or possible—as subprograms. The next section describes labels within macros, and some of the special operators available in macros.

## EXERCISES 12.2

1. Assemble Program 12.4, StackMac.ASM, and obtain the listing file. Verify that the stack is defined properly. Substitute other text for the argument, and explain what the assembler does with each case. (Use simple numbers and names, and try a bizarre expression or two as well.)
2. Explain what happens if a programmer interchanges the source and destination arguments when using the MulTenW macro.
▶3. Revise a copy of the MulTenW macro so that it operates on byte operands instead of word operands, and change its name to MulTenB. Revise Program 12.6 to use your new macro. (Be careful using GetDec and PutDec in your driver that tests your macro; these procedures use word arguments.)
▶4. Write a macro definition that converts a measurement in feet and inches into one in centimeters. The original measurement should be arguments to the macro; the measurement in centimeters should be left in the AX register. Your macro should work with parameters that are variables in memory or in registers, as well as parameters given as constants (immediate operands). Write a program that tests it completely.

## 12.3 MORE ABOUT MACROS

This section covers some of the more advanced features of macros. These features are not necessarily hard to use, and they make assembly-language programming less tedious. The features of this section are not used outside this chapter so as to provide some flexibility in the order in which material is presented.

## Labels

So far, we have not used any jump instructions in our macros. Using the guidelines for structured programming advocated in this book, it would be unlikely to need to transfer control from within a macro to an instruction outside the macro—except using the `call` instruction, of course. But it would be necessary to include jumps within a macro if that macro includes any control structures, and such jumps would require labels defined within the macro. There is a potential problem with labels in macros. Consider a definition that includes the label ENDIF01. When expanding this macro the first time, the assembler will copy the label from the definition into the program as part of the expansion. When expanding the macro a second time, it will use the exact same label—but we cannot use the same label twice in a module.

The solution is to use a new feature of macros: *local labels*. A label is declared local to a macro by the LOCAL directive. During macro expansion, local labels are replaced by unique labels generated by the assembler; local labels do not appear in the expansion. Note that the use of the term *local* for labels within macros is different from the meaning used when discussing data that is defined within a subprogram.

There is an important restriction: LOCAL, if used, must appear before any other text in the macro definition (after the MACRO directive), including comments. Some assemblers do not allow even a blank line between the MACRO directive and the LOCAL directive; the error messages for this event are not very clear.

The labels that the assembler generates for local labels during macro expansion will be unique. Typically, these labels consist of two question marks followed by a 4-digit hexadecimal number, like ??0000 and ??00C2. The assembler maintains a counter, which it starts at zero, that it uses for the numerical portion of the generated labels. Each time it needs a new label, it simply appends the value of the counter to ?? to form the label and increments the counter. This implies a limit of FFFFh unique labels; a limit we need not be concerned with.

As an example, consider finding the absolute value of a signed number. The 8086 does not have an absolute value instruction. We can write a short selection structure to implement this calculation as

```
IF num < 0
THEN num := -num
ENDIF
```

We define a macro that implements this structure in Program 12.7. The label ENDIF_ABS is declared local to the macro definition; the assembler will substitute a unique label in place of ENDIF_ABS every time it expands the AbsVal macro.

### Program 12.7

```
; Program 12.7    AbsVal
; Macro definition from file MACROS.INC

AbsVal MACRO num
LOCAL ENDIF_ABS
;;converts num to its absolute value
```

## Program 12.7 (continued)

```
;;IF_ABS num < 0
    cmp     num, 0
    jnl     ENDIF_ABS

;;THEN_ABS
;;  num := -num
    neg     num
  ENDIF_ABS:
ENDM
```

Program 12.8 illustrates use of the `AbsVal` macro. This program uses the `AbsVal` macro twice. The local label is replaced by unique labels each time it is expanded.

## Program 12.8

```
; Program 12.8        AbsMac.ASM
; Illustrate a macro with a local label.

; Get definitions of macros:
;   DefineStack     declares a stack segment
;   SetUpDS         establishes ds register
;   ExitToDos       terminates with return code 0
;   AbsVal          computes absolute value
INCLUDE MACROS.INC

DOSSEG

    DefineStack 100h

_DATA SEGMENT word public 'data'
    TestVal     dw      ?
    PromptMsg   db      "Enter number to test:"
    PromptLen   dw      $ - PromptMsg
    ResultMsg   db      "Absolute value is "
    ResultLen   dw      $ - ResultMsg
_DATA ENDS

_TEXT SEGMENT word public 'code'
    assume  cs: _TEXT
    extrn   PutStr: PROC, PutCrLf: PROC
    extrn   PutDec: PROC, GetDec: PROC

AbsMac:

    SetUpDS

; test #1: using TestVal variable
; print ("Enter number to test:")
    mov     cx, PromptLen
    mov     bx, offset PromptMsg
    call    PutStr
```

## 12.3 More About Macros

**Program 12.8 (continued)**

```
    ; read (TestVal)
        call    GetDec
        mov     TestVal, ax

    ; TestVal := ABS(TestVal)
        AbsVal  TestVal

    ; print ("Absolute value is", TestVal)
        mov     cx, ResultLen
        mov     bx, offset ResultMsg
        call    PutStr
        mov     ax, TestVal
        call    PutDec
        call    PutCrLf
        call    PutCrLf

    ; test #2: using ax
    ; print ("Enter number to test: ")
        mov     cx, PromptLen
        mov     bx, offset PromptMsg
        call    PutStr
        call    GetDec

    ; test value := ABS(test value)
        AbsVal  ax

    ; print ("Absolute value is", test value)
        mov     cx, ResultLen
        mov     bx, offset ResultMsg
        call    PutStr
        call    PutDec
        call    PutCrLf

        ExitToDos

_TEXT ENDS
END     AbsMac
```

### The Substitute Operator

In some situations, we need to include a parameter in the macro definition at a point where we want the argument to be substituted during expansion, yet some circumstance will prevent the assembler from doing so. This situation occurs when an argument is embedded in a string. For example, given the simple (but incorrect) macro defined as

```
DefChar MACRO ACode     ;;incorrect
        db      "ASCII ACode is ", ACode
ENDM
```

the assembler does not identify the parameter within the string. We would like

```
        DefChar 80
```

## Chapter 12 Macroinstructions

to be expanded as

```
        db      "ASCII 80 is ", 80
```

but instead the assembler expands this as

```
        db      "ASCII ACode is ", 80
```

The *substitute operator* directs the assembler to substitute the corresponding argument for the parameter that follows the operator, regardless of the context in which the parameter occurs. The substitute operator is the ampersand (&). To write this macro definition so that it works in the way we want, we put the substitute operator in front of the parameter within the string. See Program 12.9. Now, using the correct definition of DefChar, the line

```
        DefChar 80
```

will be expanded as

```
        db      "ASCII 80 is ", 80
```

---

### Program 12.9

```
; Program 12.9       DefChar
; Macro definition from file MACROS.INC

DefChar MACRO ACode
;;defines a string with an ASCII character and its code
        db      "ASCII &ACode is ", ACode
ENDM
```

---

If you study complicated nested macros, you will discover that it is sometimes necessary to use multiple substitute operators in succession to get the effect desired. We will not pursue examples of that here.

Program 12.10 contains two instances of the DefChar macro. It also introduces another assembler directive. We cannot use a name in the label field of a macro that will be expanded. That is, an attempt to use

```
PiMsg   DefChar 227
```

will not work. Instead we must define the label PiMsg with the LABEL directive, as

```
PiMsg   LABEL   byte
```

The operand specifies the size (byte, word, doubleword, and so on) associated with the label. The value of the label—the object with which the label is associated—is given on the line following the LABEL directive. See Program 12.10.

---

### Program 12.10

```
; Program 12.10      ASCIIMac.ASM
; Illustrate a simple macro with the substitute operator.
```

### 12.3 More About Macros

**Program 12.10 (continued)**

```
; Get definitions of macros:
;   DefineStack     declares a stack segment
;   SetUpDS         establishes ds register
;   ExitToDos       terminates with return code 0
;   DefChar         defines string containing an ASCII code
INCLUDE MACROS.INC

DOSSEG

        DefineStack 100h

_DATA SEGMENT word public 'data'
    HalfMsg     LABEL   byte
                DefChar 171
    HalfLen     dw      $ - HalfMsg
    ParaMsg     LABEL   byte
                DefChar 20
    ParaLen     dw      $ - ParaMsg
_DATA ENDS

_TEXT SEGMENT word public 'code'
        assume  cs: _TEXT
        extrn   PutStr: PROC, PutCrLf: PROC

ASCIIMac:

    SetUpDS

; display text generated by macros
        mov     cx, HalfLen
        mov     bx, offset HalfMsg
        call    PutStr
        call    PutCrLf

        mov     cx, ParaLen
        mov     bx, offset ParaMsg
        call    PutStr
        call    PutCrLf

    ExitToDos

_TEXT ENDS
END     ASCIIMac
```

In some situations, we need a second substitute operator immediately following the parameter. For example, consider the PutStr procedure. We want to simplify its use by writing a macro that puts the arguments into the registers and calls the procedure. We have generally used the convention that the text of a string is named ending in Msg, as in PromptMsg, and the length is named the same except ending in Len, as in PromptLen. We want to write a macro so that we can use just the base part of the name as a single argument, as in

```
PrintStr  Prompt
```

to move the arguments for the procedure call into the appropriate registers and call PutStr. The problem is that if we define the macro with a parameter named string, then &string is recognized, but &stringLen and &stringMsg are not. By putting a second substitute operator following the parameter name, the assembler can detect and isolate the parameter name. Thus &string&Msg is expanded into PromptMsg.

Program 12.11 shows two macros that use a second substitute operator this way. One of them is the PrintStr macro just discussed. There is one additional line in PrintStr: It declares PutStr as an external procedure. If the PrintStr macro is expanded more than once, some assemblers might warn about redefining PutStr. However, since the definition is identical each time, there really is no problem with this. Including the external declaration makes using the macro more convenient; the user (the application programmer, in this case) need not be concerned about such declarations, and only those routines actually called are declared.

**Program 12.11**

```
; Program 12.11    DefStr & PrintStr
; Macro definitions from file MACROS.INC

DefStr MACRO string,value
;;defines names for a string value and its length, for
;;use with the PutStr procedure and the PrintStr macro
    &string&Msg db      value
    &string&Len dw      $ - &string&Msg
ENDM

PrintStr MACRO string
;;sets up register arguments for PutStr and calls it
    extrn   PutStr: PROC
    mov     cx, &string&Len
    mov     bx, offset &string&Msg
    call    PutStr
ENDM
```

The other macro in Program 12.11 is DefStr. It carries the idea of generating both of the names used for the text and length of a string one step further: The line

DefStr Prompt, "Enter your age "

will be expanded by the assembler into the two lines of declarations

```
PromptMsg db       "Enter your age "
PromptLen dw       $ - PromptMsg
```

Program 12.12 uses these two macros to define and print two different strings. Additionally, it uses three of the other macros we have been employing, and PrintLn, which advances the output to a new line (much like Pascal's Writeln). The PrintLn macro is defined in the include file; it declares PutCrLf and then calls it. The include file also has definitions of PrintNum, ReadNum, and ReadChar, corresponding to PutDec,

## 12.3 More About Macros

GetDec, and GetChar. Note how using macros makes the code segment of this program shorter and more concise.

**Program 12.12**

```
; Program 12.12    StrngMac.ASM
; Illustrate macros with substitute operators before and
; after the parameter names.

; Get definitions of macros:
;    DefineStack    declares a stack segment
;    SetUpDS        establishes ds register
;    ExitToDos      terminates with return code 0
;    DefStr         defines string and its length
;    PrintStr       sets up arguments and call PutStr
;    PrintLn        advances output to new line
INCLUDE MACROS.INC

DOSSEG

   DefineStack 100h

_DATA SEGMENT word public 'data'
            DefStr Welcome, "Welcome to macro land ..."
            DefStr FareWell, "... farewell, programmer."
_DATA ENDS

_TEXT SEGMENT word public 'code'
      assume   cs: _TEXT

StrngMac:

   SetUpDS

; display messages
      PrintStr    Welcome
      PrintLn
      PrintStr    FareWell
      PrintLn

   ExitToDos

_TEXT ENDS
END      StrngMac
```

There are several other operators available for use in macros. Although not difficult, they are not pursued here.

### EXERCISES 12.3

1. Assemble Program 12.8, AbsMac.ASM, and obtain a listing file. Verify the substitution of the unique label for the local label.
▶2. Modify Program 12.8 (AbsMac.ASM) by removing the LOCAL directive, and assemble it. What error messages does the assembler give?

▶3. What data types (byte, word, doubleword) can the AbsVal macro work with? What operand types (register, memory, immediate, indirect) can the AbsVal macro work with? Modify Program 12.8, and execute it to verify your answers.

▶4. Combine the DefChar macro of Program 12.9 with the DefStr macro of Program 12.11. Your new DefChar macro should define the string and its length.

▶5. Write a macro that converts a word containing a 2-digit hexadecimal number as a character string into an unsigned byte value. For example

    HexToByte "B4"

should convert the characters "B" and "4" into the unsigned value B4h in the AL register.

6. Consider the claim that Program 12.12 looks as if it is written in a language "higher" than assembly language because of its use of macros. Discuss the issue, noting that one of the attributes of a high-level language is that statements in it represent potentially many machine instructions.

## 12.4 CONDITIONAL ASSEMBLY

Macros provide a means of adding significant extensions to assembly language. Another powerful feature of assemblers is conditional assembly, which provides for assembly-time execution of control structures that affect the code generated. The discussion begins with an example that uses information on the command line to control the assembly process.

### Using Assembler Symbols

Consider writing a program that is to run on machines that use either 8086 or 80286 processors. We might use some of the newer instructions of the 80286 where possible; however, we must ensure that the program will run on an 8086. To do so requires two versions of the program: one for the 8086 and one for the 80286. **Conditional assembly** allows us to have just one source file, from which we can have the assembler generate two object files (in two different runs of the assembler, of course): one for the 8086 and another for the 80286.

We can control which version is assembled by a symbol we define on the command line. Such a symbol is defined following the /D option, as in

MASM /DProcModel=286 progname;

The syntax is similar with other assemblers. In this example, the symbol ProcModel is defined and assigned the value 286. We can use this to control the generation of 80286 instructions in our object file.

The default behavior of the assembler is to generate only 8086 instructions (the 8088 instructions are identical to those of the 8086). If our program is to generate instructions for the 80286, we must include a directive to the assembler to specifically allow that. The directive that does so is .286. This directive must be written before the beginning of any segment in which code specific to the 80286 is written.

Before we get to the rest of this example, we need to introduce an 80286-specific instruction. Consider imul. In the 8086 formats, the destination operand is implied as either AX or DX:AX, and the source operand is either a register or memory operand. If

## 12.4 Conditional Assembly

we want to multiply the value of a word variable named Num by 12 without losing the value in the DX register, we might write

```
    push    dx
    mov     ax, 12
    imul    Num
    mov     Num, ax
    pop     dx
```

Here, we save DX on the stack before imul and restore it afterward. There are other formats for imul on the 80186 and newer processors. In one of these, we can multiply any register by an immediate operand. The equivalent sequence using this imul instruction can be written

```
    mov     ax, Num
    imul    ax, 12
    mov     Num, ax
```

Not only is this sequence shorter, it executes faster than the preceding version. However, it is available only on 80186 and newer processors.

Now, we reach the conditional assembly part of this example. If we define the symbol ProcModel on the command line, we can have the assembler test its value and assemble the appropriate sequence of instructions. The IF, ELSE, and ENDIF directives implement this, as in

```
IF ProcModel EQ 286
    (instructions for 80286)
ELSE
    (instructions for 8086)
ENDIF
```

Note the use of EQ to represent a test for equality in the condition of the IF directive. See Program 12.13. If ProcModel is defined and has value 286, the condition in the IF directive is true, and the sequence following it is assembled; if ProcModel is defined and has any other value, the condition is false, and the sequence following ELSE is assembled instead; and if ProcModel is not defined, the assembler generates an error message and does not produce an object file.

## Program 12.13

```
;  Program 12.13     MulBy12.ASM
;  Illustrate conditional assembly based on a symbol
;  defined on the command line.

;  Get definitions of macros:
;     DefineStack     declares a stack segment
;     SetUpDS         establishes ds register
;     ExitToDos       terminates with return code 0
;     DefStr          defines a string and its length
;     PrintStr        sets up arguments and calls PutStr
;     PrintNum        set up arguments and calls PutDec
;     PrintLn         calls PutCrLf
;     ReadNum         calls GetDec and saves value returned
INCLUDE MACROS.INC
```

## Program 12.13 (continued)

```
DOSSEG

    DefineStack 100h

_DATA SEGMENT word public 'data'
            DefStr   Prompt, "Enter number to multiply "
            DefStr   Result, "Twelve times that is "
    TestVal  dw       ?
_DATA ENDS

    .286    ;enable instructions for 80286 processors

_TEXT SEGMENT word public 'code'
      assume  cs: _TEXT

Mul12:

    SetUpDS

; read TestVal
    PrintStr    Prompt
    ReadNum     TestVal

; ResultVal := 12 * TestVal
    IF ProcModel EQ 286
        mov     ax, TestVal     ;80286 sequence ...
        imul    ax, 12
        mov     TestVal, ax
    ELSE
        push    dx              ;8086 sequence ...
        mov     ax, 12
        imul    TestVal
        mov     TestVal, ax
        pop     dx
    ENDIF

; print ("Twelve times that is ", TestVal)
    PrintLn
    PrintStr    Result
    PrintNum    TestVal
    PrintLn

    ExitToDos

_TEXT ENDS
END     Mul12
```

When assembling this program, we must be careful to include the /D option with ProcModel= and a value. If we omit it, the assembler fails. We can provide a default definition of ProcModel, should this field be omitted. We should not, however, simply write

```
ProcModel equ    8086
```

## 12.4 Conditional Assembly

in the source file; if the user then includes the /D option in the command, the assembler would interpret this directive as redefining a symbol, which is not allowed. Instead, we need a way to test whether the user defined the symbol ProcModel on the command line.

The IFDEF and IFNDEF directives test whether a symbol is defined. We can use an IFNDEF directive for our needs here and can write the conditional as

```
IFNDEF ProcModel
   ProcModel equ        8086
ENDIF
```

before the code segment. With this in our program, ProcModel will default to 8086 unless the user includes the /D option with ProcModel and a value as part of the command to invoke the assembler. The conditional above is included in Program 12.14.

### Program 12.14

```
; Program 12.14      MulBy12C.ASM
; Illustrate conditional assembly based on a symbol
; defined on the command line. If the symbol is omitted,
; this program provides a default value.

; Get definitions of macros:
;    DefineStack     declares a stack segment
;    SetUpDS         establishes ds register
;    ExitToDos       terminates with return code 0
;    DefStr          defines a string and its length
;    PrintStr        sets up arguments and calls PutStr
;    PrintNum        set up arguments and calls PutDec
;    PrintLn         calls PutCrLf
;    ReadNum         calls GetDec and saves value returned
INCLUDE MACROS.INC

DOSSEG

    DefineStack 100h

_DATA SEGMENT word public 'data'
            DefStr   Prompt, "Enter number to multiply "
            DefStr   Result, "Twelve times that is "
    TestVal     dw      ?
_DATA ENDS

    .286    ;enable instructions for 80286 processors

IFNDEF ProcModel
   ProcModel    equ     8086
ENDIF

_TEXT SEGMENT word public 'code'
    assume   cs: _TEXT

Mul12:

    SetUpDS
```

**Program 12.14 (continued)**

```
    ; read TestVal
        PrintStr    Prompt
        ReadNum     TestVal

    ; ResultVal := 12 * TestVal
        IF ProcModel EQ 286
            mov     ax, TestVal     ;80286 sequence ...
            imul    ax, 12
            mov     TestVal, ax
        ELSE
            push    dx              ;8086 sequence ...
            mov     ax, 12
            imul    TestVal
            mov     TestVal, ax
            pop     dx
        ENDIF

    ; print ("Twelve times that is ", TestVal)
        PrintLn
        PrintStr    Result
        PrintNum    TestVal
        PrintLn

        ExitToDos

    _TEXT ENDS
    END     Mul12
```

There are other ways to pass symbols to the assembler and to control the translation process. They will not be pursued here.

## Conditionals in Macros

We can use conditional assembly within macro definitions to control how a macro is expanded based on the value of a (constant) parameter to the macro. In high-level languages, conditions—as Boolean expressions—are used to control selection structures and repetition structures; we can have these structures within a macro definition too.

It should be clear from the last examples that we can write IF, ELSE, and ENDIF directives to control the assembler. Nothing prevents their use in macros. We can also have the condition in the IF directive test the value of an argument to the macro. An example is given shortly.

We can also build repetition into a macro definition. For example, to shift the contents of a register or variable in memory more than one bit position, either we must load the shift count into CL and use that as the second operand, or we must execute a number of shifts with 1 as the second operand. A macro that generates a variable number of shift

## 12.4 Conditional Assembly

instructions can be written as

```
ShLeft MACRO reg, count
    REPT    count
      shl     reg, 1
    ENDM
ENDM
```

The new directive, REPT, has the assembler generate the text following it, up to the matching ENDM directive, the number of times specified by its operand. Thus

```
    ShLeft  bx, 3
```

expands to

```
    shl     bx, 1
    shl     bx, 1
    shl     bx, 1
```

Note that the first ENDM terminates the REPT directive, and the second terminates the macro definition.

Even though it is useful, the ShLeft macro could be better. First, we want to use a selection structure so that if the shift count is large, CL is used for the shift count with a single shift instruction. Second, we want one macro to work with any of the shift and rotate instructions; we prefer to not define a separate macro for each one. Both of these features—the selection structure and the use of any shift instruction—are easy to implement. See Program 12.15.

### Program 12.15

```
; Program 12.15      RepShft
; Macro definition from file MACROS.INC

RepShft MACRO op,reg,count
;;shifts register reg the number of bits specified by count,
;;using the shift instruction specified as the first parameter.
    IF count LE 4
      REPT count              ;;generate up to 4 copies of
        op      reg, 1        ;;   one-bit shift instruction
      ENDM
    ELSE
      mov     cl, count       ;;generate one instruction
      op      reg, cl         ;;   with shift count in cl
    ENDIF
ENDM
```

The RepShft macro has three parameters: the mnemonic of the shift or rotate operation, the register or variable in memory to shift, and the shift count. If the shift count is 4 or less, the macro uses REPT to generate a number of 1-bit shifts; otherwise, it moves the shift count into CL and generates just one shift instruction. Thus

```
    RepShft rol,  ax, 2
```

expands to

```
    rol     ax, 1
    rol     ax, 1
```

whereas

```
    RepShft sar, NoPages, 5
```

expands to

```
    mov     cl, 5
    sar     NoPages, cl
```

Program 12.16 tests this macro with three expansions. When using this macro, we modify our indentation scheme; one approach is used in Program 12.16, in which we unindent by two spaces and write the mnemonic one space following the macro name.

## Program 12.16

```
; Program 12.16     Shifts.ASM
; Illustrate use of RepShft macro.

; Get definitions of macros:
;   DefineStack     declares a stack segment
;   SetUpDS         establishes ds register
;   ExitToDos       terminates with return code 0
;   DefStr          defines a string and its length
;   PrintStr        sets up arguments and calls PutStr
;   PrintNum        set up arguments and calls PutDec
;   ReadNum         calls GetDec and saves value returned
;   PrintLn         advances output to a new line
;   RepShft         generates multiple shifts or shift w/ CL
INCLUDE MACROS.INC

DOSSEG

    DefineStack 100h

_DATA SEGMENT word public 'data'
            DefStr  Prompt, "Enter a number: "
            DefStr  Result8, " x 8 = "
            DefStr  Result32, " x 32 = "
            DefStr  Result16, " / 16 = "
    Num         dw      ?
    NumX8       dw      ?
    NumX32      dw      ?
    NumBy16     dw      ?
_DATA ENDS

_TEXT SEGMENT word public 'code'
    assume  cs: _TEXT
    extrn   PutStr: PROC        ;PrintStr does not define this

Shifts:

    SetUpDS
```

### 12.4 Conditional Assembly

**Program 12.16 (continued)**

```
        ; read a test value as input
            PrintStr    Prompt
            ReadNum     Num
            PrintLn

        ; NumX8 := Num * 8
            mov         ax, Num
      RepShft sal,      ax, 3
            mov         NumX8, ax

        ; NumX32 := Num * 32
            mov         ax, Num
            mov         NumX32, ax
      RepShft sal,      NumX32, 5

        ; NumBy16 := Num / 16
            mov         ax, Num
      RepShft sar,      ax, 4
            mov         NumBy16, ax

        ; print (Num, "x 8 = ", NumX8)
            PrintNum    Num
            PrintStr    Result8
            PrintNum    NumX8
            PrintLn

        ; print (Num, "x 32 = ", NumX32)
            PrintNum    Num
            PrintStr    Result32
            PrintNum    NumX32
            PrintLn

        ; print (Num, "/ 16 = ", NumBy16)
            PrintNum    Num
            PrintStr    Result16
            PrintNum    NumBy16
            PrintLn

            ExitToDos

_TEXT ENDS
END     Shifts
```

---

The `RepShft` macro uses 4 in the condition to determine whether to generate multiple 1-bit shifts or one multiple-bit shift. Why 4? There are two things to consider: memory required for the instructions and the time required to execute them. On an 8086 processor, one multiple-bit shift of a register will always take longer to execute than the equivalent sequence of 1-bit shifts; the memory used for three or more 1-bit shifts is larger than the memory used for a mov and one multiple-bit shift. Four seems like a fair compromise. On an 80286 processor, one multiple-bit shift of a register will be faster (including the

**440** Chapter 12 Macroinstructions

mov to set up CL) than separate 1-bit shifts if the shift count is more than 7; the memory requirements are the same as for the 8086. Four again seems like a fair compromise.

## EXERCISES 12.4

1. Assemble Program 12.13, and obtain a listing file. Verify that using the /D option to define ProcModel does control the sequence of instructions generated. Also verify that just one sequence is indeed generated.
2. What happens when assembling Program 12.13 (or 12.14) if the .286 directive is deleted? Try assembling with /DProcModel=286 and /DProcModel=8086.
▶3. Modify the RepShft macro so that it examines the symbol Opt specified on the command line. If Opt is 'size', the macro should generate the multiple-bit shift whenever the count is 3 or more; if Opt is 'speed', the macro should generate a sequence of 1-bit shifts; if Opt is 'both' or not defined, RepShft should work as defined in Program 12.15.
▶4. Propose and implement a macro that uses the REPT directive for something other than shift instructions.
▶5. Propose and implement a macro that uses the IF and ELSE directives for something other than processor model or shift instructions.

## KEY POINTS

- A macroinstruction, or more simply a macro, is a named fragment of program text.
- Macros must be defined within each module before the first use of the macro. Definitions can contain any text, including instructions, directives, operands, labels, and conditionals.
- The assembler replaces each occurrence of the macro identifier in a program with the text of that macro's definition.
- Comments in macros can be included in each expansion on the listing file or restricted so that they appear only in the macro definition.
- Macros can have parameters, which are replaced by argument values during expansion.
- Macros can have local labels, which are replaced by unique labels during expansion.
- There are a number of operators that can be used within macro definitions to control parameter substitution and evaluation during assembly.
- Most assemblers can import text from a file into the source file being processed during translation. This facility is useful for managing common data and macro definitions.
- Macros and subprograms are both useful in larger programming projects, but their differences are very important. Each instance of a macro in a program is expanded into a distinct copy of the macro definition; each invocation of a subprogram uses the same copy of the subprogram. Each execution of a macro introduces no overhead, whereas calling a subprogram involves passing parameters and transferring control twice. Thus, macros require more memory, and subprograms require more time.
- Conditional assembly provides assembly-time execution of control structures that determine what is assembled. The values that control the assembler's behavior can be defined on the command line or in the source program.
- Conditional assembly can be combined with macros.

## PC SYSTEM SUMMARY

- Macro definitions are written between MACRO and ENDM directives. They can include any text.
- Comments in a macro that start with one semicolon are included in the listing of the expansion; those that start with two semicolons appear only within the definition.
- The INCLUDE directive causes the assembler to process the contents of a separate file as if it appeared in the program. Include files are useful in organizing macro definitions.
- The LOCAL directive defines a label as local to the macro; in each expansion of the macro, local labels are replaced by unique labels of the form ??hhhh, where hhhh is a 4-digit hexadecimal number.
- The substitute operator, &, forces the assembler to substitute an argument in a context where it might not recognize a parameter otherwise. In some contexts, a second substitute operator is needed following the parameter.
- The LABEL directive can define a label in contexts where writing a label is not allowed, such as with macro identifiers within a program. The label so defined is associated with the object defined on the line following the LABEL directive.
- Symbols used in conditional assembly can be defined on the command line that invokes the assembler.
- Conditional assembly selection structures use the IF, ELSE, and ENDIF directives; IFDEF and IFNDEF can be used in place of IF to test whether a symbol is defined.
- Conditional assembly repetition structures use the REPT and ENDM directives. REPT takes an integer operand that specifies how many times the text between REPT and ENDM is expanded.

Directives presented in this chapter:

Macros
- MACRO — begins definition of macro
- ENDM — ends definition of macro
- INCLUDE — inserts contents of file into the source program
- LABEL — defines a label

Conditional assembly
- IF, ELSE, ENDIF — define assembly-time selection structures
- IFDEF — tests whether a symbol is defined
- IFNDEF — tests whether a symbol is not defined
- REPT, ENDM — define assembly-time repetition structures

# 13

# Arrays

- **Representation**
- **Addressing**
- **Operations**
- **Arrays as Arguments**
- **Multi-Dimensional Arrays**
- **The SET Data Type**

One of the simplest and most commonly used data structures is the array. Many problems that involve simple, ordered collections of data can be solved readily using arrays.

The use of an array requires being able to access any element at any time by referring to its position within the array. This feat is easily accomplished with indexed addressing. In this chapter, how to define an array and how to access it using indexed addressing are presented. Operations involving every element or just individual elements are considered, as is passing an array as an argument to a subprogram.

Some problems require using arrays with two or more dimensions. We examine the ways in which arrays with two or more dimensions are represented and the means by which individual elements of such arrays are accessed. In the final section, one means by which sets can be implemented as arrays of binary values is briefly considered.

## 13.1 REPRESENTATION

A one-dimensional array is a structure that contains values of one data type, ordered so that individual elements can be accessed by their relative position in the structure. The relative position is written in brackets or parentheses and is called a **subscript**. For example, in Pascal an array of ten integers can be defined as

```
VAR  List: ARRAY [1..10] OF Integer;
```

Individual elements of the array can be accessed using a subscript written in brackets, as in this fragment for finding the sum of the ten elements:

```
Sum := 0;
FOR Subscr := 1 TO 10 DO
  Sum := Sum + List[Subscr];
```

Consider first how arrays are represented in memory and how they are declared in assembly language.

## Declaring Arrays

The elements of the array declared above have subscripts from 1 to 10. This arrangement suggests that the ten values could be stored in a block of ten contiguous words of memory and that the subscript could specify which word in the block an element occupies. In assembly language, a block of ten words is used to store the array, and the label List is assigned to the first word of the block.

High-level-language declarations of arrays include the data type of the elements and the range of subscripts. The subscripts may be restricted to a subrange of integers, or they may be an ordinal data type. The range of subscripts may be specified as just an upper bound with an implied lower bound (usually 0 or 1) or as explicit lower and upper bounds.

Assembly-language declarations of arrays include the size of the elements and the number of elements in the array. The programmer must convert between ranges of subscripts and number of elements. Consider first the special case of 0 as the lower bound. Data defined as

```
VAR   List: ARRAY [0..50] OF Integer
```

is stored in a block of memory that would be defined in assembly language as

```
    List        dw      51 dup (?)
```

Note that $N + 1$ words of memory are needed for an array with a lower bound of 0 and an upper bound of $N$, assuming each element requires one word. Modern practice is to name constants, so these declarations are rewritten in Pascal as

```
CONST  HiBound = 50;
VAR    List: ARRAY [0..HiBound] OF Integer;
```

and in assembly language as

```
    HiBound     equ     50
    List        dw      HiBound+1 dup (?)
```

Consider accessing an element of such an array. For now it is desirable merely to determine the displacement in bytes of an element of the array. For an array of words with a lower bound of zero, the $N$th element is $2N$ bytes from the beginning of the array; the quantity $2N$ is the needed displacement. To access List[5], List+10 is used as an operand.

## Arrays with Explicit Lower Bounds

It is sometimes easier to use arrays with a lower subscript bound other than zero. Consider an example of reading vehicle registration data and counting how many of the registered cars were built in each of the years 1950 through 1992. In Pascal an array of counters can be defined for this problem as

```
CONST  FirstYear = 1950;
       LastYear  = 1992;
VAR    Cars: ARRAY [FirstYear..LastYear] OF Integer;
```

The year a car was built can be used directly as the subscript when counting. In assembly language, this array can be declared as

```
FirstYr    equ    1950
LastYr     equ    1992
ListSize   equ    LastYr-FirstYr+1
Cars       dw     ListSize dup (?)
```

An expression is used to calculate the number of elements in the array; if the program is later revised to work with a different range of years, only the first two directives may need to be changed.

Consider accessing an element of this array. For now, only the displacement in bytes of an element of the array needs to be determined. The displacement of the $N$th element of the array is $2N$ bytes from the beginning of the array. But what is meant by $N$? In the following discussion, Cars[Year] is written to refer to an element of the array as defined in Pascal, where Year should be in the range from 1950 to 1992 in order to be meaningful. CARS[YEAR] is written to refer to an element of the array as defined in assembly language, where YEAR is the displacement in bytes of Cars[Year] from Cars[FirstYear]. That is, Cars[1950] and CARS[0] refer to the same element, as do Cars[1951] and CARS[2], Cars[1952] and CARS[4], and so on. The formula for computing the displacement YEAR that corresponds to Cars[Year] is

$$\text{YEAR} = (\text{Year} - \text{FirstYear} + 1) \times 2$$

The factor of two adjusts for word elements.

This formula can be written more generally; consider an array defined as

```
LoBound    equ    m
HiBound    equ    n
ListSize   equ    HiBound-LoBound+1
SomeList   d_     ListSize dup (?)
```

where m and n are constants and d_ represents a directive for declaring the size of each element. To access an element with subscript Sub in the range from LoBound to HiBound, the displacement can be computed as

$$\text{displacement} = (\text{Sub} - \text{LoBound}) \times \text{element\_size}$$

where element_size is 1 for arrays defined with db, 2 with dw, 4 with dd, and so on. The displacement and the offset of the start of the array are then specified in an instruction.

### Arrays with Initial Values

In some high-level languages it is possible to specify initial values for the elements of an array. For example, in FORTRAN the statements

```
INTEGER WKSTYPE (4), COUNTS(1900:2000)
DATA WKSTYPE /1000, 2103, 2104, 4402/
DATA COUNTS /1001*0/
```

can be written to define an array named WKSTYPE containing four integers, and an array named COUNTS containing 1001 integers. WKSTYPE(1) is initialized to 1000,

WKSTYPE(2) to 2103, WKSTYPE(3) to 2104, and WKSTYPE(4) to 4402. All 1001 elements of COUNTS are initialized to zero. The same thing can be accomplished in assembly language (assuming the FORTRAN integers are stored as doublewords) using the statements

```
WksType    dd    1000,2103,2104,4402
LoCount    equ   1900
HiCount    equ   2000
CountSize  equ   HiCount-LoCount+1
Counts     dd    CountSize dup (0)
```

In this section, it's been shown how one-dimensional arrays are declared in assembly language. It's also been shown how to compute the displacement in bytes of an arbitrary element of an array and to initialize the array in the declaration. In the next section, the way to use the displacements to access individual elements of an array is examined.

## EXERCISES 13.1

1. For each of the following, write the assembly-language declarations according to the guidelines presented in this section:
   (a) an array of bytes, subscripts range 0 to 100
   (b) an array of words, subscripts range $-30$ to $+30$
   (c) an array of bytes, subscripts range 750 to 900
   (d) an array of quadwords, subscripts range 3 to 31
   (e) an array of words, subscripts range from 60 to 100

2. For each of the arrays in Exercise 1, write the formula for the displacement in bytes of the element with subscript Sub, where Sub is in the given subscript range.

3. Write a fragment of 8086 assembly-language code to compute the displacement of an element in an array, using
   $$\text{displacement} = (\text{Sub} - \text{LoBound}) \times \text{element\_size}$$
   Assume element_size is defined in an equ directive.

4. The size of an element of an array is often a power of two (a word is two bytes, a doubleword is four bytes, and a quadword is eight bytes). How can this fact be exploited when computing displacements?

5. For each of the arrays in Exercise 1, rewrite part of the declaration so that every element is initialized to zero.

## 13.2 ADDRESSING

Consider the problem of finding the sum of a list of ten integers stored in ten contiguous words of memory beginning at List and saving the sum in a word labeled Sum. How can a program fragment to accomplish this task be written? Several solutions are pursued in this section using direct, indirect, and indexed addressing techniques.

### Using Direct Addresses with Arrays

A simple solution is to write instructions to add the ten values to Sum one at a time, using a direct address for each integer. This approach, illustrated in Program 13.1, is easy to understand and executes quickly. However, it is neither elegant nor easily modified to allow the sum of a longer list to be computed.

## Program 13.1

```
; Program 13.1      AddList.ASM
; Add a list of ten integers together.

; DOS function and status parameters
  DosFunc     equ      21h
  ExitToDos   equ      4Ch
  NoErrors    equ      00h

DOSSEG

_STACK SEGMENT para stack 'stack'
            dw       100h dup (?)
_STACK ENDS

_DATA SEGMENT word public 'data'
  List        dw       5,10,15,20,15,10,5,3,6,9
  Sum         dw       ?
  ResultMsg   db       "Sum is "
  ResultLen   dw       $ - ResultMsg
_DATA ENDS

_TEXT SEGMENT word public 'code'
      assume  cs: _TEXT
      extrn   PutStr: PROC, PutCrLf: PROC, PutDec: PROC

AddList:

; set up ds register to point to _DATA
      mov     ax, seg _DATA
      mov     ds, ax
      assume  ds: _DATA

; Sum := sum of ten integers in List
      mov     ax, List          ;Sum := 5
      add     ax, List + 2      ;     + 10
      add     ax, List + 4      ;     + 15
      add     ax, List + 6      ;     + 20
      add     ax, List + 8      ;     + 15
      add     ax, List + 10     ;     + 10
      add     ax, List + 12     ;     + 5
      add     ax, List + 14     ;     + 3
      add     ax, List + 16     ;     + 6
      add     ax, List + 18     ;     + 9
      mov     Sum, ax

; print ("Sum is ", Sum)
      mov     cx, ResultLen
      mov     bx, offset ResultMsg
      call    PutStr
      mov     ax, Sum
      call    PutDec
      call    PutCrLf
```

## 13.2 Addressing

**Program 13.1 (continued)**

```
; exit to DOS
      mov     ah, ExitToDos
      mov     al, NoErrors
      int     DosFunc

_TEXT ENDS
END     AddList
```

An important observation about Program 13.1 is that the nine add instructions differ from each other in only one operand field. The variation from one add instruction to the next is simple and regular: The offset increases by 2. It is worthwhile to consider ways of writing an add instruction with an operand that has a variable offset and then executing it in a loop.

### Using Indirect Addresses with Arrays

Consider using an indirect pointer to access the ten integers in List. The pointer can be initialized with the offset of the element, and on each iteration a value of 2 can be added to the pointer so that it refers to the next integer in the list. This concept is implemented in Program 13.2.

**Program 13.2**

```
; Program 13.2      AddPtr.ASM
; Add a list of ten integers together.
;    Uses indirect addressing.

; DOS function and status parameters
  DosFunc     equ     21h
  ExitToDos   equ     4Ch
  NoErrors    equ     00h

DOSSEG

_STACK SEGMENT para stack 'stack'
            dw      100h dup (?)
_STACK ENDS

_DATA SEGMENT word public 'data'
  List        dw      5,10,15,20,15,10,5,3,6,9
  Sum         dw      ?
  ResultMsg   db      "Sum is "
  ResultLen   dw      $ - ResultMsg
_DATA ENDS

_TEXT SEGMENT word public 'code'
     assume   cs: _TEXT
     extrn    PutStr: PROC, PutCrLf: PROC, PutDec: PROC
```

**Program 13.2 (continued)**

```
        AddPtr:

        ; set up ds register to point to _DATA
                mov     ax, seg _DATA
                mov     ds, ax
                assume  ds: _DATA

        ; SUM := sum of ten integers in List
                sub     ax, ax          ;Sum := 0
                mov     bx, offset List ;set up pointer

        ; FOR01 cx := 10 TO 1 STEP -1
                mov     cx, 10
        DO01:
        ;       sum (in ax) := sum + next element of LIST
                add     ax, [bx]

        ;       advance pointer and repeat
                add     bx, 2
                loop    DO01
        ; ENDFOR01

        ; save sum (in ax) in Sum
                mov     Sum, ax

        ; print ("Sum is ", Sum)
                mov     cx, ResultLen
                mov     bx, offset ResultMsg
                call    PutStr
                mov     ax, Sum
                call    PutDec
                call    PutCrLf

        ; exit to DOS
                mov     ah, ExitToDos
                mov     al, NoErrors
                int     DosFunc

        _TEXT ENDS
        END     AddPtr
```

The instructions

```
        sub     ax, ax
        mov     bx, offset List
```

clear the AX register for use as the sum and set up the pointer to List in the BX register. The body of the FOR loop consists of just two instructions: one to add an element of the list to the sum and the other to modify the indirect pointer. During the first iteration, BX has the offset of the first word of List. The instruction

```
        add     ax, [bx]
```

### 13.2 Addressing

adds the first element of the list to the sum in AX. The instruction

    add      bx, 2

advances the indirect pointer to the next word of List. During the first iteration, it changes BX to the offset of the second word of List. During the second iteration, these instructions add the second word of List to the sum in AX and change BX to the offset of the third word. This process continues through ten iterations.

One more observation about the last program: When the loop terminates, the indirect pointer refers to the location following the last word of List. Rather than controlling the loop with the CX register that counts from 10 to 1, the indirect pointer could be used as the loop control variable, varying from the offset of the first word of List to the offset of the last word of List. Doing so combines advancing the pointer with incrementing the loop control variable. The algorithm becomes

```
SUM := 0
FOR POINTER := offset of first word TO offset of last word
DO
   SUM := SUM + [POINTER]
ENDFOR
```

Implementation of this algorithm has been left as an exercise.

## Index Registers and Indexed Addressing

Another way to combine advancing a pointer into the list with incrementing the loop control variable is to leave the loop control variable in the program and add it to the offset of List in the add instruction. But how can the effective address of the add instruction be adjusted based on the value of the loop control variable? Since List+4 and List+6 are valid operand forms, something like

    add      ax, LIST+[cx]    ;not legal

might seem worth trying, but there are two problems with this attempt. The CX register varies from ten to one. Looking back at Program 13.1, it can be seen that the integer added to the effective address of List should vary from 0 to 18 in steps of 2. This first problem can be solved by subtracting CX from 10 and multiplying the result by 2. The second problem is that the CX register cannot be used as shown in the above instruction—there is no way to code this in the 8086 format. However, index registers can be used in a way that accomplishes the same objective.

An **index register** provides a displacement that can be added during the computation of an effective address. The 8086 has two index registers, named SI and DI. The "I" in the mnemonic stands for index, while "S" and "D" stand for source and destination. These registers have specific purposes in some operations on strings, but either can be used for the purposes of this chapter.

Any arithmetic operation that can be performed with the four general registers (AX, BX, CX, and DX) can also be performed with the index registers. There are no special instructions to manipulate index registers. Assemblers for the 8086 allow indexing to be specified in more than one way; brackets may be used around an index register that modifies an operand coded as a displacement. That is, the instruction

```
add     Result[si], ax
```

specifies indexing of the first operand. The effective address of this first operand is the sum of the effective address of Result and the contents of the SI register when the instruction is executed. The similarity to subscripts in high-level languages is intentional. Unlike high-level-language index expressions, however, only an index register can be included in the brackets.

Consider again the problem of adding a list of ten integers. An index register can be used to vary the effective address of the source operand of an add instruction from the first element of List to the last. Such an instruction is written

```
add     ax, List[si]
```

When this instruction is executed, the contents of the SI register are added to the offset of List, and the result is added to the shifted DS segment register to determine the address of the operand. Thus, when SI is 0, the instruction is effectively

```
add     ax, List
```

When SI is 2, the instruction is effectively

```
add     ax, List+2
```

and so on.

Program 13.3 uses indexing to add the ten integers of List. It uses CX to control the FOR loop and varies the SI register from 0 to 18 in steps of 2. Other common operations on arrays, using indexing, are examined in the next section.

## Program 13.3

```
;  Program 13.3        AddIndex.ASM
;  Add a list of ten integers together.
;    Uses indexed addressing.

;  DOS function and status parameters
    DosFunc     equ     21h
    ExitToDos   equ     4Ch
    NoErrors    equ     00h

DOSSEG

_STACK SEGMENT para stack 'stack'
            dw      100h dup (?)
_STACK ENDS

_DATA SEGMENT word public 'data'
    List        dw      5,10,15,20,15,10,5,3,6,9
    Sum         dw      ?
    ResultMsg   db      "Sum is "
    ResultLen   dw      $ - ResultMsg
_DATA ENDS
```

## 13.2 Addressing

**Program 13.3 (continued)**

```
        _TEXT SEGMENT word public 'code'
            assume  cs: _TEXT
            extrn   PutStr: PROC, PutCrLf: PROC, PutDec: PROC

AddIndex:

; set up ds register to point to _DATA
            mov     ax, seg _DATA
            mov     ds, ax
            assume  ds: _DATA

; Sum := sum of ten integers in List
            sub     ax, ax          ;Sum := 0
            mov     si, ax          ;index := 0

; FOR01 cx := 10 TO 1 STEP -1
            mov     cx, 10

  DO01:
;   sum (in ax) := sum + List[index]
            add     ax, List[si]

;   advance index and repeat
            add     si, 2
            loop    DO01
; ENDFOR01

; save sum (in ax) in Sum
            mov     Sum, ax

; print ("Sum is ", Sum)
            mov     cx, ResultLen
            mov     bx, offset ResultMsg
            call    PutStr
            mov     ax, Sum
            call    PutDec
            call    PutCrLf

; exit to DOS
            mov     ah, ExitToDos
            mov     al, NoErrors
            int     DosFunc

        _TEXT ENDS
        END     AddIndex
```

## EXERCISES 13.2

1. Compare the memory requirements of Programs 13.1–13.3. How do the requirements change as the list is increased to 20 or 30 or more elements? Which programs are most affected by the size of the list? Which are least affected?

**452**  Chapter 13 Arrays

2. How could a computer support an operand expression like `List+[Count]`, where `Count` is a variable? How is this expression different from `List[indexreg]`? How does the difference affect the machine representation of the instruction?

3. In many computers that use one-operand instructions, a load instruction with an indexed address for the operand is written

   ```
   LDA     VALUE,X
   ```

   where X specifies the index register. This syntax does not work with assembly languages that allow two or more operands. Why not? Give an example that illustrates the problem.

▶4. Write a program that finds the sum of a list of integers using a loop in which the pointer to the elements of the array also controls the loop, as outlined in this section.

## 13.3 OPERATIONS

In this section, operations that access every element in an orderly way are first considered, followed by those that access just one selected element.

### Processing a Whole Array

In some programming languages, selected operations can be performed on every element of an array by using the array name as part of a statement; in other languages, these operations must be written using a loop in which the operation is performed on one element at a time. Unless equipped with special vector or array processors, computers actually perform the operations on one element at a time in both cases.

Some possible operations on all elements of an array are

- Clearing an array to zeros
- Reading an array
- Displaying an array
- Finding the sum of all elements in an array

The sum of the elements in an array was already considered in Section 13.2, so it will not be considered further.

For illustration purposes, consider an arbitrary array of words defined using the directives

```
LoBound     equ     m
HiBound     equ     n
ListSize    equ     HiBound-LoBound+1
List        dw      ListSize dup (?)
```

where m and n are constants.

To clear every element of an array to 0, consider the program fragment

```
Index := 0
FOR Subscr := LoBound TO HiBound
DO
  List[Index] := 0
  Index := Index + 2
ENDFOR
```

## 13.3 Operations

Note the use of Index to represent a displacement from the start of the array in memory and Subscr to represent a subscript of an element of the array. Since the subscript serves no real purpose other than to document that every element is being accessed, the above loop is easier to implement if the FOR statement is rewritten as

FOR cx := ListSize TO 1 STEP -1

In assembly language, an index register (SI or DI) can be used for Index; this idea is written as

```
; index := 0
      sub     si, si
; FOR01  cx := ListSize TO 1 STEP -1
      mov     cx, ListSize
  DO01:
;     List[Index] := 0
      mov     List[si], 0
      add     si, 2
      loop    DO01
; ENDFOR01
```

Values for every element of the array can be read, assuming an appropriate prompt has already been printed, by simply replacing the mov instruction following DO01 with the pair of instructions

```
      call    GetDec
      mov     List[si], ax
```

To insert a prompt that prints the current index in the loop would require running the loop control variable in the same direction as the displacements.

Every element of the array can be displayed simply by replacing the mov instruction following DO01 with the pair of instructions

```
      mov     ax, List[si]
      call    PutDec
```

Of course, the output will not be very neat unless some text or spaces are also included with the numbers.

It is not a coincidence that the same loop structure and array operand are useful in all of the examples so far: Once a method to process every element of an array in order is available, it should be able to be used in many tasks involving every element of an array in order.

A slightly more complex problem is that of sorting an array of values into ascending order. A bubble sort can be used, which requires accessing every adjacent pair of elements in the array. For a bubble sort, start with the last element in the array and compare each element (except the first) with the element before it. Exchange two elements of the array if they are out of order with respect to each other. On the first pass, this process adjusts some pairs of elements and moves the smallest value to the first element. A second pass moves the second smallest value to the second element and makes more local adjustments elsewhere. Once repeated enough times, this method sorts the list into ascending order.

The bubble sort implemented here avoids making more than one pass through the data once the array is properly sorted. It uses a flag to indicate whether any pairs of values are exchanged in a pass. This flag is cleared before each pass. When two values are exchanged, the flag is set. This section of code is nested in a conditional loop that repeats until the flag remains cleared at the end of a pass. The design can be written in pseudocode as

```
REPEAT
  clear Exchange
  FOR Subscr := HiBound TO LoBound+1 STEP -1
  DO
    IF List[Subscr] < List[Subscr-1]
    THEN
      swap List[Subscr] with List[Subscr-1]
      set Exchange
    ENDIF
  ENDFOR
UNTIL Exchange remains cleared
```

Consider the array references within the algorithm. As seen earlier, List[Subscr] must be implemented using the displacement in an index register. However, there is a problem with the references to List[Subscr-1]. In assembly language, arithmetic on the value in the index register cannot be specified when it is used to specify an indexed address. There are three ways to approach this problem. The first is to modify the index register before the instruction that specifies indexed addressing; doing so is not practical because both index values (that is, SI and SI − 2, for example) are needed during the comparison and exchange. The second method is to use a second index register with a value that is 2 less; this approach is good if the second index register is available and if the effort needed to maintain two index registers is acceptable. The third method is to rewrite the illegal reference to List[si-2] as (List-2)[si], which is legal. This third approach is used in Program 13.4.

This program includes the loop given earlier to read values for every element of the array prior to the sort, as well as another loop to display the value of every element after the sort. In between, the bubble sort described above is implemented. The AL register is used as the exchange flag. In each iteration of the REPEAT-UNTIL loop, the flag is

## Program 13.4

```
; Program 13.4      BubSort.ASM
; Sort a list of integers into ascending order, using bubble sort.

; Constants
LoBound        equ     -3
HiBound        equ     11
ListSize       equ     HiBound-LoBound+1

; DOS function and status parameters
DosFunc        equ     21h
ExitToDos      equ     4Ch
NoErrors       equ     00h

DOSSEG

_STACK SEGMENT para stack 'stack'
               dw      100h dup (?)
_STACK ENDS
```

## 13.3 Operations

**Program 13.4 (continued)**

```
_DATA SEGMENT word public 'data'
  List          dw       ListSize dup (?)
  PromptMsg     db       " numbers:"
  PromptLen     dw       $ - PromptMsg
  ResultMsg     db       "Sorted list: "
  ResultLen     dw       $ - ResultMsg
_DATA ENDS

_TEXT SEGMENT word public 'code'
      assume    cs: _TEXT
      extrn     PutStr: PROC, PutCrLf: PROC, PutChar: PROC
      extrn     PutDec: PROC, GetDec: PROC

BubSort:

; set up ds register to point to _DATA
      mov       ax, seg _DATA
      mov       ds, ax
      assume    ds: _DATA

; Read list of numbers to be sorted.
; print (ListSize, " numbers:")
      mov       ax, ListSize
      call      PutDec
      mov       cx, PromptLen
      mov       bx, offset PromptMsg
      call      PutStr
      call      PutCrLf

; si := 0
      sub       si, si

; FOR01 cx := ListSize TO 1 STEP -1
      mov       cx, ListSize

  DO01:
;   read (List[si])
      call      GetDec
      mov       List[si], ax
;   si := si + 2
      add       si, 2

      loop      DO01
; ENDFOR01

; Sort List, using bubble sort.
  REPEAT02:
;   clear exchange flag (in al)
      sub       al, al

;   FOR03 cx := ListSize - 1 TO 1 STEP -1
      mov       cx, ListSize
      dec       cx
```

## Program 13.4 (continued)

```
                DO03:
;           convert subscript in cx to index in si
                mov     si, cx
                shl     si, 1

;           IF04 List[si] < (List-2)[si]
                mov     bx, List[si]
                cmp     bx, (List-2)[si]
                jnl     ENDIF04

;           THEN04
;             swap List[si] with (List-2)[si]
                xchg    bx, (List-2)[si]
                mov     List[si], bx

;             set exchange flag
                mov     al, 1
                ENDIF04:

                loop    DO03
;       ENDFOR03

;   TEST02
            cmp     al, 0
            jne     REPEAT02
;   UNTIL02 exchange flag clear


; Print sorted List.
; print ("Sorted list:")
            mov     cx, ResultLen
            mov     bx, offset ResultMsg
            call    PutStr
            call    PutCrLf

; move a space into dl for printing between elements of List
            mov     dl, " "

; si := 0
            sub     si, si

; FOR05 cx := ListSize TO 1 STEP -1
            mov     cx, ListSize

    DO05:
;     print (List[si], " ")
            mov     ax, List[si]
            call    PutDec
            call    PutChar
            call    PutChar

;     si := si + 2
            add     si, 2
```

## 13.3 Operations

**Program 13.4 (continued)**

```
        loop    DO05
; ENDFOR05

; exit to DOS
        mov     ah, ExitToDos
        mov     al, NoErrors
        int     DosFunc

_TEXT ENDS
END     BubSort
```

---

cleared; when the end of the loop is reached, the flag is tested: If AL is not 0, an exchange has taken place, so the loop repeats.

Nested in this section of code is a FOR loop that uses the CX register to control the number of iterations. In the algorithm given earlier, Subscr varies from HiBound down to LoBound+1; the displacements that will be used must vary from 2∗(ListSize-1) down to 2. CX varies from ListSize-1 down to 1, and it is multiplied by 2 when being copied into an index register. The body of the FOR loop is an IF statement that compares an element of the array with the element before it using the instructions

```
        mov     si, cx
        shl     si, 1
        mov     bx, List[si]
        cmp     bx, (List-2)[si]
```

The value in CX is first copied into SI, and the shl instruction doubles it to compute the displacement. The last two instructions copy an element of List to the BX register and then compare it to the preceding element.

The instructions in the THEN clause,

```
        xchg    bx, (List-2)[si]
        mov     List[si], bx
```

exchange the two values if they are not in the right order. The first of these instructions exchanges the value of List[si], which is in BX, with the value of (List-2)[si]; it then stores the value that was just copied into the BX register from (List-2)[si] into List[si]. The AL register is then set to indicate that an exchange has been made.

Other sorting methods, such as an insertion sort or a selection sort, also need to access an array at two different places. Unlike the bubble sort, however, the two index values in these other sorts are not related in a simple way.

### Processing Individual Elements

In Section 13.1, when an array with an explicit lower bound other than 0 was considered, an array declared as

```
FirstYr    equ     1950
LastYr     equ     1992
ListSize   equ     LastYr-FirstYr+1
Cars       dw      ListSize dup (?)
```

## Chapter 13 Arrays

was introduced. This array could be used to count the number of registered cars built in each of the years from 1950 to 1992. Cars[Year] referred to an element of the array, with Year in the range from FirstYr to LastYr, and CARS[YEAR] referred to the same element, with YEAR in the range from 0 to the displacement of the last element of the array.

Consider the number of cars built in 1975, which is stored in Cars[1975] in Pascal. This value corresponds to the twenty-sixth word of memory allocated for CARS. In assembly language, this count could be accessed as CARS[SI] where index register SI is 50—that is, the twenty-sixth element is 50 bytes from the beginning of the block of memory used for the array.

An application of this array might include the fragment

```
Readln (RegistrationFile, Year,...);
IF (Year >= FirstYear) AND (Year <= LastYear)
   THEN Cars[Year] := Cars[Year] + 1;
```

This code reads a value for Year, as well as other data from the file RegistrationFile. It then checks whether Year is valid; if so, it adds 1 to the corresponding element of the Cars array. To illustrate accessing arbitrary elements of an array, this selection structure and assignment statement have been implemented in assembly language in Program 13.5.

## Program 13.5

```
; Program 13.5        CarReg.ASM
; Count the number of registered cars built in each year.

; Constants
    FirstYr     equ     1950        ;first year for which we have data
    LastYr      equ     1992        ;last year for which we have data
    ListSize    equ     LastYr - FirstYr + 1

; DOS function and status parameters
    DosFunc     equ     21h
    ExitToDos   equ     4Ch
    NoErrors    equ     00h

DOSSEG

_STACK SEGMENT para stack
            dw      100h dup (?)
_STACK ENDS

_DATA SEGMENT word public 'data'
    Cars        dw      ListSize dup (?)
    Year        dw      ?
    PromptMsg   db      "Enter Year:"
    PromptLen   dw      $ - PromptMsg
    ResultMsg   db      "Final Counts "
    ResultLen   dw      $ - ResultMsg
_DATA ENDS

_TEXT SEGMENT word public 'code'
    assume  cs: _TEXT
    extrn   PutStr: PROC, PutCrLf: PROC, PutChar: PROC
    extrn   PutDec: PROC, GetDec: PROC
```

### 13.3 Operations

**Program 13.5 (continued)**

```
      CarReg:

      ; set up ds register to point to _DATA
            mov     ax, seg _DATA
            mov     ds, ax
            assume  ds: _DATA

      ; Clear Cars array to zeros.
      ; si := 0
            sub     si, si

      ; FOR01 cx := ListSize TO 1 STEP -1
            mov     cx, ListSize

        DO01:
      ;   Cars[si] := 0
            mov     Cars[si], 0

      ;   advance si and repeat
            add     si, 2
            loop    DO01
      ; ENDFOR01

      ; Read and count how many cars for each year.
      ; print ("Enter Year:")
            mov     cx, PromptLen
            mov     bx, offset PromptMsg
            call    PutStr

      ; read (Year)
            call    GetDec

        WHILE02: ;Year > 0
            cmp     ax, 0
            jng     ENDWHL02

      ; DO02
      ;   IF03 (Year >= FirstYr) AND (Year <= LastYr)
            cmp     ax, FirstYr
            jnge    ENDIF03
            cmp     ax, LastYr
            jnle    ENDIF03

      ;     THEN03
      ;       Cars[Year] := Cars[Year] + 1
              sub     ax, FirstYr
              shl     ax, 1
              mov     si, ax
              inc     Cars[si]
      ;     ENDIF03:
```

**Program 13.5 (continued)**

```
;       print ("Enter Year:")
        mov     cx, PromptLen
        mov     bx, offset PromptMsg
        call    PutStr

;       read (Year)
        call    GetDec

        jmp     WHILE02
   ENDWHL02:

; Print Cars array.
; print ("Final Counts ")
        mov     cx, ResultLen
        mov     bx, offset ResultMsg
        call    PutStr
        call    PutCrLf

; set up space for printing between values
        mov     dl, " "

; si := 0
        sub     si, si

; FOR04 cx := ListSize TO 1 STEP -1
        mov     cx, ListSize

   DO04:
;       print (Cars[si], " ")
        mov     ax, Cars[si]
        call    PutDec
        call    PutChar
        call    PutChar

;       advance pointer and repeat
        add     si, 2
        loop    DO04
; ENDFOR04

; exit to DOS
        mov     ah, ExitToDos
        mov     al, NoErrors
        int     DosFunc

_TEXT ENDS
END     CarReg
```

After setting up the DS register, Program 13.5 clears every element of the array to 0. Then, in a WHILE loop, the program reads values for Year (using GetDec) and implements the selection structure and assignment statement discussed above. The value of Year, in the AX register, is used in an IF statement that uses two conditional jumps to

## 13.3 Operations

implement the compound condition. If the restrictions on the value of Year are satisfied, AX still contains the value of Year when the THEN clause is entered.

The value in the AX register, which is in the range from FirstYr to LastYr, is then converted into a displacement from the start of the array. The number of words in this displacement is simply Year - FirstYr, which must be doubled to become the displacement in bytes; this value can then be used as the index. These calculations are performed by the instructions

```
        sub     ax, FirstYr
        shl     ax, 1
        mov     si, ax
```

The element in the array is then incremented by

```
        inc     Cars[si]
```

The rest of the program prints the values of the Cars array, ten per line.

In summary, to access an arbitrary element of an array, convert the subscript into a displacement, load the displacement into an index register, and use indexed addressing with the operand. The next section will show some more examples of this technique in subprograms with array parameters.

## EXERCISES 13.3

▶1.  Modify Program 13.4 so that it prints the array one element per line, along with the array name and subscript. For example, the first couple lines of output might be

```
List (    45) =    12
List (    46) =    15
```

▶2.  Modify Program 13.5 so that it prints the array one element per line, as in Exercise 1. Do not print any years for which no cars are registered.

▶3.  Modify Program 13.5 so that it also prints the total number of cars registered. Do so two ways:
(a) Increment the total count whenever a valid year is read.
(b) Add together all of the values in the Cars array as they are printed.

4.  Compare your two solutions from Exercise 3. Which uses fewer bytes of memory for instructions? Which executes fewer instructions? What other criteria can you suggest for comparing them, and how do they compare using those criteria?

▶5.  Write a program that reads values into one array, copies that array into another with the same range of subscripts but with the elements in reverse order, then prints both arrays, one element of each array on each line of the display.

▶6.  Write a program that reads values into an array, computes the average of the values, then determines and prints how many values are above the average and how many are below.

▶7.  Modify the bubble sort program so that it uses the second index register rather than the expression (List-2)[si]. Compare the original version with the modified version. Which executes fewer instructions?

## 13.4 ARRAYS AS ARGUMENTS

The key to using arrays as arguments is understanding what information is available in a subprogram. One observation applies to all conventions: Any element of an array can be accessed if it is known where the first element is stored, and a displacement can be computed for the element desired.

### Passing Arrays by Reference

Passing an array with a 0 lower bound by reference is the simplest case. The address of the first element of the array—which is associated with the array name—is passed like any other argument passed by reference. Depending on the language, memory model, and so on, the address could be a near pointer or a far pointer; in Turbo Pascal, for example, a far pointer is passed for any array not exactly one, two, or four bytes long.

Subscript range information may be declared (possibly indirectly) in the formal parameter list in some languages. For example, to pass an array as a parameter in Pascal, it must be declared with a named type or as a conformant array parameter. The procedure or function that accepts the array parameter has access to the declaration of the type, so subscript bounds do not have to be passed as parameters.

Subscript range information must be passed as separate arguments in other languages, including assembly language. For example, consider the array defined by

```
List : ARRAY [0..HiBound] OF Integer;
```

Consider what happens when this array is passed from a Pascal program to an assembly-language function that finds the largest value in the array and returns its subscript as the function value. The Pascal program pushes a far pointer to List and the value of HiBound as arguments, then calls the function.

The function ListMax0 is given in Program 13.6. The first three instructions after setting up the BP register,

```
les   bx, LIST
mov   dx, es:[bx]
sub   ax, ax
```

initialize the DX register, which will keep track of the largest value in the list, to the first element of List; they also initialize the AX register, which will keep track of the subscript of the largest value, to 0.

**Program 13.6**

```
; Program 13.6      ListMax0.ASM
; Determine subscript of largest element in List.
; Can be called from Turbo Pascal, as
;     Function ListMax0 (List: ListType;
;                        HiBound: Integer): Integer;
;     where ListType = ARRAY [0..HiBound] OF Integer;
```

### 13.4 Arrays as Arguments

**Program 13.6 (continued)**

```
        ; Parameters:
          List        equ     dword ptr [bp + 6]
          HiBound     equ      word ptr [bp + 4]

        _TEXT SEGMENT word public 'code'
            assume  cs: _TEXT
            public  ListMax0

        ListMax0 PROC

        ; set up bp register to point to parameters
            push    bp
            mov     bp, sp

        ; Find subscript of largest element.
        ; maxElt (in dx) := List[0]
            les     bx, List
            mov     dx, es:[bx]

        ; maxSub (in ax) := 0
            sub     ax, ax

        ; FOR01 cx := HiBound TO 1 STEP -1
            mov     cx, HiBound

          DO01:
        ;   IF02 List[cx] > maxElt
            mov     si, cx
            shl     si, 1
            cmp     es:[bx][si], dx
            jng     ENDIF02

        ;   THEN02
        ;       maxElt := List[cx]
                mov     dx, es:[bx][si]

        ;       maxSub := cx
                mov     ax, cx
          ENDIF02:

            loop    DO01
        ; ENDFOR01:

        ; restore bp register, return maxSub in ax
            pop     bp
            ret     6

        ListMax0 ENDP
        _TEXT ENDS
        END
```

**464** Chapter 13 Arrays

The rest of the function consists of a selection structure within a loop to scan all other elements of the array and save the value (in DX) and subscript (in AX) of any element that is larger than the value in DX. The operand in the cmp instruction and in the first mov instruction in the THEN clause that refers to the array is es:[bx][si]. To compute the effective address of this operand, the processor adds the contents of the BX register (the offset of List from ES) and the SI register (the displacement) to the shifted segment number in ES.

When the loop terminates, the subscript in AX is returned as the function value. A Pascal program to test this function, not shown here, is included on the disk. An assembly language program that pushes a far pointer to the array and the value of HiBound as arguments can also be written to test this function; note, however, that since Turbo Pascal conventions are being used, the general and index registers are not saved by the function.

Consider the case where the lower bound is not 0. The lower bound must now be passed to the function. Pascal pushes a far pointer to List and values of both bounds as arguments, then calls the revised function given in Program 13.7. This version differs from the function of Program 13.6 in that the loop is implemented using the CX register but not using the loop instruction. The reason for this difference is that the program must be able to execute the loop for values of CX from LoBound+1 to HiBound without stopping at 0. Also, the invoking program expects a subscript in the range from LoBound to HiBound for the function value, but the index register must have a displacement in the range of 0 to the displacement of the last element.

## Program 13.7

```
; Program 13.7      ListMaxL.ASM
; Determine subscript of largest element in List.
; Can be called from Turbo Pascal, as
;     Function ListMax (List: ListType;
;                       LoBound, HiBound: Integer): Integer;
;     where ListType = ARRAY [LoBound..HiBound] OF Integer;

; Parameters:
  List         equ     dword ptr [bp + 8]
  LoBound      equ     word ptr [bp + 6]
  HiBound      equ     word ptr [bp + 4]

_TEXT SEGMENT word public 'code'
      assume  cs: _TEXT
      public  ListMaxL

ListMaxL PROC

; set up bp register to point to parameters
      push    bp
      mov     bp, sp

; Find subscript of largest element.
; (cx is subscript into List, si is corresponding index)
; maxElt (in dx)   := List[LoBound]
      les     bx, List
      mov     dx, es:[bx]
```

### 13.4 Arrays as Arguments

**Program 13.7 (continued)**

```
        ; maxSub (in ax) := LoBound
              mov     ax, LoBound

        ; FOR01 cx := LoBound+1 TO HiBound
              mov     cx, LoBound
              inc     cx

           TEST01:
              cmp     cx, HiBound
              jg      ENDFOR01

        ; DO01
        ;    IF02 List[cx] > maxElt
              mov     si, cx
              sub     si, LoBound
              shl     si, 1
              cmp     es:[bx][si], dx
              jng     ENDIF02

        ;    THEN02
        ;       maxElt := List[cx]
              mov     dx, es:[bx][si]

        ;       maxSub := cx
              mov     ax, cx
           ENDIF02:

              inc     cx
              jmp     TEST01
           ENDFOR01:

        ; restore bp register, return maxSub in ax
              pop     bp
              ret     8

        ListMaxL ENDP
        _TEXT ENDS
        END
```

The computation of the index (in SI) from the subscript (in CX) is accomplished by the instructions

```
        mov     si, cx
        sub     si, LoBound
        shl     si, 1
```

The subtraction adjusts for the lower bound, and the shl instruction adjusts for the size of the array elements.

The programs presented so far use just one index register and access all elements of the array. A problem requiring the use of both index registers is one in which the values of two elements in an array are swapped. Unlike the bubble sort case, the elements to be swapped are not related to each other by position.

## Chapter 13 Arrays

Program 13.8 is a procedure that swaps two elements of an array. The array, the lower bound, and the subscripts of the elements to swap are all parameters. After setting up the BP register, the procedure copies the pointer to the array into the ES:BX registers. Then it converts the subscripts into displacements in index registers using sequences like

```
mov     si, Sub1
sub     si, LoBound
shl     si, 1
```

which first adjusts for the lower bound, then adjusts for the size of each element. The actual exchange is then performed by the sequence

```
mov     ax, es:[bx][si]
xchg    ax, es:[bx][di]
mov     es:[bx][si], ax
```

### Program 13.8

```
; Program 13.8        Swap.ASM
; Exchange List[Sub1] and List[Sub2].
; Can be called from Turbo Pascal, as
;     Procedure Swap (VAR List: ListType;
;                     LoBound, Sub1, Sub2: Integer);
;     where ListType = ARRAY [LoBound..HiBound] OF Integer;

; Parameters:
  List          equ     dword ptr [bp + 10]
  LoBound       equ     word ptr [bp + 8]
  Sub1          equ     word ptr [bp + 6]
  Sub2          equ     word ptr [bp + 4]

_TEXT SEGMENT word public 'code'
        assume  cs: _TEXT
        public  Swap

Swap PROC

; set up bp register to point to parameters
        push    bp
        mov     bp, sp

; es:bx := pointer to List
        les     bx, List

; si := displacement of Sub1
        mov     si, Sub1
        sub     si, LoBound
        shl     si, 1

; di := displacement of Sub2
        mov     di, Sub2
        sub     di, LoBound
        shl     di, 1
```

### 13.4 Arrays as Arguments

**Program 13.8 (continued)**

```
; swap List[si] with List[di]
    mov     ax, es:[bx][si]
    xchg    ax, es:[bx][di]
    mov     es:[bx][si], ax

; restore bp register and return
    pop     bp
    ret     10

Swap ENDP
_TEXT ENDS
END
```

## Passing Arrays by Value

When a simple argument is passed by value, the calling program makes a copy of the value and passes the copy to the subprogram. When an array is passed by value, the entire array is copied into another region of memory; a pointer to the first element of the copy is passed just like a pointer to the first element of an array passed by reference. Working with a copied array, then, is no different than working with the original array, except that changes made to the copy do not affect the original array.

Copying an array requires time and memory not directly related to the problem being solved. Many programmers routinely pass all arrays by reference to avoid the overhead in making the copy. This practice requires care to keep from making unintended changes to the array.

## Passing Part of an Array

There are two more important points regarding passing arrays as arguments. The first involves passing a single element. To pass List[42] to a subprogram, simply write List[42] as an argument in a high-level language. To pass it by reference in assembly language, something like

```
    mov     bx, 42
    sub     bx, LoBound
    shl     bx, 1
    add     bx, offset List
    push    bx
```

could be used, assuming List is an array of words and Lobound is defined as in our other examples.

In the subprogram, the parameter is accessed just like any simple parameter. The argument is either a single integer (passed by value) or the offset of a single integer (passed by reference). No information about the array, its bounds, or the index or displacement of this element is passed to or needed by the subprogram.

## Chapter 13 Arrays

A procedure to swap two elements of an array, where both elements are passed by reference, would look no different than a procedure to exchange the values of two simple integer variables. Assuming the parameters are declared as

```
Second      equ     word ptr [bp+6]
First       equ     word ptr [bp+4]
```

the body of such a procedure could be written as

```
    mov     bx, First
    mov     ax, [bx]
    mov     bx, Second
    xchg    ax, [bx]
    mov     bx, First
    mov     [bx], ax
```

Note that this fragment does not use indexing.

The second point regarding passing arrays as arguments has to do with passing a subrange of an array. Consider an array defined with indexes in the range of −30 to +50. The intention is to pass the portion of the array with subscripts in the range of +10 to +35. There are several ways to accomplish this task; two are presented here. One is generally the best method, and the other is a popular but flawed method. The preferred method requires passing the name of the array, its explicit lower bound, and the bounds that define the portion of interest. The subprogram will "know" about the entire array, but it will access only the elements in the desired range.

To illustrate this method, the function from Program 13.7 that finds the largest element in an array is revised so that the search is restricted to a portion of the array. The modified function is given in Program 13.9. The subscripts that define the range of elements to check are called LoRange and HiRange. Most of the changes involve setting initial values for the largest element and the corresponding subscript. In Program 13.7, List[LoBound] was chosen as the smallest value initially; since List[LoBound] was passed to represent the array, this concept was very easy to implement. In Program 13.9, List[LoRange] is chosen as the smallest value initially; this choice requires computing the displacement of this element from the beginning of the array.

## Program 13.9

```
; Program 13.9         ListMaxR.ASM
; Determine subscript of largest element in a portion of List.
; Can be called from Turbo Pascal, as
;     Function ListMax (List: ListType;
;                       LoBound, LoRange, HiRange: Integer): Integer;
;     where ListType = ARRAY [LoBound..HiBound] OF Integer;
;     and LoRange..HiRange define range of List to search.

; Parameters:
    List        equ     dword ptr [bp + 10]
    LoBound     equ     word ptr [bp + 8]
    LoRange     equ     word ptr [bp + 6]
    HiRange     equ     word ptr [bp + 4]

_TEXT SEGMENT word public 'code'
        assume  cs: _TEXT
        public  ListMaxR
```

## 13.4 Arrays as Arguments

**Program 13.9 (continued)**

```
        ListMaxR PROC

        ; set up bp register to point to parameters
            push    bp
            mov     bp, sp

        ; Find subscript of largest element.
        ; (cx is subscript into List, si is corresponding index)
        ; maxElt (in dx) := List[LoRange]
            les     bx, List
            mov     si, LoRange
            sub     si, LoBound
            shl     si, 1
            mov     dx, es:[bx][si]

        ; maxSub (in ax) := LoRange
            mov     ax, LoRange

        ; FOR01 cx := LoRange+1 TO HiRange
            mov     cx, LoRange
            inc     cx

          TEST01:
            cmp     cx, HiRange
            jg      ENDFOR01

        ; DO01
        ;   IF02 List[cx] > maxElt
            mov     si, cx
            sub     si, LoBound
            shl     si, 1
            cmp     es:[bx][si], dx
            jng     ENDIF02

        ;   THEN02
        ;       maxElt := List[cx]
            mov     dx, es:[bx][si]

        ;       maxSub := cx
            mov     ax, cx
          ENDIF02:

            inc     cx
            jmp     TEST01
          ENDFOR01:

        ; restore bp register, return maxSub in ax
            pop     bp
            ret     10

        ListMaxR ENDP
        _TEXT ENDS
        END
```

The other major change to restrict the search to a subrange of the array involves the loop control expressions. The statement

```
FOR cx := LoBound+1 TO HiBound
```

is changed to

```
FOR cx := LoRange+1 TO HiRange
```

to control this loop. The limits of the range are passed by value, so this change is very easy to implement.

The other method for passing a portion of an array to a subprogram requires no changes to the subprogram, a fact that accounts for its popularity. The idea is to pass a pointer to the first element in the desired range as if that element were the first one in the array. Depending on how the range of subscripts is passed, if at all, fake values might need to be passed for those arguments. As odd as this might seem, if ListMax0 (see Program 13.6) were called with a far pointer to List[10] for List and a value of 26 for HiBound, that function would work as if List[10] through List[35] were renamed List[0] through List[25].

The problem with this method and its variations is that it uses an element of the array as something other than just a simple integer in the array. Such use leads to confusion as to what the parameters represent. This method, unfortunately, is quite popular in some languages because it allows the use of the same subprogram for either the whole array or just part of it.

## EXERCISES 13.4

▶1. A popular simple sorting algorithm is the selection sort. A selection sort that arranges List into descending order using function ListMaxR and procedure Swap can be written

```
FOR Pos = LoBound TO HiBound-1
DO
  MaxSub := ListMaxR (List, LoBound, Pos, HiBound)
  Swap (List, LoBound, Pos, MaxSub)
ENDFOR
```

Implement this algorithm in assembly-language, using the two subprograms provided in this section.

▶2. Implement the selection sort of Exercise 1 in a high-level language, using the subprograms provided in this section (or versions modified to work with your language).

▶3. Rewrite Program 13.8 to use only one index register.

▶4. Write a function that accepts two arrays with the same range of subscripts and returns a value representing how many elements of the two arrays are the same. Two elements are the same if they have the same value and are in the same position in the arrays.

▶5. Write a subprogram that accepts two arrays with the same range of subscripts. The subprogram is to copy the values from the first array into the second array in reverse order.

▶6. Write a function that accepts an array, its range of subscripts, and a key value. The function is to return the lowest subscript of an element in the array with the key value; if the key does not occur in the array, the function should return a value of one less than the lower bound.

▶7. Write a subprogram that accepts two arrays. One array is a list of integer data; its length is also passed as an argument. The subprogram should count the number of times each digit from 0 through 9 occurs in the units position of the list. The second array has ten elements, to which your program is to assign the counts. That is, Count[0] is to be the number of times a zero occurs in the units position in the first list, and so on.

▶8. Write an assembly-language procedure to exchange two simple integer variables, as discussed in this section. Write a high-level-language program to test it; pass simple variables as well as elements of an array to it. Be careful; many languages pass all variable parameters as far pointers.

▶9. Write an assembly-language procedure that accepts an array and the corresponding bounds on its subscripts. The procedure should initialize each element of the array with its subscript.

▶10. Write an assembly-language function that computes the sum of the elements in an array. The bounds on the array should also be passed to the function.

## 13.5 MULTI-DIMENSIONAL ARRAYS

One-dimensional arrays have a direct mapping to computer memory. Both use a sequential organization, and both number successive elements or locations in order.

With arrays of more than one dimension, the mapping is less direct. When working with a multi-dimensional array, a single displacement must be computed from the combination of subscripts. To pass a multi-dimensional array as an argument, more information about subscript bounds must be passed.

Most of this section will deal with two dimensions to illustrate these concerns; the discussion will be extended to three or more dimensions later.

### Declaring Two-Dimensional Arrays

In a high-level language, there may be a couple of ways to define a two-dimensional array. An array can be defined with two subscripts in the declaration, as in

Table : ARRAY [1..3, 1..4] OF Integer;

With this style of declaration, the first subscript is usually thought of as specifying a row within a table, with the second subscript specifying a column. This array may be pictured as shown in Figure 13.1. The integer in the second row and third column is accessed by Table[2,3].

Another way to declare a two-dimensional array is as a one-dimensional array of one-dimensional arrays. A sample declaration can be written as

FiveRows : ARRAY [1..5] OF ARRAY [1..3] OF Integer;

Table: ARRAY [1..3, 1..4] OF Integer;

| Table[1,1] | Table[1,2] | Table[1,3] | Table[1,4] |
| Table[2,1] | Table[2,2] | Table[2,3] | Table[2,4] |
| Table[3,1] | Table[3,2] | Table[3,3] | Table[3,4] |

**Figure 13.1** Model of Two-Dimensional Array

We can interpret this arrangement as five rows with three integers each. The second integer in the fourth row, for example, is accessed by `FiveRows[4][2]`. A reference with just one subscript refers to a one-dimensional array. `FiveRows[2]`, for example, refers to the array of three integers in the second row.

The declaration of `FiveRows` could also be written as

```
TYPE   Row = ARRAY [1..3] OF Integer;
VAR    FiveRows : ARRAY [1..5] OF Row;
```

This version provides more documentation but is otherwise equivalent to the previous declaration.

To reserve space for a two-dimensional array of integers in assembly language, the number of words of memory needed is computed and used as the operand of a `dw` directive with the name of the array for the directive's label. Memory for the two examples above would be reserved with the directives

```
Table      dw      12 dup (?)
FiveRows   dw      15 dup (?)
```

## Representation in Memory

Consider next how to compute the displacement of an element in a two-dimensional array from its subscripts. TABLE[0] in assembly language is expected to correspond to `Table[1,1]` by the same convention used earlier. So, where is `Table[2,3]`? What is stored in TABLE[10]?

There are two ways to arrange the elements of a two-dimensional array in memory. The first is to store the first row of the array at the beginning of a block of memory, followed by the second row, and so on. This order is called *row-major order*. The second is to store the first column of the array at the beginning of a block of memory, followed by the second column, and so on. This order is called *column-major order*. Figure 13.2 shows the array of Figure 13.1 stored both ways.

A formula is needed to compute the displacement of an element given its row and column subscripts. For an array stored in row-major order, it is clear from Figure 13.2 that the way to access an element in some given row is to skip over the rows prior to the given row and then skip over the elements in that row prior to the desired element. The formula for converting subscripts of `Table[row,col]` to the displacement in TABLE[disp] is

$$\text{disp} = [(\text{row} - 1) \times 4 + (\text{col} - 1)] \times \text{elt\_size} \tag{13.1}$$

The (row − 1) × 4 term is the product of the number of rows to skip and the number of elements in one row. The (col − 1) term is the number of elements to skip in the target row. If each element of the array occupies more than one byte, the displacement needs to be multiplied by the size of each element, as is done by elt_size in Equation 13.1.

Equation 13.1 can be modified so that it applies to other two-dimensional arrays stored in row-major order. There are three constants that should be replaced with symbols: The constant 4 is the number of elements in a row, and the two 1 values are the lower bounds on the row and column subscripts. To make the notation more general, the array declaration is written as

```
Table : ARRAY [lo₁..hi₁, lo₂..hi₂] OF Integer;
```

## 13.5 Multi-Dimensional Arrays

Table: ARRAY [1..3, 1..4] OF Integer;

| Row-major order |
|---|
| Table[1,1] |
| Table[1,2] |
| Table[1,3] |
| Table[1,4] |
| Table[2,1] |
| Table[2,2] |
| Table[2,3] |
| Table[2,4] |
| Table[3,1] |
| Table[3,2] |
| Table[3,3] |
| Table[3,4] |

| Column-major order |
|---|
| Table[1,1] |
| Table[2,1] |
| Table[3,1] |
| Table[1,2] |
| Table[2,2] |
| Table[3,2] |
| Table[1,3] |
| Table[2,3] |
| Table[3,3] |
| Table[1,4] |
| Table[2,4] |
| Table[3,4] |

**Figure 13.2  Two-dimensional Array as Stored in Memory**

Now the displacement of Table[row,col] can be computed as

$$\text{disp} = [(\text{row} - \text{lo}_1) \times (\text{hi}_2 - \text{lo}_2 + 1) + (\text{col} - \text{lo}_2)] \times \text{elt\_size} \tag{13.2}$$

To access an element of a two-dimensional array, just compute the displacement using Equation 13.2, move the displacement into an index register, and use the index register with the pointer to the array as the operand.

For an array stored in column-major order, it is necessary to skip over columns to get to the desired column and then skip over elements in the target column to get the desired element. Using the same declarations and notation of Eq. 13.2, the formula for the displacement is

$$\text{disp} = [(\text{col} - \text{lo}_2) \times (\text{hi}_1 - \text{lo}_1 + 1) + (\text{row} - \text{lo}_1)] \times \text{elt\_size} \tag{13.3}$$

The only difference in accessing an array stored in row-major order and one stored in column-major order lies in the arrangement of terms in the formula for computing the displacement. It is essential that the correct formula be used; the wrong formula will give unpredictable results.

## Two-Dimensional Arrays as Arguments

Now consider working with a two-dimensional array passed as an argument to a subprogram. It is clear that in order to access an element of such an array, it is necessary to have both a pointer to the block of memory containing the array and the displacement of the desired element. To compute the displacement, the proper equation to use (Equation 13.2 or 13.3) must be decided upon, and values for all of the variables in the equation are needed. In practice, a subprogram to be called from a high-level language would use the same storage order as the high-level language; it would not have a parameter to specify order, but it would be written to use a specific storage order.

To compute the displacement, the subprogram needs the lower bounds on both subscripts and the upper bound on one subscript but not the other. If the array is stored in row-major order, for example, the upper bound on the row subscript is not needed; it does not appear in Equation 13.2. However, if the subprogram is to check for valid subscript values, all bounds are needed.

## Examples

Consider a program that passes a two-dimensional array to two subprograms. Program 13.10, the main program, is written in Turbo Pascal. It reads car registration information from a file and tallies how many of the cars were built in each of the years from 1950 through 1992 for each of the codes 1 through 5 (which could refer to country, size, insurance rating, or something else; it doesn't matter here). The tally is kept in a two-dimensional array with type defined as

`ARRAY [FirstYear..LastYear, FirstCode..LastCode] OF Integer;`

The array itself is named `Tally`, so `Tally[1975,3]` is the number of cars built in 1975 with code 3.

### Program 13.10

```
{ Program 13.10     Survey.PAS                                  }
{ Analyze a survey of car registrations.  The input file        }
{ includes the year and country code for each car currently     }
{ registered.  This program reads the data and                  }
{   1 - accumulates it in a two-dimensional array;              }
{   2 - prints total number of cars for each year;              }
{ Assembly language routines increment the elements of the      }
{ array as data is read and compute totals for each row.        }

PROGRAM Survey (CarFile, Input, Output);

CONST
  FirstYear = 1950;
  LastYear  = 1992;
  FirstCode =    1;
  LastCode  =    5;

TYPE
  TallyType   = ARRAY [FirstYear..LastYear, FirstCode..LastCode]
                  OF Integer;
  RowSumType  = ARRAY [FirstYear..LastYear] OF Integer;

VAR
  CarFile     : Text;        { data to be analyzed }
  CarFileName : String;      { path/file name of CarFile }
  Tally       : TallyType;   { counts of cars by year & country code }
  RowSums     : RowSumType;  { number of cars by year }
  Year        : Integer;     { year subscript }
  Code        : Integer;     { country code subscript }
```

### 13.5 Multi-Dimensional Arrays

**Program 13.10 (continued)**

```
            PROCEDURE Increment (VAR A: TallyType;
                                 LoRow, HiRow, LoCol, HiCol,
                                 RowNo, ColNo: Integer); External;
         {$L Incrment.OBJ }

            PROCEDURE SumRows (VAR A: TallyType;
                               LoRow, HiRow, LoCol, HiCol: Integer;
                               VAR B: RowSumType); External;
         {$L SumRows.OBJ }

         BEGIN { Survey }
           { clear survey data }
           FOR Year := FirstYear TO LastYear DO
             FOR Code := FirstCode TO LastCode DO
               Tally[Year,Code] := 0;

           { get filename and open file }
           Write  ('Path\filename? ');
           Readln (CarFileName);
           Assign (CarFile, CarFileName);
           Reset  (CarFile);

           { read file, tally cars by year and country code }
           Readln (CarFile, Year, Code);
           WHILE NOT Eof(CarFile) DO
           BEGIN
             Increment (Tally, FirstYear, LastYear, FirstCode, LastCode,
                        Year, Code);
             Readln (CarFile, Year, Code)
           END;

           { print tally array }
           Writeln;
           Writeln ('              -------- Code ------- ');
           Writeln ('Year          1    2    3    4    5 ');
           Writeln ('----         ---- ---- ---- ---- ----');
           FOR Year := FirstYear TO LastYear DO
           BEGIN
             Write (Year:4, '   ');
             FOR Code := FirstCode TO LastCode DO
               Write (Tally[Year,Code]:5);
             Writeln
           END;

           { compute totals for each year }
           SumRows (Tally, FirstYear, LastYear, FirstCode, LastCode, RowSums);

           { print row sums }
           Writeln;
           Writeln ('Year    Total');
           FOR Year := FirstYear TO LastYear DO
             Writeln (Year:4, RowSums[Year]:8);
           Writeln
         End. { Survey }
```

The program begins by clearing `Tally` to zero by using nested FOR loops in Pascal. It then asks for the name of the input file, reads the name, and opens the file for input. The file contains one value for `Year` and one for `Code` on each line. After opening the file, the program reads the file one line at a time in a loop until the end of the file is reached. With each pair of `Year` and `Code` values read, the program calls an assembly-language procedure to increment `Tally[Year,Code]`. Of course, it is not mandatory to use assembly language to accomplish this task; the Pascal statement

`Tally[Year, Code] := Tally[Year, Code] + 1`

works fine. The purpose here is to show what is involved in implementing that Pascal statement and how to check the subscripts for valid values. The rest of Program 13.10 will be examined later, after the `Increment` procedure is examined.

The assembly-language `Increment` procedure is given in Program 13.11. It requires seven arguments: a pointer to the array, the four bounds on the subscripts, and the two subscripts of the element to increment. Although only three of the bounds are needed to compute the displacement, all four are needed for the subprogram to check that the subscripts are valid. The subprogram is written for an array stored by rows, in accordance with how Pascal stores arrays.

After setting up the stack frame, the program checks that the subscripts of the element to increment are in the range specified by the bounds. It does so using four pairs of compare and conditional jump instructions. The jumps skip over the rest of the procedure if either subscript is out of bounds.

## Program 13.11

```
; Program 13.11     Incrment.ASM
; Increment an element of a two-dimensional array.
; Can be called from Turbo Pascal, as
;     Procedure Increment (VAR A: TallyType;
;                          LoRow, HiRow, LoCol, HiCol,
;                          RowNo, ColNo: Integer);
;     where TallyType = ARRAY [LoRow..HiRow, LoCol..HiCol]
;                       OF Integer;
;     and [RowNo, ColNo] specify element to increment.
;     If RowNo or ColNo is out of range, no action is taken.

; Parameters:
        A         equ    dword ptr [bp + 16]
        LoRow     equ    word ptr [bp + 14]
        HiRow     equ    word ptr [bp + 12]
        LoCol     equ    word ptr [bp + 10]
        HiCol     equ    word ptr [bp + 8]
        RowNo     equ    word ptr [bp + 6]
        ColNo     equ    word ptr [bp + 4]

_TEXT SEGMENT word public 'code'
      assume  cs: _TEXT
      public  Increment
```

### 13.5 Multi-Dimensional Arrays

## Program 13.11 (continued)

```
Increment PROC

; set up bp regster to point to parameters
      push    bp
      mov     bp, sp

; IF01 LoRow<=RowNo<=HiRow AND LoCol<=ColNo<=HiCol
      mov     ax, RowNo
      cmp     ax, LoRow
      jnge    ENDIF01          ;RowNo < LoRow
      cmp     ax, HiRow
      jnle    ENDIF01          ;RowNo > HiRow
      mov     cx, ColNo
      cmp     cx, LoCol
      jnge    ENDIF01          ;ColNo < LoCol
      cmp     cx, HiCol
      jnle    ENDIF01          ;ColNo > HiCol

; THEN01
;   A[RowNo,ColNo] := A[RowNo,ColNo] + 1
;   si = ((HiCol-LoCol+1)*(RowNo-LoRow) + Colno-LoCol) * elt_size
      mov     dx, HiCol        ;rowsize (in dx) := HiCol-LoCol+1
      sub     dx, LoCol
      inc     dx

      sub     ax, LoRow        ;disp := (rowsize * (RowNo-LoRow)
      mul     dx

      add     ax, ColNo        ;          + ColNo - LoCol)
      sub     ax, LoCol
      sal     ax, 1            ;          * elt_size
      mov     si, ax           ; si := ...

      les     bx, A            ; es:bx := far pointer to array
      inc     word ptr es:[bx][si]    ;increment desired element

   ENDIF01:

; restore bp register and return
      pop     bp
      ret     16

Increment ENDP
_TEXT ENDS
END
```

If the subscripts are valid, the procedure computes the displacement from Equation 13.2 using the arguments for all bounds and subscripts. After the displacement is computed and placed in the SI register, the far pointer to the array is moved into ES:BX, and the array element is incremented by the instruction

```
inc    word ptr es:[bx][si]
```

Since the only operand of the `inc` instruction is specified as an indexed indirect far pointer, `word ptr` must be used with the operand to specify the size data. The last two instructions are just a normal return.

After the subprogram returns to the Pascal program, another line of the file is read, and the process is repeated. When the main program reaches the end of the file, it prints the `Tally` array with simple headings; again, this process uses nested FOR statements in Pascal.

The Pascal program then invokes another assembly-language procedure to compute the sums in each row of `Tally`. These sums are to be returned in a second array, with type defined as

```
ARRAY [FirstYear..LastYear] OF Integer;
```

and named `RowSums`. The two arrays and their relationship are illustrated in Figure 13.3. The sum of each row can be computed in Pascal using

```
FOR Year := FirstYear TO LastYear DO
BEGIN
   Total := 0;
   FOR Code := FirstCode TO LastCode DO
      Total := Total + Tally[Year, Code];
   RowSums[Year] := Total
END
```

Using the simple variable `Total` for the sum of each row as the sum is computed avoids the indexed accesses to the array. However, an even more efficient method is available in assembly language.

The assembly-language procedure in Program 13.12 computes the sum of each row as described above and illustrated in Figure 13.3. However, note that the above Pascal fragment accesses the elements of `Tally` by row in the same order as `Tally` is stored. It

| Year | \multicolumn{5}{c}{Tally : ARRAY [1950..1992, 1..5] OF Integer} | RowSums : ARRAY [1950..1992] OF Integer |
|------|---|----|----|----|----|-----|
| 1950 | 3 | 2  | 1  | 6  | 3  | 15  |
| 1951 | 5 | 3  | 2  | 1  | 3  | 14  |
| 1952 | 1 | 1  | 3  | 4  | 0  | 9   |
| 1953 | 3 | 11 | 2  | 0  | 10 | 26  |
|      | . | .  | .  | .  | .  | .   |
|      | . | .  | .  | .  | .  | .   |
|      | . | .  | .  | .  | .  | .   |
| 1992 | 31| 27 | 58 | 20 | 19 | 155 |

**Figure 13.3** Computing RowSums from Tally

## 13.5 Multi-Dimensional Arrays

also accesses the elements of RowSums in the order stored. Taking this fact into account, the displacement calculations can be eliminated, and the algorithm can be rewritten as

```
TallyDisp := 0
SumsDisp := 0
FOR Year := FirstYear TO LastYear
DO
  Total := 0
  FOR Code := FirstCode TO LastCode
  DO
    Total := Total + Tally[TallyDisp]
    TallyDisp := TallyDisp + 2
  ENDFOR
  RowSums[SumsDisp] := Total
  SumsDisp := SumsDisp + 2
ENDFOR
```

This algorithm is implemented in Program 13.12. More general names are used for the parameters and arrays in the program, and registers are used for all local variables and displacements. The program itself is straightforward, using just one or two instructions for each step in the above algorithm.

---

**Program 13.12**

```
; Program 13.12      SumRows.ASM
; Calculates the sum of each row of a two-dimensional array
; and saves it in an element of a one-dimensional array.
; Can be called from Turbo Pascal, as
;     Procedure SumRows (VAR A: TallyType;
;                        LoRow, HiRow, LoCol, HiCol: Integer
;                        VAR B: RowSumType);
;     where TallyType = ARRAY [LoRow..HiRow, LoCol..HiCol]
;                       OF Integer;
;     and   RowSumType = ARRAY [LoRow..HiRow] OF Integer.

; Parameters:
    A         equ       dword ptr [bp + 16]
    LoRow     equ       word ptr [bp + 14]
    HiRow     equ       word ptr [bp + 12]
    LoCol     equ       word ptr [bp + 10]
    HiCol     equ       word ptr [bp + 8]
    B         equ       dword ptr [bp + 4]

_TEXT SEGMENT word public 'code'
    assume  cs: _TEXT
    public  SumRows

SumRows PROC

; set up bp register to point to parameters
    push    bp
    mov     bp, sp
```

**Program 13.12 (continued)**

```
        ; clear displacements into both arrays
            mov     si, 0
            mov     di, 0

        ; FOR01 row (in cx) := LoRow TO HiRow DO
            mov     cx, LoRow

        TEST01:
            cmp     cx, HiRow
            jnle    ENDFOR01

        ; DO01
        ;   Total (in ax) := 0
            sub     ax, ax

        ;   es:[bx] := pointer to start of A
            les     bx, A

        ;   FOR02 Col (in dx) := LoCol TO HiCol DO
            mov     dx, LoCol

        TEST02:
            cmp     dx, HiCol
            jnle    ENDFOR02

        ;   DO02
        ;     Total := Total + A[Row,Col]
            add     ax, word ptr es:[bx][si]

        ;     advance pointer in A
            add     si, 2

            inc     dx
            jmp     TEST02
        ENDFOR02:

        ;   B[Row] := Total
            les     bx, B
            mov     word ptr es:[bx][di], ax

        ;   advance displacement in B
            add     di, 2

            inc     cx
            jmp     TEST01
        ENDFOR01:

        ; restore bp register and return
            pop     bp
            ret     16

SumRows ENDP
_TEXT   ENDS
        END
```

### 13.5 Multi-Dimensional Arrays

Note the use of ES:BX as the far pointer to both arrays. Only BX or BP can be used for indirect pointers when indexing is also specified. BP is needed to reference the stack. So, ES:BX is loaded with the pointer to Tally before entering the inner loop (after clearing Total), and ES:BX is changed to the pointer to RowSums (before saving Total after leaving the inner loop).

Consider the main program (Program 13.10) again. When the SumRows procedure terminates, the main program prints the row sums in a second report using another FOR loop. The exercises for this section explore revisions and extensions to this program.

## Arrays with More than Two Dimensions

The concepts for processing a two-dimensional array apply to processing arrays with more dimensions. Consider a three-dimensional array declared as

Cube : ARRAY [$L_1$..$H_1$,$L_2$..$H_2$,$L_3$.. $H_3$] OF Integer;

Think of a two-dimensional array as a table; this concept can be extended to thinking of a three-dimensional array as a collection of tables, perhaps as a book of tables, with a separate table on each page (each table with the same layout as all other tables). In this analogy, the first subscript specifies the page, the second specifies the row on that page, and the third specifies the column in that row.

The term column-major now implies that all of the first columns are stored in sequence, followed by all of the second columns, and so on. The term row-major is sometimes used for the other principal order, which is an order by pages and by rows within pages. In this latter organization, the order of the elements of the array in memory is such that the rightmost subscript varies the most quickly and the leftmost subscript varies the most slowly. For example, a 3 × 3 × 3 array is shown stored by pages in Figure 13.4.

The formula to compute the displacement of an element, given its three subscripts, of an array stored as shown in Figure 13.4 involves skipping over a number of pages, then skipping over a number of rows on the target page, then skipping over a number of elements in the target row. For the declaration of Cube given above, the displacement of Cube[P,R,C] is given by

$$\text{disp} = [(P - L_1) \times (H_2 - L_2 + 1) \times (H_3 - L_3 + 1) + (R - L_2) \\ \times (H_3 - L_3 + 1) + (C - L_3)] \times \text{elt\_size} \tag{13.4}$$

The first term in Equation 13.4 computes the number of elements on the pages to skip over to get to page P. The second term computes the number of elements to skip over on that page to get to row R. And the third term computes the number of columns to skip in that row. The factor elt_size is applied to the sum of the three terms.

To access an element of a three-dimensional array requires more work to compute the displacement from the subscripts and bounds. But a single displacement must be computed and put in an index register to access an element of the array.

The above concepts also extend to arrays with more than three dimensions. If the analogy of a three-dimensional array as a book of tables is continued, then an increase in the number of dimensions can be represented by a row (a shelf) of such books, then bookcases (shelves of books), then rows of bookcases, and so on. The displacement formulas become correspondingly larger as the number of dimensions increases, but they are only factored polynomials of higher and higher degree.

Cube : ARRAY [1..3, 1..3, 1..3] OF Integer:

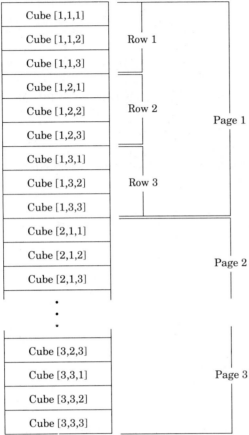

**Figure 13.4 Three-Dimensional Array as Stored in Memory, by Pages**

## EXERCISES 13.5

1. Given the array declaration

    ```
    Ex1 : ARRAY [5..20, -3..3] OF Integer;
    ```

    Compute the displacements of the following elements, assuming that the array is stored in row-major order and that each element occupies one word.
    - (a) Ex1[5,0]
    - (b) Ex1[6,0]
    - (c) Ex1[10,-3]
    - (d) Ex1[10,3]
    - (e) Ex1[19,2]
    - (f) Ex1[19,0]
    - (g) Ex1[20,-3]
    - (h) Ex1[20,3]

2. Repeat Exercise 1, assuming instead that the array is stored in column-major order.

3. For the array of Exercise 1, which element is stored in the word at each of the following displacements?
   (a) 0 (b) 2
   (c) 20 (d) 90
   (e) 44 (f) 98
   (g) 100 (h) 110
4. Repeat Exercise 3, assuming instead that the array is stored in column-major order.
5. How can the formulas of Equations 13.2 and 13.3 be modified for arrays where the subscripts are characters? Give the equation for the displacement of an element of the array

   ```
   Ex5 : ARRAY ['A'..'M', 'b'..'k'] OF Integer;
   ```

   stored in row-major order. Assume each integer occupies one word.

If you are not using Turbo Pascal, modify the programs in this section for the language you are using. Use the modified versions in exercises that reference `Tally`.

▶6. Write a subprogram to find the position of the largest element in a two-dimensional array. The subprogram should return the row and column subscripts of the largest element. Modify Program 13.10 to pass `Tally` to this subprogram and to print the subscripts of the largest value as well as the value itself.

▶7. Write a subprogram to clear all elements of a two-dimensional array to zero. Modify Program 13.10 to use this subprogram rather than the nested loops at the beginning of the program. Pass the array name and all subscript bounds.

▶8. Repeat Exercise 7, except that the parameters should be only the name of the array and the number of elements it contains. Treat the array as one-dimensional.

9. Compare the subprograms you wrote for Exercises 7 and 8. How are they similar? How are they different?

10. In Program 13.11, each subscript is compared to its bounds separately. Why would it be incorrect to compute the displacement corresponding to those subscripts and check that it is not larger than the size of the array?

11. Imagine rewriting Program 13.11 so that it computes the displacement for every combination of valid `Row` and `Col` subscripts. Outline the parts of the program that would be different. Estimate the number of additional instructions such a program would execute.

12. Examine the code produced by your compiler for the Pascal (or equivalent) program that computes row sums based on the Pascal fragment given in this section. Does that code more closely resemble Program 13.12 or the code for Exercise 11?

▶13. Write a subprogram that computes the sum of each of the columns of a two-dimensional array stored in row-major order. Try to take advantage of the fixed distance between elements in the same column rather than computing displacements from scratch each time. Revise Program 13.10 to pass `Tally` to your subprogram and to then print the number of cars with each code.

## 13.6 THE SET DATA TYPE

A set is an unordered collection of values of one type. Each possible member of a set can be either present or absent, which requires only one bit to record. The bits that represent the potential members of a set are stored in an order implied by the values of those members. Once an order is chosen in which to map each element of the set onto a unique bit in a block of memory, a set can be implemented using an array of bits. Thus, the SET data type presents an interesting variation on indexed addressing.

In this section, a simple set, some of the operations on sets, and an application for sets are all considered.

## Representation

A set can be implemented as an array of bits. However, there is no directive for declaring a single bit, nor is there any simple way to access a single bit in memory. The smallest unit that can be defined and addressed conveniently is the byte. A set can be implemented using an array of bytes, using each byte for eight elements.

For example, say we want to determine which characters are used in some document. We don't need to count them; we just want to know which ones are used at least once. An array of bits can be defined such that each bit records whether a corresponding character appears in the document. Since there are 256 characters in the extended ASCII character set, 256 bits are needed in this array. This requires $256 \div 8 = 32$ bytes.

The ordinal values of the characters, found by interpreting the codes as unsigned 8-bit numbers, range from 0 to 255. A character's ordinal value can be used as its bit displacement. For example, the character 'A' is coded as $01000001_2$, or 65 in decimal notation. Whether or not an 'A' appears in the document is recorded in the bit that is 65 bits from the start of the block.

To access a particular bit, first determine which byte it is in, then use the bit operations of Chapter 6 on that byte. The byte displacement can be determined with a simple division. For the character 'A' (which has an ordinal value of 65), the appropriate calculation is $65 \div 8 = 8$ with remainder 1. The quotient is the byte displacement, and the remainder is the displacement of the bit within the byte. So the existence of 'A' in the document is indicated by the second bit (displacement 1) of the ninth byte (displacement 8) of the array. See Figure 13.5.

Now that a set can be stored, consider operations on sets.

## Operations

The operations on a set include

- Clearing a set
- Forming the union of two sets
- Forming the intersection of two sets
- Forming the difference of two sets
- Testing for membership in a set
- Inserting an element into a set
- Removing an element from a set
- Testing whether a set is a subset of another

Each of these operations will be discussed in terms of the implementation just described, but writing functions or procedures for most operations will be left as exercises.

## 13.6 The SET Data Type

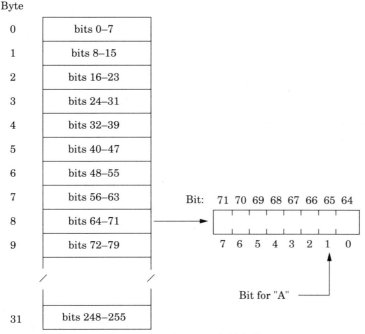

Figure 13.5 Implementation of a Set of 256 Characters

A set is cleared by storing a zero in each byte of the set. A subprogram that can be called from Pascal to perform this task is given later in this section.

Forming the union of two sets also proceeds one byte at a time. Instead of moving a zero into the destination array, the union of corresponding bytes of two input sets is formed and moved into the destination set. The union of two bytes is found using an or instruction. For example, the assignment

```
SetC := SetA union SetB
```

can be implemented by performing

```
mov     al, SetA[si]
or      al, SetB[si]
mov     SetC[si], al
```

with SI taking on the values 0 through the displacement of the last byte needed to represent the set.

Forming the intersection of two sets is similar to forming the union, using and in place of or.

Forming the difference of two sets is a little more work. The set difference is the set of all elements of the first set that are not in the second. To calculate the difference of two sets, $A - B$, it is necessary to perform the operation shown in Table 13.1 on each corresponding pair of potential set members. Note that the result is 1 only when $A$ is 1

**Table 13.1 Set Difference Operation**

| A−B | B 0 | B 1 |
|---|---|---|
| A 0 | 0 | 0 |
| A 1 | 1 | 0 |

and $B$ is not 1; the set difference $A - B$ can be implemented as (not B) and A by performing

```
mov   al, SetB[si]
not   al
and   al, SetA[si]
mov   SetC[si], al
```

with every byte of the sets.

To test whether a value is a member of a set, assuming the type of the value is compatible with the set definition, it is necessary to isolate the bit corresponding to the value. A function that returns the desired bit as a Boolean value to a Pascal program is given later in this section.

Inserting a value into a set can be done in two ways. One way is to make a set that contains only the value to be inserted and then form the union of that set with the original set. This is the way that Pascal programmers code it, but the question of how to insert the element into a new set remains. The second method, which is later implemented in a subprogram, is to use an or instruction with a mask corresponding to the value to be inserted.

Removing an element of a set can be done by clearing the bit in the set that corresponds to the value to be removed. To clear a bit, use an and instruction with a mask that has 0 in the position to be cleared and 1 in all other positions.

Determining whether one set is a subset (or proper subset) of another can be done using the union and difference operations. $B$ is a subset of $A$ if the union of $A$ and $B$ is the same as $A$; $B$ is a proper subset of $A$ if it is a subset of $A$ and if the difference $A - B$ is not empty.

## An Application

Consider again the idea of using a set to record which characters are present in some document. The set for this problem should be declared as an array of 32 bytes; each byte represents the presence or absence of eight values in the set, as shown in Figure 13.5.

Program 13.13 is a Turbo Pascal program that reads one or more lines of text from the keyboard and prints a list of all the characters in that text. It uses a set declared as

```
CharSetType = ARRAY [0..31] of Byte;
```

rather than Pascal's own SET data type to focus on the implementation of a set as an array of bits.

### 13.6 The SET Data Type

---

**Program 13.13**

```
{ Program 13.13      SetOps.PAS                              }
{ Determines which characters are used in a sentence.        }
{ Uses assembly language routines for SET operations, for    }
{ illustration purposes, rather than Pascal's SET operators. }

PROGRAM SetOps (Input, Output);

CONST
  LoControl = 0;
  HiControl = 31;
  LoGraphic = 32;
  HiGraphic = 255;

TYPE
  CharSetType = ARRAY [0..31] OF Byte;

VAR
  CharSet : CharSetType;
  CharIn  : Char;

PROCEDURE ClearSet (VAR S: CharSetType); External;
{$L ClearSet.OBJ }
PROCEDURE InsertInSet (VAR S: CharSetType; Ch: Char); External;
{$L InsrtSet.OBJ }
FUNCTION  IsElementOf (VAR S: CharSetType; Ch: Char):
          Boolean; External;
{$L IsEltOf.OBJ }

BEGIN { SetOps }
  { clear set to empty }
  ClearSet (CharSet);

  { read text and save characters in the set }
  Writeln ('Enter text, terminate with number sign "#".');
  Writeln;
  Read (CharIn);
  WHILE CharIn <> '#' DO
    BEGIN
      InsertInSet (CharSet, CharIn);
      Read (CharIn)
    END;

  { print heading for output }
  Writeln;
  Writeln ('CHARACTERS USED');
  Writeln;

  { print control characters as 'Ctrl-' and a capital letter }
  FOR CharIn := Chr(LoControl) TO Chr(HiControl) DO
    IF IsElementOf (CharSet, CharIn)
      THEN Writeln ('Ctrl-', Chr(Ord(CharIn)+64));
```

**488** Chapter 13 Arrays

**Program 13.13 (continued)**

```
    { print all other characters as their graphic symbol }
    FOR CharIn :=  Chr(LoGraphic) TO Chr(HiGraphic) DO
      IF IsElementOf (CharSet, CharIn)
        THEN Writeln ('   ', CharIn);
END. { SetOps }
```

The Pascal program starts by using the `ClearSet` procedure to clear the set. It then prompts the user for input terminated with a number sign. As it reads the input stream, it uses the `InsertInSet` procedure to insert each character in the set. When the number sign is read, the program terminates the input and proceeds to print the contents of the set. It does so by using the `IsElementOf` function to check whether each possible value is in the set and printing those that are. The character codes 0 through 31 are printed as control codes; if the user taps the ENTER key, the list contains both CTRL-J (LF) and CTRL-M (CR).

The `ClearSet` procedure is shown in Program 13.14. It moves zeros into the set one word at a time in a loop. Since the set is passed by reference, a far pointer is needed to access it. The pointer is advanced on each pass through the loop rather than making use of a separate index register.

**Program 13.14**

```
; Program 13.14       ClearSet.ASM
; Clears a set of 256 elements to an empty set.  The set
; is implemented as an array of 32 bytes, with each byte of
; the array representing eight elements of the set.
; Can be called from Turbo Pascal, as
;     Procedure ClearSet (VAR CharSet: SetType)
;     where SetType = ARRAY [0..31] of Byte;

; Parameter:
  CharSet    equ     dword ptr [bp + 4]

_TEXT SEGMENT word public 'code'
    assume  cs: _TEXT
    public  ClearSet

ClearSet PROC

; set up bp register to point to parameter
    push    bp
    mov     bp, sp

; es:[bx] := pointer to CharSet
    les     bx, CharSet

; make a word of zeros
    mov     ax, 0
```

## 13.6 The SET Data Type

**Program 13.14 (continued)**

```
; FOR01    cx := 16 DOWNTO 1
    mov     cx, 16

  DO01:
;   clear next word of set and advance pointer
    mov     es:[bx], ax
    add     bx, 2

    loop    DO01
; ENDFOR01

; restore bp register and return
    pop     bp
    ret     4

ClearSet ENDP
_TEXT ENDS
END
```

---

The `InsertInSet` procedure is shown in Program 13.15. After setting up the stack frame and the far pointer to the set, it computes by division the displacements of the desired byte from the start of the set and of the desired bit within the byte. The sequence

```
mov     ax, CharCode
mov     dl, 8
div     dl
```

leaves the quotient in AL and the remainder in AH. As shown in Figure 13.5, the quotient is the byte displacement, and the remainder is the bit displacement. The remainder (which will be in the range 0 to 7) is used as a shift count in the sequence

```
mov     cl, ah
mov     dl, 1
shl     dl, cl
```

which creates a mask in DL with a single 1-bit at the displacement specified in AH. The quotient, after being extended to a word, is used as an index into the array containing the set in the sequence

```
mov     ah, 0
mov     si, ax
```

Finally, this index is used to access the desired byte of the set. That byte is combined with the mask in DL using

```
or      es:[bx][si], dl
```

This statement makes the bit corresponding to `CharCode` in the set a 1. Note that if that bit is already 1, this procedure has no effect; it is quicker to just make the bit a 1 than to bother checking whether or not it already is 1.

## Program 13.15

```
; Program 13.15      InsrtSet.ASM
; Inserts a character into a set.  The set is implemented
; as an array of 32 bytes, with eight elements per byte.
; Can be called from Turbo Pascal, as
;     Procedure InsertInSet (VAR CharSet: SetType; CharCode: Char)
;     where SetType = ARRAY [0..31] of Byte;

; Parameters:
  CharSet     equ     dword ptr [bp + 6]
  CharCode    equ     word ptr [bp + 4]

_TEXT SEGMENT word public 'code'
     assume  cs: _TEXT
     public  InsertInSet

InsertInSet PROC

; set up bp register to point to parameters
     push    bp
     mov     bp, sp

; es:[bx] := pointer to CharSet
     les     bx, CharSet

; Determine bit within set by dividing CharCode by 8:
; quotient  = displacement of desired byte in array
; remainder = displacement of desired bit within byte
     mov     ax, CharCode
     mov     dl, 8
     div     dl

; Build mask for selected bit from bit displacement
     mov     cl, ah        ;use remainder as shift count
     mov     dl, 1         ;start with one bit in mask
     shl     dl, cl        ;shift it into position

; Copy byte displacement into si as index into array.
     mov     ah, 0
     mov     si, ax

; Set selected bit
     or      es:[bx][si], dl

; restore bp register and return
     pop     bp
     ret     6

InsertInSet ENDP
_TEXT ENDS
END
```

### 13.6 The SET Data Type

The `IsElementOf` function is shown in Program 13.16. It uses the same steps to find the byte and bit displacements as the preceding program. However, once it has moved the bit displacement into CL for later use as a shift count and has moved the byte displacement into SI for accessing the byte in the set, it proceeds with the sequence

```
mov     al, es:[bx][si]
shr     al, cl
and     al, 01h
```

This sequence copies the byte that contains the bit for CharCode, the character being tested for membership in the set, into AL; it shifts the byte so that the bit corresponding to CharCode is in the least significant position and clears the rest of AL. Thus, the presence of CharCode in the set is converted into a Boolean TRUE, and its absence is converted into FALSE.

## Program 13.16

```
; Program 13.16      IsEltOf.ASM
; Determines whether a character is present in a set.
; Can be called from Turbo Pascal, as
;    Function IsElementOf (VAR CharSet: SetType;
;                                  CharCode: Char): Boolean;
;    where SetType = ARRAY [0..31] of Byte;

; Parameters:
   CharSet     equ      dword ptr [bp + 6]
   CharCode    equ      word ptr [bp + 4]

_TEXT SEGMENT word public 'code'
     assume   cs: _TEXT
     public   IsElementOf

IsElementOf PROC

; set up bp register to point to parameters
     push     bp
     mov      bp, sp

; es:[bx] := pointer to CharSet
     les      bx, CharSet

; Determine bit within set by dividing CharCode by 8:
; quotient = displacment of desired byte in array,
; remainder = displacment of desired bit within that byte
     mov      ax, CharCode
     mov      dl, 8
     div      dl

; Save bit displacement as shift count for later use
     mov      cl, ah

; Copy byte displacement into si as index into array
     mov      ah, 0
     mov      si, ax
```

## Program 13.16 (continued)

```
; Move desired bit to position 0 of al, clear rest of al
        mov     al, es:[bx][si]     ;desired byte
        shr     al, cl              ;shift bit into position 0
        and     al, 01h             ;clear other bits

; restore bp, return with Boolean result in al
        pop     bp
        ret     6

IsElementOf ENDP
_TEXT ENDS
END
```

## EXERCISES 13.6

1. Another way to implement a set is as an unordered list of the values in the set. To determine whether a value is a member of the set, the value would be searched for in the data structure used. What underlying data structures might you use to implement such a set? Compare such an implementation to the array of bits used in the examples in this section.

▶2. Write an assembly-language function to return the number of elements in a set. See Section 6.6 for methods of counting the number of 1-bits in a word. Modify Program 13.13 to use this function and to print the number of different characters that were entered.

▶3. Write a procedure that accepts three sets (each of the same size and base type) as parameters. This procedure should form the union of the first two sets and save it in the third set. Write a main program in a high-level language to test your procedure.

▶4. Write a procedure similar to that of Exercise 3 that forms the intersection of the first two sets and saves it in the third.

▶5. Write a procedure similar to that of Exercise 3 that forms the set difference (first set − second set).

▶6. Revise Program 13.15 to remove an element from a set rather than insert it. Also modify the ClearSet procedure so that it initializes the set with every element present. Then use your modified procedures to determine which characters are not entered.

▶7. Write a Boolean function in assembly language with two sets of the same type and size as parameters. It should determine whether the first set is a subset of the second. Write a main program in a high-level language to test it.

▶8. Modify the function of Exercise 7 to test for a proper subset.

9. Use a debugging tool to inspect how set operations are implemented in some high-level language. Compare to the descriptions in this section.

## KEY POINTS

- An array is a data structure, containing values of one type, stored in a contiguous block of memory. An individual element can be referenced by a subscript that gives its position in the block.

**Key Points**

- The displacement of an element of a one-dimensional array in the block of memory can be computed from its subscript, the lower bound on the subscript, and the size of an element as

  $$\text{displacement} = (\text{subscript} - \text{lobound}) \times \text{elementsize}$$

- Direct addressing can be used to access an element of an array. However, doing so precludes using variable subscripts.
- Indirect addressing can be used to access an element of an array by adding the displacement of the desired element to the pointer that refers to the beginning of the array. This process can be useful when accessing all elements of the array in order.
- Indexed addressing can be used to access an element of an array by putting the displacement of the desired element in an index register and then using it in the address expression for the operand.
- In indexed addressing, the contents of an index register are added to the offset specified by the rest of the operand when computing an effective address.
- Some common operations involving all elements of an array are clearing an array, reading and printing an array, and finding the sum of all elements in an array. At the machine level, these operations are performed on the elements one at a time.
- For an array argument passed by reference, a pointer to the first element is passed to the subprogram. The pointer may be near or far.
- Subscript range information needed for computing displacements must be passed as arguments to subprograms (or made available some other way).
- For an array argument passed by value, a pointer to the first element of a copy of the array is passed.
- When a single array element is passed as an argument, it is treated like a simple variable of the same type.
- When passing a portion of an array, the array should be passed as usual, and subscripts that define the portion of the array to be processed should also be passed.
- Multi-dimensional arrays are stored in a contiguous block of memory. The formula for the displacement of an element depends on the storage order used.
- Two-dimensional arrays can be stored by rows (row-major order) or by columns (column-major order).
- Formulas for displacements are factored polynomials with degree the same as the number of dimensions. The displacement of Table[row,col] in an array with subscripts $[lo_1..hi_1, lo_2..hi_2]$ stored in row-major order is given by

  $$\text{disp} = [(\text{row} - lo_1) \times (hi_2 - lo_2 + 1) + (\text{col} - lo_2)] \times \text{elt\_size}$$

  For the same array stored in column-major order, the displacement is given by

  $$\text{disp} = [(\text{col} - lo_2) \times (hi_1 - lo_1 + 1) + (\text{row} - lo_1)] \times \text{elt\_size}$$

- Sets can be implemented as arrays of bits, where each bit represents whether a potential member of a set is actually present. In practice, the set array is accessed as an array of bytes, each byte representing eight elements of the set.
- Operations that involve a single set element require dividing the bit displacement by eight to get a byte displacement (the quotient) and a displacement within the byte (the remainder).

## PC SYSTEM SUMMARY

- The 8086 has two index registers: SI and DI.
- The arithmetic operations that can be performed on all of the general registers can also be performed on the index registers.
- Assemblers for the 8086 allow indexing to be written several ways; the convention of writing the index register enclosed in brackets [ ] following the array name or pointer has been adopted.
- The only registers that can be used as base registers in an indexed indirect address are BX and BP.

# Records

**14**

- ◆ **Representation**
- ◆ **Addressing**
- ◆ **Linked Lists**

The array data structure discussed in the previous chapter is quite useful when all values in a collection of data have the same type. However, such is not always the case. The record data structure is a collection of logically related values that do not necessarily have the same type. The separate values in a record are called fields. In a high-level language, fields are specified by using a name that qualifies the reference to the record. To access a field of a record in memory, however, the displacement of the field from the start of the record is needed. The displacement can be used with indexed addressing.

In this chapter we examine how records are declared and stored, how fields within a record are accessed, and how records passed as arguments are used. An important application of records is in defining other data structures. The general idea of a linked list is considered, and a few operations on a linked list using pointer variables are examined.

## 14.1 REPRESENTATION

A record is a data structure that contains several logically related values. The individual elements of a record are called fields. Unlike the elements of an array, all of the fields of a record need not have the same data type; the data type of each field can be defined as whichever type helps solve the problem. Each field in a record has a name that we can use to access the field.

Records may be collected and stored as a file. Such files may be processed individually or as part of a database. Except for the material in Chapter 9, file and database processing are not within the intended scope of this book. However, a small file may be read into an array of records and processed using a combination of array and record techniques. An example is presented in Section 14.2.

### Declaring Records

We define record data structures in a high-level language with a name for the record and a separate name for each field. For example, a record in an inventory file might include a one-letter part number prefix, a part number, the quantity on hand, the reorder point, a one-letter reorder code, and a supplier number. (Since we have only integer, logical, and single-character data types so far, our record cannot contain description, price [with a fraction], and supplier name fields.) Such a record could be defined in Pascal as

```
TYPE
  InvRecord = RECORD
    PartNoPrefix : Char;
    PartNo       : Integer;
    QtyOnHand    : Integer;
    ReorderPt    : Integer;
    OrderCode    : Char;
    SupplierNo   : Integer
  END; {InvRecord }
VAR
  Inventory : InvRecord;
```

This record structure occupies 10 consecutive bytes of memory, as shown in Figure 14.1.

Using just the assembly-language features we have seen so far, we can reserve memory for a record by using a db directive with the size of the record as operand. The memory for one of our inventory records could be reserved as

```
Inventory      db      10 dup (?)
```

since it contains 10 bytes of data. This declaration does not associate a name with each field of the record. To do so, we could define each field in a separate db or dw directive. But that is not a good idea: Defining each field separately destroys the record concept and would require passing each field as a separate argument rather than passing the entire record as a single argument.

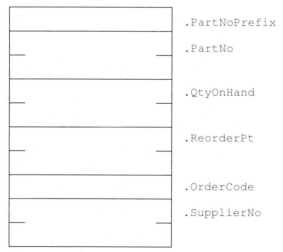

**Figure 14.1 Inventory Record in Memory**

## 14.1 Representation

Consider how the field names might be used to access the values within the record. To access an element of an array, no matter how that array is defined and how many dimensions it has, we must compute the displacement of the desired element in the array structure. The situation is similar with records. To access a field in a record, we must determine the displacement of the desired field within the record structure. Each field name can be associated with the displacement of the field within the record. For our inventory record, we can find the displacements from Figure 14.1 and write

```
; Inventory record displacements, types
    PartNoPrfx  equ     0       ;char
    PartNo      equ     1       ;integer
    QtyOnHand   equ     3       ;integer
    ReorderPt   equ     5       ;integer
    OrderCode   equ     7       ;char
    SupplierNo  equ     8       ;integer
```

Exactly how to use these displacements is shown in the next section.

Even though we have displacements associated with names, there is still more information about the fields that we would like to have, namely the data type of each field. We included comments with the types in the example above, but more is needed. Although most assemblers support only limited type information (byte vs. word vs. doubleword and so on) in general, we would like at least that information for each field to be in a form that the assembler can use. There is no practical way to do this with just the assembly-language features described up to this point.

Some assemblers for 8086 processors include a directive for defining a record (although they typically use C language terminology and refer to a record as a "structure"). The STRUC (or STRUCT) directive acts like a type definition, providing a convenient way to specify the names and types of fields in a record. By itself, it does not reserve memory for an instance of the record it defines. To define our inventory record using STRUC we would write

```
InvRecord STRUC
    PartNoPrfx  db      ?       ;char
    PartNo      dw      ?       ;integer
    QtyOnHand   dw      ?       ;integer
    ReorderPt   dw      ?       ;integer
    OrderCode   db      ?       ;char
    SupplierNo  dw      ?       ;integer
InvRecord ENDS
```

The name of the record type, InvRecord, is written as a label on both the STRUC directive and the ENDS directive. This convention is similar to having segment names written on both SEGMENT and ENDS directives. Also the same directive is used to terminate a segment or a structure; the assembler matches ENDS to SEGMENT or STRUC from the context. The STRUC definition can be written outside of segment definitions, so that the structure is not associated with any particular segment; this is the preferred placement. We will write them just before the data segment.

We used InvRecord for the name of the structure to parallel our TYPE declaration in Pascal given earlier. To actually define a variable of this type we wrote

```
Inventory : InvRecord;
```

within the VAR section in the Pascal program. To define a variable of this type in assembly language we write

```
Inventory     InvRecord     <>
```

in the data segment. The structure name is used as a directive. The operand field can include initial values (which we discuss next) enclosed in <>; the < and > are required even when no values are specified.

## Records with Initial Values

Sometimes we want to define initial values for the fields in a record. To do this for an inventory record using just db and dw directives, we could replace the declaration

```
Inventory   db     10 dup (?)
```

with

```
; inventory record values
    Inventory   db      "P"      ;part no. prefix
                dw      1234     ;part no.
                dw      56       ;qty on hand
                dw      65       ;reorder pt
                db      "O"      ;order code
                dw      4321     ;supplier no.
; end of Inventory record
```

Here we write a comment line before and after declarations and a comment field following each record value to suggest the record structure.

Initial values can be specified for records defined with STRUC. For example, to set up the same values using a structure, we replace

```
Inventory  InvRecord  <>
```

with

```
Inventory  InvRecord  <"P",1234,56,65,"O",4321>
```

in the data segment. We must be careful to include the values in the correct order.

The STRUC directive allows us to specify default values, which we may or may not use when defining an actual record in the data segment. For example, consider the record type defined as

```
SomeType STRUC
    Field1      db      "A"
    Field2      db      "B"
    Field3      db      ?
    Field4      db      ?
SomeType ENDS
```

and the actual record defined as

```
SomeRec    SomeType   <"W",,"C">
```

## 14.2 Addressing

The first three fields are initialized to the values "W", "B", and "C" respectively, whereas the fourth field is uninitialized. The values in the record definition override the default values in the type definition.

The next section examines how to access the individual fields in a record structure.

## EXERCISES 14.1

1. A student registration record might contain the student identification number (a doubleword integer), a major code (an integer), class (a letter), number of credits completed (an integer), and an array of up to 10 section codes (each an integer) listing the classes for which the student wants to register. Define a record type for this data, and declare a record variable of that type.
2. Use a db directive to reserve memory for a record variable like the one of Exercise 1.
3. Write the equ directives to associate field names with displacements for the record of Exercise 1.
4. Define a record type for the record of Exercise 1 using the STRUC directive. All fields should have undefined values.
5. Define a record with initial values (make up your own data and codes, but use 0 for any extra section codes). Use db and dw directives.
6. Repeat Exercise 5, using the structure of Exercise 4.

## 14.2 ADDRESSING

Now that you have seen how records are defined and how they are organized in memory, we turn to methods of accessing fields in records. We do this in three stages: accessing the fields of a record defined within the program, then accessing the fields of a record passed as an argument, and finally accessing an array of records passed as an argument.

### Accessing Fields

Consider the inventory record defined in Pascal earlier. To check whether it is time to order more of the item that this record refers to, we could use the test

```
IF Inventory.QtyOnHand < Inventory.ReorderPt
```

Here, the field names QtyOnHand and ReorderPt are separated from the record name Inventory by a period. The field names qualify the record name. This section shows how fields are accessed in assembly language and at the register level.

It has already been mentioned that we must determine the displacement of a field from the start of the record in order to access it. We also associated the field names with the displacements of the fields using equ directives. Now we use those displacements in an example.

Consider a direct—that is, neither indexed nor indirect—reference to an operand in memory. The operand is usually written symbolically; the operand is coded in the instruction as an offset from a segment register. To access the first field of a record, we can just use the name of the record as the symbolic operand. However, to access any other field of the record, we must arrange for the displacement to be added to the offset. It could be added by putting the displacement in an index register and specifying that register as part of the operand. However, since the displacement is a constant known during program translation, we can have the assembler add it to the offset as it builds the instruction. Having the assembler do it makes the program more efficient.

For example, consider the OrderCode field of our Inventory record. It has displacement 7 in the record. We can copy it into the DL register with the instruction

```
        mov     dl, Inventory+7
```

Because we so carefully associated the displacements with the field names, we can also write this as

```
        mov     dl, Inventory+OrderCode
```

This is exactly how we copy this field into DL for printing with PutChar in Program 14.1, which prints selected fields of a record defined within the program.

## Program 14.1

```
; Program 14.1          Rec1.ASM
; Prints selected fields of a record...

; Inventory record displacements, types
    PartNoPrfx  equ     0       ;char
    PartNo      equ     1       ;integer
    QtyOnHand   equ     3       ;integer
    ReorderPt   equ     5       ;integer
    OrderCode   equ     7       ;char
    SupplierNo  equ     8       ;integer

; DOS function and status parameters
    DosFunc     equ     21h
    ExitToDos   equ     4Ch
    NoErrors    equ     00h

DOSSEG

_STACK SEGMENT para stack 'stack'
            dw      100h dup (?)
_STACK ENDS

_DATA SEGMENT word public 'data'
; inventory record values (keep these fields in order):
    INVENTORY   db      "P"     ;part no. prefix
                dw      1234    ;part no.
                dw      56      ;qty on hand
                dw      65      ;reorder point
                db      "O"     ;order code
                dw      4321    ;supplier no.
; end of inventory record

    HeadingMsg  db      "Part No    Code    Supplier"
    HeadingLen  dw      $ - HeadingMsg
    Blanks      db      "      "
    BlankLen    dw      $ - Blanks
_DATA ENDS
```

## 14.2 Addressing

**Program 14.1 (continued)**

```
_TEXT   SEGMENT word public 'code'
        assume  cs: _TEXT
        extrn   PutStr: PROC, PutCrLf: PROC
        extrn   PutDec: PROC, PutChar: PROC

PrintRec:

; set up ds register to point to _DATA
        mov     ax, seg _DATA
        mov     ds, ax
        assume  ds: _DATA

; print ("Part No    Code     Supplier")
        mov     cx, HeadingLen
        mov     bx, offset HeadingMsg
        call    PutStr
        call    PutCrLf

; print (PartNo, "      ", OrderCode, "     ", Supplier)
        mov     dl, Inventory+PartNoPrfx
        call    PutChar
        mov     ax, word ptr Inventory+PartNo
        call    PutDec
       ⎡mov     cx, BlankLen
       ⎨mov     bx, offset Blanks
       ⎣call    PutStr
        mov     dl, Inventory+OrderCode
        call    PutChar
        mov     bx, offset Blanks
        call    PutStr
        mov     ax, word ptr Inventory+SupplierNo
        call    PutDec
        call    PutCrLf

; exit to DOS
        mov     ah, ExitToDos
        mov     al, NoErrors
        int     DosFunc

_TEXT   ENDS
        END     PrintRec
```

There is one small problem with this method of accessing fields of a record: The type (that is byte, word, doubleword, and so on) of all fields is determined by the type of the first field. In the Inventory example, since the first field is a byte, the assembler assumes all references to Inventory are byte references. To access the PartNo field, for example, using

```
        mov     ax, Inventory+PartNo
```

generates a warning message: The first operand is clearly a word, and the second is assumed to be a byte. To rectify this, we need to inform the assembler that the second operand is indeed a word. We do this with the `ptr` operator, as in

```
        mov     ax, word ptr Inventory+PartNo
```

The `ptr` operator is used with both word fields printed in Program 14.1.

In the previous section, we saw how to define a record type using STRUC (in MASM 6.0, STRUCT is preferred, but STRUC is recognized). The STRUC directive also associates displacements with field names, so the examples just given would also work with records defined this way. Furthermore, fields defined in STRUC directives are also correctly typed when used as operands. The assemblers that support the STRUC directive also allow use of the period to specify addition. So, combining these features, the last example can be written as

```
        mov     ax, Inventory.PartNo
```

Although this code resembles the Pascal (and C) syntax, it really just implies a type for the `PartNo` field and specifies addition of the displacement of the `PartNo` field to the offset of the `Inventory` record. Program 14.2 is a copy of Program 14.1 revised to use the capabilities of the STRUC directive.

## Program 14.2

```
; Program 14.2     SRec1.ASM
; Prints selected fields of a record... using STRUC

; DOS function and status parameters
  DosFunc       equ     21h
  ExitToDos     equ     4Ch
  NoErrors      equ     00h

DOSSEG

_STACK SEGMENT para stack 'stack'
                dw      100h dup (?)
_STACK ENDS

; Inventory Record structure (type definition)
InvRecord STRUC
    PartNoPrfx  db      ?       ;char
    PartNo      dw      ?       ;integer
    QtyOnHand   dw      ?       ;integer
    ReorderPt   dw      ?       ;integer
    OrderCode   db      ?       ;char
    SupplierNo  dw      ?       ;integer
InvRecord ENDS

_DATA SEGMENT word public 'data'
    Inventory   InvRecord   <"P",1234,56,65,"O",4321>
    HeadingMsg  db      "Part No    Code    Supplier"
    HeadingLen  dw      $ - HeadingMsg
    Blanks      db      "       "
    BlankLen    dw      $ - Blanks
_DATA ENDS
```

### 14.2 Addressing

**Program 14.2 (continued)**

```
_TEXT SEGMENT word public 'code'
    assume  cs: _TEXT
    extrn   PutStr: PROC, PutCrLf: PROC
    extrn   PutDec: PROC, PutChar: PROC

PrintRec:

; set up ds register to point to _DATA
    mov     ax, seg _DATA
    mov     ds, ax
    assume  ds: _DATA

; print ("Part No    Code     Supplier")
    mov     cx, HeadingLen
    mov     bx, offset HeadingMsg
    call    PutStr
    call    PutCrLf

; print (PartNo, "    ", OrderCode, "     ", Supplier)
    mov     dl, Inventory.PartNoPrfx
    call    PutChar
    mov     ax, Inventory.PartNo
    call    PutDec
    mov     cx, BlankLen
    mov     bx, offset Blanks
    call    PutStr
    mov     dl, Inventory.OrderCode
    call    PutChar
    mov     bx, offset Blanks
    call    PutStr
    mov     ax, Inventory.SupplierNo
    call    PutDec
    call    PutCrLf

; exit to DOS
    mov     ah, ExitToDos
    mov     al, NoErrors
    int     DosFunc

_TEXT ENDS
END     PrintRec
```

In both programs, the reference to the first field included the field displacement. The field displacement was not necessary in Program 14.1, as it is zero; it was included for consistency. However, in Program 14.2, any reference to Inventory without a displacement (field name) will be interpreted as a reference to the entire record, resulting in a warning that the operand types differ.

Accessing fields of a record defined in the same program is fairly straightforward. Next, accessing fields of a record passed as an argument is discussed.

## Record Arguments

Program 14.3 is a Turbo Pascal program that reads a file containing inventory records with the same data as the fields of our example record. The record structure defined in Program 14.3 is the same as the one given earlier in this chapter; the record variable is named InvLine, representing one line of the inventory data. Other than the record declaration, the interesting part of the program is the loop that reads all records and prints those with QtyOnHand less than ReorderPt. The Readln and IF statements are in a block defined by a WITH statement, which allows us to use just the field names without the record name.

**Program 14.3**

```
{ Program 14.3      RecArg.PAS                         }
{ Example of passing a record as an argument.          }

PROGRAM RecArg (Input, Output, InvData);

TYPE
  InvRecord = Record
    PartNoPrefix : Char;
    PartNo       : Integer;
    QtyOnHand    : Integer;
    ReorderPt    : Integer;
    OrderCode    : Char;
    SupplierNo   : Integer
  END; { InvRecord }

VAR
  InvData: Text;
  InvFileName: String;
  InvLine : InvRecord;
  BlankRead: Char;

PROCEDURE PrintRec (InvRec: InvRecord); External;
{$L PrintRec.OBJ }
{$I \INC\IO.INC --- include i/o routines for PrintRec to use. }

BEGIN { RecArg.PAS }
  Writeln ('INVENTORY REORDER PROGRAM');
  Writeln;

  { open input file }
  Write ('Name of inventory file? ');
  Readln (InvFileName);
  Assign (InvData, InvFileName);
  Reset  (InvData);

  { write headings for list to reorder }
  Writeln;
  Writeln ('Items to reorder ...');
  Writeln ('Part No    Code     Supplier');
```

**Program 14.3 (continued)**

```
    { check each inventory record, write those to reorder }
    WHILE NOT Eof(InvData) DO
      WITH InvLine DO
        BEGIN
          Readln (InvData, PartNoPrefix, PartNo, QtyOnHand,
                  ReorderPt, BlankRead, OrderCode, SupplierNo);
          IF QtyOnHand < ReorderPt
             THEN PrintRec (InvLine)
        END;

    { close file and terminate }
    Close (InvData);
    Writeln;
    Writeln ('End of report.')
END.
```

Selected fields of some records are printed by the assembly-language routine `PrintRec`. The only argument to `PrintRec` is `InvLine`, the record variable, passed by value. Turbo Pascal passes a far pointer for the record argument. (Actually, record arguments that are one, two, or four bytes are copied onto the stack when passed by value; all other record arguments, whether passed by value or by reference, are passed as far pointers to the structure.)

Before we pursue the `PrintRec` procedure, note the $I directive following the declaration of `PrintRec` in Program 14.3. The $L directive identifies the object file for `PrintRec`; the $I directive identifies the object file for the external routines used by `PrintRec`. Turbo Pascal needs this information to link our I/O routines into the executable program for `PrintRec` to use. We also used this directive in Chapter 8.

Now consider the `PrintRec` procedure. See Program 14.4. Like Program 14.2, it uses `STRUC` to define the record as `InvRecord`. The parameter, a far pointer to `InvLine`, is named `Inventory` and is defined using an `equ` directive. Unlike Program 14.2, we cannot simply write `Inventory.OrderCode` to access the order code field. Instead, we must copy the far pointer into a segment and base or index register. We do this with the instruction

```
les     di, Inventory
```

which copies the segment into ES and the offset into DI. Now the reference `es:[di]` as an operand refers to the beginning of the argument record. To access a field, we must use the field name as a qualifier; however, the field name must qualify a record name, not a register. One way to write this reference that is compatible with MASM 5.1 and 6.0 and TASM 2.0 is

```
mov     dl, es:[di]+InvRecord.PartNo
```

Note that, since `InvRecord` was defined with `STRUC` in the procedure, this instruction is equivalent to

```
mov     dl, word ptr es:[di]+1
```

where 1 is the displacement of the `PartNo` field. The rest of Program 14.4 is similar to Program 14.2.

## Program 14.4

```
;   Program 14.4        PrintRec.ASM
;   Prints selected fields of a record passed as an argument.
;   Can be called by Turbo Pascal, as
;       Procedure PrintRec (Inventory: InvRecord);
;       where InvRecord is defined in the STRUC declaration below.

; Parameter:
    Inventory   equ     dword ptr [bp + 4]

; Inventory Record structure
InvRecord STRUC
    PartNoPrfx  db      ?       ;char
    PartNo      dw      ?       ;integer
    QtyOnHand   dw      ?       ;integer
    ReorderPt   dw      ?       ;integer
    OrderCode   db      ?       ;char
    SupplierNo  dw      ?       ;integer
InvRecord ENDS

_DATA SEGMENT word public 'data'
    Blanks      db      "     "
    BlankLen    dw      $ - Blanks
_DATA ENDS

_TEXT SEGMENT word public 'code'
    assume  cs: _TEXT
    assume  ds: _DATA
    extrn   PutStr: PROC, PutCrLf: PROC
    extrn   PutDec: PROC, PutChar: PROC
    public  PrintRec

PrintRec PROC

; set up bp register to point to parameter
    push    bp
    mov     bp,sp

; print (PartNo, "     ", OrderCode, "     ", Supplier)
    les     di, Inventory
    mov     dl, es:[di]+InvRecord.PartNoPrfx
    call    PutChar
    mov     ax, es:[di]+InvRecord.PartNo
    call    PutDec
    mov     cx, BlankLen
    mov     bx, offset Blanks
    call    PutStr
    mov     dl, es:[di]+InvRecord.OrderCode
    call    PutChar
    mov     bx, offset Blanks
    call    PutStr
    mov     ax, es:[di]+InvRecord.SupplierNo
    call    PutDec
    call    PutCrLf
```

## 14.2 Addressing

**Program 14.4 (continued)**

```
    ; restore bp register and return
        pop     bp
        ret     4

PrintRec ENDP
_TEXT ENDS
END
```

Now that we know how to access fields of a record passed as an argument, we consider working with an array of records passed as an argument.

## Arrays of Records

To illustrate processing an array of records passed as an argument, we modify Programs 14.3 and 14.4 so that the main program reads all inventory records (there will be fewer than 50 of them) into an array and passes the array to the procedure. The procedure examines all records one at a time and prints selected fields for items that should be reordered.

The revised main program is shown in Program 14.5. There are changes to the declarations to define an array of records and to the declaration of the external procedure. The procedure is named ReOrder and expects two arguments: the array and the number of records in it. The earlier version of the main program checked each record as it was read and called PrintRec with each record to be printed; the new version reads all records into an array and passes the whole structure to the ReOrder procedure.

The ReOrder procedure must access every record in the array; although the order may not matter, we prefer to access the records in order of increasing subscript. With each record, the procedure must compare the quantity on hand to the reorder point and possibly print selected other fields. As with any array, to access an element with a particular

**Program 14.5**

```
{ Program 14.5      Inventory.PAS              }
{ Example of passing an array of records...    }

PROGRAM Inventory (Input, Output, InvData);

CONST
  MaxRecords = 50;

TYPE
  InvRecord = Record
    PartNoPrefix : Char;
    PartNo       : Integer;
    QtyOnHand    : Integer;
    ReorderPt    : Integer;
    OrderCode    : Char;
    SupplierNo   : Integer
  END; { InvRecord }
  InvList = ARRAY [1..MaxRecords] OF InvRecord;
```

**Program 14.5 (continued)**

```
VAR
  InvData: TEXT;
  InvFileName: String;
  InvItems : InvList;
  ItemIndex: 0..MaxRecords;
  BlankRead: Char;

PROCEDURE ReOrder (InvRecords: InvList; NoItems: Integer); External;
{$L ReOrder.OBJ }
{$I \INC\IO.INC --- include i/o routines for ReOrder to use. }

BEGIN { Inventry.PAS }
  Writeln ('    INVENTORY REORDER PROGRAM ');
  Writeln;

  { open input file }
  Write ('Name of inventory file? ');
  Readln (InvFileName);
  Assign (InvData, InvFileName);
  Reset (InvData);

  { read input file into array of records }
  ItemIndex := 0;
  WHILE NOT Eof(InvData) AND (ItemIndex < MaxRecords) DO
    BEGIN
      ItemIndex := ItemIndex + 1;
      WITH InvItems[ItemIndex] DO
        Readln (InvData, PartNoPrefix, PartNo, QtyOnHand,
                ReorderPt, BlankRead, OrderCode, SupplierNo);
    END;

  { close file }
  Close (InvData);

  { print inventory reorder report }
  ReOrder (InvItems, ItemIndex);

  Writeln;
  Writeln ('End of program.')
END.
```

---

subscript, we must determine the displacement of the element based on the size of a record. To do this, we use the formula

$$\text{displacement} = (\text{subscript} - 1) \times \text{record size}$$

Assuming that the CX register (which we could use to control the loop, too) has the subscript and that a named constant `RecSize` has been defined, we can implement this calculation as

```
mov    ax, cx
dec    ax
mov    dx, RecSize
mul    dx
```

leaving the displacement in AX.

## 14.2 Addressing

We need to combine the index register with a far pointer to the beginning of the structure and with the field displacement. We can use

```
les     di, Inventory
```

to copy the far pointer passed as an argument into ES:DI. Now we can add the displacement of the desired record, left in AX by the computation above, using

```
add     di, ax
```

Then, to copy the QtyOnHand field into AX, we can write the instruction

```
mov     ax, es:[di]+InvRecord.QtyOnHand
```

Although there are other approaches to implementing this reference, this one reduces the amount of calculation performed at runtime and uses the fewest registers. This is the approach used in Program 14.6.

An advantage of this approach is that the addition of the displacement to the desired record is performed only once per record; the disadvantage is that the argument pointer must be loaded into ES:DI for each record. The exercises suggest another approach that loads ES:DI only once and that adds the displacement to each record only once.

## Program 14.6

```
; Program 14.6       ReOrder.ASM
; Procedure ReOrder (Inventory: InvList; NoItems: Integer);
; Prints a report of items to be reordered from an array of
;    records (see description below) passed as an argument.

; Parameters:
    Inventory     equ      dword ptr [bp + 6]
    NoItems       equ      word ptr [bp + 4]

; Inventory record structure and size:
InvRecord STRUC
    PartNoPrfx    db       ?         ;char
    PartNo        dw       ?         ;integer
    QtyOnHand     dw       ?         ;integer
    ReorderPt     dw       ?         ;integer
    OrderCode     db       ?         ;char
    SupplierNo    dw       ?         ;integer
InvRecord ENDS

    RecSize       equ      10        ;size of one record

_DATA SEGMENT word public 'data'
    HeadingMsg    db       "Part No    Code      Supplier"
    HeadingLen    dw       $ - HeadingMsg
    Blanks        db       "          "
    BlankLen      dw       $ - Blanks
_DATA ENDS

_TEXT SEGMENT word public 'code'
    assume   cs: _TEXT
    assume   ds: _DATA
    extrn    PutStr: PROC, PutCrLf: PROC
    extrn    PutDec: PROC, PutChar: PROC
    public   ReOrder
```

**Program 14.6 (continued)**

```
ReOrder PROC

; set up bp register to point to arguments
    push    bp
    mov     bp, sp

; print ("Part No   Code      Supplier")
    mov     cx, HeadingLen
    mov     bx, offset HeadingMsg
    call    PutStr
    call    PutCrLf

; FOR01 cx := 1 TO NoItems DO
    mov     cx, 1

  TEST01:
    cmp     cx, NoItems
    jg      ENDFOR01

; DO01
;   IF02 Inventory[cx].QtyOnHand < Inventory[cx].ReorderPt
        mov     ax, cx              ;compute displacement
        dec     ax                  ; of Inventory[cx] as
        mov     dx, RecSize         ; (cx-1)*RecSize
        mul     dx
        les     di, Inventory       ;es:[di] := start of array +
        add     di, ax              ;        displacement of record
        mov     ax, es:[di]+InvRecord.QtyOnHand   ;compare fields
        cmp     ax, es:[di]+InvRecord.ReorderPt
        jnl     ENDIF02

;     THEN02
;       print (PartNo, "   ", OrderCode, "      ", Supplier)
        mov     dl, es:[di]+InvRecord.PartNoPrfx
        call    PutChar
        mov     ax, es:[di]+InvRecord.PartNo
        call    PutDec
        push    cx                  ;save cx for next iteration
        mov     cx, BlankLen
        mov     bx, offset Blanks
        call    PutStr
        mov     dl, es:[di]+InvRecord.OrderCode
        call    PutChar
        mov     bx, offset Blanks
        call    PutStr
        mov     ax, es:[di]+InvRecord.SupplierNo
        call    PutDec
        call    PutCrLf
        pop     cx                  ;restore cx for next iteration
  ENDIF02:
```

### 14.3 Linked Lists

**Program 14.6 (continued)**

```
; next record
        inc     cx
        jmp     TEST01
ENDFOR01:

; restore bp register and return
        pop     bp
        ret     6

ReOrder ENDP
_TEXT   ENDS
        END
```

---

### EXERCISES 14.2

▶1. For the record type defined in the exercises at the end of Section 14.1, write a program that prints one record defined within the program. Use two calls to PutDec to print the student identification number (unless you have a procedure that prints a doubleword integer handy).

▶2. For the record type defined in the exercises of Section 14.1, write a procedure that prints one record passed as an argument. Also write an appropriate main program to test your procedure.

▶3. Modify the main program of Exercise 2 to use an array of student registration records. Write a procedure that examines the array and prints a list of those students who are registering for more than three sections of classes. Print their identification numbers only.

▶4. Consider Program 14.6. A method of accessing all records in order without loading ES:DI for each record is to load ES:DI once before the loop. Then, after each iteration of the loop, add RecSize to DI to advance it to the next record. Modify a copy of Program 14.6 to use this method.

5. Compare the number of instructions executed by both Program 14.6 and by the program for Exercise 4.

6. Propose an example of an array of records in which one of the fields is another array of other records. Discuss what is necessary to access the various fields of the outer records and what is necessary to access the various fields of the inner records. How might the restriction of using a single base register and a single index register in an operand affect processing such a structure?

## 14.3 LINKED LISTS

The last topic of this chapter is linked lists. Much of what there is to say about linked lists is outside the scope of this book; the discussion is confined to examining the pointer data type, implementing simple operations on a linked list, and looking briefly at dynamic memory allocation.

## Record Description

A linked list is an ordered collection of records. The records are often called *nodes*. At least one field in each node is a pointer to another node; in some lists, nodes have several pointers to other nodes. The remaining fields in each node contain some data values. Linked lists also have a *header node*. This node has no data fields, only a pointer to the beginning of the list (or pointers to the ends of more complex lists). There is a special pointer constant, called NIL, which represents a pointer that has not been assigned a reference to another node. Usually, the last node in a linked list has this constant as its pointer to the next record. NIL is an end-of-list marker.

As an example of a linked list, consider the problem of counting how many times each character occurs in some text. One way to record these counts is to use a linked list in which each node contains a character, an integer count of how many times that character occurs, and a pointer to the next node. (Yes, this problem can be solved more easily using an array of integers with character subscripts; we want a simple list with two data types for our example, and this is a convenient list.) A portion of such a list is shown in Figure 14.2. The nodes shown in the figure indicate that e occurs five times, m once, and t three times. Not shown are the header node or the last node of the list.

The list of Figure 14.2 can be declared in Pascal as

```
TYPE
   NodePtr  = ^NodeType;
   NodeType = RECORD
      Ch    : Char;
      Count : Integer;
      Next  : NodePtr;
   END;
```

Note that this is only a type declaration; we do not declare variables to represent nodes. Nodes in the list are allocated as needed and are disposed of when no longer needed. The header node, a variable, is declared with type `NodePtr`. It allows us access to the other nodes in the list.

Program 14.7 defines a linked list using the declarations above. It also includes a Pascal procedure to set up values for the list. Rather than actually scanning some text and building the list—we do not want to let such an algorithm get in our way here—procedure `BuildList` requests data for consecutive nodes as character and count pairs. For each pair the user enters, `BuildList` requests a node using the New procedure. When the user enters # for the character, `BuildList` terminates.

Program 14.7 invokes two assembly-language routines, which are discussed in detail shortly. The first prints the data in all nodes in the list and is invoked just once by the main program when `BuildList` terminates. The second searches the list for a node that contains a selected character and returns either a pointer to it or NIL as the function value; this is invoked repeatedly until the user enters # to terminate. In both assembly-language routines, the first argument is the header node, which is just the pointer to the list.

**Figure 14.2** Portion of a Linked List

## 14.3 Linked Lists

**Program 14.7**

```pascal
{ Program 14.7      LetFreq.PAS                      }
{ Counts frequency distribution of characters,       }
{ using a linked list.                               }

PROGRAM LetFreq (Input, Output);

TYPE
  NodePtr = ^NodeType;
  NodeType = RECORD
    Ch    : Char;         { character from input     }
    Count : Integer;      { no. times Ch occurs      }
    Next  : NodePtr       { pointer to next node     }
  END;

VAR
  List,                   { Pointer to list of input chars }
  SearchRes : NodePtr;    { pointer to search result }
  SearchCh  : Char;       { character to search for in List }

PROCEDURE BuildList (var List: NodePtr);
{ Builds a list of characters and counts for use in     }
{ testing list procedures; values are provided by user. }

VAR
  InChar   : Char;        { character from input        }
  InCount  : Integer;     { count for InChar from input }
  NewNode,                { pointer for node being built }
  LastNode : NodePtr;     { pointer to last node of list }

BEGIN { BuildList }
  { initialize List for first node }
  List := NIL;

  { get data for first node }
  Write ('Character & Count (#0 to stop)? ');
  Readln(InChar, InCount);

  WHILE InChar <> '#' DO
    BEGIN  { build a new node }
      New(NewNode);
      NewNode^.Ch := InChar;
      NewNode^.Count := InCount;
      NewNode^.Next := NIL;

      { insert new node into list }
      IF List = NIL
        THEN   {first node}
          List := NewNode
        ELSE   {not first node}
          LastNode^.Next := NewNode;

      { update pointer to end of list }
      LastNode := NewNode;
```

**Program 14.7 (continued)**

```
            { get data for next node }
            Write ('Character & Count (#0 to stop)? ');
            Readln (InChar, InCount)
         END;
   END;    { BuildList }

PROCEDURE PrintList (List: NodePtr); External;
{$L PrintLis.OBJ }
{$I \INC\IO.INC --- include i/o routines for PrintList to use. }

FUNCTION LetterPtr (List: NodePtr; SearchCh: Char): NodePtr; External;
{$L LetterPtr.Obj }

BEGIN {LetFreq.PAS }
   { read text and build list }
   BuildList (List);

   { test PrintList procedure }
   PrintList (List);

   { test LetterPtr function }
   { get character to search for }
   Writeln;
   Write ('Character to search for? ');
   Readln (SearchCh);

   WHILE SearchCh <> '#' DO
      BEGIN
         { search for it }
         SearchRes := LetterPtr (List, SearchCh);

         { print result of search }
         Write ('There are ');
         IF SearchRes = NIL
            THEN Write ('no ')
            ELSE Write (SearchRes^.Count:1, ' ');
         Writeln (SearchCh:1, '''s in the list.');
         Writeln;

         { repeat test for another character }
         Write ('Character to search for (# to stop)? ');
         Readln (SearchCh);
      END;
END.    { LetFreq.PAS }
```

## Pointer Variables

There is little new about pointer variables. Recall that in passing an argument by reference, the parameter is a far pointer to the argument. We have used such pointers enough that we should be comfortable with them. A *pointer variable* is just a far pointer to a node. In a program that uses a linked list with dynamic allocation of the nodes, the only memory local to the program—that is, not accessed by a far pointer—is the header node. All nodes allocated during execution are accessed through far pointers.

### 14.3 Linked Lists

Our first assembly-language routine that works with a linked list prints the data fields of every node, in the order in which they are linked. The PrintList procedure is shown in Program 14.8.

**Program 14.8**

```
; Program 14.8      PrintLis.ASM
; Prints the data fields of all records in a linked list.
; Can be called from Turbo Pascal, as
;     Procedure PrintList (List: NodePtr);
;     List contains nodes as defined by the STRUC below

; Parameter:
    List            equ     dword ptr [bp + 4]

; List Record structure:
NodeType STRUC
    Chr             db      ?       ;char
    Count           dw      ?       ;integer
    Next            dd      ?       ;far pointer
NodeType ENDS

_DATA SEGMENT word public 'data'
    HeadingMsg      db      "  Char     Count"
    HeadingLen      dw      $ - HeadingMsg
    Blanks          db      "     "
    BlanksLen       dw      $ - Blanks
_DATA ENDS

_TEXT SEGMENT word public 'code'
    assume          cs: _TEXT
    assume          ds: _DATA
    extrn           PutStr: PROC, PutCrLf: PROC
    extrn           PutDec: PROC, PutChar: PROC
    public          PrintList

PrintList PROC

; set up bp register to point to parameter
    push    bp
    mov     bp, sp

; print ("  Char     Count")
    mov     cx, HeadingLen
    mov     bx, offset HeadingMsg
    call    PutStr
    call    PutCrLf

; NodePtr (in es:[di]) := List
    les     di, List

  WHILE01: ;NodePtr <> NIL
    mov     ax, es
    or      ax, di
    jz      ENDWHL01
```

**Program 14.8 (continued)**

```
;       DO01
;         print (NodePtr^.Chr, NodePtr^.Count)
          mov     cx, BlanksLen
          mov     bx, offset Blanks
          call    PutStr
          mov     dl, es:[di]+NodeType.Chr
          call    PutChar
          call    PutStr
          mov     ax, es:[di]+NodeType.Count
          call    PutDec
          call    PutCrLf

;         NodePtr := NodePtr^.Next
          les     di, es:[di]+NodeType.Next

;       repeat
          jmp     WHILE01
ENDWHL01:

; restore registers and return
          pop     bp
          ret     4

PrintList ENDP
_TEXT  ENDS
END
```

---

Note the record description using the STRUC directive:

```
NodeType STRUC
    Chr     db      ?       ;char
    Count   dw      ?       ;integer
    Next    dd      ?       ;far pointer
NodeType ENDS
```

Other than using Chr for the character data in the node (CH is reserved as a register name in assembly language, and Chr and Char are reserved in Pascal), this is the same as the Pascal declaration of NodeType.

The algorithm used in the PrintList procedure, with List representing the argument and NodePtr representing a local copy of the pointer, is

```
print headings
NodePtr := List
WHILE NodePtr <> Nil
DO
   print (NodePtr^.Chr, NodePtr^.Count)
   NodePtr := NodePtr^.Next
ENDWHILE
```

In Program 14.8, we use ES:DI as the far pointer NodePtr, and copy List into it using an les instruction.

## 14.3 Linked Lists

Testing that a pointer is NIL is interesting. The NIL pointer is just two words of zeros. A convenient way to test for a NIL pointer is to combine the two words using or and compare the result to zero: A zero can result only when the segment and offset are both zero. The instructions that implement the test in the WHILE statement are thus

```
mov     ax, es
or      ax, di
jz      ENDWHL01
```

The instructions to print the data fields use the record notation to specify the addition of the field displacements to the far pointer in ES:DI. To advance the pointer to the next node in the list, we copy the Next field of the current node into ES:DI using

```
    les     di, es:[di]+NodeType.Next
```

Note that the address of the source operand is fully determined before the destination operand is changed.

The second assembly-language routine is a function that searches the linked list for a node with a given value in the character field. If found, the function returns a pointer to the node; if not, the function returns the NIL pointer. Using List and SearchCh for the arguments, NodePtr for a local pointer, and Found as a local Boolean variable, the search algorithm we use is

```
NodePtr := List
Found := False
WHILE NodePtr <> Nil AND Not Found
DO
  IF NodePtr^.Chr = SearchCh
  THEN
    Found := True
  ELSE
    NodePtr := NodePtr^.Next
  ENDIF
ENDWHILE
IF Found
THEN
  return NodePtr
ELSE
  return NIL
ENDIF
```

This algorithm is implemented in Program 14.9. The declaration of the node structure is the same as in the previous program. We use ES:DI for NodePtr again and the CL register for the logical variable Found. The condition for the loop is implemented using the same test for a NIL pointer as in Program 14.8, followed by a test for CL not zero. The processing within the loop is simple enough that it needs no explanation.

---

**Program 14.9**

```
; Program 14.9      LettrPtr.ASM
; Search a linked list, return a pointer to the node that contains
; a specified character. Can be called from Turbo Pascal, as
;       Function LetterPtr (List: NodePtr; SearchCh: Char): NodePtr;
;       List has nodes defined as in the STRUC below.
```

## Program 14.9 (continued)

```
        ; Parameters:
          List         equ       dword ptr [bp + 6]
          SearchCh     equ       byte ptr [bp + 4]

        ; List Record structure
        NodeType STRUC
          Chr          db        ?           ;char
          Count        dw        ?           ;integer
          Next         dd        ?           ;pointer to next node
        NodeType ENDS

        _TEXT SEGMENT word public 'code'
            assume    cs: _TEXT
            public    LetterPtr

        LetterPtr PROC

        ; set up bp register to point to parameter
            push      bp
            mov       bp, sp

        ; NodePtr (in es:di) := List
            les       di, List

        ; Found (in cl) := False
            mov       cl, 0

          WHILE01: ;NodePtr <> NIL AND NOT Found
            mov       ax, es
            or        ax, di
            jz        ENDWHILE01
            cmp       cl, 0
            jnz       ENDWHILE01

        ; DO01
        ;   IF02 NodePtr^.Chr = SearchCh
            mov       dl, es:[di]+NodeType.Chr
            cmp       dl, SearchCh
            jne       ELSE02
        ;   THEN02
        ;     Found := True
            mov       cl, 1
            jmp       ENDIF02
          ELSE02:
        ;     NodePtr := NodePtr^.Next
            les       di, es:[di]+NodeType.Next
          ENDIF02:

        ;   repeat
            jmp       WHILE01
          ENDWHILE01:
```

## 14.3 Linked Lists

**Program 14.9 (continued)**

```
; IF03 Found
      cmp       cl, 1
      jne       ELSE03
; THEN03
;     return NodePtr (es:di) in dx:ax
      mov       dx, es
      mov       ax, di
      jmp       ENDIF03
  ELSE03:
;     return NIL in dx:ax
      mov       dx, 0
      mov       ax, 0
  ENDIF03:

; restore bp register and return
      pop       bp
      ret       6

LetterPtr ENDP
_TEXT ENDS
END
```

The new feature of Program 14.9 is the way that the function returns a pointer value. Turbo Pascal expects the pointer in DX:AX. To return NodePtr, implemented using ES:DI, we simply copy it into the other registers

```
mov       dx, es
mov       ax, di
```

To return a NIL pointer, we simply clear DX and AX to zero.

### Dynamic Memory Allocation

This section closes with a few words about *dynamic memory allocation*. When we request a node using the New procedure in Pascal, for example, the memory for the node is allocated, and a pointer to that node is returned in the parameter.

Running under DOS, the Pascal run-time environment has a region of memory, called the *heap*, that is used for dynamic variables. At any time, part of the heap is in use as nodes allocated to applications dynamically, and the rest of the heap is free (that is, it is available for use). The free regions of the heap may not be contiguous; the heap manager keeps all free regions linked in what is called a free list. As requests for nodes of various sizes are processed, the heap manager allocates memory from the free list. As nodes are disposed, the memory they used is returned to the free list.

When allocating memory dynamically, some systems search the free list for a node that is the size requested to allocate, whereas others allocate part of the first node of the free list that is large enough. When returning memory to the free list, the heap manager usually checks whether the returned memory is adjacent to nodes already on the free list; if so, it merges it with the adjacent free node(s); if not, it links the returned memory into the free list.

When a program terminates, the entire heap is made available to the operating system to allocate to the next program that needs memory. That is why it is not necessary to dispose of all nodes before terminating a program.

Heap management is complex enough and varies enough from one system to another that application programs should use the heap manager for all allocations and de-allocations of dynamic memory. Writing other procedures that manipulate the free list in any way is just begging for problems. When linking assembly routines with a high-level language, the assembly-language routines should use the same memory allocation procedures and functions as the high-level language.

## EXERCISES 14.3

▶1. Write an assembly-language procedure that scans the linked list used in this section and returns the total of all counts. Modify Program 14.7 to invoke your procedure and print the result.

▶2. Write an assembly-language function that scans the linked list used in this section and returns a pointer to the node with the largest count field. Modify Program 14.7 to invoke your function and print the result.

▶3. Write a Pascal function that calls New and returns the pointer as the function value. The argument to your procedure should be a pointer. This function is an intermediate routine that can be called from assembly language; New cannot be called directly from assembly language. Modify a copy of Program 14.7 so that rather than return a NIL pointer when SearchCh is not found it invokes New (through the intermediate Pascal function) and links the new node, with SearchCh and 0 for data, into the end of the list.

▶4. Write an assembly-language procedure that accesses all of the nodes in a linked list (such as the one from Program 14.9) in order and prints the address of each node in the form ssss:oooo, where ssss is the segment number and oooo is the offset, in hexadecimal.

## KEY POINTS

- A record is a collection of related data fields. The fields of a record may be different data types.
- Memory for a record variable can be reserved with data definition directives. Initial values can be assigned.
- To access a field in a record, the displacement of that field from the start of the record is added to the offset of the record.
- It is useful to associate the field names with the type of each field and the displacement of each field from the start of the record.
- When a record is passed as an argument, the subprogram must be able to determine the displacement and type of each field in the record. The record declaration in the subprogram can provide this information.
- To access a field within a record in an array of records, the displacement of the desired record within the array and the displacement of the desired field within the record are added to the starting address of the block of memory used for the structure.
- A linked list is a collection of records, called nodes, that are connected by pointers. Each node contains at least one pointer to another node. There is also a header containing only a pointer to the first node.

- To access a node in a linked list, the pointer to it is copied to a segment and base (or index) register pair, and those registers are used as an indirect operand.
- A region of memory, called the heap, is used for dynamic memory allocation. When memory is allocated, the run-time system partitions the heap and provides a pointer to the area allocated. When memory is disposed, the run-time system links the returned block into the free list. The run-time system needs the size of the block requested or disposed; some high-level languages hide this need.

## PC SYSTEM SUMMARY

- STRUC and ENDS define a record data type, including an explicit type and an implicit displacement for each field, and a name for the record type.
- Record variables are written using the record type name (the label on the STRUC directive) following the label of the record variable. This is followed by <, any initial values for the fields, and >.
- Default initial values for fields can be included in the record type definition written with STRUC.
- Pointer variables are implemented as far pointers, as a 16-bit segment and a 16-bit offset.

Directives presented in this chapter:
    STRUC    Declares the start of a record data type
    ENDS    Declares the end of a record data type

# 15 Character Strings

- **Representation**
- **Specification**
- **Operations**
- **Instructions**

Much of the data processed by computer systems is represented as character strings. User input is entered as character strings at a keyboard. Output is produced as character strings on a video display or a printer. Data processed in business applications are character strings or a closely related form of decimal number. Source programs are character strings. In many activities, our computers do not compute as much as they manipulate strings.

The common operations on character strings are simple to describe and use in a high-level language. Since character strings usually cannot fit in a register all at once, implementing the common operations on strings is another matter. Unlike addition or comparison of integer data, most string operations require manipulating parts of a string in some sequence, often repeating several instructions for each character in a string.

This chapter examines how strings are represented and reviews common operations on strings. To help the reader better understand and appreciate string operations, this chapter shows how to implement some of the operations using only the instructions we have already seen. It then examines the 8086's powerful string instructions and how they can be used to implement the operations more efficiently.

## 15.1 REPRESENTATION

Characters are stored in computer memory and transmitted between various devices using six, seven, or eight bits for each. By interpreting the bits that represent a character as an unsigned byte integer, we can associate a number with each character. In a high-level language, the unsigned integer that corresponds to a character is often called the ordinal value of the character.

### Character Codes

There are several codes used to represent characters. Two of the more commonly used codes are the *American Standard Code for Information Interchange* (*ASCII*) and *Extended Binary Coded Decimal Interchange Code* (*EBCDIC*). The standard ASCII code uses seven

## 15.1 Representation

bits; the extended version of ASCII used in PCs uses eight bits. The EBCDIC code uses eight bits.

The number of characters that can be represented in a code depends on the number of bits used. The 7-bit ASCII code can represent 128 different characters—enough for capital and lower case letters, digits, punctuation, some special symbols, and a number of control codes. The 8-bit EBCDIC code can represent 256 different characters—essentially most of the ASCII characters plus a few more special symbols and control codes. The 8-bit extended ASCII code used in PCs contains the seven-bit ASCII code with a leading zero bit, and another 128 codes with a leading one bit for graphics and foreign language characters. A table for this code is given in Appendix 2. Other 8-bit extended ASCII codes incorporate the 128 codes for the standard character set and different sets of 128 additional codes.

In the extended ASCII code used by PCs, the first 32 codes, 00h through 1Fh, represent control codes. For example, codes 02h and 03h, STX (Start TeXt) and ETX (End TeXt), are used to delimit the text of a message transmitted using certain protocols. More familiar codes include the following:

07h (BEL): sounds the bell or speaker

08h (BS, BackSpace): moves the cursor back one character

0Ah (LF, LineFeed): advances output to the next line

0Ch (FF, FormFeed): advances output to a new page

0Dh (CR, Carriage Return): returns the output device to the start of the line

1Bh (ESC, ESCape): signals the start of a sequence of control codes

Another important code is 00h, the NUL character. It is used to fill memory used for strings when the string is shorter than the memory allocated to it. NUL characters do not generally cause any noticeable effect when included in output.

The next 95 codes, 20h through 7Eh represent the standard ASCII graphic characters. (The term "graphic character," as used here, simply means that there is a standard symbol that can be displayed or shown on a keycap.) The code for a blank, 20h, is the first of these.

The digits are represented by codes 30h through 39h. The difference between a digit represented as an ASCII character and as a binary number is 30h. To convert a digit from a character code to a number represented in binary, we can subtract 30h from the code. In a high-level language, conversion from a character to a number might be written as

```
Number := ORD(Digit) - ORD('0')
```

which merely subtracts 30h from the representation of Digit. To convert the other way, we add 30h. These conversions can be performed as addition and subtraction, or as and and or operations with appropriate masks.

The capital letters of the English alphabet use the 26 consecutive codes 41h through 5Ah. The lowercase letters of the English alphabet use the 26 consecutive codes 61h through 7Ah. The difference between the two forms of the same letter is 20h. To convert a letter from lowercase to capital, we can subtract 20h from the code. In a high-level language, conversion of a letter from lowercase to capital might be written as

```
Capital := CHR(ORD(Lower) - ORD('a') + ORD('A'))
```

This can be explained as computing the displacement of Lower from 'a' and adding it to 'A' in some sense. But the conversion can be rewritten as

```
Capital := CHR(ORD(Lower) - (ORD('a') - ORD('A')))
```

Here the difference of the last two terms is 20h.

The code 7Fh is a control character, but is treated like bs (code 08h) under DOS. The codes 80h through FEh represent selected graphic characters from several other natural languages, some mathematics symbols, background shading, and line-drawing characters.

## Strings in Memory

Character strings are represented in memory as a sequence of the bytes that contain the codes for each character of the string in sequence. In addition to the codes for the characters, length information or a special end-of-string code may also be stored.

When each byte of memory has a unique address, the individual characters within a string can be accessed simply. When memory is addressed as words containing two or more characters, how we access individual characters within a string depends on whether the string is packed or unpacked (Figure 15.1). A **packed character string**, declared as a packed array of characters or as a string type in high-level languages, is stored with as many characters per word as fit. This uses the minimum amount of storage for the string, but requires extra processing to access individual characters. An **unpacked character string**, declared as an array of characters, is stored with one character per word. This provides convenient access to individual characters in the string, but uses more memory than a packed string.

| T | h | i | s |
|---|---|---|---|
|   | i | s |   |
| a |   | p | a |
| c | k | e | d |
|   | c | h | a |
| r | a | c | t |
| e | r | s |   |
| t | r | i | n |
| g | . |   |   |

| U |
|---|
| n |
| p |
| a |
| c |
| k |
| e |
| d |
| . |

**Figure 15.1  Strings Packed Four Characters per Word, and Unpacked**

## 15.1 Representation

Computers that address memory as bytes can access each character in a string separately, yet do not leave any memory unused. These machines have the advantages of both packed and unpacked representations.

### String Length

It is often necessary to know how many characters are in a string. This dimension is called the length of the string. The maximum length of a string in a high-level language is available to the compiler, and is used for checking assignments to the string during execution. Strings can be classified into three types based on length: fixed-length, bounded-length, and variable-length. Each of these types is used in some high-level language.

In a **fixed-length string**, the declaration of the string specifies its length. Values assigned to the string, either by assignment statements or by input operations, must contain the number of characters specified in the declaration. The string may be extended with spaces or NUL characters if it is too short, or truncated if it is too long. With fixed-length strings, any reference to the length of the string returns the constant used in the declaration.

In a **bounded-length string**, the declaration of the string specifies the longest string value that can be assigned. A string of any length up to and including the limit can be assigned, without supplying trailing spaces or NUL characters. Longer strings are truncated when assigned. As with fixed-length strings, a fixed amount of memory is allocated for a bounded-length string. A reference to the length of the string returns the length of the value most recently assigned to the string.

In a **variable-length string**, the declaration does not include length information. There is usually a limit to the length of a string, typically 1 less than some power of 2, such as 255 or 65535 characters. (Sometimes the limit applies not to each string, but to the combined lengths of all strings in the program.) Typically, the memory associated with each string variable consists of two parts: a static part that contains the length of the string and a pointer to the actual string, and a dynamic part where the actual string is stored. When an assignment is made, memory is allocated dynamically for the string value from a separate area of memory reserved for strings. See the discussion of dynamic memory allocation in Section 14.3 for more on this subject.

## EXERCISES 15.1

1. Code the following strings in ASCII. Write your answers in hexadecimal.
   (*a*) "Pi aren't square!"
   (*b*) "7% of 25 is 1.75."
   (*c*) "[bx], 0Eh"
   (*d*) "Len := 0;"
   (*e*) "word ptr [bx]"

2. Decode the following messages, which are coded in ASCII:
   (*a*) 50 69 20 61 72 65 20 72 6F 75 6E 64 3F
   (*b*) 36 20 2A 20 37 20 3D 20 34 32 2E
   (*c*) 53 73 72 2C 20 65 73 3A 64 69
   (*d*) 57 72 69 74 65 20 28 22 3E 22 29 3B
   (*e*) 50 75 74 44 65 63 3A 20 50 52 4F 43

3. The character code used on some supercomputers uses only six bits. That code does not include lowercase letters. How does this affect the applications that run on these computers? How does it affect sharing information between these computers and others that use ASCII or EBCDIC?

▶4. Write an assembly-language function that reads a character using GetChar. If the character is a lowercase letter, return the corresponding capital letter; otherwise, return the character as the function result.

▶5. Write an assembly-language program that reads a number less than 256 and prints the ASCII character that it codes. For control codes (00h through 31h), print the word Ctrl- and the graphic character from the range 40h through 5Fh. That is, it should print Ctrl-A for input value 1, and Ctrl-] for input value 29.

## 15.2 SPECIFICATION

This text has been using strings with PutStr to display prompt messages and to label output. These strings have been defined as string constants in the data segment. This section reviews these declarations and examines how string variables are specified.

### String Constants

The typical string constant in this book has been defined as in the following example:

```
StringMsg  db      "This is a literal string."
StringLen  dw      $ - StringMsg
```

Strings declared with the db directive are stored in consecutive bytes of memory, one character per byte. The expression $ - StringMsg represents the length of the string, computed during assembly.

It might occasionally be desirable to include a control character as part of a string. The 8086 assemblers allow use of the ordinal values of characters separated by commas as well as the characters in quotation marks. For example, the declaration

```
XNUL       db      "X",0
```

defines a string of two characters in ASCII: an X followed by the code for NUL. More than one control character can be included in the string, as can more than one literal value. For example, to shift one popular brand of dot-matrix printers from normal text to superscript text requires sending the ESC code followed by "S" and NUL; sending the ESC code followed by "T" cancels superscript mode. To define the string "$X^2$ =" we could use

```
XSqStr     db      "X",27,"S",0,"2",27,"T ="
XSqLen     dw      $ - XSqStr
```

The shift to superscript requires three codes: ESC specified by 27, the letter "S", and NUL specified by 0. These appear in the example between "X" and "2". The shift back to normal text requires two codes: ESC specified by 27, and the letter "T". These follow "2" in the example.

## 15.2 Specification

## String Variables

Consider reserving memory for string variables. There are many possible conventions that can be used, depending on whether the string has a fixed length, a bounded length, or a variable length.

For fixed-length strings, it is recommended that the length of the string be defined as a named constant and that that name be used in a db directive. For example, to reserve memory for a 20-character string called NameStr, we would use

```
NameLen   equ    20
NameStr   db     NameLen dup (?)
```

The named constant is available as an immediate operand that can be used in the program and can be passed as an argument to a subprogram. To refer to individual characters, we treat the string as an array of bytes; NameStr[si] with SI = 0 refers to the first character, and with SI = 19 refers to the last. (Alteratively, (NameStr-1)[si] could be used for the operand, so that the index register, SI, can have the same number as the relative position of the character.) FORTRAN uses fixed-length strings, and allows substrings to be accessed using subscripts.

For bounded-length strings, if we assume that we do not need strings longer than 255 characters, then we need one byte for the actual length of the string and one byte for each character. Again, a named constant is used for the maximum length of the string. For example, if NameStr is a string up to 20 characters long, memory for it can be reserved as a bounded-length string with the declarations

```
NameMax   equ    20
NameStr   db     0, NameMax dup (?)
```

NameMax is the maximum length of the string. The first byte of memory reserved in the second line is the actual length of the string; this has been cleared to 0 as there is no value assigned to the string yet. The string itself is stored in the next 20 bytes of memory. To refer to individual characters, we again treat the string as an array of bytes, but recognize that the leading byte contains the length. This is how strings are stored in many of the versions of Pascal that provide a string type as an extension of the language.

If strings are longer than 255 characters, the length requires a word rather than a byte. In some applications, using a word for the length is convenient even if the string is small. In these cases, it is recommended that a separate name be used for the actual length. The example becomes

```
NameMax   equ    20
NameLen   dw     ?
NameStr   db     NameMax dup (?)
```

The characters of NameStr are accessed relative to the first character using indexing, just like a fixed-length string. The next section presents a procedure, GetStr, that uses strings defined this way.

For variable-length strings, we use dynamic memory allocation and store a pointer to the string. In 8086 systems, the pointer is a far pointer into the heap used for storing all strings. The maximum length of a string is determined by the largest available block of memory in the heap. The length of the actual string does not need to be stored as a number; usually, the end of the string is marked by a NUL character. However, the heap manager needs the length to allocate memory and to reclaim memory no longer needed. To access individual characters in the string, we can use the pointer with an index register or we can modify the pointer as we proceed through the string. The C language uses variable-length strings that terminate with a NUL character; some versions of BASIC use variable-length strings with the length and pointer stored in a record associated with the name of the string variable.

The next section examines the operations typically provided in a high-level language and shows how they can be implemented at the machine level.

## EXERCISES 15.2

1. Some applications on a personal computer allow you to enter an extended ASCII character (those with codes 80h through FEh) by holding down an ALT key while typing the ordinal value of the character as a three-digit decimal number on the numeric keypad. Can you enter extended characters this way in an assembly-language source program? Can you enter extended characters this way as data read by an assembly-language program?
2. As a programmer working in a high-level language, what do you think are some of the advantages of using fixed-length strings? Some of the disadvantages?
3. As a programmer working in a high-level language, what do you think are some of the advantages of using bounded-length strings? Some of the disadvantages?
4. As a programmer working in a high-level language, what do you think are some of the advantages of using variable-length strings? Some of the disadvantages?
5. How does your favorite high-level language store string variables? Can you tell from the declarations and syntax rules?
6. In many high-level languages, to include a string delimiter within a string constant we must write two consecutive delimiters. For example, in FORTRAN we write `'Don''t ask,'` to specify the string `"Don't ask,"` in a program. Can we use this trick to include a NUL within a string when NUL is used to mark the end of the string? Explain.

## 15.3 OPERATIONS

There are many operations that can be performed on strings. We need only consider some of the capabilities of a word processor or text editor to identify more operations than we care to implement in assembly language. Many editing tasks can be implemented using a fairly small set of operations. Such a set is considered here.

### Input and Output

We have already seen one of the most useful operations involving a string: printing it. The `PutStr` procedure prints a string by extracting its characters one at a time and passing them on to a DOS function that prints them. The arguments to `PutStr` are the length of the string in the CX register, and the offset of the first character in the BX register. The

## 15.3 Operations

DOS Display Character function expects its argument in DL. The heart of the PutStr procedure is the loop body:

```
    DO21:
;       display character from string
            mov     dl, [bx]
            int     DosFunc
;       advance to next character of string, repeat
            inc     bx
            loop    DO21
    ENDFOR21:
```

See the listing in Appendix 1. The mov instruction copies a character from the string into DL, in preparation for DOS to print it. The inc instruction advances the pointer to the next character in the string.

As a complement to the PutStr procedure, a procedure can be written to read a string. To be consistent with PutStr, the arguments to this procedure are the maximum length for the string in CX and the offset of the string in BX. The procedure should read characters from the keyboard, store them in the string, and return in the CX register the number of characters actually read.

Before writing this procedure, it is necessary to decide how the user can terminate a string if he or she wants to enter fewer than the maximum number of characters, and what the procedure should do when the user enters more than the number of characters specified in CX. The procedure shown here will terminate string input when the user taps the ENTER key or when the maximum number of characters has been read. Any input beyond this maximum will be ignored, but it will be kept in the keyboard buffer for later use. (Actually, depending on what the calling program does after reading the string, the user will usually know when the program stops reading characters because something else will be happening.)

Our GetStr procedure is given in Program 15.1. The algorithm used to read the string is

```
clear counter
REPEAT
   read a character
   append character to string
   advance pointer in string
   increment counter
UNTIL (character is CR) OR (max. chars read)
IF character is CR
THEN
   decrement counter
ENDIF
```

The procedure uses the CX register to control how many characters are read and the DX register to count the characters as they are copied to the argument string.

The loop in Program 15.1 is implemented using the loopne instruction. The test of whether the character just read into the AL register is CR is performed by the cmp instruction before the loopne instruction. The loopne instruction decrements CX and jumps back to the start of the loop if the zero flag is cleared (that is, if the character is not CR) and the CX register is not zero (that is, the maximum number of characters has not been read).

# Program 15.1

```
;   Program 15.1       GetStr.ASM
;   Reads a string, terminated by CR or when the max. number
;     of characters specified in cx have been read.
;   Input parameters:
;     bx = offset of memory into which string is to be read
;     cx = maximum length of string
;   Output parameters:
;     bx = offset of memory into which string was read
;     cx = number of characters read (not counting Enter)

_TEXT SEGMENT word public 'code'
        assume  cs: _TEXT
        extrn   GetChar: PROC
        public  GetStr

GetStr PROC

; save caller's registers
        push    ax
        push    bx
        push    dx

; clear counter
        mov     dx, 0

  REPEAT01:
;     read a character
        call    GetChar

;     append it to string and advance pointer
        mov     [bx], al
        inc     bx

;     increment counter
        inc     dx

; TEST01
        cmp     al, 0Dh
        loopne  REPEAT01
; UNTIL01 (character is CR) OR (max. chars read)

; replace max. count with actual count
        mov     cx, dx

; IF02 last character read was CR
        jne     ENDIF02

; THEN02
;     decrement actual count by one
        dec     cx
  ENDIF02:
```

## Program 15.1 (continued)

```
; restore caller's registers and return
    pop     dx
    pop     bx
    pop     ax
    ret

GetStr ENDP
_TEXT ENDS
END
```

The selection structure following the loop adjusts the counter when the last character read is CR. As the mov instruction in the loop copies every character read into the string, the inc instruction following it adds one to DX for every character read, including CR. The CX register is adjusted so that the calling program gets the length of the string without the CR (if present).

## Finding the Length of a String

Usually, there isn't much work involved in finding the length of a string. For fixed-length and bounded-length strings, the length is either an immediate constant defined in the program or a variable; for some variable-length strings, the length is stored in the record containing the pointer to the string; and for other variable-length strings, a function is needed to determine the length.

The basic strategy is to search the string and look for the code that defines the end of the string. During the search, we simply count the number of characters scanned; when the end of the string is found, we return the count as the function value. We must be clear whether the length should include the end-of-string code, and possibly adjust the count accordingly. (Searching for the code that marks the end of a string is a special case of matching a substring, which will be considered in detail later in this section.)

## Copying a Substring

A **substring** is simply a part of a string. We need three items to define a substring: the original string and information to specify the two ends of the substring. The latter can be specified in a number of ways. In the examples that follow, it is assumed that the original string is "concatenate" and that a substring of it is desired. The ends of the substring can be specified using the position of the first and last characters in the original string. For example, the substring "cat" contains the fourth through sixth characters. We can specify the number of characters and the position of the first. For example, "ten" contains three characters starting with the sixth character. We can specify the number of characters and the position of the last character. For example, "on" contains two characters ending at the third character. We can specify the number of characters from the beginning of the string. For example, "con" consists of the first three characters. The starting position is implied.

## 532 Chapter 15 Character Strings

We can also specify the number of characters from the end of the string. For example, "ate" consists of the last three characters. The ending position is implied.

Actually, if we can find the length of a string and are willing to do some simple arithmetic, a routine that implements the first method, specifying a substring by the starting and ending positions in the original string, can be used to implement all of the other methods. Therefore, only the first method will be discussed further.

Consider a substring of Source specified by the positions of the First and Last characters. Assuming that $1 \leq \text{First} \leq \text{Last} \leq \text{length(Source)}$, and that the memory reserved for the substring is large enough, the algorithm for copying the substring to Result can be written

```
length(Result) := Last - First + 1
di := 1
si := First
FOR cx := length(Result) DOWNTO 1
DO
  Result[di] := Source[si]
  si := si + 1
  di := di + 1
ENDFOR
```

When we implement this, we need to consider where the length of the substring will be stored, and we might have to adjust the indexes by 1. In the algorithm it is assumed that, when an index is 1, the reference is to the first character of the string; in the computer, this reference is to the second byte of memory reserved for the string.

Program 15.2 implements this algorithm as a function using Pascal strings. Turbo Pascal pushes a far pointer for the result of a string function onto the stack before pushing the arguments to the function. The first two equ directives define far pointers for Result and Source. These strings are stored with the length in the first byte (at index zero). The positions of the first and last characters of the substring are also unsigned byte arguments to the function (recall that byte arguments are actually pushed as words, with the argument byte at an even displacement from BP).

## Program 15.2

```
        ; Program 15.2       SubStr.ASM
        ; Returns a substring specified by first and last position.
        ; Can be called from Turbo Pascal, as
        ;    SubString (Source: String; First, Last: Byte): String;

        ; Pointer to result, parameters:
           Result      equ      dword ptr [bp + 12]
           Source      equ      dword ptr [bp + 8]
           First       equ      byte ptr [bp + 6]
           Last        equ      byte ptr [bp + 4]

        _TEXT SEGMENT word public 'code'
            assume    cs: _TEXT
            public    Substring

SubString PROC
```

## 15.3 Operations

**Program 15.2 (continued)**

```
            ; set up bp register to point to result and parameters
                push    bp
                mov     bp, sp

            ; set up pointers to strings
                push    ds                      ;save caller's ds
                les     di, Result
                lds     si, Source

            ; check starting position, save correct position in bl
            ; IF01 First <= 1
                mov     al, First
                cmp     al, 1
                jnbe    ELSE01

            ; THEN01
            ;   starting position (in bl) := 1
                mov     bl, 1
                jmp     ENDIF01

              ELSE01:
            ;   IF02 First > length(Source)
                cmp     al, ds:[si]
                jna     ELSE02

                THEN02:
            ;     starting position (in bl) := length(Source) + 1
                mov     bl, ds:[si]
                inc     bl
                jmp     ENDIF02

                ELSE02:
            ;     starting position (in bl) := First
                mov     bl, First
              ENDIF02:
              ENDIF01:

            ; determine length of substring in al
            ; IF03 Last < starting position
                mov     al, Last
                cmp     al, bl
                jnb     ELSE03

            ; THEN03
            ;   length(Result) := 0
                sub     al, al
                jmp     ENDIF03

              ELSE03:
            ;   IF04 Last <= length(Source)
                cmp     al, ds:[si]
                jnbe    ELSE04
```

**Program 15.2 (continued)**

```
;       THEN04
;          length(Result) := Last - starting position + 1
           sub     al, bl
           inc     al
           jmp     ENDIF04

        ELSE04:
;          length(Result) := length(Source) - starting position + 1
           mov     al, ds:[si]
           sub     al, bl
           inc     al
        ENDIF04:
     ENDIF03:

; save length in Result[0]
           mov     es:[di], al

; advance indexes to start of substrings
           sub     bh, bh
           add     si, bx
           inc     di

; Copy substring.
; FOR05 cx := length(Result) TO 1 STEP -1
           mov     cl, al
           sub     ch, ch
           jcxz    ENDFOR05

        DO05:
;          Result[di] := Source[si]
           mov     al, ds:[si]
           mov     es:[di], al

;          advance indexes to next characters
           inc     si
           inc     di

        loop    DO05
     ENDFOR05:

; restore caller's registers and return
           pop     ds
           pop     bp
           ret     8

SubString ENDP
_TEXT ENDS
END
```

## 15.3 Operations

Although function `SubString` cannot verify that the substring it returns will fit in the string defined for the function result, it can and does check that `First` and `Last` define a substring of `Source`. The first pair of nested selection structures verifies that `First` is within the string and determines a starting position accordingly:

```
IF First <= 1
THEN
  Start := 1
ELSE
  IF First > length(Source)
  THEN
    Start := length(Source) + 1
  ELSE
    Start := First
  ENDIF
ENDIF
```

After determining the starting position, a second pair of nested selections determines the length of the substring:

```
IF Last < Start
THEN
  length(Result) := 0
ELSE
  IF Last <= length(Source)
  THEN
    length(Result) := Last - Start + 1
  ELSE
    length(Result) := length(Source) - Start + 1
  ENDIF
ENDIF
```

Note that if `First` is greater than the length of the `Source` string, `Start` is made 1 greater than that length; in the second pair of selections, the length of the result will be made 0 by either the first THEN clause (when `Last` is valid) or the second ELSE clause (when `Last` is also greater than the length of the source string). The net effect of these tests is that, if the function is asked for the fourth through tenth characters of an 8-character string, for example, the function returns a substring consisting of the fourth through eighth characters.

The arguments for `First` and `Last` are bytes, and the lengths of `Source` and `Result` are the first bytes referenced by the far pointers. The nested selections and length calculations use unsigned byte arithmetic and conditional jumps and are straightforward.

The part of the function that makes the actual copy starts by adding `Start` to SI and 1 to DI. This positions the far pointer to the appropriate starting positions in the strings. The function then copies the length of the substring into CX and tests that it is indeed greater than 0. Then the loop

```
DO05:
    mov     al, ds:[si]
    mov     es:[di], al
    inc     si
    inc     di
    loop    DO05
```

copies the characters from `Source` to `Result` one at a time, using the AL register.

## Concatenating Two Strings

Joining one string onto the end of another is called **concatenation**. For example, if we concatenate the strings "break" and "fast", we get "breakfast"; if we concatenate them as "fast", " ", and "break", we get "fast break" instead.

Often the two strings being joined are specified as substrings of other strings. For example, if the string FullName has a person's name as "Smith, John Q." we might write an expression that extracts substrings and rebuilds FullName as "John Q. Smith".

Concatenation is implemented as a series of (sub)string copy operations. Essentially, Program 15.2 can be modified so that, when we finish copying the part of the first source string that we're interested in, we proceed to copy the relevant part of the second source string, continuing in the same destination string. We must be careful with the length byte, however. Concatenation of two strings will be implemented after the 8086 string instructions have been introduced later in this chapter.

## Comparing Strings

There are three possible relationships between two strings: They can be equal; the first can be less than the second; or the first can be greater than the second. What does it mean, though, to say that one string is less than another? Actually, since the ordinal values of the individual characters are compared, and since these are unsigned numbers, we should be asking what it means for one string to be below another. As neither "less than" nor "below" sound quite right in this context, the phrases "is before" and "is after" will be adopted when comparing strings.

For strings of all capital letters or all lowercase letters, one string is before another if it precedes it alphabetically. For example, "ANNA" is before "ARTHUR" since "N" is before "R" in the alphabet. For strings made up of mixed capital and lowercase letters, or that contain other characters, the outcome of the comparison depends on the code used. In ASCII, the string "Arthur" is before the string "arthur" because the ordinal value of "A" is below the ordinal value of "a".

Strings are compared by comparing the characters in each position, from left to right, until the relationship between the strings is determined. As long as the two characters compared at each succesive step are the same, it is impossible to determine whether one string is before the other or whether they are the same string. It is when we find two different characters in the same position, or when we reach the end of one of the strings without finding a difference, that we can determine the relation. In the former case, the result of comparing the different characters gives the relationship between the strings. In the latter case, the lengths of the strings give the relationship.

Before implementing string comparisons, we must decide how we want to code the result. One option is to write three Boolean functions, one for each of the possible relationships. However, it is more convenient to have six functions, combining relationships and writing tests for "is before or equal" and so on.

Comparison of two strings can also be implemented as a single function that returns one of three values according to the relation of the first string to the second. This requires the calling program to test the result further. Whether we choose to write one function or six, however, the processing needed to compare the two strings byte by byte is the same.

## 15.3 Operations

Rather than write the same code six times, we write only one function that returns one of three values.

The algorithm for comparing strings is implemented in the function of Program 15.3. The function is called from Pascal, and is passed from the far pointers to the strings. It returns −1 if the first string is before the second, 0 if they are the same, and +1 if the first string is after the second.

**Program 15.3**

```
; Program 15.3        CompStr.ASM
; Compares two strings; returns -1 if Str1 < Str2,
;    0 if Str1 = Str2, or +1 if Str1 > Str2.
; Can be called from Turbo Pascal, as
;    CompStr (Str1, Str2: String): Integer;

; Parameters and local variables:
  Str1      equ    dword ptr [bp + 8]
  Str2      equ    dword ptr [bp + 4]
  Str1Len   equ    byte ptr [bp - 1]
  Str2Len   equ    byte ptr [bp - 2]

_TEXT SEGMENT word public 'code'
      assume   cs: _TEXT
      public   CompStr

CompStr PROC

; set up bp register to point to parameters
      push     bp
      mov      bp, sp

; allocate stack space for local variables
      sub      sp, 2

; set up pointers to strings
      push     ds                ;save caller's ds
      lds      si, Str1
      les      di, Str2

; save lengths of string for later use
      mov      al, ds:[si]
      mov      Str1Len, al
      mov      al, es:[di]
      mov      Str2Len, al

; Find shorter length, for use in cx to control loop.
; IF01 Str1Len <= Str2Len
      cmp      Str1Len, al
      jnbe     ELSE01

; THEN01
;    cx := Str1Len
      mov      cl, Str1Len
      sub      ch, ch
      jmp      ENDIF01
```

**Program 15.3 (continued)**

```
        ELSE01:
;           cx := Str2Len
            mov     cl, Str2Len
            sub     ch, ch
        ENDIF01:

; Compare characters from strings, up to the length
; of the shorter string, or until a difference is found.
; IF02 shorter string is not empty
        jcxz    ENDIF02

; THEN02
        REPEAT03:
;           advance indexes to next pair of characters
            inc     di
            inc     si

;           TEST03 Str1[si] = Str2[di]
            mov     al, ds:[si]
            cmp     al, es:[di]
            loope   REPEAT03
;       UNTIL03 end of shorter string OR difference found
        ENDIF02:

; If a difference is found, it determines the relationship
; between the strings... check this next
; IF04 a difference is found
        je      ELSE04

; THEN04
;       IF05 Str1[] < Str2[]
        jnb     ELSE05

;       THEN05 Str1 < Str2
;           return -1
            mov     ax, -1
            jmp     ENDIF05

        ELSE05: ;Str1 > Str2
;           return +1
            mov     ax, 1
        ENDIF05:
        jmp     ENDIF04

        ELSE04: ;No difference found, check lengths.
;       IF06 Str1Len < Str2Len
            mov     al, Str1Len
            cmp     al, Str2Len
            jnb     ELSE06

;       THEN06 Str1 is shorter, so it comes before Str2
;           return -1
            mov     ax, -1
            jmp     ENDIF06
```

### 15.3 Operations

**Program 15.3 (continued)**

```
            ELSE06:
;               IF07 Str1Len > Str2Len
                    jna         ELSE07

;               THEN07 Str1 is longer, so it comes after Str2
;                  return +1
                    mov         ax, 1
                    jmp         ENDIF07

                ELSE07:  ;strings are same length, so they are the same
;                  return 0
                    mov         ax, 0
                ENDIF07:
            ENDIF06:
        ENDIF04:

    ; restore caller's registers and stack, then return
            pop         ds
            add         sp, 2
            pop         bp
            ret         8

CompStr ENDP
_TEXT ENDS
END
```

Program 15.3 uses two bytes of local storage on the stack for the string lengths. These are defined in equ directives as Str1Len and Str2Len. The stack pointer is adjusted to allocate space for these by the instruction

```
    sub     sp, 2
```

after establishing the BP register. Then, once the pointers to the argument strings are set up, the lengths are copied from the first bytes of the strings into the bytes allocated on the stack.

The function determines the length of the shorter string and assigns it to CX in the first selection structure. The part of the function that actually compares the two strings consists of a REPEAT-UNTIL loop implemented with a loope instruction. If the shorter string is not empty, this loop advances the pointers and compares characters of the two strings until unequal characters are found or the end of the shorter string is reached. This is implemented by the instructions

```
        REPEAT03:
            inc     di
            inc     si
;       TEST03 Str1[si] = Str2[di]
            mov     al, ds:[si]
            cmp     al, es:[di]
            loope   REPEAT03
;       UNTIL end of shorter string OR difference
```

The `loope` instruction transfers control to REPEAT03 after the `cmp` instruction sets the zero flag—to indicate that the two characters are the same—and the CX register is not 0. When the characters differ, `cmp` clears the zero flag, and sets or clears the carry flag according to whether the character from Str1 is below the character from Str2; in this case, `loope` does not transfer control. When CX becomes 0, all characters of the shorter string have been compared, and `loope` does not transfer control.

When the loop terminates, for either reason, the zero and carry flags remain as set or cleared by the last `cmp` instruction. The states of these flags indicate the relationship between the strings determined so far.

The program then checks, at IF04, whether the last pair of characters compared differ. If the characters differ, the IF05 selection structure determines which string is before the other and loads AX with the corresponding code. If the last pair of characters compared are the same, nested selections IF06 and IF07 load AX according to which string is shorter or whether they are the same length.

Although long, the program is straightforward. The next section will present some instructions that simplify string comparison.

## Matching a Substring

Another operation commonly available in implementations of high-level languages that provide a string data type is the finding of the starting position of one string within another. This is often implemented as a function named INDEX. It is a *pattern-matching* operation. The string we are searching for is called the **pattern string**, while the string we are searching in is called the source string, or **object string**. The **index** of a pattern string in a source string is the position at which the first complete copy of the pattern occurs in the source, or 0 if the pattern does not occur.

For example, the index of "ate" in "concatenate" is 5, since the first copy of "ate" occurs in the fifth through seventh characters. The occurrence of "ate" in the ninth through eleventh characters is not recognized unless we restart the search after the fifth character position. The index of "cant" in "concatenate" is zero, since the string "cant" does not occur. That the characters in "cant" occur individually within the object, even in the right order, is irrelevant, because they do not appear as a substring without intervening characters.

The basic pattern-matching algorithm is reasonably straightforward. Starting with the first character in the object string, we compare a substring of the same length as the pattern string to the pattern. If they match, return 1 as the index. Otherwise, start the substring with the second character of the object string, and then with the third, and so on. Each time the comparison of the substring fails to match the pattern, advance the starting position within the object string one character. When a copy of the pattern is found, return the starting position within the object as the index. If no copy of the pattern is found before advancing the starting position in the object to the point where the object has fewer remaining characters than the pattern—no copy of the pattern exists within the object—return 0 as the index. This can be written in more detail as in Figure 15.2.

There are several faster algorithms known, but they will not be investigated here. Even this version will not be implemented. Rather, a slightly different algorithm will be implemented following the examination of the 8086's string instructions.

### 15.3 Operations

```
i := 1
Found := false
WHILE NOT Found AND i <= length(Object) - length(Pattern) + 1
DO
   j := i
   k := 1
   WHILE Object[j] = Pattern[k] AND k <= length(Pattern)
   DO
       j := j + 1
       k := k + 1
   ENDWHILE
   IF Object[j] = Pattern[k]
     THEN Found := true
     ELSE i := i + 1
   ENDIF
ENDWHILE
IF Found
  THEN return i
  ELSE return 0
ENDIF
```

**Figure 15.2** Algorithm for Locating Pattern in Object

## EXERCISES 15.3

▶1. Modify `GetStr.ASM` so that it continues to accept characters until the ENTER key is tapped. It should ignore any characters beyond the maximum length specified in CX.

▶2. Write a function that finds the last nonblank character in a string that might be padded with blanks. The function should return the position as the function value; it should not change the length argument.

3. Trace the execution of `CompStr` for each of the pairs of argument strings below. Give the outcome of all `cmp` instructions; use the labels on the control structures to indicate the path taken.

   (a)  Str1 = 4, "AbcD"
        Str2 = 4, "AbCd"
   (b)  Str1 = 0, ""
        Str2 = 3, "XXX"
   (c)  Str1 = 5, "ABC  "
        Str2 = 3, "ABC"
   (d)  Str1 = 2, " X"
        Str2 = 1, " "
   (e)  Str1 = 0, ""
        Str2 = 0, ""
   (f)  Str1 = 2, "co"
        Str2 = 3, "con"

▶4. Implement the pattern-matching algorithm given in the last section. Use a high-level language and comparisons of single characters.

▶5. Implement the pattern-matching algorithm given in the last section. Use 8086 assembly language.

▶6. Write an assembly-language procedure that has two string arguments. It is to copy the first string into the second string, replacing any lowercase letters with the corresponding capital letter.

▶7. Write an assembly-language procedure that has one string argument. It is to replace all occurrences of more than one space by a single space and to change the length to reflect the length of the result.

## 15.4 INSTRUCTIONS

String processing is so common that many computers have special instructions to support it. Making memory addressable by bytes also simplifies string operations while using memory effectively. This section examines the 8086 string instructions.

### String Pointers

To work with a string, we need a pointer to its first byte. The PutStr procedure uses the offset from DS as a near pointer. The programs of the previous section use a far pointer. To access individual characters of the string in a loop, one option is to load the offset portion of the pointer into a base register and increment that register as we process characters. We could also use an index register as a displacement into the string.

The 8086 processor has a set of string instructions. Some of these instructions work with one string; others work with two strings of the same length. The two index registers, SI and DI, have special purposes with the string instructions. SI is the offset into the source string, relative to DS, and DI is the offset into the destination string, relative to ES. The source and destination operands of the string instructions are always implied to be DS:SI and ES:DI, respectively.

Many of the string instructions are available in three different forms in assembly language. In two of the forms, the size of the data is specified in the instruction mnemonic, using b for byte data and w for word data. In the third form, an explicit operand is used to determine the size of the data; even if an operand is specified, the source and destination are still implied in DS:SI and ES:DI. The third form also provides a means to override using DS to specify the source operand, but this capability will not be needed here. The two forms that specify the data size in the mnemonic are presented, but the form with an explicit operand is not.

### Direction Flag

Consider the string "aabbccdd" and a program that copies the substring consisting of the first six characters into the last six bytes. If this is done with increasing addresses, the first character is copied to the third byte (giving "aaabccdd"), the second character is then copied to the fourth byte (giving "aaaaccdd"), and so on. The final value of the string is "aaaaaaaa". On the other hand, if this is done with decreasing addresses, the sixth character is copied into the eighth byte (giving "aabbccdc"), the fifth character is copied into the seventh byte (giving "aabbcccc"), and so on. In this case the final value of the string is "aaaabbcc".

The direction flag specifies the direction in which string transfers occur. When DF is cleared, string operations proceed in order of increasing addresses, as in the first example. When DF is set, string operations proceed in order of decreasing addresses, as in the second example. The cld and std instructions can be used to specify a value for DF and to control the direction of string operations.

## 15.4 Instructions

---

**CLear Direction flag**
- syntax: `cld`
- action: DF := 0 {use increasing indexes}
- flags: .D...... cleared
  O.ITSZAPC unchanged

**SeT Direction flag**
- syntax: `std`
- action: DF := 1 {use decreasing indexes}
- flags: .D...... set
  O.ITSZAPC unchanged

---

## Repeat Prefixes

We have used the CX register and the `loop` or `loope` instruction to repeat a sequence of instructions for each character in a string. The string instructions can also use the CX register and the zero flag to repeat their operation on every character in a string.

To have a string instruction repeat automatically, a special prefix is written before the instruction. The CX register, and optionally the zero flag, control the repetition. The repeat prefixes create implied loops much like the `loop` and conditional loop (`loope`, `loopne`) instructions. The displays that describe the repeat prefixes list the string instructions with which they are used; the instructions themselves are presented later in this section. The unconditional repeat prefix is as follows:

---

**unconditional REPeat**
- syntax: `rep stringinstruction`
- action: execute `stringinstruction` the number of times specified by cx
- flags: as per `stringinstruction`

used with `movsb`, `movsw`, `stosb`, `stosw` instructions

---

The CX register must be loaded with the number of times that the string instruction is to be executed. After each execution of the string instruction, the CX register is decremented (without affecting the flags). When CX reaches 0, the repetition stops. For example, to execute a `stosb` instruction (which will be presented soon) the number of times specified by `StringLen`, we can write the loop

```
; FOR cx := StringLen DOWNTO 1
      mov     cx, StringLen
  DO:
      stosb
      loop    DO
; ENDFOR
```

The same result can be achieved using the `rep` prefix on the `stosb` instruction, as

```
; FOR cx := StringLen DOWNTO 1
      mov      cx, StringLen
; DO
      rep stosb
; ENDFOR
```

The `stosb` instruction is executed the number of times specified by CX in both examples.

The conditional repeat prefixes test the zero flag as well as the CX register after each execution of the string instruction:

---

**REPeat if Equal**
    syntax:    `repe stringinstruction`

**REPeat if Zero**
    syntax:    `repz stringinstruction`
    action:    execute `stringinstruction` the number of times specified by cx, but only while the zero flag is set

**REPeat if Not Equal**
    syntax:    `repne stringinstruction`

**REPeat if Not Zero**
    syntax:    `repnz stringinstruction`
    action:    execute `stringinstruction` the number of times specified by cx, but only while the zero flag is cleared

    flags:    as per `stringinstruction`
used with `cmpsb`, `cmpsw`, `scasb`, `scasw` instructions

---

The CX register must be loaded with the number of times that the string instruction is to be executed. After each execution of the string instruction, the CX register is decremented (without affecting the flags). When CX reaches 0, or if the zero flag is set (`repne`, `repnz`) or cleared (`repe`, `repz`), the repetition stops. For example, to execute a `cmpsb` instruction (which will be presented soon) at most `StringLen` times, but only while ZF = 1, we can write the loop

```
; FOR cx := StringLen DOWNTO 1
      mov      cx, StringLen
  DO:
      cmpsb
      loope    DO
; ENDFOR
```

The same result can be achieved using the `repe` prefix on the `cmpsb` instruction, as

```
; FOR cx := StringLen DOWNTO 1
      mov      cx, StringLen
; DO
      repe cmpsb
; ENDFOR
```

## 15.4 Instructions

### Move Instructions

Some string instructions copy bytes or words from the source to the destination. They move data between a register and memory or within memory. There are three move instructions, one for each path: memory to register, register to memory, and memory to memory. There are byte and word forms for each instruction.

The first instruction copies part of a source string from memory into a register and adjusts the pointer to the source string so that it points to the next part of the source string. The adjustment takes into consideration the direction flag and the type of data.

**LOaD String Byte**
- syntax: `lodsb`
- action: (1) al := ds:[si];
  (2) if DF = 0 then si := si + 1
  else si := si − 1

**LOaD String Word**
- syntax: `lodsw`
- action: (1) ax := ds:[si];
  (2) if DF = 0 then si := si + 2
  else si := si − 2
- flags: ODITSZAPC unchanged

These instructions copy a byte or word from a string into the AL or AX register and update the pointer accordingly. Although a repeat prefix can be specified with the load string instructions, there is no reason to do so since each load will replace the data previously loaded.

The second string instruction copies a register into a destination string. It then adjusts the pointer to that string according to the direction flag and the type of data stored:

**STOre String Byte**
- syntax: `stosb`
- action: (1) es:[di] := al;
  (2) if DF = 0 then di := di + 1
  else di := di − 1

**STOre String Word**
- syntax: `stosw`
- action: (1) es:[di] := ax;
  (2) if DF = 0 then di := di + 2
  else di := di − 2
- flags: ODITSZAPC unchanged

These instructions copy a byte or word from the AL or AX register into a string and update the pointer. The store string instructions can be used with the `rep` prefix. This is useful to fill a region of memory with some value. For example, suppose we define the block

```
InBuffer   db      100 dup (?)
```

within the segment named _DATA. If we want to fill it with 100 copies of the NUL character, we could write

```
mov     ax, seg _DATA
mov     es, ax
mov     di, offset InBuffer
mov     cx, 100
mov     al, 00h
rep stosb
```

This would copy the NUL character from the AL register into each byte of `InBuffer` one at a time. This could be made faster by using words instead of bytes, replacing the last three instructions with

```
mov     cx, 50
mov     ax, 0000h
rep stosw
```

Since only the size of an operand is checked, this last fragment can be used in other contexts. For example, if we needed to zero an array of fifty 16-bit integers, we could use the last fragment with the name of the array in place of `InBuffer`.

The combination of load string and store string instructions can be used to copy a string or substring from one location in memory to another. After we set up DS:SI to point to the source string and ES:DI to point to the destination and we set or clear DF, we could write a loop like the following:

```
; FOR each character in Source
        mov     cx, SourceLen
DO:     lodsb
        stosb
        loop    DO
; ENDFOR
```

Note that we cannot use a repeat prefix with this example, as we need to alternate between `lodsb` and `stosb`.

There is a simpler method for copying a string, using a move string instruction with a repeat prefix. The move string instruction combines the actions of the load string and store string instructions, without using AX.

---

**MOVe String Byte**

syntax:    movsb

action:    (1) es:[di] := ds:[si];
           (2) if DF = 0 then si := si + 1,
                         di := di + 1
                 else si := si − 1,
                         di := di − 1

### 15.4 Instructions

**MOVe String Word**
    syntax:    movsw
    action:    (1) es:[di] := ds:[si];
                    (2) if DF = 0 then si := si + 2,
                                       di := di + 2
                          else si := si − 2,
                                       di := di − 2
    flags:     ODITSZAPC unchanged

To move a string or a substring from one location in memory to another, we set up DS:SI to point to the source string, ES:DI to point to the destination, clear the direction flag, load the length of the string into CX, and use a move string instruction with the repeat prefix. The substring move of Program 15.2 is rewritten to use this in Program 15.4.

## Program 15.4

```
; Program 15.4       SubStr86.ASM
; Returns a substring specified by first and last position.
; Can be called from Turbo Pascal, as
;    SubString (Source: String; First, Last: Byte): String;

; Pointer to result, parameters:
    Result      equ     dword ptr [bp + 12]
    Source      equ     dword ptr [bp + 8]
    First       equ     byte ptr [bp + 6]
    Last        equ     byte ptr [bp + 4]

_TEXT SEGMENT word public 'code'
    assume  cs: _TEXT
    public  SubString

SubString PROC

; set up bp register to point to result and parameters
    push    bp
    mov     bp, sp

; set up pointers to strings
    push    ds                  ;save caller's ds
    les     di, Result
    lds     si, Source

; check starting position, save correct position in bl
; IF01 First <= 1
    mov     al, First
    cmp     al, 1
    jnbe    ELSE01

; THEN01
;   starting position (in bl) := 1
    mov     bl, 1
    jmp     ENDIF01
```

**Program 15.4 (continued)**

```
        ELSE01:
;       IF02 First > length(Source)
            cmp     al, ds:[si]
            jna     ELSE02

;       THEN02:
;           starting position (in bl) := length(Source) + 1
            mov     bl, ds:[si]
            inc     bl
            jmp     ENDIF02

        ELSE02:
;           starting position (in bl) := First
            mov     bl, First
        ENDIF02:
    ENDIF01:

; determine length of substring in al
; IF03 Last < starting position
        mov     al, Last
        cmp     al, bl
        jnb     ELSE03

;   THEN03
;       length(Result) := 0
        sub     al, al
        jmp     ENDIF03

    ELSE03:
;       IF04 Last <= length(Source)
            cmp     al, ds:[si]
            jnbe    ELSE04

;       THEN04
;           length(Result) := Last - starting position + 1
            sub     al, bl
            inc     al
            jmp     ENDIF04

        ELSE04:
;           length(Result) := length(Source) - starting position + 1
            mov     al, ds:[si]
            sub     al, bl
            inc     al
        ENDIF04:
    ENDIF03:

; save length in Result[0]
        mov     es:[di], al

; advance indexes to start of substrings
        sub     bh, bh
        add     si, bx
        inc     di
```

## 15.4 Instructions

**Program 15.4 (continued)**

```
        ; direction flag := increasing addresses
            cld

        ; Copy substring.
        ; FOR05 cx := length(Result) TO 1 STEP -1
            mov     cl, al
            sub     ch, ch
            jcxz    ENDFOR05

        ; DO05
        ;   Result[di] := Source[si], advancing indexes
            rep movsb
        ENDFOR05:

        ; restore caller's registers and return
            pop     ds
            pop     bp
            ret     8

SubString ENDP
_TEXT ENDS
END
```

The only change to Program 15.2 in Program 15.4 is that the body of the loop is now simply

```
; DO05
;   Result[di] := Source[si], advancing indexes
    rep movsb
ENDFOR05:
```

This is simpler and more efficient.

The subject of concatenation was discussed earlier, but no example program was provided. Now consider a procedure that concatenates one string onto the end of another. Such a procedure might be named Append. If the strings are named Str1 and Str2, we want the procedure to append Str2 to the end of Str1. In the process, it must change the length of Str1 recorded in the first byte. In Figure 15.3, we see that the Append operation has to copy the text of the second string to the memory following Str1. If ES:DI points to Str1 initially, adding the length of Str1 (shown as L1 in the figure) to DI moves the pointer to the last byte of Str1. Adding one more to DI moves it to the start of where Str2 should be copied. However, before changing DI we want to use it to store the new length, L1+L2, into the Str1 length byte. One way to keep all this straight is to save a copy of L1, compute L1+L2, save the sum in L1, and add the copy of L1 to DI+1. This is the approach taken in Program 15.5.

After setting up the pointers to the strings, procedure Append copies the length of the first string (L1 in the figure) into AL, and the length of the second string (L2 in the figure) into CL. Then it adds CL to the length byte for the first string, making it L1+L2 in the figure. Next, the length saved in AL is converted to a word by clearing AH and then added to DI. Adding 1 more to DI then effectively moves the pointer to the byte following the last character of Str1. Adding 1 to SI also moves the second pointer to the first byte to be copied.

## 550   Chapter 15   Character Strings

BEFORE

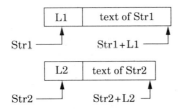

AFTER Append (Str1, Str2)

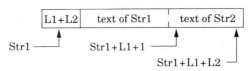

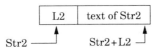

**Figure 15.3   Operation of Append**

---

## Program 15.5

```
        ; Program 15.5        Append.ASM
        ; Appends the second argument string to the first.
        ; Can be called from Turbo Pascal, as
        ;     Append (VAR Str1: String; Str2: String);

        ; Parameters:
           Str1         equ       dword ptr [bp + 8]
           Str2         equ       dword ptr [bp + 4]

    _TEXT SEGMENT word public 'code'
           assume    cs: _TEXT
           public    Append

    Append PROC

        ; set up bp register to point to parameters
           push      bp
           mov       bp, sp

        ; set up pointers to strings
           push      ds                    ;save caller's ds
           les       di, Str1
           lds       si, Str2

        ; al := original length(Str1)
           mov       al, es:[di]
```

### 15.4 Instructions

**Program 15.5 (continued)**

```
        ; cl := length(Str2)
            mov     cl, ds:[si]

        ; length(Str1) := length(Str1) + length(Str2)
            add     es:[di], cl

        ; es:di := pointer to Str1[al+1]
            sub     ah, ah      ;convert original length to word
            add     di, ax
            inc     di

        ; ds:si := pointer to Str2[1]
            inc     si

        ; direction flag := increasing addresses
            cld

        ; FOR01 cx := length(Str2) TO 1 STEP -1
            sub     ch, ch
            jcxz    ENDFOR01

        ; DO01
        ;   Str1[di] := Str2[si], advancing indexes
            rep     movsb
          ENDFOR01:

        ; restore caller's registers and return
            pop     ds
            pop     bp
            ret     8

Append   ENDP
_TEXT    ENDS
END
```

Now that the pointers are set up and the length of the destination string adjusted, we clear the carry flag. Then the text of Str2 is copied using the loop

```
; FOR01 cx := length(Str2) TO 1 STEP -1
    sub     ch, ch
    jcxz    ENDFOR01
; DO01
;   Str1[di] := Str2[si], advancing indexes
    rep     movsb
  ENDFOR01:
```

Note that CL already has the length of Str2, so it is only necessary to clear CH to set up for the loop.

Many Pascal compilers that provide a string data type also provide a function that returns a string that is the concatenation of any number of argument strings. They also support BASIC-style concatenation, which uses + as an infix operator to specify concatenation.

These capabilities can be built, like the Append procedure, using the move string instruction with repeat prefix.

## Compare Instructions

Instructions that compare two strings are similar to the cmp instruction, but with the syntax and pointer-manipulating features of the move string instruction.

**CoMPare String Byte**
- syntax: cmpsb
- action: (1) compare ds:si to es:[di], set flags
  (2) if DF = 0 then si := si + 1,
          di := di + 1
      else si := si − 1,
         di := di − 1

**CoMPare String Word**
- syntax: cmpsw
- action: (1) compare ds:[si] to es:[di], set flags
  (2) if DF = 0 then si := si + 2,
          di := di + 2
      else si := si − 2,
         di := di − 2
- flags: O...SZAPC modified for comparison
     .DIT..... unchanged

Like cmp, cmpsb and cmpsw subtract the source operand from the destination operand and set the flags according to the difference, which is not saved. The string compare instructions then increment or decrement the index registers according to the direction flag and size of the operands.

The string compare instructions are usually used with a conditional repeat prefix. To do so, we must first load the CX register with the maximum number of times the instruction is to execute. When used with a conditional repeat prefix, the string compare instruction terminates with SI and DI pointing to the position following the comparison that satisfied the repeat prefix, or past the end of the strings if the repeat prefix has not been satisfied.

With the repe (or repz) prefix, the comparison is made and the index registers updated as long as the comparison indicates equal and the CX register is not 0; this is used to find the first position where two strings do not match. With the repne (or repnz) prefix, the comparison is made and the index registers updated as long as the comparison indicates not equal and the CX register is not 0; this is used to find the first position where two strings do match.

Program 15.6 is a rewritten version of Program 15.3, which compared two strings and returned −1, 0, or +1 based on the relation between them. The length of the shorter string

## 15.4 Instructions

is found the same way as before. The THEN clause of the second selection structure and the loop are replaced with

```
; THEN02
;    advance pointers past length bytes
        inc     si
        inc     di
; REPEAT03
;    compare characters from strings
        repe cmpsb
; UNTIL03 end of shorter string OR difference
```

The rest of Program 15.6 is the same as Program 15.3.

---

## Program 15.6

```
; Program 15.6          CmpStr86.ASM
; Compares two strings; returns -1 if Str1 < Str2,
;    0 if Str1 = Str2, or +1 if Str1 > Str2.
; Can be called from Turbo Pascal, as
;    CompStr (Str1, Str2: String): Integer;

; Parameters and local variables:
   Str1         equ     dword ptr [bp + 8]
   Str2         equ     dword ptr [bp + 4]
   Str1Len      equ     byte ptr [bp - 1]
   Str2Len      equ     byte ptr [bp - 2]

_TEXT SEGMENT word public 'code'
    assume    cs: _TEXT
    public    CompStr

CompStr PROC

; set up bp register to point to parameters
    push      bp
    mov       bp, sp

; allocate stack space for local variables
    sub       sp, 2

; set up pointers to strings
    push      ds                  ;save caller's ds
    lds       si, Str1
    les       di, Str2

; direction flag := increasing addresses
    cld

; save lengths of string for later use
    mov       al, ds:[si]
    mov       Str1Len, al
    mov       al, es:[di]
    mov       Str2Len, al
```

## Program 15.6 (continued)

```
        ; Find shorter length, for use in cx to control loop.
        ; IF01 Str1Len <= Str2Len
            cmp     Str1Len, al
            jnbe    ELSE01

        ; THEN01
        ;     cx := Str1Len
            mov     cl, Str1Len
            sub     ch, ch
            jmp     ENDIF01

        ELSE01:
        ;     cx := Str2Len
            mov     cl, Str2Len
            sub     ch, ch
        ENDIF01:

        ; Compare characters from strings, up to the length
        ; of the shorter string, or until a difference is found.
        ; IF02 shorter string is not empty
            jcxz    ENDIF02

        ; THEN02
        ;     advance pointers past length bytes
            inc     di
            inc     si

        ;     REPEAT03
        ;         compare characters from strings, advancing pointers
                repe cmpsb
        ;     UNTIL03 end of shorter string OR difference found
        ENDIF02:

        ; If a difference is found, it determines the relationship
        ; between the strings... check this next
        ; IF04 a difference is found
            je      ELSE04

        ; THEN04
        ;     IF05 Str1[] < Str2[]
            jnb     ELSE05

        ;     THEN05 Str1 < Str2
        ;         return -1
            mov     ax, -1
            jmp     ENDIF05

        ELSE05:  ;Str1 > Str2
        ;     return +1
            mov     ax, 1
        ENDIF05:
            jmp     ENDIF04
```

## 15.4 Instructions

**Program 15.6 (continued)**

```
            ELSE04: ;No difference found, check lengths.
        ;      IF06 Str1Len < Str2Len
                mov     al, Str1Len
                cmp     al, Str2Len
                jnb     ELSE06

        ;      THEN06 Str1 is shorter, so it comes before Str2
        ;      return -1
                mov     ax, -1
                jmp     ENDIF06

            ELSE06:
        ;      IF07 Str1Len > Str2Len
                jna     ELSE07

        ;      THEN07 Str1 is longer, so it comes after Str2
        ;      return +1
                mov     ax, 1
                jmp     ENDIF07

            ELSE07: ;strings are same length, so they are the same
        ;      return 0
                mov     ax, 0
            ENDIF07:
            ENDIF06:
          ENDIF04:

        ; restore caller's registers and stack, then return
                pop     ds
                add     sp, 2
                pop     bp
                ret     8

CompStr ENDP
_TEXT ENDS
END
```

The compare string instructions compare two strings to each other. Now consider the problem of finding a particular character in a string. For example, when a person's name is written in the last-name-first format there is often a comma following the last name. If we could find the comma, we could then extract the first and last names as substrings. The scan string instructions search a destination string for a specific character or pair of characters.

**SCAn String Byte**
- syntax:    scasb
- action:    (1) compare al to es:[di], set flags
             (2) if DF = 0 then di := di + 1
                         else di := di − 1

## SCAn String Word

    syntax:     scasw

    action:     (1) compare ax to es:[di], set flags
                        (2) if DF = 0 then di := di + 2
                                  else di := di − 2

    flags:      O...SZAPC modified for comparison
                     .DIT..... unchanged

Like the compare string instructions, the scan string instructions are usually used with a conditional repeat prefix. The CX register is used for the maximum number of times the scan instruction is to execute. It will stop when the condition in the prefix is satisfied, with ES:DI pointing to the byte after the match or nonmatch.

The matter of matching substrings was discussed earlier. This can be accomplished using the scan string and compare string instructions in a modified version of the algorithm presented earlier. In this algorithm, Object is the string we scan looking for a copy of Pattern (Figure 15.4). We start by determining the number of positions in Object at which there are enough characters to match Pattern. We also initialize a flag that records the state of the entire match to False. These two values control a conditional loop.

In each iteration of the loop, we scan Object looking for an occurrence of Pattern[1]. When this is found, we check whether the pattern is longer than a single character. If it is, we attempt to match the rest of Pattern beginning at the next position of Object. If the string compare succeeds, or if the Pattern only had one character, the Pattern has been found. Otherwise, we repeat the scan, starting with the next starting position in Object. When the loop terminates, the index in Object where Pattern first occurs can be computed

```
compute number of starting positions for match
Found := false
WHILE NOT Found AND more starting positions
DO
  scan object for Pattern[1]
  IF scan is successful
  THEN
    IF length(Pattern) > 1
    THEN
      compare rest of Pattern to next part of Object
    ENDIF
    IF compare is successful OR length(Pattern) = 1
    THEN
      Found := true
    ENDIF
  ENDIF
ENDWHILE
IF Found
THEN
  compute position from pointers
ELSE
  position := 0
ENDIF
```

**Figure 15.4** Modified Algorithm for Locating Pattern

## 15.4 Instructions

from the restored scan state and the offset of the start of the Object string. (The outline in Figure 15.4 necessarily omits many details involving the pointers and lengths that must be considered in an actual implementation.)

An example will help to clarify the algorithm. Assume that the Object string is "aaabbaaabbbbaa" and that the Pattern is "bbb" (Figure 15.5). The object contains 14 characters and the pattern 3 characters, so there are at most $14-3+1=12$ positions where there are enough characters in the object to match the pattern; this is computed in the first step. The scan at the start of the WHILE loop locates the first "b" in the fourth position of the object; this scan has examined and rejected three characters of Object. It therefore also reduces the number of start positions by three, to nine. Since the Pattern is

```
        Object:   a a a b b a a a b b b b a a
        Pattern:        b b b
```

Result of first scan:

```
        Object:   a a a b b a a a b b b b a a
        Pattern:        b ? ?
                  └──────────── Found at position 4
```

Result of first string compare:

```
        Object:   a a a b b a a a b b b b a a
        Pattern:        b b ?
                          └──── Fails
```

Result of second scan:

```
        Object:   a a a b b a a a b b b b a a
        Pattern:          b ? ?
                          └──────── Found at position 5
```

Result of second string compare:

```
        Object:   a a a b b a a a b b b b a a
        Pattern:          b b ?
                              └──── Fails
```

Result of third scan:

```
        Object:   a a a b b a a a b b b b a a
        Pattern:                  b ? ?
                                  └──── Found at position 9
```

Result of third string compare:

```
        Object:   a a a b b a a a b b b b a a
        Pattern:                  b b b
                                     └ Succeeds
```

**Figure 15.5** Operation of Pattern-Matching Algorithm

longer than a single character, we now attempt to match the rest of it using a string compare. This compare string fails, so we must execute the loop again.

The second scan is successful at position 5. This scan reduces the number of start positions by one, to eight. We attempt another match, using a string compare; it fails immediately. The third scan is successful at position 9. This scan reduces the number of start positions to four. We attempt another match, using a string compare; this time, however, the match is also successful. This is recorded in the Boolean variable Found. The loop terminates when it finds a copy of the pattern or when it exhausts all possible starting positions without finding the pattern. In the former case, the pointer into the object refers to the position of the match of the first character of the pattern; we can subtract the pointer to the first character of the object to get the relative position in the object of the first character of the pattern. This calculation must account for the length byte. In the case when the pattern is not found, we simply move a 0 into Position.

This algorithm is implemented in Program 15.7. The string scan and match have been written as simple statements rather than documented as loops. The program necessarily includes several instructions to determine lengths, set up pointers, and clear DF, but it otherwise implements the algorithm outlined in Figure 15.4 directly. Although it is lengthy, there are only a few details that need to be discussed.

One subtlety in the program involves computing the number of possible starting positions. Even though the lengths are unsigned (positive) numbers, the number of starting positions must be calculated as a signed number to guard against searching for patterns that are longer than the object. The alternative is to test for this situation and nest most of Program 15.7 in another selection structure.

## Program 15.7

```
; Program 15.7      MatchStr.ASM
; Search the first argument string for a copy of the
; second argument string, return its starting position.
; Can be called from Turbo Pascal, as
;    MatchStr (Object, Pattern: String): Integer;

; Parameters and local variable:
    Object     equ    dword ptr [bp + 8]
    Pattern    equ    dword ptr [bp + 4]
    Remains    equ    word ptr [bp - 2]     ;length of Pattern - 1

_TEXT SEGMENT word public 'code'
    assume   cs: _TEXT
    public   MatchStr

MatchStr PROC

; set up bp register to point to parameters
    push     bp
    mov      bp, sp

; allocate stack space for local variable
    sub      sp, 2
```

### 15.4 Instructions

**Program 15.7 (continued)**

```
        ; set up pointers to strings
            push    ds              ;save caller's ds
            les     di, Object
            lds     si, Pattern

        ; direction flag := increasing addresses
            cld

        ; save length of Pattern less one, for use in string compare
            mov     cl, ds:[si]
            sub     ch, ch
            dec     cx
            mov     Remains, cx

        ; compute number of possible starting positions for match
            mov     al, es:[di]
            sub     al, ds:[si]
            cbw
            inc     ax
            mov     cx, ax

        ; advance pointer to first character of Object
            inc     di

        ; Found (in ah) := false
            mov     ah, 0

          WHILE01: ;(NOT Found) AND cx > 0
            cmp     ah, 0
            jne     ENDWHL01
            cmp     cx, 0
            jng     ENDWHL01

        ; DO01
        ;   set ds:si to Pattern[1]
                lds     si, Pattern
                inc     si

        ;   scan Object for Pattern[1]
                mov     al, ds:[si]
                repne scasb

        ;   IF02 scan is successful
                jnz     ENDIF02

        ;   THEN02
        ;       save cx for next scan (if needed)
                push    cx

        ;       IF03 Pattern longer than 1 character
                mov     cx, Remains
                jcxz    ENDIF03
```

## Program 15.7 (continued)

```
;           THEN03
;             advance pointer in Pattern and compare strings
              push    di              ;save next scan position
              inc     si
              repe cmpsb
              pop     di              ;restore next scan position
            ENDIF03:

;           IF04 compare is successful OR Pattern only 1 char long
              jnz     ENDIF04

;           THEN04
;             Found (in ah) := true
              mov     ah, 1
            ENDIF04:

;           restore cx for next scan (if needed)
              pop     cx
          ENDIF02:
          jmp       WHILE01
        ENDWHL01:

; IF05 pattern found
        cmp     ah, 1
        jne     ELSE05

; THEN05
;   position := offset of start of Pattern in Object -
;               offset of start of Object
        mov     ax, di          ;save offset of start of Pattern ...
        les     di, Object      ;get offset of start of Object
        inc     di              ;skip length byte
        sub     ax, di
        jmp     ENDIF05

    ELSE05:
;   position := 0
        sub     ax, ax
    ENDIF05:

; restore caller's registers and stack, then return
        pop     ds
        add     sp, 2
        pop     bp
        ret     8

MatchStr ENDP
_TEXT ENDS
END
```

## 15.4 Instructions

The CX register is used to control the repeat prefix of both the scan string and compare string instructions. For scan, CX is just the number of possible starting positions that are left. For compare, it is the number of characters in Pattern following the first. It is necessary to save CX before the compare and to restore it afterward. We must also save the pointer in Object before the compare string, so that we can start the next scan at the same place. The rest of the program follows from the outline and the usual setup for the string operations. There are more sophisticated algorithms for matching a pattern, but these are left to texts on algorithm design and analysis.

### Conversion Instruction

The last instruction in this section converts a byte from one code to another. Such an instruction is useful when, for example, a computer that normally uses ASCII receives a file that was transmitted in EBCDIC, or vice versa. The instruction requires a table of target bytes where each element contains the byte that we want to substitute for the index. For example, if the first three bytes of the table contain the characters "a", "b", and "c", when we translate a byte containing 01h, we get "b", and so on. The location of this table is specified by DS:BX.

**X transLATe**
syntax:   xlat

**X transLATe Byte**
syntax:   xlatb
action:   al := ds:[bx + al]
flags:    ODITSZAPC unchanged

As an application of this instruction, consider printing a 16-bit word as four hexadecimal digits. We can use a table that contains the characters "0", "1", ..., "9", "A", ..., "F". As each 4-bit chunk of the word is isolated, it is used as the index into the table to retrieve the character to print (Program 15.8).

## Program 15.8

```
; Program 15.8      PutHex.ASM
; Prints a sixteen-bit word in hexadecimal.
; Can be called from Turbo Pascal, as
;     PutHex (HexWord: word);

; Parameter
  HexWord       equ     word ptr [bp + 4]

_DATA SEGMENT word public 'data'
  ByteTable     db      "0123456789ABCDEF"
_DATA ENDS

_TEXT SEGEMNT word public 'code'
    assume  cs: _TEXT
    extrn   PutChar: PROC
    public  PutHex
```

## Program 15.8 (continued)

```
PutHex PROC
; set up bp register to point to parameter, and copy it
        push    bp
        mov     bp, sp
        mov     ax, HexWord

; set up pointer to table for xlat instruction
        assume  ds: _DATA
        mov     bx, offset ByteTable

; Print word as four hexadecimal characters.
; FOR01 cx := 4 TO 1 STEP -1
        mov     cx, 4

  DO01:
;       shift bits 4*cx-1 through 4*(cx-1) into positions 3..0
        rol     ax, 1
        rol     ax, 1
        rol     ax, 1
        rol     ax, 1

;       save shifted argument for next iteration
        push    ax

;       clear bits 7..4 of al, and convert to hex character
        and     al, 0Fh
        xlat

;       PutChar (al)
        mov     dl, al
        call    PutChar

;       restore shifted argument and repeat
        pop     ax
        loop    DO01
; ENDFOR01

; restore caller's registers and return
        pop     bp
        ret     2

PutHex ENDP
_TEXT ENDS
END
```

The table is included as a string named `ByteTable`. The offset of this table is loaded into the BX register in preparation for the processing in the loop. In the loop, we rotate the four most significant bits of the argument into bits 3...0 of AL, clear bits 7...4, and translate them into a character with `xlat`. We pass that character to `PutChar`. We repeat this for all four 4-bit pieces of the argument.

The table in Program 15.8 is only 16 bytes long. There are only 16 hexadecimal digits, and the value in the AL register is in the range 0 to 15, so the table needs only 16 elements.

**Key Points**

It is up to the programmer to ensure that the value in the AL register when an xlat instruction is executed lies within the range of the table pointed to by DS:BX. If it does not, the xlat instruction will reach beyond the table as if it were larger and retrieve whatever happens to be in the byte of memory it reaches.

An interesting use for this instruction is to convert lowercase letters in a text to capitals, or vice versa. For example, to convert an ASCII string containing mixed capitals and lowercase letters, and other characters, to one in which all letters are capitals, we can use a table that contains the capital letters in positions indexed by the lowercase letters. For example, the ordinal value of "A" in ASCII is 65 and the ordinal value of "a" is 97. The conversion table would contain "A" in both the sixty-fifth and ninety-seventh bytes, as "a" should be converted to "A".

## EXERCISES 15.4

1. Can the word version of the scan string instruction (scasw) be used in Program 15.9 to speed up the program? Explain.
▶2. Rewrite Program 15.4 (MovStr.ASM) so that it moves the string a word at a time instead of a byte at a time. If there is an odd number of characters, the last word should be padded with a NUL character.
3. Compare the program you wrote for Exercise 2 with Program 15.4. Which program is smaller (in bytes of assembled code)? Which program executes faster?
▶4. Write a function that returns a string of the characters in the argument string reversed. For example, if the argument is "abcde" the function should return "edcba".
▶5. Write a procedure to rotate the characters in a string one position toward the first character, with the first one becoming the last ("STOP" becomes "TOPS").
▶6. Modify Program 15.7 so that the pattern can contain wildcard characters. Use the question mark for the wildcard in the pattern, and let it match any one character in the object. For example, the pattern "a?c" should match "aac", "abc", "a-c", and so on.
▶7. Modify Program 15.7 so that the pattern can contain arbitrary substrings. Use the *at* sign (@) for the arbitrary string in the pattern, and let it match any number of consecutive characters in the object. The pattern "a@c" should match "ac", "abbbc", "autoexec", and so on. Hint: Use a scan string instruction to find the character specified after @ in the pattern.
▶8. Write a subprogram that has arguments representing an array of fixed-length strings, the length of the strings, and the number of such strings in the array. The subprogram is to sort the strings into ascending order. Adapt the bubble sort used in Chapter 13.
▶9. Some alphanumeric data sorts do not distinguish between capital and lowercase letters. Modify your sort of Exercise 8 to work this way. (See the discussion of xlat just before the exercises.)
▶10. Write a Boolean-valued function that has a string parameter. The function is to determine whether the string is a palindrome (a word that is spelled the same forward and backward, like "LEVEL" or "NOON"). The string should contain all capital letters and have no spaces.

## KEY POINTS

- Characters in memory are coded as unsigned byte integers.
- The 7-bit ASCII (American Standard Code for Information Interchange) code can represent 128 different characters; an 8-bit extended ASCII code can represent 256 characters.

- The 8-bit EBCDIC (Extended Binary Coded Decimal Interchange Code) code can represent 256 different characters.
- Computers that are word-addressed might store strings packed with as many characters per word as can fit, which uses memory efficiently, or unpacked, which simplifies string processing.
- Computers that are byte-addressed make efficient use of memory and offer simpler string processing.
- A string's length is the number of characters it contains.
- A fixed-length string uses a declared number of bytes of memory. Values assigned to it are padded with spaces or truncated, as needed.
- A bounded-length string uses a declared number of bytes of memory, but the length of the string's actual value is also saved in memory. Values assigned to it are not padded with spaces, but may be truncated.
- A variable-length string has no declared length and is not stored in a fixed location in memory. There is a fixed part of the string that contains a pointer to the actual string. The fixed part may also contain the length of the string.
- For fixed-length strings, one byte of memory must be reserved for each character; a constant can be used for the length.
- For bounded-length strings, one byte of memory needs to be reserved for each character in the longest value, and either a byte or word for the actual length; a constant can be used for the maximum length.
- For variable-length strings, dynamic memory allocation must be used for the string itself; memory is reserved for a pointer and sometimes for the length.
- Operations on a single string, such as reading or printing, can be implemented as the operation on a single character repeated for each character in the string.
- Finding the length of a variable-length string where the length is not stored requires searching for the character that marks the end of the string.
- Copying a substring requires copying characters from a selected portion of one string to another string.
- Concatenating two strings requires copying the characters of the second string onto the end of the first.
- Comparing strings requires comparing characters from one string to those of the other one character at a time, from left to right. When a difference is found, the relation between the two strings can be determined; if no differences are found, the strings are equal.
- Searching an object string for an instance of a pattern string can be performed by scanning for the first character of the pattern in the object and then attempting to match the rest of the pattern with the object string starting at the next character.

## PC SYSTEM SUMMARY

- PCs use an 8-bit extended ASCII code.
- String constants, as operands of the db directive, are written as character strings enclosed in quotation marks or as ordinal values of the characters.
- Memory is reserved for string variables by the db directive and the dup operator. Lengths, if stored, are reserved with either db or dw.

# PC System Summary

- The direction flag controls whether string instructions use increasing or decreasing memory addresses.
- String instructions use DS:SI to point to the source operand and ES:DI to point to the destination operand.
- String instructions adjust the offsets in the index registers according to the size of the operand and the state of the direction flag, in preparation for the next string instruction.
- String instructions can have a repeat prefix. The CX register specifies the maximum number of times the string instruction will repeat.
- Conditional repeat prefixes test the zero flag as well as CX to control repetition of a string instruction.

Instructions presented in this chapter:

Direction flag:
- `cld`     clear direction flag
- `std`     set direction flag

Move string:
- `lodsb`     load string byte
- `lodsw`     load string word
- `stosb`     store string byte
- `stosw`     store string word
- `movsb`     move string byte
- `movsw`     move string word

Compare string:
- `cmpsb`     compare string bytes
- `cmpsw`     compare string words

Scan string:
- `scasb`     scan string byte
- `scasw`     scan string word

Translate:
- `xlat`     translate
- `xlatb`     translate byte

Repetition prefixes presented in this chapter:
[synonyms in brackets]

Unconditional: (used with `movs_` and `stos_`)
- `rep`     repeat

Conditional: (used with `cmps_` and `scas_`)
- `repe`     repeat if equal     [repz]
- `repne`     repeat if not equal     [repnz]

# 16 Decimal Data

- ◆ **Representation**
- ◆ **Specification**
- ◆ **Operations**
- ◆ **Instructions and Procedures—Unpacked BCD**
- ◆ **Instructions and Procedures—Packed BCD**

Integers are very useful, but there are applications where other numeric data types are needed. Two other numeric data types will be examined in this text: decimal in this chapter and floating-point in the next.

The decimal data type is used to represent numbers in which each decimal digit is coded separately in binary format. Such representations require fewer operations for reading and writing than numbers represented as binary integers, and they allow for a greater range of values than binary integers. The trade-off is in calculation effort: Each digit must be operated upon separately, so multidigit numbers require loops for even simple operations. Decimal numbers are commonly used in business applications which have substantially more input and output operations than arithmetic operations.

In this chapter, the way decimal digits can be represented in binary, the way such numbers are specified in programs, and the way common operations on numbers represented in decimal notation can be implemented are all discussed.

## 16.1 REPRESENTATION

Many business applications require that numeric data have certain properties not readily provided by binary integers. For example, monetary amounts must have at least an implied decimal point and a greater range of values than binary integers typically provide. Furthermore, business applications tend to perform relatively more input and output operations than arithmetic operations, so it is desirable to have numbers that are easy to convert to and from character strings.

Representations that meet this requirement leave the numbers in decimal notation and code each digit separately in binary. Although there are several variations, these representations are collectively referred to as **Binary Coded Decimal**, or BCD. The two BCD representations supported by the 8086 will be examined. First though, consider working with decimal numbers represented as character strings.

## Strings of Digits

In the previous chapter, character string representation and some common operations on strings were examined. One thing not considered was how to perform arithmetic on strings that contain only digits. For example, can the two strings "123" and "68" be added to get the string "191"? In the ASCII table in Appendix 2, it is shown that the codes for the ten digits 0 through 9 are 30h through 39h. The hypothetical addition problem posed above would be represented by adding the codes 31 32 33h (corresponding to "123") and 36 38h (corresponding to "68") to get 31 39 31h for the sum. If a simple right-to-left addition is tried, the hexadecimal and binary results are

```
  31  32  33h     0011  0001  0011  0010  0011  0011
      36  38h                 0011  0110  0011  1000
  ─────────────   ──────────────────────────────────
  31  68  6Bh     0011  0001  0110  1000  0110  1011
```

This formulation is clearly not right, since the hexadecimal result 31 68 6Bh corresponds to the string "1hk".

There are two problems with the above attempt. First, the left four bits of each character should always be 0011; these should not be added but rather just copied into the sum. Second, as the right four bits are added, the sum should be checked to make sure it does not exceed 9. If it does, subtract 10 from it and carry 1 into the next byte. Reworking the example, the first addition gives

```
  31  32  33h     0011  0001  0011  0010  0011  0011
      36  38h                 0011  0110  0011  1000
  ─────────────   ──────────────────────────────────
          Bh                                    1011
```

The sum exceeds 9, so it is adjusted. The next four bits are copied into the sum. The second addition, with the carry indicated, gives

```
              1                                 1
  31  32  33h     0011  0001  0011  0010  0011  0011
      36  38h                 0011  0110  0011  1000
  ─────────────   ──────────────────────────────────
       9  31h                             1001  0011  0001
```

This sum is 9; no carry is generated. The next four bits are copied into the sum. The last addition gives

```
  0   1           0     1
  31  32  33h     0011  0001  0011  0010  0011  0011
      36  38h                 0011  0110  0011  1000
  ─────────────   ──────────────────────────────────
  1   39  31h           0001  0011  1001  0011  0001
```

Then the next four bits are copied into the sum, giving the correct result 31 39 31h—the string "191".

A sequence of instructions could be written to add character strings this way. In doing so, it would probably be easier to first clear the left four bits of each byte, which is how numbers are represented in unpacked BCD.

## Unpacked BCD

The ASCII codes for the characters "0" through "9" are 30h through 39h. In **unpacked BCD** the first four bits of each byte are cleared, so that decimal digits are represented by 00h through 09h. The number 153 is thus represented in unpacked BCD as 010503h. There is no limit on the length of unpacked BCD numbers other than the size of memory. It is preferable to store the digits in order from most significant to least significant in bytes with increasing offsets; this order is the same as the digits would appear in a string.

There is no provision for a sign as part of an unpacked BCD number. However, one can be implemented by the programmer willing to invest the effort. For example, a sign could be coded in an extra leading byte, using 00h for positive and 80h for negative. This byte would have to be checked before most operations, and the operations would be modified accordingly. A sign is not included in the examples and procedures in this chapter; implementing a sign is left for the exercises.

## Packed BCD

In unpacked BCD format, numbers are stored one digit per byte, with the first four bits of the byte cleared. In **packed BCD** format, numbers are stored two digits per byte. The representation of 153 in two bytes is simply 01h 53h.

There is a special 10-byte form of packed BCD used by the 8087 math coprocessor. To use the math coprocessor with packed decimals, the operands must be in this 10-byte format. The 10-byte packed BCD form uses one byte for a sign, coded as 00h for positive numbers and 80h for negative numbers. Using one byte for the sign leaves space for 18 digits in the packed BCD format. Like most multibyte data in the 8086, the bytes are stored in reverse order with the least significant digits in the first byte and the most significant digits in the ninth byte. The digits in each byte, however, are not reversed. The sign is stored in the last byte.

## Numbers with Fractions

There is no provision for a decimal point as part of either type of BCD number, but one is needed in business applications for things like interest rates or for amounts that include cents but that are expressed as dollars. However, numbers can always be scaled by powers of 10 to make them whole numbers. For example, 6875 could be used for 6.875 percent and 123450 for $1234.50. Consider adding 6.875 percent to $1234.50 by multiplying 1234.50 by (1 + .06875). Keeping all digits, the product of 123450 and 106875 is computed as 13193718750. The five least significant digits can then be removed, leaving 131937 to represent $1319.37. The decimal data types provide enough digits so that overflow will not be a problem. However, the programmer has the burden of keeping track of the decimal point.

## EXERCISES 16.1

1. Show using hexadecimal notation how each of the following numbers would be represented in unpacked BCD, using six bytes for each number.

   (a) 123                 (b) 468
   (c) 5000                (d) 235
   (e) 9876                (f) 8830

## 16.2 Specification

2. The following unpacked BCD numbers are written in hexadecimal. Give their decimal equivalents.
   - (a) 000004080002
   - (b) 000000040200
   - (c) 000000070700
   - (d) 000100090803
   - (e) 000000020208
   - (f) 000001090902

3. Show how each of the numbers from Exercise 1 would be represented in packed BCD, using four bytes each.

4. Show how each of the numbers from Exercise 2 would be represented in packed BCD, using four bytes each.

5. Give the value of each of the following packed BCD numbers in common notation. These are standard 10-byte numbers, written in the order in which the bytes are stored.
   - (a) 01500400000000000000
   - (b) 00005604000000000000
   - (c) 42000000000000000080
   - (d) 01000000000000000080
   - (e) 03050000000000000000
   - (f) 92120200000000000000

6. The convention proposed for representing signs in unpacked BCD numbers is borrowed from the 10-byte packed form. Propose another way to code a sign, and compare the two methods.

7. Another representation of decimal numbers uses excess-3 notation, in which each digit is represented by four bits that are the sum of the digit and 3. For example, 28 is represented as 5Bh. Addition of any two digits whose sum exceeds 10 will cause the representation of the sum to exceed 16, which automatically provides the correct carry bit. After the carry is noted, each 4-bit sum must be reduced by 3. What other advantages and disadvantages of excess-3 notation can you find?

8. A bank programmer proposes using the 10-byte packed BCD representation for account balances, which are maintained to the nearest tenth of a cent. What is the largest balance, in dollars, that can be represented if the packed BCD number represents tenths of cents?

9. The bank programmer in Exercise 8 must provide enough digits in intermediate results to multiply the balance by numbers like 1.00125. What is the largest result, in dollars, that can be computed reliably?

## 16.2 SPECIFICATION

This section presents a convention for declaring decimal data. Constants and variables in unpacked BCD format are considered first.

### Unpacked BCD

A number in unpacked BCD representation is declared just like a character string, with its length coded in the first byte. For example, to define the constant 42 as an unpacked 10-digit BCD number, just write

UnBCD42    db       10,0,0,0,0,0,0,0,0,4,2

Note that 11 bytes were used; UnBCD42[0] is the length, and the other 10 bytes each store a single digit. All of the leading zeros must be provided in the operand field. In the examples, the numbers are represented from left to right, with the least significant digit at the largest offset (highest address in memory).

## Chapter 16 Decimal Data

To reserve memory for a 15-digit BCD variable, the db directive is used to reserve 16 bytes. The first byte is for the length. The dup directive can be used for the digit positions:

```
BCD15      db      15, 15 dup (?)
```

The value can easily be initialized to 0:

```
BCD15      db      15, 15 dup (0)
```

## Packed BCD

Memory for packed BCD numbers is reserved in the same way as unpacked BCD numbers. However, since two digits are packed into each byte, it is necessary to reserve only half as many bytes as the number has digits, plus one for the length. For example, to define the constant 42 as a packed 10-digit BCD number, just write

```
Packed42   db      5,0,0,0,0,42h
```

The 8086 has a special 10-byte form for packed BCD numbers. In 10 bytes, 18 digits and a sign are coded. No length byte is needed, since the length is fixed. The 8087 math coprocessor can work with packed BCD numbers in the 10-byte format.

The dt directive can be used to allocate 10 bytes of storage for a packed BCD number. (dt can also be used for floating-point data, which is presented in the next chapter.) To reserve memory for a 10-byte packed BCD variable, simply write

```
PackedNum dt       ?
```

The dup operator can be used to reserve more than one 10-byte area, perhaps for an array of packed BCD numbers.

Ten-byte packed BCD constants or initialized variables can be defined with the dt directive as well. The statements

```
Sum        dt      0
Const325   dt      325
```

reserve two 10-byte areas of memory and initialize them to packed representations of 0 and 325. Negative values can also be used. The statement

```
NegFive    dt      -5
```

reserves 10 bytes of memory and initializes it to the packed decimal representation of $-5$.

## EXERCISES 16.2

1. Write directives to define each of the following unpacked BCD variables, using eight bytes.
   (a) Twenty1, initialized to 21
   (b) Four, initialized to 4
   (c) UnitCost, initialized to all nines
   (d) Total, initialized to 0
   (e) Taxes, not initialized
2. Rewrite the directives of Exercise 1 using packed BCD and eight digits.
3. Rewrite the directives of Exercise 1 using 10-byte packed BCD.
4. Compare the number of bits required to represent an $N$-digit decimal number in packed BCD with the number of bits needed to represent it as an unsigned binary number.

## 16.3 OPERATIONS

Operations on BCD data are considered next, including conversions between strings and unpacked BCD and between unpacked and packed BCD, arithmetic, and comparisons.

### Conversions

Given a character string that contains only digits followed by spaces or null characters (00h) and given the length of the string, suppose the goal is to convert it to unpacked BCD representation. The string and BCD number can be different lengths. For example, given the declarations

```
String    db    8, "12345   "
UnPacked  db    12, 12 dup (?)
```

the goal would be to convert "12345   " from String into the twelve bytes

00h 00h 00h 00h 00h 00h 00h 01h 02h 03h 04h 05h

following the length byte of UnPacked.

The code to do this conversion can be written using the string instructions from the previous chapter and the and instruction to mask off the first four bits of each character. An algorithm for this conversion is given in Figure 16.1.

```
{ Scan String for least significant digit  }
i := length(String)
WHILE i>1 AND String[i] is not space or null
DO
  i := i - 1
ENDWHILE

{ Convert characters to BCD and copy to UnPacked  }
j := length(UnPacked)
WHILE i>1 AND String[i] is space or null
DO
  UnPacked[j] := and(String[i], 0Fh)
  i := i - 1
  j := j - 1
ENDWHILE

{ String[1] not checked by either loop; do so now  }
IF String[i] is a digit
THEN
  UnPacked[j] := and(String[i], 0Fh)
  j := j - 1
ENDIF

{ Fill leading digits of UnPacked with 00h  }
WHILE j >= 1
DO
  UnPacked[j] := 00h
  j := j - 1
ENDWHILE
```

**Figure 16.1  Algorithm for Converting a String of Digits to Unpacked BCD**

## 572  Chapter 16  Decimal Data

The algorithm starts by finding the position of the character in String that represents the least significant digit by scanning from the end of the string toward the beginning, looking for any character other than a space or a null character. In this example, the last three characters would be scanned, stopping at the character "5" in the fifth position of String. See Figure 16.2.

The second step is to copy the BCD equivalents of the characters of String that represent digits into the last bytes of UnPacked. When completed, UnPacked would contain seven undefined bytes followed by the BCD representations of the digits 1 through 5. Note that, because of the way the algorithm is written, it is necessary to check String[i] separately when the second loop terminates with i = 1.

The final step is to load leading zeros into the rest of UnPacked. Implementing this algorithm is left as an exercise. A program using this algorithm should check for valid characters in String. Corrective action may not be possible if a character other than a digit is encountered, but at least an error message should be printed.

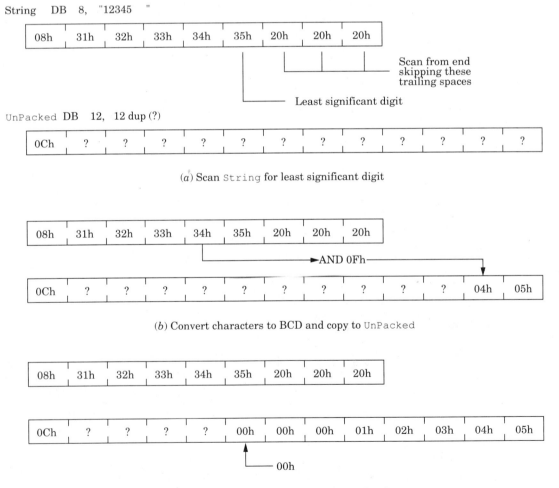

Figure 16.2  Converting Digits in String to Unpacked BCD

## 16.3 Operations

Converting a number from unpacked BCD representation to a character string is just the reverse of the above process. Depending on whether the number is to be left-justified or right-justified in the string, leading zeros need to be converted into leading spaces or trailing spaces or null characters. Doing so is left for the exercises.

Conversions between unpacked BCD and packed decimal formats are not provided by the 8086 instruction set. Procedures for these conversions are presented later in this chapter.

## Arithmetic

Decimal arithmetic may be performed on numbers in either format. The numbers are shown here in packed format for convenience, but the ideas apply to both formats.

### Addition and subtraction

Separate instructions and operations are needed for addition and subtraction. The signs of decimal numbers, however coded, affect the operation performed. Addition of two numbers with different signs requires subtracting the magnitudes; subtraction of two numbers with different signs requires adding the magnitudes. Only addition of positive numbers is considered in the following examples.

Addition of two numbers can produce a sum that is at most one digit larger than the larger of the two numbers. Addition of decimal numbers proceeds from the least significant digit to the most significant, from right to left, in groups of four bits. The sum of two 4-bit numbers (each in the range 0 through 9) can require five bits (and be in the range 0 through 18). As each group of four bits is added, the sum must be checked. If it exceeds 9, then 10 must be subtracted before saving it, and a carry of 1 must be saved for addition to the next group of four bits. If the sum does not exceed 9, it is saved, and a carry of 0 is saved for addition to the next group. This process of adding a few bits and recording a carry is similar to the earlier examples of adding multiple-word integers.

For example, the addition of the numbers 98765 and 1300 proceeds as follows. The rightmost digits are added, giving 5 with a 0 carry. The next digits to the left are added, giving 6 with a 0 carry. The next digits are added, giving a sum of 10. This sum is adjusted and recorded as 0, with 1 carried into the next step. The addition so far, in both decimal and binary, is

```
      1              1    0    0
98765     1001    1000 0111 0110 0101
 1300             0001 0011 0000 0000
-----             ---------------------
  065                  0000 0110 0101
```

The next group of four bits and the carry from the previous step are added together. This addition gives another sum of 10, which is recorded in the sum as 0, with 1 carried to the next group. In the last step, this carry is added to the most significant digit of the first number. The carry in this addition generates a new digit in the result. Thus, the complete addition is

```
   111         1    1    1    0    0
 98765            1001 1000 0111 0110 0101
  1300                 0001 0011 0000 0000
------         ------------------------------
100065         0001 0000 0000 0000 0110 0101
```

Subtraction of numbers with the same signs also proceeds from right to left, with borrowing from groups of four bits. Subtraction is left for the exercises.

## Multiplication

The product of two numbers can have as many digits as the number of digits in both numbers combined. If a sufficiently large field is not reserved for it, the most significant digits of the product are lost. Unlike multiplication of integers, where the processor puts long products in two registers, multiplication of BCD numbers requires the programmer to specify the length of the field used for the product. There is no problem working with numbers that have different signs. The product of two numbers with the same sign is positive; the product of two numbers with different signs is negative.

Multiplication can be implemented based on longhand methods with some record-keeping changes. For example, when multiplying 750 by 321, separate intermediate results for 750 $\times$ 1, 750 $\times$ 20, and 750 $\times$ 300 might be kept on different lines in the usual longhand arrangement and then added to get the final result. However, the sum in any column can easily exceed five bits, so intermediate results must be added together as they are generated. The hardest part of this process is keeping track of the current location in three separate multidigit numbers. An algorithm and a function for multiplying BCD numbers are given in the next section.

## Division

Like integer division, there are more potential problems with decimal division than with other decimal operations. The implementations of decimal division vary considerably. Most often, division yields a quotient that is a whole number. The remainder may or may not be available, depending on the computer.

Among the potential errors that can occur are those common to all decimal operations, such as an invalid digit or sign in one of the operands. There are also errors unique to division, such as division by zero or the case of a quotient exceeding the field reserved for it.

Division with decimal numbers uses the same rules for signs as arithmetic. If the dividend and divisor have the same sign, the quotient is positive; for different signs, the quotient is negative. The remainder, when computed, has the same sign as the dividend.

Division can be implemented as repeated subtraction, or an attempt can be made to implement the trial-and-error approach of the manual method. There are better methods, but they are beyond the scope of this text.

## Negation

Changing the sign of a packed decimal number requires changing only the byte that contains the sign. A positive sign is coded as 00h; a negative sign is coded as 80h. To change the sign, take the exclusive or (xor) of the first byte with 80h. Depending on how it is stored, xor and a mask may be used to negate an unpacked number.

## Shifts

Just as shifting binary numbers can be interpreted as multiplying and dividing by powers of 2, shifting packed BCD numbers by a multiple of 4 positions or unpacked BCD numbers by a multiple of 8 positions can be interpreted as multiplying and dividing by powers of 10. These shifts should be implemented so that they do not affect the sign, if present.

### Comparing Decimal Numbers

To compare two decimal numbers, first check their signs. If the signs differ, the relationship between numbers is easily determined. If the signs are the same and if the numbers have the same length, the numbers can be compared as character strings using a repeated cmpsb instruction. If the numbers are not the same length, the shorter number is treated as though it is extended with zeros between the sign and the most significant digit.

In the next sections, instructions that the 8086 provides for working with decimal numbers are introduced and used to implement a set of procedures and functions.

## EXERCISES 16.3

1. Perform the following subtractions using unpacked decimal notation. Explain how and when to borrow.
   (a) 0002030305
       − 070205
   (b) 0002030305
       − 080604

2. Carefully describe how you perform long division by hand. Try to avoid using words like "guess," and describe every step in enough detail so that someone else can implement your description.

▶3. Implement the algorithm of Figure 16.1 to convert a string of digits into an unpacked BCD number. Assume that the string is right-justified, that its length is stored in the first byte, and that the unpacked BCD variable is 18 bytes long.

4. Modify the algorithm of Figure 16.1 to include a sign character (space or "+" for positive, "−" for negative). Assume the sign is to the immediate left of the most significant digit. Code the sign as 00h for positive or 80h for negative in the first byte following the length of the unpacked number.

▶5. Develop and implement an algorithm to convert an unpacked BCD number into a character string. Use the same assumptions as in Exercise 3.

## 16.4 INSTRUCTIONS AND PROCEDURES—UNPACKED BCD

The 8086 provides instructions for addition, subtraction, multiplication, and division with single bytes of unpacked BCD numbers as well as for addition and subtraction with single bytes of packed BCD numbers. The 8087 coprocessor provides instructions for converting between the special 10-byte packed BCD numbers and the representation used within the 8087. The 8086 operations on unpacked BCD numbers are examined in this section, the 8086 operations on packed BCD numbers in the next section, and the 8087 coprocessor in the next chapter.

As each operation on unpacked BCD numbers and the instructions of the 8086 are examined, procedures and functions are given that operate on numbers 20 digits long stored as bounded-length strings. These numbers are compatible with strings in Pascal; the Turbo Pascal conventions for passing these strings as arguments and for passing function results have been adopted. This section closes with an application that uses most of the routines developed here, with versions in both assembly language and Pascal.

## Input and Output

Input and output of unpacked BCD numbers can be implemented by using separate procedures for string I/O and conversion between strings and BCD or by integrating the processes to write unpacked BCD I/O procedures. The latter method is used here.

Procedure GetBCD in Program 16.1 has two parameters: InBCD, a far pointer to a 21-byte area in which to save the unpacked BCD number, and Success, a far pointer to a Boolean variable that indicates whether the read was successful. There is also a local variable named InChars, which is used as an input buffer. After the usual setup code, GetBCD accepts characters from the keyboard, converts them to BCD, and saves them in InChars. The part of the algorithm to accomplish this task is

```
Done := false
REPEAT
   read a character
   IF character is a digit
   THEN
      convert character to BCD
      append it to InChars
   ELSE
      Done := true
   ENDIF
UNTIL Done OR 20 digits read
```

The pointer to InChars is set up by the instructions

```
mov    ax, ds
mov    es, ax
mov    di, offset InChars
```

### Program 16.1

```
;  Program 16.1        GetBCD.ASM
;  GetBCD (var InBCD : String20;
;          var Success : Boolean)
;  Reads a BCD number.  If there are no errors in input,
;  the number is returned in InBCD with Success true;
;  otherwise, zero is returned in INBCD with Success false.

;  Parameters:
   InBCD       equ      dword ptr [bp + 8]
   Success     equ      dword ptr [bp + 4]

_DATA SEGMENT word public 'data'
   InChars     db       20 dup (?)    ;BCD codes as entered
_DATA ENDS

_TEXT SEGMENT word public 'code'
      assume   cs: _TEXT
      assume   ds: _DATA
      extrn    GetChar: PROC
      public   GetBCD

GetBCD PROC
```

## 16.4 Instructions and Procedures—Unpacked BCD

**Program 16.1 (continued)**

```
        ; set up bp register to point to parameters
              push    bp
              mov     bp, sp

        ; save caller's ds register
              push    ds

        ; set up pointer to InChars
              mov     ax, ds
              mov     es, ax
              mov     di, offset InChars

        ; direction flag := increasing addresses
              cld

        ; Done (in ah) := false
              mov     ah, 0

        ; set up counters
              mov     cx, 20        ;maximum characters to read
              mov     bh, 0         ;actual characters read

        ; read characters into local variable (InChars), converting
        ; to BCD, until 20 digits or CR or illegal character read
        REPEAT01:
        ;     read a character into al
              call    GetChar

        ;     IF02 character is a digit
              cmp     al, 30h
              jl      ELSE02
              cmp     al, 39h
              jg      ELSE02

        ;     THEN02
        ;       convert character to BCD, append it to InChars
              and     al, 0Fh       ;clear left four bits
              stosb                 ;save byte
              inc     bh            ;count it
              jmp     ENDIF02

        ELSE02:
        ;     done := true
              mov     ah, 1
        ENDIF02:

              cmp     ah, 1         ;test to terminate loop
              loopne  REPEAT01
        UNTIL01:  ;done OR twenty digits read

        ; IF03 (last character is CR)  OR  (20 digits read)
              cmp     al, 0Dh       ;is it CR?
              je      THEN03
              cmp     bh, 20        ;20 digits read?
              jl      ELSE03
```

**Program 16.1 (continued)**

```
        THEN03:
;   copy digits, with leading zeros, to InBCD
;   and set Success true

;   InBCD[0] := length of string
        les     di, InBCD
        mov     al, 20
        stosb

;   put leading zeros in InBCD
        mov     al, 0           ;leading zero
        mov     cx, 20          ;number of zeros is
        sub     cl, bh          ;  20 - number of digits
        rep stosb

;   copy digits user entered into InBCD
        mov     cl, bh
        mov     si, offset InChars
        rep movsb

;   Success := true
        lds     si, Success
        mov     word ptr ds:[si], 1
        jmp     ENDIF03

      ELSE03:
;   Fill InBCD with zeros, and clear Success to false
;   InBCD[0] := length of string
        les     di, InBCD
        mov     al, 20
        stosb

;   fill InBCD with zeros
        mov     al, 0           ;zero to fill with
        mov     cx, 20          ;number of zeros to copy
        rep stosb

;   Success := false
        lds     si, Success
        mov     word ptr ds:[si], 0
      ENDIF03:

; restore caller's registers and return
        pop     ds
        pop     bp
        ret     8

GetBCD ENDP
_TEXT ENDS
END
```

### 16.4 Instructions and Procedures—Unpacked BCD 579

By using the same segment conventions used in main programs thus far, the DS register on entry to GetBCD will point to the start of _DATA in the main program, and all offsets in GetBCD will already have been adjusted by the linker. There is no need to load DS with the segment of _DATA. Fortunately, this convention also allows the use of GetBCD (and all other subprograms in this chapter) with main programs written in Turbo Pascal.

After reading a character, the process of testing whether it is a digit is performed by the instructions

```
cmp     al, 30h
jl      ELSE02
cmp     al, 39h
jg      ELSE02
```

which reject any character before "0" or after "9" in ASCII. The instruction

```
and     al, 0Fh
```

clears the left four bits of the character in AL, and then

```
stosb
```

copies it to the location pointed to by ES:DI and increments DI.

The second part of procedure GetBCD copies the digits from Inchars into InBCD, padding with leading zeros. The algorithm is

```
IF last character is CR OR 20 digits read
THEN
   put length byte in InBCD
   put leading zeros into InBCD
   copy digits of InChars to InBCD
   Success := true
ELSE
   put length byte in InBCD
   fill InBCD with zeros
   Success := false
ENDIF
```

The constant 20 is copied into the length byte of InBCD by the instructions

```
les     di, InBCD
mov     al, 20
stosb
```

in both clauses of the selection structure. Including these instructions in both clauses leaves AL intact for the test in the selection structure; it also sets ES:DI to point to the second byte of InBCD in preparation for copying either the digits or leading zeros. In the THEN clause, leading zeros, if needed, are copied into InBCD by moving 00h into the AL register, setting CX to the number of zeros needed, and storing them with a repeated stosb instruction. The digits of InChars are moved with the repeated string move instruction, movsb.

Procedure PutBCD in Program 16.2 has one parameter, OutBCD, a far pointer to the number to be displayed. After copying the pointer into DS:SI, incrementing SI to skip the length byte, and setting CX to 20, the program executes the sequence

```
mov     dl, ds:[si]
or      dl, 30h
call    PutChar
inc     si
```

**Program 16.2**

```
; Program 16.2         PutBCD.ASM
; PutBCD (OutBCD : String20);
; Displays a BCD number in a field of twenty characters.

; Parameter:
   OutBCD        equ     dword ptr [bp + 4]

_TEXT SEGMENT word public 'code'
       assume   cs: _TEXT
       extrn    PutChar : PROC
       public   PutBCD

PutBCD PROC

; set up bp register to point to argument
       push     bp
       mov      bp, sp

; set ds:si to point to first digit of OutBCD
       push     ds                ;save caller's ds
       lds      si, OutBCD
       inc      si

; FOR01 cx := 20 TO 1 STEP -1
       mov      cx, 20

  DO01:
;      print (OutBCD[si])
       mov      dl, ds:[si]       ;get digit
       or       dl, 30h           ;convert to character
       call     PutChar

;      advance to next byte
       inc      si
       loop     DO01
; ENDFOR01

; restore caller's registers and stack, return
       pop      ds
       pop      bp
       ret      4

PutBCD ENDP
_TEXT ENDS
END
```

20 times. This sequence extracts a digit of the unpacked number, converts it to a character, calls PutChar to display it, and advances the pointer to the next digit.

## Move and Clear Operations

Moving an unpacked BCD number from one region of memory to another of the same size is a simple operation. Set up ES:DI and DS:SI to point to the arguments, move

### 16.4 Instructions and Procedures—Unpacked BCD

21 into the CX register (to move the length byte, too), and then copy the BCD number with a repeated movsb instruction.

Clearing an unpacked BCD number to 0 is a special case of copying a value: Just move 0 into every digit.

## Arithmetic Instructions

Arithmetic operations on unpacked BCD data in the 8086 are performed one byte at a time. Unsigned binary arithmetic instructions are used to perform the arithmetic operations, and decimal instructions are used to adjust the results (or operands) of each arithmetic operation to represent unpacked BCD numbers. Loops must be written to perform arithmetic on multibyte data.

The rest of this section presents functions that return results as unpacked BCD numbers represented in strings 20 characters long with an initial length byte. For functions that return strings, Turbo Pascal pushes a far pointer for the result onto the stack before pushing the arguments. The function should not delete this pointer with the ret instruction, since the calling program needs it to access the function result. This convention will be followed for all of the BCD-valued functions so that they may be called from either assembly language or Turbo Pascal.

## Addition

To add two one-digit unpacked BCD numbers, move one of them into the AL register, and add the other to it. The sum might exceed 9, but the 8086 provides an instruction that inspects AL, adjusts the sum, and sets the carry and auxiliary carry flags accordingly.

**ASCII Adjust for Addition**
syntax:   aaa
action:   if al > 9 then al := al − 10;
              ah := ah + 1;
              CF and AF set
            else CF and AF cleared
flags:    ......A.C modified
          O...SZ.P. undefined
          .DIT..... unchanged

Function AddBCD in Program 16.3 adds two unpacked BCD numbers passed as arguments and returns the sum as the function value. The loop varies CX from 20 to 1, corresponding to the displacements of the digits in the string from least significant to most significant. The instructions in the body of the loop load a digit from the first argument into AL, add a digit from the second argument to it using adc and aaa instructions, then copy AL into the function result. For each reference using a far pointer, the value of CX is added to the far pointer that was passed as the argument. Since this addition of CX affects the carry flag, the flags are pushed onto the stack before the loop, popped before the adc, and pushed after the aaa. This process preserves the carry flag from one iteration to the next. Also, the carry flag is cleared before pushing the flags the first time, and the flags are popped before returning.

## Program 16.3

```
;   Program 16.3       AddBCD.ASM
;   Function AddBCD (BCD1, BCD2: String20): String20;
;   Computes and returns BCD1 + BCD2.

;   Pointer to Result, Parameters:
    Result      equ     dword ptr [bp + 12]
    BCD1        equ     dword ptr [bp + 8]
    BCD2        equ     dword ptr [bp + 4]

_TEXT SEGMENT word public 'code'
    assume   cs: _TEXT
    public   AddBCD

AddBCD PROC

;   set up bp register to point to parameters
    push    bp
    mov     bp, sp

;   save caller's ds register
    push    ds

;   clear carry flag and save it for use in first iteration
    clc
    pushf

;   add digits of BCD1 and BCD2, with carry, saving
;   the sum in the function result
;   FOR01 cx := 20 TO 1 STEP -1
    mov     cx, 20

  DO01:
;     Result[cx] := BCD1[cx] + BCD2[cx] + carry
    lds     si, BCD1
    add     si, cx
    mov     al, ds:[si]
    lds     si, BCD2
    add     si, cx
    popf                    ;get saved carry flag
    adc     al, ds:[si]
    aaa
    pushf                   ;save flag for next iteration
    les     di, Result
    add     di, cx
    mov     es:[di], al

;     repeat for next digit to left
    loop    DO01
;   ENDFOR01

;   set length of Result
    les     di, Result
    mov     byte ptr es:[di], 20
```

### 16.4 Instructions and Procedures—Unpacked BCD

**Program 16.3 (continued)**

```
    ; restore caller's registers, and return
        popf
        pop     ds
        pop     bp
        ret     8

AddBCD ENDP
_TEXT ENDS
END
```

## Subtraction

To subtract, move a 1-digit unpacked BCD number into the AL register and subtract another 1-digit unpacked BCD number from it. The difference might be negative when a borrow is needed (for example, 05h − 07h = −02h = FEh with a borrow). The 8086 provides an instruction that inspects AL, adjusts the difference, and sets the carry and auxiliary carry flags accordingly.

**ASCII Adjust for Subtraction**

syntax:  aas

action:  if al < 0 then al := al + 10;
          ah := ah − 1;
          CF and AF set
         else CF and AF cleared

flags:   ......A.C modified
         O...SZ.P. undefined
         .DIT..... unchanged

Function SubBCD, provided on the disk but not printed here, is similar to AddBCD, substituting sbb for adc and aas for aaa.

## Multiplication

To multiply two 1-digit unpacked BCD numbers, move one of them into the AL register and multiply the other by it using mul. The product could be as large as 81. The 8086 provides an instruction that converts the number in AL into a 2-digit unpacked BCD number.

**ASCII Adjust for Multiplication**

syntax:  aam

action:  al := less significant BCD digit of al
       & ah := more significant BCD digit of al

flags:   ....SZ.P. modified
         O.....A.C undefined
         .DIT..... unchanged

**584**   Chapter 16   Decimal Data

Multiplication of multidigit unpacked BCD numbers is more complicated than addition. While addition generates carries of 0 or 1, multiplication can generate carries as large as 8. Furthermore, each nonzero digit of the multiplier generates an intermediate result at least as large as the multiplicand.

Start with the simpler problem of multiplying a 20-digit unpacked BCD number by a single digit. A solution is implemented in function Mul1BCD in Program 16.4. The first

---

## Program 16.4

```
; Program 16.4      Mul1BCD.ASM
; Function Mul1BCD (SourceBCD: String20;
;                   Digit: Byte): String20;
; Computes and returns SourceBCD * Digit.

; Pointer to Result, Parameters:
Result          equ     dword ptr [bp + 10]
SourceBCD       equ     dword ptr [bp + 6]
Digit           equ     word ptr [bp + 4]

_TEXT SEGMENT word public 'code'
     assume   cs: _TEXT
     public   Mul1BCD

Mul1BCD PROC

; set up bp register to point to parameters
     push     bp
     mov      bp, sp

; save caller's ds register
     push     ds

; move Digit into bl for multiplication, clear bh for use
; as carry from previous multiply
     mov      bx, Digit
     mov      bh, 0

; multiply each digit of SourceBCD by Digit, adding
; previous carry to product and adjusting each result
; FOR01 cx := 20 TO 1 STEP -1
     mov      cx, 20

 DO01:
;    Result[cx] := SourceBCD[cx] * Source + carry
     lds      si, SourceBCD
     add      si, cx
     mov      al, ds:[si]
     mul      bl
     aam
     add      al, bh
     aaa
     les      di, Result
     add      di, cx
     mov      es:[di], al
```

### 16.4 Instructions and Procedures—Unpacked BCD

**Program 16.4 (continued)**

```
    ;   save carry for next iteration
            mov     bh, ah

    ;   repeat for next digit to left
            loop    DO01
    ; ENDFOR01

    ;   set length of Result
            les     di, Result
            mov     byte ptr es:[di], 20

    ;   restore caller's registers, and return
            pop     ds
            pop     bp
            ret     6

Mul1BCD ENDP
_TEXT   ENDS
        END
```

argument is a far pointer to a 20-digit number; the second is a byte (in the low half of a word pushed on the stack) representing a single digit. After setting up BP and saving DS, Mul1BCD loads the second argument into BL and clears BH, which is used to record the carry between multiplications. All references through far pointers refer to either the first argument or the result.

The multiplication is performed one digit at a time in a loop where CX varies from 20 to 1; CX is added to the index registers used for far pointers to reference the digits from least significant to most. In the loop, the digit from the argument is copied into AL, and then the sequence

```
mul     bl
aam
add     al, bh
aaa
```

multiplies it by the second argument, adjusts the product so that any part over 9 is moved to AH, and adds the carry from the previous multiplication, stored in BH. After saving AL in the function result, the program moves the carry from this step from AH to BH for use in the next iteration.

Consider the sequence in more detail. See Figure 16.3. Assume that the three least significant digits of the first argument are 238 and that the multiplier is 6. In the first iteration, the last digit, 08h, is copied into AL. This value is multiplied by 6, giving 30h (48) in AL. The aam instruction converts this result into 04h in AH and 08h in AL. The addition of BH (previously cleared to 0) has no effect; the aaa following it has no effect either. The 08h in AL is saved as the least significant digit of the function result. The 4-bit carry, 04h, is copied into BH for safekeeping.

In the second iteration, the next digit, 03h, is copied into AL. Multiplication by 6 gives 12h (18) in AL and clears AH. AL is then converted by aam into 01h in AH and 08h in

**586**  Chapter 16  Decimal Data

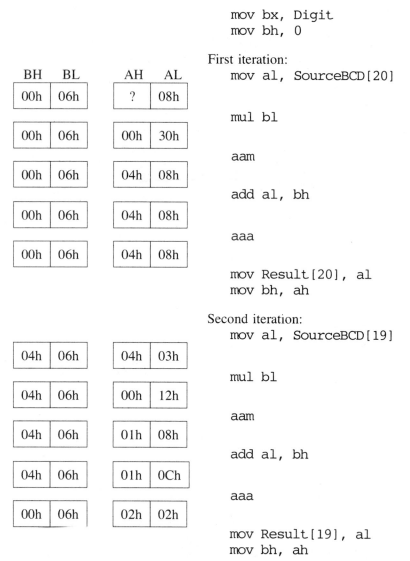

**Figure 16.3**  Multiplication of BCD Number by Single Digit

AL. The previous 4-bit carry, 04h, saved in BH, is added to AL. This step gives 0Ch. The aaa instruction detects the out-of-range value, so it adjusts AL to 02h and AH to 02h; AL is then saved as the tens digit of the result and AH as the next 4-bit carry; and so on.

Now consider multiplying by a multidigit number. Start by defining a 40-digit unpacked BCD number—large enough for the product of two 20-digit numbers—for an intermediate result, and clear it to 0. As one digit of one number is multiplied by one digit of the other number, the corresponding digit of the intermediate result can be added and adjusted for carries. The hardest part is keeping track of the current location in each of the three numbers. For example, consider multiplying 147 by 83. See Figure 16.4.

### 16.4 Instructions and Procedures—Unpacked BCD

Problem: 0...083 × 0...0147

| Steps | Intermediate result | Carry |
|---|---|---|
| Clear result, carry | 0...000000000000000 | 0 |
| 3 × 7 + result[40] + carry = 21 Save 2 as carry Save 1 as result[40] | 0...000000000000001 | 2 |
| 3 × 4 + result[39] + carry = 14 Save 1 as carry Save 4 as result[39] | 0...000000000000041 | 1 |
| 3 × 1 + result[38] + carry = 4 Save 0 as carry Save 4 as result[38] | 0...000000000000441 | 0 |
| 3 × 0 + result[37] + carry = 0 Save 0 as carry Save 0 as result[37] | 0...000000000000441 | 0 |
| (Multiplication of remaining leading zeros not shown) | | |
| Clear carry | | 0 |
| 8 × 7 + result[39] + carry = 60 Save 6 as carry Save 0 as result[39] | 0...000000000000401 | 6 |
| 8 × 4 + result[38] + carry = 42 Save 4 as carry Save 2 as result[38] | 0...000000000000201 | 4 |
| 8 × 1 + result[37] + carry = 12 Save 1 as carry Save 2 as result[37] | 0...000000000002201 | 1 |
| 8 × 0 + result[36] + carry = 1 Save 0 as carry Save 1 to result[36] | 0...000000000012201 | 0 |

(Multiplication of remaining leading zeros not shown)
(Multiplication of remaining digits not shown)

**Figure 16.4 Multidigit BCD Multiplication**

As each digit of 147 is multiplied by 3, add the products to the intermediate result to yield 0...000441. Next multiply each digit of 147 by 8, adding the digits of the intermediate result and each previous carry. Start with 7 × 8 = 56 and add the 4 in the tens position of the intermediate result, which gives 60; write the 0 in the tens position, and save the 6 as the carry. Then multiply 4 × 8 = 32, add the hundreds digit of the intermediate result (yielding 32 + 4 = 36), add the previous carry (yielding 36 + 6 = 42), save the 2 as the hundreds digit of the intermediate result and the 4 as the carry, and so on.

## Chapter 16 Decimal Data

This multiplication is implemented in function MulBCD in Program 16.5. This function uses a local variable, Prod, which is 40 bytes long, to store the intermediate result. Only the less significant half of the final value is copied to the function result. Although it is simpler to just compute all 40 digits and throw away some of the result, doing so is inefficient. The exercises suggest modifications to improve efficiency.

## Program 16.5

```
; Program 16.5      MulBCD.ASM
; Function MulBCD (BCD1, BCD2: String20): String20;
; Computes and returns BCD1 * BCD2.

; Pointer to Result, Parameters
  Result      equ      dword ptr [bp + 12]
  BCD1        equ      dword ptr [bp + 8]
  BCD2        equ      dword ptr [bp + 4]

_DATA SEGMENT word public 'data'
  M           db       ?                 ;multiplier
  Prod        db       40 dup (?)        ;intermediate results
_DATA ENDS

_TEXT SEGMENT word public 'code'
      assume   cs: _TEXT
      public   MulBCD

MulBCD PROC

; set up bp register to point to parameters
      push     bp
      mov      bp, sp

; set up ds and es registers to point to _DATA
      push     ds
      mov      ax, seg _DATA
      mov      ds, ax
      assume   ds: _DATA

; Prod := 0
      cld
      mov      es, ax
      mov      di, offset Prod
      mov      cx, 20
      mov      ax, 0
      rep stosw

; for each digit of BCD1, multiply each digit of BCD2 by it,
; accumulating the product in the temporary result Prod
; FOR01 cx := 20 TO 1 STEP -1
      mov      cx, 20
```

## 16.4 Instructions and Procedures—Unpacked BCD

**Program 16.5 (continued)**

```
     DO01:
;      get next digit of BCD1 to use as multiplier and set
;      pointer for intermediate results
;      M := BCD1[cx]
         les     di, BCD1
         add     di, cx
         mov     al, es:[di]
         mov     M, al

;      set ds:si to point to Prod[cx]
         mov     si, offset Prod
         add     si, 19
         add     si, cx

;      multiply each digit of BCD2, adding each product
;      to corresponding digits of intermediate result;
;      clear carry for first iteration
         mov     bh, 0

;      FOR02 cx := 20 TO 1 STEP -1
         push    cx               ;save FOR01 lcv
         mov     cx, 20

         DO02:
;         Prod[si] := BCD2[cx] * M + Prod[si] + carry
         les     di, BCD2
         add     di, cx
         mov     al, es:[di]
         mul     M                ;BCD2[cx] * M
         aam
         add     al, ds:[si]      ;   + Prod[si]
         aaa
         add     al, bh           ;   + carry
         aaa
         mov     ds:[si], al

;        save carry for next iteration
         mov     bh, ah

;        advance to next digit in Prod
         dec     si

;       repeat for next digit in BCD2
         loop    DO02
;      ENDFOR02

; repeat for next digit in BCD1
         pop     cx
         loop    DO01
; ENDFOR01
```

**Program 16.5 (continued)**

```
        ; copy the 20 least significant digits of Prod to Result
            mov     si, offset Prod
            add     si, 20          ;skip 20 leading digits
            les     di, Result
            inc     di              ;skip length byte
            mov     cx, 10          ;move as ten words
            rep     movsw

        ; set length of Result
            les     di, Result
            mov     byte ptr es:[di], 20

        ; restore caller's registers, and return
            pop     ds
            pop     bp
            ret     8

MulBCD  ENDP
_TEXT   ENDS
        END
```

Procedure MulBCD starts by clearing Prod to all zeros using a repeated stosw instruction. It then uses nested loops to implement the repeated multiplications. The outer loop varies CX from 20 down to 1 as it uses the digits of the first argument, BCD1, as 1-digit multipliers in order from right to left, saving each in turn in the local variable M. DS:SI are then set to point to the least significant digit in Prod that will be affected by the multiplications in this loop by means of

```
        mov     si, offset Prod
        add     si, 19
        add     si, cx
```

The addition of 19 skips over the most significant 19 digits of Prod; Prod[0] is used not for length but for the most significant digit. The addition of CX, which is 20 in the first iteration, skips to the least significant digit; as CX decreases in subsequent iterations, DS:SI point to more significant digits.

In preparation for the inner loop, BH is cleared for use as the carry. The inner loop, which also uses CX as the control variable—note the push before initializing CX to 20 and the pop before the loop instruction for the outer loop—is similar to the loop of Mul1BCD, except for the addition of a digit from the intermediate result as well as the 4-bit carry in BH. The instructions in the loop follow directly from the example in Figure 16.4 Once these nested loops complete, the 20 least significant digits of Prod are copied into the function result.

## Division

To divide a 1-digit or 2-digit dividend in unpacked BCD format by a 1-digit divisor, move the dividend into the AL or AX register, convert it to binary, and use div. The quotient can be as large as the dividend (when the divisor is 1) so it's important to be

### 16.4 Instructions and Procedures—Unpacked BCD

careful when using 2-digit dividends. The instruction that converts two unpacked digits into binary is aad.

**ASCII Adjust for Division**
- syntax: aad
- action: ax := 10 * ah + al
- flags: ....SZ.P. modified
  O.....A.C undefined
  .DIT..... unchanged

Consider dividing a multidigit unpacked BCD number by a single digit. This is implemented in function Div1BCD, in Program 16.6.

**Program 16.6**

```
; Program 16.6      Div1BCD.ASM
; Function Div1BCD (SourceBCD: String20;
;                   Digit: Byte): String20;
; Computes and returns SourceBCD / Digit.

; Pointer to Result, Parameters:
    Result      equ     dword ptr [bp + 10]
    SourceBCD   equ     dword ptr [bp + 6]
    Digit       equ     word ptr [bp + 4]

_TEXT SEGMENT word public 'code'
    assume  cs: _TEXT
    public  Div1BCD

Div1BCD PROC

; set up bp register to point to parameters
    push    bp
    mov     bp, sp

; move Digit into bl, and clear carry (in ah)
; in preparation for first iteration
    mov     bx, Digit
    mov     ah, 0

; set up pointers to most significant digits
    push    ds                      ;save caller's ds register
    lds     si, SourceBCD
    inc     si
    les     di, Result
    inc     di

; FOR01 cx := 20 TO 1 STEP -1
    mov     cx, 20
```

**Program 16.6 (continued)**

```
            D001:
        ;       Result[di] := (SourceBCD[si] + 10 * carry) / Digit
                mov     al, ds:[si]
                aad
                div     bl
                mov     es:[di], al

        ;       advance pointers to next digits to right and repeat
                inc     si
                inc     di
                loop    D001
        ;   ENDFOR01

        ; set length of Result
                les     di, Result
                mov     byte ptr es:[di], 20

        ; restore caller's registers, and return
                pop     ds
                pop     bp
                ret     6

        Div1BCD ENDP
        _TEXT   ENDS
        END
```

After saving the caller's registers, the divisor is copied into the BL register for easier access (the word pushed for the parameter is copied into BX; the meaningful part will be in BL). Clear the AH register, which will be used for the 4-bit remainder from one division step; this value becomes the more significant digit of the next dividend.

Unlike other operations, division proceeds from left to right. Div1BCD sets DS:SI to point to the most significant digit of the 20-digit argument. Then the instructions

```
    mov     al, ds:[si]
    aad
    div     bl
    mov     es:[di], al
    inc     si
    inc     di
```

are executed 20 times.

Consider, for example, dividing 237 by 5. The leading zeros will be skipped in this discussion. AH is initialized to 0 before the loop; it will still be 0 when the first nonzero digit in the dividend is reached. In the first iteration that does useful work, the first mov instruction above copies the 2 into AL. The aad instruction forms $10 \times 0 + 2 = 2$ in the AL register. The div instruction gives quotient 0 in AL and remainder 2 in AH. The quotient is saved in the function result. The next time through the loop, the 3 is moved into AL. This 3 is combined with the 2 in AH by the aad instruction to form 23 (as a binary integer) in AL, which is then divided by 5. And so on. When 237 is divided by 5 in longhand, essentially the same steps are performed.

### 16.4 Instructions and Procedures—Unpacked BCD

To divide by a multidigit divisor is much more complicated. It is left to the interested reader to research division algorithms.

## Decimal shifts

Since unpacked BCD numbers do not have decimal points, it may be necessary to keep track of an implied decimal point and adjust results by powers of 10. Division by powers of 10 can be implemented as right shifts and multiplication by powers of 10 as left shifts.

Recall the introduction to shifts in Chapter 6. Two questions formed the basis for the discussion: what is shifted into vacated positions, and what happens to bits shifted out. For the unpacked BCD shifts, substitute groups of four bits—representing digits—for the bits in the earlier discussion. Since the numbers are unsigned, the goal is to shift 00h into vacated digits and discard digits that are shifted out.

The decimal shifts are implemented as two functions that take an unpacked BCD number and an integer shift count as arguments; the function result is the BCD number shifted. The left shift is implemented in function ShLBCD in Program 16.7. It sets ES:DI to point to the most significant digit of the result and DS:SI to point to the digit in the argument that will end up there after the shift. After computing how many digits of the argument survive the shift, ShLBCD moves them into their final positions of the result. ShLBCD

**Program 16.7**

```
; Program 16.7      ShLBCD.ASM
; Function ShLBCD (SourceBCD: String20;
;                  ShiftCt: Integer): String20;
; Returns SourceBCD shifted left by ShiftCt places,
;   which computes Result := SourceBCD * 10^ShiftCt

; Pointer to Result, Parameters:
    Result      equ     dword ptr [bp + 10]
    SourceBCD   equ     dword ptr [bp + 6]
    ShiftCt     equ     word ptr [bp + 4]

_TEXT SEGMENT word public 'code'
      assume   cs: _TEXT
      public   ShLBCD

ShLBCD PROC

; set up bp register to point to parameters
      push     bp
      mov      bp, sp

; set es:di to point to most significant digit of Result,
; set ds:si to point to digit of SourceBCD to shift into
; most significant position of Result
      les      di, Result
      inc      di
      push     ds                ;save caller's ds register
      lds      si, SourceBCD
      inc      si
      add      si, ShiftCt
```

## Program 16.7 (continued)

```
                ; direction flag := increasing addresses
                    cld

                ; copy bytes of SourceBCD into final position in Result
                ; FOR01 cx := 20 - ShiftCt TO 1 STEP -1
                    mov     cx, 20
                    sub     cx, ShiftCt
                    cmp     cx, 1
                    jl      ENDFOR01

                ; DO01
                ;   Result[1..20-ShiftCt] := SourceBCD[ShiftCt+1..20]
                    rep movsb
                ENDFOR01:

                ; fill vacant positions of Result with zeros;
                ; the number of vacant positions is ShiftCt, except when
                ; ShiftCt > 20, the whole number should be cleared
                ;   IF02 ShiftCt > 20
                    mov     cx, ShiftCt
                    cmp     cx, 20
                    jng     ENDIF02

                ;   THEN02
                ;       cx := 20
                    mov     cx, 20
                ENDIF02:

                ;   Result[20-ShiftCt+1..20] := 0
                    mov     al, 0
                    rep stosb

                ; set length of Result
                    les     di, Result
                    mov     byte ptr es:[di], 20

                ; restore caller's registers, and return
                    pop     ds
                    pop     bp
                    ret     6

ShLBCD ENDP
_TEXT ENDS
END
```

then computes how many digits of the result need to be filled with zeros, checks that it is no more than 20 (in case the shift count is larger than the length of the number), and stores zeros in the remaining digits of the result. Finally, it sets the length of the result and returns.

The right shift is implemented in function ShRBCD, which is provided on the disk but not printed here. It is similar to ShLBCD, except it works from least significant digit of the result toward the most significant.

## 16.4 Instructions and Procedures—Unpacked BCD

## Compare Operations

Conditional loops and selection structures can be controlled using BCD numbers by using functions that compare two decimal numbers and return a Boolean value. Although six distinct functions could be written, one for each relation provided in high-level languages, only two are given here.

The first function that compares two unpacked BCD numbers, BelowBCD, is given in Program 16.8. After it copies the pointers to the arguments into DS:SI and ES:DI and adjusts them to point to the most significant digits, the function executes a cmpsb instruction with a conditional repeat prefix.

### Program 16.8

```
; Program 16.8       BelowBCD.ASM
; Function BelowBCD (BCD1, BCD2: String20): Boolean;
; Returns BCD1 < BCD2.

; Parameters:
  BCD1            equ     dword ptr [bp + 8]
  BCD2            equ     dword ptr [bp + 4]

_TEXT SEGMENT word public 'code'
    assume   cs: _TEXT
    public   BelowBCD

BelowBCD PROC

; set up bp register to point to parameters
    push     bp
    mov      bp, sp

; direction flag := increasing addresses
    cld

; compare parameters by computing BCD1-BCD2 using cmpsb
; set es:di to point to first digit of BCD2, and
; set ds:si to point to first digit of BCD1
    push     ds              ;save caller's ds
    lds      si, BCD1
    inc      si
    les      di, BCD2
    inc      di

; do comparison
    mov      cx, 20
    repe cmpsb

; return carry flag (which records unsigned "below") in al
    lahf
    and      ah, 01h
    mov      al, ah

; restore caller's registers, and return
    pop      ds
```

**Program 16.8 (continued)**

```
        pop     bp
        ret     8

BelowBCD ENDP
_TEXT  ENDS
END
```

When the cmpsb instruction completes, the carry and zero flags are set or cleared accordingly. To finish, the BelowBCD function simply copies the carry flag into the least significant bit of AL, and clears the rest of AL. This task is done with the three instructions

```
lahf
and     ah, 01h
mov     al, ah
```

The second Boolean function, EqualBCD (provided on the disk but not printed here), returns an indication of whether two BCD numbers are equal. This function uses the same pointers and string comparison as BelowBCD but returns the zero flag in AL as the function value. To perform this task, the three instructions given above are replaced by the four instructions

```
lahf
and     ax, 4000h
rol     ax, 1
rol     ax, 1
```

This is the last of the routines provided for working with unpacked BCD numbers. On the disk is included a Pascal driver program that tests them. An example program is considered next; both assembly-language and Pascal implementations are included on the disk.

## Computing with BCDs

The quintessential example of a business calculation is the computation of wages for a week's work. This calculation involves two formulas: one for those who work less than 40 hours and another for those who work more than 40 hours (and thus receive overtime pay); either formula can be used for those who work exactly 40 hours. The calculation computes regular wages separately from overtime wages, since these wages are usually itemized on the paycheck stub. The algorithm is

```
IF Hours < 40
THEN
   RegularPay := Hours * Rate
   OvertimePay := 0
ELSE
   Regularpay := 40 * Rate
   Overtimepay := (Hours - 40) * Rate * 1.5
ENDIF
TotalPay := RegularPay + OvertimePay
```

## 16.4 Instructions and Procedures—Unpacked BCD

Start by considering exactly what each number represents. Take the hourly rate: Assume that all monetary amounts are in cents, so that a rate of $4.75 per hour is represented as 475. Assume that the number of hours worked is recorded to the nearest tenth of an hour, so 38.5 hours is represented as 385. The three computed amounts should be represented in cents. For example, a typical pay amount might be 38.5 × $4.75, or $182.87. In this calculation, one half of a cent was truncated from the true product. This truncation raises an important issue: The product of 385 × 475 is 182875, which represents an amount not in cents but in tenths of a cent. It is necessary to shift off the least significant digit to arrive at 18287.

The multiplication by 1.5 in the calculation of overtime pay is implemented as a multiplication by 3 followed by a division by 2.

Program 16.9, in assembly language, implements this algorithm using this chapter's unpacked BCD routines. It is rather long compared to a program for the same calculation with integers, but nearly every operation requires three instructions to push each unpacked BCD argument and result. The program is so long that only a fragment of it is discussed; the rest on the disk is left for the reader to examine.

## Program 16.9

```
; Program 16.9         Wages.ASM
; Demonstrates computation using unpacked BCD numbers
;    with implied decimal points.
       .
       .
       .
       Hours       db      0, 20 dup (?)         ;hours worked - input
       Rate        db      0, 20 dup (?)         ;hourly rate -- input
       RegPay      db      0, 20 dup (?)         ;pay for first 40 hours
       OTPay       db      0, 20 dup (?)         ;pay for hours over 40
       TotalPay    db      0, 20 dup (?)         ;regular + overtime pay
       WorkBCD     db      0, 20 dup (?)         ;intermediate results
       Forty       db      20, 18 dup (0), 4, 0            ;constant 40
       FortyPtZero db      20, 17 dup (0), 4, 0, 0         ;constant 40.0
       .
       .
       .
;      OTPay := (Hours - 40.0) * Rate * 3 / 2
       mov     ax, offset OTPay       ; push far pointer to OTPay
       push    ds                     ; for final result
       push    ax
       mov     ax, offset WorkBCD     ; push far pointers to WorkBCD
       push    ds                     ; for result of / 2
       push    ax
       push    ds                     ; for result of * 3
       push    ax
       push    ds                     ; for result of * Rate
       push    ax
       push    ds                     ; for result of Hours - 40.0
       push    ax
```

**Program 16.9 (continued)**

```
;          WorkBCD := Hours - 40.0
           mov     ax, offset Hours
           push    ds
           push    ax
           mov     ax, offset FortyPtZero
           push    ds
           push    ax
           call    SubBCD

;          WordBCD := (Hours - 40.0) * Rate
           mov     ax, offset Rate
           push    ds
           push    ax
           call    MulBCD

;          WorkBCD := (Hours - 40.0) * Rate * 3
           mov     ax, 3
           push    ax
           call    Mul1BCD

;          WorkBCD := (Hours - 40.0) * Rate * 3 / 2
           mov     ax, 2
           push    ax
           call    Div1BCD

;          OTPAY := ShRBCD (WorkBCD, 1)
           mov     ax, 1
           push    ax
           call    ShRBCD
           add     sp, 4        ; discard pointer for result
   ENDIF01:
           .
           .
           .
```

In the calculation of OTPay in the ELSE clause, the assignment statement

OTPay := (Hours - 40.0) * Rate * 3 / 2

is implemented using six blocks of code and a variable named WorkBCD for intermediate results. The first block pushes the far pointer to OTPay onto the stack for the final assignment operation, then pushes four pointers to WorkBCD for the four intermediate results. Note that each intermediate result will be one source operand for the next operation. The last operation, not written explicitly in the formula, is the shift to adjust the position of the implied decimal point. See Figure 16.5 for diagrams of the stack during the computation.

The second block computes (Hours - 40.0) in the variable WorkBCD, using the constant FortyPtZero, which is 400 and has an implied decimal point in the same position as the one in Hours. The third through fifth blocks multiply WorkBCD by Rate, multiply that result by 3, and divide that result by 2. The final block pushes 1 onto the stack and calls ShRBCD to adjust the implied decimal point of WorkBCD. The result of this shift is put in OTPay. The last block then adds 4 to SP to remove the far pointer to OTPay.

```
OTPay := (Hours - 40.0) * Rate * 3/2
```
with `Hours` = 0...00440 (represents 44.0 hours)
and `Rate` = 0...00500 (represents $5.00)

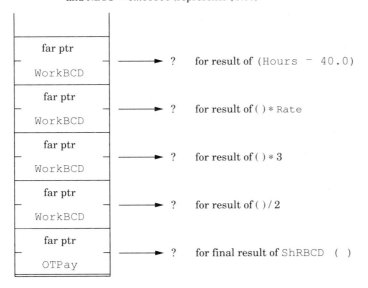

(*a*) Stack after pushing pointers for function results

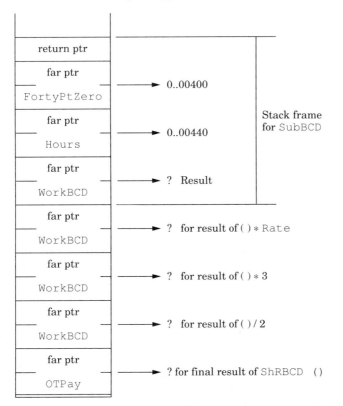

(*b*) Stack on entry to SubBCD

**Figure 16.5** Computation of `OTPay` in Program 16.9

**600** Chapter 16 Decimal Data

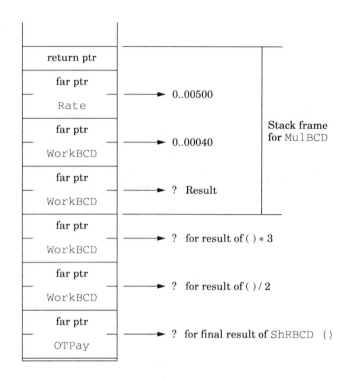

(c) Stack on entry to MulBCD

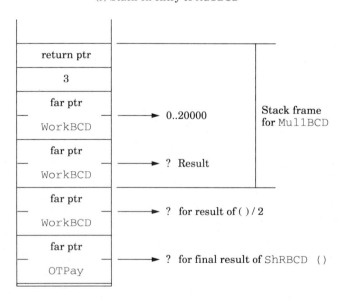

(d) Stack on entry to Mul1BCD

**Figure 16.5** (*continued*)

### 16.4 Instructions and Procedures—Unpacked BCD

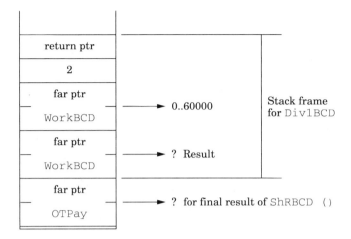

(e) Stack on entry to Div1BCD

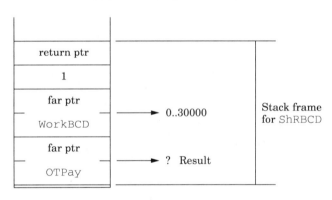

(f) Stack on entry to ShrBCD

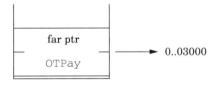

(g) Stack after computation of OTPay

**Figure 16.5** (*continued*)

A Turbo Pascal version of the Wages program is available on the disk. The calculation of OTPay discussed above is implemented in the Pascal version as

```
WorkBCD := SubBCD (Hours, FortyPtZero);
WorkBCD := MulBCD (WorkBCD, Rate);
WorkBCD := Mul1BCD (WorkBCD, 3);
WorkBCD := Div1BCD (WorkBCD, 2);
OTPay := ShRBCD (WorkBCD, 1)
```

The rest of this program is left for the reader to examine.

## EXERCISES 16.4

1. Trace execution of `MulBCD` with arguments 2047 and 853. Use Figure 16.4 as a guide. Show enough steps to illustrate your understanding of the function; it is not necessary to show all of the steps.
2. How could you use a packed BCD number to control a count-controlled loop? Discuss the restrictions of your answer.
▶3. Modify function `Div1BCD` so that it rounds the quotient. For example, the revised `Div1BCD (27, 4)` should return 7 and `Div1BCD (27, 5)` should return 5.
▶4. Write a function with two parameters: a 20-digit unpacked BCD number and an unsigned byte integer. The function is to return the BCD value rounded at the digit position specified by the second parameter. For example, if `InBCD` is 0...0013579, `Round(InBCD,2)` should return 0...0013600.
▶5. Write a procedure that clears an unpacked BCD number to 0. The procedure should have one argument: a far pointer to the number. Assume the number is 20 digits long, with the length stored in the first byte.
▶6. Using the unpacked BCD procedures and functions of this section, write a program that prints a table showing the balance in a savings account each month for one year. The program should read the balance as of January 1 and the annual interest rate. The formula for the new balance each month is

$$\text{new balance} = \text{old balance} \times (1 + \text{monthly rate})$$

where the monthly rate is 1/12 of the annual rate. [Hint: To divide by 12, divide first by 4, then by 3; use at least four or five implied decimal places in intermediate computations.] Write your program in Pascal.
▶7. Do Exercise 6 in assembly language.
▶8. Using the unpacked BCD procedures and functions of this section, write a program that computes and prints values of $N!$ for $N$ from 1 to 20. $N!$ is the product $1 \times 2 \times 3 \times \cdots \times N$. Write your program in Pascal.
▶9. Do Exercise 8 in assembly language.
▶10. Modify function `MulBCD` so that the inner loop is not executed when the multiplier M is zero. Compare the execution times of the original version and your revised version.
▶11. Modify function `MulBCD` as in Exercise 10, and so that the inner loop also terminates when all remaining multiplications involve only leading zeros. Compare the execution times of this version with the other two.
▶12. Revise the functions of this section to use bounded-length unpacked BCD numbers. Function results should be the shortest length that includes all significant digits. For example, the call `AddBCD (0034, 5)` should return 39 with length 2.

## 16.5 INSTRUCTIONS AND PROCEDURES—PACKED BCD

The 8086 supports limited operations on packed BCD numbers, so only a few operations will be implemented on them here. Procedures are given that convert between the 20-digit unpacked BCD format used in the previous section and the 10-byte packed BCD format. A function for adding two 10-byte packed BCD numbers is also given.

### 16.5 Instructions and Procedures—Packed BCD

## Conversions

The conversions between unpacked BCD and packed BCD formats use no new instructions. Procedure BCD2PD, in Program 16.10, converts the unpacked BCD number in its second argument into a packed BCD number in its first argument. After the usual setup, BCD2PD loads DS:SI with a pointer to the third most significant digit of SrcBCD, the unpacked number, and loads ES:DI with a pointer to the first byte of DestPD, the packed number. Recall that the 10-byte number is stored in typical 8086 order, with the least significant byte first. The two most significant digits of SrcBCD are skipped since they will not fit in the 18 digits of DestPD.

## Program 16.10

```
; Program 16.10       BCD2PD.ASM
; Procedure BCD2PD (var DestPD: TenBytes; SrcBCD: String20);
; Converts an unpacked BCD number into a packed BCD number.
; Assumes the number is positive, and has fewer than 18 digits.

; Parameters:
  DestPD        equ     dword ptr [bp + 8]
  SrcBCD        equ     dword ptr [bp + 4]

_TEXT SEGMENT word public 'code'
      assume  cs: _TEXT
      public  BCD2PD

BCD2PD PROC

; set up bp register to point to parameters
      push    bp
      mov     bp, sp

; set up pointers to most significant digits of arguments
      push    ds              ;save caller's ds register
      lds     si, SrcBCD
      add     si, 3           ;skip length byte, two digits
      les     di, DestPD
      add     di, 9           ;ten-byte stored backwards

; clear sign of DestPD (assume number is positive)
      mov     es:[di], byte ptr 0
      dec     di

; FOR01 cx := 9 TO 1 STEP -1
      mov     cx, 9

  DO01:
;     move one digit into left four bits of al
        mov     al, ds:[si]
        shl     al, 1
        shl     al, 1
        shl     al, 1
        shl     al, 1
```

## Program 16.10 (continued)

```
    ; move second digit into right four bits of ah
            inc     si
            mov     ah, ds:[si]
            and     ah, 0Fh

    ; combine digits and save
            or      al, ah
            mov     es:[di], al

    ; advance pointers and repeat
            inc     si
            dec     di
            loop    DO01
    ; ENDFOR01

    ; restore caller's ds register, and return
            pop     ds
            pop     bp
            ret     8

BCD2PD  ENDP
_TEXT   ENDS
        END
```

The sign byte of DestPD is cleared, and the pointer is changed to point to the most significant digit. This step is followed by a loop that executes nine times, each time packing two digits from two consecutive bytes of SrcBCD into one byte of DestPD. The first of the two digits is copied into the left four bits of AL by the instructions

```
mov     al, ds:[si]
shl     al, 1
shl     al, 1
shl     al, 1
shl     al, 1
```

The next digit of SrcBCD is copied into the right four bits of AH by the instructions

```
inc     si
mov     ah, ds:[si]
and     ah, 0Fh
```

Note that these sequences clear the four bits of each register not occupied by the BCD digit. Although this step is not necessary when the SrcBCD argument is indeed an unpacked BCD number, doing so allows the conversion of a 20-character string directly to packed decimal (assuming all the characters are digits) without converting it to unpacked BCD first.

The two digits are combined into one byte and saved in DestPD by the instructions

```
or      al, ah
mov     es:[di], al
```

The pointers are then advanced to the next more significant digits, and the process is repeated.

### 16.5 Instructions and Procedures—Packed BCD

Procedure PD2BCD, in Program 16.11, converts the packed BCD number in its second argument into an unpacked BCD number in its first argument. It sets DS:SI to point to the last byte—the sign—of SrcPD, and it sets ES:DI to point to the length byte of DestBCD. It then moves 20 into that length byte and advances the pointer. The sign byte of SrcPD is treated like two zeros; thus the sign and 18 digits of SrcPD are unpacked and copied into DestBCD two at a time in a loop that executes 10 times.

## Program 16.11

```
; Program 16.11      PD2BCD.ASM
; Procedure PD2BCD (var DestBCD: String20; SrcPD: TenBytes);
; Converts a packed BCD number into an unpacked BCD number.
; The sign byte of the packed BCD number is treated like
; two leading zero digits, assuming the number is positive.

; Parameters:
  DestBCD       equ     dword ptr [bp + 8]
  SrcPD         equ     dword ptr [bp + 4]

_TEXT SEGMENT word public 'code'
    assume  cs: _TEXT
    public  PD2BCD

PD2BCD PROC

; set up bp register to point to parameters
    push    bp
    mov     bp, sp

; set up pointers to most significant digits of arguments
    push    ds              ;save caller's ds register
    lds     si, SrcPD
    add     si, 9
    les     di, DestBCD

; put 20 in length byte of DestBCD
    mov     al, 20
    mov     es:[di], al
    inc     di

; FOR01 cx := 10 TO 1 STEP -1
    mov     cx, 10

  DO01:
;   move left digit of PD into BCD
    mov     al, ds:[si]     ;get left digit
    shr     al, 1           ;shift it
    shr     al, 1           ;   into the
    shr     al, 1           ;       right end
    shr     al, 1           ;           of byte
    mov     es:[di], al
```

## Program 16.11 (continued)

```
;       move right digit of PD into BCD
        mov     al, ds:[si]     ;get right digit
        and     al, 0Fh         ;clear left digit
        inc     di
        mov     es:[di], al
;       advance pointers, repeat
        dec     si
        inc     di
        loop    DO01
; ENDFOR01
;       restore caller's ds register and stack, return
        pop     ds
        pop     bp
        ret     8

PD2BCD  ENDP
_TEXT   ENDS
        END
```

The first digit of each pair is moved from the left four bits of the byte of SrcPD to the right four bits of the next byte of DestBCD by the instructions

```
mov     al, ds:[si]
shr     al, 1
shr     al, 1
shr     al, 1
shr     al, 1
mov     es:[di], al
```

The second digit is moved from the right four bits of the same byte of SrcPD into the right four bits of the next byte of DestBCD by the instructions

```
mov     al, ds:[si]
and     al, 0Fh
inc     di
mov     es:[di], si
```

Then the pointers are advanced to the next less significant digits, and the loop repeats.

## Arithmetic Instructions

Unsigned binary addition and subtraction instructions can be used with packed BCD data one byte at a time. The 8086 provides instructions for adjusting the results to represent packed BCD numbers. It is necessary to write loops to work with data longer than one byte.

## Addition

To add packed BCD numbers, move one byte of one number into the AL register, and add the corresponding byte of the other number, plus the carry from the previous addition

## 16.5 Instructions and Procedures—Packed BCD 607

(if any), to it. The sum might exceed 9 in each digit; furthermore, the sum of the less significant digits might carry into the sum of the more significant ones. The 8086 provides an instruction that inspects AL and adjusts the sum to ensure that the sum is represented by two correct packed BCD digits with any additional carry recorded in the carry flag.

**Decimal Adjust for Addition**
syntax:   daa
action:   (see description that follows)
flags:    ....SZAPC modified
          O........ undefined
          .DIT..... unchanged

The add instruction sets the carry flag when there is a carry out of the most significant digit in a sum. It also sets the auxiliary carry when there is a carry from bit three to bit four in computing the sum. This carry from bit three to bit four indicates that the sum of the four lower bits exceeds 16. When working with decimal numbers, a sum that exceeds 10 in any four bits requires an extra addition of 6 to force the carry into the next digit and adjust the sum correctly.

Consider adding decimal values 28 and 19. In packed BCD (in binary), this addition is given by

```
         111          carries
     0010  1000
   + 0001  1001
   ─────────────
     0100  0001
```

The unadjusted sum looks like 41, but the correct sum of 28 and 19 is 47. The carry from bit three to bit four looks like a decimal carry of 10, but it is really a binary carry of 16. To adjust for this carry, the daa instruction adds 6 to the lower digit when the auxiliary carry flag is set by the addition.

Now consider adding decimal values 28 and 43. In packed BCD (in binary), this addition is given by

```
     0010  1000
   + 0100  0011
   ─────────────
     0110  1011
```

There is no carry from bit three to bit four, but the sum cannot be interpreted as a decimal number. The daa instruction also detects this fact and adds 6 to the lower four bits. The addition of 6 to the sum

```
        1   11      carries
     0110  1011
   +       0110
   ─────────────
     0111  0001
```

gives decimal value 71, which is the expected answer. If the result of the addition does not set the auxiliary carry flag and if the lower four bits do represent a decimal digit, no adjustment is added.

The daa instruction also detects whether the higher four bits exceed 9 after any adjustments that are applied to the lower four bits. If necessary, daa also adds 6 to the higher four bits to adjust them and records a carry out of bit seven in the carry flag.

In summary, then, the daa instruction adjusts the contents of the AL register to two packed decimal digits and a possible carry of 1 following the addition of two packed decimal numbers.

A function to add two 10-byte packed decimals, AddPD, is given in Program 16.12. The function assumes that both packed decimal numbers have the same sign.

**Program 16.12**

```
; Program 16.12      AddPD.ASM
; Function AddPD (PD1, PD2: TenBytes): TenBytes;
;    Returns PD1 + PD2.
;    Assumes PD1 and PD2 have the same sign.

; Pointer to Result, Parameters:
  Result        equ     dword ptr [bp + 12]
  PD1           equ     dword ptr [bp + 8]
  PD2           equ     dword ptr [bp + 4]

_TEXT SEGMENT word public 'code'
       assume   cs: _TEXT
       public   AddPD

AddPD PROC

; set up bp register to point to parameters
       push     bp
       mov      bp, sp

; save caller's ds register
       push     ds

; Add digits of PD1 and PD2, one byte at a time, with carry,
; saving the sum in result.
; clear carry flag
       clc

; clear index register (least significant digits of tenbyte
; data are stored with smaller offsets, so index increases...)
       mov      si, 0

; FOR21 cx := 9 TO 1 STEP -1
       mov      cx, 9
```

## 16.5 Instructions and Procedures—Packed BCD

**Program 16.12 (continued)**

```
        DO21:
;       Result[si] := PD1[si] + PD2[si] + carry
        lds     bx, PD1
        mov     al, [bx+si]
        lds     bx, PD2
        adc     al, [bx+si]
        daa
        lds     bx, Result
        mov     [bx+si], al

;       adjust index to next more significant digits
        inc     si
        loop    DO21
; ENDFOR21

; copy sign of PD1 to sign of Result
        lds     bx, PD1
        mov     al, [bx+si]
        lds     bx, Result
        mov     [bx+si], al

; restore caller's registers and stack, return
        pop     ds
        pop     bp
        ret     8

AddPD   ENDP
_TEXT   ENDS
        END
```

AddPD has two parameters named PD1 and PD2; it returns the sum as the function value. Like AddBCD, it follows Turbo Pascal calling conventions, expecting a far pointer to the function result pushed onto the stack before the arguments. After setting up BP and saving DS, AddBCD clears both the carry flag and SI. SI is used as an index register; the packed BCD numbers are accessed using DS:BX+SI. The function then executes the sequence

```
        lds     bx, PD1
        mov     al, [bx+si]
        lds     bx, PD2
        adc     al, [bx+si]
        daa
        lds     bx, Result
        mov     [bx+si], al
        inc     si
```

nine times. Note the use of adc to add the previous carry—0 the first time, 0 or 1 as set by the previous daa instruction thereafter—to each sum. The sign of the first argument is also copied to the result.

## Subtraction

To subtract bytes of packed decimal numbers, move one of them into the AL register and subtract the other from it. The difference is adjusted to two decimal digits in a manner similar to the daa instruction; the auxiliary carry flag now indicates a borrow from bit four to bit three.

**Decimal Adjust for Subtraction**
syntax:   das
action:   (see description of daa above)
flags:    ....SZAPC modified
          O....... undefined
          .DIT..... unchanged

Writing a function to subtract 10-byte BCD numbers is left as an exercise.

Program 16.13 is a simple assembly-language program that tests the three procedures described in this section. It reads an unpacked BCD number using GetBCD from the previous section, packs it, adds a constant to it, and then unpacks and prints the sum using PutBCD. Each operation in Program 16.13 requires pushing far pointers and calling a procedure or function, making it a long program but not one difficult to read.

## Program 16.13

```
; Program 16.13      PDMain.ASM
; Tests packed decimal (PD) routines.

; DOS function and status parameters
    DosFunc     equ     21h
    ExitToDos   equ     4Ch
    NoErrors    equ     00h

DOSSEG

_STACK SEGMENT para stack 'stack'
        dw      100h dup (?)
_STACK ENDS

_DATA SEGMENT word public 'data'
    Unpacked    db      0, 20 dup (?)       ;unpacked BCD variable
    Packed      dt      ?                   ;packed BCD variable
    Con1        dt      2042                ;packed BCD constant
    Sum         dt      ?                   ;sum of Packed + Con1
    Success     dw      ?                   ;flag for succssful read
    PromptMsg   db      "Enter unpacked number:  "
    PromptLen   dw      $ - PromptMsg
    SumMsg      db      "Your number + 2042 is "
    SumLen      dw      $ - SumMsg
_DATA ENDS

_TEXT SEGMENT word public 'code'
    assume  cs: _TEXT
```

## 16.5 Instructions and Procedures—Packed BCD

**Program 16.13 (continued)**

```
        ; IO procedures
            extrn   PutStr: PROC, PutCrLf: PROC

        ; Unpacked BCD procedures
            extrn   PutBCD: PROC, GetBCD: PROC

        ; Packed BCD procedures
            extrn   BCD2PD: PROC, PD2BCD: PROC, AddPD: PROC

PDMain:
        ; set up ds register to point to _DATA
            mov     ax, seg _DATA
            mov     ds, ax
            assume  ds: _DATA

        ; print ("Enter unpacked number:  ")
            mov     cx, PromptLen
            mov     bx, offset PromptMsg
            call    PutStr

        ; read (UnPacked)
            mov     ax, offset UnPacked
            push    ds
            push    ax
            mov     ax, offset Success
            push    ds
            push    ax
            call    GetBCD
            call    PutCrLf

        ; convert UnPacked to Packed
            mov     ax, offset Packed
            push    ds
            push    ax
            mov     ax, offset UnPacked
            push    ds
            push    ax
            call    BCD2PD

        ; Sum := Packed + Con1
            mov     ax, offset Sum
            push    ds
            push    ax
            mov     ax, offset Packed
            push    ds
            push    ax
            mov     ax, offset Con1
            push    ds
            push    ax
            call    AddPD
            add     sp, 4       ; discard pointer for result
```

**Program 16.13 (continued)**

```
    ; convert Sum to UnPacked
        mov     ax, offset UnPacked
        push    ds
        push    ax
        mov     ax, offset Sum
        push    ds
        push    ax
        call    PD2BCD

    ; print ("Your number + 2042 is ", UnPacked)
        mov     cx, SumLen
        mov     bx, offset SumMsg
        call    PutStr
        mov     ax, offset UnPacked
        push    ds
        push    ax
        call    PutBCD
        call    PutCrLf

    ; exit to DOS
        mov     ah, ExitToDos
        mov     al, NoErrors
        int     DosFunc

_TEXT ENDS
END     PDMain
```

## Other Operations

The complexity of adjusting intermediate results of multidigit multiplication or division of packed BCD numbers is beyond the scope of this text. The 8086 has no provision for adjusting such terms. If the goal is to multiply or divide packed decimals, there are three choices: use only the instructions seen so far, and write some fairly complex routines; convert the packed decimal numbers to unpacked BCD numbers, and do the arithmetic in unpacked form; or use the math coprocessor if available.

Clear and move operations on packed decimals can be implemented as string moves. Input and output are not normally performed on packed BCD; these operations are performed on unpacked data. Compare operations must first compare the sign bytes; if the signs are the same, the rest of the packed decimal numbers can be compared as strings. If the signs of both numbers are negative, the carry flag of an unequal result must be complemented. Such operations are not considered further here.

**EXERCISES 16.5**

1. Test whether Procedure BCD2PD really can convert strings of digits to packed BCD. What restrictions are there on the strings that can be successfully converted?

▶2. Write a function that subtracts packed BCD numbers. The function should use the 10-byte format and return the difference computed as the first argument minus the second argument. Assume both numbers have the same sign.

▶3. Revise AddBCD and your subtraction function from Exercise 2 so that, if the arguments have different signs, the other function is invoked with the magnitudes of the arguments. Then put the correct sign on the result.

▶4. Write a function that converts a doubleword integer to a 10-byte packed BCD number.

▶5. Write a function that converts a 10-byte packed BCD number into a doubleword integer. If the 10-byte number is too large, your function should keep the least significant 32 bits and set the overflow flag. Otherwise, it should clear the overflow flag.

▶6. Write a procedure that reads a 10-byte packed BCD number. It should return the value it reads as well as a Boolean value that indicates whether the read was successful.

▶7. Write a procedure that prints a 10-byte packed BCD number passed to it as an argument.

## KEY POINTS

- Numbers in unpacked BCD format are stored as the binary representation of each digit, using one byte for each.
- Numbers in packed decimal format are stored as the binary representation of each digit, using four bits for each, with two digits packed in each byte.
- Numbers in BCD formats do not include a decimal point; programmers can manage an implied decimal point.
- Converting between strings and unpacked BCD requires masking off or inserting the leading four bits of the character representation. Other issues for consideration involve length and whether the string is right- or left-justified.
- Addition and subtraction of BCD numbers proceed right to left, with a carry or borrow generated after adding or subtracting each pair of digits.
- Multiplication of BCD numbers can be implemented from right to left, multiplying one pair of digits at a time; all intermediate results should be added as they are generated.
- Division of BCD numbers, when not supported by the instruction set, can be implemented using repeated subtraction.
- Negation of BCD numbers can be performed using an xor instruction with an appropriate mask.
- Shifts of BCD numbers by multiples of four (packed BCD) or eight (unpacked BCD) bits are equivalent to multiplication and division by powers of 10.
- Comparison of two BCD numbers of the same length proceeds much like string comparisons—from right to left, looking for digits that differ. If the numbers have different lengths, the shorter is treated as though it is extended with leading zeros.
- When computing with BCD numbers and implied decimal points, it is necessary to consider what each number and each intermediate result represent as well as the location of the implied decimal point in each number.

## PC SYSTEM SUMMARY

- The 8086 supports two forms of decimal numbers: unpacked BCD, in which each digit is represented by four bits and occupies a whole byte, and packed BCD, in which two digits are packed in each byte.
- To define a constant in unpacked BCD, use the db directive, and write every digit (including a length byte, if used) in the operand field.

**Chapter 16   Decimal Data**

- To reserve memory for an unpacked BCD variable, use the db directive and the dup operator to specify the number of bytes desired.
- The dt directive can be used to define 10-byte packed decimal numbers. These numbers have a sign coded in the last byte, leaving room for 18 digits. An initial value can be included in the operand field.
- The 8086 has instructions for adjusting the result of unpacked addition, subtraction, and multiplication and for preparing an unpacked dividend for division. The actual operations are performed using unsigned binary instructions.
- The 8086 has instructions for adjusting the result of packed addition and subtraction. The actual operations are performed using unsigned binary instructions.
- There is no provision for implied decimal points in decimal numbers, either packed or unpacked.
- The numeric coprocessor can convert between 10-byte packed decimal numbers and the internal numeric representation used by the coprocessor.

Instructions presented in this chapter:

Unpacked BCD:
      aas    ASCII adjust for subtraction
      aam   ASCII adjust for multiplication
      aad    ASCII adjust for division

Packed Decimal:
      daa    decimal adjust for addition
      das    decimal adjust for subtraction

# Floating-Point Data 17

- **Representation**
- **Specification**
- **Operations**
- **The 8087 Coprocessor**
- **Instructions**
- **Applications**

The two numeric data types discussed so far, integer and BCD, do not directly support fractions or very large numbers. They do, however, provide exact arithmetic within the range of values supported. There are many applications where fractions or very large numbers are indispensable, even if exact arithmetic must be sacrificed to get them.

The floating-point data type provides both fractions and a great range of values. It uses a discrete subset of the real numbers of mathematics. Because they are represented in finite computers, however, the range of floating-point numbers is neither infinitely large nor infinitely dense. One consequence is that operations on them may give a result that is not a floating-point number. Instructions usually give an approximate result that is a floating-point number; the difference between the true result and its floating-point representation is an error that needs to be understood. This and other errors require more careful programming when computing with floating-point numbers. This chapter considers the representation of floating-point numbers, the 8087 coprocessor, and its operations on floating-point numbers.

## 17.1 REPRESENTATION

Engineers and scientists work with numbers in a form called *scientific notation*, in which the numbers are written as a sign, a number between 1 and 10, and a power of 10. For example, the number 42.5 is represented in scientific notation as $4.25 \times 10^1$; 0.001 is represented as $1.0 \times 10^{-3}$; and $-3350$ is represented as $-3.35 \times 10^3$. To multiply these three numbers together, we first compute $4.25 \times 3.35$—we don't bother multiplying by 1.0—to arrive at 14.2375. Since the original numbers have only three significant digits, we truncate the product to 14.2. We convert this intermediate result to scientific notation, getting $1.42 \times 10^1$. Then we account for the exponents of the three factors by simply adding them to the exponent of the product, getting $1.42 \times 10^{1+1-3+3} = 1.42 \times 10^2$. Finally, we account for the sign, and write the result as $-1.42 \times 10^2$.

The idea of representing numbers in something like scientific notation is attractive. Computers can use a similar form called floating-point representation. This section will examine floating-point representations after showing how to convert fractions from one base to another.

## Converting Real Numbers

We are interested in writing **normalized floating-point numbers**, a format consisting of a sign, a significand, and an integral power of the radix. The **significand** is a number greater than or equal to 1.0 and less than the radix. In base 10, the significand of a normalized floating-point number must be in the range from 1 to less than 10. For example, the number 42.5 is represented as $+4.25 \times 10^1$.

More generally, a number in radix $b$ is written in floating-point form as

$$+d_0.d_1d_2d_3\ldots \times b^e$$

where $d_i$ is a digit in base $b$ ($0 \leq d_i < b$), except that $d_0$ cannot be 0. Thus, the following are normalized floating-point numbers in base 10:

$+1.23456789 \times 10^{-1}$
$-9.87654321 \times 10^{12}$
$+5.0 \times 10^0$

The following are not, for the reasons given:

| | |
|---|---|
| $+11.3 \times 10^3$ | significand > radix |
| $-0.002 \times 10^7$ | significand < 1.0 |
| $-4.0 \times 10^{\frac{1}{2}}$ | exponent not integer |

With few exceptions, floating-point numbers are normalized when represented in a computer. One exception is 0, which cannot be normalized. Other exceptions will be introduced when operations on floating-point numbers are discussed.

We are interested in floating-point numbers in other bases, especially binary. A normalized floating-point number in binary is written as a sign, a significand written as $1.f$ where $1.0 \leq 1.f < 2.0$ (that is, $f$ is a fraction), and an exponent representing a power of 2. For example, the following numbers are both in normalized floating-point form:

$+1.00101 \times 2^3$
$-1.110 \times 2^{-7}$

By convention, everything except the significand is written in base 10.

Just how big is $1.00101_2 \times 2^3$, and how small is $-1.110_2 \times 2^{-7}$? To answer these questions, the numbers are converted to base 10.

### Binary to decimal

To convert a floating-point number from binary to base 10, we must convert the significand to base 10 and multiply by the power of 2 specified by the exponent. These tasks can be done in either order. Both orders are demonstrated using the first example given above.

A fraction can be expanded as negative powers of the radix. For example, in base 10 the fraction 0.237 is

$$0.237 = 2 \times 10^{-1} + 3 \times 10^{-2} + 7 \times 10^{-3}$$

## 17.1 Representation

We can expand fractions in other bases the same way. The binary significand in the example is

$$1.00101_2 = 1 \times 2^0 + 0 \times 2^{-1} + 0 \times 2^{-2} + 1 \times 2^{-3} + 0 \times 2^{-4} + 1 \times 2^{-5}$$

or

$$1.00101_2 = 1 + \tfrac{0}{2} + \tfrac{0}{4} + \tfrac{1}{8} + \tfrac{0}{16} + \tfrac{1}{32}$$

Now writing a common denominator and dropping zero terms,

$$1.00101_2 = \tfrac{32}{32} + \tfrac{4}{32} + \tfrac{1}{32}$$
$$= \tfrac{37}{32}$$
$$= 1.15625$$

(Decimals can be used instead of fractions in the expansion, but that is sometimes more cumbersome.) Our example number is $1.00101_2 \times 2^3$, so the intermediate result must be multiplied by $2^3$:

$$1.00101_2 \times 2^3 = 1.15625 \times 8 = 9.25$$

Note that it would be easier to multiply by 8 before rewriting $\tfrac{37}{32}$ as a decimal:

$$1.00101_2 \times 2^3 = \left(\tfrac{37}{32}\right) \times 8 = \tfrac{37}{4} = 9\tfrac{1}{4} = 9.25$$

We can also multiply by the power of 2 before expanding the fraction. This is easy, since multiplying a binary number by a power of 2 just shifts the binary point within the number. The same example becomes

$$1.00101_2 \times 2^3 = 1001.01 \times 2^0$$

The exponent can now be dropped, since $2^0$ is 1. To convert $1001.01_2$ to decimal, simply expand it in powers of 2.

## Decimal to binary

To convert a decimal number to binary, start by shifting the decimal point and adjusting the exponent so that the exponent is 0. For example, $3.4625 \times 10^1$ is easier to work with if we rewrite it as $34.625 \times 10^0$, or simply $34.625$. The whole number part is converted as an integer, using the methods discussed in Chapter 1. To convert the fraction, a new technique is introduced here that seems nebulous at first but is easily verified. The method is as follows. Start with the fraction in base 10 and multiply it by 2:

$$2 \times .625 = 1.25$$

Now save the whole number part of the product for later use. Take the fraction part of the product and multiply it by 2:

$$2 \times .25 = 0.5$$

Again save the whole number part and multiply the fraction part by 2, and repeat this process until the fraction in the product is 0. In the example here, only one more multiplication is needed:

$$2 \times .5 = 1.0$$

Now collect the whole number parts, writing them from left to right in the order they were obtained, preceded by a binary point. Thus, we get

$$.625 = .101_2$$

Including the whole number parts, we have

$$34.625 = 100010.101_2$$

Now shift the binary point to normalize the number, and get

$$34.625 = 1.00010101_2 \times 2^5$$

Here is another example. Consider the number $1.23125 \times 10^1$. First adjust the decimal point to get rid of the exponent:

$$1.23125 \times 10^1 = 12.3125$$

Then convert the whole number part to binary:

$$12 = 1100_2$$

Then convert the fraction to binary:

$$2 \times .3125 = 0.625$$
$$2 \times .625 = 1.25$$
$$2 \times .25 = 0.5$$
$$2 \times .5 = 1.0$$

so that $0.3125 = 0.0101_2$. Next combine the whole number and the fraction:

$$12.3125 = 1100.0101_2$$

Finally, shift the binary point to normalize the number:

$$12.3125 = 1.1000101_2 \times 2^3$$

The preceding two examples have binary fractions that terminate after only a few bits. The next example is not as simple. When we convert 0.6 to binary using the multiplication algorithm, we get the sequence

$$2 \times 0.6 = 1.2$$
$$2 \times 0.2 = 0.4$$
$$2 \times 0.4 = 0.8$$
$$2 \times 0.8 = 1.6$$
$$2 \times 0.6 = 1.2$$

## 17.1 Representation

and so on. The sequence repeats forever; in the binary representation of 0.6, the four bits 1001 repeat forever:

$$0.6 = 0.1001100110011001\ldots_2$$

This phenomenon is similar to that of trying to represent $\frac{1}{3}$ as a decimal. This repeating nature of the binary fraction causes some problems, which will be discussed later.

## Floating-Point Numbers in Memory

Now that we know how to convert real numbers to binary, and how to write them in normalized floating-point form, we can consider how floating-point numbers are represented in computer memory.

There are three components of a normalized floating-point number to include in the representation: the sign, the significand, and the exponent. These are packed into some number of consecutive bytes. The 32-bit format used with the 8087 coprocessor is presented first; other formats will be considered later. The 32-bit floating-point data type is often called **single-precision** real (or just single) as well as short real.

First consider how to partition 32 bits into the three fields needed. The sign requires one bit. The sign and significand are represented separately, much like sign and magnitude notation. (Some computer systems combine them into a single field and represent it using a complement representation.) The sign of a positive number is 0 and the sign of a negative number is 1.

### Coding the significand

Using one bit for the sign leaves 31 bits for the significand and exponent. The more bits used for the significand, the more precisely the number can be represented. The more bits used for the exponent, the greater the range of numbers that can be represented. The 8087 uses 23 bits for the significand and 8 bits for the exponent.

The first bit will always be 1 in a normalized significand, so it is not actually necessary to store it. All 23 bits can be used for the most significant part of the fraction.

### Representation error

Some real numbers are represented exactly, others only approximately. Clearly, if 23 bits are used for the fraction, any floating-point number that requires more than 24 bits in its significand cannot be represented exactly, but will be approximated by a number that can be represented—either the nearest or the next smaller one, depending on the processor. It is natural to ask how much error can be expected when this happens. The answer is usually expressed as a relative error or as the number of significant digits.

The largest error occurs when an exact number is represented by the next smaller number that can be represented, and the bits that are lost represent as large a number possible compared to the smallest number possibly retained. In binary, this worst case occurs when we try to represent a number with the significand

$$1.00000000000000000000000111111111111\ldots$$

where the value retained is 1.0, and the part that is lost is an infinitely long string of 1 bits. These 1 bits together represent a value just under $2^{-23}$. To see this, note that these bits represent $2^{-24}, 2^{-25}, 2^{-26}$, and so on. If we add them and factor out $2^{-23}$, we get

$$2^{-23} \times \left(\frac{1}{2} + \frac{1}{4} + \frac{1}{8} + \frac{1}{16} + \cdots\right)$$

The terms in parentheses are a geometric series whose sum is 1.0. The largest error is therefore a little less than $2^{-23}$.

What is this error in decimal? Using logarithms, we can show that $2 \approx 10^{0.30103}$, so $2^n \approx 10^{0.30103n}$, which gives

$$2^{-23} \approx 10^{-0.30103 \times 23}$$
$$\approx 10^{-6.9237}$$
$$\approx 10^{0.0763} \times 10^{-7}$$
$$\approx 1.2 \times 10^{-7}$$

Thus, the representation error is about 0.00001 percent. Another interpretation of this is to say that we can represent a real number with almost seven digits of precision. This is adequate for many applications.

## Coding the exponent

Eight bits are left for the exponent in single-precision floating-point representation. With eight bits, 256 different exponents are possible. The 8087 uses **biased exponents** in which the number in the 8-bit field is the exponent plus 127. That is, using $e$ for the 8-bit integer in the exponent field, and $E$ for the exponent of the floating-point number, $e = E + 127$.

One advantage of using a biased exponent is that all exponents are coded as positive integers. This simplifies some of the operations that the hardware must perform. Since $e$ can take on values from 0 to 255, it would seem that the exponent $E$ can take on values between $-127$ and $+128$. But the cases where $e = 0$ and $e = 255$ have special meanings in the 8087, which will be explained shortly. The effective range of exponents for floating point numbers is thus $-126$ to $+127$.

## Range of numbers

The range of floating-point numbers that can be represented is simple to derive. First, the largest normalized number that can be represented has a significand containing all 1-bits. This represents the number

$$1 \times 2^0 + 1 \times 2^{-1} + 1 \times 2^{-2} + \cdots + 1 \times 2^{-23}$$

which is $2.0 - 2^{-23}$. If we combine this with the largest exponent $E = +127$, we get $(2 - 2^{-23}) \times (2^{127})$, which is $2^{128} - 2^{104}$. Converting to decimal, we find that

$$2^{128} \approx 10^{0.30103 \times 128}$$
$$\approx 10^{38.532}$$
$$\approx 10^{0.532} \times 10^{38}$$
$$\approx 3.4 \times 10^{38}$$

## 17.1 Representation

The smallest positive number that can be represented has significand 1.0 and exponent $E = -126$. Converting to decimal, we find that

$$2^{-126} \approx 10^{-0.30103 \times 126}$$
$$\approx 10^{-37.930}$$
$$\approx 10^{0.070} \times 10^{-38}$$
$$\approx 1.2 \times 10^{-38}$$

In summary, the short real representation provides a precision of almost seven significant digits and a range of magnitudes from $1.2 \times 10^{-38}$ to $3.4 \times 10^{38}$. This is adequate for most purposes.

### Arrangement of fields

Most arithmetic operations need to separate the sign, fraction, and exponent as the operation proceeds. The move operations, however, do not need to separate the fields. The negate instruction changes only the sign bit. These operations are not affected by the order of fields in a floating-point number.

Now consider the comparison of two floating-point numbers. To compare two numbers, we first check their signs. If they are different, we know the relationship between the two numbers. If the signs are the same, we must consider the exponents. If the exponents are the same, we consider the fractions. It is possible to combine comparing exponents and fractions into one operation by taking advantage of the bias on the exponent. Simply store the biased exponent in front of the fraction so that the exponent and fraction form a 31-bit field, with the exponent in the more significant bits. Since all biased exponents are positive, the comparison is simple: These 31-bit fields compare correctly as unsigned integers. Note that the fractions affect the outcome only if the exponents of the two numbers are the same. The organization of floating-point numbers in this 32-bit format is shown in Figure 17.1.

Let's look at how some floating-point numbers are stored in this format. Consider 1.0. First convert it to binary:

$$1.0_{10} = +1.0_2 \times 2^0$$

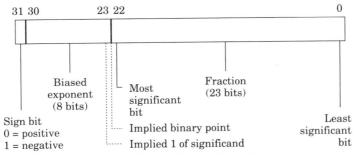

**Figure 17.1** Format of Short Floating-Point Numbers

**622** Chapter 17 Floating-Point Data

We have
$$\text{sign} = 0$$
$$\text{biased exponent} = 0 + 127 = 0111\ 1111_2$$
$$\text{significand} = 1.000\ 0000\ 0000\ 0000\ 0000\ 0000_2$$

Putting these together according to Figure 17.1, we get
$$0\ 0111\ 1111\ 000\ 0000\ 0000\ 0000\ 0000\ 0000$$

or 3F800000h. The fields are separated with an extra space to make it easier to read. Note that the leading 1 of the significand is not stored.

Now consider $-12.4375$. In binary, normalized floating-point, it is
$$-12.4375 = -1.1000111_2 \times 2^3$$

We have
$$\text{sign} = 1$$
$$\text{biased exponent} = 3 + 127 = 1000\ 0010_2$$
$$\text{significand} = 1.100\ 0111\ 0000\ 0000\ 0000\ 0000_2$$

Putting these together, we get
$$1\ 1000\ 0010\ 100\ 0111\ 0000\ 0000\ 0000\ 0000$$

or C1470000h.

## Long reals

In addition to the 32-bit floating-point numbers, the 8087 also supports a 64-bit floating-point type (Figure 17.2). This type is called **double-precision** real (or just double) as well as long real. It uses one bit for the sign, 11 bits for the exponent, and 52 bits for the significand. The leading 1 of the significand is not stored. The order of the fields is the same as in short reals.

The largest error in representing an exact real number in a long real is a little less than $2^{-52}$, or $2.2 \times 10^{-16}$. The long reals have slightly over 15 significant digits.

The exponent in a long real number is biased by 1023 rather than 127, and the smallest and largest exponents are again reserved for special cases. The range of magnitudes that can be represented is between $2^{-1022}$ and $2^{1024}$, or about $2.2 \times 10^{-308}$ to $1.8 \times 10^{308}$.

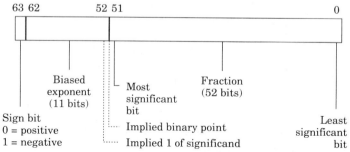

Figure 17.2  Format of Long Floating-Point Numbers

## 17.1 Representation

### Extended reals

In addition to the 32-bit and 64-bit formats for floating-point numbers, the 8087 also supports an **extended-precision** real (or just extended) format that uses 80 bits (Figure 17.3). Although values in this format can be used as constants and variables in the same way as the other two formats, the extended format is intended for intermediate results within the 8087. The extended reals are intended to provide a few extra digits of precision in calculations so that the inevitable errors in the least significant bits do not affect the values ultimately stored in short or long real variables.

The extended real format uses one bit for the sign, 15 bits for the exponent, and 64 bits for the significand. Unlike the other formats, the leading 1 of the significand is present in the extended format. The largest error in representing an exact real value in extended floating-point is a little less than $2^{-64}$, or about $5.4 \times 10^{-20}$. Thus, the extended format has more than 19 significant digits. The exponent in an extended number is biased by 16383, and the smallest and largest exponents are again reserved for special cases. The range of extended numbers is from $2^{-16382}$ to $2^{16384}$, or about $3.4 \times 10^{-4932}$ to $1.2 \times 10^{4932}$. The coprocessor performs all calculations using extended precision. The range and precision is adequate to ensure accurate results whether the application program represents the data as integers, short or long reals, or 10-byte (18-digit) BCD numbers.

Figure 17.4 shows how the numbers $-12.4375$ and $0.1$ are represented in each of the three formats. The short format representation of the former of these has been described already. The other examples follow directly. Note that the leading 1 of the significand is stored in the extended format but not in the others. Note also that one-tenth does not terminate in binary. Its representation is shown with the trailing bits of the significand discarded. Some assemblers (and compilers) round the representation rather than truncate; rounding will be discussed shortly.

### Special representations

In all three formats, the smallest and largest biased exponents are reserved for special cases. The following discussion will use single precision where the smallest and largest biased exponents are $e = 0$ and $e = 255$. The exponent $e = 0$ will be considered first. Note that we do not yet have zero in floating-point. Since 0.0 cannot be normalized, we need some exceptional coding for it. The usual choice is $e = 0$ and $f = 0$. In this case, the first bit of the significand, which we normally assume is 1 and is not saved, is also 0. Note that with this representation there is a negative 0 as well as a positive 0.

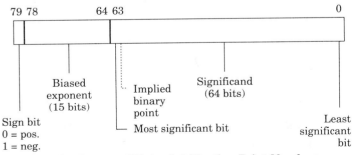

**Figure 17.3 Format of Extended Floating-Point Numbers**

$-12.4375 = -1100.0111_2$

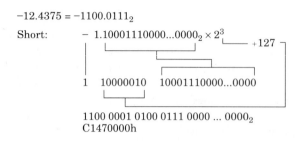

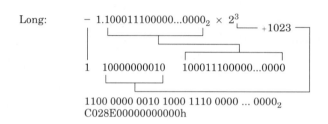

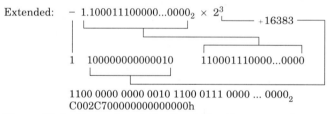

**Figure 17.4** Examples of Floating-Point Representation

There is also another use for $e = 0$. Consider trying to represent $1.01_2 \times 2^{-130}$ in short format. We cannot have an exponent less than $-126$, but if we shift the binary point three places, we get $0.00101_2 \times 2^{-127}$. Now the number is not normalized, but it has the special exponent $E = -127$ that corresponds to $e = 0$. Numbers with $e = 0$ are called **denormalized numbers**. They are too small to represent in normalized form, but may be represented in denormalized form. For example, we can store $1.01_2 \times 2^{-130}$ as a denormalized number with the 23-bit fraction $001010...0$ and biased exponent 0. The result of a calculation with a mix of denormalized and normalized numbers will have fewer significant digits than the result of a calculation with only normalized numbers.

Any single-precision floating-point number represented with $e = 255$, or an unbiased exponent of $+127$, is not a number in the conventional sense. The special codes with $e = 255$ and $f = 0$ represent positive infinity and negative infinity, depending on the sign bit. Infinity is not a number, of course, but this code is used for the result of a calculation that is too large in magnitude to represent.

Other numbers represented with $e = 255$ and $f > 0$ are not numbers either. Such a code is called a **NaN**, which stands for Not a Number. A NaN is the result of an undefined operation, such as adding positive infinity to negative infinity. The subject of infinities and NaNs will be explored in more detail later.

## 17.1 Representation

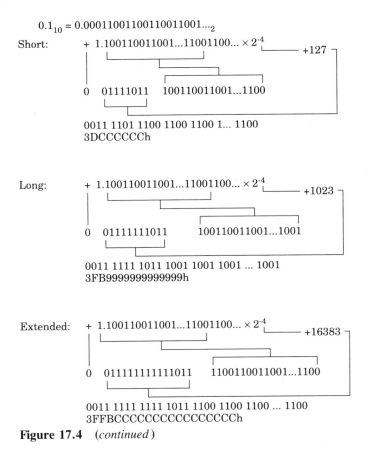

**Figure 17.4** (*continued*)

## EXERCISES 17.1

1. Convert the following base 10 numbers to binary.
    (a) 13.8125
    (b) 17.15625
    (c) 7.24
    (d) 9.3
    (e) 5.0
    (f) 0.515625
    (g) 100.0
    (h) 0.0125
2. Convert the following binary numbers to base 10.
    (a) 1001.00111
    (b) 11100.11011
    (c) 100.1001
    (d) 100.000001
    (e) 100.000000001
    (f) 10.111111111
    (g) 0.00011
    (h) 100.01000001

3. Show how the numbers in Exercise 1 would be stored using the short floating-point format of Figure 17.1.
4. Interpret each of the following numbers according to the floating-point format of Figure 17.1.
   (a) 01000100100100000000000000000000
   (b) 11000100100100000000000000000000
   (c) 00111101111000000000000000000000
   (d) 01000000000000000000000000000000
   (e) 01000000100000000000000000000000
   (f) 00111111100000000000000000000000
   (g) 00000000000110000000000000000000
   (h) 11111111100000000000000000000000
5. Show how the numbers in Exercise 1 would be stored in the long floating-point format of Figure 17.2.
6. Show how the numbers in Exercise 1 would be stored in the extended floating-point format of Figure 17.3.
7. How many digits are there in the decimal expansion of $2^{-n}$? State your answer in terms of $n$.
8. Explain why the method used to convert fractions from base 10 to base 2 works.
9. Floating-point representation uses a discrete subset of the real numbers. The real numbers include rational numbers and irrational numbers. Are any irrational numbers represented exactly in floating-point representation? Explain.
10. How many different normalized values can be represented in each of the three floating-point formats?

## 17.2 SPECIFICATION

In those cases where floating-point numbers can be written in assembly-language programs (see below), they are written in much the same way as in high-level languages: as a number with a decimal point and an optional exponent. Some assemblers do not require a decimal point if an exponent is provided, and some do. Some assemblers use the exponent (or lack of it) to determine the precision of constants. Floating-point numbers can also be written in hexadecimal for the purposes of working with internal representation.

Assemblers for the 8086 support several formats for floating-point numbers, including at least the three used by the 8087 coprocessor. Other formats that might be supported are usually used with the libraries of high-level languages that provide floating-point operations when a coprocessor is not available. Such formats will not be considered here, however; this discussion will cover only the three 8087 formats.

Assemblers for the 8086 do not allow floating-point numbers as immediate operands. All constants must be defined as initialized variables. The format used for a floating-point constant or variable is determined by the directive used to define it: dd specifies short or single precision, dq specifies long or double precision, and dt specifies ten-byte or extended precision. To declare named floating-point constants, we use one of the directives with the constant in the operand field. The constant should have a decimal point and may have an exponent. The following are all valid declarations of constants:

```
ShortOne   dd    1.0
LongOne    dq    1.0
Pi         dd    0.314159265E1
IntRate    dt    13.25E-4
```

## 17.2 Specification

The first two directives declare two floating-point numbers, both with value 1.0 but with different lengths. The third directive specifies a value for $\pi$, declared as a single-precision number. The value contains nine digits, which exceeds the precision of the short format. Some assemblers would truncate the binary representation of $\pi$ by simply discarding all bits after the twenty-third bit of the fraction, while others would round the fraction properly to 23 bits. The last constant is 0.001325, which the assembler builds in 10-byte extended precision.

To reserve memory for floating-point variables, we use the same directives with a question mark in the operand field. For example, the declarations

```
Mass      dd    ?
CoefFric  dq    ?
Temp      dt    ?
```

reserve memory for a single-precision variable named Mass, a double-precision variable named CoefFric, and an extended-precision variable named Temp. Normally, extended-precision variables are not used except to save intermediate results temporarily when all of the registers in the coprocessor are needed for another computation.

## EXERCISES 17.2

1. Create a module containing only a data segment. In it, write the values from Exercise 1 of Section 17.1 as operands of dd, dq, and dt directives. Assemble it and obtain a listing file. Verify your answers to Exercises 3, 5, and 6 of Section 17.1.

2. In what order are the bytes of a floating-point number written on the listing file generated by your assembler? Consider all three formats.

3. In what order are the bytes of a floating-point number stored in memory? Consider all three formats. Explain how you have determined your answer.

4. Write the directives necessary to define each of the following floating-point constants, with the precision specified.
   (a) 42.0 in short precision
   (b) 42.0 in long precision
   (c) 42.0 in extended precision
   (d) −1.2E+5 in long precision
   (e) +2.1E−3 in short precision
   (f) −4.7E−11 in extended precision

5. What is the difference between "precision" and "accuracy" when discussing numerical computing?

6. Define a record data structure in a high-level language that could be used for the three components of a floating-point number written in base 10. Your structure should provide a range and precision between that of short and long reals. (Hint: Use an array of digits to represent the fraction.)

7. For the data structure defined in Exercise 6, write a procedure (in the high-level language) to read a floating-point number and store it into the record. Make reasonable simplifying assumptions, but document them clearly.

8. For the data structure defined in Exercise 6, write a procedure (in the high-level language) to print in scientific format a floating-point number.

## 17.3 OPERATIONS

The operations on floating-point numbers include copying them from one location in memory to another; converting between different floating-point formats and between floating-point and integer formats; arithmetic; and comparing two numbers. Input and output operations, which involve a little of everything, will be covered only in the exercises.

### Moving and Rounding

The simplest operation is copying a floating-point number from one memory location to another. If the source and destination operands are the same length, the number can be copied, as is, using a few mov instructions or a repeated string move.

When the source and destination fields are different lengths, the floating-point number must be converted from one format to another. Converting a single-precision number to double-precision format involves copying the sign bit, copying the fraction bits, and extending them with extra zeros to fill the larger field. Since the bias differs between formats, the difference $1023 - 127 = 896$ must be added to the exponent during the conversion.

Converting a double-precision number to single-precision format is not as simple. If there are more significant bits in the double-precision value than there are bits in the single-precision fraction field, the fraction should be rounded. There are four ways to round; these will be discussed shortly. The difference in bias, 896, must also be subtracted from the exponent of the double-precision number. If the result is in the range of 1 to 254, it can be copied to the exponent field of the single-precision number. But if the result is less than 1, there is underflow; if the result is greater than 254, there is overflow. Underflow and overflow will be discussed in detail after the other operations.

There are four basic rounding strategies. Assume that some value is computed with infinite precision, but must be rounded to a finite number that can be represented. By default, the 8087 rounds to the nearest representable number. If the source is exactly between two consecutive representable numbers, the one in which the least significant bit is 0 is chosen. While this sounds fairly complicated, it is really quite simple.

Consider rounding a fraction where the first bit that does not fit in the fraction field of the destination is 0. This number is rounded simply by discarding all fraction bits that do not fit. For example, let's round the floating-point number with fraction

$$00001111000011110000111\ 01010\ldots$$

to fit in a single-precision fraction field (there is a space between the twenty-third and twenty-fourth bits). Since the twenty-fourth bit is 0, the bits beyond the twenty-third will be discarded by the rounding operation.

When the first bit that is discarded is a 1, it is necessary to inspect the other bits that are not discarded: If any of them are ones, we add one to the least significant bit that is retained. For example, if the fraction before rounding is

$$00001111000011110000111\ 100010\ldots$$

we discard all bits beyond the twenty-third, to which we add 1, making the fraction

$$00001111000011110001000$$

## 17.3 Operations

When only the first bit to be discarded is 1, we add 1 to the least significant retained bit only if it also is 1. Consider rounding

$$00001111000011110000111\ 100000\ldots$$

where all bits following those shown are zeros. In this case, the least significant retained bit is 1. After rounding, the fraction becomes

$$00001111000011110001000$$

If the fraction before rounding is

$$00001111000011110000110\ 10000\ldots$$

where all bits following those shown are again zeros, the least significant bit retained is 0. After rounding, the fraction is just

$$00001111000011110000110$$

These examples all round to the number closest in value that can be represented. This is called **round to nearest**. Another common rounding technique is to **round toward zero**. This is the same as truncating or chopping the fraction of the source number to the length of the destination field. Chopping is the simplest form of rounding to implement in hardware.

The other two strategies are to **round toward positive infinity** and to **round toward negative infinity**. In the former, the result is the representable number closest to but not less than the source value. In the latter, the result is the representable number closest to but not greater than the source number.

## Conversions

We need to be able to convert floating-point numbers from one precision to another, and between floating-point and other representations. Conversions between floating-point formats with different precision are usually performed as part of copying a value from one location or register to another. These conversions have already been discussed.

The integer and floating-point data types cannot be freely mixed in an operation. We have seen instructions for adding two integers. We will see instructions for adding two floating-point numbers. But to add an integer and a floating-point number together, one of them must be converted to the other format and the addition instruction for that type used. Usually, the integer is converted to floating-point.

Conversions between floating-point and integer formats are fraught with problems. Consider first the conversion from floating-point to integer. The potential problems include a magnitude too large to represent as an integer (**overflow**), a magnitude too small to represent as an integer (**underflow**), and a loss of the fractional part of the floating-point value (**inexact result**). If no problems occur, conversion of a floating-point value to integer format proceeds by copying the significand, including the leading 1-bit, into a work area. The binary point is shifted and the exponent adjusted, so that the exponent becomes zero. For example, if the significand of a positive number is

$$1.1110000000000000000000$$

and the exponent is 7, we shift the binary point seven places to the right, leaving

$$11110000.0000000000000000$$

The bits to the right of the binary point are discarded, and the value to the left of the binary point is rounded accordingly. Leading 0-bits are supplied to make the result the length of an integer. If the floating-point number is negative, the integer is complemented. Overflow occurs if, after shifting the binary point to make the exponent 0, the number in the work area exceeds the range of values that can be represented by the integer type. Underflow occurs if, after shifting, all of the 1-bits in the work area are still to the right of the binary point. Usually, this merely generates a 0 result. An inexact result occurs if there are 1-bits on both sides of the binary point after shifting. The whole-number part of the floating-point number is copied to the integer, but the nonzero fraction part is lost. Note that even when rounding occurs during the conversion from floating-point to integer format, an inexact result is generated.

Conversion from integer to floating-point format also has a potential problem. It cannot generate overflow, because the range of floating-point numbers is far greater than the range of integers. It cannot generate underflow, because integers cannot represent any numbers between 0 and 1. But there is the possibility of an inexact result if the integer representation has more significant digits than the floating-point representation. That occurs, for example, when the 32-bit integer

$$00001111000011110000111100001111$$

becomes

$$1.111000011110000111000 \times 2^{27}$$

in floating-point representation. In base 10, this integer is 252,645,135; the floating-point number is $2.5264512 \times 10^8$. Even though this loss is not likely to ruin an otherwise good calculation, the result is inexact.

## Arithmetic

Arithmetic with floating-point numbers is more complicated than arithmetic with integers. In addition to the errors arising from overflow and division by zero, we have to be concerned with underflow, inexact results, and invalid operations. These will be considered in detail after the operations.

## Addition

To add two floating-point numbers, it may first be necessary to adjust one of their exponents. For example, working in base 10, consider adding $2.34 \times 10^3$ and $8.8 \times 10^2$. If we write them without exponents, we get 2340 and 880. Clearly, the sum should be 3220, or $3.22 \times 10^3$. Note that the exponent of the sum is the same as the exponent of the larger operand. This suggests that we should adjust the number with the smaller exponent. The example becomes

$$\begin{array}{r} 2.34 \times 10^3 \\ +0.88 \times 10^3 \\ \hline 3.22 \times 10^3 \end{array}$$

## 17.3 Operations

Sometimes the sum must be normalized by adjusting the exponent and shifting the decimal point. For example,

$$\begin{array}{r} 6.22 \times 10^8 \\ +\ 3.93 \times 10^8 \\ \hline 10.15 \times 10^8 \end{array}$$

To normalize this sum, the decimal point is shifted and the exponent is adjusted, making it $1.015 \times 10^9$.

Addition can signal overflow, underflow, and inexact results; these are discussed in detail following the remaining arithmetic operations.

## Subtraction

Like addition, subtraction may also require shifting the significand and adjusting the exponent of the number with the smaller exponent. For example, using the same numbers as in the first addition example, $2.34 \times 10^3 - 8.8 \times 10^2$ would be computed as

$$\begin{array}{r} 2.34 \times 10^3 \\ -0.88 \times 10^3 \\ \hline 1.46 \times 10^3 \end{array}$$

The difference following a subtraction may need to be normalized by shifting the decimal point to the right and decrementing the exponent. Consider the difference

$$\begin{array}{r} 6.44 \times 10^4 \\ -6.23 \times 10^4 \\ \hline 0.21 \times 10^4 \end{array}$$

There is a need to normalize this significand and adjust the exponent. The difference is $2.1 \times 10^3$.

Subtraction can signal overflow, underflow, and inexact results. There is a potential problem with subtraction that the hardware cannot signal. In the example above, the difference has one less significant digit than do the operands. If we start with only three or four significant digits—which is what we can expect with most common measurements—and lose one or two of them in subtraction like this, the final result of the calculation may not be precise enough to be useful. There are often ways to restate a formula or write an expression to avoid the loss of the most significant digits, but detecting the problem is not always easy.

## Multiplication

Unlike addition and subtraction, multiplication does not require that both of its factors have the same exponent. There is nothing to be gained by adjusting the exponent of a factor prior to multiplication; doing so could actually cause a loss of significance.

Consider multiplying $2.4 \times 10^{-3} \times 6.3 \times 10^2$. In algebra, we learned that this expression can be rewritten as

$$(2.4 \times 6.3) \times (10^{-3} \times 10^2)$$

We multiply the first two factors together:
$$2.4 \times 6.3 = 15.12$$
We add the exponents of the last two factors:
$$10^{-3} \times 10^2 = 10^{(-3+2)} = 10^{-1}$$
Now we put these together and normalize:
$$2.4 \times 10^{-3} \times 6.3 \times 10^2 = 15.12 \times 10^{-1}$$
$$= 1.512 \times 10^0$$

Thus we find the product of two floating-point factors as the product of their significands with an exponent that is the sum of the factor's exponents, adjusted for normalization.

The computer does this calculation essentially the same way in binary. When it adds the exponents, it must adjust for the bias—the sum should not include the bias twice. Multiplication can signal overflow, underflow, and inexact results.

## Division

Division of a floating-point number by another gives just a floating-point quotient. Consider the calculation $1.86 \times 10^{13} \div 7.44 \times 10^5$. This can be written as

$$\frac{1.86 \times 10^{13}}{7.44 \times 10^5} = \frac{1.86}{7.44} \times 10^{13-5}$$

We then divide the significand of the dividend by the significand of the divisor, which gives 0.25. We then subtract the exponent of the divisor from the exponent of the dividend, which gives $10^8$. Putting the significand of the quotient together with its exponent and normalizing gives

$$1.86 \times 10^{13} \div 7.44 \times 10^5 = 0.25 \times 10^8$$
$$= 2.5 \times 10^7$$

The computer also does this in binary, and it adds the bias to the difference of the exponents. Division can signal overflow, underflow, inexact results, and attempts to divide by 0.

## Remainder

Division of floating-point numbers gives a floating-point quotient. In some applications we would like to compute a quantity, called the remainder, which represents the difference between the dividend and the product of the quotient rounded to the nearest integer and the divisor. That is, the value of ($s$ REM $t$), where $s$ and $t$ are floating-point numbers and REM is the remainder operator, is given by the expression

$$s \text{ REM } t = s - t \times \text{NINT}(s/t)$$

Here, NINT returns the integer closest to its argument. In the event that the quotient $\frac{s}{t}$ is exactly midway between two integers, NINT returns the even integer. NINT is implemented as the normal conversion to integer format with rounding.

Let's compute a few remainders to see how this expression works. The first example is 3.2 REM 1.5. We start by computing 3.2/1.5, which is 2.1333.... The integer nearest

## 17.3 Operations

this quotient is 2, so NINT (3.2/1.5) is 2. The value of the expression is $3.2 - 1.5 \times 2$, or $3.2 - 3.0$, which is just 0.2. So we find that (3.2 REM 1.5) = 0.2.

Here are two more examples:

$$\begin{align} 20.0 \text{ REM } 4.5 &= 20.0 - 4.5 \times \text{NINT } (20.0/4.5) \\ &= 20.0 - 4.5 \times \text{NINT } (4.44\ldots) \\ &= 20.0 - 4.5 \times 4 \\ &= 20.0 - 18.0 \\ &= 2.0 \end{align}$$

and

$$\begin{align} 21.0 \text{ REM } 4.5 &= 21.0 - 4.5 \times \text{NINT } (21.0/4.5) \\ &= 21.0 - 4.5 \times \text{NINT } (4.66\ldots) \\ &= 21.0 - 4.5 \times 5 \\ &= 21.0 - 22.5 \\ &= -1.5 \end{align}$$

The result of the remainder operation has a magnitude less than or equal to one-half of the divisor. Its sign is not necessarily the same as the sign of either the divisor or dividend. However, in the event that the magnitude of the remainder is 0, its sign is taken as the same as the sign of the dividend. The remainder operation can signal an attempt to divide by 0. Overflow, underflow, and inexact results cannot occur.

## Comparing Floating-Point Numbers

When we compare two floating-point numbers, there are four possible relations. Three of these are the familiar relations: less than, equal to, and greater than. The fourth relation is unordered, sometimes called incomparable. It is the result of a comparison involving one or more NaNs. A NaN is a code that is used for the result of invalid operations, and for results of operations on undefined values. Since NaNs are not numbers, they cannot be ordered among the numbers.

Comparison of two floating-point numbers can be implemented by subtracting one from the other and checking the result using floating-point arithmetic. Alternatively, the fields can be checked separately. The signs are compared, and if they are different, the relation is determined. If the signs are the same, the biased exponents are compared; if they differ, the number with the larger exponent is larger if the signs are positive, smaller if the signs are negative. If the signs and exponents are the same, the fractions are compared; the relation between the numbers is determined from the fractions in the same way as with the exponents. If the exponent is stored with a bias and is positioned before the fraction, as in the 8087 formats, the exponent and fraction fields need not be partitioned, since any difference in the exponents will be more significant in this arrangement than a difference in the fractions.

If either of the values being compared is a NaN, the relation is *unordered*. Note that, although it is possible to combine relations like *less than* and *equal to* to make a *less than or equal to* predicate, *unordered* relations cannot be combined with other relations unless they are coded separately from the sign and zero flags. Although a predicate like *less than or unordered* might not appear terribly useful, unordered should be considered when complementing a relation: The complement of *less than or equal to* is *greater than or unordered*, for example.

## Exceptions

A number of errors can occur during floating-point operations, including

    overflow
    underflow
    inexact result
    division by zero
    denormalized operand
    invalid operation

When any of these errors occur, the operation signals an exception, either setting a bit in the status register, generating an interrupt so another routine can take corrective action, or both. We can usually check the status bits, although it is not as simple as checking for overflow in integer operations.

### Overflow

Each operation generates an intermediate result, which is rounded to the precision of the destination. If the intermediate value is too large to fit in the destination—that is, if its exponent is too large—overflow is signaled. Overflow can occur during an arithmetic operation only if the result exceeds the range of the extended-precision format, such as addition of the largest extended number to itself. However, it can also occur when converting an extended value to another format. Overflow is usually not a problem when all application data consist of short or long reals and computations are performed in extended precision.

In the absence of an interrupt handler to take corrective action, the value assigned to the destination field is infinity with the same sign as the true result.

### Underflow

When the magnitude of the result of a floating-point operation is too small to represent in the destination format, but the result is not 0, underflow is signaled. The value assigned to the destination field when underflow occurs might be 0 or the denormalized representation of the result. The 8087 creates a denormalized number when it can, but resorts to 0 if the result is too small even for a denormalized number.

### Inexact result

Each operation generates an exact result, but if the exact result cannot be represented in extended precision, an inexact result exception occurs. Usually this exception is masked, so all values are rounded to numbers that can be represented in extended precision.

## Division by zero

Division by zero is undefined. If the processor detects a zero divisor and a nonzero dividend, it signals a division by zero exception. Like overflow, this exception usually causes an interrupt. If this exception is masked, a quotient of infinity with the correct sign is generated.

## Denormalized operand

Underflow generates a result that is a denormalized number if the underflow exception is masked. If we then try to use that denormalized number as an operand of another operation, the denormalized operand exception is raised. If this exception is also masked, the result of the operation can be zero (a valid result); it can be another denormalized number if small enough; it can be a normal result if the reduced precision of the denormalized operand does not affect the result; it can be an unnormal number (a number that is too big to be denormalized but that has reduced precision). In some circumstances, an operation on denormalized numbers will signal an invalid operation exception.

## Invalid operation

There are several errors that signal an invalid operation exception, the most serious exception. Usually this exception is not masked, but when it is, the result of the operation is a NaN.

The result of most operations involving a NaN is also a NaN. No NaN as an operand can ever generate a numeric result—the error in the program that produced the first NaN will propagate as a NaN. The comparison of a NaN with another value always yields an unordered (incomparable) result.

Invalid operation exceptions are signaled by operating on a NaN, adding or subtracting two infinities, multiplying or dividing with infinity as one operand and 0 as the other, and dividing infinity by itself. These operations are clearly invalid.

## EXERCISES 17.3

1. Perform the following operations, using base 10 arithmetic, maintaining exactly four significant digits, and rounding to nearest at each step.
    - (a) $1.234 \times 10^4 + 5.670 \times 10^2$
    - (b) $5.670 \times 10^4 + 1.234 \times 10^2$
    - (c) $1.234 \times 10^4 + 5.670 \times 10^{-2}$
    - (d) $1.234 \times 10^4 - 5.670 \times 10^2$
    - (e) $5.670 \times 10^4 - 1.234 \times 10^2$
    - (f) $1.234 \times 10^4 - 5.670 \times 10^{-2}$
    - (g) $2.468 \times 10^3 * 6.420 \times 10^{-1}$
    - (h) $1.357 \times 10^7 * 7.410 \times 10^2$
    - (i) $1.470 \times 10^4 / 4.555 \times 10^3$
    - (j) $9.876 \times 10^3 / 2.365 \times 10^8$

2. Is addition of floating-point numbers commutative? Associative? Explain.

3. Is multiplication of floating-point numbers commutative? Associative? Explain.
4. Does the distributive law $[a(b + c) = ab + ac]$ hold for floating-point numbers? Explain.
▶5. Discuss some of the challenges of reading and writing floating-point numbers. Design an algorithm for reading, and implement it in a high-level language.
▶6. For floating-point numbers stored in the record format you designed in Exercise 6 of Section 17.2, write separate functions for implementing the following operations:
   (*a*) addition of two floating-point numbers
   (*b*) subtraction of one floating-point number from another
   (*c*) multiplication of a floating-point number by another
   (*d*) division of a floating-point number by another.

## 17.4 THE 8087 COPROCESSOR

The 8086 cannot directly operate on floating-point data. The optional 8087 (or 80287 or 80387) numeric coprocessor is designed to supplement the 8086 (or 80286 or 80386) by providing floating-point capabilities. (The 80486 includes the capabilities of the 80387, as does the 80487SX; the 80486SX does not.)

Many compilers include a library of routines to emulate the 8087 if the coprocessor is not available. If few floating-point computations are needed, or if speed is not critical, such emulators may be adequate. Writing an emulator library is beyond the scope of this discussion. This section examines the registers and operation of the 8087 coprocessor.

### Data Registers

The 8087 coprocessor has 13 registers. Eight of these are 10-byte numeric registers used for manipulating data in the extended-precision format. These registers are named ST(0), ST(1), and so on through ST(7). ST(0) is also referred to as ST.

The data registers can be accessed as a stack, with ST as the top, ST(1) just below it, and so on with ST(7) at the bottom. They can also be accessed individually by name, although instructions that take two register operands require that one of them be ST. Both modes of accessing the numeric registers are always in effect. This makes the register names relative to the current top of the stack. For example, if we load a number into ST(3) and then pop the stack, the number moves into ST(2). The number in parentheses following ST is the displacement (in units of 10-byte registers) from the top of the stack.

Although it is not what really happens, it may be useful to pretend that pushing or popping the stack causes all of the data in the other registers to move. We will see how the stack is implemented when we examine the 8087 status register.

### Control, Status, and Tag Registers

In addition to the eight numeric registers, there are also three 16-bit registers. These are the tag, control, and status registers. Figure 17.5 shows the layout of the fields in these three registers. The tag register contains a two-bit tag for each of the eight numeric registers.

## 17.4 The 8087 Coprocessor

| 15 | 14 | 13 | 12 | 11 | 10 | 9 | 8 | 7 | 6 | 5 | 4 | 3 | 2 | 1 | 0 |
|----|----|----|----|----|----|---|---|---|---|---|---|---|---|---|---|
| tag 7 | | tag 6 | | tag 5 | | tag 4 | | tag 3 | | tag 2 | | tag 1 | | tag 0 | |

8087 tag register

| | 12 | 11 | 10 | 9 | 8 | | 5 | 4 | 3 | 2 | 1 | 0 |
|---|----|----|----|---|---|---|---|---|---|---|---|---|
| | IC | RC | | PC | | | PM | UM | OM | ZM | DM | IM |

8087 control register

| 15 | 14 | 13 | | 11 | 10 | 9 | 8 | 7 | | 5 | 4 | 3 | 2 | 1 | 0 |
|----|----|----|---|----|----|---|---|---|---|---|---|---|---|---|---|
| B | $C_3$ | | ST | | $C_2$ | $C_1$ | $C_0$ | ES | | PE | UE | OE | ZE | DE | IE |

8087 status register

**Figure 17.5  8087 Tag, Control, and Status Registers**

The tag records, for the 8087's benefit, the state of each register. The meaning of the tag field is as follows:

| tag | meaning |
|-----|---------|
| 00  | valid (finite nonzero number) |
| 01  | zero |
| 10  | invalid (infinity or NaN) |
| 11  | empty |

The tag is inspected before each push or pop to check for stack overflow and stack empty conditions. The tag is also used internally in arithmetic operations to check for invalid operations and the like.

The control register has six exception mask bits in positions 0 through 5. If a mask bit is cleared and the corresponding exception occurs, the program is suspended and an interrupt is generated for the 8086. The interrupt handler may take corrective action or display an error message and terminate the program. If a mask bit is set and the corresponding exception occurs, the exception value is produced as previously described. For example, if bit 5, the Precision Mask, is set and a result cannot be exactly represented in extended-precision format, the result is rounded to a value that can be represented. This is the normal mode for the precision mask. On the other hand, if bit 2, the Zero-divide Mask, is cleared and a division instruction encounters a zero divisor, the division is suspended and the 8086 is interrupted.

The control register also has three control fields. These control rounding and the type of infinity used. Bits 8 and 9 are the Precision Control field, interpreted as

| PC | desired rounded length |
|----|------------------------|
| 00 | single-precision |
| 01 | (not used) |
| 10 | double-precision |
| 11 | extended-precision |

The default is extended-precision. Bits 10 and 11 are the Rounding Control field, interpreted as

| RC | direction to round |
|----|---------------------|
| 00 | to nearest |
| 01 | toward negative infinity |
| 10 | toward positive infinity |
| 11 | toward zero |

The default is to round toward nearest. Bit 12 is the Infinity Control field. When this bit is cleared, the default, projective mode is used; when set, affine mode is used. The significance of these infinity modes is beyond the scope of this text; it is sufficient to note that projective mode is more conservative.

The status register has six exception flags that correspond to the six exception masks in the control register. These flags are set when a numeric exception occurs, whether or not that exception is masked. Unlike the 8086 flags, the 8087 flags remain set until explicitly cleared. Normally, a program can clear the 8087 flags, do its calculations, and check whether anything went wrong during the calculation. This is easier than writing exception handlers that are invoked when exceptions occur.

Bit 7 of the 8087 status register is the Error Summary flag. It indicates whether the most recently executed 8087 instruction resulted in an unmasked exception. Bits 8, 9, 10, and 14 are the condition code bits. These record the result of comparisons and tests, much like some of the flags in the 8086 flags register. The meaning of each bit, and the reason for this peculiar layout, will be discussed when we examine the compare instructions in the next section.

Bits 11 through 13 of the status register are the Stack Top field. It keeps track of which numeric register is the current top of stack. To see how this works, consider the eight numeric registers as numbered 0 through 7, these numbers fixed. The three-bit ST field is then the number of one of these registers. A reference to ST(0) is to the numeric register specified by the ST field. A reference to ST(3) is to the numeric register specified by ST+3 mod 8. Note that the programmer always specifies a numeric register by its displacement from the current top of stack, not by its physical register number.

Bit 15, the Busy bit, is set when the 8087 is executing an instruction or signaling an interrupt and is cleared when the 8087 is idle. This is used by the 8086 to coordinate the two processors.

## Exception Pointers

The 8087 also has two 32-bit registers that point to the last instruction executed by the coprocessor, and to the operand specified in that instruction. This information is useful when writing exception handlers—routines that the 8086 interrupt mechanism will invoke when the corresponding 8087 exception occurs. The information in these pointers is needed because, while the instruction that produces the exception is executing, the 8086 can also execute instructions, changing the 8086's instruction pointer, and possibly changing registers that were used in fetching the operand for the 8087 instruction. Without this information, there are few clues about what caused the exception. Writing this type of interrupt routine is beyond the scope of this discussion.

### Coordinating 8086 with 8087

Programs contain a mix of 8086 instructions and 8087 instructions. All input, output, procedure call, and control structure operations use 8086 instructions. Unless an emulation library is used, all floating-point operations use 8087 instructions.

The 8087 is called a coprocessor because it works in conjunction with the 8086. Since they are separate processors, they should be able to execute instructions concurrently. However, there are potential problems that require some coordination and cooperation.

Consider a program that contains an 8087 instruction that modifies an integer in memory, followed by an 8086 instruction that uses that integer in some manner. If the 8087 instruction does not store the new value for the integer before the 8086 instruction accesses it, the 8086 instruction will use the old value, not the one produced by the 8087. This problem is avoided by forcing the 8086 to wait for the 8087 to finish its instruction before executing the next 8086 instruction. This is the purpose of the Busy bit in the 8087 status register: There is an 8086 instruction that waits for the Busy bit to clear before proceeding to the next instruction.

Whenever the 8086 processor encounters an 8087 instruction, it should check the Busy bit of the 8087 status register before attempting to pass the instruction on to the 8087. Unfortunately, the 8086 does not do this automatically, so most assemblers insert an explicit instruction to force the 8086 to wait for the Busy bit to clear before every 8087 instruction. The 80286 and 80386 do check the Busy bit automatically.

### EXERCISES 17.4

1. Compare the implementation of the register stack in the 8087 with a stack implemented in a circular queue; if possible, refer to an implementation of a queue you might have used in a data structures course.
2. What conventions might you adopt for using the eight data registers in the 8087? Consider such things as use by subprograms and functions that return floating-point values.
3. Consider a calculation involving more floating-point numbers than there are registers. What policies might you use to decide how to allocate the registers?
4. There are several manufacturers that make numeric coprocessors that are compatible with the 8087. Would it benefit a manufacturer to provide more than eight data registers? Explain your answer carefully.
5. At least one manufacturer makes a numeric coprocessor that is not compatible with the 8087. What problems does this introduce for programmers?

## 17.5 INSTRUCTIONS

The 8087 coprocessor instructions for working with floating-point numbers can be grouped into five classes:

- move
- arithmetic
- compare
- control
- transcendental

Most of the move, arithmetic, and compare instructions, as well as a few of the control instructions, are presented; the 8087 transcendentals are discussed only briefly. All instructions for the coprocessor have mnemonics that start with the letter f.

Some instructions treat the floating-point registers as a stack; others treat them as a set of named registers; some allow both methods. We have already seen how pushing and popping affect the names of the registers; this behavior of the coprocessor must be considered when selecting each instruction.

All values in the numeric registers are in extended precision. Instructions that load values from memory into the registers, or that store register values into memory, convert between the extended format and the format of the operand in memory. Some instructions appear to operate on integer or packed BCD operands, but such operands are converted to extended format as part of the operation.

The coprocessor instructions do not affect the 8086 flags register. However, this discussion will examine in detail how the various compare instructions affect the 8087 status register.

## Move Instructions

The move instructions copy values between memory and a numeric register, or between two numeric registers. Those that include a memory operand can convert between the extended format and single- or double-precision real; 16-, 32-, or 64-bit integer; and 10-byte packed BCD formats. There are also instructions for pushing selected constants into the top numeric register.

The load instructions convert an operand in memory to extended precision (if it is not already an extended real), and push it onto the top of the numeric register stack.

**Floating LoaD**

    syntax:    fld *source*

    action:    convert *source* to extended real;
                 push onto numeric stack

    operands:   *freg*    *mem* {short, long, extended real}

**Floating Integer LoaD**

    syntax:    fild *source*

    action:    convert *source* to extended real;
                 push onto numeric stack

    operand:   *mem* {16-, 32-, 64-bit integer}

**Floating packed Bcd LoaD**

    syntax:    fbld *source*

    action:    convert *source* to extended real;
                 push onto numeric stack

    operand:   *mem* {10-byte packed BCD}

## 17.5 Instructions

The store instructions copy the value in the top of the numeric register stack into memory, converting it from extended precision to the format of the memory operand if necessary. The numeric register stack may be unchanged, or the value on the top may be popped.

### Floating STore
- syntax:     fst *destination*
- action:     *destination* := ST, converted
- operand:     *freg*     *mem* {short, long real}

### Floating STore and Pop
- syntax:     fstp *destination*
- action:     (1) *destination* := ST, converted as needed; (2) pop numeric stack
- operand:     *freg*     *mem* {short, long, extended real}

### Floating Integer STore
- syntax:     fist *destination*
- action:     *destination* := ST, converted
- operand:     *mem* {16-, 32-bit integer}

### Floating Integer STore and Pop
- syntax:     fistp *destination*
- action:     (1) *destination* := ST, converted; (2) pop numeric stack
- operand:     *mem* {16-, 32-, 64-bit integer}

### Floating packed Bcd STore and Pop
- syntax:     fbstp *destination*
- action:     (1) *destination* := ST, converted; (2) pop numeric stack
- operand:     *mem* {10-byte packed BCD}

The exchange instruction swaps the values of the top numeric register with another numeric register. If no operand is specified, it swaps the top two registers.

### Floating eXCHange
- syntax:     fxch
- action:     ST := ST(1) & ST(1) := ST
- syntax:     fxch *destination*
- action:     ST := *destination* & *destination* := ST
- operand:     *freg*

There are instructions that push selected constants onto the top of the numeric register stack. Some of the constants are useful when working with transcendental functions; these are not included here but are mentioned later.

**Floating LoaD 1**
    syntax:    `fld1`
    action:    push 1.0 onto numeric stack

**Floating LoaD Zero**
    syntax:    `fldz`
    action:    push 0.0 onto numeric stack

To clear a floating-point register, push 0 onto the top of the stack, and store-and-pop it into the desired register. For example, to clear ST(3) to 0 without changing any other register, assuming that the register stack is not full, we would use

```
fldz
fstp    ST(4)
```

Note that the first instruction renames ST(3) to ST(4). The operand of the second instruction is ST(4). Following the pop, this again becomes ST(3). To clear a real variable in any length to 0, the same pair of instructions can be used with the memory operand on the `fstp`. We could also just move two, four, or five words of zeros using the 8086 `stosw` instruction with a repeat prefix.

## Arithmetic Instructions

There are many floating-point arithmetic instructions. The addition, subtraction, multiplication, and division instructions can treat the numeric registers as a stack as well as access individual registers directly; operands can be specified in a numeric register, a memory location, or implied on the stack; memory operands can be integers as well as reals; and the subtraction and division operations have normal as well as reversed forms.

## Addition

Floating-point addition instructions that use the numeric register stack for both source and destination operands allow both operands to be implied, as in a classic stack-based machine, or both specified explicitly. When both operands are specified, one of them must be the top register, ST.

**Floating ADD**
    syntax:    `fadd`
    action:    (1) ST(1) := ST(1) + ST;
                (2) pop ST

## 17.5 Instructions

**Floating ADD**

| | |
|---|---|
| syntax: | `fadd` *destination, source* |
| action: | *destination* := *destination* + *source* |
| operands: | ST, *freg*    *freg*, ST |

**Floating ADD and Pop**

| | |
|---|---|
| syntax: | `faddp` *destination*, ST |
| action: | (1) *destination* := *destination* + ST; <br> (2) pop ST |
| operand: | *freg*, ST |

The floating addition instructions can also add a real number or integer stored in memory to the top of the stack:

**Floating ADD**

| | |
|---|---|
| syntax: | `fadd` *source* |
| action: | ST := ST + *source* |
| operand: | *mem* {short, long real} |

**Floating Integer ADD**

| | |
|---|---|
| syntax: | `fiadd` *source* |
| action: | ST := ST + *source* |
| operand: | *mem* {16-, 32-bit integer} |

## Subtraction

The subtraction instructions have the same forms as the addition instructions.

**Floating SUBtract**

| | |
|---|---|
| syntax: | `fsub` |
| action: | (1) ST(1) := ST(1) − ST; <br> (2) pop ST |

**Floating SUBtract**

| | |
|---|---|
| syntax: | `fsub` *destination, source* |
| action: | *destination* := *destination* − *source* |
| operands: | ST, *freg*    *freg*, ST |

**Floating SUBtract and Pop**

| | |
|---|---|
| syntax: | `fsubp` *destination*, ST |
| action: | (1) *destination* := *destination* − ST; <br> (2) pop ST |
| operand: | *freg*, ST |

**644**  Chapter 17  Floating-Point Data

The floating subtraction instructions can also subtract a real number or integer stored in memory from the top of the stack:

**Floating SUBtract**
- syntax: `fsub` *source*
- action: $ST := ST - source$
- operand: *mem* {short, long real}

**Floating Integer SUBtract**
- syntax: `fisub` *source*
- action: $ST := ST - source$
- operand: *mem* {16-, 32-bit integer}

Since subtraction is not commutative, the 8087 provides reversed forms of the subtraction instructions. Where the above forms subtract the source operand from the destination operand, the reversed forms subtract the destination from the source.

**Floating SUBtract Reversed**
- syntax: `fsubr`
- action: (1) $ST(1) := ST - ST(1)$;
  (2) pop ST

**Floating SUBtract Reversed**
- syntax: `fsubr` *destination, source*
- action: $destination := source - destination$
- operands: ST, *freg*    *freg*, ST

**Floating SUBtract Reversed and Pop**
- syntax: `fsubrp` *destination*, ST
- action: (1) $destination := ST - destination$;
  (2) pop ST
- operand: *freg*, ST

There are also reversed floating subtraction instructions that subtract a real number or integer stored in memory from the top of the stack.

**Floating SUBtract Reversed**
- syntax: `fsubr` *source*
- action: $ST := source - ST$
- operand: *mem* {short, long real}

## 17.5 Instructions

**Floating Integer SUBtract Reversed**

    syntax:      `fisubr` *source*
    action:       ST := *source* − ST
    operand:    *mem* {16-, 32-bit integer}

## Multiplication

The multiplication instructions also parallel the addition instructions:

**Floating MULtiply**

    syntax:      `fmul`
    action:       (1) ST(1) := ST(1) × ST;
                   (2) pop ST

**Floating MULtiply**

    syntax:      `fmul` *destination, source*
    action:       *destination* := *destination* × *source*
    operands:   ST, *freg*    *freg*, ST

**Floating MULtiply and Pop**

    syntax:      `fmulp` *destination, ST*
    action:       (1) *destination* := *destination* × ST;
                   (2) pop ST
    operand:    *freg*, ST

The floating multiply instructions can also multiply the top of the stack by a real number or integer stored in memory:

**Floating MULtiply**

    syntax:      `fmul` *source*
    action:       ST := ST × *source*
    operand:    *mem* {short, long real}

**Floating Integer MULtiply**

    syntax:      `fimul` *source*
    action:       ST := ST × *source*
    operand:    *mem* {16-, 32-bit integer}

## Division

The division instructions compute only a quotient. They have the same forms as the subtraction instructions.

**Floating DIVide**

   syntax:      `fdiv`
   action:      (1) ST(1) := ST(1) / ST;
                    (2) pop ST

**Floating DIVide**

   syntax:      `fdiv` *destination, source*
   action:      *destination* := *destination* / *source*
   operands:  ST, *freg*    *freg*, ST

**Floating DIVide and Pop**

   syntax:      `fdivp` *destination*, ST
   action:      (1) *destination* := *destination* / ST;
                    (2) pop ST
   operand:   *freg*, ST

The floating division instructions can also divide the top of the numeric stack by a real number or integer stored in memory.

**Floating DIVide**

   syntax:      `fdiv` *source*
   action:      ST := ST / source
   operand:   *mem* {short, long real}

**Floating Integer DIVide**

   syntax:      `fidiv` *source*
   action:      ST := ST / source
   operand:   *mem* {16-, 32-bit integer}

Since division is not commutative, the 8087 provides reversed forms of the division instructions.

**Floating DIVide Reversed**

   syntax:      `fdivr`
   action:      (1) ST(1) := ST / ST(1);
                    (2) pop ST

**Floating DIVide Reversed**

   syntax:      `fdivr` *destination, source*
   action:      *destination* := *source* / *destination*
   operands:  ST, freg    *freg*, ST

## 17.5 Instructions

**Floating DIVide Reversed and Pop**

    syntax:    `fdivrp` *destination*, ST
    action:    (1) *destination* := ST / *destination*;
               (2) pop ST
    operand:  *freg*, ST

**Floating DIVide Reversed**

    syntax:    `fdivr` *source*
    action:    ST := *source* / ST
    operand:  *mem* {short, long real}

**Floating Integer DIVide Reversed**

    syntax:    `fidivr` *source*
    action:    ST := *source* / ST
    operand:  *mem* {16-, 32-bit integer}

## Remainder

The 8087 includes an instruction that computes the partial remainder from division. It does this computation by repeated subtraction; if after 64 subtractions it has not found the remainder, it stops anyway—this allows interrupts a chance to get the 8087's attention. Since the instruction might terminate before it finds the remainder, the result is called a partial remainder. It is a simple matter to test whether the instruction has completed and to repeat it until it does.

The remainder operation as implemented on the 8087 and 80287 does not meet the standard definition. The calculation of the partial remainder uses the formula

$$\text{remainder} = ST - ST(1) \times \text{quotient}$$

In the 8087 and 80287, the quotient is the value obtained by rounding ST/ST(1) toward 0. According to the standard, the quotient should be rounded to the nearest integer; this is implemented in the 80387 as a separate instruction.

**Floating Partial REMainder**

    syntax:    `fprem`
    action:    if reduction complete
               then   ST := ST − ST(1) × quotient;
                         $C_2$ of status word := 0
               else   ST := partial result;
                         $C_2$ of status word := 1

## Scaling

Scaling multiplies the value in the top numeric register by a power of 2. The power of 2 is taken from the integer in ST(1), which is rounded toward 0 (truncated) if it is not already an integer. This value must be a 16-bit integer or the result will be undefined. Scaling is the floating-point analog of a binary arithmetic shift.

**648** Chapter 17 Floating-Point Data

---
**Floating SCALE**
syntax:    fscale
action:    ST := ST * $2^{trunc(ST(1))}$

---

## Decomposition

In some applications, it is useful to separate a floating-point number into its significand and exponent. This can be done using 8086 instructions on a copy of the number in memory, but we would most likely want these components in registers in the coprocessor. The extract instruction separates the number in ST into its exponent and significand.

---
**Floating eXTRACT exponent and significand**
syntax:    fxtract
action:    (1) separate ST into exponent and significand fields;
           (2) ST := exponent;
           (3) push significand

---

`fxtract` essentially removes the significand of ST and pushes it on top of the exponent. Note that following `fxtract` with `fscale` restores the floating-point number in ST; this combination of instructions, however, leaves the exponent in ST(1).

## Negation

The negation instruction changes the sign of the value in the top numeric register:

---
**Floating CHange Sign**
syntax:    fchs
action:    ST := -ST

---

## Absolute Value

The absolute value instruction makes the value in the top numeric register positive:

---
**Floating ABSolute value**
syntax:    fabs
action:    ST := |ST|

---

## Round to Integer

The round to integer instruction rounds the value in the top numeric register to an integer. The Rounding Control field of the 8087 control register specifies the rounding mode.

## 17.5 Instructions

---
**Floating RouND to INTeger**
syntax: `frndint`
action: ST := *round*(ST)

---

## Square Root

The square root instruction computes the square root of the value in the top numeric register. The value in ST must be positive or 0; the instruction returns −0 as the square root of −0.

---
**Floating SQuare RooT**
syntax: `fsqrt`
action: ST := square root of ST

---

## Comparison Instructions

Comparison of floating-point numbers sets the condition codes—bits $C_0$, $C_1$, $C_2$, and $C_3$ of the status register—to record the outcome of the comparison. The 8087 condition codes can be used indirectly to control 8086 conditional jumps, but they must first be copied into the 8086 flags register. There is no single instruction for doing this. There is, however, an instruction to copy the status register to a word of memory.

---
**Floating STore Status Word**
syntax: `fstsw` *destination*
action: *destination* := status register
operands: *mem* {word}   ax (80287 and 80387 only)

---

After using this instruction to copy the status register to memory, we can copy the 8087 condition codes into the 8086 flags register. The sequence we use is

```
fstsw   StatusReg
mov     ax, StatusReg
sahf
```

Figure 17.6 shows the correspondence between the condition code bits and the flags. It also shows which conditional jump instruction to use in order to mimic a jump based on 8087 condition codes. $C_1$ doesn't map to any flag bit; fortunately, most of the comparisons do not affect $C_1$. Note that $C_2$, which signals completion of the partial remainder operation, maps onto the parity flag.

The floating compare instruction has more forms than any other instruction. It always compares one floating-point number to the number in ST. It works by subtracting the source operand from ST to set the condition codes, but doesn't save the difference. If either the explicit operand or ST is a NaN, the comparison generates an invalid operation

## Chapter 17 Floating-Point Data

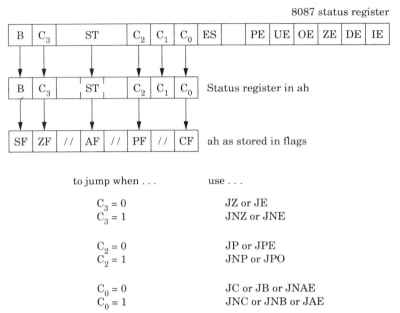

**Figure 17.6** Mapping of 8087 Condition Codes onto 8086 Flags

exception (which can be masked). The result of the floating compare instruction is coded as follows (? means undefined):

| relation | $C_3$ | $C_2$ | $C_1$ | $C_0$ |
|---|---|---|---|---|
| ST > source | 0 | 0 | ? | 0 |
| ST = source | 1 | 0 | ? | 0 |
| ST < source | 0 | 0 | ? | 1 |
| not comparable | 1 | 1 | ? | 1 |

Combining this information with that of Figure 17.6, we can determine which conditional jump instruction to use after a floating-point comparison. The only condition that sets $C_2$ is not comparable, which arises, for example, if one or both of the operands is a NaN. To jump on this result, we can use jp or jnp, since $C_2$ maps to the parity flag. Once we eliminate not comparable, we can jump on the relationship between the two floating-point numbers using the zero flag and carry flag—these are the same flags used for comparing unsigned integers. So, even though floating-point numbers have signs, we can compare two of them, copy the condition codes into the flags register, and inspect the flags as if we had compared two unsigned integers.

The compare instruction can treat the numeric registers as a stack. It can also pop ST or ST and ST(1) after making the comparison.

---

**Floating COMpare**

    syntax:    fcom

    action:    condition codes := ST:ST(1)

## 17.5 Instructions

**Floating COMpare and Pop**

    syntax:      fcomp  
    action:      (1) condition codes := ST:ST(1);  
                   (2) pop ST

**Floating COMpare, Pop, and Pop**

    syntax:      fcompp  
    action:      (1) condition codes := ST:ST(1);  
                   (2) pop ST;  
                   (3) pop ST {former ST(1)}

The compare instruction can also use any other numeric register or floating-point value in memory as the source operand. In this form, it can also optionally pop ST after the comparison.

**Floating COMpare**

    syntax:      fcom *source*  
    action:      condition codes := ST:*source*  
    operands:   *freg*    *mem* {short, long real}

**Floating COMpare and Pop**

    syntax:      fcomp *source*  
    action:      (1) condition codes := ST:*source*;  
                   (2) pop ST  
    operands:   *freg*    *mem* {short, long real}

Finally, the compare instruction can use an integer in memory as the source operand. The integer is converted to extended precision for the comparison.

**Floating Integer COMpare**

    syntax:      ficom *source*  
    action:      condition codes := ST:*source*  
    operand:    *mem* {16-, 32-bit integer}

**Floating Integer COMpare and Pop**

    syntax:      ficomp *source*  
    action:      (1) condition codes := ST:*source*;  
                   (2) pop ST  
    operand:    *mem* {16-, 32-bit integer}

As an example, consider the fragment

```
IF X > Y
THEN ...
ENDIF
```

## 652  Chapter 17  Floating-Point Data

We can implement this with the sequence

```
fld      Y
fld      X
fcompp
fstsw    StatusReg
mov      ax, StatusReg
sahf
jna      ENDIF
```

Note the order in which we push X and Y on the stack. Had we pushed in the other order, we could use the `ja` instruction; it has been done this way to be consistent with the earlier implementation of the selection control structure.

There is an instruction that compares the top register with 0. It returns the same results in the condition codes as the floating compare instructions.

**Floating TeST**
- syntax: `ftst`
- action: condition codes := ST:+0.0

There is also an instruction that examines the contents of ST. It sets the four condition code bits so that they describe the value in ST. The condition codes following this instruction have the meanings shown in Figure 17.7. The examine instruction can be useful in numerical procedures.

**Floating eXAMine**
- syntax: `fxam`
- action: condition codes := type of value in ST (see Figure 17.7)

## Control Instructions

There are a number of instructions that give the programmer significant control over the 8087 processor. Only a few of them will be considered here.

The `wait` (or `fwait`) instruction causes the 8086 to wait for the 8087 to complete an instruction. Consider the sequence

```
fist     IntVar
mov      ax, IntVar
```

The 8086 does not normally wait for the 8087 to finish an instruction before going on. It is possible for both processors to execute instructions at the same time. However, in this example, the `mov` instruction may copy the old value of `IntVar` into AX before `IntVar` is updated by `fist`. To prevent this, we can insert a wait instruction between them.

**WAIT for coprocessor**
- syntax: `wait`
  `fwait`
- action: suspend 8086 until 8087 not busy

## 17.5 Instructions

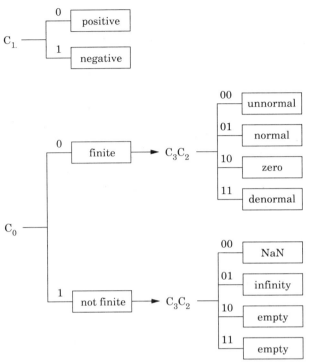

**Figure 17.7** Interpretation of Condition Codes Following FXAM Instruction

There is another application for wait: When the 8086 encounters an instruction for the 8087, it must wait for the 8087 to finish the previous instruction before passing the new instruction to it. This happens automatically in the newer processors (80286/80287, 80386/80387) but not in the 8086. As a result, it is possible for the 8086 to pass instructions to the 8087 before it is ready, with unpredictable and unwelcome results. To fix this problem, most assemblers insert an fwait instruction before each 8087 instruction. These waits are not needed with newer processors.

To ensure that the register stack is empty when beginning a calculation, there is an instruction that initializes the 8087.

**Floating INITialize coprocessor**
- syntax: finit
- action: tags register := all empty;
  control register :=
  projective infinity,
  round to nearest,
  extended precision,
  mask all exceptions;

> status register :=
>   not busy,
>   ST cleared,
>   error summary cleared,
>   exception flags cleared

The state of the condition codes depends on the processor model; to ensure portability, it is best to treat the condition codes as undefined after an initialization instruction.

There are instructions for saving and restoring the state of the coprocessor. The first two considered here save and restore the coprocessor environment. The environment requires a block of 14 bytes; the registers are copied between the coprocessor and memory in the following order, with byte displacements given in brackets: control[0], status[2], tag[4], instruction pointer[6], and operand pointer[10].

---

**Floating STore coprocessor ENVironment**
- syntax: `fstenv` *destination*
- action: *destination* := 8087 environment

**Floating LoaD coprocessor ENVironment**
- syntax: `fldenv` *source*
- action: 8087 environment := *source*
- operand: *mem* {14 bytes}

---

There are also save and restore instructions that copy the environment and all eight data registers. This requires a block of 94 bytes of memory to store the contents of all 8087 registers. The registers are copied into this block in the following order, with byte displacements given in brackets: control[0], status[2], tag[4], instruction pointer[6], operand pointer[10], and ST(0)[14] through ST(7)[84].

---

**Floating SAVE coprocessor state**
- syntax: `fsave` *destination*
- action: (1) *destination* := all 8087 registers;
  (2) initialize 8087

**Floating ReSTORe coprocessor state**
- syntax: `frstor` *source*
- action: all 8087 registers := *source*
- operand: *mem* {94 bytes}

---

The last control instructions examined here load and store the control register.

---

**Floating STore Control Word**
- syntax: `fstcw` *destination*
- action: *destination* := control register

### Floating LoaD Control Word

| | |
|---|---|
| syntax: | `fldcw` *source* |
| action: | control register := *source* |
| operand: | *mem* {2 bytes} |

The control register specifies infinity, rounding, and precision control, as well as masks for the exceptions. To change the rounding mode, for example, we could store the control word in memory, use `and` and `or` with appropriate masks to change the Rounding Control field, and store the modified word back in the control register.

## Transcendental Instructions

The 8087 includes instructions that compute values of some common transcendental functions. The mathematical background needed to write such routines is beyond that assumed in the rest of this text. The transcendental instructions are not presented here, as they are not useful without an extensive discussion of the mathematics involved and an understanding of the restrictions on operand values. Furthermore, as the technology has progressed from the 8087 to the 80287 and 80387 and 80486, the restrictions have been changed and instructions have been added and omitted.

The trigonometric instructions that are available on the 8086 can compute the following: For an angle between 0 and $\pi/4$, two numbers $Y$ and $X$ such that $\frac{Y}{X}$ is the tangent of the angle; and for any angle specified by two numbers $Y$ and $X$, the arctangent of $\frac{Y}{X}$. It can also push $\pi$ onto the stack in extended precision. From these instructions, and the supporting mathematics, values for all trigonometric functions, for all angles, can be computed.

The logarithmic and exponential instructions that are available on the 8086 can compute: for any real number $Y$ and a positive real number $X$, the value of $Y * \log_2(X)$; for any real number $Y$ and a real number $X$ that satisfies $|X| < (1 - 1/\sqrt{2})$, the value of $Y * \log_2(X + 1)$; and for a real number $X$ that satisfies $0 \leq X \leq 0.5$, the value of $2^X - 1$. There are also instructions that push four constants that are useful with the logarithmic and exponential instructions. From these instructions, and the supporting mathematics, values for $\log_2(x)$, $\log_e(x)$, $\log_{10}(x)$, $2^x$, $e^x$, $10^x$, $y^x$, the hyperbolic functions, and the inverse hyperbolic functions can be computed.

These are all of the instructions for manipulating floating-point numbers that will be discussed here. The next section will examine several concerns that arise in computing with floating-point numbers, and will present sample programs.

## EXERCISES 17.5

1. Outline the loop structure needed to implement the remainder operation using the partial remainder instruction. Be sure to include the steps needed to test for completion.
2. There are five forms of the addition, subtraction, multiplication, and division instructions (plus the reversed forms of subtraction and division). Summarize the five forms.
3. Write instructions for each of the following assignments. Assume any registers used in the expression contain normal floating-point numbers.
    (*a*)  ST(1) := ST + 1.0
    (*b*)  ST := ST(1) - 1.0

(c) ST := 2 * ST
(d) ST := ST + ST(1)
(e) ST := ST(1) + ST(2)
(f) ST(3) := ST

4. Write instructions for each of the following assignments. Assume that any registers used contain normal floating-point numbers, that IW is a 16-bit integer, and that FW is a short floating-point number.
   (a) FW := ST
   (b) FW := ST(2)
   (c) FW := ST + IW; pop ST
   (d) FW := ST + ST(1); pop ST
   (e) FW := ST(2) + FW
   (f) FW := 2*ST; pop ST

5. Write sequences of instructions that implement the following assignment statements. Assume that all registers in the coprocessor are empty, and leave them empty. All names in the statements are short floating-point variables.
   (a) `Celsius := (Fahrenheit - 32.0) / 1.8`
   (b) `Total := UnitCost * Quantity + Handling`
   (c) `Y := 2 * X * X - 4.3 * X + 1`
   (d) `Pace := |X+1| - 1`
   (e) `Height := 600.0 - 16.1 * T * T`
   (f) `Volume := π * Radius * Radius * Height / 3.0`

## 17.6 APPLICATIONS

Many programmers use floating-point numbers as freely as they use integers, with little regard for the problems that can arise. Fortunately, in most applications the floating-point numbers behave reasonably well, thanks in part to the use of extended precision. But every programmer should be aware of the potential for trouble when computing with floating-point numbers.

This section presents example programs that demonstrate computing with floating-point numbers.

### FOR Loops

Some high-level languages allow floating-point expressions to control counted loops. Consider the loop specified by the statement

`FOR R := 0.0 TO 10.0 STEP 0.1`

We anticipate that it should execute with $R=0.0$, $R=0.1$, $R=0.2$, and so on to $R=10.0$. But we also know that 0.1 is one of many numbers that is not represented exactly in a binary computer. One-tenth in binary is $0.000110011001\ldots$, where the pattern $1001_2$ repeats forever. The number that the computer uses in place of 0.1 in the counted loop depends on the precision used and rounding mode in effect. The difference between 0.1 and the actual number that the computer substitutes for it is small enough that it goes unnoticed in many applications.

In the count-controlled loop, however, the difference accumulates as the loop iterates the statement

`R := R + 0.1`

## 17.6 Applications

For example, if the number used in place of 0.1 is slightly smaller, such as $0.1 - 2^{-23}$, when we anticipate R = 1.6 the actual value of R is $16 \times (0.1 - 2^{-23})$, or $1.6 - 2^{-19}$, which is 1.5999981. This may not cause obvious problems, but the error is large enough that it could affect a sensitive computation.

Chapter 5 showed how to implement a count-controlled loop using the CX register and a loop instruction. An iteration count was computed using

$$IC = \left\lfloor \frac{\text{Limit} - \text{First}}{\text{Increment}} \right\rfloor + 1$$

This formula can also be used with floating-point values for Limit, First, and Increment. However, inexact representation can cause problems with the number of times the loop executes. For example, the loop controlled by the statement

```
FOR R := 0.0 TO 1.0 STEP 0.1
```

gives an iteration count value:

$$IC = \left\lfloor \frac{1.0 - 0.0}{0.1} \right\rfloor + 1$$

This should evaluate to 11. If 0.1 is rounded down a little, the quotient in the formula for IC becomes a little bigger than 10, which is chopped to 10, and the formula works in this case. If 0.1 is rounded up a little, the quotient becomes a little smaller than 10, which is then chopped to 9, and the loop executes one iteration fewer than expected.

The loop control variable can be computed using the statement

```
Lcv := First + (IC-X)*Increment
```

where X is IC for the first iteration, IC-1 for the second, IC-2 for the third, and so on down to 1 for the last iteration. Recall that X is typically in the CX register, and having it vary from IC down to 1 allows us to control the loop with only a loop instruction. In calculating Lcv, IC and X are integers so that computation is performed using the sub instruction. The difference is converted to real; this conversion is exact. The multiplication by Increment and addition of First each introduce a little error if these are not exact numbers.

The total error in Lcv computed this way is at most the result of three operations: conversion from integer to floating-point, multiplication, and addition. The total error in the control variable when a counted loop is implemented using the WHILE loop design increases on each iteration. In the first iteration, the error is only the representation error in First. In each following iteration, the error is increased by the addition of Increment, so that by the tenth iteration, the error can be as large as the original error in First, plus nine times the error introduced by adding Increment. For this reason, loops controlled by floating-point numbers should be implemented using the formulas for IC and Lcv.

### Testing for Equal

The earlier discussion of comparing two floating-point numbers considered the mechanics of the process and the result of comparing a NaN with another number. Another important issue is often overlooked: comparing two floating-point numbers for equality. The result of such a test depends on the numbers involved and on how they were generated. One common test for equality is to check for 0 entered as a sentinel. Since 0 has an exact representation, the values stored in the program and returned by an input routine should be identical.

Difficulties can arise when testing floating-point numbers that have been computed. Consider the test used to demonstrate selection:

IF SideA * SideA + SideB * SideB = SideC * SideC

Let's evaluate this with two different sets of data, both of which should satisfy the condition. First, let's try SideA = 3.0, SideB = 4.0, and SideC = 5.0. All three of these numbers are represented exactly in floating-point format. Their squares are also represented exactly, as is the sum of the first two squares. Since there are no inexact numbers anywhere in the evaluation of the expression, no problems are expected. Indeed, this example does evaluate correctly.

Another example is SideA = 0.3, SideB = 0.4, and SideC = 0.5. We multiplied the previous numbers by 0.1. From algebra, we know that we can multiply both sides of an equality by the same constant and not change its value. We therefore anticipate that the condition in the IF statement will still be true. If we evaluate it, we get

$$0.3 * 0.3 + 0.4 * 0.4 = 0.5 * 0.5$$

or

$$0.09 + 0.16 = 0.25$$

which is clearly true. However, 0.3 and 0.4 are not represented exactly in floating-point format; 0.5 is. There is therefore some error in evaluating the left side of the expression, and no error in evaluating the right side. Unless the errors on the left side exactly cancel out, which is not likely, the value computed will be different from 0.25. Thus, the expression yields false.

It is necessary to change the condition from "are the two numbers equal?" to "are the two numbers almost equal?" and to decide exactly what is meant by "almost equal." We might start by suggesting a test that checks whether the magnitude of the difference is small. For example, rather than the test

$$X = Y$$

we might use a test like

$$ABS(X - Y) <= 0.00001$$

Consider this test with $X = 5.499995$ and $Y = 5.500000$. The difference $X - Y$ is $-0.000005$. These two numbers would test almost equal. If we multiply two almost equal numbers by the same constant, we expect the products to be almost equal as well. However, if we multiply this $X$ and $Y$ by 100, so that we have $X = 549.9995$ and $Y = 550.0000$, their difference becomes $-0.0005$. According to the proposed test, these new values of $X$ and $Y$ are not almost equal. Before trying to revise the test, let's consider one more example. Let $X = 5.3 \times 10^{-7}$ and $Y = -2.6 \times 10^{-7}$. Their difference is $7.9 \times 10^{-7}$, which qualifies them as almost equal numbers. Yet these numbers have different signs, and the magnitude of one is twice as large as the magnitude of the other, so they are clearly not almost equal.

## 17.6 Applications

The proposed test for almost equal given above is an absolute test, in that it asks "Is the difference between two numbers small?" In many situations, the question "Is the difference between two numbers relatively small?" is more appropriate. The first question relates to decimal places, the second to significant digits. The numbers 123000.3 and 123000.9 agree to six significant digits, but no decimal places; the numbers 0.000123 and 0.000188 agree to four decimal places, but only one significant digit.

To test whether two numbers are almost equal in the relative sense, we must consider the magnitude of the numbers. The condition can be stated as

$$\text{ABS}(X - Y) <= 0.00001 * \text{ABS}(X)$$

It doesn't make much difference whether we use the magnitude of $X$ or the magnitude of $Y$ in the expression on the right, since we expect the magnitudes to be the same.

The number that was used in both of the tests for almost equal is 0.00001. There is nothing magical about this number; it is just reasonably small. If we change it to 0.1, the tests will be much less discriminating—and probably misleading. On the other hand, if we change it to $10^{-23}$, we will get a true result only when the floating-point numbers involved are exactly equal—there is not enough precision for this small tolerance, even with extended precision.

## Example Programs

Any of the available programs or subprograms that compute with integers could be rewritten to compute with floating-point numbers without great effort. Instead, new programs are presented: Two problems are numerical in nature, and one uses arrays of floating-point numbers.

## A square root function

The first program presented here is a function that computes the square root of a positive number. Normally the 8087 square root instruction would be used; the purpose here is to demonstrate programming with the coprocessor and to introduce some simple numerical techniques. Newton's method, an iterative algorithm, is used here. It's derivation, although not difficult, is beyond the scope of this text; an explanation and illustration of the method should suffice.

Let's call the number whose square root we want to compute $A$. The method needs an initial guess, $X_0$, for the square root. Any guess between 1.0 and $A$, whether $A$ is less than 1.0 or greater than 1.0, will work.

Newton's method for computing a square root computes a better approximation, $X_1$, from the guess $X_0$, using the formula

$$X_1 = (A/X_0 + X_0)/2$$

The formula for the next approximation is the same, substituting $X_1$ for $X_0$ and $X_2$ for $X_1$; all subsequent iterations are also similar. If we consider $X_0$ to be the older approximation and $X_1$ the newer approximation, we can simply repeat the computation until it converges on the square root of $A$.

Consider what happens if our guess, by some coincidence, is indeed the square root of $A$. Substituting $\sqrt{A}$ for $X_0$ in the iteration formula gives

$$X_1 = \left(A/\sqrt{A} + \sqrt{A}\right)/2$$
$$= \left(\sqrt{A} + \sqrt{A}\right)/2$$
$$= \left(2\sqrt{A}\right)/2$$
$$= \sqrt{A}$$

This method preserves the correct value when it is encountered. But what happens if our guess is not the square root? Let's consider an initial guess that is too small. The first term in parentheses, $A/X_0$, will be larger than the square root; the second term, $X_0$, will be smaller. Adding the terms and dividing by two averages these. Clearly, the average of the two numbers, one greater than the square root of $A$ and the other less than it, will be closer to the square root of $A$. That is, if we start with

$$X_0 < \sqrt{A}$$

then the terms in parentheses in the formula satisfy

$$X_0 < \sqrt{A} < A/X_0$$

Also, we get

$$X_0 < X_1 < A/X_0$$

Now these relations imply that, as we iterate, $X_1$ gets squeezed into smaller and smaller intervals. At some point, either $X_1$ becomes exactly $\sqrt{A}$ or it becomes so close that we cannot distinguish the two values in the selected precision. The case for an initial guess that is too large also gives two inequalities and the same conclusion.

Here is an example using base 10 and seven significant digits. We select a simple number, 49, whose square root we know; we also select an arbitrary initial guess, 10. The first iteration gives

$$\left(\tfrac{49}{10} + 10\right)/2 = 7.45$$

For the second iteration we substitute 7.45 and compute

$$\left(\tfrac{49}{7.45} + 7.45\right)/2 = 7.013591$$

Now substitute this and compute

$$\left(\tfrac{49}{7.013591} + 7.013591\right)/2 = 7.000013$$

One more iteration gives 7.0 after rounding to seven significant digits.

Before writing the function in assembly language, it is necessary to determine when the function will stop iterating. It is reasonable to test for convergence of the sequence of approximations. But how close do two results have to be for us to say that they have converged?

There is a limit imposed by the floating-point representation used here. Consider two approximations that differ only in the least significant bit of the fraction. Let's call them $X_i$ and $X_j$. It is possible that if we do one more iteration, computing a value for $X_k$, it

## 17.6 Applications

will be the same value as $X_i$. We could go on forever iterating between two numbers that differ in only the least significant bit. To avoid this, we must either test for it or accept a result that differs from the previous result in the last bit.

In Newton's method, the number of correct digits approximately doubles after each iteration. In practice, testing for about 21 significant bits of the two most recent results being the same will avoid problems with infinite loops, assuming that 23 significant bits of the fraction are represented in floating-point format. It is also unlikely that any further iterations would give a better result.

To test for agreement of two fractions to 21 bits, we must also make sure that the exponents are the same. Thus, we want a relative error less than about $2^{-21}$. If our two most recent results are $X$old and $X$new, we continue to iterate until we get results that satisfy

$$|X\text{new} - X\text{old}| <= X\text{new} \times 2^{-21}$$

This is the test that will be used in the function demonstrated here. The relative error is converted to base 10, as it is easier to work with. We find that $2^{-21}$ is a little less than $0.5 \times 10^{-6}$.

The last issue that must be resolved before writing the function is the selection of a first guess. We could ask the user to pass a guess as a second parameter, but how can we be sure that the user will provide a reasonable guess? A more attractive option is to have the function pick the first guess. Since the square root of any positive number is between 1.0 and itself, 1.0 can be the guess. A better first guess will be explored in the exercises.

Now the termination condition and the first guess can be combined with the iteration formula. The algorithm we get is

```
Xnew := 1.0
REPEAT
   Xold := Xnew
   Xnew := (A/Xold + Xold)/2
UNTIL Xnew*0.5E-6 > abs(Xold-Xnew)
```

This is implemented in the function of Program 17.1. The function treats the numeric registers as a stack, with all arithmetic operations using the top one or two elements of the stack. The stack is empty at the start and end of every iteration. The intermediate values of Xold and Xnew are stored in memory using `fst` instructions; their values remain on the stack as well. When Xold is compared with Xnew, `fsub` is used to compute the difference of the values that the `fst` instructions have left on the stack.

### Program 17.1

```
; Program 17.1      NewSqrt.ASM
; Computes the square root using Newton's method.
; Can be called from Turbo Pascal, as
;   Function NewSqrt (A: Single): Single;

; Parameter and local variables
    A           equ     dword ptr [bp + 4]
    Xold        equ     dword ptr [bp - 4]
    Xnew        equ     dword ptr [bp - 8]
    TestResult  equ     word ptr [bp - 10]
```

## Program 17.1 (continued)

```
_DATA SEGMENT word public 'data'
    Two       dd      2.0
    MaxRelErr dd      0.5E-6
_DATA ENDS

_TEXT SEGMENT word public 'code'
    assume  cs: _TEXT
    assume  ds: _DATA
    public  NewSqrt

NewSqrt PROC

; set up bp register to point to parameter
    push    bp
    mov     bp, sp

; allocate stack space for local variables
    sub     sp, 10

; Xnew := 1.0
    fld1
    fstp    Xnew

  REPEAT01:
;   Xold := Xnew
    fld     Xnew
    fst     Xold        ;copy of Xold remains on stack

;   Xnew := (A/Xold + Xold) / 2.0
    fld     A
    fld     Xold
    fdiv
    fld     Xold
    fadd
    fld     Two
    fdiv
    fst     Xnew        ;copy of Xnew remains on stack

;   test MaxRelErr*Xnew > abs(Xnew-Xold)
    fsub
    fabs
    fld     MaxRelErr
    fld     Xnew
    fmul
    fcompp

    fstsw   TestResult
    fwait
    mov     ax, TestResult
    sahf
    jna     REPEAT01
; UNTIL MaxRelErr*Xnew > abs(Xnew-Xold)
```

## 17.6 Applications

**Program 17.1 (continued)**

```
; return Xnew in 8087 stack, restore 8086 stack
    fld     Xnew
    add     sp, 10
    pop     bp
    ret     4

NewSqrt ENDP
_TEXT ENDS
END
```

The function result in Program 17.1 is returned to the calling program in ST. The rest of the program is left to the reader to peruse. A Pascal program that invokes this function and compares its result with that of the Pascal Sqrt function is included on the disk.

Newton's square root algorithm is implemented again as a function in Program 17.2. This time, however, we do not use memory for the values of Xold and Xnew, but rather keep these on the stack. We still do all arithmetic on the top element(s) of the stack. To help keep track of the stack, a description of the stack after each instruction executes is included in the comment field. We use < to indicate the top and ] to indicate the bottom of the stack. Note that at the start and end of each iteration, only the most recent result, Xnew, is on the 8087 stack. The last result is left there as the function value on return.

**Program 17.2**

```
; Program 17.2       NewSqrt2.ASM
; Computes the square root using Newton's method.
; Can be called from Turbo Pascal, as
;   Function NewSqrt (A: Single): Single;

; Parameter and local variable
    A           equ     dword ptr [bp + 4]
    TestResult  equ     word ptr [bp - 2]

_DATA SEGMENT word public 'data'
    Two         dd      2.0
    MaxRelErr   dd      0.5E-6
_DATA ENDS

_TEXT SEGMENT word public 'code'
    assume  cs: _TEXT
    assume  ds: _DATA
    public  NewSqrt

NewSqrt PROC

; set up bp register to point to parameter
    push    bp
    mov     bp, sp

; allocate stack space for local variable
    sub     sp, 2
```

**Program 17.2 (continued)**

```
;   Xnew := 1.0              ;8087 stack --- <top ... bottom]
        fld1                 ;<Xnew]

    REPEAT01:
;   Xold := Xnew
        fld     ST           ;<Xold, Xnew]

;   Xnew := (A/Xold + Xold) / 2.0
        fld     A            ;<A, Xold, Xnew]
        fdiv    ST, ST(1)    ;<A/Xold, Xold, Xnew]
        fadd    ST, ST(1)    ;<A/Xold+Xold, Xold, Xnew]
        fdiv    Two          ;<(A/Xold+Xold)/2, Xold, Xnew]
        fst     ST(2)        ;<(A/Xold+Xold)/2, Xold, (A/Xold+Xold)/2]
                             ;<Xnew, Xold, Xnew]

;   test MaxRelErr*Xnew > abs(Xnew-Xold)
        fsub                 ;<Xnew-Xold, Xnew]
        fabs                 ;<abs(Xnew-Xold), Xnew]
        fld     MaxRelErr    ;<MaxRelErr, abs(Xnew-Xold), Xnew]
        fmul    ST, ST(2)    ;<MaxRelErr*Xnew, abs(Xnew-Xold), Xnew]
        fcompp               ;<Xnew]

        fstsw   TestResult
        fwait
        mov     ax, TestResult
        sahf
        jna     REPEAT01
;   UNTIL MaxRelErr*Xnew > abs(Xnew-Xold)

;   return Xnew in 8087 stack, restore 8086 stack
        add     sp, 2
        pop     bp
        ret     4

NewSqrt ENDP
_TEXT   ENDS
        END
```

Figure 17.8 shows the state of the 8087 stack after each instruction that manipulates it in the first two iterations of Program 17.2. The value 49.0 has been used as the argument, and the stack contents have been shown as numbers.

## An exponential function

The next example is a function that computes $e^x$ for a given value of $x$. This is available in many high-level languages as EXP($x$). The version developed here has a few deliberate weaknesses that are left as exercises to correct.

Again the derivation of the formula used is beyond the scope of this text. The formula itself is

$$e^x = 1 + x + x^2/2! + x^3/3! + x^4/4! + \cdots$$

### 17.6 Applications

|  | first iteration | | section iteration | |
|---|---|---|---|---|
|  | top | bottom | top | bottom |
| ; Xnew := 1.0 | | | | |
|     fld1 | 1.0 | | | |
| | | | | |
| REPEAT01: | | | | |
| ; Xold := Xnew | | | | |
|     fld    ST | 1.0, 1.0 | | 25.0, 25.0 | |
| ; Xnew := ... | | | | |
|     fld    A | 49.0, 1.0, 1.0 | | 49.0, 25.0, 25.0 | |
|     fdiv   ST, ST(1) | 49.0, 1.0, 1.0 | | 1.96, 25.0, 25.0 | |
|     fadd   ST, ST(1) | 50.0, 1.0, 1.0 | | 26.96, 25.0, 25.0 | |
|     fdiv   Two | 25.0, 1.0, 1.0 | | 13.48, 25.0, 25.0 | |
|     fst    ST(2) | 25.0, 1.0, 25.0 | | 13.48, 25.0, 13.48 | |
| ; compare... | | | | |
|     fsub | 24.0, 25.0 | | −11.52, 13.48 | |
|     fabs | 24.0, 25.0 | | 11.52, 13.48 | |
|     fld    MaxRelErr | 0.5e−6, 24.0, 25.0 | | 0.5e−6, 11.52, 13.48 | |
|     fmul   ST, ST(2) | 0.125e−4, 24.0, 25.0 | | 0.689e−5, 11.52, 13.48 | |
|     fcompp | 25.0 | | 13.48 | |
| | | | | |
|     fstsw   TestResult | | | | |
|     fwait | | | | |
|     mov    ax, TestResult | | | | |
|     sahf | | | | |
|     jna    REPEAT01 | | | | |
| ; UNTIL ... | | | | |

**Figure 17.8** 8087 Data Registers During Execution of Program 17.2

This is the Maclaurin series for $e^x$. It is not the best formula known, but it provides an interesting example. Many aspects of this example also apply to other calculations based on series.

A few examples will be provided to illustrate. The first is a simple case, $e^1$. The first six terms of the series gives

$$e = 1 + 1 + \tfrac{1}{2} + \tfrac{1}{6} + \tfrac{1}{24} + \tfrac{1}{120} + \cdots$$

The sum of these six terms, to six digits, is 2.71667, which has a relative error less than 0.06 percent. Adding the seventh term, $\tfrac{1}{720}$, brings the sum to 2.71806, which decreases the error to less than 0.01 percent. Adding the eighth term, $\tfrac{1}{5040}$, brings the sum to 2.71825. Clearly, the more terms of the sum are taken, the closer the sum is to the correct value.

Now let's compute $e^3$. The first few terms give

$$e^3 = 1 + 3 + \tfrac{9}{2} + \tfrac{27}{6} + \tfrac{81}{24} + \tfrac{243}{120} + \cdots$$

These terms increase initially, then decrease, and eventually become small relative to the total. For instance, the tenth term is $3^9/9!$, or 19683/362880, which is about 0.05424; the sum approaches 20.0855, so the tenth term represents less than 0.3 percent of the sum.

The most obvious issue to address is when to stop adding terms. One approach is to add terms until they become so small that they no longer affect the sum. Recall that the number with the smaller exponent is shifted when adding. When the new term is shifted prior to adding it to the sum, and all of the significant bits of its fraction are lost, we can stop. No other terms will affect the sum. If we stop computing when a term is less than $2^{-21}$ (about $0.5 \times 10^{-6}$) times the sum, the sum should be as close to correct as this method allows with single-precision numbers.

Now consider how to compute the terms of this series. Two consecutive terms of the series are denoted as $T_{k-1}$ and $T_k$. These are

$$T_{k-1} = x^{k-1}/(k-1)!$$

and

$$T_k = x^k/(k)!$$

We assume that $x$ is positive. Now take the ratio

$$\frac{T_k}{T_{k-1}} = \frac{x^k/(k)!}{x^{k-1}/(k-1)!} = \frac{x}{k}$$

and solve for $T_k$:

$$T_k = (x/k)T_{k-1}$$

This can be used to compute each term from the previous term. It is combined with the stopping criterion developed above, and the algorithm is written as

```
K := 0
Term := 1.0
Sum := 1.0
REPEAT
   K := K + 1
   Term := Term * X / K
   Sum := Sum + Term
UNTIL abs(Term) <= abs(Sum*0.5E-6)
```

We relax our assumption that $x$ is positive, so we need to take absolute values of the expressions in the condition for the loop. There is another problem when $x$ is negative, which will be considered in the exercises.

This algorithm is implemented as the function in Program 17.3. The exponential function is implemented using operands in memory and just the top numeric register. The computations have been ordered to take advantage of the previous result left in ST as we start each new expression or statement. For example, after we compute and save a new Term, we add Sum to it.

This function works satisfactorily for positive arguments. The argument must be less than about 88.72, or the function value is too large for single-precision format. (The largest single-precision number is about $3.4 \times 10^{38}$; $\ln(3.4 \times 10^{38}) \approx 88.72$.) Noticeable errors occur with negative arguments: Function values fluctuate wildly for small changes in the argument when the argument is less than $-2$; the function may even return negative values. The exercises provide some insight into these problems.

## 17.6 Applications

**Program 17.3**

```
;   Program 17.3       MacExp.ASM
;   Computes e^x using Maclaurin Series.
;   Can be called from Turbo Pascal, as
;      Function MacExp (X: Single): Single;

;   Parameter and local variables:
        X           equ     dword ptr [bp + 4]
        K           equ     dword ptr [bp - 4]
        Term        equ     dword ptr [bp - 8]
        Sum         equ     dword ptr [bp - 12]
        TestResult  equ     word ptr [bp - 14]

_DATA SEGMENT word public 'data'
        MaxRelErr   dd      0.5E-6
_DATA ENDS

_TEXT SEGMENT word public 'code'
        assume  cs: _TEXT
        assume  ds: _DATA
        public  MacExp

MacExp PROC

;   set up bp register to point to parameter
        push    bp
        mov     bp, sp

;   allocate stack space for local variables
        sub     sp, 14

;   K := 0.0                    ;8087 stack --- <top ... bottom]
        fldz                    ;<0.0]
        fstp    K               ;<]

;   Term := 1.0,  Sum := 1.0
        fld1                    ;<1.0]
        fst     Term            ;<1.0]
        fstp    Sum             ;<]


    REPEAT01:
;       K := K + 1
        fld1                    ;<1.0]
        fadd    K               ;<K+1.0]
        fstp    K               ;<]

;       Term := Term * X / K
        fld     Term            ;<Term]
        fmul    X               ;<Term*X]
        fdiv    K               ;<Term*X/K]
        fst     Term            ;<Term]
```

**Program 17.3 (continued)**

```
;       Sum := Sum + Term
        fadd    Sum             ;<Term+Sum]
        fst     Sum             ;<Sum]

;       test abs(Term) <= abs(Sum * MaxRelErr)
        fmul    MaxRelErr       ;<Sum*MaxRelErr]
        fabs                    ;<abs(Sum*MaxRelErr)]
        fld     Term            ;<Term, abs(Sum*MaxRelErr)]
        fabs                    ;<abs(Term), abs(Sum*MaxRelErr)]
        fcompp                  ;<]

        fstsw   TestResult
        fwait
        mov     ax, TestResult
        sahf
        jnbe    REPEAT01
; UNTIL abs(Term) <= abs(Sum * MaxRelErr)

; return Sum on 8087 stack, restore 8086 stack
        fld     Sum
        add     sp, 14
        pop     bp
        ret     4

MacExp  ENDP
_TEXT   ENDS
        END
```

## Correlation coefficient

Given a set of observations $(X_i, Y_i)$, $i = 1..N$, we can compute a dimensionless quantity called the correlation coefficient that indicates how strongly the values are related. If we plot the observations and they all fall perfectly on a line with positive slope, the correlation coefficient is 1.0—the $Y$ values are proportional to the $X$ values; if they all fall on a line with negative slope, the coefficient is $-1.0$—the $Y$ values are inversely proportional to the $X$ values. Between these extremes, there are varying degrees of correlation between $X$ and $Y$. For example, a coefficient of 0.8 indicates that the $Y$ values tend to be proportional to $X$; a coefficient of 0.0 indicates that $X$ and $Y$ are unrelated.

To compute the correlation coefficient, we need the mean of all $X$ values, which we call MnX, and the mean of all $Y$ values, MnY. (We use shorter names than usual so that we can use the same style of documentation for the stack as in Program 17.2. As many as seven of the stack registers will be in use in the program we write for this problem, so we must squeeze things a little.) We know how to compute means. Once we have the means, we need three sums:

$$\text{SSDX} = \sum_{i=1}^{N} (X_i - \text{MnX})^2$$

$$\text{SSDY} = \sum_{i=1}^{N} (Y_i - \text{MnY})^2$$

## 17.6 Applications

and

$$\text{SDXDY} = \sum_{i=1}^{N}((X_i - \text{MnX})(Y_i - \text{MnY}))$$

We can then compute the correlation coefficient from the formula

$$r = \text{SDXDY}/\sqrt{(\text{SSDX} \times \text{SSDY})}$$

These computations are performed in the function of Program 17.4. There are three arguments: pointers to the arrays of single precision numbers X and Y, and an integer N passed by value. There are no local variables in memory in Program 17.4; all intermediate results are kept in the numeric registers. Two of the registers, ST and ST(1), are used as working registers. Register ST(2) is used for the sum of the X values in the first loop and then used for MnX in the second loop. Similarly, register ST(3) is used for the sum of Y values and then for MnY. In the second loop, registers ST(4), ST(5), and ST(6) are used for SSDX, SSDY, and SDXDY respectively. Using the registers this way introduces the problem of the registers' becoming renumbered whenever a load or pop occurs. The solution is to use load and pop in pairs, except as we compute the final value to be returned by the function. Thus, most `fld` instructions are preceded by an `fstp ST` instruction, which is the efficient, but not obvious, way to pop and discard the top of the numeric stack.

## Program 17.4

```
; Program 17.4      Correl.ASM
; Computes the coefficient of correlation between X and Y,
; where N values for X and Y are stored in arrays.
; Can be called from Turbo Pascal, as
;    Function Correl (var X, Y: SingleArray; N: Integer): Single;

; Parameters
    X           equ     dword ptr [bp + 10]
    Y           equ     dword ptr [bp + 6]
    N           equ     word ptr [bp + 4]

; Text substitutions
    Xi          equ     dword ptr ds:[si]       ;an element of X
    Yi          equ     dword ptr es:[di]       ;an element of Y

; Abbreviations used in internal documentation
; SX, SY        Sums of Xi, Yi    for i=1 to N
; MnX, MnY      Means of Xi, Yi   for i=1 to N
; DX, DY        Differences Xi-MnX, Yi-MnY   one value
; SSDX, SSDY    Sums of Squares of DX, DY
; SDXDY         Sum of product DX*DY

_TEXT SEGMENT word public 'code'
    assume  cs: _TEXT
    public  Correl

Correl PROC
```

## Program 17.4 (continued)

```
        ; set up bp register to point to parameters
            push    bp
            mov     bp, sp

        ; set up pointers to arrays
            push    ds                  ;save caller's ds register
            lds     si, X
            les     di, Y

        ; SX := 0; SY := 0              ;8087 stack --- <top ... bottom]
            fldz                        ;<0]
            fst     ST(2)               ;<0, ?, SX]
            fst     ST(3)               ;<0, ?, SX, SY]

        ; FOR01 cx := N TO 1 STEP -1
            mov     cx, N

        DO01:
        ;   SX := SX + X[si]
            fstp    ST                  ;<?, SX, SY]
            fld     Xi                  ;<Xi, ?, SX, SY]
            fadd    ST(2), ST           ;<Xi, ?, SX, SY]

        ; SY := SY + Y[di]
            fstp    ST                  ;<?, SX, SY]
            fld     Yi                  ;<Yi, ?, SX, SY]
            fadd    ST(3), ST           ;<Yi, ?, SX, SY]

        ;   advance to next elements of X and Y
            add     si, 4
            add     di, 4

            loop    DO01
        ; ENDFOR01

        ; MnX := SX / N
            fstp    ST                  ;<?, SX, SY]
            fild    N                   ;<N, ?, SX, SY]
            fdiv    ST(2), ST           ;<N, ?, MnX, SY]

        ; MnY := SY / N
            fdiv    ST(3), ST           ;<N, ?, MnX, MnY]

        ; set pointers to start of arrays
            lds     si, X
            les     di, Y

        ; SSDX := 0; SSDY := 0; SDXDY := 0
            fstp    ST                  ;<?, MnX, MnY]
            fldz                        ;<0, ?, MnX, MnY]
            fst     ST(4)               ;<0, ?, MnX, MnY, SSDX]
            fst     ST(5)               ;<0, ?, MnX, MnY, SSDX, SSDY]
            fst     ST(6)               ;<0, ?, MnX, MnY, SSDX, SSDY, SDXDY]
```

### 17.6 Applications

**Program 17.4 (continued)**

```
;   FOR02 cx := N TO 1 STEP -1
        mov     cx, N

    DO02:
;       compute DY and save it, add (DY)^2 to SSDY
        fstp    ST(1)           ;<0, MnX, MnY, SSDX, SSDY, SDXDY]
        fstp    ST              ;<MnX, MnY, SSDX, SSDY, SDXDY]
        fld     Yi              ;<Yi, MnX, MnY, SSDX, SSDY, SDXDY]
        fsub    ST, ST(2)       ;<DY, MnX, MnY, SSDX, SSDY, SDXDY]
        fld     ST              ;<DY, DY, MnX, MnY, SSDX, SSDY, SDXDY]
        fmul    ST, ST          ;<DY*DY, DY, MnX, MnY, SSDX, SSDY, SDXDY]
        fadd    ST(5), ST       ;<DY*DY, DY, MnX, MnY, SSDX, SSDY, SDXDY]

;       compute DX and DXDY, add (DX)^2 to SSDX
        fstp    ST              ;<DY, MnX, MnY, SSDX, SSDY, SDXDY]
        fld     Xi              ;<Xi, DY, MnX, MnY, SSDX, SSDY, SDXDY]
        fsub    ST, ST(2)       ;<DX, DY, MnX, MnY, SSDX, SSDY, SDXDY]
        fmul    ST(1), ST       ;<DX, DX*DY, MnX, MnY, SSDX, SSDY, SDXDY]
        fmul    ST, ST          ;<DX*DX, DX*DY, MnX, MnY, SSDX, SSDY, SDXDY]
        fadd    ST(4), ST       ;<DX*DX, DX*DY, MnX, MnY, SSDX, SSDY, SDXDY]

;       add DXDY to SDXDY
        fxch    ST(1)           ;<DX*DY, DX*DX, MnX, MnY, SSDX, SSDY, SDXDY]
        fadd    ST(6), ST       ;<DX*DY, DX*DX, MnX, MnY, SSDX, SSDY, SDXDY]

;       advance to next elements of X and Y
        add     si, 4
        add     di, 4

        loop    DO02
;   ENDFOR02

;   pop and discard two work registers, MnX, and MnY
        fstp    ST              ;<DX*DX, MnX, MnY, SSDX, SSDY, SDXDY]
        fstp    ST              ;<MnX, MnY, SSDX, SSDY, SDXDY]
        fstp    ST              ;<MnY, SSDX, SSDY, SDXDY]
        fstp    ST              ;<SSDX, SSDY, SDXDY]

;   compute correlation coefficient from sums
        fmul                    ;<SSDX*SSDY, SDXDY]
        fsqrt                   ;<sqrt(SSDX*SSDY), SDXDY]
        fdiv                    ;<SDXDY/sqrt(SSDX*SSDY)]

;   return with coefficient in ST
        pop     ds
        pop     bp
        ret     10

Correl ENDP
_TEXT ENDS
END
```

There are a few instructions for which the register assignments just described do not hold. The instructions in the first half of the program should be direct enough that further discussion is not needed. It is in the second loop, where we compute the three sums, that an explanation is in order.

The first two instructions following DO02 are

```
fstp    st(1)
fstp    st
```

which pop the stack twice. Since ST(1) has not been used yet, at least in the first iteration, we cannot pop ST(1) into ST and then pop ST—it is tagged as empty and cannot be popped. But the order we have used here puts ST into ST(1) and then pops it back into ST, so that the second pop is now legal. We then load Yi and subtract MnY, which is in ST(2)—note that the stack is temporarily renumbered by 1. The next instruction, fld with ST as the operand, pushes another copy of the difference onto the stack. This restores the register numbers to those described earlier, and leaves two copies of the difference in the top two registers. We then square one of them with fmul and add it to the SSDY.

The next block of instructions pops the stack and loads Xi, in effect replacing the square of the difference of Yi and MnY with Xi. The difference of this and MnX is computed in ST. The difference in Y in ST(1) is multiplied by the difference in X in ST before the difference in X in ST is squared. These products are then added to the totals in ST(6) and ST(4), respectively, although the instructions are not in that order.

The final computation first discards ST through ST(3), leaving SSDX at the top of the stack, SSDY below it, and SDXDY below that. The simple stack-based instruction sequence

```
fmul
fsqrt
fdiv
```

completes the calculation and leaves the result in the top of the stack as the function value to return.

## EXERCISES 17.6

1. Continue the trace given in Figure 17.8 for the next two iterations of Program 17.2.
2. Trace the execution of Program 17.3, using a format similar to Figure 17.8, when the argument is 7.0.
3. Trace the execution of Program 17.3, using a format similar to Figure 17.8, when the argument is −7.0.
▶4. Write a subprogram that computes the mean and sample standard deviation of a set of observations passed as an array of floating-point numbers. The size of the array is also a parameter. The sample standard deviation of the observations $X_i, i = 1, 2, .., n$, is computed as

$$s = \sqrt{\Sigma(X\text{mean} - X_i)^2/(n-1)}$$

▶5. Write a subprogram that computes the coefficients of a straight line fit to some experimental data using the method of least squares. The data are passed as two arrays, $(X_i, Y_i), i = 1, 2, .., n$; the number of data points is also passed. The coefficients we want to calculate are $a$ and $b$ in the equation $y = ax + b$ that represents the best line through the data. The formulas are

$$d = N * \Sigma(X_i^2) - (\Sigma X_i)^2$$
$$a = (N * \Sigma(X_i * Y_i) - \Sigma X_i * \Sigma Y_i)/d$$
$$b = (\Sigma(X_i^2) * \Sigma Y_i - \Sigma X_i * \Sigma(X_i * Y_i))/d$$

▶6. The EXP function in Program 17.3 uses a series. Another approximation formula is the rational equation

$$\text{EXP}(x) = \frac{1 + x/2 + x^2/12}{1 - x/2 + x^2/12}$$

Write an EXP function using this. Test it with arguments in the range $-10.0 \leq x \leq 10.0$, and compare your results with the system EXP function.

▶7. The EXP function in Exercise 6 is good only for $x$ near 0. To extend the range of values for which it can be used, include a table of values of EXP($x$) for $x = 1.0, 2.0, 3.0, .., 10.0$, use the table and the relation $e^{a+b} = e^a e^b$, to evaluate EXP($x$) for $0 \leq x \leq 10.0$. For example, to compute $e^{3.7}$, find $e^3$ in the table, compute $e^{0.7}$ from the rational equation, and multiply them together.

▶8. Extend the range of your function of Exercise 7 by using the relation $e^{-x} = 1/e^x$. That is, to compute $e^{-3.7}$, compute $e^{3.7}$ and take its reciprocal.

▶9. The square root function of Program 17.1 used 1.0 as the first guess. A closer first guess can be found quickly from the relationship

$$\sqrt{(A \cdot 2^m)} = \sqrt{A} \cdot 2^{m/2}$$

where $m$ is even. For example, $\sqrt{(4.5 \cdot 2^8)} = \sqrt{4.5} \cdot 2^4$. If $m$ is odd, multiply $A$ by 2 and reduce $m$ by 1 to make it even. Write a function that computes the first guess in this way. Be sure to consider the bias on the exponent. Modify Program 17.1 to use this first guess.

▶10. The sum of the infinite series

$$4 - \tfrac{4}{3} + \tfrac{4}{5} - \tfrac{4}{7} + \tfrac{4}{9} - \tfrac{4}{11} + \cdots$$

is $\pi$. The sum after adding a term is larger than $\pi$, and the sum after subtracting a term is smaller. Write an assembly-language function that computes and returns the sum of the first $N$ terms, where $N$ is the parameter passed to the function. Write a program that invokes your function with several values for $N$ and prints each approximation to $\pi$.

## KEY POINTS

- Floating-point numbers are represented as a sign, a significand, and an exponent.
- In a normalized number, the significand is a number greater than or equal to 1.0 and less than the radix. The integer exponent specifies the power of the radix by which to multiply the significand.
- Most computers use 2 as the radix for floating-point numbers.
- To convert a normalized floating-point number from base 2 to base 10, the significand must be converted and multiplied by the power of 2 indicated by the exponent.
- To convert a real number from base 10 to normalized floating-point format in base 2, the number is first converted to binary and then normalized by shifting the binary point while adjusting the exponent.

- The three components of a floating-point number—sign, significand or fraction, and exponent—are packed together into contiguous words of memory.
- The first bit of a significand does not need to be stored, since it is always 1. The number of bits used for the significand determines the precision.
- Exponents are stored in a biased form, where some constant is added to the actual exponent and the sum—which is always positive—is stored as an unsigned integer. The number of bits used for the exponent determines the range of values that can be represented.
- The largest and smallest biased exponents are reserved for numbers that cannot be normalized, 0, infinity, and NaNs. A NaN, which stands for Not a Number, is the result of an undefined operation.
- To convert a floating-point number from one length to another we must add trailing zeros to the fraction or truncate (or round) it, and adjust the bias on the exponent.
- The four types of rounding are to nearest number, toward 0 (also called truncation), toward positive infinity, and toward negative infinity. The rounding method used may be fixed by the system hardware or left to the programmer to specify.
- Conversions between floating-point and integer representation can produce overflow, underflow, or an inexact result.
- Addition and subtraction of floating-point numbers require that the number with the smaller exponent be denormalized so that it has the same exponent as the other number. Then the magnitudes can be added or subtracted; the result has the larger exponent, which may then be adjusted during renormalization.
- Multiplication of floating-point numbers is performed by multiplying the significands and adding the exponents. Division is performed by dividing the significands and subtracting the exponent of the divisor from the exponent of the dividend.
- The floating-point remainder is defined as the dividend minus the product of the quotient (rounded to the nearest integer) and the divisor. The magnitude of the remainder is less than one-half of the divisor, but its sign is not necessarily the same as the sign of either the dividend or the divisor.
- Comparison of two floating-point numbers can produce one of four results: less than, equal to, greater than, or unordered. Two floating-point numbers are unordered if either of them is a NaN.
- Overflow occurs when the result of a calculation is too large for the destination. Underflow occurs when the result is too small, but not 0; the result can be stored in denormalized form. These situations, as well as inexact results, attempts to divide by 0, use of a denormalized operand, or attempts to perform an invalid operation all signal exceptions.
- Floating-point numbers can be used to control FOR loops, but errors in representation may cause the loop control variable to take on unexpected values. Also, the loop might execute one time too many or too few.
- Testing whether two numbers are equal can lead to subtle problems. We should instead check whether two numbers are nearly equal; tests can be written to check for two numbers being nearly equal in either an absolute or a relative sense.

## PC SYSTEM SUMMARY

- The 8087 coprocessor provides floating-point capabilities for systems that use the 8086 processor.

# PC System Summary

- The 8087 supports floating-point numbers in three lengths. The short, or single precision, format uses 32 bits; the long, or double precision, format uses 64 bits; and the extended format uses 80 bits.
- The extended format is used in all computations; it is provided to protect data and results in the short and long formats from the inevitable errors that arise from representation errors.
- The precision and range of the three formats are

  | format | precision | range |
  |---|---|---|
  | short | <7 digits | $1.2 \times 10^{-38}$ to $3.4 \times 10^{38}$ |
  | long | >15 digits | $2.2 \times 10^{-308}$ to $1.8 \times 10^{308}$ |
  | extended | >19 digits | $3.4 \times 10^{-4932}$ to $1.2 \times 10^{4932}$ |

- Assemblers for the 8086 do not support the use of floating-point numbers as immediate operands.
- To declare floating-point data, the **dd** (short), **dq** (long), or **dt** (extended) directives are used. Constants are written in the operand field with a decimal point and an optional exponent.
- The 8087 has eight 10-byte data registers, which can be accessed either as a stack or individually by name.
- The 8087 has three 16-bit registers. The tag register records the state of each data register. The control register has masks for each exception, as well as fields for controlling rounding, precision, and infinity modes. The status register has exception flags, condition codes, and the busy bit, which signals whether the 8087 is busy or idle.
- The 8087 has two 32-bit registers, which point to the last instruction executed and to its operand. These pointers are used by exception handlers.
- The 8087 can convert between 2-, 4-, or 8-byte integer representation and extended-precision representation.
- The 8087 can also convert between 10-byte packed BCD representation and extended-precision representation.
- Results of tests and comparisons are recorded in the 8087 condition codes. The condition codes can be moved into the flags register; unsigned jumps can then be used to implement control structures.

Instructions presented in this chapter:

Move:

| | |
|---|---|
| `fld` | floating load |
| `fild` | floating integer load |
| `fbld` | floating packed BCD load |
| `fst` | floating store |
| `fstp` | floating store and pop |
| `fist` | floating integer store |
| `fistp` | floating integer store and pop |
| `fbstp` | floating packed BCD store and pop |
| `fxch` | floating exchange |
| `fld1` | floating load 1 |
| `fldz` | floating load 0 |

Arithmetic:
| | |
|---|---|
| `fadd` | floating add |
| `faddp` | floating add and pop |
| `fiadd` | floating integer add |
| `fsub` | floating subtract |
| `fsubp` | floating subtract and pop |
| `fisub` | floating integer subtract |
| `fsubr` | floating subtract reversed |
| `fsubrp` | floating subtract reversed and pop |
| `fisubr` | floating integer subtract reversed |
| `fmul` | floating multiply |
| `fmulp` | floating multiply and pop |
| `fimul` | floating integer multiply |
| `fdiv` | floating divide |
| `fdivp` | floating divide and pop |
| `fidiv` | floating integer divide |
| `fdivr` | floating divide reversed |
| `fdivrp` | floating divide reversed and pop |
| `fidivr` | floating integer divide reversed |
| `fprem` | floating partial remainder |
| `fscale` | floating scale |
| `fxtract` | floating extract |
| `fchs` | floating change sign |
| `fabs` | floating absolute value |
| `frdint` | floating round to integer |
| `fsqrt` | floating square root |

Compare:
| | |
|---|---|
| `fstsw` | floating store status word |
| `fcom` | floating compare |
| `fcomp` | floating compare and pop |
| `fcompp` | floating compare, pop, and pop |
| `ficom` | floating integer compare |
| `ficomp` | floating integer compare and pop |
| `ftst` | floating test |
| `fxam` | floating examine |

Control:
| | |
|---|---|
| `fwait` | wait for coprocessor |
| `wait` | wait for coprocessor |
| `finit` | floating initialize coprocessor |
| `fstenv` | floating store coprocessor environment |
| `fldenv` | floating load coprocessor environment |
| `fsave` | floating save coprocessor state |
| `frstor` | floating restore coprocessor state |
| `fstcw` | floating store control word |
| `fldcw` | floating load control word |

# Input and Output Routines  A.1

This appendix contains listings of the source files for the input and output routines provided with this text. The source, object, and library files are available on the disk included with the text. An include file, for use with Turbo Pascal programs that call assembly-language subprograms that use these routines, is also available. For details on the disk organization, see the "read me" file. Refer to Section 3.4 for information on using these routines and Section 9.3 for explanations of the DOS functions called.

The PutChar routine, in Program A1.1, displays the character passed to it in DL. No registers are modified.

**Program A1.1**

```
; Program A1.1     PutChar.ASM
; Displays a single character.
; Input parameters:
;   dl = character to display
; Output parameters: none

; DOS interrupt and function
  DosFunc     equ     21h
  DispChar    equ     02h

_TEXT SEGMENT word public 'code'
    assume  cs: _TEXT
    public  PutChar

PutChar PROC

; call DOS Display Character function
    push    ax
    mov     ah, DispChar
    int     DosFunc
    pop     ax

; return
    ret

PutChar ENDP
_TEXT ENDS
END
```

## Appendix 1  Input and Output Routines

The PutStr routine, in Program A1.2, displays a string. It expects the offset of the string in BX and the length of the string in CX. No registers are modified.

**Program A1.2**

```
; Program A1.2      PutStr.ASM
; Displays a character string, and leaves the cursor at the
;   end of the output (does not force new line).
; Input parameters:
;    cx = length of string
;    bx = offset of beginning of string
; Output parameters: none

; DOS interrupt and function
DosFunc     equ     21h
DispChar    equ     02h

_TEXT SEGMENT word public 'code'
    assume  cs: _TEXT
    public  PutStr

PutStr PROC

; save registers
    push    ax
    push    bx
    push    cx
    push    dx

; set up for calling DOS Display Character function
    mov     ah, DispChar

; FOR21 cx := length TO 1 STEP -1
    cmp     cx, 1
    jl      ENDFOR21

  DO21:
;   display character from string
    mov     dl, [bx]
    int     DosFunc

; advance to next character of string, repeat
    inc     bx
    loop    DO21
  ENDFOR21:

; restore registers and return
    pop     dx
    pop     cx
    pop     bx
    pop     ax
    ret

PutStr ENDP
_TEXT ENDS
END
```

**Appendix 1  Input and Output Routines**

The PutCrLf routine, in Program A1.3, sends the two codes for CR and LF to the output device. No arguments are needed, and no registers are changed.

## Program A1.3

```
; Program A1.3      PutCrLf.ASM
; Advances display to next line.
; Input parameters: none
; Output parameters: none

; DOS interrupt and function
  DosFunc     equ     21h
  DispChar    equ     02h

; ASCII codes
  Cr          equ     0Dh
  Lf          equ     0Ah

_TEXT SEGMENT word public 'code'
    assume  cs: _TEXT
    public  PutCrLf

PutCrLf PROC

; save registers
    push    ax
    push    dx

; call DOS Display Character function with <CR>, <LF>
    mov     ah, DispChar
    mov     dl, Cr
    int     DosFunc
    mov     dl, Lf
    int     DosFunc

; restore registers and return
    pop     dx
    pop     ax
    ret
PutCrLf ENDP
_TEXT ENDS
END
```

The PutDec routine, in Program A1.4, displays the signed integer in AX as a string of six characters. No registers are changed.

## Program A1.4

```
; Program A1.4      PutDec.ASM
; Displays a 16-bit integer in decimal, using a field of
;   six characters: sign and five digits, with leading
;   zeros replaced by blanks and the sign (if negative)
;   immediately before the most significant digit.
```

## A.4    Appendix 1    Input and Output Routines

**Program A1.4 (continued)**

```
        ; Input parameters:
        ;   ax = integer to display
        ; Output parameters: none.

        ; DOS interrupt and function
          DosFunc     equ      21h
          DispChar    equ      02h

        ; ASCII codes
          NullSpace   equ      0020h
          NullZero    equ      0030h

        _TEXT SEGMENT word public 'code'
              assume  cs: _TEXT
              public  PutDec

PutDec PROC

        ; save registers
              push    ax
              push    bx
              push    cx
              push    dx

        ; Put sign character in ch, and magnitude in ax.
        ; IF41 argument < 0
              cmp     ax, 0
              jnl     ELSE41

        ; THEN41
        ;   ax := magnitude of argument
              mov     bx, -1
              imul    bx

        ;   sign (in ch) := "-"
              mov     ch, "-"
              jmp     ENDIF41

          ELSE41:
        ;   sign (in ch) := " "
              mov     ch, " "
          ENDIF41:

        ; Convert digits of ax into characters, counting them. On each
        ; iteration, divide the (remaining) part of the magnitude by ten:
        ;    the remainder is the next digit to put into the string,
        ;    the quotient is the part of the magnitude left to convert.

        ; counter (in cl) := 0
              sub     cl, cl

        ; divisor (in bx) := 10
              mov     bx, 10
```

# Program A1.4 (continued)

```
        WHILE42: ;magnitude (in ax) > 0
            cmp     ax, 0
            jna     ENDWHL42

;   DO42:
;       divide remaining magnitude by ten
            sub     dx, dx          ;unsigned word to doubleword
            div     bx

;       convert remainder to character and push it onto stack
            or      dx, NullZero
            push    dx

;       increment counter and repeat
            inc     cl
            jmp     WHILE42
        ENDWHL42:

; If the argument was zero, the preceding loop terminates
; without pushing any characters; so push "0" in that case.

; IF43 no digits in string
            cmp     cl, 0
            jne     ENDIF43

; THEN43
;       push "0" and increment counter
            mov     dx, NullZero
            push    dx
            inc     cl
        ENDIF43:

; push sign and increment counter
            mov     bl, ch
            push    bx
            inc     cl

; Print (6-cl) leading spaces.
; setup DOS function number, dx := " "
            mov     ah, DispChar
            mov     dx, NullSpace

; FOR44 ch := cl+1 TO 6
            mov     ch, cl
            inc     ch

        TEST44:
            cmp     ch, 6
            jg      ENDFOR44

; DO44:
;   print " "
            int     DosFunc
```

## Program A1.4 (continued)

```
            inc     ch
            jmp     TEST44
    ENDFOR44:

; Display the string representation of the argument.
; FOR45 cx := cl DOWNTO 1
        sub     ch, ch

    DO45:
;       pop character off stack and print it
            pop     dx
            int     DosFunc

;       repeat
            loop    DO45
    ENDFOR45:

; restore registers and return
        pop     dx
        pop     cx
        pop     bx
        pop     ax
        ret

PutDec ENDP
_TEXT ENDS
END
```

The GetChar routine, in Program A1.5, accepts one character from the keyboard. If the character is an ASCII code, it returns 0 in AH and the ASCII code in AL; otherwise, it returns 1 in AH and an extended code in AL. No other registers are modified.

## Program A1.5

```
; Program A1.5       GetChar.ASM
; Accepts one character from the keyboard.
; Input parameters: none
; Output parameters:
;   al = character or extended code
;   ah = 0 if al is ASCII, 1 if al is extended character

; DOS interrupt and functions
    DosFunc     equ     21h
    ReadKbdEcho equ     01h
    DispChar    equ     02h
    ReadKbd     equ     08h

; ASCII codes
    Cr          equ     0Dh
    Lf          equ     0Ah
```

# Appendix 1  Input and Output Routines

## Program A1.5 (continued)

```
        _TEXT SEGMENT word public 'code'
            assume   cs: _TEXT
            public   GetChar

GetChar PROC

; call DOS Read Keyboard and Echo function to get a character
            mov      ah, ReadKbdEcho
            int      DosFunc

; IF51 an extended code was entered
            cmp      al, 0
            jne      ELSE51

; THEN51
;    call DOS Read Keyboard (no echo) function to get code byte
            mov      ah, ReadKbd
            int      DosFunc

;    indicate extended character
            mov      ah, 1
            jmp      ENDIF51

    ELSE51:
;    indicate ASCII character
            mov      ah, 0
    ENDIF51:

; IF52 character is <Enter>
            cmp      al, Cr
            jne      ENDIF52

; THEN52
;    send <lf> to display, using DOS Display Character function
            push     dx
            mov      ah, DispChar
            mov      dl, Lf
            int      DosFunc
            pop      dx

;    return <cr> in al register
            mov      ah, 0
            mov      al, Cr
    ENDIF52:

; return
            ret

GetChar ENDP
_TEXT ENDS
END
```

**A.8**   Appendix 1   Input and Output Routines

The GetDec routine, in Program A1.6, accepts characters from the keyboard, interprets them as a signed integer, and returns the integer in AX. No other registers are modified. If any errors are detected, the program is terminated with an error message. GetDec calls GetChar and local routines ChkDigit and IOError. IOError also calls PutStr and PutCrLf to display the error message.

## Program A1.6

```
; Program A1.6       GetDec.ASM
; Reads a signed 16-bit integer from keyboard.
;   In the event of an error in input, an error message
;   is printed and control is returned to DOS.
; Input parameters: none.
; Output parameters:
;   ax = signed integer read from keyboard

; ASCII codes
    NullSpace   equ     0020h
    NullMinus   equ     002Dh
    Cr          equ     0Dh
    Space       equ     20h

_TEXT SEGMENT word public 'code'
        assume  cs: _TEXT
        extrn   GetChar: PROC, PutStr: PROC, PutCrLF: PROC
        public  GetDec

GetDec PROC

; save registers
        push    bx
        push    cx
        push    dx

; initialize intermediate value (in dx) to zero.
        sub     dx, dx

; skip over any leading spaces in input
    REPEAT61:
; read character from input
        call    GetChar

; TEST61
        cmp     ax, NullSpace
        je      REPEAT61
; UNTIL61 input <> " "

; save -1 or +1 for sign in cl
; IF62 input = "-"
        cmp     ax, NullMinus
        jne     ELSE62

; THEN62:
;   sign (in cl) := -1
        mov     cl, -1
```

**Appendix 1  Input and Output Routines**                                A.9

**Program A1.6 (continued)**

```
        ;       read next character
                call    GetChar
                jmp     ENDIF62

        ELSE62:
        ;   sign (in cl) := +1
                mov     cl, 1
        ENDIF62:

        ; Process the digits in the input. For each digit read,
        ; shift the intermediate value to the left and add new digit.

            WHILE63: ;input is digit
                call    ChkDigit
                jc      ENDWHL63

        ; DO63:
        ;   value (in dx) := 10 * value + (Ord(digit) - Ord("0"))
                mov     bx, dx          ;       value
                shl     dx, 1           ;   2*value
                shl     dx, 1           ;   4*value
                add     dx, bx          ;   5*value
                shl     dx, 1           ;  10*value
                sub     al, "0"         ;            ord(digit)-ord("0")
                add     dx, ax          ;  10*value+ord(digit)-ord("0")

        ;       read next character and repeat
                call    GetChar
                jmp     WHILE63
            ENDWHL63:

        ; Check whether loop terminated with illegal input.

        ; IF64 character is not " " or <Enter>
                cmp     ah, 0           ; any extended code is error
                jne     THEN64
                cmp     al, Space       ; " " is okay
                je      ENDIF64
                cmp     al, Cr
                je      ENDIF64         ; <Enter> is okay

            THEN64:
        ;   print error message and terminate
                call    IOError

            ENDIF64:

        ; ax := result of conversion
                mov     ax, dx

        ; IF65 "-" read earlier
                cmp     cl, 0
                jnl     ENDIF65
```

**Program A1.6 (continued)**

```
; THEN65
;    complement the result
        neg     ax
  ENDIF65:

; restore registers and return
        pop     dx
        pop     cx
        pop     bx
        ret

GetDec ENDP

;;;;;;;;;;;;;;;;;;;;;; Function ChkDigit ;;;;;;;;;;;;;;;;;;;;;

; Checks whether character in ax is a digit.
; Input parameters:
;    ax = character or extended code
; Output parameters:
;    CF = 0 if ax is digit, 1 if ax is not digit

        public  ChkDigit

ChkDigit PROC

; IF71 input character is not a digit
        cmp     ah, 0       ; any extended character is an error
        jne     THEN71
        cmp     al, "9"     ; any character after "9" is an error
        jg      THEN71
        cmp     al, "0"     ; a character after "0" (before "9")
        jge     ELSE71      ;   is okay

  THEN71:
;    set carry flag
        stc
        jmp     ENDIF71

  ELSE71:
;    clear carry flag
        clc
  ENDIF71:

; return
        ret

ChkDigit ENDP
_TEXT ENDS

;;;;;;;;;;;;;;;;;;;;;; Function IOError ;;;;;;;;;;;;;;;;;;;;;;

; Display an error message and terminate to DOS
; Input parameters: none
; Output parameters: -1 returned as DOS return code
```

**Appendix 1   Input and Output Routines**

**Program A1.6 (continued)**

```
        ; DOS interrupt, function, and parameters
        DosFunc     equ     21h
        ExitToDos   equ     4Ch
        ErrorCode   equ     0FFh

_DATA SEGMENT word public 'data'
        ErrorMsg    db      "ERROR - invalid input character in GetDec."
        ErrorLen    dw      $ - ErrorMsg
_DATA ENDS

_TEXT SEGMENT
        assume  cs: _TEXT
        public  IOError

IOError PROC

        ; set up ds register to point to _DATA
        mov     ax, seg _DATA
        mov     ds, ax
        assume  ds: _DATA

        ; print ("ERROR - invalid input character in GetDec.")
        call    PutCrLf
        mov     cx, ErrorLen
        mov     bx, offset ErrorMsg
        call    PutStr
        call    PutCrLf

        ; terminate with DOS error code
        mov     ah, ExitToDos
        mov     al, ErrorCode
        int     DosFunc

IOError ENDP
_TEXT ENDS
END
```

# A.2 Extended ASCII Character Set

| Ordinal Value | | | | Ordinal Value | | | |
|---|---|---|---|---|---|---|---|
| Decimal | Binary | Hexadecimal | Character | Decimal | Binary | Hexadecimal | Character |
| 0 | 0000 0000 | 00 | NUL | 32 | 0010 0000 | 20 | space |
| 1 | 0000 0001 | 01 | SOH | 33 | 0010 0001 | 21 | ! |
| 2 | 0000 0010 | 02 | STX | 34 | 0010 0010 | 22 | " |
| 3 | 0000 0011 | 03 | ETX | 35 | 0010 0011 | 23 | # |
| 4 | 0000 0100 | 04 | EOT | 36 | 0010 0100 | 24 | $ |
| 5 | 0000 0101 | 05 | ENQ | 37 | 0010 0101 | 25 | % |
| 6 | 0000 0110 | 06 | ACK | 38 | 0010 0110 | 26 | & |
| 7 | 0000 0111 | 07 | BEL | 39 | 0010 0111 | 27 | ' |
| 8 | 0000 1000 | 08 | BS | 40 | 0010 1000 | 28 | ( |
| 9 | 0000 1001 | 09 | HT | 41 | 0010 1001 | 29 | ) |
| 10 | 0000 1010 | 0A | LF | 42 | 0010 1010 | 2A | * |
| 11 | 0000 1011 | 0B | VT | 43 | 0010 1011 | 2B | + |
| 12 | 0000 1100 | 0C | FF | 44 | 0010 1100 | 2C | , |
| 13 | 0000 1101 | 0D | CR | 45 | 0010 1101 | 2D | - |
| 14 | 0000 1110 | 0E | SO | 46 | 0010 1110 | 2E | . |
| 15 | 0000 1111 | 0F | SI | 47 | 0010 1111 | 2F | / |
| 16 | 0001 0000 | 10 | DLE | 48 | 0011 0000 | 30 | 0 |
| 17 | 0001 0001 | 11 | DC1 | 49 | 0011 0001 | 31 | 1 |
| 18 | 0001 0010 | 12 | DC2 | 50 | 0011 0010 | 32 | 2 |
| 19 | 0001 0011 | 13 | DC3 | 51 | 0011 0011 | 33 | 3 |
| 20 | 0001 0100 | 14 | DC4 | 52 | 0011 0100 | 34 | 4 |
| 21 | 0001 0101 | 15 | NAK | 53 | 0011 0101 | 35 | 5 |
| 22 | 0001 0110 | 16 | SYN | 54 | 0011 0110 | 36 | 6 |
| 23 | 0001 0111 | 17 | ETB | 55 | 0011 0111 | 37 | 7 |
| 24 | 0001 1000 | 18 | CAN | 56 | 0011 1000 | 38 | 8 |
| 25 | 0001 1001 | 19 | EM | 57 | 0011 1001 | 39 | 9 |
| 26 | 0001 1010 | 1A | SUB | 58 | 0011 1010 | 3A | : |
| 27 | 0001 1011 | 1B | ESC | 59 | 0011 1011 | 3B | ; |
| 28 | 0001 1100 | 1C | FS | 60 | 0011 1100 | 3C | < |
| 29 | 0001 1101 | 1D | GS | 61 | 0011 1101 | 3D | = |
| 30 | 0001 1110 | 1E | RS | 62 | 0011 1110 | 3E | > |
| 31 | 0001 1111 | 1F | US | 63 | 0011 1111 | 3F | ? |

Note: The two- and three-letter entries represent control codes. For example, VT is the Vertical Tab code for a printer.

## Appendix 2  Extended ASCII Character Set

| Ordinal Value | | | | Ordinal Value | | | |
|---|---|---|---|---|---|---|---|
| Decimal | Binary | Hexadecimal | Character | Decimal | Binary | Hexadecimal | Character |
| 64 | 0100 0000 | 40 | @ | 112 | 0111 0000 | 70 | p |
| 65 | 0100 0001 | 41 | A | 113 | 0111 0001 | 71 | q |
| 66 | 0100 0010 | 42 | B | 114 | 0111 0010 | 72 | r |
| 67 | 0100 0011 | 43 | C | 115 | 0111 0011 | 73 | s |
| 68 | 0100 0100 | 44 | D | 116 | 0111 0100 | 74 | t |
| 69 | 0100 0101 | 45 | E | 117 | 0111 0101 | 75 | u |
| 70 | 0100 0110 | 46 | F | 118 | 0111 0110 | 76 | v |
| 71 | 0100 0111 | 47 | G | 119 | 0111 0111 | 77 | w |
| 72 | 0100 1000 | 48 | H | 120 | 0111 1000 | 78 | x |
| 73 | 0100 1001 | 49 | I | 121 | 0111 1001 | 79 | y |
| 74 | 0100 1010 | 4A | J | 122 | 0111 1010 | 7A | z |
| 75 | 0100 1011 | 4B | K | 123 | 0111 1011 | 7B | { |
| 76 | 0100 1100 | 4C | L | 124 | 0111 1100 | 7C | | |
| 77 | 0100 1101 | 4D | M | 125 | 0111 1101 | 7D | } |
| 78 | 0100 1110 | 4E | N | 126 | 0111 1110 | 7E | ~ |
| 79 | 0100 1111 | 4F | O | 127 | 0111 1111 | 7F | DEL |
| 80 | 0101 0000 | 50 | P | 128 | 1000 0000 | 80 | Ç |
| 81 | 0101 0001 | 51 | Q | 129 | 1000 0001 | 81 | ü |
| 82 | 0101 0010 | 52 | R | 130 | 1000 0010 | 82 | é |
| 83 | 0101 0011 | 53 | S | 131 | 1000 0011 | 83 | â |
| 84 | 0101 0100 | 54 | T | 132 | 1000 0100 | 84 | ä |
| 85 | 0101 0101 | 55 | U | 133 | 1000 0101 | 85 | à |
| 86 | 0101 0110 | 56 | V | 134 | 1000 0110 | 86 | å |
| 87 | 0101 0111 | 57 | W | 135 | 1000 0111 | 87 | ç |
| 88 | 0101 1000 | 58 | X | 136 | 1000 1000 | 88 | ê |
| 89 | 0101 1001 | 59 | Y | 137 | 1000 1001 | 89 | ë |
| 90 | 0101 1010 | 5A | Z | 138 | 1000 1010 | 8A | è |
| 91 | 0101 1011 | 5B | [ | 139 | 1000 1011 | 8B | ï |
| 92 | 0101 1100 | 5C | \ | 140 | 1000 1100 | 8C | î |
| 93 | 0101 1101 | 5D | ] | 141 | 1000 1101 | 8D | ì |
| 94 | 0101 1110 | 5E | ^ | 142 | 1000 1110 | 8E | Ä |
| 95 | 0101 1111 | 5F | _ | 143 | 1000 1111 | 8F | Å |
| 96 | 0110 0000 | 60 | ` | 144 | 1001 0000 | 90 | É |
| 97 | 0110 0001 | 61 | a | 145 | 1001 0001 | 91 | æ |
| 98 | 0110 0010 | 62 | b | 146 | 1001 0010 | 92 | Æ |
| 99 | 0110 0011 | 63 | c | 147 | 1001 0011 | 93 | ô |
| 100 | 0110 0100 | 64 | d | 148 | 1001 0100 | 94 | ö |
| 101 | 0110 0101 | 65 | e | 149 | 1001 0101 | 95 | ò |
| 102 | 0110 0110 | 66 | f | 150 | 1001 0110 | 96 | û |
| 103 | 0110 0111 | 67 | g | 151 | 1001 0111 | 97 | ù |
| 104 | 0110 1000 | 68 | h | 152 | 1001 1000 | 98 | ÿ |
| 105 | 0110 1001 | 69 | i | 153 | 1001 1001 | 99 | Ö |
| 106 | 0110 1010 | 6A | j | 154 | 1001 1010 | 9A | Ü |
| 107 | 0110 1011 | 6B | k | 155 | 1001 1011 | 9B | ¢ |
| 108 | 0110 1100 | 6C | l | 156 | 1001 1100 | 9C | £ |
| 109 | 0110 1101 | 6D | m | 157 | 1001 1101 | 9D | ¥ |
| 110 | 0110 1110 | 6E | n | 158 | 1001 1110 | 9E | ₧ |
| 111 | 0110 1111 | 6F | o | 159 | 1001 1111 | 9F | ƒ |

# A.14 Appendix 2 Extended ASCII Character Set

| Ordinal Value | | | | Ordinal Value | | | |
|---|---|---|---|---|---|---|---|
| Decimal | Binary | Hexadecimal | Character | Decimal | Binary | Hexadecimal | Character |
| 160 | 1010 0000 | A0 | á | 208 | 1101 0000 | D0 | ⊥ |
| 161 | 1010 0001 | A1 | í | 209 | 1101 0001 | D1 | ╤ |
| 162 | 1010 0010 | A2 | ó | 210 | 1101 0010 | D2 | ╥ |
| 163 | 1010 0011 | A3 | ú | 211 | 1101 0011 | D3 | ╙ |
| 164 | 1010 0100 | A4 | ñ | 212 | 1101 0100 | D4 | ╘ |
| 165 | 1010 0101 | A5 | Ñ | 213 | 1101 0101 | D5 | ╒ |
| 166 | 1010 0110 | A6 | ª | 214 | 1101 0110 | D6 | ╓ |
| 167 | 1010 0111 | A7 | º | 215 | 1101 0111 | D7 | ╫ |
| 168 | 1010 1000 | A8 | ¿ | 216 | 1101 1000 | D8 | ╪ |
| 169 | 1010 1001 | A9 | ⌐ | 217 | 1101 1001 | D9 | ┘ |
| 170 | 1010 1010 | AA | ¬ | 218 | 1101 1010 | DA | ┌ |
| 171 | 1010 1011 | AB | ½ | 219 | 1101 1011 | DB | ■ |
| 172 | 1010 1100 | AC | ¼ | 220 | 1101 1100 | DC | ▬ |
| 173 | 1010 1101 | AD | ¡ | 221 | 1101 1101 | DD | ▌ |
| 174 | 1010 1110 | AE | « | 222 | 1101 1110 | DE | ▐ |
| 175 | 1010 1111 | AF | » | 223 | 1101 1111 | DF | ▀ |
| 176 | 1011 0000 | B0 | ░ | 224 | 1110 0000 | E0 | $\alpha$ |
| 177 | 1011 0001 | B1 | ▒ | 225 | 1110 0001 | E1 | $\beta$ |
| 178 | 1011 0010 | B2 | ▓ | 226 | 1110 0010 | E2 | $\Gamma$ |
| 179 | 1011 0011 | B3 | │ | 227 | 1110 0011 | E3 | $\pi$ |
| 180 | 1011 0100 | B4 | ┤ | 228 | 1110 0100 | E4 | $\Sigma$ |
| 181 | 1011 0101 | B5 | ╡ | 229 | 1110 0101 | E5 | $\sigma$ |
| 182 | 1011 0110 | B6 | ╢ | 230 | 1110 0110 | E6 | $\mu$ |
| 183 | 1011 0111 | B7 | ╖ | 231 | 1110 0111 | E7 | $\tau$ |
| 184 | 1011 1000 | B8 | ╕ | 232 | 1110 1000 | E8 | $\Phi$ |
| 185 | 1011 1001 | B9 | ╣ | 233 | 1110 1001 | E9 | $\Theta$ |
| 186 | 1011 1010 | BA | ║ | 234 | 1110 1010 | EA | $\Omega$ |
| 187 | 1011 1011 | BB | ╗ | 235 | 1110 1011 | EB | $\delta$ |
| 188 | 1011 1100 | BC | ╝ | 236 | 1110 1100 | EC | $\infty$ |
| 189 | 1011 1101 | BD | ╜ | 237 | 1110 1101 | ED | $\varphi$ |
| 190 | 1011 1110 | BE | ╛ | 238 | 1110 1110 | EE | $\epsilon$ |
| 191 | 1011 1111 | BF | ┐ | 239 | 1110 1111 | EF | $\cap$ |
| 192 | 1100 0000 | C0 | └ | 240 | 1111 0000 | F0 | $\equiv$ |
| 193 | 1100 0001 | C1 | ┴ | 241 | 1111 0001 | F1 | $\pm$ |
| 194 | 1100 0010 | C2 | ┬ | 242 | 1111 0010 | F2 | $\geq$ |
| 195 | 1100 0011 | C3 | ├ | 243 | 1111 0011 | F3 | $\leq$ |
| 196 | 1100 0100 | C4 | ─ | 244 | 1111 0100 | F4 | ⌠ |
| 197 | 1100 0101 | C5 | ┼ | 245 | 1111 0101 | F5 | ⌡ |
| 198 | 1100 0110 | C6 | ╞ | 246 | 1111 0110 | F6 | $\div$ |
| 199 | 1100 0111 | C7 | ╟ | 247 | 1111 0111 | F7 | $\approx$ |
| 200 | 1100 1000 | C8 | ╚ | 248 | 1111 1000 | F8 | ° |
| 201 | 1100 1001 | C9 | ╔ | 249 | 1111 1001 | F9 | • |
| 202 | 1100 1010 | CA | ╩ | 250 | 1111 1010 | FA | · |
| 203 | 1100 1011 | CB | ╦ | 251 | 1111 1011 | FB | $\sqrt{\phantom{x}}$ |
| 204 | 1100 1100 | CC | ╠ | 252 | 1111 1100 | FC | $^n$ |
| 205 | 1100 1101 | CD | CD | ═ | 253 | 1111 1101 | FD | $^2$ |
| 206 | 1100 1110 | CE | ╬ | 254 | 1111 1110 | FE | ■ |
| 207 | 1100 1111 | CF | ╧ | 255 | 1111 1111 | FF | |

# A.3 Instructions

The tables in this appendix summarize all instructions presented in this text (but not all 80x86 and 80x87 instructions).

Table A3.1 presents the 8086 instructions in alphabetical order. For each instruction, the following is included:

- Required syntax
- Description
- Operation, as assignments
- Allowed operand forms:
    X = Allowed
    A = Allowed; instruction uses a special format for accumulator (AH or AX)
- Effect on flags:
    0 = Cleared
    1 = Set
    X = Modified for result of instruction
    − = Unchanged
    U = Undefined

The abbreviations used for possible operand forms in Table A3.1, both singly and in pairs, are

   R = register
   M = memory
   I = immediate
   L = label
   S = segment register

# Table A3.1  8086 Instructions

| Instruction | Description | Operation | R | M | I | L | S | R,R | R,M | R,I | M,R | M,I | O | D | I | T | S | Z | A | P | C |
|---|---|---|---|---|---|---|---|---|---|---|---|---|---|---|---|---|---|---|---|---|
| AAA | ASCII Adjust for Addition | if AL > 9 then AL := AL − 10, aH := AH + 1, CF := 1, AF := 1 else CF := 0, AF := 0 | | | | | | | | | | | U | – | – | – | U | U | X | U | X |
| AAD | ASCII Adjust for Division | AX := 10 * AH + AL | | | | | | | | | | | U | – | – | – | X | X | U | X | U |
| AAM | ASCII Adjust for Multiplication | AL := less significant digit of AL; & AH := more significant digit of AL | | | | | | | | | | | U | – | – | – | X | X | U | X | U |
| AAS | ASCII Adjust for Subtraction | if AL < 0 then AL := AL + 10, AH := AH − 1, CF := 1, AF := 1 else CF := 0, AF := 0 | | | | | | | | | | | U | – | – | – | U | U | X | U | X |
| ADC dest,source | ADd integers with Carry | dest := dest + source + CF | | | | | | X | X | A | X | X | X | – | – | – | X | X | X | X | X |
| ADD dest,source | ADD integers | dest := dest + source | | | | | | X | X | A | X | X | X | – | – | – | X | X | X | X | X |
| AND dest,source | logical AND | dest := dest AND source | | | | | | X | X | A | X | X | 0 | – | – | – | X | X | U | X | 0 |
| CALL dest | CALL subprogram | (1) SP := SP − 2; (2) SS:SP := IP; (3) IP := dest | X | X | X | | | | | | | | – | – | – | – | – | – | – | – | – |
| CBW | Convert Byte to Word | ax := al, sign extended | | | | | | | | | | | – | – | – | – | – | – | – | – | – |
| CLC | CLear Carry flag | CF := 0 | | | | | | | | | | | – | – | – | – | – | – | – | – | 0 |
| CLD | CLear Direction flag | DF := 0 | | | | | | | | | | | – | 0 | – | – | – | – | – | – | – |
| CLI | CLear Interrupt flag | IE := 0 | | | | | | | | | | | – | – | 0 | – | – | – | – | – | – |
| CMC | CoMplement Carry flag | CF := 1 − CF | | | | | | | | | | | – | – | – | – | – | – | – | – | X |
| CMP dest,source | CoMPare two values | compute (dest−source), set/clear flags | | | | | | X | X | A | X | | X | – | – | – | X | X | X | X | X |
| CMPSB[a] | CoMPare String Byte | (1) compare DS:[SI] to ES:[DI]; (2) if DF = 0 then SI: = SI + 1, DI: = DI + 1 else SI := SI − 1, DI := DI − 1 | | | | | | | | | | | X | – | – | – | X | X | X | X | X |
| CMPSW[a] | CoMPare String Word | (1) compare DS:[SI] to ES:[DI]; (2) if DF = 0 then SI: = SI + 2, DI: = DI + 2 else SI := SI − 2, DI := DI − 2 | | | | | | | | | | | X | – | – | – | X | X | X | X | X |
| CWD | Convert Word to Double | dx:ax := ax, sign extended | | | | | | | | | | | – | – | – | – | – | – | – | – | – |
| DAA | Decimal Adjust for Addition | adjust AL to two packed decimal digits and set/clear CF following ADD | | | | | | | | | | | U | – | – | – | X | X | X | X | X |
| DAS | Decimal Adjust for Subtraction | adjust AL to two packed decimal digits and set/clear CF following SUB | | | | | | | | | | | U | – | – | – | X | X | X | X | X |
| DEC dest | DECrement integer | dest := dest − 1 | X | X | | | | | | | | | X | – | – | – | X | X | X | X | – |
| DIV source | DIVide unsigned | al : = quotient of ax ÷ source & ah := remainder of ax ÷ source or ax := quotient of dx:ax ÷ source & dx := remainder of dx:ax ÷ source | X | X | | | | | | | | | U | – | – | – | U | U | U | U | – |
| IDIV source | Integer DIVide signed | al := quotient of ax ÷ source & ah := remainder of ax ÷ source or ax := quotient of dx:ax ÷ source & dx := remainder of dx:ax ÷ source | X | X | | | | | | | | | U | – | – | – | U | U | U | U | U |

Notes:

a. String instructions also allow a memory operand that specifies only the size of the operands; a segment override for the source string can also be specified with the memory operand.

**Table A3.1** *(continued)*

| Instruction | Description | Operation | Operand Form | | | | | | | | | | Flags | | | | | | | | |
|---|---|---|---|---|---|---|---|---|---|---|---|---|---|---|---|---|---|---|---|---|---|---|
| | | | R | M | I | L | S | R,R | R,M | R,I | M,R | M,I | O | D | I | T | S | Z | A | P | C |
| IMUL source | Integer MULtiply signed | ax := al * source or dx:ax := ax * source | X | X | . | . | . | . | . | . | . | . | X | - | - | - | U | U | U | U | X |
| IN acc,port[b] | INput from port | acc := port | . | . | . | . | . | . | . | . | . | . | - | - | - | - | - | - | - | - | - |
| INC dest | INCrement integer | dest := dest + 1 | X | X | . | . | . | . | . | . | . | . | X | - | - | - | X | X | X | X | - |
| INT number | INTerrupt | invoke interrupt handler specified by number | . | . | X | . | . | . | . | . | . | . | - | - | 0 | 0 | - | - | - | - | - |
| IRET | Interrupt RETurn | (1) pop IP (2) pop CS (3) pop flags | . | . | . | . | . | . | . | . | . | . | X | X | X | X | X | X | X | X | X |
| JA dest | Jump if Above | if CF = 0 and ZF = 0 then IP := dest | . | . | . | X | . | . | . | . | . | . | - | - | - | - | - | - | - | - | - |
| JAE dest | Jump if Above or Equal | if CF = 0 then IP := dest | . | . | . | X | . | . | . | . | . | . | - | - | - | - | - | - | - | - | - |
| JB dest | Jump if Below | if CF = 1 then IP := dest | . | . | . | X | . | . | . | . | . | . | - | - | - | - | - | - | - | - | - |
| JBE dest | Jump if Below or Equal | if CF = 1 or ZF = 1 then IP := dest | . | . | . | X | . | . | . | . | . | . | - | - | - | - | - | - | - | - | - |
| JC dest | Jump if Carry | if CF = 1 then IP := dest | . | . | . | X | . | . | . | . | . | . | - | - | - | - | - | - | - | - | - |
| JCXZ dest | Jump if CX is Zero | if CX = 0 then IP := dest | . | . | . | X | . | . | . | . | . | . | - | - | - | - | - | - | - | - | - |
| JE dest | Jump if Equal | if ZF = 1 then IP := dest | . | . | . | X | . | . | . | . | . | . | - | - | - | - | - | - | - | - | - |
| JG dest | Jump if Greater | if ZF = 0 or SF = OF then IP := dest | . | . | . | X | . | . | . | . | . | . | - | - | - | - | - | - | - | - | - |
| JGE dest | Jump if Greater or Equal | if SF = OF then IP := dest | . | . | . | X | . | . | . | . | . | . | - | - | - | - | - | - | - | - | - |
| JL dest | Jump if Less | if SF <> OF then IP := dest | . | . | . | X | . | . | . | . | . | . | - | - | - | - | - | - | - | - | - |
| JLE dest | Jump if Less or Equal | if ZF = 1 or SF <> OF then IP := dest | . | . | . | X | . | . | . | . | . | . | - | - | - | - | - | - | - | - | - |
| JMP dest | JuMP unconditionally | IP := dest | X | X | . | X | . | . | . | . | . | . | - | - | - | - | - | - | - | - | - |
| JNA dest | Jump if Not Above | if CF = 1 or ZF = 1 then IP := dest | . | . | . | X | . | . | . | . | . | . | - | - | - | - | - | - | - | - | - |
| JNAE dest | Jump if Not Above or Equal | if CF = 1 then IP := dest | . | . | . | X | . | . | . | . | . | . | - | - | - | - | - | - | - | - | - |
| JNB dest | Jump if Not Below | if CF = 0 then IP := dest | . | . | . | X | . | . | . | . | . | . | - | - | - | - | - | - | - | - | - |
| JNBE dest | Jump If Not Below or Equal | If CF = 0 and ZF = 0 then IP := dest | . | . | . | X | . | . | . | . | . | . | - | - | - | - | - | - | - | - | - |
| JNC dest | Jump if Not Carry | If CF = 0 then IP := dest | . | . | . | X | . | . | . | . | . | . | - | - | - | - | - | - | - | - | - |
| JNE dest | Jump if Not Equal | if ZF = 0 then IP := dest | . | . | . | X | . | . | . | . | . | . | - | - | - | - | - | - | - | - | - |
| JNG dest | Jump if Not Greater | if ZF = 1 or SF <> OF then IP := dest | . | . | . | X | . | . | . | . | . | . | - | - | - | - | - | - | - | - | - |
| JNGE dest | Jump if Not Greater or Equal | if SF <> OF then IP := dest | . | . | . | X | . | . | . | . | . | . | - | - | - | - | - | - | - | - | - |
| JNL dest | Jump if Not Less | if SF = OF then IP := dest | . | . | . | X | . | . | . | . | . | . | - | - | - | - | - | - | - | - | - |
| JNLE dest | Jump if Not Less or Equal | if ZF = 0 or SF = OF then IP := dest | . | . | . | X | . | . | . | . | . | . | - | - | - | - | - | - | - | - | - |
| JNO dest | Jump if No Overflow | if OF = 0 then IP := dest | . | . | . | X | . | . | . | . | . | . | - | - | - | - | - | - | - | - | - |
| JNP dest | Jumple if No Parity | if PF = 0 then IP := dest | . | . | . | X | . | . | . | . | . | . | - | - | - | - | - | - | - | - | - |
| JNS dest | Jump if Not Sign | if SF = 0 then IP := dest | . | . | . | X | . | . | . | . | . | . | - | - | - | - | - | - | - | - | - |
| JNZ dest | Jump if Not Zero | If ZF = 0 then IP := dest | . | . | . | X | . | . | . | . | . | . | - | - | - | - | - | - | - | - | - |
| JO dest | Jump if Overflow | If OF = 1 then IP := dest | . | . | . | X | . | . | . | . | . | . | - | - | - | - | - | - | - | - | - |
| JP dest | Jump if Parity | if PF = 1 then IP := dest | . | . | . | X | . | . | . | . | . | . | - | - | - | - | - | - | - | - | - |
| JPE dest | Jump if Parity Even | if PF = 1 then IP := dest | . | . | . | X | . | . | . | . | . | . | - | - | - | - | - | - | - | - | - |
| JPO dest | Jump if Parity Odd | if PF = 0 then IP := dest | . | . | . | X | . | . | . | . | . | . | - | - | - | - | - | - | - | - | - |
| JS dest | Jump if Sign | if SF = 1 then IP := dest | . | . | . | X | . | . | . | . | . | . | - | - | - | - | - | - | - | - | - |

Notes:
b. IN allows two operand forms:
accum, immed    accum, DX

**Table A3.1** (continued)

| Instruction | Description | Operation | Operand Form ||||||||| Flags |||||||||
|---|---|---|---|---|---|---|---|---|---|---|---|---|---|---|---|---|---|---|
| | | | R | M | I | L | S | R,R | R,M | R,I | M,R | M,I | O | D | I | T | S | Z | A | P | C |
| JZ dest | Jump if Zero | if ZF = 1 then IP := dest | . | . | . | X | . | . | . | . | . | . | – | – | – | – | – | – | – | – | – |
| LAHF | Load AH from Flags | AH := bits 0..7 of flags | . | . | . | . | . | . | . | . | . | . | – | – | – | – | – | – | – | – | – |
| LDS dest, source | Load far pointer into DS | DS := segment of source; & dest := offset of source | . | . | . | . | . | . | X | . | . | . | – | – | – | – | – | – | – | – | – |
| LES dest source | Load far pointer into ES | ES := segment of source: & dest := offset of source | . | . | . | . | . | . | X | . | . | . | – | – | – | – | – | – | – | – | – |
| LODSB[a] | LOaD String Byte | (1) AL := DS:[SI]; (2) if DF = 0 then SI := SI + a else SI := SI − 1 | . | . | . | . | . | . | . | . | . | . | – | – | – | – | – | – | – | – | – |
| LODSW[a] | LOaD String Word | (1) AX := DS:[SI]; (2) if DF = 0 then SI := SI + 2 else SI := SI − 2 | . | . | . | . | . | . | . | . | . | . | – | – | – | – | – | – | – | – | – |
| LOOP dest | LOOP | (1) CX := CX − 1; (flags unchanged) (2) if CX <> 0 then IP := dest | . | . | . | X | . | . | . | . | . | . | – | – | – | – | – | – | – | – | – |
| LOOPE dest | LOOP if Equal | (1) CX := CX − 1; (flags unchanged) (2) if CX <> 0 and ZF = 1 then IP := dest | . | . | . | X | . | . | . | . | . | . | – | – | – | – | – | – | – | – | – |
| LOOPNE dest | LOOP if Not Equal | (1) CX := CX − 1; (flags unchanged) (2) if CX <> 0 and ZF = 1 then IP := dest | . | . | . | X | . | . | . | . | . | . | – | – | – | – | – | – | – | – | – |
| LOOPNZ dest | LOOP if Not Zero | (1) CX := CX − 1; (flags unchanged) (2) if CX <> 0 and ZF = 1 then IP := dest | . | . | . | X | . | . | . | . | . | . | – | – | – | – | – | – | – | – | – |
| LOOPZ dest | LOOP if Zero | (1) CX := CX − 1; (flags unchanged) (2) if CX <> 0 and ZF = 1 then IP := dest | . | . | . | X | . | . | . | . | . | . | – | – | – | – | – | – | – | – | – |
| MOV dest,source[c] | MOVe data | dest := source | . | . | . | . | . | X | A | X | A | X | – | – | – | – | – | – | – | – | – |
| MOVSB[a] | MOVe String Byte | (1) ES:[DI] := DS:[SI]; (2) if DF = 0 then SI := SI + 1, DI := DI + 1 else SI := SI − 1, DI:DI−1 | . | . | . | . | . | . | . | . | . | . | – | – | – | – | – | – | – | – | – |
| MOVSW[a] | MOVe String Word | (1) ES:[DI] := DS:[SI] (2) if DF = 0 then SI := SI + 2, DI := DI + 2 else SI := SI − 2, DI := DI − 2 | . | . | . | . | . | . | . | . | . | . | – | – | – | – | – | – | – | – | – |
| MUL source | MULtiply unsigned | ax := al * source or dx := ax * source | X | X | . | . | . | . | . | . | . | . | X | – | – | – | U | U | U | U | X |
| NEG dest | NEGate | dest := 0 − dest | X | X | . | . | . | . | . | . | . | . | X | – | – | – | X | X | X | X | X |
| NOP | NO oPeration | (does nothing) | . | . | . | . | . | . | . | . | . | . | – | – | – | – | – | – | – | – | – |
| NOT dest | logical complement | dest := NOT dest | X | X | . | . | . | . | . | . | . | . | – | – | – | – | – | – | – | – | – |
| OR dest, source | inclusive OR | dest := dest OR source | . | . | . | . | . | X | X | A | X | X | O | – | – | – | X | X | U | X | O |
| OUT port, acc[d] | OUTput to port | port := acc | . | . | . | . | . | . | . | . | . | . | – | – | – | – | – | – | – | – | – |

Notes:

a. String instructions also allow a memory operand that specifies only the size of the operands; a segment override for the source string can also be specified with the memory operand.

c. MOV also allows the following four operand forms:

segreg,reg     reg, segreg
segreg,mem     mem, segreg

d. OUT allows two operand forms:

immed, accum     DX, accum

A.18

Table A3.1 (continued)

| Instruction | Description | Operation | Operand Form | | | | | | | | Flags | | | | | | | |
|---|---|---|---|---|---|---|---|---|---|---|---|---|---|---|---|---|---|---|
| | | | R | M | I | L | S | R,R | R,M | R,I | M,R | M,I | O | D | I | T | S | Z | A | P | C |

| Instruction | Description | Operation | R | M | I | L | S | R,R | R,M | R,I | M,R | M,I | O | D | I | T | S | Z | A | P | C |
|---|---|---|---|---|---|---|---|---|---|---|---|---|---|---|---|---|---|---|---|---|---|
| POP dest | POP operand from stack | (1) dest := SS:[SP]; (2) SP := SP + 2 | X | X | – | – | X | – | – | – | – | – | – | – | – | – | – | – | – | – | – |
| POPA | POP All registers | pop DI, SI, BP, SP, BX, DX, CX, AX off stack in that order | – | – | – | – | – | – | – | – | – | – | – | – | – | – | – | – | – | – | – |
| POPF | POP Flags | pop stack into flags register | – | – | – | – | – | – | – | – | – | – | X | X | X | X | X | X | X | X | X |
| PUSH source | PUSH operand onto stack | (1) SP := SP – 2; (2) SS:[SP] :source | X | X | – | – | X | – | – | – | – | – | – | – | – | – | – | – | – | – | – |
| PUSHA | PUSH ALL registers | push AX, CX, DX, BX, SP, BP, SI, DI | – | – | – | – | – | – | – | – | – | – | – | – | – | – | – | – | – | – | – |
| PUSHF | PUSH Flags | push flags register onto stack | – | – | – | – | – | – | – | – | – | – | – | – | – | – | – | – | – | – | – |
| RCL dest, 1[e] | Rotate with Carry Left | dest[N..1] := dest[N – 1...0] onto stack in that order | – | – | – | – | – | – | – | – | – | – | X | – | – | – | – | – | – | – | X |
| RCL dest,CL[f] | Rotate with Carry Left | dest[N..CL] := dest[N – CL..0] & dest[CL – 1] := CF & dest[CL – 2..0] := dest[N..N – CL + 2] & CF := dest[N – CL + 1] | – | – | – | – | – | – | – | – | – | – | U | – | – | – | – | – | – | – | X |
| RCR dest,1[e] | Rotate with Carry Right | dest[N – 1..0] := dest[N..1] & dest[N] := CF | – | – | – | – | – | – | – | – | – | – | X | – | – | – | – | – | – | – | X |
| RCR dest,CL[f] | Rotate with Carry Right | dest[N – CL..0] := dest[N..CL] & dest[N – CL + 1] := CF & dest[N..N – CL + 2] := dest[CL – 2..0] & CF := dest[CL – 1] | – | – | – | – | – | – | – | – | – | – | U | – | – | – | – | – | – | – | X |
| REP instr[g] | unconditional REPeat | execute instruction the number of times specified by CX; flags modified by instruction | – | – | – | – | – | – | – | – | – | – | – | – | – | – | – | – | – | – | – |
| REPE instr[h] | REPeat if Equal | execute instruction the number of times specified by CX, but only while ZF = 1; flags modified by instruction | – | – | – | – | – | – | – | – | – | – | – | – | – | – | – | – | – | – | – |
| REPNE instr[h] | REPeat if Not Equal | execute instruction the number of times specified by CX, but only while ZF = 0; flags modified by instruction | – | – | – | – | – | – | – | – | – | – | – | – | – | – | – | – | – | – | – |
| REPNZ instr[h] | REPeat if Not Zero | execute instruction the number of times specified by CX, but only while ZF = 0; flags modified by instruction | – | – | – | – | – | – | – | – | – | – | – | – | – | – | – | – | – | – | – |

Notes:
e. Shift operands for shift count = 1:
reg, 1        mem, 1
f. Shift operands for variable shift count:
reg, CL       mem, CL
g. Used with MOVSB, MOVSW, STOSB, and STOSW instructions.
h. Used with CMPSB, CMPSW, SCASB, and SCASW instructions.

A.19

Table A3.1  (*continued*)

| Instruction | Description | Operation | R | M | I | L | S | R,R | R,M | R,I | M,R | M,I | O | D | I | T | S | Z | A | P | C |
|---|---|---|---|---|---|---|---|---|---|---|---|---|---|---|---|---|---|---|---|---|---|
| REPZ instr[h] | REPeat if Zero | execute instruction the number of times specified by CX, but only while ZF = 1; flags modified by instruction | | | | | | | | | | | – | – | – | – | – | – | – | – | – |
| RET | REturn to calling program | (1) IP := SS:[SP]; (2) SP := SP + 2 | | | | | | | | | | | – | – | – | – | – | – | – | – | – |
| RET source | RETurn and adjust stack | (1) IP := SS:[SP]; (2) SP := SP + 2 + source | | | | | | | | | | | – | – | – | – | – | – | – | – | – |
| ROL dest, 1[e] | ROtate Left | dest[N..1] := dest[N – 1..0] & dest[0] := dest[N] | | | | | | | | | | | X | – | – | – | – | – | – | – | X |
| ROL dest, CL[f] | ROtate Left | dest[N..CL] := dest[N – CL..0] & dest[CL – 1..0] := dest[N..N – CL + 1] | | | | | | | | | | | U | – | – | – | – | – | – | – | X |
| ROR dest, 1[e] | ROtate Right | dest[N – 1..0] := dest[N..1] & dest[N] := dest[0] | | | | | | | | | | | X | – | – | – | – | – | – | – | X |
| ROR dest, CL[f] | ROtate Right | dest[N – CL..0] := dest[N..CL + 1] := dest[CL – 1..0] | | | | | | | | | | | U | – | – | – | – | – | – | – | X |
| SAHF | Store AH into Flags | bits 0..7 of flags := AH | | | | | | | | | | | – | – | – | – | X | X | X | X | X |
| SAL dest, 1[e] | Shift Arithmetic Left | dest[N..1] := [N – 1..0] & dest[0] := 0 | | | | | | | | | | | X | – | – | – | X | X | U | X | X |
| SAL dest, CL[f] | Shift Arithmetic Left | dest[N..CL] := dest[N – CL..0] & dest[CL – 1..0] := 0 | | | | | | | | | | | U | – | – | – | X | X | U | X | X |
| SAR dest, 1[e] | Shift Arithmetic Right | dest[N – 1..0] := dest[N..1] & dest[N] unchanged | | | | | | | | | | | 0 | – | – | – | X | X | U | X | X |
| SAR dest, CL[f] | Shift Arithmetic Right | dest[N – CL..0] := dest[N..CL] & dest[N..N – CL+1] := dest[N] | | | | | | | | | | | 0 | – | – | – | X | X | U | X | X |
| SBB dest, source | SuBtract integers with Borrow | dest := dest – source – CF | | | | | | X | X | A | X | X | X | – | – | – | X | X | X | X | X |
| SCASB[a] | SCAn String Byte | (1) compare AL to ES:[DI]; (2) if DF = 0 then DI := DI + 1 else DI := DI – 1 | | | | | | | | | | | X | – | – | – | X | X | X | X | X |
| SCASW[a] | SCAn String Word | (1) compare AX to ES:[DI]; (2) if DF = 0 then DI := DI + 2 else DI := DI – 2 | | | | | | | | | | | X | – | – | – | X | X | X | X | X |
| SHL dest, 1[e] | SHift Left | dest[N..1] := dest[N – 1..0] & dest[0] := 0 | | | | | | | | | | | X | – | – | – | X | X | U | X | X |

Notes:

a. String instructions also allow a memory operand that specifies only the size of the operands; a segment override for the source string can also be specified with the memory operand.

e. Shift operands for shift count = 1:

    reg, 1        mem, 1

f. Shift operands for variable shift count:

    reg, CL        mem, CL

h. Used with CMPSB, CMPSW, SCASB, and SCASW instructions.

**Table A3.1** (continued)

| Instruction | Description | Operation | Operand Form | | | | | | | | | Flags | | | | | | | |
|---|---|---|---|---|---|---|---|---|---|---|---|---|---|---|---|---|---|---|---|
| | | | R | M | I | L | S | R,R | R,M | R,I | M,R | M,I | O | D | I | T | S | Z | A | P | C |
| SHL dest,CL[f] | SHift Left | dest[N..CL] := dest[N − CL..0] & dest[CL − 1..0] := 0 | . | . | . | . | . | . | . | . | . | . | X | – | – | – | X | X | U | X | X |
| SHR dest,1[e] | SHift Right | dest[N − 1..0] := dest[N..1] & dest[N] := 0 | . | . | . | . | . | . | . | . | . | . | X | – | – | – | X | X | U | X | X |
| SHR dest,CL[f] | SHift Right | dest[N − CL..0] := dest[N..CL] & dest[N..N − CL + 1] := 0 | . | . | . | . | . | . | . | . | . | . | X | – | – | – | X | X | U | X | X |
| SHR dest,1[e] | SHift Right | dest[N − 1..0] := dest[N..1] & dest[N] := 0 | . | . | . | . | . | . | . | . | . | . | X | – | – | – | X | X | U | X | X |
| SHR dest,CL[f] | SHift Right | dest[N − CL..0] := dest[N..CL] & dest[N..N − CL + 1] := 0 | . | . | . | . | . | . | . | . | . | . | X | – | – | – | X | X | U | X | X |
| STC | SeT Carry flag | CF := 1 | . | . | . | . | . | . | . | . | . | . | – | – | – | – | – | – | – | – | 1 |
| STD | SeT Direction flag | DF := 1 | . | . | . | . | . | . | . | . | . | . | – | 1 | – | – | – | – | – | – | – |
| STI | SeT Interrupt flag | IF := 1 | . | . | . | . | . | . | . | . | . | . | – | – | 1 | – | – | – | – | – | – |
| STOSB[a] | STOre String Byte | (1) ES:[DI] := AL; (2) if DF=0 then DI := DI + 1 else DI := DI − 1 | . | . | . | . | . | . | . | . | . | . | – | – | – | – | – | – | – | – | – |
| STOSW[a] | STOre String Word | (1) ES:[DI] := AX; (2) if DF=0 then DI := DI + 2 else DI := DI − 2 | . | . | . | . | . | . | . | . | . | . | – | – | – | – | – | – | – | – | – |
| SUB dest,source | SUBtract integers | dest := dest − source | . | . | . | . | . | X | X | A | X | X | X | – | – | – | X | X | X | X | X |
| TEST dest,source | logical compare | compute (dest AND source), set/clear flags | . | . | . | . | . | X | X | A | X | X | 0 | – | – | – | X | X | U | X | 0 |
| WAIT | WAIT for coprocessor | suspend 8086 until 8087 not busy | . | . | . | . | . | . | . | . | . | . | – | – | – | – | – | – | – | – | – |
| XCHG dest1,dest2 | eXCHange data | dest1 := dest2 & dest2 := dest1 | . | . | . | . | A | X | . | . | X | . | – | – | – | – | – | – | – | – | – |
| XLAT | transLATe | AL := DS:[BX + AL] | . | . | . | . | . | . | . | . | . | . | – | – | – | – | – | – | – | – | – |
| XLATB | transLATe Byte | AL := DS:[BX + AL] | . | . | . | . | . | . | . | . | . | . | – | – | – | – | – | – | – | – | – |
| XOR dest,source | eXclusive OR | dest := dest XOR source | . | . | . | . | . | X | X | A | X | X | 0 | – | – | – | X | X | U | X | 0 |

Notes:

a. String instructions also allow a memory operand that specifies only the size of the operands; a segment override for the source string can also be specified with the memory operand.

e. Shift operands for shift count = 1:

    reg,1      mem,1

f. Shift operands for variable shift count:

    reg,CL     mem,CL

A.21

### Appendix 3 Instructions

Table A3.2 presents the 8087 instructions in alphabetical order. For each instruction, the following is included:

- Required syntax
- Description
- Operation, as assignments
- Allowed operand forms:
  X = allowed

The abbreviations used for possible operand forms in Table A3.2 are

    ST = top 8087 data register
    STn = any 8087 data register
    R32 = short (32-bit) floating-point operand in memory
    R64 = long (64-bit) floating-point operand in memory
    R80 = extended (80-bit) floating-point operand in memory
    I16 = word (16-bit) signed integer operand in memory
    I32 = doubleword (32-bit) signed integer operand in memory
    I64 = quadword (64-bit) signed integer operand in memory
    D80 = tenbyte (80-bit) packed BCD operand in memory

Table A3.2  8087 Instructions

| Instruction | Description | Operation | STn | ST,STn | STn,ST | R32 | R64 | R80 | I16 | I32 | I64 | D80 |
|---|---|---|---|---|---|---|---|---|---|---|---|---|
| FABS | Floating ABSolute value | ST := \|ST\| | . | . | . | . | . | . | . | . | . | . |
| FADD | Floating ADD | (1) ST(1) := ST(1) + ST; (2) pop ST | . | . | . | . | . | . | . | . | . | . |
| FADD dest,source | Floating ADD | dest := dest + source | . | . | X | . | . | . | . | . | . | . |
| FADD source | Floating ADD | ST := ST + source | . | . | . | X | X | . | . | . | . | . |
| FADDP dest,ST | Floating ADD and Pop | (1) dest := dest + ST; (2) pop ST | . | . | X | . | . | . | . | . | . | . |
| FBLD source | Floating BCD LoaD | push source onto 8087 stack | . | . | . | . | . | . | . | . | . | X |
| FBSTP dest | Floating BCD STore and Pop | (1) dest := ST; (2) pop 8087 stack | . | . | . | . | . | . | . | . | . | X |
| FCHS | Floating CHange Sign | ST := − ST | . | . | . | . | . | . | . | . | . | . |
| FCOM | Floating COMpare | condition codes := ST:ST(1) | X | . | . | . | . | . | . | . | . | . |
| FCOM source | Floating COMpare | condition codes := ST:source | . | . | . | . | . | . | . | . | . | . |
| FCOMP | Floating COMpare and Pop | (1) condition codes := ST:ST(1); (2) pop ST | X | . | . | . | . | . | . | . | . | . |
| FCOMP source | Floating COMpare and Pop | (1) condition codes := ST:source; (2) pop ST | . | . | . | . | . | . | . | . | . | . |
| FCOMPP | Floating COMpare, Pop, and Pop | (1) condition codes := ST:ST(1); (2) pop ST (3) pop ST (former ST(1)) | . | . | . | . | . | . | . | . | . | . |
| FDIV | Floating DIVide | (1) ST(1) := ST(1) ÷ ST; (2) pop ST | . | . | . | . | . | . | . | . | . | . |
| FDIV dest,source | Floating DIVide | dest := dest ÷ source | . | X | . | . | . | . | . | . | . | . |
| FDIV source | Floating DIVide | ST := ST ÷ source | . | . | . | X | X | . | . | . | . | . |
| FDIVP dest,ST | Floating DIVide and Pop | (1) dest := dest ÷ ST; (2) pop ST | . | . | X | . | . | . | . | . | . | . |
| FDIVR | Floating DIVide Reversed | (1) ST(1) := ST ÷ ST(1); (2) pop ST | . | . | . | . | . | . | . | . | . | . |
| FDIVR dest,source | Floating DIVide Reversed | dest := source ÷ dest | . | X | . | . | . | . | . | . | . | . |
| FDIVR source | Floating DIVide Reversed | ST := source ÷ ST | . | . | . | X | X | . | . | . | . | . |
| FDIVRP dest,ST | Floating DIVide Reversed and Pop | (1) dest := ST ÷ dest; (2) pop ST | . | . | X | . | . | . | . | . | . | . |
| FIADD source | Floating Integer ADD | ST := ST + source | . | . | . | . | . | . | X | X | . | . |
| FICOM source | Floating Integer COMpare | condition codes := ST:source | . | . | . | . | . | . | X | X | . | . |
| FICOMP source | Floating Integer COMpare and Pop | (1) condition codes := ST:source; (2) pop ST | . | . | . | . | . | . | X | X | . | . |
| FIDIV source | Floating Integer DIVide | ST := ST ÷ source | . | . | . | . | . | . | X | X | . | . |
| FIDIVR source | Floating Integer DIVide Reversed | ST := source ÷ ST | . | . | . | . | . | . | X | X | . | . |
| FILD source | Floating Integer LoaD | push source onto 8087 stack | . | . | . | . | . | . | X | X | X | . |
| FIMUL source | Floating Integer MULtiply | ST := ST * source | . | . | . | . | . | . | X | X | . | . |

Table A3.2 (continued)

| Instruction | Description | Operation | \|  | Operand Forms |  |  |  |  |  |  |  |  |
|---|---|---|---|---|---|---|---|---|---|---|---|---|
|  |  |  | STn | ST,STn | STn,ST | R32 | R64 | R80 | I16 | I32 | I64 | D80 |
| FINIT | Floating INITialize coprocessor | initializes coprocessor (see text) |  |  |  |  |  |  |  |  |  |  |
| FIST dest | Floating Integer STore | dest := ST; |  |  |  |  |  |  | X | X |  |  |
| FISTP dest | Floating Integer STore and Pop | (1) dest := ST; (2) pop 8087 stack |  |  |  |  |  |  | X | X | X |  |
| FISUB source | Floating Integer SUBtract | ST := ST − source |  |  |  |  |  |  | X | X |  |  |
| FISUBR source | Floating Integer SUBtract Reversed | ST := source − ST |  |  |  |  |  |  | X | X |  |  |
| FLD source | Floating LoaD | push source onto 8087 stack | X |  |  | X | X | X |  |  |  |  |
| FLD1 | Floating LoaD 1 | push 1.0 onto 8087 stack |  |  |  |  |  |  |  |  |  |  |
| FLDCW source | Floating LoaD Control Word | control register := source |  |  |  |  |  |  | X |  |  |  |
| FLDENV source[a] | Floating LoaD ENVironment | control register := source; status register := source + 2; tags register := source + 4; instruction pointer := source + 6; operand pointer := source + 10 |  |  |  |  |  |  |  |  |  |  |
| FLDZ | Floating LoaD Zero | push 0.0 onto 8087 stack |  |  |  |  |  |  |  |  |  |  |
| FMUL | Floating MULtiply | (1) ST(1) := ST(1) * ST; (2) pop ST |  | X |  |  |  |  |  |  |  |  |
| FMUL dest,source | Floating MULtiply | dest := dest * source |  | X |  |  |  |  |  |  |  |  |
| FMUL source | Floating MULtiply | ST := ST * source | X |  |  | X | X |  |  |  |  |  |
| FMULP dest,ST | Floating MULtiply and Pop | (1) dest := dest * ST; (2) pop ST |  |  | X |  |  |  |  |  |  |  |
| FPREM | Floating Partial REMainder | if reduction complete then ST := ST − ST(1) * quotient, C2 of status word := 0 else ST := partial result, C2 of status word := 1 |  |  |  |  |  |  |  |  |  |  |
| FRNDINT | Floating RouND to INTeger | ST := round(ST) |  |  |  |  |  |  |  |  |  |  |
| FRSTOR source[b] | Floating ReSTORe coprocessor state | all 8087 registers := source[0..93] |  |  |  |  |  |  |  |  |  |  |
| FSAVE dest[b] | Floating SAVE coprocessor state | (1) dest[0..93] := all 8087 registers; (2) initialize 8087 |  |  |  |  |  |  |  |  |  |  |
| FSCALE | Floating SCALE | ST := ST * 2^trunc(ST(1)) |  |  |  |  |  |  |  |  |  |  |
| FSQRT | Floating SQuare RooT | ST := √ST |  |  |  |  |  |  |  |  |  |  |
| FST dest | Floating STore | dest := ST | X |  |  | X | X |  |  |  |  |  |
| FSTCW dest | Floating STore Control Word | dest := control register |  |  |  |  |  |  | X |  |  |  |

Notes:
a. Operand is a 14-byte block of memory.
b. Operand is a 94-byte block of memory.

A.24

Table A3.2 (continued)

| Instruction | Description | Operation | Operand Forms | | | | | | | | | |
|---|---|---|---|---|---|---|---|---|---|---|---|---|
| | | | STn | ST,STn | STn,ST | R32 | R64 | R80 | I16 | I32 | I64 | D80 |
| FSTENV source[a] | Floating STore ENVironment | source := control register; source + 2 := status register; source + 4 := tags register; source + 6 := instruction pointer source + 10 := operand pointer; | | | | | | | | | | |
| FSTP dest | Floating STore and Pop | (1) dest := ST; (2) pop 8087 stack | X | | | X | X | X | | | | |
| FSTSW dest[c] | Floating STore Status Word | dest := 8087 status register | | | | | | | X | | | |
| FSUB | Floating SUBtract | (1) ST(1) := ST(1) − ST; (2) pop ST | | | | | | | | | | |
| FSUB dest,source | Floating SUBtract | dest := dest − source | | X | | X | X | | | | | |
| FSUB source | Floating SUBtract | ST := ST − source | | | | X | X | | | | | |
| FSUBP dest,ST | Floating SUBtract and Pop | (1) dest := dest − ST; (2) pop ST | | | X | | | | | | | |
| FSUBR | Floating SUBtract Reversed | (1) ST(1) := ST − ST(1); (2) pop ST | | | | | | | | | | |
| FSUBR dest,source | Floating SUBtract Reversed | dest := source − dest | | X | | X | X | | | | | |
| FSUBR source | Floating SUBtract Reversed | ST := source − ST | | | | X | X | | | | | |
| FSUBRP dest,ST | Floating SUBtract Reversed and Pop | (1) dest := ST − dest; (2) pop ST | | | X | | | | | | | |
| FTST | Floating TeST | condition codes := ST : + 0.0 | | | | | | | | | | |
| FWAIT | WAIT for coprocessor | suspend 8086 until 8087 not busy | | | | | | | | | | |
| FXAM | Floating eXAMine | condition codes := type of value in ST | | | | | | | | | | |
| FXCH | Floating eXCHange | ST := ST(1) & ST(1) := ST | | | | | | | | | | |
| FXCH dest | Floating eXCHange | ST := dest; & dest := ST | X | | | | | | | | | |
| FXTRACT | Floating eXTRACT exponent and significand | (1) extract significand of ST; (2) ST := exponent of ST; (3) push significand (from step 1) | | | | | | | | | | |

Notes:
a: Operand is a 14-byte block of memory.
c. AX is allowed as operand on 80287 and later processors.

A.25

# A.4 Directives and Operators

## DIRECTIVES

The syntax and a description of each of the directives that are presented in this text are summarized in this section.

**ASSUME segmentregister:segmentname**
Associates a segment register with a segment name. This allows the assembler to use offsets from that segment register during program translation, but does not initialize the segment register.

**[name] DB value[,value]...**
Allocates one or more bytes of memory. If a name is supplied, that name is associated with the first byte. Initial values may be either specified or left undefined by using ? as operand.

**[name] DD value[,value]...**
Allocates one or more doublewords of memory. If a name is supplied, that name is associated with the first byte. Initial values may be either specified or left undefined by using ? as operand.

**DOSSEG**
Specifies that segments are to be placed in the executable file in the order that DOS uses.

**[name] DQ value[,value]...**
Allocates one or more quadwords of memory. If a name is supplied, that name is associated with the first byte. Initial values may be either specified or left undefined by using ? as operand.

**[name] DT value[,value]...**
Allocates one or more 10-byte blocks of memory. If a name is supplied, that name is associated with the first byte. Initial values may be either specified or left undefined by using ? as operand.

**[name] DW value[,value]...**
Allocates one or more words of memory. If a name is supplied, that name is associated with the first byte. Initial values may be either specified or left undefined by using ? as operand.

**ELSE**
Assembles statements up to ENDIF only if the expression in the preceding IF (or IF ____) directive was false (zero).

### Directives

**END [label]**
Defines the end of a module. The label, if specified, indicates where execution is to begin (used for main programs only).

**ENDIF**
Terminates a block defined by IF, IF ____, or ELSE.

**ENDM**
Defines the end of a macro definition or a repeat block.

**name ENDP**
Defines the end of a procedure.

**name ENDS**
Defines the end of a segment or structure.

**name EQU expression**
Assigns the text of the expression to the name, an assembly-time constant.

**EXTRN name:type[,name:type]...**
Defines one or more external symbols and their types.

**IF expression**
Assembles statements up to ENDIF (or optional ELSE if used) only if the expression is true (nonzero).

**IFDEF name**
Assembles statements up to ENDIF (or optional ELSE if used) only if the name is already defined.

**IFNDEF name**
Assembles statements up to ENDIF (or optional ELSE if used) only if the name is not yet defined.

**INCLUDE pathname**
Processes the contents of the named file as if it were part of the source file during assembly.

**name LABEL type**
Defines the name as a label and specifies its type; the name is associated with the object defined on the next line.

**LOCAL name[,name]...**
Declares a label that is to be replaced by a unique, assembler-defined label during macro expansion.

**name MACRO [parameter[,parameter]...]**
Begins the definition of a macro and specifies its parameters.

**PAGE [[length],width]**
Sets the dimensions of a page for the listing file.

**name PROC [type]**
Declares the start of a procedure; type may be NEAR (default) if in the same segment, or FAR if in another segment.

**PUBLIC name[,name]...**
Makes one or more symbols defined in a module available to other modules.

**REPT expression**
Evaluates the expression and generates that number of copies of the text between it and the next ENDM directive.

**name SEGMENT [alignment] [combine] [size] ['class']**
Defines the start of a segment with the given name. If included, the operands specify the following: the alignment of the segment in memory on a byte, word, doubleword, paragraph, or page boundary; the combine type (how segments with the same name from different modules are combined) as PUBLIC, STACK, COMMON, or PRIVATE; the size of a word operand as either 16-bit or 32-bit (used with 80386 and 80486 processors only); and the class name (to associate segments with different names but similar purposes).

**name STRUC       (MASM 5.1, TASM)**
**name STRUCT     (MASM 6.0)**
Defines the start of a data structure.

## OPERATORS

The syntax and a description of each of the operators that are presented in this text are summarized in this section.

**expression1 + expression2**
Returns the sum of the expressions.

**expression1 − expression2**
Returns the difference of the expressions.

**expression1 ∗ expression2**
Returns the product of the expressions.

**expression1 / expression2**
Returns the quotient of the expressions.

**segment:expression**
Overrides the default segment so that the offset of expression is computed relative to the given segment register.

**&parameter**
Forces substitution of the parameter following & with the corresponding argument in a macro.

**count DUP (value[,value] . . . )**
Specifies a list of values that is to be repeated count times. A question mark can be used when values are undefined.

**OFFSET expression**
Returns the offset of expression. The value is an immediate operand, determined during linking.

**type PTR expression**
Specifies that the expression is to be treated as a value of the specified type.

**SEG expression**
Returns the segment of expression. The value is an immediate operand, determined when the program is loaded.

# Microsoft Software A.5

This Appendix discusses briefly the tools available from Microsoft for working in assembly language. These tools include MASM (5.1 and 6.0), LINK, LIB, DEBUG, CodeView (2.2 and 3.14), and the Programmer's Workbench. Section 3.5 of the text describes how to use MASM 5.1 and LINK, and how to read the listing, cross-reference, and map files. This appendix summarizes that discussion and presents other options.

## MASM 5.1

Version 5.1 of MASM can be either invoked with all file specifications and options on the command line or used interactively. The full command line, with optional entries in [] (but assuming all files will be specified), is

MASM [options] source,object,listing,crossref

where

| | |
|---|---|
| options | are codes that control assembler activity |
| source | is the name of the source file (.ASM extension assumed) |
| object | is the name of the object file (.OBJ extension assumed) |
| listing | is the name of an optional listing file (.LST extension assumed) |
| crossref | is the name of an optional cross-reference file (.CRF extension assumed) |

Any of the three output files can be suppressed by specifying NUL for the filename; the default listing and cross-reference filenames are NUL. If the default names are acceptable, the field can be skipped, but the separating comma must be supplied. All trailing commas can be omitted if a semicolon is used in place of the first trailing comma. For example,

MASM PROG,,PROG;

reads PROG.ASM as the source file, assembles PROG.OBJ by default, creates a listing file named PROG.LST (overriding the default NUL), and suppresses the cross-reference file (the semicolon implies use of all remaining defaults, which is just NUL for the cross-reference file).

The interactive form is initiated by typing MASM and any options (other than /H) without any filenames. The assembler asks for the filenames one at a time, with the prompts

```
Source filename  [.ASM]:
Object filename  [source.OBJ]:
Source listing   [NUL.LST]:
Cross-reference  [NUL.CRF]:
```

In response to each prompt, MASM 5.1 accepts a filename without an extension (it appends the extension shown in the prompt), a filename with a different extension, or no entry (it uses the default filename and extension shown in the prompt). At any time, typing a semicolon terminates the interaction; MASM 5.1 then uses defaults for the remaining filenames. MASM 5.1 also prompts for filenames when an incomplete command line not terminated with a semicolon is entered.

There are many options that can be included on the MASM 5.1 command line. Some options are listed in Table A5.1.

In Section 3.5, the listing file was examined, and CREF was used to examine the cross-reference file in detail. Refer to that section for information about the files produced by the assembler.

## MASM 6.0

Release 6.0 of the Microsoft Macro Assembler introduced many new features which are of interest to professional programmers who write extensively in assembly language. Few of the new features affect the needs of this text.

With the new release, Microsoft provides a utility to convert a program written for MASM 5.1 so that it will be compatible with MASM 6.0. For convenience, they named the new utility MASM to make it possible to assemble older programs using what looks like the older setup. All of the programs in this text assemble under version 6.0 without conversion.

This release has a new command line and new options. The assembler invokes the linker automatically, unless the option that disables this feature is specified. The complete command line is

ML [options] filenames [[options] filenames]...[/link linkoptions]

where the entries in [] are optional and the ellipsis points indicate that the [[options] filenames] entry may be repeated any number of times. Options apply to all files that

Table A5.1  Selected Options for MASM 5.1 Command Line

| Option | Action |
|---|---|
| /H | Displays a help screen consisting of command line syntax and a list of all options; no other options or filenames should be used with /H. |
| /T | Suppresses display of free symbol space and numbers of warnings and errors. |
| /V | Displays the number of lines and symbols processed in addition to free symbol space and numbers of warnings and errors. |
| /W0 | Reports only severe errors. |
| /W1 | Reports serious warnings and severe errors (default). |
| /W2 | Reports advisory warnings, serious errors, and severe errors. |
| /Z | Displays lines containing errors along with the error messages on the screen. |
| /ZD | Writes line number information to object file, for use with some debuggers. |
| /ZI | Writes line number and symbolic information to object file, for use with CodeView. |
| /Dsymbol[= value] | Defines the symbol and optionally assigns a string value to it. |
| /MU | Converts all lowercase letters in names to capitals (default). |
| /MX | Makes all public and external names case-sensitive. |
| /ML | Makes all names case-sensitive. |

follow the option specification, up to the next set of options. All files that have .ASM extensions are assembled, and the resulting object files are linked with all .OBJ and .LIB files to form an executable file. Filenames with no extensions are assumed to have .OBJ extensions.

To assemble and link WELCOME.ASM, a simple assembly-language program from Chapter 3, use the command

ML WELCOME.ASM \LIB\IO.LIB

The system displays a series of self-explanatory messages as it assembles and links the program. The last message concerns a definitions file, which is used with Microsoft Windows and OS/2 applications only and will not be considered here.

To assemble and link a main program and the subprograms it invokes, such as NestdMax with Max2Fn and Max3Fn from Chapter 8, include all of the source files in the command. For example,

ML NESTDMAX.ASM MAX2FN.ASM MAX3FN.ASM \LIB\IO.LIB

assembles a main program and two subprograms and links them with IO.LIB to make NESTDMAX.EXE.

There are many options that can be included on the ML command line. These options are case-sensitive; in some instances, typing the option in lowercase gives different results from typing it in capital letters. Some options are listed in Table A5.2.

**Table A5.2 Selected Options for ML Command Line (MASM 6.0)**

| Option | Action |
| --- | --- |
| -? | Displays a help screen consisting of command line syntax and a list of all options; no other options or filenames should be used with -?. |
| /help | Invokes the QuickHelp utility. |
| /Fo[filename] | Specifies name of object file; if filename omitted, or if option omitted, the source filename is used with the .OBJ extension. |
| /Fe[filename] | Specifies name of executable file; if filename omitted, or if option omitted, the source filename is used with the .EXE extension. |
| /Fl[filename] | Specifies creation and name of listing file; if filename omitted, the source filename is used with the .LST extension. |
| /Fm[filename] | Specifies creation and name of map file; if filename omitted, the source filename is used with the .MAP extension. |
| /W0 | Reports only fatal and severe errors. |
| /W1 | Reports fatal and severe errors and some warnings (default). |
| /W2 | Reports fatal and severe errors and more warnings than /W1. |
| /W3 | Reports all errors and warnings. |
| /Zs | Checks for syntax errors only; does not generate object or executable files. |
| /Zd | Writes line number information to object file, for use with some debuggers. |
| /Zi | Writes line number and symbolic information to object file, for use with CodeView. |
| /Dsymbol[=value] | Defines the symbol and optionally assigns a string value to it. |
| /Cu | Converts all lowercase letters in identifiers to capitals. |
| /Cx | Preserves case of identifiers declared in PUBLIC, EXTERN, and PROC directives (and other directives not discussed in this text); (default). |
| /Cp | Preserves case of all identifiers. |
| /c | Assembles .ASM files but does not invoke linker. |
| /link [linkoptions] [libraries] | Specifies options for linker and libraries for linker to use; these options are not case-sensitive, but they must be given after all other filenames. |

The cross-reference files and utility (CREF) of earlier versions of the assembler have been replaced with a Browser utility integrated into the Programmer's Workbench.

The listing file, if requested by the /Fl option, is very similar to the MASM 5.1 listing file explained in Section 3.5. The differences, other than minor changes in spacing and page numbering, are the lack of line numbers (previously used with CREF), the omission of statistics at the end of the listing, and the addition of a size attribute in the Segments and Groups table. This size attribute of a segment specifies whether a word within the segment is 16 or 32 bits long; this value is always 16 for the 8086 through 80286 processors, but it can be 32 for the 80386 and 80486 processors.

## LINK

The Microsoft Linker, LINK, has a command line structure similar to the version 5.1 assembler in that the filenames can be specified either on the command line or in response to prompts. The full command line is

LINK [options] objects,executable,map,libraries

where

| | |
|---|---|
| options | are codes that control linker activity |
| objects | are the names of the object files to combine (.OBJ extension assumed) |
| executable | is the name of the executable file to create (.EXE extension assumed) |
| map | is the name of the map file to create (.MAP extension assumed) |
| libraries | are the names of any library files to be linked to the object files (.LIB extension assumed) |

The name of the first object file is used for the executable file and the map file (if created) with appropriate extensions unless other names are provided. If the default names are acceptable, the field can be skipped, but the separating comma must be supplied. All trailing commas can be omitted if a semicolon is used in place of the first trailing comma; however, doing so affects the creation of the map file. For example,

LINK MAIN SUB1,,,IO

links MAIN.OBJ, SUB1.OBJ, and IO.LIB to create the executable MAIN.EXE and a map file MAIN.MAP. Or

LINK MAIN SUB1 IO;

links MAIN.OBJ, SUB1.OBJ, and IO.OBJ to create the executable MAIN.EXE; no listing file is created when the comma following its position is omitted. To suppress creation of the map file when a library must be linked, use NUL in the map field.

The interactive form is initiated by typing LINK and any options (other than /HE) without any filenames. The linker asks for the filenames one at a time; to enter more than one object or library file, separate them with either a space or a plus sign (+), or end the line with a plus sign to repeat the prompt. The series of prompts are

```
Object Modules [.OBJ]:
Run File [filename.EXE]:
List File [NUL.MAP]:
Libraries [.LIB]:
```

Typing a semicolon in response to any of the prompts except the first uses the defaults for the remaining prompts. LINK also prompts for filenames when an incomplete command line not terminated with a semicolon is entered.

The new linker provided with MASM 6.0 adds one more entry to the end of the command line and another prompt to the interactive form. The new entry is for the name of a definitions file to be used with Windows and OS/2.

There are many options that can be included on the LINK command line. Some options are listed in Table A5.3.

The map file produced by LINK for the Welcome program was examined in Section 3.5. Refer to that discussion for information about the map.

## LIB

The Microsoft LIB utility is used to create and modify libraries. To make sense of the operations involved, it is necessary to distinguish between object files and object modules. Both contain object code produced by a compiler or an assembler, but an object file is an independent file, whereas an object module is part of a library. For example, PUTSTR.OBJ and PUTCRLF.OBJ are separate object files; the IO.LIB library includes both the PUTSTR and PUTCRLF object modules, among others.

One advantage of using libraries is that it simplifies the commands needed to link a program. For example, by specifying the IO.LIB library when linking, any of the object modules in it that are referenced are linked into the executable file. If the library is not used, it will be necessary to list each needed object file separately when linking.

The use of object files instead of libraries could be facilitated by combining the source code for all routines into one single source file and assembling into one large object file, but there are two drawbacks with this approach. First, all source files to be combined must be written in the same language; second, even if only one routine in the object file is needed, all routines in the file, as well as all routines that they invoke, must be included

Table A5.3   Selected Options for LINK

| Option | Action |
|---|---|
| /HE | Older versions: displays a help screen of command line syntax and a list of all options; Newer versions: invokes the QuickHelp utility; no other options or filenames should be used. |
| /? | Newer versions only: displays a help screen of command line syntax and a list of all options. |
| /CO | Writes line number and symbolic data to executable file for use with the CodeView debugger. |
| /M | Includes all public symbols defined in the object files in the map; the listing is included twice, once sorted by name and once sorted by location; without this option, the map includes only a list of segments. |
| /LI | Includes line number information in the map file if included in the object files. |

in the executable file. With libraries, only the object modules that are needed are included in the executable file.

An object module contains all of the routines that the object file from which it was created contains. Note that if we start with all code for several routines in one source file, create a single object file from that source file, and create an object module from that object file, the object module will contain all of the routines. When linked, all routines in the module will be included in the executable file. However, if each routine is in a separate source file, the library ultimately will contain separate modules for each routine, and only those routines actually invoked will be included in the executable file.

The LIB utility can be invoked either with all filenames, options, and commands on one line or in interactive mode, as with MASM 5.1 and LINK. Only the interactive mode is presented in this appendix. LIB is started by typing LIB at the DOS prompt. The first prompt is

Library name:

In response, type the filename of the library you want to create or modify. A disk and path can be included; the default extension .LIB will be supplied. If the file specified in response to this prompt does not exist, LIB prompts whether you want to create it. Respond Y to create it or N to terminate LIB.

The second prompt is

Operations:

In response, type one or more commands. The commands are listed in Table A5.4. If you have many commands to enter, or if you want to enter commands one per line, follow the last command on each line with an ampersand (&), and LIB will repeat this prompt and accept more commands. If you do not specify any operations, LIB checks the existing library and terminates.

The third prompt is

List file:

In response, type the name of a file where LIB can write two reports: a list of all public symbols in alphabetical order and a list of all modules in the library. These lists are cross-referenced to each other. There is no default filename or extension. If you do not type a filename here, LIB suppresses the listing file.

Table A5.4  Commands Used with LIB

| Command | Operand | Action |
|---|---|---|
| + | Object file | Adds object module to current library. |
| + | Library file | Copies the contents of the specified library to current library. |
| - | Module name | Deletes module from current library. |
| -+ | Module name | Replaces module from current library with one from object file with same name in the current directory. |
| * | Module name | Copies the module into an object file with the same name and .OBJ extension in the current directory. |
| -* | Module name | Moves the module into an object file with the same name and .OBJ extension in the current directory. |

The fourth and final prompt is

Output library:

LIB provides the current library name (given in response to the first prompt) as the default name; type a filename to have LIB leave the current library unchanged and write the revised library to a new library.

As an example of using LIB, the following dialogue adds a module to IO.LIB. The module is derived from the file GETSTR.OBJ, which has been created from GETSTR.ASM in Chapter 15 and copied to the same directory as IO.LIB:

```
Library name: io.lib
Operations: +getstr
List file: io.lis
Output library:
```

This sequence modifies IO.LIB to include the GETSTR module and writes the lists of modules and public symbols to the file IO.LIS.

## DEBUG

The DEBUG utility, supplied with DOS, allows the user to inspect and modify the memory used by a program and to execute a program either one instruction at a time or until a previously set breakpoint is encountered.

DEBUG can be invoked from the DOS prompt with or without a filename. If a filename is included, the file is loaded; arguments to the program being inspected can be included on the command line as well. If DEBUG is started without a filename, a filename can be specified with the Name command and loaded with the Load command.

A demonstration of DEBUG is included in Section 3.6. Refer to that discussion for examples of some of the commands. Table A5.5 lists the commands used in Section 3.6 and several other commands that are useful in examining memory. Refer to your DOS user's reference manual for more information on other features of DEBUG.

## CODEVIEW 2.2

CodeView is a window-oriented symbolic debugging tool. Two slightly different versions of CodeView are examined here. Version 2.2 was supplied with MASM 5.1. Version 3.14 is supplied with MASM 6.0. Version 2.2 is considered first.

To prepare a program written entirely in assembly language for use with CodeView 2.2, there are three requirements. First, the class name of the segment with the instructions must be 'CODE' in order to debug using the source statements; without this class name, CodeView 2.2 can show only an unassembled version of the program. The second requirement is that the source file must be assembled with the /Zi option. Doing so writes the symbolic data for CodeView 2.2 to the object file. Then, the object file must be linked with the /CO option, which copies the symbolic data to the executable file. Note that the resulting executable is larger when it includes the information for CodeView. The final requirement is that the source file must be in the same directory as the executable file when CodeView is invoked.

### Table A5.5 DEBUG Commands

| Command | Action |
|---|---|
| Nfilename[filename...] | Sets name of file to be examined and optional filename arguments. |
| L[address] | Loads a file into memory at the address specified or at CS:100h if no address specified; BX:CX is set to the number of bytes loaded. |
| D[range] | Displays the contents of the specified range of memory in hexadecimal and ASCII. |
| U[range] | Displays the contents of the specified range as unassembled code. |
| R[register] | Displays the contents of the selected register then prompts for a new value for the register (tap ENTER to not change it); if no register specified, the contents of all registers are only displayed; if F is typed, all flags are displayed as two-letter codes, and it prompts for new flag values, which can be entered as two-letter codes. |
| T[=address][number] | Executes one or more instructions and displays the contents of all registers, flags, and the instruction after each. Execution starts at the specified address or following the previously executed instruction. The second parameter specifies the number of instructions to execute and defaults to 1. |
| P[=address][number] | Similar to the T command, but it executes loops, repeated string instructions, called procedures, and interrupt handlers in their entirety without stopping. |
| G[=address[addresses]] | Executes the program as if run from the command prompt. The "=address" specifies the starting address; the other addresses (up to 10 of them) specify breakpoints. If any breakpoints are set, execution proceeds until one of them is encountered or the program terminates normally. When a breakpoint is encountered, all breakpoints are cleared. |
| Q | Terminates DEBUG. |

Notes:

1. Addresses are specified as a segment register followed by a colon and an offset in hexadecimal; in some commands, the CS register is assumed by default and need not be specified; in most commands, a default address is assumed if one is not specified.
2. Ranges are specified as two addresses or as an address and a length following the letter L; in some commands, a default length is assumed if one is not specified.
3. The two-letter codes for the flags register are

| flag | cleared | set |
|---|---|---|
| overflow | NV | OV |
| direction | UP | DN |
| interrupt | DI | EI |
| sign | PL | NG |
| zero | NZ | ZR |
| auxiliary carry | NA | AC |
| parity | PO | PE |
| carry | NC | CY |

The command line to invoke CodeView 2.2 is

CV [options] executablefile [arguments]

The options control how CodeView 2.2 starts on various computers; the only option presented here is /W. On some systems, CodeView 2.2 starts in "sequential mode," in which there are no windows; only a dialogue much like that with DEBUG is present. Using the /W option on some of those systems will force the preferred window mode. If CodeView 2.2 still starts in sequential mode with the /W option, refer to the CodeView

2.2 manual or a local system expert for assistance. This appendix assumes that CodeView 2.2 starts in window mode.

The arguments specified on the command line (following the name of the executable file that is to be examined) are present in the PSP as a copy of the command line (see Section 11.5).

When started in window mode with a program originally written in assembly language, CodeView 2.2 displays three windows and a menu bar. For example, see Figure A5.1, which shows CodeView 2.2 started with the DayTime program of Chapter 4. The top line is the menu bar; it shows titles of menus and commands. The largest window contains the source statements of the program, with the line of the next instruction to be executed highlighted and line numbers along the left side. To its right is the register window, showing the contents (unless specified otherwise, all numbers are hexadecimal) of the registers and the state of all flags except TF, using the same two-letter codes as in DEBUG (see the notes to Table A5.5). Along the bottom is the dialog window, where a > prompt appears below the copyright notice. The boundary between the program and dialog windows can be moved to partition the screen differently. The contents of both windows can also be scrolled.

There are three modes of interaction with CodeView 2.2. Two of them are related to the window-like nature of the display and use the mouse or keyboard. The third is related to the dialog window specifically, where commands such as those in DEBUG are typed. Describing all modes for all commands and options and all language possibilities would require a fairly large reference manual; this appendix is restricted to a subset of commands that would be useful for someone learning assembly language and to simple modes of interaction.

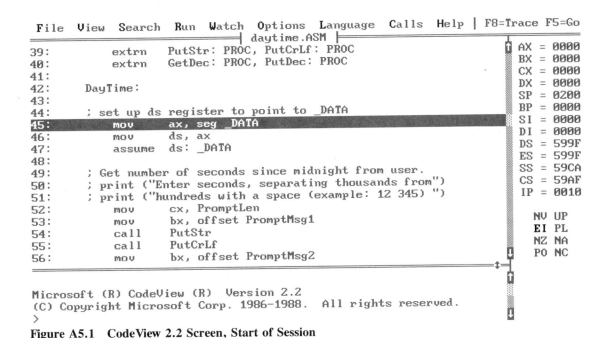

Figure A5.1  CodeView 2.2 Screen, Start of Session

## Appendix 5  Microsoft Software

To use the menus, select the word of the menu title either by clicking the mouse on it or by pressing the ALT key in conjunction with the first letter of the title. A menu will then drop down. To select the desired entry in the menu, either click the mouse on it, use the arrow keys to move the highlight to it and tap ENTER, or tap the highlighted letter of the menu item. Some menu entries have a shortcut listed following their names; such commands can be selected directly by typing the shortcut. For example, CTRL+W is the shortcut for selecting Add Watch... from the Watch menu.

To type commands in the dialogue area, just type, and the command will be echoed to the next line. The response to the command may appear in the dialogue area or may alter the contents of one or more windows, depending on the command. Some commands, especially those that cause one or more instructions of the program to execute, are not echoed, but their execution affects the display in other ways.

Some of the menu options and what they do are listed in Table A5.6. Some of the entries in the table may not be clear on a first reading; more details will be presented in an extended example shortly.

The function keys provide shortcuts for many menu functions and dialog commands. Table A5.7 lists the function keys and their uses.

Finally, there are few keys used for moving around the display. These keys are listed in Table A5.8. A mouse can also be used to move around the display. Clicking in any window positions the cursor in that window. Dragging (clicking and holding the button down while moving the mouse) the double line between the program and dialog windows

**Table A5.6  Some Menu Selections of CodeView 2.2**

| Menu Title | Selected Option | Action |
|---|---|---|
| File | Exit | Terminates CodeView 2.2 session. |
| View | Source | Displays source file in program window. |
|  | Mixed | Displays source and assembled code together in program window. |
|  | Assembly | Displays assembled code in program window. |
|  | Registers | Toggles register window on and off. |
|  | Output | Switches display to program output; tap any key to return to CodeView 2.2 display. |
| Run | Start | Runs the program from its beginning to its end or until a breakpoint reached; same as Restart + Go; |
|  | Restart | Resets CodeView 2.2 to the beginning of the program; does not affect breakpoints or watch statements. |
|  | Execute | Runs the program in slow motion until its end, a breakpoint is reached, or any key is tapped. |
|  | Clear Breakpoints | Clears all breakpoints; does not affect watch statements. |
| Watch | Add Watch | Asks for a watch expression and adds that expression to the watch window. |
|  | Delete Watch | Displays all current watch expressions; highlighting one and tapping ENTER deletes that expression. |
|  | Delete All Watch | Deletes all expressions from watch window. |
| Help | — | Provides on-line help for using CodeView 2.2. |
| Trace | — | Executes the next instruction of the program (see F8 in Table A5.7). |
| Go | — | Executes program, continuing from last instruction executed, until its end or a breakpoint is reached (see F5 in Table A5.7). |

**Table A5.7  Function Keys in CodeView**

| Key | Action |
| --- | --- |
| F1 | Invokes on-line help; same as Help on menu. |
| F2 | Toggles register window on and off; same as View/Registers on menu. |
| F3 | Cycles program window through source, mixed, and assembly displays; same as View/Source, View/Mixed, and View/Assembly on menu. |
| F4 | Switches display to program output; any key returns to CodeView 2.2 display; same as View/Output on menu. |
| F5 | Executes from next instruction through end of program or until breakpoint reached. Same as Go on menu (mouse users: click Go using either button). |
| F6 | Moves cursor between dialog and program display windows. |
| F7 | Sets a temporary breakpoint at the cursor and executes program; (mouse users: point to line and click right button). |
| F8 | Executes next line (viewing source) or instruction (viewing assembly) of program; traces into called routines (viewing assembly or viewing source and the called routine's symbolic information is available); (mouse users: point to Trace on menu and click left button). |
| F9 | Sets or clears breakpoint at cursor; (mouse users: point to line and click left button). |
| F10 | Executes next line (viewing source) or instruction (viewing assembly) of program; executes called routines to completion as if a single instruction; (mouse users: point to Trace on menu and click right button). |

moves it to change the sizes of these windows. The program and dialog windows also have simple scroll bars, and the usual ways of using a mouse with a scroll bar are supported.

Consider using CodeView 2.2 to execute the instructions in programs one at a time (or rapidly up to a breakpoint) and to show the contents of the registers and selected memory locations. The register window is displayed by default when examining an assembly-language program, but it can be toggled off and on with the F2 function key. Displaying the contents of selected memory locations, however, requires a little more work. Three options are discussed here: setting watches, evaluating expressions, and displaying memory dumps.

**Table A5.8  Cursor Move and Window Scroll in CodeView 2.2**

| Keys | Action |
| --- | --- |
| F6 | Moves cursor between dialog and program display windows (window with cursor is "current window"). |
| CTRL+G | Enlarges current window, shrinks other window. |
| CTRL+T | Shrinks current window, enlarges other window. |
| UP | Scrolls current window up one line. |
| DOWN | Scrolls current window down one line. |
| PAGEUP | Scrolls current window up the size of the window. |
| PAGEDOWN | Scrolls current window down the size of the window. |
| HOME | Scrolls to top of file (if program display window is current) or top of command buffer (if dialog window is current). |
| END | Scrolls to bottom of file or command buffer. |

Notes for mouse users:

1. Dragging the double line that separates the program display and dialog windows changes the sizes of the windows.
2. The contents of the current window can be scrolled using its scroll bar.

## A.40  Appendix 5  Microsoft Software

There is another window available on the CodeView 2.2 display called the watch window. CodeView 2.2 can display the values of selected memory locations in the watch window; every time the value of a watched location changes, CodeView 2.2 automatically updates the value shown in the watch window. A few ways to specify watches are illustrated in the following example.

Refer again to Figure A5.1. Move the cursor to the program window (using F6) and scroll up (using the HOME and arrow keys) to the data segment. Then move the cursor back to the dialog window. Using the dialog WI command, add KSec and USec to the watch window. The "I" in the WI command specifies the integer format, so the values are interpreted as signed numbers and are displayed in base 10. See Figure A5.2. Note the two commands in the dialog window. The watch window is open between the program window and the menu bar; the watch window is sized automatically but cannot contain more than 10 lines. In the watch window, KSec and USec are listed along with their addresses and current values.

To add the next watch, use the menu. First select Watch from the menu bar (ALT+W). The Watch menu appears as shown in Figure A5.3. The first entry of the menu, Add Watch..., is already highlighted, so just tap ENTER to select it. Also note that CTRL+W could be typed to select this option. Once added, a watch stays in effect until deleted with Delete Watch... on this menu (CTRL+U) or until all watches are deleted with the last selection of the Watch menu.

The ellipsis points in the menu selection mean that there is another entry to be made. In the case of Add Watch..., that entry is the expression to be added to the window. When Add Watch... is selected, the Watch menu is removed, and a dialogue box appears with a prompt; the cursor also appears in the box. The expression to be watched can then be

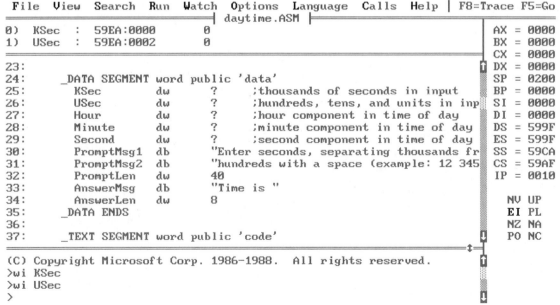

**Figure A5.2**  CodeView 2.2 Screen, after Setting Two Watch Expressions using Dialog Commands

# CodeView 2.2                                                              A.41

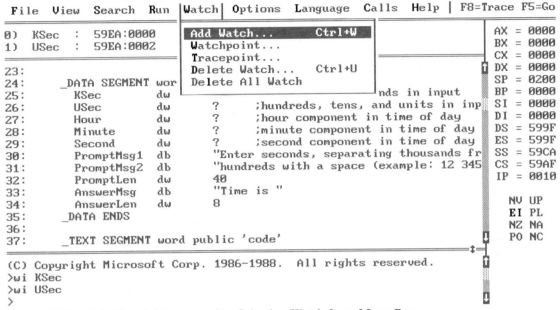

**Figure A5.3**  CodeView 2.2 Screen, after Selecting Watch from Menu Bar

typed. In Figure A5.4, typing Hour,i tells CodeView 2.2 to watch the variable Hour and to display its value as a signed integer in base 10.

Use CTRL+W to enter Minute and Second into the watch window with integer formats, too. Execute the instructions of the program up to but not including the instruction

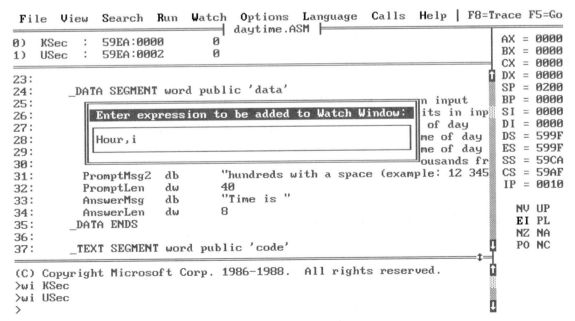

**Figure A5.4**  CodeView 2.2 Screen, Setting Watch Expression

in line 84 (press F8 to single step, or move the cursor to line 84 in the program window and tap F7 to set a breakpoint and then execute to that point). See Figure A5.5. KSec and USec now contain 15 and 678, respectively. The program has converted 15,678 seconds into 4 hours (the 4 is still in AX and will be saved in Hour when the next instruction executes), 21 minutes (in Minute), and 18 seconds (in Second). Note that the last instruction executed saved the contents of DX (0015h) in Minute.

The next instruction will save AX in Hour. There is another item displayed in Figure A5.5. The instruction that is highlighted has an operand in memory, specified as Hour in the source statement. In the lower right corner, CodeView 2.2 displays the address of this operand as DS:0004. Below that, it displays the value stored there, 0000.

With watches, as F8 is tapped, the effect of each instruction can be seen. To skip over boring sections, set a breakpoint just before an interesting part, use F5 to execute to the breakpoint, and then single step.

Watches entered through the menu consist of an expression followed optionally by a comma and a format. If no format is specified, the previously entered watch format is used. The expression is usually a symbolic name; other expressions are allowed, but it is preferable to use the dialog window when entering other expressions. The formats that CodeView 2.2 allows, in general, are listed in Table A5.9. The case used to enter the X and E formats is used for the letters (A through F of a hexadecimal number, or E of a floating-point number, respectively) of the output.

Watches can be entered in the dialog window in two forms:

W? expression[,format]

or

W<type> range

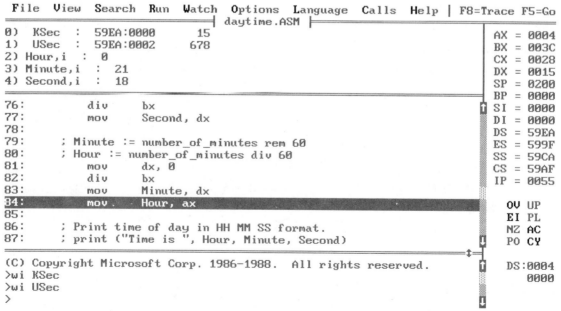

**Figure A5.5** CodeView 2.2 Screen, during Execution of Program

**Table A5.9  Format Specifiers for CodeView 2.2 Watch, Display, and Dump Commands**

| Specifier | Format |
| --- | --- |
| D or I | Signed integer, base 10 |
| U | Unsigned integer, base 10 |
| X | Hexadecimal |
| F | Floating-point number, no exponent |
| E | Floating-point number, scientific notation |
| C | Single character |
| S | Character string terminated with NUL (00h) |

In the first form, the expression can include several operators. However, the expressions are evaluated using the rules of the C language; the operators are either C operators or hybrids not used elsewhere. A few examples of such expressions are given here; the enterprising reader can probably figure out how to write a needed expression with a little experimentation and patience.

In the second form, <type> is a single letter that specifies the data type. Possible types are listed in Table A5.10. We have already seen the I type. A range is an expression that refers to a location in memory, a space, the letter L, and the number of data elements to watch. The output of each watch statement is allocated only one line of the watch window, so an array of more than a few elements should be split into several watch statements.

For example, if List is an array of 10 words, the first half of that array could be watched by issuing the command

```
ww  List   l5
```

where WW specifies a watch of word data type. The range starts at List and contains five words. The output generated by this watch is the address followed by five words in hexadecimal. Then, to watch the second half of the array, issue the command

```
ww &List+a l5
```

The ampersand (&) is the C operator that returns the address of its operand. To this address, add 10 (which is A in hexadecimal). Codeview 2.2 then watches five words starting

**Table A5.10  Types for CodeView 2.2 Watch and Dump Commands**

| Specifier | Type | Display |
| --- | --- | --- |
| B | Byte | Hexadecimal and ASCII characters |
| A | ASCII | Character string |
| I | Integer | Signed, base 10 |
| U | Unsigned | Base 10 |
| W | Word | Hexadecimal |
| D | Doubleword | Hexadecimal |
| S | Short real | Hexadecimal and scientific |
| L | Long real | Hexadecimal and scientific |
| T | 10-byte real | Hexadecimal and scientific |

at the resulting address. Without the ampersand, CodeView 2.2 would add 10 to the value stored in the first word of `List` and then use that modified value in computing the starting address of the range to display.

Now consider the value referenced by a near pointer, which is accessed with a sequence like the following:

```
mov     bx, offset List
add     bx, 6
mov     ax, [bx]
```

Use an expression like

```
w? WO bx
```

which is in the first form given above. WO is a hybrid operator, the same as `word ptr` in assembly language. This expression watches not the contents of BX (which is already watched in the register display) but rather the contents of the word of memory to which BX points. Figure A5.6 summarizes some of the more useful operators and the details of writing expressions for watch (and display) commands.

To watch the value of an argument passed on the stack, issue watch commands like

```
ww WO ss:bp+4
```

This expression displays the contents of the last argument passed before calling the subprogram.

While watches are very useful, the values of expressions can also be displayed in the dialog window. If the `W` is omitted from a watch expression that would normally start with W?, the expression will be evaluated once, and the result will be displayed in the dialog window. The result will not be updated after each instruction. The advantage of this response is that CodeView 2.2 need not evaluate the expression and update the display after each instruction. This method is especially handy when you are not sure how to write some expression and want to experiment without filling the watch window with erroneous expressions.

- To specify the size of an operand in an expression, use
  BY in place of `byte ptr`
  WO in place of `word ptr`
  DW in place of `dword ptr`
- To specify the type of a symbol, use
  (char) symbol in place of `byte ptr` symbol
  (int) symbol in place of `word ptr` symbol
  (long) symbol in place of `dword ptr` symbol
- Use the & operator in place of OFFSET.
- To specify based, indexed, or based-indexed addressing, use + in place of []; for example use
  BY bp+8+si  in place of `byte ptr [bp+8][si]`.
- All numbers are interpreted in hexadecimal.

**Figure A5.6  Notes on Expressions and Operators**

CodeView 2.2 can also dump a region of memory to the dialog area. The commands to accomplish this task are much like the watch commands that start with W and a letter for the data type, followed by a range, except that D is substituted for W. If a range is not specified, CodeView 2.2 dumps 128 bytes for db but just one value for the other formats.

The last command presented here is simply 7. This command dumps the contents of the 8087 registers, writing these contents in the dialog window. The format of the display reflects the structure of the 8087 processor, except that each line begins with the letter c if an 8087 is installed or the letter e if an emulator is used.

## CODEVIEW 3.14

The requirements for building an executable file from assembly language that can be examined with the new version of CodeView are the same as for the old version: The class name of the instruction segment must be 'CODE', the executable file must contain symbolic information, and the source file must be in the same directory as the executable file. With the compile and link capabilities of the ML command, the /Zi option not only specifies inclusion of symbolic information in the object file but also issues the /CO option when it invokes the linker.

CodeView 3.14 can be invoked from the command line using the same command that the earlier version uses.

When started for the first time at a new installation, CodeView 3.14 uses default options for number and size of windows, radix, and a few other features. However, the combinations of windows, their sizes, and so forth are saved when CodeView 3.14 terminates; these values are used as the defaults the next time CodeView 3.14 starts. Some commands have been used to set up in a particular manner the display shown here; it is unlikely that any other copy of CodeView 3.14 will start exactly as shown here, so do not be concerned if your first display appears different.

The CodeView display has been redesigned, and some of the user interface has been changed, too. When starting CodeView 3.14 with the DayTime program, the result is the display shown in Figure A5.7. Compare this display to Figure A5.1. The new display has four windows: watch, source1, and command (from top to bottom on the left side), and registers (along the right side).

The top line of the display is the menu bar; it shows titles of menus. The bottom line of the display lists several of the more useful keys in different situations. The watch window is empty when CodeView 3.14 is started. The source1 window contains the source statements of the program, with the line of the next instruction to be executed highlighted and the line numbers along the left side. The command window, which replaces the dialog window of the earlier version, is also empty when CodeView 3.14 starts. The register window on the right shows the contents of the registers and the state of all flags except TF.

Every boundary between windows can be moved to partition the screen differently. The contents of all windows can also be scrolled.

There are still three modes of interaction with CodeView 3.14. To use the menus, select the word of the menu title either by clicking the mouse on it or by tapping the ALT key in conjunction with the first letter of the title. A menu will then drop down. To select the desired entry in the menu, either click the mouse on it, use the arrow keys to move the

### A.46  Appendix 5  Microsoft Software

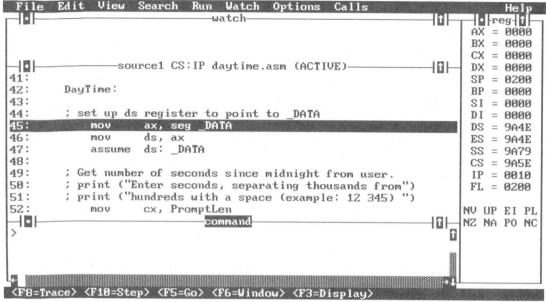

**Figure A5.7**  CodeView 3.14 Screen with Watch, Source1, Command, and Register Windows

highlight to it and tap ENTER, or tap the highlighted letter of the menu item. Some menu entries have a shortcut listed following their names. For example, CTRLW is the shortcut for selecting ADD WATCH... from the Watch menu.

To type commands, just type, and the command will be echoed to the next line of the command window. The response to the command may appear in the command window or may alter the contents of one or more windows, depending on the command. Some commands, especially those that cause one or more instructions of the program to execute, are not echoed, but their execution affects the display in other ways.

Some of the menu options and what they do are given in Table A5.11. Although some of the menu options are the same as in previous versions of CodeView, there are enough differences that a new table is worthwhile.

The function keys provide shortcuts for many menu functions and commands. All of the functions listed earlier in Table A5.7 apply to the new version. Some additional functions are listed in Table A5.12.

There are more ways to move around the display and alter the windows than in previous versions of CodeView. Some of these ways are listed in Table A5.13. A mouse is especially convenient. Clicking in any window positions the cursor in that window. Dragging (clicking and holding the button down while moving the mouse) the line between any two windows moves the line and changes the window sizes. Every window, when active, also has two scroll bars, and the usual ways of using a mouse with scroll bars are supported.

CodeView 3.14 can be used to execute the instructions in programs one at a time (or rapidly up to a breakpoint) and display the contents of the registers and selected memory locations. The register window displays the registers. Selected memory locations can be displayed as either watches or memory dumps; both of these arrangements are updated

**Table A5.11  Some Menu Selections of CodeView 3.14**

| Menu Title | Selected Option | Action |
|---|---|---|
| File | Exit | Terminates CodeView 3.14 session. |
| View | Source | Opens a second source window. |
|  | Memory | Opens memory window. |
|  | Register | Opens register window. |
|  | 8087 | Opens 8087 register window. |
|  | Watch | Opens watch window. |
|  | Command | Opens command window. |
|  | Output | Switches display to program output; tap any key to return to CodeView 3.14 display. |
|  | Maximize | Enlarges active window to full screen (menu entry changes to Restore). |
|  | Restore | Restores display to multiple windows (menu entry changes to Maximize). |
|  | Size | Initiates sequence to change the size of the active window. |
|  | Close | Closes the active window. |
| Run | Restart | Resets CodeView 3.14 to the beginning of the program; does not affect breakpoints of watch statements. |
|  | Animate | Runs the program in slow motion until its end, a breakpoint is reached, or a key is tapped. |
| Watch | Add Watch... | Asks for a watch expression and adds that expression to the watch window. |
|  | Delete Watch... | Displays all current watch expressions; highlighting one and tapping ENTER deletes that expression. Includes option to delete all watches. |
|  | Set BreakPoint... | Sets breakpoints and options to control breakpoint. |
|  | Edit BreakPoints... | Adds, removes, modifies, enables, disables, and clears breakpoints and options that control breakpoint. |
| Options | Source Window... | Selects mode in which source is displayed (Source, Assembly, or Mixed). |
|  | Memory Window... | Selects format for contents of memory window. |
| Help | — | Provides on-line help on using CodeView 3.14. |


**Table A5.12  Additional Function Keys in CodeView 3.14**

| Key | Action |
|---|---|
| F1 | Invokes context-sensitive help, which displays information on token at cursor position. |
| F3 | Cycles source window through source, mixed, and assembly displays. |
| SHIFT+F3 | Cycles memory window through all available formats. |
| CTRL+F4 | Closes current window. |
| F6 | Moves cursor to next window. |
| SHIFT+F6 | Moves cursor to previous window. |
| CTRL+F8 | Initiates sequence to change size of current window. An arrow key selects side of window to move; arrow keys then move that side; ENTER terminates size operation. |
| CTRL+F10 | Toggles between maximize current window and restore multiple window display. |

Table A5.13  Cursor Move and Window Scroll in CodeView 3.14

| Keys | Action |
| --- | --- |
| F6 | Moves cursor to next window. |
| SHIFT+F6 | Moves cursor to previous window. |
| UP | Moves cursor up one line, scrolling if necessary. |
| DOWN | Moves cursor down one line, scrolling if necessary. |
| CTRL+UP | Scrolls active window up one line. |
| CTRL+DOWN | Scrolls active window down one line. |
| PAGEUP | Scrolls current window up the size of the window. |
| PAGEDOWN | Scrolls current window down the size of the window. |
| HOME | Moves cursor to beginning of line. |
| END | Moves cursor to end of line. |
| CTRL+HOME | Scrolls to top of file or command buffer. |
| CTRL+END | Scrolls to bottom of file or command buffer. |

Notes for mouse users:
1. Dragging the line that separates any two (or more) windows changes the sizes of the windows.
2. The contents of the current window can be scrolled in both directions using the scroll bars.

as execution proceeds. The previous examples using CodeView 2.2 are repeated here for version 3.14.

Referring back to the situation shown in Figure A5.7, two commands must be typed to watch KSec and USec. The first of these commands is entered as

```
w? KSec,i
```

The W? command is used to enter a watch expression; the trailing comma and i specify the format as a signed integer to be displayed in base 10.

To add the third watch, use the menu. First select Watch from the menu bar (using ALT+W). The Watch menu appears. The first entry of the menu, Add Watch..., is already highlighted, so just tap ENTER to select it. Also note that CTRL+W could be used to select this option. The ellipsis points in the menu selection mean that there is another entry to be made. In the case of Add Watch..., that additional entry is the expression to be added to the window. When Add Watch... is selected, the Watch menu is removed, and a dialog box appears with a prompt; the cursor also appears in the box. Type the expression to be watched. In Figure A5.8, typing Hour,i tells CodeView 3.14 to watch the variable Hour and display its value as a signed integer in base 10. Note at the bottom of the Add Watch window that there are three buttons. The <OK> button is highlighted by default. When ENTER is pressed, it is selected; it can also be selected with the mouse. The other two buttons cancel the Add Watch... command or display help. Note also that on the very bottom of the screen, there are directions for using the Add Watch window.

Use CTRL+W to enter Minute and Second into the watch window with integer formats, too. Then execute the instructions of the program up to but not including the instruction in line 84. This task can be performed by moving the cursor to line 84 in the source1 window, tapping F9 to set a breakpoint, and tapping F5 to execute to that point. See Figure A5.9. Note the output in the command window regarding the breakpoint. In the watch window, KSec and USec now contain 15 and 678, respectively. The program has converted 15,678 seconds into 4 hours (still in AX; 4 will be saved in Hour when the

CodeView 3.14  A.49

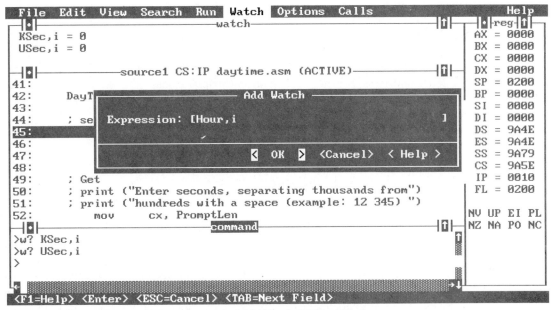

**Figure A5.8** CodeView 3.14 Screen with Add Watch Dialog Window

next instruction executes), 21 minutes (in Minute), and 18 seconds (in Second). Note that the last instruction executed saved the contents of DX (0015h) in Minute.

The next instruction saves AX in Hour. There is another item displayed in Figure A5.9. The instruction that is highlighted has an operand in memory, specified as Hour in the

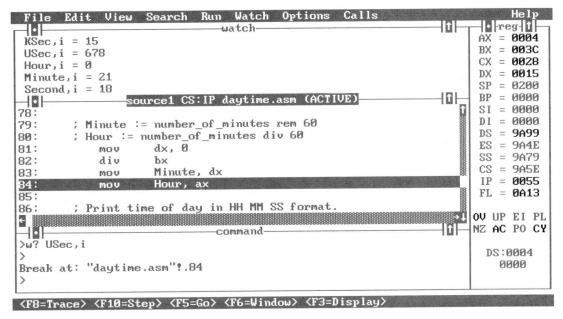

**Figure A5.9** CodeView 3.14 Screen, with Watch Expressions after BreakPoint Encountered

source statement. In the lower right corner, CodeView 3.14 displays the address of this operand as DS:0004. Below that, it displays the value stored there, 0000.

Blocks of memory can be viewed conveniently in a memory window. If invoked from the menus, the first of the two possible memory windows displays the block starting at CS:0000; to view a different region, move the cursor to the address in the memory window (along the left), and type in a new segment and displacement. It is more convenient to specify the start of the block symbolically when requesting the memory window by using the dialog command. The syntax is

vm<type> expression

where <type> is a one-letter data type (see Table A5.10). For example, to view an array of words named List, issue the command

vmw List

This command opens the first memory window between the source1 window and the command window and displays in it the contents of memory starting at List. To view more of the contents of memory, scroll the window.

There are many features of CodeView 3.14 that have not been explored here. Hopefully enough has been presented to enable you to start using CodeView; the on-line help and reference manual should enable you to explore many other features that you might find useful.

## PROGRAMMER'S WORKBENCH

Microsoft includes their integrated program-development environment, the Programmer's Workbench, with MASM 6.0. This environment, which uses an interface much like that for CodeView 3.14, provides a text editor, context-sensitive help, CodeView, build (assemble and link) facilities, and a source code Browser. It is not necessary to use this environment to work with MASM 6.0. The interested reader should consult the reference manual and spend some time becoming familiar with the environment before planning productive use.

Microsoft also provides a number of other useful tools with their assembler. These tools are beyond the scope of this text.

# Borland Software A.6

In this appendix, tools available from Borland International for working in assembly language are briefly examined. These tools include Turbo Assembler (TASM), the cross-reference utility TCREF, Turbo Link (TLINK), Turbo Librarian (TLIB), Turbo Debugger (TD), and the file-dumping utility TDUMP.

## TASM

TASM is invoked with all file specifications and options on the command line. Although multiple file sets can be included, each with different options and wildcards in filenames, this discussion is limited to assembling a single file. The syntax of the command line is

TASM [options] source[,object][,listing][,crossref]

where

| | |
|---|---|
| options | are codes that control assembler activity |
| source | is the name of the source file (.ASM extension assumed) |
| object | is the name of the object file (.OBJ extension assumed) |
| listing | is the name of an optional listing file (.LST extension assumed) |
| crossref | is the name of an optional cross-reference file (.XRF extension assumed) |

The listing and cross-reference files are created only if requested. For example,

TASM PROG,,WORK

reads PROG.ASM as the source file, assembles PROG.OBJ, and creates a listing file named WORK.LST. The command

TASM PROG,,,

reads PROG.ASM as the source file, assembles PROG.OBJ, and creates both PROG.LST and PROG.XRF.

TASM reports the name of the file it is assembling along with any error and warning messages. When the assembler finishes, it displays the number of error messages, the number of warning messages, the number of passes it made, and the remaining memory.

There are many options that can be included on the TASM command line. Some options are listed in Table A6.1.

A.51

Table A6.1  Selected Options for TASM Command

| Option | Action |
| --- | --- |
| /H | Displays a help screen consisting of command line syntax and a list of all options; no other options or filenames should be used with /H; entering TASM with no other options or filenames also displays the help screen. |
| /W | Enables generation of "mild" warnings. |
| /W- | Disables generation of all warnings. |
| /W+ | Enables generation of all warnings. |
| /Z | Displays lines containing errors along with the error messages. |
| /ZD | Writes line number information to object file for use with some debuggers. |
| /ZI | Writes line number and symbolic information to object file for use with Turbo Debugger. |
| /Dsymbol[ = value] | Defines the symbol and optionally assigns a string value to it. |
| /MU | Converts all lowercase letters in names to capitals (default). |
| /MX | Makes all public and external names case-sensitive. |
| /ML | Makes all names case-sensitive. |

The listing file created by TASM when assembling program Welcome.ASM of Chapter 3 is shown in Figure A6.1. As in Chapter 3, a PAGE 56,100 directive was inserted at the beginning of the file so that it would be printed in a form that would reproduce well; TASM does not include that directive in the listing file.

The first section of the listing file shows the source program, the code generated for each line, and the offset of that code. It also shows a line number for use with the tables at the end of the file. For example, line 64 of the listing file is essentially

```
64  001F  A3 0000r         mov    Languages, ax
```

The mov instruction is assembled in the code segment at displacement 001Fh; it is coded as A30000h, where A3h specifies the operation on the AX register and 0000h is the displacement of the memory operand relative to the data segment. The "r" following the displacement indicates a relative displacement that may be changed when the linker combines this data segment with others. An instruction assembled with 0000e for the displacement is a reference to an external symbol; these displacements must be resolved by the linker.

The final section of Figure A6.1 shows the symbol table and the groups and segments table. In the symbol table, every name used in the program and some names provided by TASM are listed along with their type and value. Values for names and labels are given as a segment name and displacement or as just a segment for external names. The symbol table includes a cross-reference table, showing where every instance of a symbol occurs. The references use the line numbers on the listing, not the line numbers in the file. Note how line 18 of the source file generates five lines on the listing, so source line 19 is listing line 23. Where a # appears in the cross-reference, the symbol is defined on that line.

## TCREF

The assembler can create a cross-reference file named with the .XRF extension. This file is coded in binary; to display its contents, use the TCREF utility. TCREF takes two parameters: a list of object files separated with plus signs and the name of an output file.

TCREF                                                                    A.53

Turbo Assembler   Version 2.0      02/17/92 20:45:38      Page 1
welcome.ASM


```
 1                                  ; Program 3.1      Welcome.ASM
 2                                  ; Prints a welcome message, reads how many languages the
 3                                  ;   user knows, and prints a message increasing it by 1.
 4
 5                                  ; DOS function and status parameters
 6        = 0021                    DosFunc     equ     21h
 7        = 004C                    ExitToDos   equ     4Ch
 8        = 0000                    NoErrors    equ     00h
 9
10                                          DOSSEG
11
12 0000                             _STACK SEGMENT para stack 'stack'
13 0000  0100*(????)                            dw      100h dup (?)
14 0200                             _STACK ENDS
15
16 0000                             _DATA SEGMENT word public 'data'
17 0000  ????                       Languages   dw      ?
18 0002  57 65 6C 63 6F 6D 65+      HelloMsg    db      "Welcome to 8086 Assembly Language."
19       20 74 6F 20 38 30 38+
20       36 20 41 73 73 65 6D+
21       62 6C 79 20 4C 61 6E+
22       67 75 61 67 65 2E
23 0024  0022                       HelloLen    dw      34
24 0026  48 6F 77 20 6D 61 6E+      PromptMsg   db      "How many languages do you know? "
25       79 20 6C 61 6E 67 75+
26       61 67 65 73 20 64 6F+
27       20 79 6F 75 20 6B 6E+
28       6F 77 3F 20
29 0046  0020                       PromptLen   dw      32
30 0048  20 69 73 20 61 20 67+      ReplyMsg    db      " is a good start.  Soon you'll know "
31       6F 6F 64 20 73 74 61+
32       72 74 2E 20 20 53 6F+
33       6F 6E 20 79 6F 75 27+
34       6C 6C 20 6B 6E 6F 77+
35       20
36 006C  0024                       ReplyLen    dw      36
37 006E                             _DATA ENDS
38
39 0000                             _TEXT SEGMENT word public 'code'
40                                          assume  cs: _TEXT
41                                          extrn   PutStr: PROC, PutCrLf: PROC
42                                          extrn   GetDec: PROC, PutDec: PROC
43
44 0000                             Welcome:
45
46                                  ; set up ds register to point to _DATA
47 0000  B8 0000s                           mov     ax, seg _DATA
48 0003  8E D8                              mov     ds, ax
49                                          assume  ds: _DATA
50
51                                  ; print ("Welcome to 8086 Assembly Language.")
```

**Figure A6.1   Listing File Created by TASM when Assembling** Welcome.ASM

```
Turbo Assembler         Version 2.0        02/17/92 20:45:38      Page 2
welcome.ASM


52 0005  8B 0E 0024r              mov     cx, HelloLen
53 0009  BB 0002r                 mov     bx, offset HelloMsg
54 000C  E8 0000e                 call    PutStr
55 000F  E8 0000e                 call    PutCrLf
56
57                        ; print ("How many languages do you know? ")
58 0012  8B 0E 0046r              mov     cx, PromptLen
59 0016  BB 0026r                 mov     bx, offset PromptMsg
60 0019  E8 0000e                 call    PutStr
61
62                        ; read (Languages)
63 001C  E8 0000e                 call    GetDec
64 001F  A3 0000r                 mov     Languages, ax
65
66                        ; print (Languages, " is a good start.  Soon you'll know ")
67 0022  E8 0000e                 call    PutCrLf
68 0025  E8 0000e                 call    PutDec
69
70 0028  8B 0E 006Cr              mov     cx, ReplyLen
71 002C  BB 0048r                 mov     bx, offset ReplyMsg
72 002F  E8 0000e                 call    PutStr
73
74                        ; Languages := Languages + 1
75 0032  FF 06 0000r              inc     Languages
76
77                        ; print (Languages)
78 0036  A1 0000r                 mov     ax, Languages
79 0039  E8 0000e                 call    PutDec
80 003C  E8 0000e                 call    PutCrLf
81
82                        ; exit to DOS
83 003F  B4 4C                    mov     ah, ExitToDos
84 0041  B0 00                    mov     al, NoErrors
85 0043  CD 21                    int     DosFunc
86
87 0045                   _TEXT   ENDS
88                        END     Welcome
```

**Figure A6.1**  (*continued*)

For example, Chapter 8 presents a simple main program and two separate functions that are linked (along with the input and output routines) to form one program. If these routines are assembled with TASM and cross-reference files are requested, TCREF can be used to combine the three .XRF files into a single .REF file, which can then be examined. To accomplish this task, issue the command

TCREF NESTDMAX+MAX2FN+MAX3FN,NESTDMAX

## TLINK

Turbo Link, also called TLINK, expects all options and filenames to be specified on the command line as

LINK [options] objects,executable,map,libraries

**TLINK** A.55

```
Turbo Assembler      Version 2.0      02/17/92 20:45:38      Page 3
Symbol Table
```

| Symbol Name | Type | Value | Cref (defined at #) |
|---|---|---|---|
| ??DATE | Text | "02/17/92" | |
| ??FILENAME | Text | "welcome " | |
| ??TIME | Text | "20:45:37" | |
| ??VERSION | Number | 0200 | |
| @CPU | Text | 0101H | |
| @CURSEG | Text | _TEXT | #12  #16  #39 |
| @FILENAME | Text | WELCOME | |
| @WORDSIZE | Text | 2 | #12  #16  #39 |
| DOSFUNC | Number | 0021 | #6  85 |
| EXITTODOS | Number | 004C | #7  83 |
| GETDEC | Near | _TEXT:---- Extern | #42  63 |
| HELLOLEN | Word | _DATA:0024 | #23  52 |
| HELLOMSG | Byte | _DATA:0002 | #18  53 |
| LANGUAGES | Word | _DATA:0000 | #17  64  75  78 |
| NOERRORS | Number | 0000 | #8  84 |
| PROMPTLEN | Word | _DATA:0046 | #29  58 |
| PROMPTMSG | Byte | _DATA:0026 | #24  59 |
| PUTCRLF | Near | _TEXT:---- Extern | #41  55  67  80 |
| PUTDEC | Near | _TEXT:---- Extern | #42  68  79 |
| PUTSTR | Near | _TEXT:---- Extern | #41  54  60  72 |
| REPLYLEN | Word | _DATA:006C | #36  70 |
| REPLYMSG | Byte | _DATA:0048 | #30  71 |
| WELCOME | Near | _TEXT:0000 | #44  88 |

| Groups & Segments | Bit | Size | Align | Combine | Class | Cref (defined at #) |
|---|---|---|---|---|---|---|
| _DATA | 16 | 006E | Word | Public | DATA | #16  47  49 |
| _STACK | 16 | 0200 | Para | Stack | STACK | #12 |
| _TEXT | 16 | 0045 | Word | Public | CODE | #39  40 |

**Figure A6.1**  (*continued*)

where

| options | are codes that control linker activity |
|---|---|
| objects | are the names of the object files to combine (.OBJ extension assumed) |
| executable | is the name of the executable file to create (.EXE extension assumed) |
| map | is the name of the map file to create (.MAP extension assumed) |
| libraries | are the names of any library files to be linked to the object files (.LIB extension assumed) |

The name of the first object file is used for the executable and map files (if created) with appropriate extensions unless other names are provided. If the default names are acceptable, the field can be skipped, but the separating comma must be supplied. For example,

```
TLINK MAIN SUB1,,,\LIB\IO
```

links `MAIN.OBJ`, `SUB1.OBJ`, and `IO.LIB` to create the executable `MAIN.EXE` and a listing file `MAIN.MAP`. Or

```
TLINK MAIN SUB1 IO
```

links `MAIN.OBJ`, `SUB1.OBJ`, and `IO.OBJ` to create the executable `MAIN.EXE` and a listing file `MAIN.MAP`. To suppress the map file, the /x option must be used.

There are many options that can be included on the LINK command line. Some options are listed in Table A6.2.

The default map includes a table of all segments giving the segment name, its start and end displacements, its length, and its class name. The map also includes tables of all public symbols, sorted by name and by value, and the entry point of the program.

## TLIB

The TLIB utility is used to create and modify libraries. To make sense of the operations involved, it is necessary to distinguish between object files and object modules. Both contain object code produced by a compiler or an assembler, but an object file is an independent file, whereas an object module is part of a library. For example, `PUTSTR.OBJ` and `PUTCRLF.OBJ` are separate object files; the `IO.LIB` library includes both the `PUTSTR` and `PUTCRLF` object modules, among others.

One advantage of using libraries is that doing so simplifies the commands needed to link a program. For example, by specifying the `IO.LIB` library when linking, any of the object modules in it that are referenced are linked into the executable file. If the library is not used, it will be necessary to list each needed object file separately when linking.

The use of object files instead of libraries could be facilitated by combining the source code for all routines into one single source file and assembling them into one large object file, but there are two drawbacks to this approach: First, all source files to be combined must be written in the same language; second, even if only one routine in the object file is needed, all routines in the file, as well as all routines that they invoke, must be included in the executable file. With libraries, only the needed object modules are included in the executable file.

An object module contains all of the routines of the object file from which it was created. Note that if we start with all code for several routines in one source file, create a single object file from that source file, and then create an object module from that object file, the object module will contain all of the routines. When linked, all of the routines in the module will be included in the executable file. However, if each routine is in a separate source file, the library will ultimately contain separate modules for each routine, and only those routines actually invoked will be included in the executable file.

Table A6.2  Selected Options for TLINK

| Option | Action |
|---|---|
|  | Entering TLINK with no options or filenames displays a help screen consisting of command line syntax and a list of all options. |
| /X | Suppresses creation of map file. |
| /M | Includes all public symbols defined in the object files in the map. |
| /C | Makes all public and external names case-sensitive. |
| /V | Includes symbolic and line number information in the executable file for use with Turbo Debugger. |

The TLIB utility is invoked with all filenames, options, and commands on one line. The syntax of the command line is

TLIB libname [options] [operations] [,listfile]

The two options are for advanced uses; they will not be considered here. The name of the library to create or modify is required; it is assumed to have a .LIB extension if none is provided. The list file, if requested, has a default extension of .LST and will contain a list of each module in the library and each public symbol in that library.

The operations for the TLIB utility are listed in Table A6.3. The operations can be given on the command line in any order; they are always performed in this order: all extractions (*) first, then all removals (−), then all additions (+). If no operations are specified, a list file can still be created.

As an example of using TLIB, the following command adds a module to IO.LIB:

TLIB IO + GETSTR, IO.LST

The module is derived from the file GetStr.OBJ, which has been created from GetStr.ASM in Chapter 15 and copied to the same directory as IO.LIB. This command modifies IO.LIB to include the GETSTR module and writes the lists of modules and public symbols to the file IO.LST.

## TURBO DEBUGGER

Turbo Debugger (TD) is a window-oriented symbolic debugging tool. It is a very powerful and flexible tool; its treatment here, by necessity, is limited to few of its features. There are typically three or four ways of doing everything in order to accommodate mouse users and individual work habits. One way of performing the operations is presented here, illustrating several of the work styles you can develop; the mouse is not used in this example, because those users with a mouse can readily adapt to a keyboard approach. The presentation here is more like a tutorial than a reference; the on-line help is a useful reference.

To prepare a program written entirely in assembly language for use with Turbo Debugger, the source file must be assembled with the /zi option, and the object file must be linked with the /v option. These options copy symbolic data and line number information to the executable file for TD to use.

The command line to invoke Turbo Debugger is

TD [options] [progname [arguments]]

Table A6.3  Commands Used with TLIB

| Command | Operand | Action |
| --- | --- | --- |
| + | Object file | Adds object module to library. |
| + | Library file | Adds all object modules of operand to library. |
| − | Module name | Deletes module from library. |
| * | Module name | Creates a file and copies the module to it. |
| −+ | Module name | Replaces module from library with one from corresponding file. |
| *− | Module name | Creates a file, copies module into it, then deletes module from library. |

The options are described in the Turbo Debugger reference guide and are listed when TD is started with the -? option. No options are needed for the presentation here; if some option is needed to adjust for local circumstances, check with a local expert or see the reference guide. The arguments that follow the name of the program are present in the PSP as a copy of the command line (see Section 11.5).

The startup screen that TD displays contains a menu bar across the top; a Module window filling most of the screen; a small, empty Watches window; and a helpful list of keys across the bottom line. The Module window is the active window, indicated by the double-line border and the scroll bars along its right and bottom edges. The list of keys along the bottom of the screen are context-sensitive, changing when different windows and commands are selected. Holding down ALT or CTRL displays other lists, which are also context-sensitive. Figure A6.2 shows the TD startup screen when invoked with Daytime.ASM of Chapter 4 as the program to debug.

The first thing to do is to set watches for the variables in this program. Do this using PageUp and the arrow keys to scroll through the Module window until the _DATA segment is on the screen and the cursor is on the name Second (anywhere on the name is okay). Type CTRL+W, which copies Second into the Watches window. CTRL+F7 could also be typed, which displays a dialog window with Second already typed in; the expression could then be modified and ENTER could be tapped to have the expression entered in the Watches window. Alternatively, F10 could be tapped to activate the menu bar, D could be tapped to select the Data menu, and then the option to add a watch could be selected, which brings up the same dialog window as CTRL+F7.

Following either choice, move the cursor up one line so that it is on Minute and tap CTRL+W to enter Minute in the Watches window. Note that new watches are added at

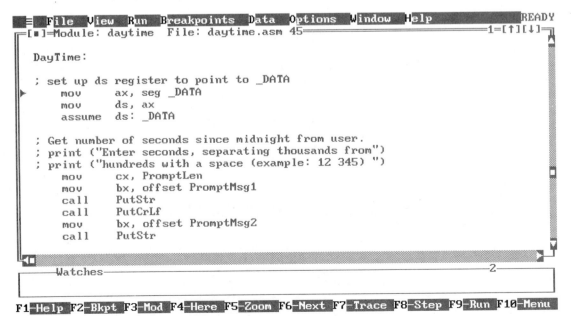

**Figure A6.2** Turbo Debugger, Initial Display

the top of the window; by entering them from bottom to top within the _DATA segment, the variables will appear in the Watches window in the same order. The Watches window is enlarged automatically as new expressions are added to it. Its size and position can be controlled (those commands will be discussed shortly). After adding the remaining variables to the Watches window, the screen appears as in Figure A6.3. Note that values are displayed as words (the variables are defined with dw) in both base 10 and base 16.

Next, it is desired to add the Registers window to the display. Do this by tapping F10 to activate the menu and then selecting View from the menu bar and Registers from the menu. This sequence displays the Register window, as shown in Figure A6.4. Note that the Register window is active (it has a double-line border but no scroll bars).

The Register window is not at a desirable on-screen location. If we leave it there and switch to the Module window, the portion of the Module window that overlaps the Register window will overwrite, blocking the view of half of the registers. So it's a good idea to move the Register window. To do so, tap F10 to activate the menu bar, select the Window menu, and select Size/move from that menu; also note that that menu suggests CTRL+F5 as a shortcut. When Size/move is selected from the menu, the list of keys at the bottom of the screen changes to those keys used in moving and resizing the window. Tap the right and up arrow keys and a single line outline of the Register window moves. Continue moving it until the outline is in the top right corner of the screen. See Figure A6.5, which also shows the active command in the top right corner and the keys used to move and resize a window along the bottom. When ENTER is tapped, the Register window moves to the position where the outline was moved. Note in Figure A6.5 that the left edge of the outline is under the space

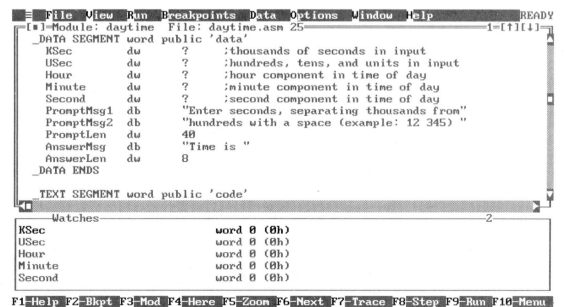

**Figure A6.3** Turbo Debugger Display with Five Watch Variables

### A.60 Appendix 6 Borland Software

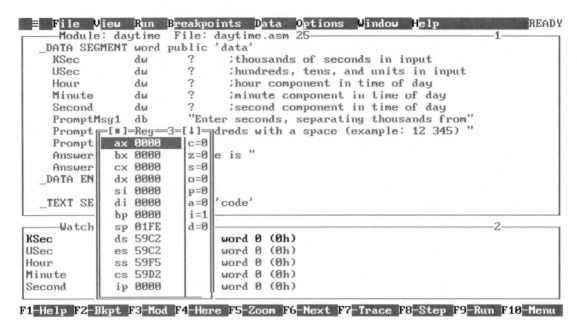

**Figure A6.4** Turbo Debugger Display after Opening Register Window

**Figure A6.5** Turbo Debugger Display during Move of Register Window

following Help in the menu bar. Now, the next step is to shrink the Module window so that it does not overlap the Register window. To do so, first tap F6 twice to make the Module window active. Then the Size/move command is again needed, but use CTRL+F5 to invoke it. Then hold down SHIFT and tap the left arrow key to shrink the window. While doing so, the right edge of an outline moves to the left. When the outline reaches the "p" in Help, tap ENTER. The Module window is then reduced to the size of the outline, as shown in Figure A6.6.

Now that the windows are configured as desired, proceed to execute the program. The intention is to execute up to the instruction

```
mov     Hour, ax
```

on line 84. Set a breakpoint there by moving the cursor to line 84 using the PAGEDOWN and arrow keys, then tap F2. The F2 key toggles the breakpoint at the line in the Module window; when the breakpoint is set, the line is underlined or displayed in a different color. With the breakpoint set, tap F9 to execute the program up to the breakpoint. Or, rather than setting a breakpoint, execute the instructions one at a time using F7 and F8. These two keys work the same way, except when a call instruction is encountered; F7 will attempt to trace into the called procedure or function, whereas F8 will step over it (the procedure or function is executed as a single step). As the program executes, watch the values of the variables and in the registers change. When execution reaches line 84, the display is as shown in Figure A6.7.

Note in Figure A6.7 that Ksec and Usec contain 15 and 678 respectively. The program has converted 15,678 seconds into 4 hours (still in AX, to be saved in Hour by the next instruction), 21 minutes (0015h, still in DX, too), and 18 seconds.

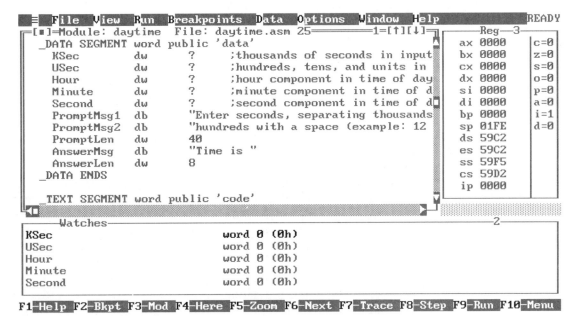

**Figure A6.6** Turbo Debugger Display after Move of Register Window

## A.62 Appendix 6 Borland Software

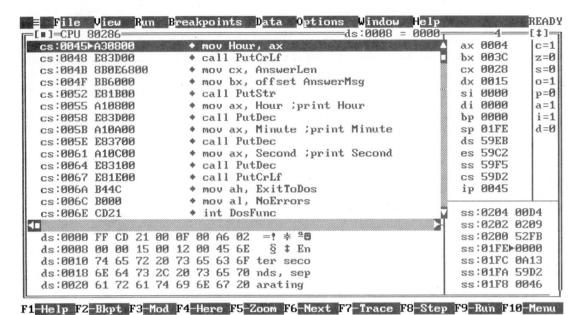

**Figure A6.7** Turbo Debugger Display after Executing to Line 84

There is another useful display. Tapping F10 to activate the menu bar, selecting View from the menu bar, and selecting CPU from the menu displays a window with five panes. Then tapping F5 (note the entry on the bottom line of most TD figures) "zooms" the window to full screen. The result is shown in Figure A6.8.

The largest pane in the CPU window is the code pane. In Figure A6.8, the code pane is the active pane, indicated by the presence of a highlighted line and scroll bars. The code pane contains the assembly-language source statements with all extra spaces edited out, the actual machine code in hexadecimal, and the offset of the code relative to CS. The contents of this pane can be rotated through several optional displays using ALT+F10 to activate the local menu (F10 always activates the menu bar at the top of the screen; ALT+F10 activates a context-sensitive local menu) and then selecting Mixed until the desired format is listed.

With the CPU pane displayed, F8 steps over not only called procedures and functions, treating them as a single instruction, but also int and loop and repeated string instructions.

The TAB key moves the highlight from one pane to another, changing the active pane. Tapping it once makes the register pane active. Tapping it again makes the flags pane active. Tapping it again makes the stack pane in the bottom right corner active. Note the position of the triangle in the stack pane; it points to the top of the stack. The stack pane can be scrolled to allow other portions of the stack to be seen.

One more tap of the TAB key makes the dump pane below the code pane active. Look at the dump pane. Holding down CTRL with the dump pane active brings up a list of hot keys for modifying the dump pane. To change the starting address of the dump, tap CTRL+G. A dialog window appears, prompting for an address. The address can be entered using a segment name like DS:0100. To change the display format of the dump, tap CTRL+D. A menu appears with the possible formats; select one and tap ENTER.

# TDUMP

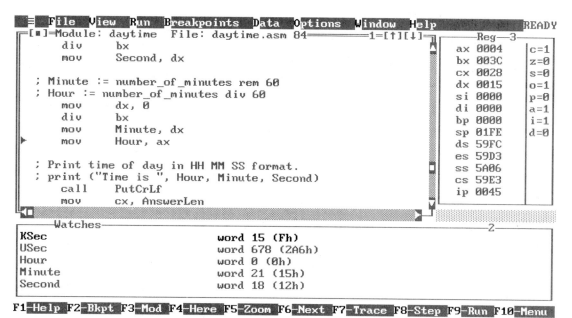

**Figure A6.8** Turbo Debugger Display with CPU Window

The CPU window can be resized and moved just like any other window. If symbolic information for a program is not available, TD starts with the CPU window rather than the Module or Watches windows.

To exit TD, tap F10 to activate the menu bar, select File from the menu bar, and select Quit from the File menu. Or tap ALT+X.

Watch expressions in TD are sensitive to the scope of identifiers. If a symbol used in an expression is not defined within a procedure or function, the Watches window will show the value as ????. This mode of operation is useful in debugging high-level languages, but it makes watching arguments in assembly language rather awkward. One way to watch arguments is to display the CPU window and examine the arguments in the stack pane and the values passed by reference in the dump pane. It also helps to watch the registers, particularly BP, when debugging involves the arguments.

There are many other commands and options; the presentation here should enable the reader to begin using Turbo Debugger. When using TD, remember that holding down CTRL or ALT changes the list of hot keys and that ALT+F10 displays a local menu. Memorizing all of the commands and options is not an easy task, so learn to explore TD as you use it. For reference, the commands used in this section, as well as a few more, are summarized in Tables A6.4 and A6.5.

## TDUMP

The file-dumping utility TDUMP is useful for inspecting the contents of binary files. With TDUMP, any file can be displayed as a hexadecimal or ASCII dump; object, library,

**Table A6.4  Some Menu Selections for Turbo Debugger**

| Menu title | Selected option | Hot key | Action |
|---|---|---|---|
| File | Open... | | Opens a new program to debug. |
| | Quit | ALT+X | Terminates TD. |
| View | Watches | | Displays watch-selected variables. |
| | Module | | Displays program source module. |
| | CPU | | Displays window containing code, data, registers, flags, and stack panes. |
| | Dump | | Displays a region of memory. |
| | Registers | | Displays registers and flags. |
| | Numeric Processor | | Displays coprocessor or emulator registers. |
| Run | Run | F9 | Runs program to its end or until a breakpoint reached. |
| | Go To Cursor | F4 | Runs program to the current cursor location. |
| | Trace Into | F7 | Executes one source line or one instruction. |
| | Step Over | F8 | Executes one source line or instruction, stepping over CALLs and repeated instructions. |
| | Animate... | | Runs the program in slow motion until its end, a breakpoint is reached, or any key is tapped. |
| | Program Reset | CTRL+F2 | Resets TD to the start of the program; does not affect breakpoints or watches. |
| Breakpoints | Toggle | F2 | Toggles breakpoint at cursor location. |
| | Delete All | | Deletes all breakpoints. |
| Data | Evaluate/Modify... | CTRL+F4 | Evaluates an expression. |
| | Add Watch... | CTRL+F7 | Adds variable to the watch window. |
| Options | Save Options... | | Saves screen layout and other options to file on disk. |
| | Restore Options... | | Restores previously saved options from file on disk. |
| Window | Zoom | F5 | Zooms window to full screen or back to previous size. |
| | Next | F6 | Makes next window active. |
| | Next Pane | Tab | Makes next pane in window active. |
| | Size/move | CTRL+F5 | Changes the size and position of a window. |
| | Close | ALT+F3 | Closes the active window. |
| | User Screen | ALT+F5 | Displays the user screen; any keystoke returns to TD display. |

and executable files can also be dumped according to their internal record formats. The command line for TDUMP is

TDUMP [options] infile [outfile]

If no options are specified, the extension of the input file determines the type of dump generated. If no output file is specified, the output is displayed on the user's screen. If no options or filenames are specified, TDUMP displays the command line syntax and a list of options. Some of the useful options discussed in Chapter 11 are listed in Table A6.6. Refer to Chapter 11 for a discussion of object, library, and executable file formats.

Borland International provides several other tools that are of interest to users of assembly language; they are beyond the scope of this text.

**Table A6.5   Function and Hot Keys in Turbo Debugger**

| Key | Action |
|---|---|
| F1 | Provides context-sensitive help. |
| F2 | Toggles breakpoint at cursor location. |
| F4 | Executes program to cursor location. |
| F5 | Zooms active window to full screen or reduces it to previous size. |
| F6 | Makes next window active. |
| F7 | Executes next instruction, tracing into calls. |
| F8 | Executes next instruction, stepping over calls and repeated instructions. |
| F9 | Executes program to end or breakpoint. |
| F10 | Activates menu bar at top of display. |
| ALT+F3 | Closes active window. |
| ALT+F5 | Shows the user screen. |
| ALT+F10 | Activates and displays local menu. |
| ALT+1 | Makes window #1 active. |
| ⋮ | ⋮ |
| ALT+9 | Makes window #9 active. |
| ALT+X | Terminates TD. |
| CTRL+F2 | Resets TD to start of program. |
| CTRL+F4 | Evaluates an expression. |
| CTRL+F5 | Changes the size and position of active window. |
| CTRL+F7 | Adds variable to Watches window. |
| TAB | Makes next pane active or moves to next field in dialog box. |
| SHIFT+TAB | Makes previous pane active or moves to previous field in dialog box. |

**Table A6.6   Options for TDUMP**

| Option | Meaning |
|---|---|
| /a | Dumps file as ASCII characters, substituting "." for all nonprinting characters. |
| /h | Dumps file in hexadecimal, with ASCII interpretation appended on right. |
| /o | Dumps file in special object record format. |
| /l | Dumps file in special library record format. |
| /e | Dumps file in special executable record format. |

# A.7 High-Level-Language Information

This appendix summarizes some of the requirements for linking routines written in assembly language to a program written in a high-level language. It does not consider assembly language calls to high-level-language routines. This appendix is not exhaustive, but it does serve as a guide that should be useful in conjunction with the course of study pursued in the text.

The appendix is organized by language. Within each language, the following topics are discussed:

- Name conventions (case and length)
- Representation of data types
- Segment conventions
- Register usage conventions
- Argument-passing conventions
- Function value return conventions

The details of three Pascal implementations are presented since Pascal is the language most likely to be used in the setting for which this text is intended. In addition, C and FORTRAN are generically presented.

Many fine compilers for Pascal, C, FORTRAN, and a number of other languages are available for 80x86 computers. The treatment in this appendix should not be taken as an endorsement or a criticism of any product.

## PASCAL

### Names

Identifiers in Pascal are not case-sensitive; all lowercase letters are converted to capital letters. There is no standard limit on the length of identifiers; Turbo Pascal and Microsoft QuickPascal recognize the first 63 characters; Microsoft Pascal recognizes the first 8 characters.

### Data Types

Table A7.1 summarizes the numeric data types and their variations. The 6-byte Real data type is not supported by the 80x87 coprocessor but instead is implemented by routines provided in the Pascal library.

The Boolean data type is represented using one byte, with `False` represented as 00h and `True` as 01h.

Values of type `Char` are stored one per byte, as are elements of arrays of `Char`. Although strings are not included in standard Pascal, most implementations provide a string type. The String type of Turbo Pascal and QuickPascal and the LString type of

# Pascal

Table A7.1  Numeric Data Types in Pascal

| Internal Representation | Turbo Pascal | Microsoft Pascal | Microsoft QuickPascal |
|---|---|---|---|
| 8-bit unsigned | Byte | Byte | |
| 8-bit signed | ShortInt | | Byte, ShortInt |
| 16-bit unsigned | Word | Word | Word |
| 16-bit signed | Integer | Integer2 | Integer |
| 32-bit signed | LongInt | Integer4 | LongInt |
| 32-bit (short) | Single | Real4 | Single |
| 48-bit (not 8087) | Real | | Real |
| 64-bit (long) | Double | Real8 | Double |
| 80-bit (temp) | Extended | | Extended |

Microsoft Pascal use a bounded-length string, with the length stored in the first byte. The String type of Microsoft Pascal uses a fixed-length representation; the CString type of QuickPascal uses the C representation.

The elements of an array are stored in contiguous memory locations. Multidimensional arrays are stored in row-major order (last subscript varies fastest). The fields of a record are stored in contiguous memory locations.

## Segments

Turbo Pascal does not produce .OBJ files, but it can link external routines assembled as .OBJ files. The conventions regarding segments in assembly-language routines to be linked with Turbo Pascal 6.0 state that

- The code segment must be named CODE or CSEG or have a name that ends in _TEXT
- Any segment with initialized data must be named CONST or have a name that ends in _DATA
- Any segment with uninitialized data must be named DATA or DSEG or have a name that ends in _BSS
- The stack segment is managed by Turbo Pascal

Any other segment names are ignored; attributes such as alignment and class are overridden or ignored, so they need not be specified. Routines declared in the implementation part of a unit, or in a program, use a near call and return; those declared in the interface part of a unit use a far call and return.

Microsoft Pascal uses the large memory model, which expects the following:

- The code segment name ends in _TEXT and has the class name 'CODE'
- The segment with initialized data is named _DATA and has the class name 'DATA'
- The segment with uninitialized data is named _BSS and has the class name 'BSS'
- The stack segment is named STACK and has the class name 'STACK'

For all segments other than STACK, the alignment is WORD and the combine type is PUBLIC; the STACK segment is PARA aligned and has the combine type STACK. The programmer must manage far and near references.

## Register Use

The registers that must be preserved by assembly-language routines called from Pascal include BP, SP, SS, and DS, for all versions. Microsoft Pascal also requires that SI and DI be preserved and that SS not be changed.

## Arguments

Arguments in Pascal are pushed onto the stack from left to right. In Turbo Pascal, value parameters that are 1, 2, or 4 bytes long, regardless of type, are pushed onto the stack. All floating-point value parameters are also pushed onto the stack. Strings, records, and arrays that are not 1, 2, or 4 bytes long are always passed as variable parameters. All variable parameters are passed as far pointers. All multiword data that are pushed onto the stack are pushed with the most significant word first and the least significant word last. QuickPascal uses very much the same conventions as Turbo Pascal.

In Microsoft Pascal, all value parameters are pushed onto the stack. Variable parameters declared with either VAR or CONST are pushed as near pointers (offset only); those declared with VARS or CONSTS are pushed as far pointers. Two additional bytes are passed for the maximum length of all String and LString parameters.

## Function Results

Many function results are returned in registers: Byte values are returned in AL, word values in AX, and doubleword values in DX:AX. In Turbo Pascal, pointer results are also returned in DX:AX, and floating-point results are returned in ST. For string results, Turbo Pascal passes a far pointer to a block of memory reserved for the result; this pointer is pushed onto the stack before the other parameters and must be left on the stack for the caller to access the function result.

Microsoft Pascal also uses the AL, AX, and DX:AX registers for many function results. However, it uses a "long return" for floating-point and other values larger than 4 bytes. In the long-return method, the caller pushes the offset of a block to receive the function value onto the stack after all other arguments are pushed. This offset is relative to SS. The function writes its result in that block and then must copy the offset to AX and SS to DX, so that DX:AX is a far pointer to the result value. The offset is removed from the stack along with the other arguments when the called routine returns.

QuickPascal also uses AL, AX, and DX:AX for many function results. For string and floating-point (other than Real) results, a pointer to storage for the result is pushed onto the stack before the other arguments. This pointer should not be removed by the called routine.

# C

## Names

Identifiers in C are case-sensitive, so the assembly-language routines should be assembled with the option to preserve the case of external and public names. C also inserts a leading underscore (_) in front of each function and external name. C recognizes the first 31 characters of a name.

## Data Types

Table A7.2 summarizes the data types available in C. The identifier associated with a string, an array, or a structure is a pointer to the item. Strings are stored as variable-length strings terminated with a NUL (00h) character. Array elements are stored in contiguous memory, in row-major order. The fields in a structure are also stored in contiguous memory.

## Segments

The C program and the assembly-language functions it calls should use the same memory model. The large memory model uses the following conventions:

- The code segment name ends in _TEXT and has the class name 'CODE'
- The segment with initialized data is named _DATA and has the class name 'DATA'
- The segment with uninitialized data is named _BSS and has the class name 'BSS'
- The stack segment is named STACK and has the class name 'STACK'

For all segments other than STACK, the alignment is WORD and the combine type is PUBLIC; the STACK segment is PARA aligned and has the combine type STACK. Alternatively, the small model used for programs written entirely in assembly language in this text can also be used with smaller programs. For full details, refer to your C reference manual.

## Register Use

The registers that must be preserved by assembly-language routines called from C include BP, SP, SS, DS, SI, and DI.

Table A7.2  Data Types in C

| Data type | Internal representation |
|---|---|
| unsigned char | 8-bit unsigned |
| char | 8-bit signed |
| unsigned short | 16-bit unsigned |
| unsigned int | 16-bit unsigned |
| int | 16-bit signed |
| short | 16-bit signed |
| unsigned long | 32-bit unsigned |
| long | 32-bit signed |
| float | 32-bit floating-point |
| double | 64-bit floating-point |
| long double | 80-bit floating-point |

## Arguments

Arguments in C are pushed onto the stack from right to left. All arguments other than arrays are passed by value; to pass arguments by reference, pointers must be passed. Arrays are always passed using a pointer. Depending on the memory model in use, pointers may be near or far; refer to your C reference manual for details on memory models used by your compiler. Arguments should not be removed from the stack by the called routine, but rather, by the calling program.

## Function Results

Many function results are returned in registers: char values are returned in AL; int, short, and near values in AX; and long and far values in DX:AX. To return a structure, copy the structure to a global variable and return a pointer to it. The type of pointer needed depends on the memory model and how the pointer is declared; the pointer is returned in DX:AX.

# FORTRAN

## Names

Identifiers in FORTRAN are not case-sensitive; all lowercase letters are converted to capital letters. Although the FORTRAN 77 standard specifies a limit of 6 characters, many compilers allow as many as 31 characters in names.

## Data Types

Table A7.3 summarizes the data types available in FORTRAN.

Strings in FORTRAN are implemented as arrays of characters; they follow fixed-length string conventions. Although the length of a string argument is available in a FORTRAN subroutine or function, the location where the length is stored is not generally available to assembly-language procedures. The string length can be passed as an explicit integer argument.

The elements of an array are stored in contiguous memory locations. Multidimensional arrays are stored in column-major order (first subscript varies fastest). Lower bounds other than the default bound of 1 can be specified.

## Segments

The FORTRAN program and the assembly-language procedures it calls should use the same memory model. The large memory model uses the following conventions:

- The code segment name ends in _TEXT and has the class name 'CODE'.
- The segment with initialized data is named _DATA and has the class name 'DATA'
- The segment with uninitialized data is named _BSS and has the class name 'BSS'
- The stack segment is named STACK and has the class name 'STACK'.

# FORTRAN

Table A7.3  Data Types in FORTRAN

| Data type | Internal representation |
|---|---|
| CHARACTER*1 | 8-bit unsigned |
| INTEGER*1 | 8-bit signed |
| INTEGER*2 | 16-bit signed |
| INTEGER*4 | 32-bit signed |
| REAL*4 | 32-bit floating-point |
| REAL*8 | 64-bit floating-point |
| DOUBLE PRECISION | 64-bit floating-point |
| LOGICAL*2, *4 | 8-bit (1 = true, 0 = false) followed by unused byte(s) |

For all segments other than STACK, the alignment is WORD and the combine type is PUBLIC; the STACK segment is PARA aligned and has the combine type STACK. Other memory models are also used with FORTRAN. For details, refer to your FORTRAN reference manual.

## Register Use

The registers that must be preserved by assembly-language routines called from FORTRAN include BP, SP, SS, DS, SI, and DI.

## Arguments

By default, FORTRAN programs compiled with the large memory model pass all arguments by reference, using far pointers. In memory models where all data share one segment, near pointers are used. Many compilers have extensions for forcing near pointers and for passing arguments by value. Like Pascal, FORTRAN arguments are pushed onto the stack from left to right in the argument list.

## Function Results

FORTRAN uses the AL, AX, and DX:AX registers for many function results. The way in which results longer than a doubleword are returned depends on the compiler. Microsoft FORTRAN uses a "long return" for floating-point and other values larger than four bytes. In the long-return method, the caller pushes the offset of a block to receive the function value onto the stack after all other arguments are pushed. This offset is relative to SS. The function writes its result in that block and then must copy the offset to AX and SS to DX, so that DX:AX is a far pointer to the result value. The offset is removed from the stack along with the other arguments when the called routine returns.

# Glossary

**abstract machine**  A model of a computer as specified by a programming language.

**abstract data type**  A specification of the properties and operations provided for a data type, where the actual implementation is hidden from the user of the type.

**accumulator**  A general-purpose data register used in integer arithmetic operations (in the 8086, AX or AL).

**actual argument**  See *arguments*.

**actual parameter**  See *arguments*.

**address**  A number associated with a memory location, used to access it.

**AF**  In the 8086, the Auxiliary carry Flag; records whether a decimal operation caused a carry within AL.

**AH**  In the 8086, the high-order half of the AX register.

**AL**  In the 8086, an 8-bit accumulator; the low-order half of the AX register.

**algorithm**  A sequence of unambiguous and executable steps that solves a specific class of problems in a finite amount of time.

**arguments**  Data that a program passes to a subprogram. The subprogram refers to the value of an argument through the use of a *parameter*.

**arithmetic logic unit**  The part of the processor that performs arithmetical, relational, and logical operations.

**arithmetic shift**  A shift operation in which the operand is treated as a signed integer; the bits shifted out are lost; values provided for vacated bit positions depend on the representation used for negative integers. Arithmetic shifts are used to multiply or divide by powers of two.

**ASCII**  American Standard Code for Information Interchange. A standard code that uses seven bits to represent a character. Extended versions of ASCII use eight bits to represent a character. See Appendix 2.

**assembler**  A program that reads a file containing the text of an assembly-language program and generates a file containing the equivalent machine instructions coded in binary.

**assembler directive**  A command or information for the assembler to use when translating an assembly-language program into machine instructions.

**attribute byte**  A byte that is associated with each file on a disk and contains information about the basic charactertistics of a file.

**auxiliary storage**  Provides long-term storage for programs and data, typically magnetic disk and tape.

**AX**  In the 8086, a 16-bit accumulator. See also AH and AL.

**base register**  A register that contains (at least part of) an operand address and is used in register-indirect addressing.

**BH**  The high-order half of the BX register.

**BIOS**  The Basic Input/Output System, usually provided in ROM with the computer system.

**biased exponent**  The exponent that is stored as part of a floating-point number. The bias is added to the actual exponent so that only positive integers are coded in the exponent field.

A.73

**Binary Coded Decimal (BCD)**  See *packed BCD* and *unpacked BCD*.

**binary number system**  A positional number system with just two digits, 0 and 1.

**binding**  The process of associating values with attributes. Binding can occur during translation, linking, loading, and execution.

**bit**  (from *b*inary dig*it*) A single digit, 0 or 1, of the binary number system.

**BL**  In the 8086, the low-order half of the BX register.

**bounded-length string**  A sequence of characters stored in memory with a fixed maximum number of characters specified when the string is declared. The actual number of characters in the string is also stored.

**BP**  In the 8086, a 16-bit register that contains the offset, relative to SS, of a reference point in the stack frame.

**breakpoint**  A place where a program is stopped during execution so that memory can be examined by a debugging utility.

**bus**  The collection of electrical paths that connect all of the internal components of a computer system.

**BX**  In the 8086, a 16-bit register used as a base register with indirect addressing. See also BH and BL.

**byte**  (from *b*inary *te*rm) A group of bits that represents a character; usually eight bits.

**cache memory**  Very fast, associative storage. The system tries to anticipate what data and instructions will be needed next and keeps that information in cache memory in an attempt to increase system throughput.

**call by name**  A method of passing arguments in which the argument expression is evaluated by a parameterless routine each time the subprogram refers to the corresponding parameter.

**call by reference**  A method of passing arguments in which the parameter gets the address of the argument.

**call by value**  Method of passing arguments in which the parameter gets a copy of the value of the argument.

**cell**  See *memory cell*.

**central processing unit (CPU)**  The part of the computer that executes the instructions in a program; consists of the control unit and the arithmetic logic unit.

**CF**  In the 8086, the Carry Flag; records the carry out of a result.

**CH**  In the 8086, the high-order half of the CX register.

**circular shift**  See *rotate*.

**CL**  In the 8086, the low-order half of the CX register.

**class name**  A segment attribute that specifies how segments are combined when linked.

**code segment**  The segment that contains a program's instructions.

**combine type**  A segment attribute that specifies how segments with the same name from different modules are to be combined by the linker.

**comments**  Remarks written in a natural language within a program to explain or document the program.

**compiler**  A program that reads another program, written in a high-level language, and generates an equivalent set of machine instructions.

**concatenation**  The joining of one string to the end of another string.

**conditional assembly**  The ability of an assembler to include or exclude sequences of instructions based on conditions evaluated during translation.

**conditional jump**  An instruction that inspects the flags and transfers control only if some condition is satisfied.

**control unit**  The part of the processor that fetches instructions and operands from memory, decodes the instructions, and generates the signals for the other components to carry out the specified operations.

**controller**  A device located between the processor and a peripheral device. It converts the codes sent by the processor into the signals that control the peripheral device.

**CS**  In the 8086, the 16-bit segment register that contains the selector for the code (instruction) segment.

**CX**  In the 8086, a 16-bit register used as a counter in iterative and conditional instructions. See also CH and CL.

**cylinder**  In a disk drive with more than one recording surface, the set of tracks at the same position of the read/write heads.

**data abstraction**  The separation of how data are represented, and how data structures are implemented, from the applications of those data.

**data segment**  The segment containing data used by the program.

**denormalized number**  A floating-point number that is too small to be represented in normalized form. Such numbers cannot be represented with the same precision as a normalized number.

**device driver**  The software interface between an application (or DOS) and a peripheral device.

**DF**  In the 8086, the Direction Flag; used to control the direction of string operations.

**DH**  In the 8086, the high-order half of the DX register.

**DI**  In the 8086, a 16-bit index register; this is the destination index with string instructions.

**direct access**  Property that allows locations in memory or sectors on the disk to be accessed in any order.

**direct addressing**  An addressing mode in which the offset is coded in the operand field of an instruction.

**direct memory access (DMA)**  The use of a controller that can copy data between memory and a port associated with a fast peripheral device, so that the processor need not be involved with transferring every byte or word of data to the peripheral device.

**directive**  See *assembler directive*.

**displacement**  The number of addresses between a reference address and the effective address of an operand.

**DL**  In the 8086, the low-order half of the DX register.

**DMA**  See *direct memory access*.

**double-precision**  Long format for floating-point numbers. Compared to single-precision, numbers in double precision have a greater range of values and about twice as many digits of precision. Also called *long*.

**dummy argument**  See *parameter*.

**DS**  In the 8086, the 16-bit segment register that contains the selector for the data segment.

**DX**  In the 8086, a 16-bit register used for data in input and output operations, and in multiplication and division. See also DH and DL.

**dynamic data** Memory that is allocated as it is needed, and made available for other uses as soon as no longer needed. See also *static data*.

**effective address** The computed address of an operand in memory.

**emulator** A program that interprets a machine or assembly-language program written for a different computer.

**ES** In the 8086, an extra 16-bit segment register.

**exclusive OR** Boolean operator that combines two operands. The result is true if either operand is true, but false if both are true. Compare *inclusive OR*.

**extended precision** A 10-byte form of floating-point number used by the 8087 math coprocessor.

**external interrupt** An interrupt generated by an event occurring outside of the processor. External interrupts can be generated by input, output, and storage devices and by system timers.

**external subprogram** A subprogram that is defined in a module other than the one that contains the calling program.

**far jump** A jump to an instruction in another segment. The instruction must specify a segment and an offset.

**far pointer** A segment and offset pair used as an indirect pointer to an item in another segment.

**FCB** See *file control block*.

**fetch-execute cycle** The sequence of operations repeated by the control unit in executing the instructions of a program: (1) fetching the instruction referenced by the IP register; (2) incrementing the IP register; (3) decoding and executing the instruction.

**file control block** A region of memory used by an application and by DOS to manage an open file.

**fixed-length string** A sequence of characters stored in memory as a string that always contains the same number of characters.

**flags register** A register that contains bits that record selected status information, and that provides control over some operations.

**formal parameter** See *parameter*.

**frame** See *physical segment*.

**fully reentrant** A program segment in which no changes occur during execution. A fully reentrant program can be invoked even when another invocation of it is suspended.

**general register** A register used for operands and results of integer arithmetic, logical, and string instructions.

**global data** Data that can be accessed by any main program or subprogram within the same module.

**handle** An integer index used by a program to reference a file.

**head** An electromagnet used to read and write magnetic patterns on the surface of a disk.

**hexadecimal number system** A positional number system that uses 16 as the radix. It has 16 digits (0 through 9 and A through F) and represents numbers as sums of powers of 16. Used for representing groups of four bits with a single hexadecimal digit.

**IF** In the 8086, the Interrupt Flag; controls whether maskable interrupts will be recognized.

**immediate operand** A constant specified as an operand, coded directly as part of the instruction.

**implied operand** A constant that an instruction always uses as an operand without the constant being provided explicitly.

**inclusive OR** Boolean operator that combines two values. The result is true if either or both of its operands is true. Compare to *exclusive OR*.

**index** The displacement of an element in an array.

**index register** A register that contains a displacement into a data structure; it is used with indexed addressing.

**indexed addressing** An addressing mode in which the contents of an index register are added during the calculation of the effective address.

**indirect addressing** An addressing mode in which the offset of an operand cannot be determined solely from the information coded in the instruction.

**indirect pointer** A location in memory, or a register, that contains the address of an operand.

**indirection** See *indirect addressing*.

**inexact result** The exception that occurs when the result of a calculation involving floating-point numbers cannot be represented exactly as a floating-point number.

**input device** A hardware component that allows the user to enter data and programs to a computer system.

**input port** See *port*.

**instruction pointer (IP)** A register that contains the offset in the code segment of the instruction to be executed.

**internal interrupt** An interrupt generated within the processor, by an error or an instruction intended to signal an interrupt. Interrupts caused by errors are also called *traps*.

**internal subprogram** A subprogram that is in the same module as the program that calls it.

**interpreter** A program that reads another program written in a high-level language and performs the specified operations as it analyzes the program.

**interrupt** A signal to the processor that an event that needs immediate attention has occurred.

**interrupt service routine** A program invoked when an interrupt occurs. It saves enough information about the running program to restart it later, then performs whatever processing is required by the interrupt. If it does not terminate the program, the service routine eventually returns control to the interrupted program.

**IP** In the 8086, a 16-bit register (the instruction pointer) that contains the offset of the next instruction to be executed.

**iteration count** The number of times a FOR loop is to execute. The iteration count can be computed from the control expressions and used with an index register or with autodecrement instructions to control the loop.

**K** A measure of memory capacity. When not qualified, 1K is 1024 bytes of memory.

**label** A symbol used to associate an address with an instruction.

**linear memory mode** Addressing mode introduced with the 80386, in which a 16-bit segment selector is used as an index into a table of 32-bit base addresses, and a 32-bit offset is added to the base address.

**linkage editor** A system program that combines program units that have been translated separately into a single unit. It binds the external references in each program to the objects that the references name.

**linker** See *linkage editor*.

**linking loader** A system program that performs the processing of a linkage editor and a loader. The load module is usually built directly in memory rather than as a separate file on disk.

**load module**  The final executable version of a program as produced by a linkage editor; also called a *run image*.

**loader**  A system program that copies a run image (or load module) from storage into memory and arranges for it to execute.

**local data**  Data that can be accessed only by the program or subprogram in which they are defined.

**location counter**  The displacement of the next available byte in a segment during program translation.

**logical complement**  Representation of integers using the magnitude if the number is positive, or taking the bit-by-bit complement of the magnitude if the number is negative. Also called *one's complement*.

**logical record**  The data a program transfers between memory and a storage device. Compare *physical record*.

**logical segment**  A region of memory used for instructions or data.

**logical shift**  A shift operation in which each bit in the operand is treated as a separate logical value; the bits shifted out of one end of a register are lost, and zeros are provided for the vacated positions on the other end.

**long**  See *double-precision*.

**M**  A measure of memory capacity. When not qualified, 1M is 1024K, or 1,048,576 bytes.

**macroinstruction**  A named fragment of program text, often containing a sequence of instructions. It can include operands, labels, conditionals, and special macro operators; during expansion, arguments can be substituted for parameters.

**main memory**  Storage for programs, and the data they use, while the programs are executing.

**mask**  A bit pattern that specifies which individual bits in an operand are to be used in an instruction. Used with Boolean operators (AND, OR, XOR).

**maskable interrupt**  An interrupt that can be disabled by setting a control flag.

**memory cell**  A unit of memory used in a high-level language to store one value.

**mnemonic**  A symbolic name that represents an instruction, an assembler directive, or the name of a macroinstruction.

**module**  The program units contained within a file, either from the start to the first END directive, or between END directives, translated at the same time.

**NaN (Not a Number)**  A special code that represents the result of an undefined operation.

**near jump**  A jump to another instruction in the same segment. The instruction specifies the destination as a word displacement relative to IP.

**near pointer**  An offset used as an indirect pointer to an item in the same segment.

**non-maskable interrupt**  An interrupt that cannot be disabled by a control flag.

**non-reentrant program**  A program segment that is modified during execution so that it cannot be used a second time unless a new copy of it is loaded into memory.

**normalized floating-point number**  A number consisting of a sign, a significand, and an integer power of the radix.

**object file**  The file that contains the object program.

**object program**  The version of a program coded as machine instructions, generated by a compiler or assembler.

**object string**  A character string that is searched for a copy of a given *pattern string*.

**Glossary** **A.79**

**OF**  In the 8086, the Overflow Flag; indicates whether a result is too large or too small to represent.

**offset**  The displacement from the start of a segment to a specified location within the segment.

**one's complement**  See *logical complement*.

**opcode**  See *operation code*.

**operand**  A value, or the location of a value, that an instruction uses; the location where the result of an operation is to be stored.

**operation code**  The part of an instruction, coded in binary, that specifies the operation. Also called an *opcode*.

**output device**  A hardware component that presents the results of a program to the user.

**output port**  See *port*.

**overflow**  An error that occurs when the result of an arithmetic operation is too large to be stored in the destination specified in an instruction. Compare *underflow*.

**packed BCD**  A representation for numbers that uses four bits for each digit, stored as two digits per byte. Compare *unpacked BCD*.

**packed character string**  A sequence of characters arranged with two or more per word, to minimize the number of words of memory needed.

**page**  In the 8086, a unit of memory that contains 256 bytes.

**paragraph**  In the 8086, a unit of memory that contains 16 bytes.

**paragraph boundary**  A physical address that is a multiple of 16.

**parameter**  The name a subprogram uses to refer to an argument.

**pattern string**  A string of characters, or rules for forming such a string, that is searched for in another string (called the *object string*).

**peripheral**  An input, output, or storage device.

**PF**  In the 8086, the Parity Flag; records whether the low-order byte of a result has an even number of 1-bits.

**physical address**  The address of a location in memory, specified as a displacement from the start of memory. This is the address written to the address bus in accessing the location.

**physical record**  The data transferred in one access of a storage device. Compare *logical record*.

**physical segment**  A region of addressable memory; 64K in the 8086.

**pointer register**  A register that contains an offset, used with indirect addressing.

**port**  A register mapped to a memory address, used in transferring data between main memory and a peripheral device.

**positional number system**  A system of writing numbers in which the position of a digit affects its value.

**preprocessor**  A program that translates features not implemented by a compiler or assembler into statements that can then be translated by the compiler or assembler.

**procedural abstraction**  Separation of how operations in a programming language are implemented from the syntax needed to use those operations.

**program end**  The logically last statement in a program.

**program heading**  A reference that specifies where program execution is to begin.

**prologue**  The introductory comments in a program, stating the purpose of the program, its development history, or other information about it.

**protected mode**  The addressing mode introduced with the 80286 processor, in which a 16-bit segment selector is used to find a 24-bit base address in a table, and a 16-bit offset is added to the base address.

**pure code segment**  A segment containing only constants and instructions that do not change during execution.

**radix**  The base of a number system. It determines the number of digits in a system and is the base used in the expansion of a number.

**radix complement**  Representation of integers using the magnitude if the number is positive, or the difference between the magnitude of the number and the number that is one greater than the largest that can be represented with the specified number of digits if the number is negative.

**RAM**  See *random access memory*.

**random access memory (RAM)**  Memory that can be read or written in any order.

**read-only memory (ROM)**  Memory that can be read but not written to. Access may occur in any order.

**real mode**  The segmented addressing mode, with 16-bit segment selectors and 16-bit offsets combined to form a 20-bit address, used by the 8086.

**recursive program**  A program that invokes itself or that invokes another that in turn invokes it.

**reentrant program**  See *serially reentrant* and *fully reentrant*.

**register**  A small, high-speed storage unit within the processor; it can be accessed directly by the control and arithmetic/logic units.

**register direct operand**  An operand specified as the contents of a register.

**register indirect operand**  An operand specified by an indirect pointer stored in a register.

**relative address**  An address specified in an instruction as a displacement from a reference address. In the 8086, jump instructions use relative addresses with displacements from IP.

**return address**  The address of the instruction to which control passes when a subprogram terminates.

**ROM**  See *read-only memory*.

**rotate**  A shift operation in which the bits shifted out one end of the operand are shifted back into the vacated positions at the other end. Also called a *circular shift*.

**round to nearest**  A rounding strategy that converts a real number to the floating-point number that is nearest it.

**round toward negative infinity**  A rounding strategy that converts a real number to the largest floating-point number that is less than or equal to it.

**round toward positive infinity**  A rounding strategy that converts a real number to the smallest floating-point number that is greater than or equal to it.

**round toward zero**  A rounding strategy that converts a real number to the nearest floating-point number that is smaller in magnitude. Also called chopping, or truncating, the number.

**run image**  The executable version of a program produced by a linkage editor; also called a *load module*.

**scan code**  A code generated by the keyboard hardware whenever a key is pressed or released.

**sector**  A portion of a track on a magnetic disk.

**segment**  (1) A unit of memory. Locations within a segment are usually accessed using an offset from the start of the segment. Also called a *physical segment*. (2) A portion of a program.

Programs are usually partitioned into segments according to the logical structure of the program, with separate segments for data and instructions. Also called a *logical segment*.

**segment register**   A register used for storing a segment selector. In the 8086, the CS, DS, ES, and SS registers are segment registers.

**segment selector**   (1) In real mode, the high-order portion of the paragraph boundary where a segment starts. (2) In protected and linear modes, an index into a set of tables that give the address of the start of a segment.

**segment table**   The table of segments and their attributes that is built by an assembler in its first pass.

**serially reentrant**   Describes a program segment that is reentrant only if each invocation is allowed to run to completion before another invocation begins. Serially reentrant segments modify themselves during execution, but initialize or restore the changed values.

**SF**   In the 8086, the Sign Flag; records the sign of a result.

**shift count**   The number of bit positions that a bit moves in a shift or rotate operation.

**shift operation**   Operation in which bits in a register or memory location move left or right within the register or memory location. See also *logical shift*, *arithmetic shift*, and *rotate*.

**short**   See *single-precision*.

**short jump**   A jump to another instruction in the same segment. The instruction specifies the destination as a byte displacement relative to IP.

**SI**   In the 8086, a 16-bit index register; this is the source index with string instructions.

**sign and magnitude**   Representation of integers as a sign coded in the first bit (0 for +, 1 for −) and the magnitude of the integer in the remaining bits.

**sign bit extension**   The repetition of the sign bit in the most significant positions of an integer represented in a complement form.

**significand**   A positive number greater than or equal to 1.0 and less than the radix of the system in which the number is written.

**single-precision**   Short format for floating-point numbers. Also called *short*.

**source file**   The file that contains the source program.

**source program**   The program, written in a high-level or assembly language, entered by the programmer.

**SP**   In the 8086, a 16-bit register that contains the offset of the top of the current stack.

**SS**   In the 8086, the 16-bit segment register that contains the selector for the stack segment.

**stack**   A list structure in which all insertions and deletions are performed on the same end. Items are inserted by the push operation and removed by the pop operation.

**stack frame**   A block of memory allocated on the stack as part of a subprogram call; it is used for the return address, for saving the caller's registers, for passing arguments, and for data local to the subprogram.

**stack segment**   The portion of memory allocated for a stack structure used in transfer of control and communication with subprograms.

**statement**   A line containing an optional label, an instruction or directive or macroinstruction definition or macroinstruction call, any operands needed, and an optional comment.

**static data**   A region of memory used for data that is allocated when a program is loaded; it remains available to the program for its entire execution. See also *dynamic data*.

**storage** Provides external, long-term storage for inactive programs and data.

**subprogram** A function or procedure, written as a separate program, that is invoked by another program.

**subscript** An integer that specifies the relative position of an element in an array.

**substring** A sequence of consecutive characters from another string.

**symbol** A name used to represent a constant, an address, a register, an operation, a directive, or a macroinstruction.

**symbol table** The table of symbols and their attributes that is built by an assembler in its first pass.

**tail recursion** A special form of recursion in which the recursive call is the last operation in a program. The call can be implemented as a jump to the entry point (or a point following any prologue code) without the need to allocate a new stack frame.

**TF** In the 8086, the Trap Flag; controls generation of an interrupt after each instruction is executed.

**track** On magnetic tape, a single recording path along the length of tape. On a magnetic disk, a circular path on the surface of a platter.

**trap** An internal interrupt caused by an error.

**trap handler** A routine provided to service an internal interrupt.

**two's complement** Representation of an integer using radix complement with 2 as the radix.

**two-pass assembler** An assembler that reads the source file twice. In the first pass, it builds symbol and segment tables. In the second pass, it generates the object file and the optional listing and cross-reference files.

**underflow** An error that occurs when the magnitude of a nonzero result of an arithmetic operation is too small to be stored in the destination specified in an instruction. Compare *overflow*.

**unpacked BCD** A representation for numbers that uses four bits for each digit, with the leading four bits of each byte cleared. Compare *packed BCD*.

**unpacked character string** A sequence of characters stored with one per word, even though two or more characters can fit into a single word.

**value parameter** A parameter that corresponds to an argument passed by value.

**variable-length string** A sequence of characters stored in a region of memory dedicated only to variable-length strings. A fixed part of the string contains the actual length and a pointer to the start of the current value.

**variable parameter** A parameter that corresponds to an argument passed by reference.

**virtual machine** See *abstract machine*.

**virtual memory** The use of auxiliary storage to store inactive segments (or pages) of a program while only the active segments (or pages) are in main memory. Virtual memory systems support programs that are arbitrarily large (up to the capacity of auxiliary storage).

**word** A fixed number of bits that represents a number or an instruction. Word sizes vary from 8 to over 60 bits.

**ZF** In the 8086, the Zero Flag; records whether a result is zero.

# Bibliography

Baase, Sara. *Computer Algorithms: Introduction to Design and Analysis.* Reading, Mass.: Addison-Wesley, 1978.
Borland International, Inc., *Turbo Assembler Quick Reference Guide.* Scotts Valley, Calif., 1990.
———. *Turbo Assembler Reference Guide.* Scotts Valley, Calif., 1988.
———. *Turbo Assembler User's Guide.* Scotts Valley, Calif., 1989.
———. *Turbo Debugger User's Guide.* Scotts Valley, Calif., 1990.
———. *Turbo Pascal Verison 6.0: Programmer's Guide.* Scotts Valley, Calif., 1990.
Calingaert, Peter. *Program Translation Fundamentals: Methods and Issues.* Rockville, Md.: Computer Science Press, 1988.
Dale, Nell, and Susan C. Lilly. *Pascal Plus Data Structures, Algorithms, and Advanced Programming.* 3d ed. Lexington, Mass.: D C Heath & Co, 1991.
Deitel, Harvey M. *An Introduction to Operating Systems.* rev. 1st ed. Reading, Mass.: Addison-Wesley, 1984.
Eckert, Richard R. "Kicking Off a Course in Computer Organization and Assembly/Machine Language Programming." *SIGCSE Bulletin* 19 (December 1987): 2–9.
Fletcher, G. Yates, Larry F. Hodges, and Stephen G. Worth, III. "MANIAC: A Preliminary Machine Approach to the ACM CS 3 Course." *SIGCSE Bulletin* 16 (February 1984): 26–33.
Gear, C. William. *Computer Organization and Programming.* 3d ed. New York: McGraw-Hill, 1980.
Gerald, Curtis F., and Patrick O. Wheatley. *Applied Numerical Analysis.* 3d ed. Reading, Mass.: Addison-Wesley, 1984.
Graham, Neill. *Introduction to Computer Science: Programming and Problem Solving with Pascal.* 4th ed. St. Paul, Minn.: West Publishing, 1988.
Hayes, Frank. "The Spirit of the '86s." *Byte* 15 (March 1990): 266–70.
Heuring, Vincent P. "The Teaching of Assembly Language to Computer Science and Computer Engineering Majors." *SIGCSE Bulletin* 16 (December 1984): 12–14.
Hogan, Thom. *The Programmer's PC Sourcebook.* Redmond, Wash.: Microsoft Press, 1988.
Holtzman, Jeff. "Expanding the Limits." *Byte* 15 (March 1990): 205–214.
Institute of Electrical and Electronics Engineers, *IEEE Standard for Radix-Independent Floating-Point Arithmetic.* (ANSI/IEEE Std 854–1987). New York, 1987.
Johnston, Robert L. *Numerical Methods: A Software Approach.* New York: John Wiley & Sons, 1982.
Lawson, Harold W., Jr. *Understanding Computer Systems.* Rockville, Md.: Computer Science Press, 1982.
Leeper, Robert R., and Karl O. Rehmer. "Structured Assembly Language in VAX-11 MACRO." *SIGCSE Bulletin* 18 (February 1986): 53–60.
Little, R. Rainey, and Mark K. Smotherman. "Assembly Language Courses in Transition." *SIGCSE Bulletin* 20 (February 1988): 95–99.
Mano, M. Morris. *Computer Engineering: Hardware Design.* Englewood Cliffs, N.J.: Prentice Hall, 1988.
Microsoft Corporation, *Macro Assembler 6.0 Programmer's Guide.* Redmond, Wash., 1991.
———. *Macro Assembler 5.1 Programmer's Guide.* Redmond, Wash., 1987.
———. *Macro Assembler 6.0 Reference.* Redmond, Wash., 1991.
———. *Macro Assembler 5.1 Reference.* Redmond, Wash., 1987.

———. *Microsoft CodeView and Utilities*. Redmond, Wash., 1987.
———. *Mixed-Language Programming Guide*. Redmond, Wash., 1987.
———. *Microsoft MS-DOS Programmer's Reference*. Redmond, Wash., 1988.
———. *Microsoft MS-DOS User's Reference*. Redmond, Wash., 1988.
Moote, Robert. "Virtual Memory: The Next Generation." *Byte* 14 (November 1989): 342–50.
Morse, Stephen P., and Douglas J. Albert. *The 80286 Architecture*. New York: John Wiley & Sons, 1986.
Page, Rex, Rich Didday, and Elizabeth Alpert. *FORTRAN 77 for Humans*. 3d ed. St. Paul, Minn.: West Publishing, 1986.
Peterson, James L. *Computer Organization and Assembly Language Programming*. New York: Academic Press, 1978.
Pfleeger, Charles P. *Machine Organization: An Introduction to the Structure and Programming of Computing Systems*. New York: John Wiley & Sons, 1982.
Phoenix Technologies Ltd. *System BIOS for IBM PC/XT/AT Computers and Compatibles*. Reading, Mass.: Addison-Wesley, 1989.
Ratzer, Gerald F. G. *Micros to Supermicros: An Overview*. Englewood Cliffs, N.J.: Prentice Hall, Reston, 1987.
Reges, Stuart. *Building Pascal Programs: An Introduction to Computer Science*. Boston: Little, Brown, 1987.
Schulman, Andrew, Raymond J. Michels, Jim Kyle, Tim Paterson, David Maxey, and Ralf Brown. *Undocumented DOS: A Programmer's Guide to Reserved MS-DOS Functions and Data Structures*. Reading, Mass.: Addison-Wesley, 1990.
Silver, James L., Jr., and Robert R. Leeper. "Schemata for Teaching Structured Assembly Language Programming." *SIGCSE Bulletin* 15 (February 1983): 128–32.
Smotherman, Mark. "On the Use of Naming and Binding in Early Courses." *SIGCSE Bulletin* 19 (February 1987): 79–83.
Stein, Marvin L. and William D. Munro. *Introduction to Machine Arithmetic*. Reading, Mass.: Addison-Wesley, 1971.
Walker, Terry M. *Introduction to Computer Science: An Interdisciplinary Approach*. Boston: Allyn & Bacon, 1972.

# Index

$ location counter symbol, 227
$I directive (Turbo Pascal), 284–85, 505
$L directive (Turbo Pascal), 283, 505
& in instruction displays, 110
& substitute operator, 427–30
. in record notation, 502
; in instruction displays, 110
; in macros, 416
;; in macros, 416
? in data declarations, 68
[ ] with indirection, 218
/D assembler option, 432

09h keyboard interrupt, 318
10h BIOS video interrupt, 320
16h keyboard interrupt, 319
25h Set Interrupt Vector function, 309–12
31h Keep Process function, 309–12
35h Get Interrupt Vector function, 308–12
4Bh DOS loader function, 407
8086
    coordinating with 8087, 638, 651–52
    instructions, A.15–A.20
    interrupts, 304–6
    survey of family, 40
8087, 40, 47, 635–38
    floating-point number
        specifications, 625
    instructions, 638–54, A.21–A.24
    register stack documentation, 662
80186, 256, 433
80286, 40, 355–58
80287, 40
80386, 40, 204–5, 211, 358–60
80387, 40
80486, 40

aaa instruction, 581
aad instruction, 591
aam instruction, 583
aas instruction, 583
Absolute value, floating-point
   instruction, 647
Abstraction, 5–7

Access arm in disk drive, 331
Accumulator, 32, 44
adc instruction, 116
add instruction, 116
Addition
   BCD, 573–74
   binary, 15
   floating-point, 629–30
   hexadecimal, 18
   integer, 103–4
Addition instructions
   floating-point, 641–42
   integer, 115–17
   packed BCD, 606–8
   unpacked BCD, 581–83
Address bus, 38, 216–18
Addresses, 28–31, 215–18
   linear mode (80386), 358–60
   protected mode (80286), 355–58
   real mode, 351–54
AF flag, 34
AH register, 32
Algorithms, 2
Alignment in SEGMENT directive, 66
AL register, 32
AND Boolean operation, 196–97
and instruction, 199
Argument lists, 232, 235, 238–39
Arguments
   arrays, 462–70, 473–74
   far pointers, 265
   and linking with high-level
      languages, 281
   in macros, 418–24
   passing by reference, 235–39
   passing by value, 231–35
   records, 504–7
   use of stack, 243, 248–49
Arithmetic
   on character strings, 567
   floating-point, 629–32
   integer, 102–9
   with logical complement notation, 99
   using shifts, 189

A.85

Arithmetic instructions
    floating-point, 638–54
    integer, 115–20
    packed BCD, 606–12
    unpacked BCD, 581–95
Arithmetic logic unit, 31
Arrays
    accessing elements of, 445–449
    as arguments, 462–70
    declaring, 443–45, 471–81
    multi-dimensional, 471–82
    operations on, 452–61
    of records, 507–10
    representation, 442–45
    representing a set with, 484
ASCII character code, 522–23, A.12–A.14
ASCIZ string, 333
Assembler, 77
    algorithm for first pass, 380–83
    algorithm for second pass, 391–93
    and binding, 367
    and external references, 267, 268
    one pass, 393
    operations in first pass, 372–83
    operations in second pass, 383–93
Assembly, conditional, 432–40
`assume` directive, 67
Attributes
    and binding, 367
    segment, 66–67, 372
    symbol, 372
Auxiliary storage. *See* Storage
AX register, 32

Base pointer. *See* BP register
Basic input/output system. *See* BIOS services
BCD
    operands with 8087 instructions, 639
    operations, 571–75, 595–96, 612
    representation, 566–68
    specification, 569–70
    unpacked I/O, 576–80
BH register, 32
Binary coded decimal. *See* BCD
Binary number system, 13–16
Binding, 367–68
Binding time, 367
BIOS services
    disk, 342–44
    in general, 306–8
    keyboard, 318–20
    video, 320–30
Bits, 13, 25
Bit scan instructions (80386), 211
BL register, 32
Boolean data, 192–95, 204–6
Borrow with integer subtraction, 104
BP register, 32, 246–48, 253, 290
Branch instructions. *See* jump instructions
Breakpoints, 93
Bubble sort, 453–57
Bus, 38–39
Busy bit, 637, 638
BX register, 32, 219, 226
Bytes, 26

C (language), 281, A.67–A.69
Cache memories, 362–63
Calculator example, 21–24
Call by name, 239
Call by reference, 231
Call by value, 231
Calling program, 221
`call` instruction, 121, 242–43
Canonic frame number, 41
Carry flag. *See* CF flag
Carry with integer addition, 103
CASE statement, 157
`cbw` instruction, 115
Central processing unit, 8, 9, 31–34
CF flag, 34
    assigning a value, 116
    comparison of unsigned data, 139–41
    integer arithmetic, 104, 106, 108–9
    shift instructions, 186–91
Character codes, 522–24
Character strings
    instruction repeat prefixes, 543–44
    instructions, 542–63
    operations, 528–41
    pointers, 542
    representation, 524–25
    specification, 526–28
ChkDigit procedure, A.8, A.10
CH register, 32
Class name in `SEGMENT` directive, 67
`clc` instruction, 116
`cld` instruction, 542–43
`cli` instruction, 305
CL register, 32

Cluster, 332
cmc instruction, 116
cmp instruction, 136
cmpsb instruction, 552
cmpsw instruction, 552
Code optimization, 396
Code segment, 32
CodeView 2.2, A.34–A.44
CodeView 3.14, A.44–A.49
Column-major order, 472
Combine type in SEGMENT directive, 66
COM executable program, 352
Command line in PSP, 410
Comment record in object file, 380
Comments, 4, 60, 416–17
common combine type, 67
Communications, 345–48
Compare instruction, 136
Compiler, 3, 10, 394–95
Computed GOTO statement, 157
Concatenation, 536, 549–52
Conditional assembly, 432–40
Conditionals, in macros, 436–40
Condition codes (8087), 637, 648–49, 651–52
Control characters, 526
Controllers, 346–47
Control register (8087), 635–37
Control structures, 135, 148
Control unit, 31
Conversions
   binary to decimal, 13–14, 615–16
   binary to hexadecimal, 16
   capital to lowercase letter, 523–24, 563
   characters to digits, 523
   character string to unpacked BCD, 571–72
   decimal to binary, 14–15, 616–18
   decimal to hexadecimal, 17–18
   digits to characters, 523
   flags to Boolean values, 204–6
   floating-point precision, 627–28
   floating-point to integer, 628–29
   hexadecimal to binary, 16–17
   hexadecimal to decimal, 17
   integer to floating-point, 629
   long integer to short integer, 105
   lowercase to capital letter, 523–24, 563
   packed to unpacked BCD, 605–6
   short integer to long integer, 107
   unpacked BCD to character string, 573
   unpacked to packed BCD, 603–4

Correlation coefficient example, 667–71
Count-controlled loop. *See* FOR loop
CPU. *See* Central processing unit
Cross-reference file, 84
CS register, 32
Current directory, 337
cwd instruction, 115
CX register, 32, 146–47, 543–44
Cylinder on disk, 36, 331

$d$ (direction bit), in instruction, 52
daa instruction, 607
das instruction, 610
Data bus, 38, 216–18
Data declaration directives, 68–69
Data registers (8087), 635
Data segment, 32
Data transfer area. *See* DTA
Data types, high-level languages, 280, A.65–A.66, A.68–A.70
db directive, 63, 68, 374
dd directive, 625–26
DEBUG, 88–93, A.34
Debuggers, 368, 411
Decimal number system, 12–13
dec instruction, 117
Decomposition instruction, 647
Deleting element from set, 486
Denormalized floating-point numbers, 624
Denormalized operand exception, 634
Device drivers, 307
DF flag, 34, 542–43
DH register, 32
Difference of sets, 485–86
Digit representation in ASCII, 523
Direct access, 36, 332
Direct address, 53, 445–47
Direction flag. *See* DF flag
Directives, 61, A.25–A.27
   conditional, 433–47
   data declaration, 68–69
   external definition, 69, 267–68
   macro, 415
   module termination, 70
   procedure, 268–69
   segment, 66
   Turbo Pascal, 283–85, 505
Direct memory access, 348
Directory services, DOS, 337–38
DI register, 32, 449, 542

Disk drives, 36–38, 330–32
Disk operating system. *See* DOS
Disk services, BIOS, 342–44
Displacement
   array, 443–44, 472–73, 481
   record, 497, 508
`div` instruction, 119
Division
   BCD, 574, 612
   floating-point, 631
   integer, 106–7
   using arithmetic shifts, 182–84
Division by zero, 107, 303, 634
Division instructions
   floating-point, 644–46
   integer, 118–20
   unpacked BCD, 590–91
DL register, 32
DMA, 348
DOS
   directory services, 337–38
   DTA services, 337–38
   file services, 332–34
   I/O services, 315–18
   services, in general, 306–8
   standard devices, 315–18
`DosFunc` constant, 75
`DOSSEG` directive, 66, 404
Double-precision. *See* Long floating-point format
Doubleword, 27
`dq` directive, 625–26
DRAM, 361
DS register, 32, 262, 284, 542
DTA, 337–39
`dt` directive, 625–26
Dummy arguments. *See* Parameters
`dup` operator, 68–69
`dw` directive, 63, 68
`dword` type used with `ptr`, 284
DX register, 32
Dynamic data, 254
Dynamic memory allocation, 519–20
Dynamic RAM. *See* DRAM

EBCDIC character code, 522–23
EEMS memory. *See* Expanded memory
Effective address, 215
ELSE clause, 149
`ELSE` directive, 433, 436
EMS memory. *See* Expanded memory

Emulator, 93
END=, FORTRAN read option, 135
`END` directive, 70
`ENDIF` directive, 433, 436
`ENDM` directive, 415, 437
`ENDP` directive, 269
`ENDS` directive, 66, 497
Enumerated data records, 383–84
EOF Pascal function, 135
EQ operator, 433
`equ` directive, 69, 193, 249–50
Errors, in floating-point representation, 618–19
Error summary flag (8087), 637
ES register, 32, 262, 542
Exception flags (8087), 637
Exception masks (8087), 636
Exception pointers (8087), 637
Exceptions, floating-point, 633–34
Executing from DOS prompt, 87
`ExitToDos` constant, 75
Expanded memory, 353–54
Exponent, floating-point, 619
Exponential function, example program, 663–67
Exponentiation, 103
Expressions as operands, 65
Extended ASCII code, 523
Extended codes returned by `GetChar`, 72, 317
Extended floating-point format, 622–23
Extended integer arithmetic, 108–9
Extended memory, 357
`External`, in Pascal declaration, 282
External interrupt, 302–3
External names record in object file, 380
External subprograms, 267–72
External symbols, 69, 267–68
Extra segment, 32
`extrn` directive, 69, 267–68

`fabs` instruction, 647
`fadd` instruction, 641–42
`faddp` instruction, 642
Far jumps, 147, 261
Far pointers, 261–62, 265, 304
FAR procedure type, 269
FAT. *See* File allocation table
`fbld` instruction, 639
`fbstp` instruction, 640
FCB. *See* File control block

# Index

fchs instruction, 647
fcom instruction, 649–50
fcomp instruction, 650
fcompp instruction, 650
fdiv instruction, 645
fdivp instruction, 645
fdivr instruction, 645–46
fdivrp instruction, 646
Fetch-execute cycle, 33
fiadd instruction, 642
ficom instruction, 650
ficomp instruction, 650
fidiv instruction, 645
fidivr instruction, 646
Fields
   of assembly-language statement, 60
   in records, 495
fild instruction, 639
File allocation table, 342
File attribute byte, 332–33
File control block, 332
File services, DOS, 332–34
fimul instruction, 644
finit instruction, 652–53
fist instruction, 640
fistp instruction, 640
fisub instruction, 643
fisubr instruction, 644
Fixup record, 386
Fixups
   linker, 405–7
   loader, 408–9
Flags
   converting to Boolean values, 204–6
   copying to AX, 257–58
   in instruction displays, 111
   saving in subprogram, 257
   and test results, 136–37
fld1 instruction, 641
fldcw instruction, 653–54
fldenv instruction, 653
fld instruction, 639
fldz instruction, 641
Floating-point
   arithmetic, 629–32
   comparison, 632–33, 649
   constants, 625–26
   denormalized numbers, 624
   exceptions, 633–34
   extended, 622–23
   FOR loops, 655–56

infinity, 624
instructions, 638–54
long, 621–22
move operations, 627–28
normalized numbers, 615
precision, 674
range, 619–20, 674
representation error, 618–19
rounding, 627–28
short, 618–24
testing for equal, 656–58
variables, 626
zero, 624
fmul instruction, 644
fmulp instruction, 644
FOR loop, 164–72, 655–56
FORTRAN
   arithmetic IF statement, 158
   computed GOTO statement, 157
   END= option in READ, 135
   information for linking with, A.69–A.70
fprem instruction, 646
Fractions, in BCD numbers, 568
Frame, 352, 403
Free list in dynamic memory allocation, 519
frndint instruction, 648
frstor instruction, 653
fsave instruction, 653
fscale instruction, 647
fsqrt instruction, 648
fstcw instruction, 653–54
fstenv instruction, 653
fst instruction, 640
fstp instruction, 640
fstsw instruction, 648
fsub instruction, 642–43
fsubp instruction, 642
fsubr instruction, 643
fsubrp instruction, 643
ftst instruction, 651
Full evaluation of Boolean expressions, 206
Fully reentrant subprograms, 288, 299
Function results, 232, 281, 519, 532
Functions as interrupts, 308
fwait instruction, 651–52
fxam instruction, 651
fxch instruction, 640
fxtract instruction, 647

G, unit of memory capacity, 28
GetChar procedure, 72, 317, A.6–A.7

GetDec procedure, 72–73, 106, 189, A.8–A.11
Get Interrupt Vector, DOS function, 308–12
Global data, 224

Handle, file access method, 332
Hardware, 8–10, 25–40, 315, 330–32, 361–63
Head, in disk drive, 331
Header node, in linked list, 512
Header record, in object file, 379
Heap, 519
Hexadecimal number system, 16–19
High-level languages, 3, 279–85, 394–97, A.65–A.70

IC. *See* Iteration count
idiv instruction, 119
IFDEF directive, 435
IF directive, 433, 436
IF flag, 34, 304–5
IFNDEF directive, 435
IF-THEN-ELSE structure, 148–50
IF-THEN structure, 152
Immediate operands, 51, 54, 65
Implied operands, 51, 54, 64
imul instruction, 118, 433
inc instruction, 116
Include files, 417–18
Indexed addressing, 449–51
Index registers, 449–51
Indirect address, 53, 220–21, 447–49
Indirect jump, 225
Indirect pointers, 216, 218–20, 226, 481
Inexact result, 628–29, 633
Infinity, floating-point representation, 624
Infinity control field (8087), 637
in instruction, 345
Input devices, 8, 9, 302, 315
Input procedures, 70–73, A.6–A.11
Inserting element into set, 486
Instruction display notation, 110–11
Instruction pointer. *See* IP register
Instructions
    8087 control, 651–54
    Boolean, 199–204
    character string, 542–63
    coding, 52–54, 83, 89–90
    floating-point, 638–51, 654
    integer, 114–20
    jump, 143–46

move, 111–14
one-operand, 44–47
packed BCD, 602–12
shift, 186–91
three-operand, 42–44
two-operand, 44
unpacked BCD, 581–95
zero-operand, 47–48
Instruction table, assembler, 370
Integers
    arithmetic operations, 102–9
    arithmetic using shifts, 189
    conversions, 105, 107
    extended arithmetic, 108–9
    instructions, 110–31
    operands with 8087 instructions, 639
    representation, 97–101
Interpreters, 3, 395–96
Interrupts, 39–40, 302–6, 308, 347
int instruction, 121
Invalid operation, 303, 634
IO.LIB, 70, 86, 401–3
I/O devices, 8–10. *See also* Input devices; Output devices
IOError procedure, A.8, A.10–A.11
I/O services
    BIOS, 318–30
    DOS, 315–18
IP register, 31, 32–33, 142, 147
iret instruction, 305
Iterated data records, 383–84
Iteration count, 172, 656
Iteration versus recursion, 298–99

jae instruction, 144
ja instruction, 144
jbe instruction, 144
jb instruction, 144
jc instruction, 146
jcxz instruction, 146
je instruction, 143–44
jge instruction, 145
jg instruction, 145
jle instruction, 145
jl instruction, 145
jmp instruction, 143
jnae instruction, 144
jna instruction, 144
jnbe instruction, 144
jnb instruction, 144
jnc instruction, 146

# Index

jne instruction, 144
jnge instruction, 145
jng instruction, 145
jnle instruction, 145
jnl instruction, 145
jno instruction, 145–46
jnp instruction, 146
jns instruction, 145–46
jnz instruction, 144
jo instruction, 145–46
jpe instruction, 146
jp instruction, 146
jpo instruction, 146
js instruction, 145–46
Jumps, 143–47, 166, 225, 261, 649
jz instruction, 143–44

K, unit of memory capacity, 28
Keep Process, DOS function, 309–12
Keyboard, 34–35, 308, 315, 318–20
Keystroke buffer, 319

LABEL directive, 428
Labels, in macros, 425
lahf instruction, 205
LCV. *See* Loop control variable
lds instruction, 262–63
les instruction, 262–63
LIB, A.32–A.34
Library file, 401
LIM memory. *See* Expanded memory
Linear memory mode, 358–60
Line numbers in listing file, 79–81
LINK, A.31–A.32
Linkage editor. *See* Linker
Linked lists, 511–20
Linker, 11
   and binding, 367
   and external names record, 380
   and external references, 267–68
   fixup records, 386, 405–7
   logical segments, 352
   operation, 398–404
   and public names record, 380
Linking example, 85–87
Linking loader, 11, 398
Listing file, 79–84
Loaders, 11, 307, 407–10
Load map, 11
Load module, 11, 407, 411
Local data, 224, 252–53

LOCAL directive, 425
Location. *See also* Addresses
Location counter symbol, 227–28
Location in fixup record, 386
lodsb instruction, 545
lodsw instruction, 545
Logical complement notation, 98–99
Long floating-point format, 621–22
Long integers
   printing in two parts, 127–28
   reading in two parts, 130
Loop body, 158
Loop control variable, 172, 656
loope instruction, 147, 172
loop instruction, 146–47, 168
loopne instruction, 147, 172
loopnz instruction, 147, 172
Loops
   FOR, 164–72
   mixed, 172–75
   REPEAT-UNTIL, 162–64
   WHILE, 159–61
loopz instruction, 147, 172

M, unit of memory capacity, 28
Maclaurin series for $e^x$, 664–65
MACRO directive, 415
Macroinstructions. *See* Macros
Macros
   comments, 416–17
   compared to subprograms, 423–24
   concept, 414–18
   conditionals in, 436–40
   labels in, 425
   parameters, 418–24
   side effects in, 422–23
   substitute operator, 427–30
Main memory. *See* Memory
Map file, 87
MASM 5.1, 77–79, A.28–A.29
MASM 6.0, A.29–A.31
Membership in a set, 486
Memory, 8–10, 25–31
   cache, 362–63
   capacity, 28
   hardware, 361–63
Memory cells in high-level-language model, 9
Memory management unit, 216
Memory models, compiler, 352
Memory operands, 50–51, 63–64

Memory units, 25–27
Mnemonic, 60
*mod*
   instruction field, 53
   integer operation, 106–7
Module, 222
Module termination directive, 70
mov instruction, 111–13
movsb instruction, 546–47
movsw instruction, 546–47
mul instruction, 118
Multiplication
   BCD, 574
   binary, 16
   floating-point, 630–31
   integer, 104–6
   using arithmetic shifts, 182–84
Multiplication instructions
   floating-point, 644
   integer, 118
   unpacked BCD, 583–84
Multiprogram systems, 289, 302, 304, 358

Name field, in assembly-language
   statement, 60
Names record, in object file, 379
NaN, 624, 632, 634, 648–49
Near jumps, 147, 261
Near pointers, 261
NEAR procedure type, 268–69
Negation, 107–8, 574
Negation instructions, 120, 647
neg instruction, 120
Newton's method for square roots, 658–60
NIL pointer, 512, 517
Nodes, in linked list, 511–12
NoErrors constant, 75
Non-reentrant procedures, 286–88
nop instruction, 389
NOT (Boolean operation), 198
not instruction, 203
NUL character, 523, 528
NUL filename, 78

Object file, 10, 79
   compared to object modules,
      A.32–A.33, A.55
   records from assembler first pass, 379–80
   records from assembler second pass, 391
Object modules, A.32–A.33, A.55
Object program, 3

Object string, in pattern matching, 540
OF flag, 34
   and arithmetic shift instructions, 189
   and comparison of signed data, 137–39
   and integer instructions, 103, 105, 108
   and rotate instructions, 190
Offset
   in address, 29
   in fixup record, 386
offset operator, 75
One's complement. *See* Logical
   complement notation
Opcode, 52
Operand field, in assembly-language
   statement, 61
Operands, 42, 48–51, 63–65
   in instruction displays, 111
   memory, 50–51, 63–64
   register, 48–50, 63, 218–20
Operation code, 52
Operations
   array, 452–61
   BCD, 571–75
   Boolean, 196–98
   character string, 528–41
   floating-point, 627–34
   integer, 102–9
   move, 102
   set, 484–86
   shift, 181–85
Operators, 68–69, 75, 228–30, 249, 266,
   433, 502, A.27
OR (Boolean operation), 197
or instruction, 202, 517
out instruction, 345
Output devices, 8, 315
   and external interrupts, 302
Output procedures, 70–72, A.1–A.6
Overflow
   floating-point, 628–29, 633
   integer, 103–5, 107
   internal interrupt, 303
Overflow flag. *See* OF flag
Overlays, 408

PAGE directive, 79
Page memory unit, 27
Pages, in linear memory mode, 359
Paragraph
   boundary, 29, 405
   unit of memory, 27

Parameters
    in macros, 418–24
    with subprograms, 231–39
Parameters, actual. *See* Arguments
Partial evaluation of Boolean expressions, 207
Partial remainder, floating-point, 646
Pascal, 476, A.65–A.66. *See also* Turbo Pascal
Pattern string, in pattern matching, 540
Peripherals, 34–38
PF flag, 34
Pointers, 261–66, 514–19
popa instruction, 256
popf instruction, 257
pop instruction, 242
Ports, 345–46
Precision, of floating-point formats, 674
Precision control field (8087), 636–37
Preprocessors, 396–97
Printer, 35, 315
private combine type, 66–67
PROC directive, 268–69
PROC external symbol type, 69
Program format, assembly language, 61–62
Program header, 408
Programmable ROM. *See* PROM
Programmer's Workbench, A.49
Program segment prefix. *See* PSP
PROM, 362
Protected mode, 355–58
Pseudo-operations. *See* Directives
PSP, 312, 409–10
ptr operator, 228–30, 249, 266, 502
public combine type, 66
public directive, 268
Public names record, in object file, 380
Pure code, 289, 362
pusha instruction, 256
pushf instruction, 257
push instruction, 241–42
PutChar procedure, 71, A.1
PutCrLf procedure, 71–72, A.3
PutDec procedure, 72, A.3–A.6
PutStr procedure, 71, 529, A.2

Quadword, unit of memory, 27

Radix, 12, 68
Radix complement notation, 100–101
RAM, 361–62
Random access memory. *See* RAM
rcl instruction, 190–91
rcr instruction, 191
Read-only memory. *See* ROM
Real mode addresses, 351–54
Real numbers. *See* Floating-point
Record, disk I/O, 38
Record data structure, 495–507
    arrays of, 507–10
    and linked lists, 511–12
Recursion, 289–99
Reentrant procedures, 288–89
*reg* field, in instruction, 52–53
Registers, 22, 31
    clearing, 114, 117
    conventions with subprograms, 255–58
    index, 449–51
    initialized by loader, 409
    as operands, 48–50, 63
Relative addresses, in jump instructions, 147–48
Remainder, 106, 631–32, 646
Repeat prefixes, 543–44
REPEAT-UNTIL, 162–64, 175
repe instruction prefix, 544
Repetition, within a macro, 436–37
Repetition control structures, 158–75. *See also* Loops
rep instruction prefix, 543
repne instruction prefix, 544
repnz instruction prefix, 544
Representation
    Boolean, 192–93
    character string, 522–26
    decimal data types, 566–68
    floating-point, 614–24
    integer, 97–101
    one-dimensional array, 442–45
    records, 495–99
    set, 484
    two-dimensional array, 472–73
REPT directive, 437
repz instruction prefix, 544
retf instruction, 266
ret instruction, 243, 249, 266
retn instruction, 266
Return address, 225–27
*r/m* field, in instruction, 53
rol instruction, 190
ROM, 361–62
ror instruction, 190
Rotate instructions, 189–91

Rotate operations, 184–85
Rounding, 122, 627–28, 647–48
Rounding control field (8087), 637
Row-major order, 472
Run image, 11

`sahf` instruction, 205
`sal` instruction, 188
`sar` instruction, 188
`sbb` instruction, 117
Scaling, floating-point, 646–47
Scan code, keyboard, 34
`scasb` instruction, 555–56
`scasw` instruction, 555–56
Scientific notation, 614
Scope of identifiers, 221–25
Sectors, disk, 36, 331
Segment, 27, 29–31
    addressing directives, 67–68
    alignment, 66
    attributes, 372
    combine type, 66
    descriptor, in protected mode, 355
    logical, 352, 403–4
    memory unit, 27
    order directive, 66
    physical, 352, 403
    selector, 29
Segment definitions record, in object file, 379
**SEGMENT** directive, 66–67, 372
Segment order, in executable file, 404
Segments
    and linking with high-level languages, 280
    in real mode addressing, 351–52
Segments table, 84, 370
`seg` operator, 75
Selection
    arithmetic IF, 158
    block IF with one sequence, 152
    block IF with two sequences, 148–50
    CASE statement, 157
    computed GOTO, 157
    nested block IF structures, 155
Serially reentrant subprograms, 288
`set`, 80386 condition instructions, 204–5
Set data type, 483–92
Set Interrupt Vector, DOS function, 309–12
SF flag, 34, 137–39
Shadow registers (80286), 357
Shift circular. *See* Rotate operations
Shift count, 181, 186

Shift instructions, 186–91
Shift operations, 180–85, 593–95
`shl` instruction, 187
Short floating-point format, 618–24
Short jumps, 147, 261
`shr` instruction, 187
Side effects, in macros, 422–23
Sign and magnitude notation, 98
Sign bit extension, 101
Signed data, comparing, 137–39
Sign flag. *See* SF flag
Significand, 615, 618
Signs, in BCD numbers, 568
Single-precision. *See* Short floating-point format
SI register, 32, 449, 542
Software, 10–11
Sorting, 2, 453
Source file, 10
SP register, 32, 240
Square root, 648, 658–63
SRAM, 361, 363
SS register, 32, 240
Stack
    accessing with BP register, 246–48
    argument transfer, 243
    frames with subprograms, 253–54
    and interrupt handlers, 305
    local variables, 252–53
    operations on, 241–42
    removing arguments, 249
    segment, 32, 240–41
    switching segments, 306
    transfer of control with subprograms, 242–43
    with zero-operand instructions, 47
Stack (8087), 635, 662
`stack` combine type, 66–67
Stack top field (8087), 637
Standard devices in DOS, 315
Statements
    assembly-language, 60–61
    high-level-language, 3–4
Static data, in data and code segment, 254
Static RAM. *See* SRAM
Status register (8087), 635–37
`stc` instruction, 116
`std` instruction, 542–43
`sti` instruction, 305
Storage, 8–9
`stosb` instruction, 545–46

# Index

stosw instruction, 545–46
ST register (8087), 635
Strings. *See* Character strings
STRUC directive, 497
STRUCT directive, 497
Structures. *See* Record data structure
sub instruction, 117
Subprograms, 4, 221–24
  active, 289
  compared to macros, 423–24
  external, 267–72
  nested calls, 273–79
  recursive, 289–99
  reentrant, 286–89
  stack frames, 253–54
Subscript, used with arrays, 442
Subset operation, 486
Substitute operator, in macros, 427–30
Substring, 531–32, 540–41, 556–61
Subtraction
  BCD, 573–74
  binary, 15
  floating-point, 630
  hexadecimal, 18–19
  integer, 104
Subtraction instructions
  floating-point, 642–44
  integer, 117–18
  packed BCD, 610
  unpacked BCD, 583
Swapping two values with xchg
  instruction, 113
Symbols, 60, 372
Symbols defined on command line, 432–36
Symbol table, 84, 370

Tag register (8087), 635–37
Tail recursion, 295–98
TASM, A.50–A.51
TCREF, A.51–A.53
TD, A.56–A.63
TDUMP, A.63–A.64
Template
  FOR loop, 166
  FOR loop using loop instruction, 169
  FOR loop with loop instruction and
    formulas, 173
  IF-THEN, 152
  IF-THEN-ELSE, 149
  REPEAT-UNTIL, 162
  WHILE, 159

Ten-byte type as packed BCD, 568
Terminate-and-stay-resident, 309–12
test instruction, 200
Tests
  for equal floating-point numbers, 656–58
  in high-level languages, 135
  interpreting results, 137–42
  saving results, 136
TF flag, 34
THEN clause, 149
Timers and external interrupts, 303
TLIB, A.55–A.56
TLINK, A.53–A.55
Track, on disk, 36, 331
Transfer of control
  with far pointers, 266
  within program, 142
  with subprograms, 225–30
  using stack, 242–43
Traps, 39. *See also* Interrupts
TSR. *See* Terminate-and-stay-resident
Turbo Debugger, A.56–A.63
Turbo Pascal, A.65–A.66
  $I directive, 284–85, 505
  $L directive, 283, 505
  arguments, 281, 505
  array parameter, 462
  and assembly language, 279–282
  data types, 280–81
  DS register, 284
  function result, 519, 532, 581
Two's complement. *See* Radix complement

Unconditional jump with indirect
  pointer, 226
Underflow, 628–29, 633
Uninitialized variables, 83
Union of sets, 485
Unordered floating-point relation, 632–33
Unsigned data, comparing, 139–41

Video adapters, 320
Video display, 35–36, 315
Video services, BIOS, 320–30
Virtual memory
  80286, 357–58
  80386, 359–60

$w$ (word/byte bit), in instruction, 52
wait instruction, 651–52
WHILE structure, 159–61

word data type with ptr, 249
Word size in SEGMENT directive, 67
Word unit of memory, 26
xchg instruction, 113–14
xlatb instruction, 561
xlat instruction, 561

XOR (Boolean operation), 197–98
xor instruction, 202–3

Zero, in floating-point, 624
Zero flag. *See* ZF flag
ZF flag, 34, 137–41, 543–44

**IMPORTANT: PLEASE READ BEFORE OPENING THIS PACKAGE**
**THIS PACKAGE IS NOT RETURNABLE IF SEAL IS BROKEN.**

West Services, Inc.
620 Opperman Drive
P.O. Box 64779
St. Paul, Minnesota 55164-0779

*Programs/Input-Output library disk*

**LIMITED USE LICENSE**

Read the following terms and conditions carefully before opening this diskette package. Opening the diskette package indicates your agreement to the license terms. If you do not agree, promptly return this package unopened to West Services for a full refund.

By accepting this license, you have the right to use this Software and the accompanying documentation, but you do not become the owner of these materials.

This copy of the Software is licensed to you for use only under the following conditions:

**1. PERMITTED USES**

You are granted a non-exclusive limited license to use the Software under the terms and conditions stated in this license. You may:

   a. Use the Software on a single computer.
   b. Make a single copy of the Software in machine-readable form solely for backup purposes in support of your use of the Software on a single machine. You must reproduce and include the copyright notice on any copy you make.
   c. Transfer this copy of the Software and the license to another user if the other user agrees to accept the terms and conditions of this license. If you transfer this copy of the Software, you must also transfer or destroy the backup copy you made. Transfer of this copy of the Software, and the license automatically terminates this license as to you.

**2. PROHIBITED USES**

You may not use, copy, modify, distribute or transfer the Software or any copy, in whole or in part, except as expressly permitted in this license.

**3. TERM**

This license is effective when you open the diskette package and remains in effect until terminated. You may terminate this license at any time by ceasing all use of the Software and destroying this copy and any copy you have made. It will also terminate automatically if you fail to comply with the terms of this license. Upon termination, you agree to cease all use of the Software and destroy all copies.

**4. DISCLAIMER OF WARRANTY**

Except as stated herein, the Software is licensed "as is" without warranty of any kind, express or implied, including warranties of merchantability or fitness for a particular purpose. You assume the entire risk as to the quality and performance of the Software. You are responsible for the selection of the Software to achieve your intended results and for the installation, use and results obtained from it. West Services does not warrant the performance of nor results that may be obtained with the Software. West Services does warrant that the diskette(s) upon which the Software is provided will be free from defects in materials and workmanship under normal use for a period of 30 days from the date of delivery to you as evidenced by a receipt.

Some states do not allow the exclusion of implied warranties so the above exclusion may not apply to you. This warranty gives you specific legal rights. You may also have other rights which vary from state to state.

**5. LIMITATION OF LIABILITY**

Your exclusive remedy for breach by West Services of its limited warranty shall be replacement of any defective diskette upon its return to West at the above address, together with a copy of the receipt, within the warranty period. If West Services is unable to provide you with a replacement diskette which is free of defects in material and workmanship, you may terminate this license by returning the Software, and the license fee paid hereunder will be refunded to you. In no event will West be liable for any lost profits or other damages including direct, indirect, incidental, special, consequential or any other type of damages arising out of the use or inability to use the Software even if West Services has been advised of the possibility of such damages.

**6. GOVERNING LAW**

This agreement will be governed by the laws of the State of Minnesota.

You acknowledge that you have read this license and agree to its terms and conditions. You also agree that this license is the entire and exclusive agreement between you and West and supersedes any prior understanding or agreement, oral or written, relating to the subject matter of this agreement.

West Services, Inc.

## Instructions Grouped by Function (*continued*)

| Group | Instruction | Description |
|---|---|---|
| **String** | CLD | CLear Direction flag |
| | CMPSB | CoMPare String Byte |
| | CMPSW | CoMPare String Word |
| | LODSB | LOaD String Byte |
| | LODSW | LOaD String Word |
| | MOVSB | MOVe String Byte |
| | MOVSW | MOVe String Word |
| | REP instr | unconditional REPeat |
| | REPE instr | REPeat if Equal |
| | REPNE instr | REPeat if Not Equal |
| | REPNZ instr | REPeat if Not Zero |
| | REPZ instr | REPeat if Zero |
| | SCASB | SCAn String Byte |
| | SCASW | SCAn String Word |
| | STD | SeT Direction flag |
| | STOSB | STOre String Byte |
| | STOSW | STOre String Word |
| | XLAT | transLATe |
| | XLATB | transLATe Byte |
| **Decimal** | AAA | ASCII Adjust for Addition |
| | AAD | ASCII Adjust for Division |
| | AAM | ASCII Adjust for Multiplication |
| | AAS | ASCII Adjust for Subtraction |
| | DAA | Decimal Adjust for Addition |
| | DAS | Decimal Adjust for Subtraction |
| **8087 move** | FBLD source | Floating BCD LoaD |
| | FBSTP dest | Floating BCD STore and Pop |
| | FILD source | Floating Integer LoaD |
| | FIST dest | Floating Integer STore |
| | FISTP dest | Floating Integer STore and Pop |
| | FLD source | Floating LoaD |
| | FLD1 | Floating LoaD 1 |
| | FLDZ | Floating LoaD Zero |
| | FST dest | Floating STore |
| | FSTP dest | Floating STore and Pop |
| | FXCH | Floating eXCHange |
| | FXCH dest | Floating eXCHange |
| **8087 control** | FINIT | Floating INITialize coprocessor |
| | FLDCW source | Floating LoaD Control Word |
| | FLDENV source | Floating LoaD ENVironment |
| | FRSTOR source | Floating ReSTORe coprocessor state |
| | FSAVE dest | Floating SAVE coprocessor state |
| | FSTCW dest | Floating STore Control Word |
| | FSTENV source | Floating STore ENVironment |
| | FWAIT | WAIT for coprocessor |
| | WAIT | WAIT for coprocessor |